W9-CFR-954

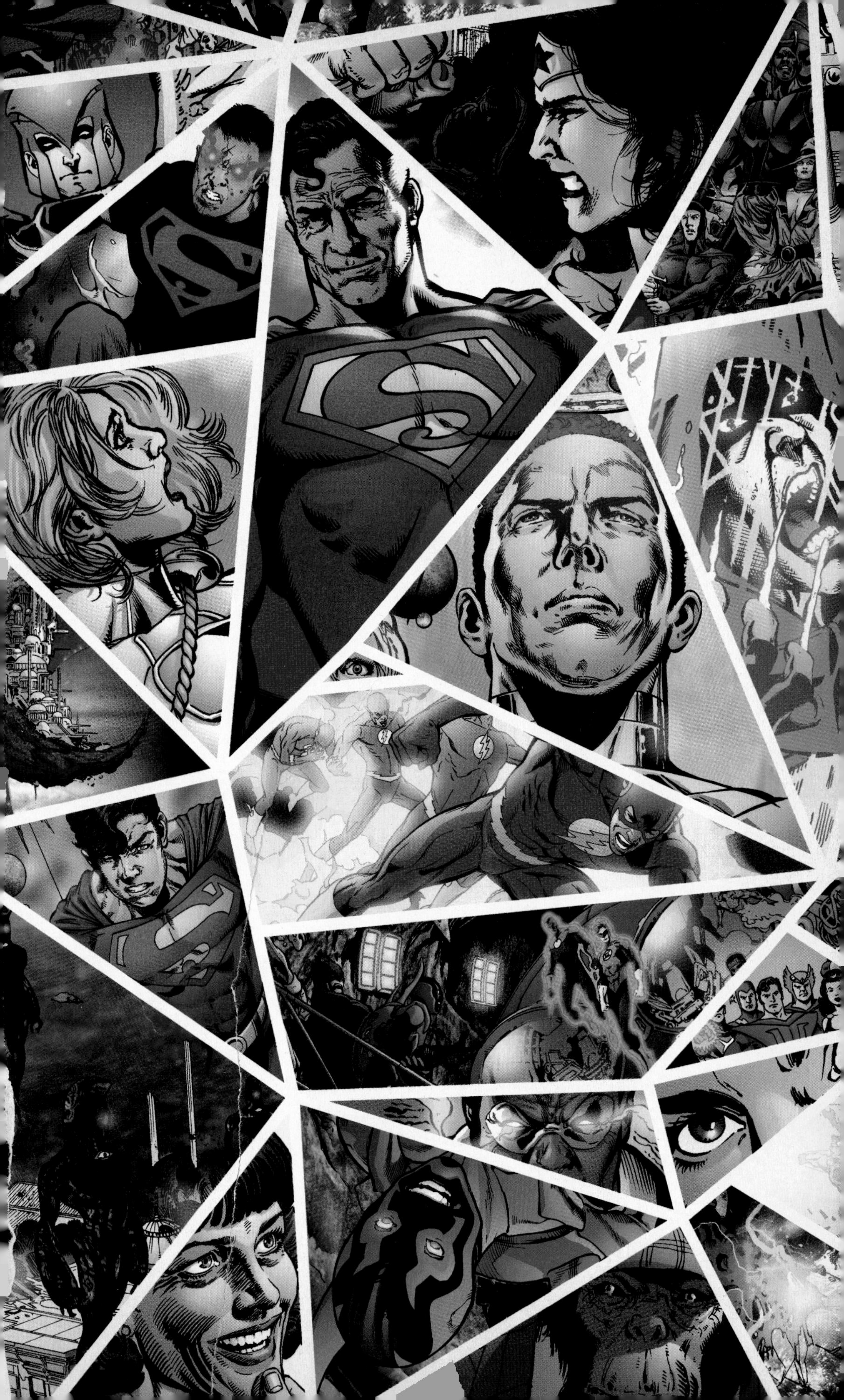

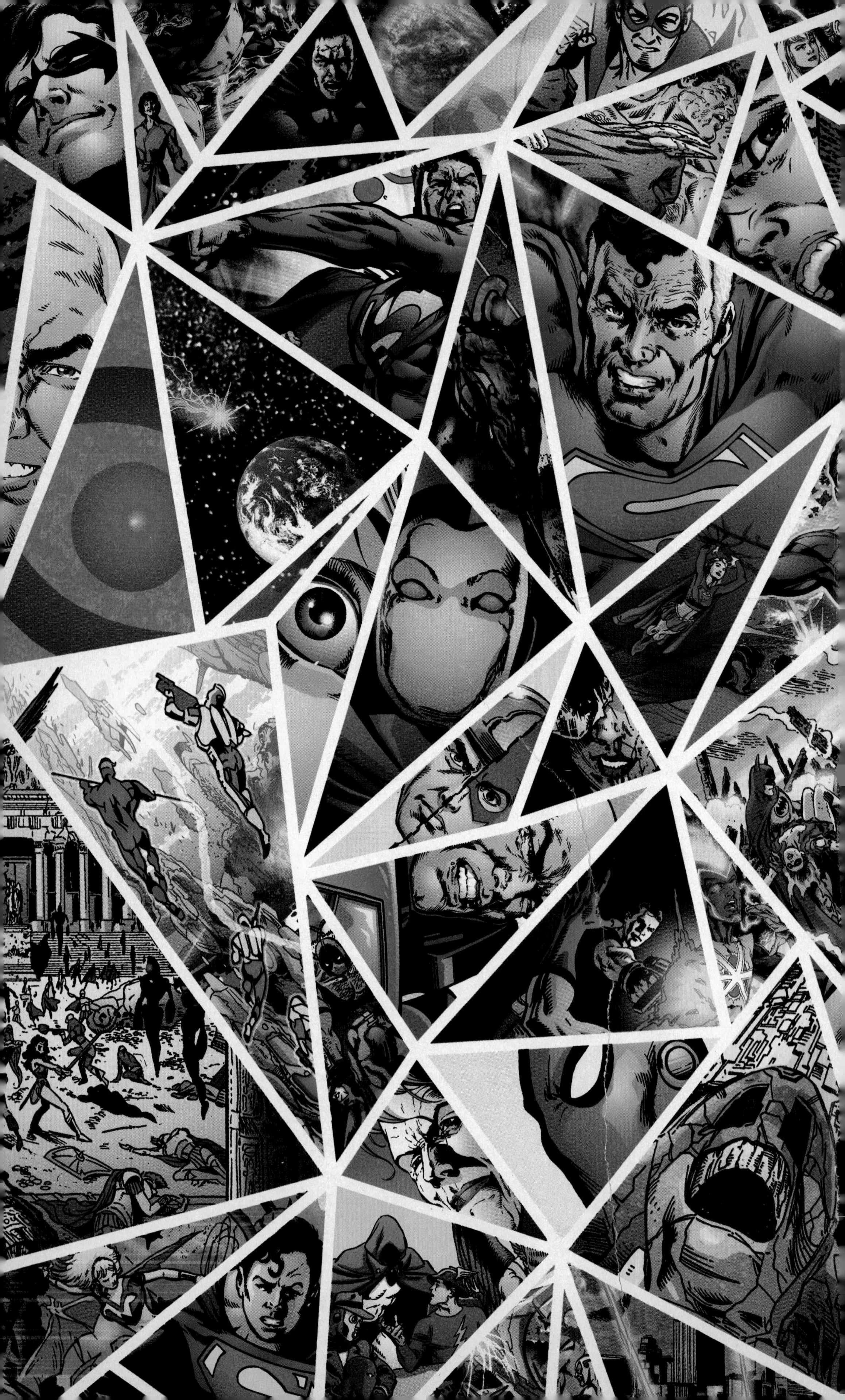

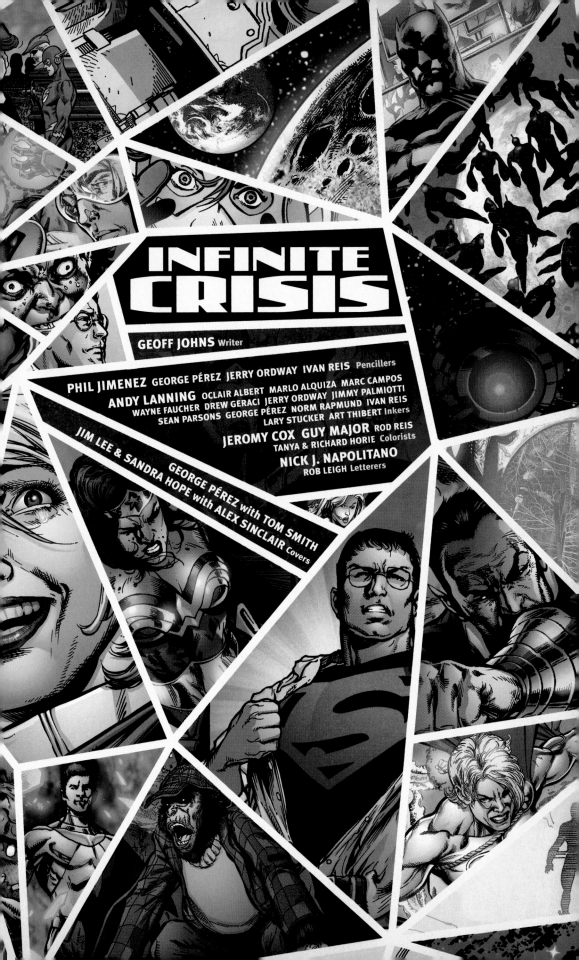

INFINITE CRISIS

GEOFF JOHNS Writer

PHIL JIMENEZ GEORGE PÉREZ JERRY ORDWAY IVAN REIS Pencillers

ANDY LANNING OCLAIR ALBERT MARLO ALQUIZA MARC CAMPOS
WAYNE FAUCHER DREW GERACI JERRY ORDWAY JIMMY PALMIOTTI
SEAN PARSONS GEORGE PÉREZ NORM RAPMUND IVAN REIS
LARY STUCKER ART THIBERT Inkers

JEROMY COX GUY MAJOR ROD REIS
TANYA & RICHARD HORIE Colorists

NICK J. NAPOLITANO
ROB LEIGH Letterers

JIM LEE & SANDRA HOPE with ALEX SINCLAIR Covers
GEORGE PÉREZ with TOM SMITH

DAN DIDIO SENIOR VP-EXECUTIVE EDITOR **EDDIE BERGANZA** EDITOR-ORIGINAL SERIES

JEANINE SCHAEFER ASSISTANT EDITOR-ORIGINAL SERIES **ANTON KAWASAKI** EDITOR-COLLECTED EDITION

ROBBIN BROSTERMAN SENIOR ART DIRECTOR **LOUIS PRANDI** ART DIRECTOR **PAUL LEVITZ** PRESIDENT & PUBLISHER

GEORG BREWER VP-DESIGN & DC DIRECT CREATIVE **RICHARD BRUNING** SENIOR VP-CREATIVE DIRECTOR

PATRICK CALDON EXECUTIVE VP-FINANCE & OPERATIONS **CHRIS CARAMALIS** VP-FINANCE

JOHN CUNNINGHAM VP-MARKETING **TERRI CUNNINGHAM** VP-MANAGING EDITOR

STEPHANIE FIERMAN SENIOR VP-SALES & MARKETING **ALISON GILL** VP-MANUFACTURING

HANK KANALZ VP-GENERAL MANAGER, WILDSTORM **LILLIAN LASERSON** SENIOR VP & GENERAL COUNSEL

JIM LEE EDITORIAL DIRECTOR-WILDSTORM **PAULA LOWITT** SENIOR VP-BUSINESS & LEGAL AFFAIRS

DAVID McKILLIPS VP-ADVERTISING & CUSTOM PUBLISHING **JOHN NEE** VP-BUSINESS DEVELOPMENT

GREGORY NOVECK SENIOR VP-CREATIVE AFFAIRS **CHERYL RUBIN** SENIOR VP-BRAND MANAGEMENT

JEFF TROJAN VP-BUSINESS DEVELOPMENT, DC DIRECT **BOB WAYNE** VP-SALES

INFINITE CRISIS Published by DC Comics. Cover, introduction and compilation copyright © 2006
DC Comics. All Rights Reserved. Originally published in single magazine form in INFINITE CRISIS #1-7.
Copyright © 2005, 2006 DC Comics. All Rights Reserved. All characters, their distinctive likenesses
and related elements featured in this publication are trademarks of DC Comics. The stories, characters
and incidents featured in this publication are entirely fictional. DC Comics does not read or accept
unsolicited submissions of ideas, stories or artwork. DC Comics, 1700 Broadway, New York, NY 10019.
A Warner Bros. Entertainment Company. Printed in Canada. First Printing.
HC ISBN: 1-4012-0959-9 ISBN13: 978-1-4012-0959-9
SC ISBN: 1-4012-1060-0 ISBN13: 978-1-4012-1060-1
Special thanks to Greg Rucka, Simon Colby and Joe Prado. And eternal gratitude to
Marv Wolfman and George Pérez for building the foundation that all super-hero epics
have come from. Cover by Phil Jimenez & Andy Lanning with Jeromy Cox.

INTRODUCTION By Dan DiDio

Julie Schwartz said that every ten years or so you needed to give the universe an enema. You know, clear out all the old stories, and make way for new tales rife with infinite possibilities. Smart man, that Julie Schwartz.

Over the years, individual characters have changed directions, and origins have been rebooted to keep more in line with the times, but up until 1985, stories like that never occurred on a universal scale. CRISIS ON INFINITE EARTHS changed that. As the saying goes, worlds lived, worlds died, and nothing would ever be the same. The original Crisis became a seminal event for all comics fans, one cosmic series that touched upon every book and showed the DC universe to be one shared universe. Other series have tried to achieve the scope of Crisis, and all have gone by the wayside.

Flash forward eighteen years. The twentieth anniversary of Crisis was on the horizon, and all of DC Editorial agreed we should do something to commemorate it. The question was, would we do something to highlight the past event, or would we be foolish enough to plan something that built on the original and attempt to surpass it? There were many discussions and even some arguments, but it always came down to two people: Geoff Johns and Phil Jimenez.

Several writers were instrumental in the planning of INFINITE CRISIS, from the COUNTDOWN TO INFINITE CRISIS Special and through the four lead-in miniseries (DAY OF VENGEANCE; THE OMAC PROJECT; RANN-THANAGAR WAR; VILLAINS UNITED), but when it came down to who would execute the actual series, there was only one choice, Geoff Johns. Geoff is that rare breed of writer who can straddle the two worlds of classic and contemporary storytelling, pay tribute to the past while launching the characters and story into the future. Needless to say, that was exactly what we needed for this series. For the art we turned to the one man who seemed born to take on this project, Phil Jimenez. Phil, like his CRISIS predecessor and idol George Pérez, was most comfortable when he was drawing a cast of thousands, and that was only panel one.

With the primary creative team in place, all attention was placed on the story. This, of course, presented a huge problem. I mean, in the original series, thousands of universes were destroyed, timelines were reshaped and some of our greatest heroes died, never to be seen again. It is hard to imagine what you could do as an encore. Over the years several sequels were pitched, some by the best talent in the business, but ultimately, all were rejected. It wasn't until we looked at where the first series ended that we saw where the next series could begin.

Now forgive me if my memory isn't the sharpest on the exact details; I always lose the "who said what first" in the swirl of the creative process. But as the "legend" goes, nearly three

years prior to the first issue of this epic series seeing print, Geoff Johns, Greg Rucka, Judd Winick, editor Eddie Berganza and myself locked ourselves away and mapped out a course for the DC Universe that would take us from COUNTDOWN TO CRISIS. At the end of the three-day summit, each writer had his assignment. Geoff was handed this series, which he promptly tucked under his arm and started to run with. And over the next three years, he continued to run with it, continually working the ideas and the story until the final issue hit the stands.

It's usually the case with sequels that they up the ante — you know, bigger explosions, higher body counts. Unfortunately, in following the original Crisis, it's hard to go that level of wholesale destruction and change one better. So, rather than look at the physical change of the universe, we explored the emotional. Remember, this story was crafted in a post 9/11 world at a time when most Americans were feeling vulnerable and in need of heroes. We saw a world were the human spirit was pushed to the limit, and against overwhelming odds, people persevered and heroes emerged — sadly, at the cost of their own lives. And although we work in fantasy, the question became "Should we expect less from comics' greatest heroes?" The answer, of course, is "No." So, while the series has all the requisite death and destruction, the true story is the measure of determination and self-sacrifice necessary to be a hero in the DC Universe. It was a great central theme, but we were still unclear about where to hang the actual story. So, like I said earlier, we looked to the ending to find the beginning.

Now I would argue that there were no real villains in INFINITE CRISIS. After all, the four returning characters, the Earth-Two Superman and Lois Lane, Alex Luthor of Earth-Three, and the Superboy of Earth-Prime all walked off stage at the end of CRISIS ON INFINITE EARTHS sacrificing their lives so that others could live. They were true heroes in every sense of the word. So with their return, we had to make it clear that their plans and machinations were set in motion because they truly believed they were doing the right thing. But as the saying goes, the road to hell is paved with good intentions. And in no case is that truer than with the tragic descent of Superboy Prime.

Geoff Johns was presented with the difficult task of balancing both sides of the story so that at any given moment one side might be more right than the other. I think he did an amazing job bringing this complex tale together. I hope you agree.

In bringing this to a close, I want to give some special thanks to some special people. First to DC's President Paul Levitz who, rather than accept what we gave him, constantly pushed the team to reach for higher goals. Although he is our publisher, it's clear he approached this project with the eyes of an editor, writer and fan as well. I would also like to thank George Pérez and Jerry Ordway, the art team on the original series. Geoff created special scenes for both of these accomplished artists to draw so that they could be part of the celebration and help us through deadlines. And speaking of deadlines, a separate thanks to Ivan Reis, who stepped in time and time again, helping out on the art whenever we needed him. And last, a big and important thank-you to Marv Wolfman. While his name may not be in the credits, his guiding presence was felt on every page.

For me and the cast of hundreds also involved in producing this series, it was the culmination of so many months, weeks and hours of work. Judging by the final product and the reactions to it, trust me when I say it was time well spent.

Dan DiDio
Senior VP-Executive Editor
August, 2006

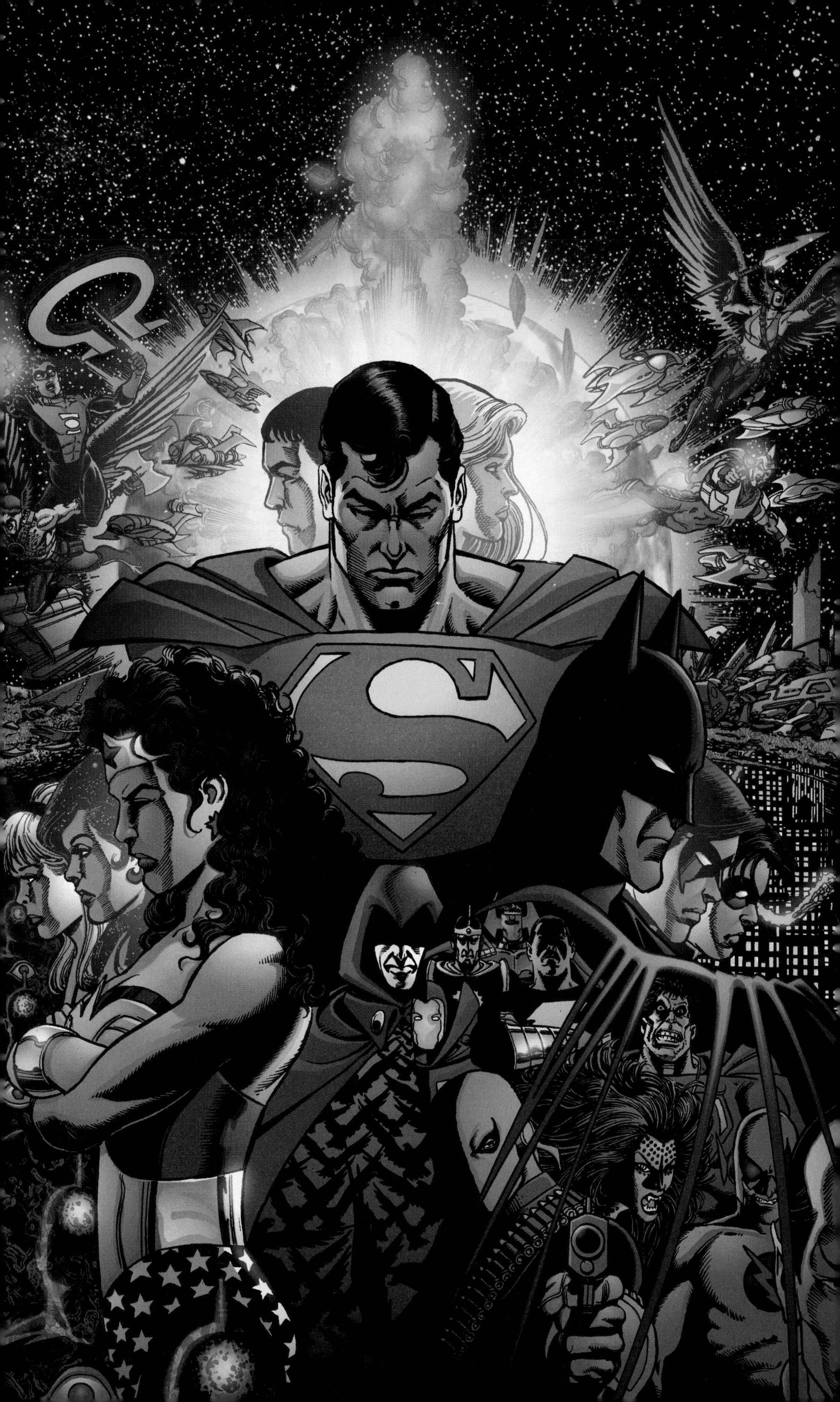

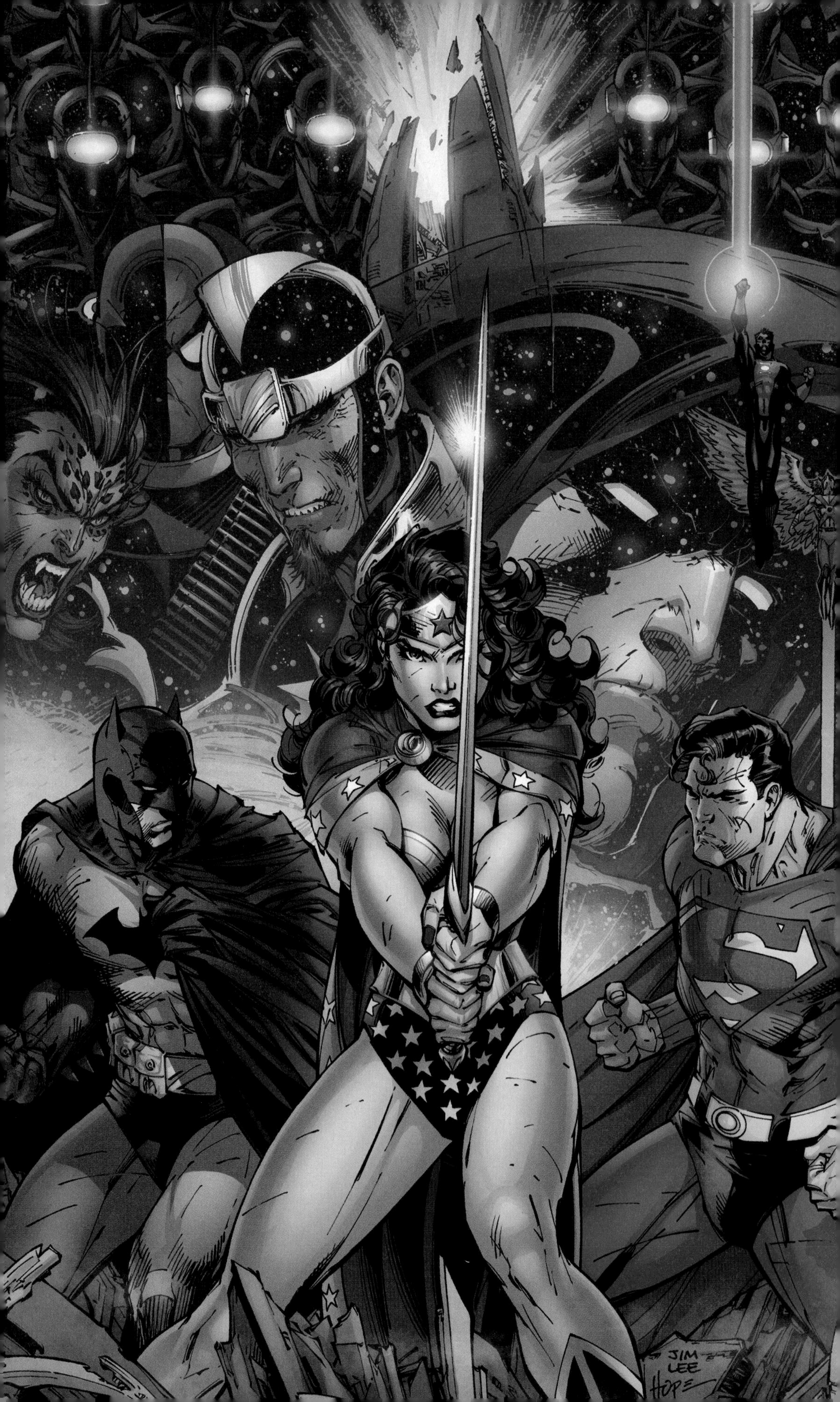
JIM LEE
HOPE

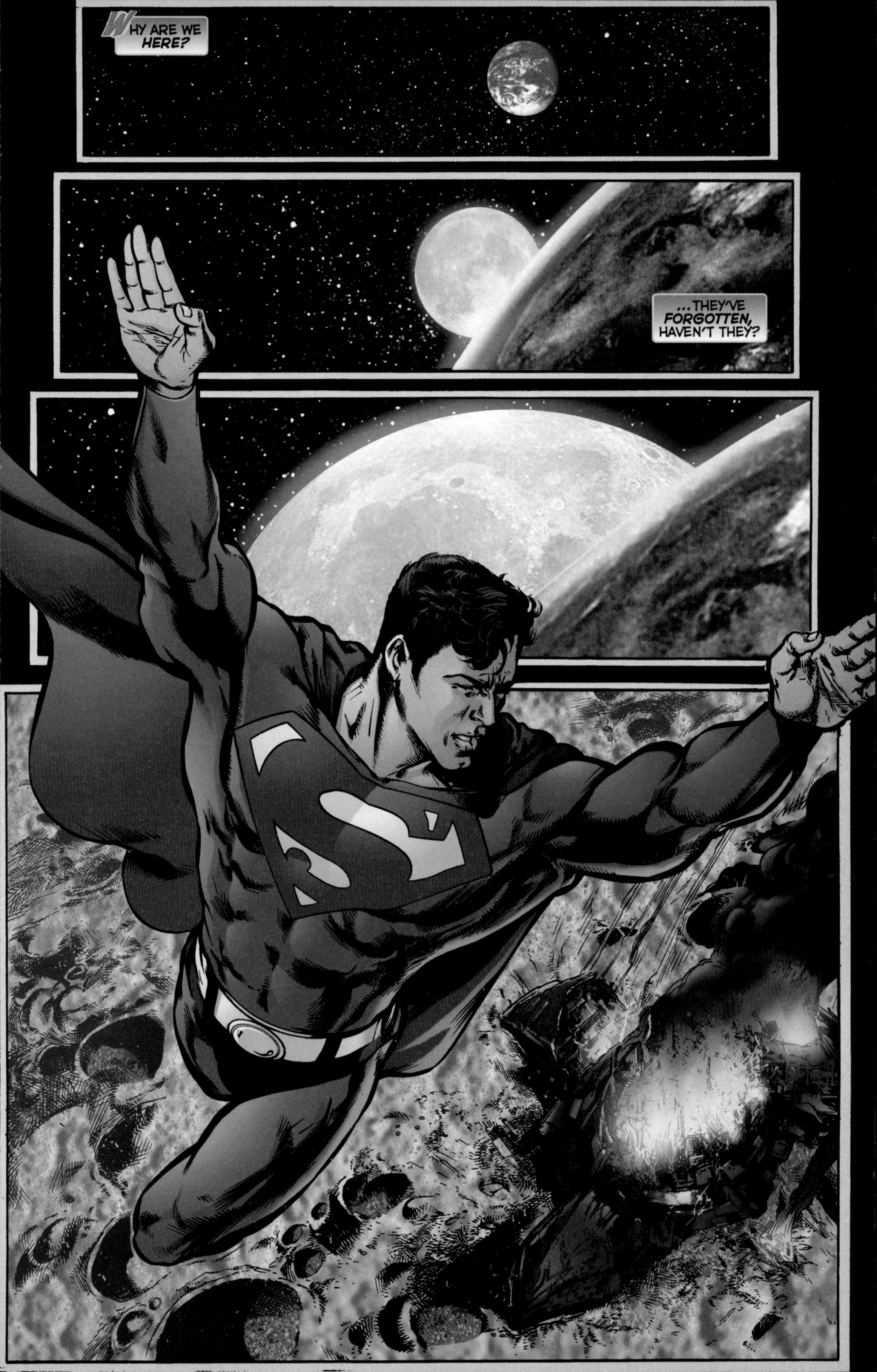
WHY ARE WE HERE?
...THEY'VE FORGOTTEN, HAVEN'T THEY?

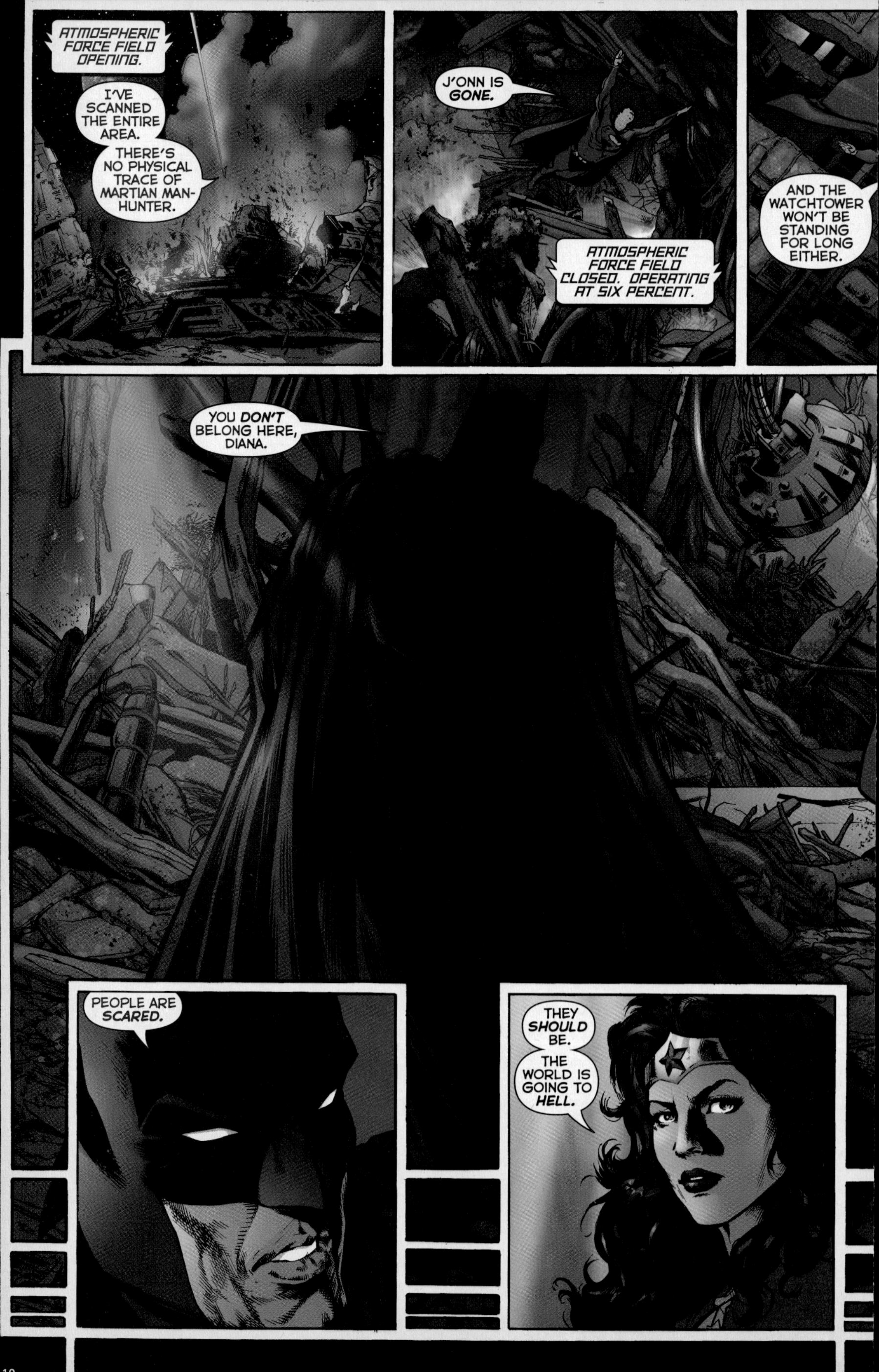
ATMOSPHERIC FORCE FIELD OPENING.
I'VE SCANNED THE ENTIRE AREA.
THERE'S NO PHYSICAL TRACE OF MARTIAN MAN-HUNTER.
J'ONN IS GONE.
ATMOSPHERIC FORCE FIELD CLOSED. OPERATING AT SIX PERCENT.
AND THE WATCHTOWER WON'T BE STANDING FOR LONG EITHER.
YOU DON'T BELONG HERE, DIANA.
PEOPLE ARE SCARED.
THEY SHOULD BE.
THE WORLD IS GOING TO HELL.

THE TELE-PORTATION CHAMBER WAS ACTIVATED LESS THAN NINE *SECONDS* BEFORE THE TOWER EXPLODED.

SOMEONE WAS HERE. SOMEONE *DID* THIS.

WHAT'S *THAT*?

A *BLACK BOX.*

IT'S GHOSTED OUR SECURITY CAMERAS AND RECORDED EVERY-THING ON OUR MONITOR SCREENS FOR THE LAST TWO YEARS.

IT SHOULD TELL ME WHO'S RESPONSIBLE FOR THIS.

MORE SPYING?

THAT *SATELLITE* WASN'T *ENOUGH?*

DON'T BE *NAÏVE,* CLARK. THIS IS SIMPLE *SECURITY.*

NOTHING'S SIMPLE.

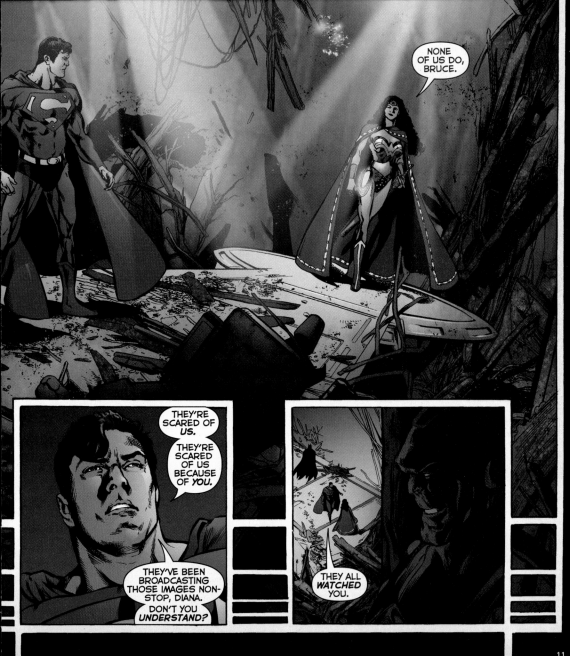

NONE OF US DO, BRUCE.

THEY'RE SCARED OF *US.*

THEY'RE SCARED OF US BECAUSE OF *YOU.*

THEY'VE BEEN BROADCASTING THOSE IMAGES NON-STOP, DIANA. DON'T YOU *UNDERSTAND?*

THEY ALL *WATCHED* YOU.

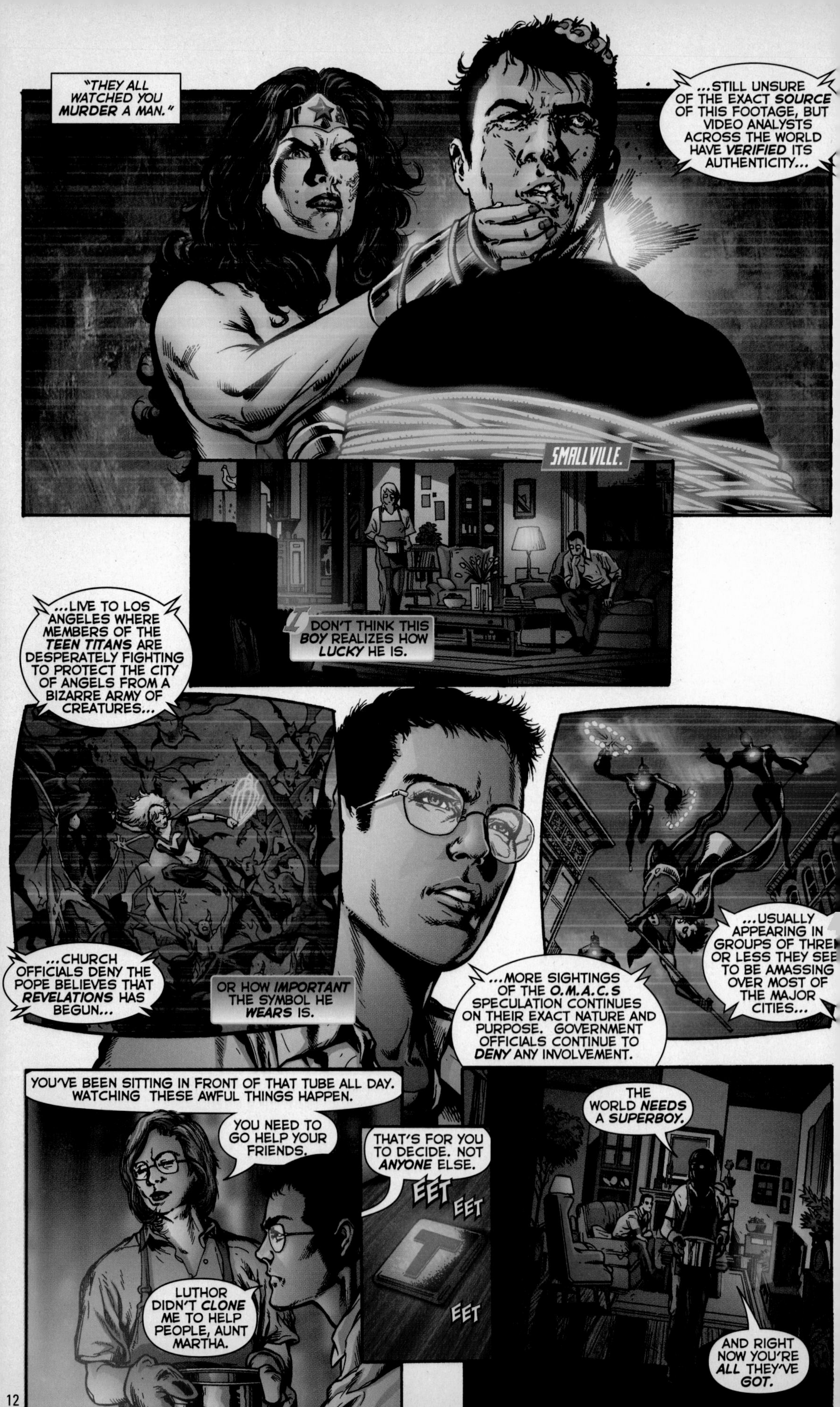
"THEY ALL WATCHED YOU MURDER A MAN."
...STILL UNSURE OF THE EXACT SOURCE OF THIS FOOTAGE, BUT VIDEO ANALYSTS ACROSS THE WORLD HAVE VERIFIED ITS AUTHENTICITY...
SMALLVILLE.
...LIVE TO LOS ANGELES WHERE MEMBERS OF THE TEEN TITANS ARE DESPERATELY FIGHTING TO PROTECT THE CITY OF ANGELS FROM A BIZARRE ARMY OF CREATURES...
I DON'T THINK THIS BOY REALIZES HOW LUCKY HE IS.
...CHURCH OFFICIALS DENY THE POPE BELIEVES THAT REVELATIONS HAS BEGUN...
OR HOW IMPORTANT THE SYMBOL HE WEARS IS.
...MORE SIGHTINGS OF THE O.M.A.C.S SPECULATION CONTINUES ON THEIR EXACT NATURE AND PURPOSE. GOVERNMENT OFFICIALS CONTINUE TO DENY ANY INVOLVEMENT.
...USUALLY APPEARING IN GROUPS OF THRE OR LESS THEY SEE TO BE AMASSING OVER MOST OF THE MAJOR CITIES...
YOU'VE BEEN SITTING IN FRONT OF THAT TUBE ALL DAY. WATCHING THESE AWFUL THINGS HAPPEN.
YOU NEED TO GO HELP YOUR FRIENDS.
LUTHOR DIDN'T CLONE ME TO HELP PEOPLE, AUNT MARTHA.
THAT'S FOR YOU TO DECIDE. NOT ANYONE ELSE.
EET
EET
EET
THE WORLD NEEDS A SUPERBOY.
AND RIGHT NOW YOU'RE ALL THEY'VE GOT.

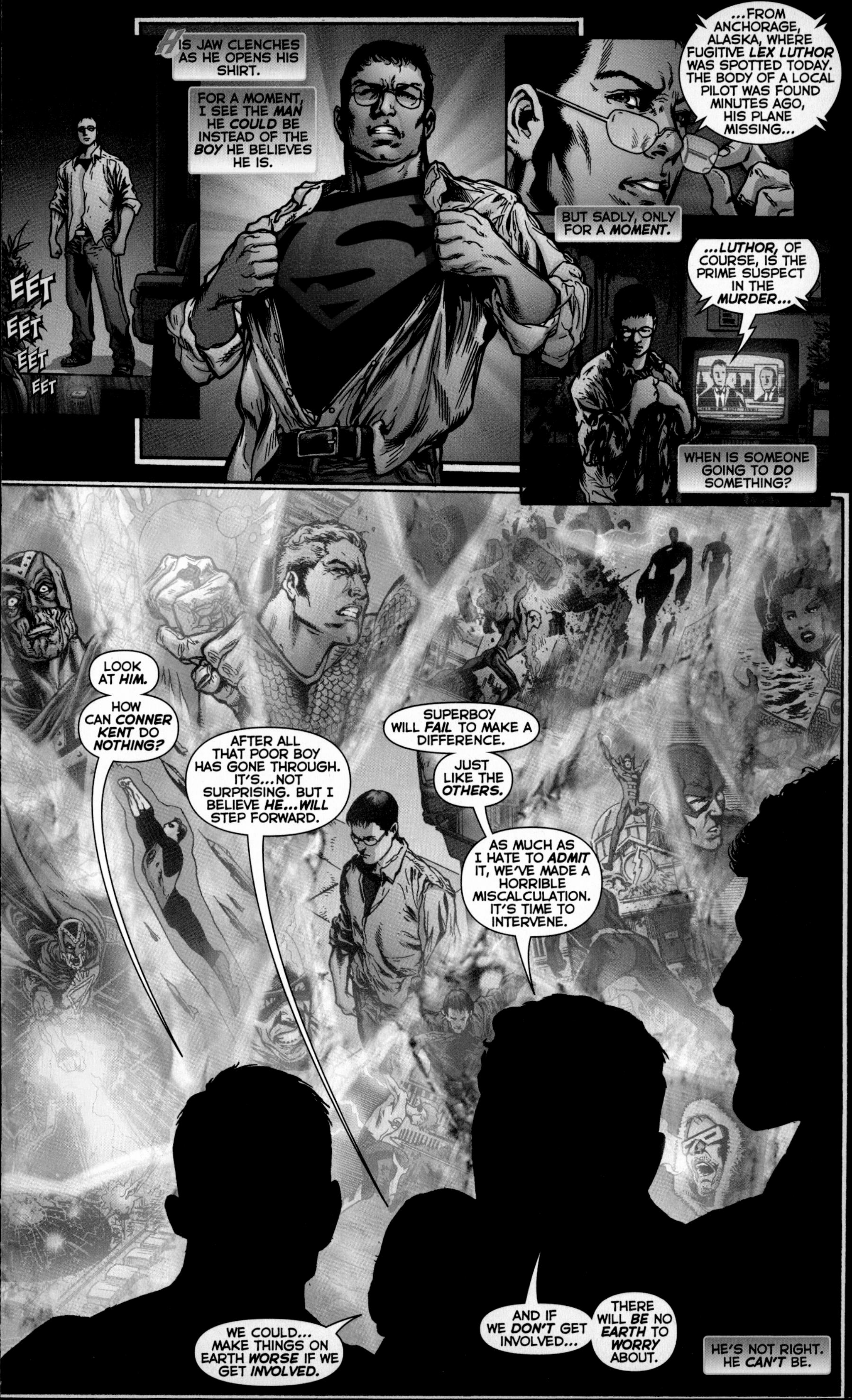
HIS JAW CLENCHES AS HE OPENS HIS SHIRT.
FOR A MOMENT, I SEE THE MAN HE COULD BE INSTEAD OF THE BOY HE BELIEVES HE IS.
EET EET EET EET
...FROM ANCHORAGE, ALASKA, WHERE FUGITIVE LEX LUTHOR WAS SPOTTED TODAY. THE BODY OF A LOCAL PILOT WAS FOUND MINUTES AGO, HIS PLANE MISSING...
BUT SADLY, ONLY FOR A MOMENT.
...LUTHOR, OF COURSE, IS THE PRIME SUSPECT IN THE MURDER...
WHEN IS SOMEONE GOING TO DO SOMETHING?
LOOK AT HIM.
HOW CAN CONNER KENT DO NOTHING?
AFTER ALL THAT POOR BOY HAS GONE THROUGH. IT'S...NOT SURPRISING. BUT I BELIEVE HE...WILL STEP FORWARD.
SUPERBOY WILL FAIL TO MAKE A DIFFERENCE.
JUST LIKE THE OTHERS.
AS MUCH AS I HATE TO ADMIT IT, WE'VE MADE A HORRIBLE MISCALCULATION. IT'S TIME TO INTERVENE.
WE COULD... MAKE THINGS ON EARTH WORSE IF WE GET INVOLVED.
AND IF WE DON'T GET INVOLVED...
THERE WILL BE NO EARTH TO WORRY ABOUT.
HE'S NOT RIGHT. HE CAN'T BE.

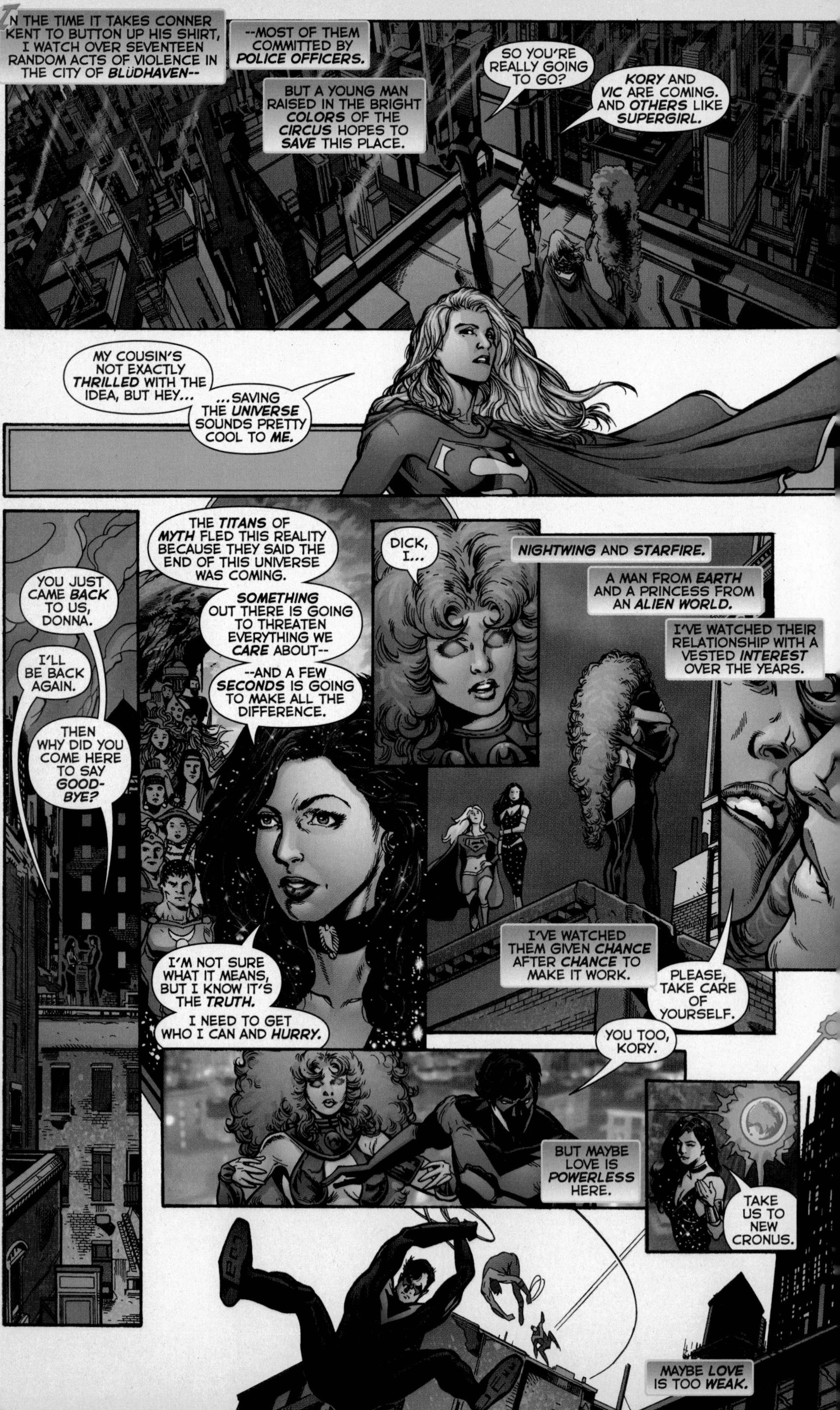
IN THE TIME IT TAKES CONNER KENT TO BUTTON UP HIS SHIRT, I WATCH OVER SEVENTEEN RANDOM ACTS OF VIOLENCE IN THE CITY OF BLÜDHAVEN--
--MOST OF THEM COMMITTED BY POLICE OFFICERS.
BUT A YOUNG MAN RAISED IN THE BRIGHT COLORS OF THE CIRCUS HOPES TO SAVE THIS PLACE.
SO YOU'RE REALLY GOING TO GO?
KORY AND VIC ARE COMING. AND OTHERS LIKE SUPERGIRL.
MY COUSIN'S NOT EXACTLY THRILLED WITH THE IDEA, BUT HEY...
...SAVING THE UNIVERSE SOUNDS PRETTY COOL TO ME.
YOU JUST CAME BACK TO US, DONNA.
I'LL BE BACK AGAIN.
THEN WHY DID YOU COME HERE TO SAY GOOD-BYE?
THE TITANS OF MYTH FLED THIS REALITY BECAUSE THEY SAID THE END OF THIS UNIVERSE WAS COMING.
SOMETHING OUT THERE IS GOING TO THREATEN EVERYTHING WE CARE ABOUT--
--AND A FEW SECONDS IS GOING TO MAKE ALL THE DIFFERENCE.
I'M NOT SURE WHAT IT MEANS, BUT I KNOW IT'S THE TRUTH.
I NEED TO GET WHO I CAN AND HURRY.
DICK, I...
NIGHTWING AND STARFIRE.
A MAN FROM EARTH AND A PRINCESS FROM AN ALIEN WORLD.
I'VE WATCHED THEIR RELATIONSHIP WITH A VESTED INTEREST OVER THE YEARS.
I'VE WATCHED THEM GIVEN CHANCE AFTER CHANCE TO MAKE IT WORK.
PLEASE, TAKE CARE OF YOURSELF.
YOU TOO, KORY.
BUT MAYBE LOVE IS POWERLESS HERE.
TAKE US TO NEW CRONUS.
MAYBE LOVE IS TOO WEAK.

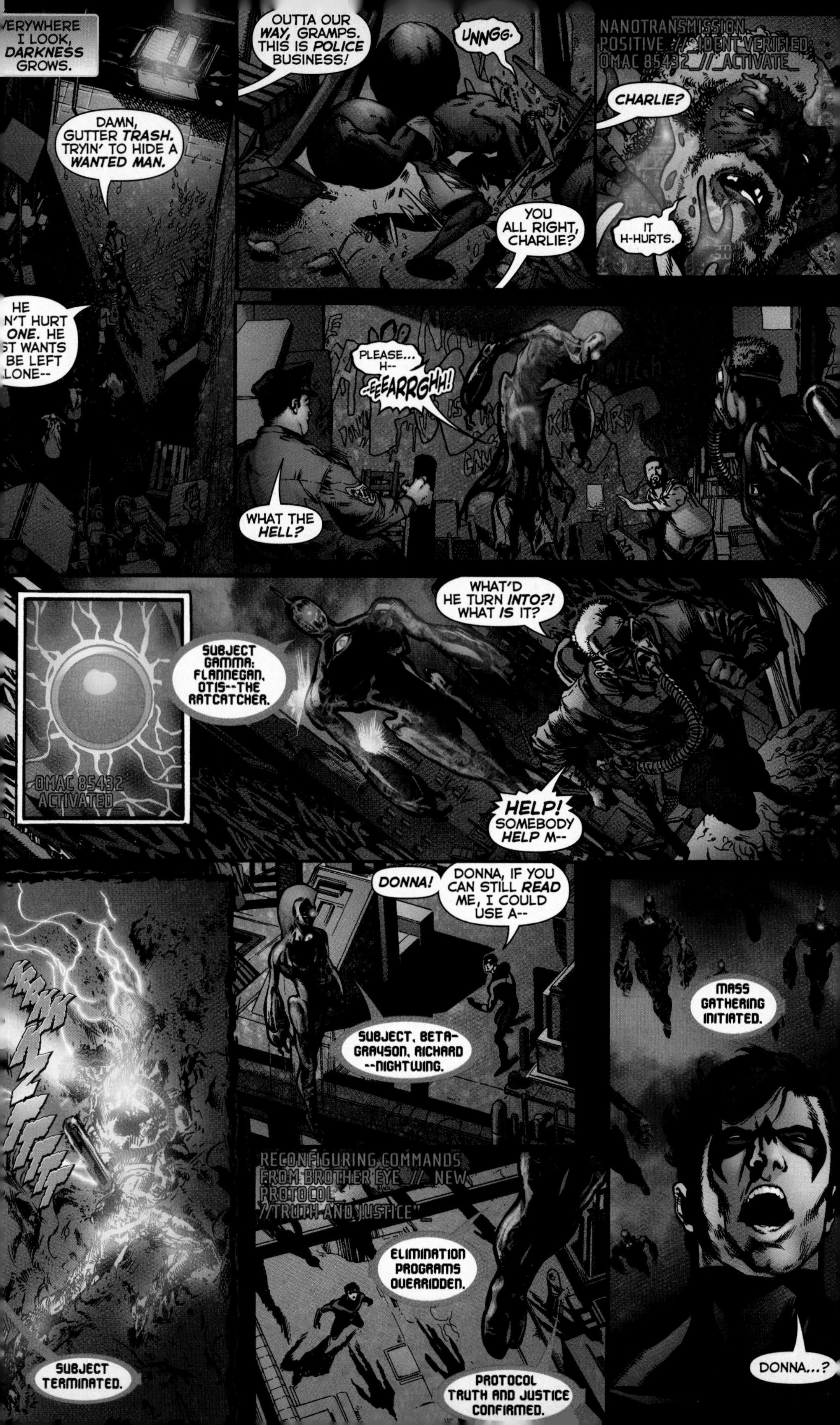

VERYWHERE I LOOK, DARKNESS GROWS.
DAMN, GUTTER TRASH. TRYIN' TO HIDE A WANTED MAN.
HE N'T HURT ONE. HE ST WANTS BE LEFT LONE--
OUTTA OUR WAY, GRAMPS. THIS IS POLICE BUSINESS!
UNNGG.
YOU ALL RIGHT, CHARLIE?
NANOTRANSMISSION POSITIVE_//_IDENT VERIFIED: OMAC 85432_//_ACTIVATE_
CHARLIE?
IT H-HURTS.
PLEASE... H--
EEEARRGHH!
WHAT THE HELL?
SUBJECT GAMMA: FLANNEGAN, OTIS--THE RATCATCHER.
OMAC 85432 ACTIVATED_
WHAT'D HE TURN INTO?! WHAT IS IT?
HELP! SOMEBODY HELP M--
SUBJECT TERMINATED.
DONNA!
DONNA, IF YOU CAN STILL READ ME, I COULD USE A--
SUBJECT, BETA-GRAYSON, RICHARD --NIGHTWING.
RECONFIGURING COMMANDS FROM BROTHER EYE // NEW PROTOCOL //TRUTH AND JUSTICE"_
ELIMINATION PROGRAMS OVERRIDDEN.
PROTOCOL TRUTH AND JUSTICE CONFIRMED.
MASS GATHERING INITIATED.
DONNA...?

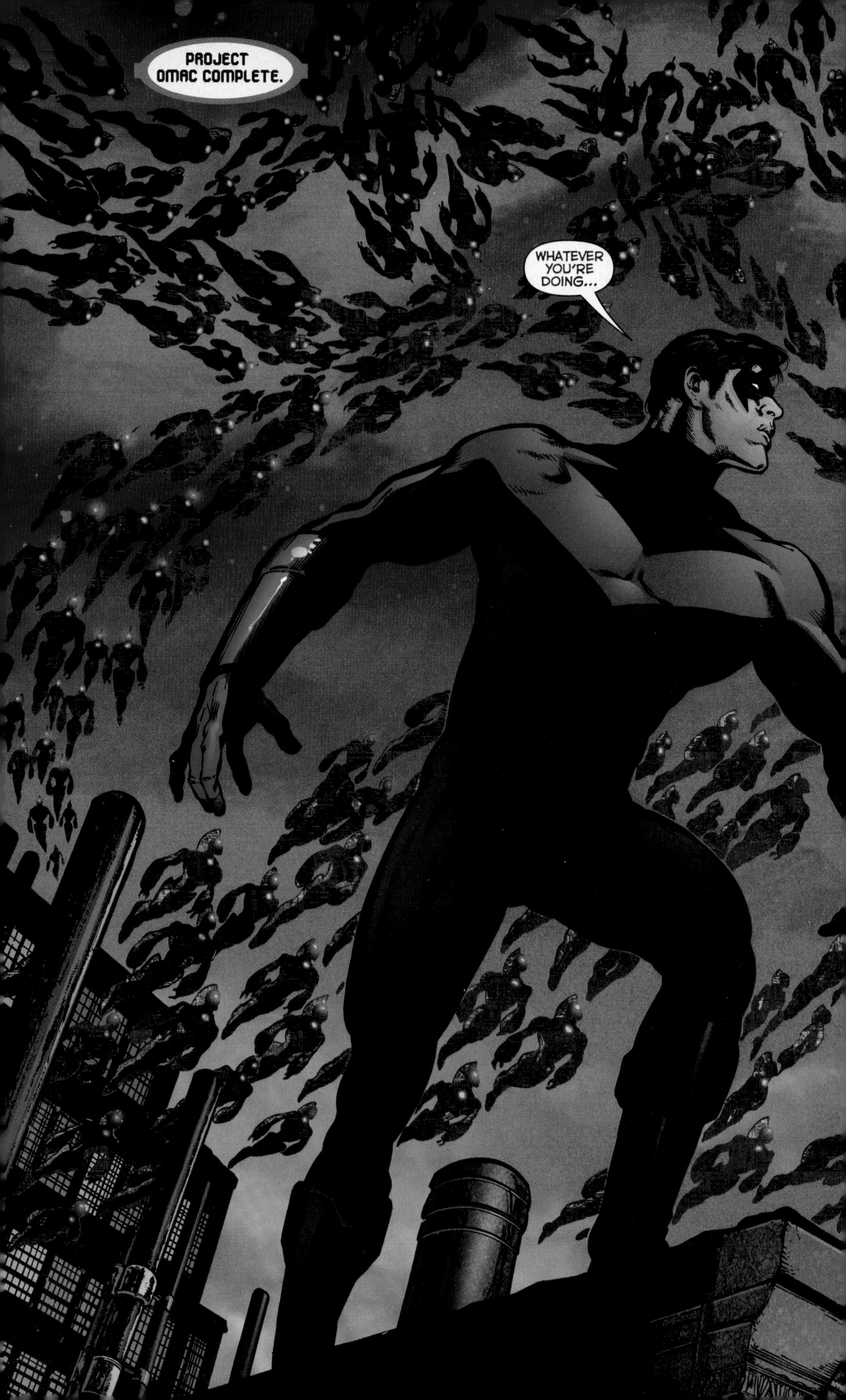
PROJECT OMAC COMPLETE.
WHATEVER YOU'RE DOING...

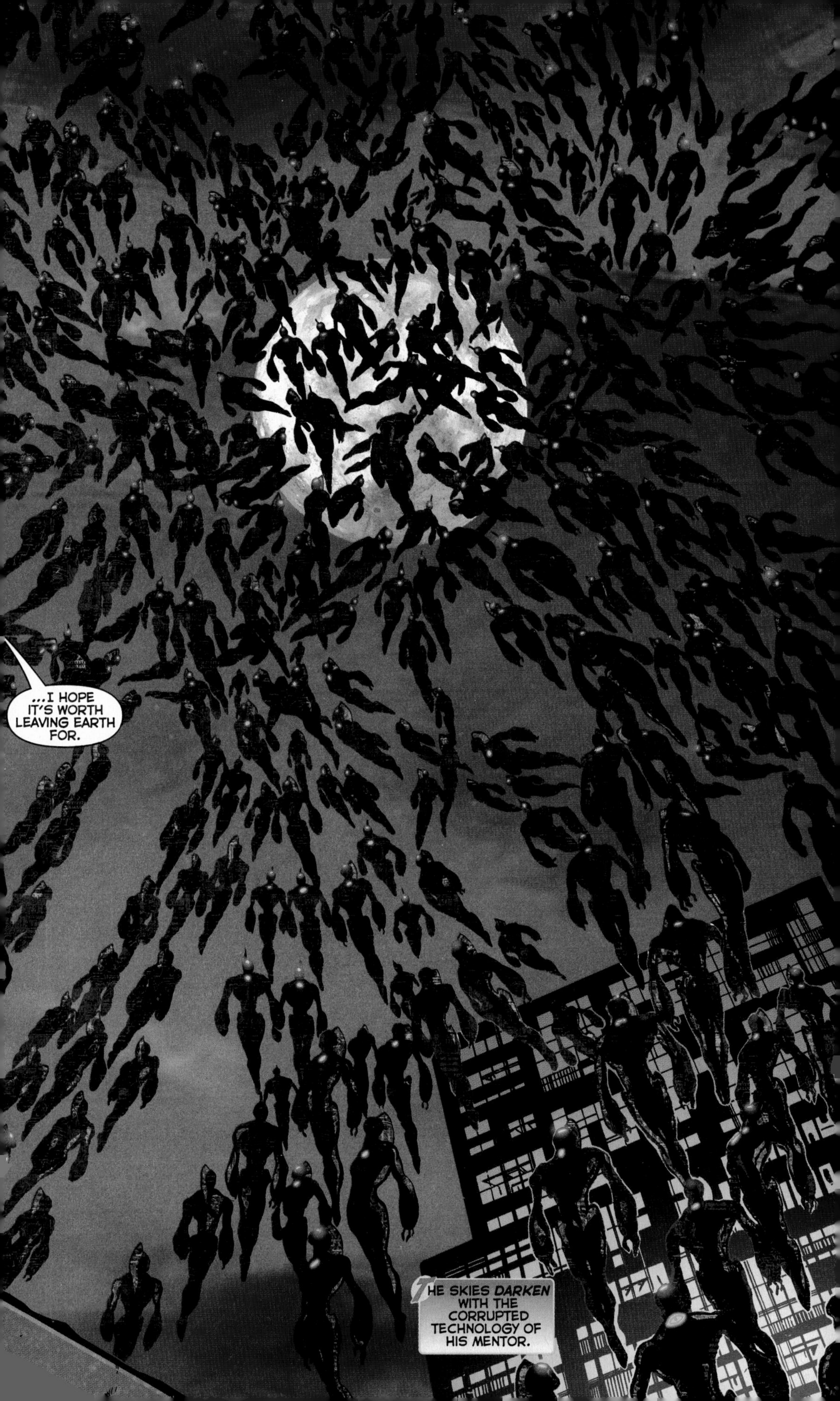
...I HOPE IT'S WORTH LEAVING EARTH FOR.
THE SKIES DARKEN WITH THE CORRUPTED TECHNOLOGY OF HIS MENTOR.

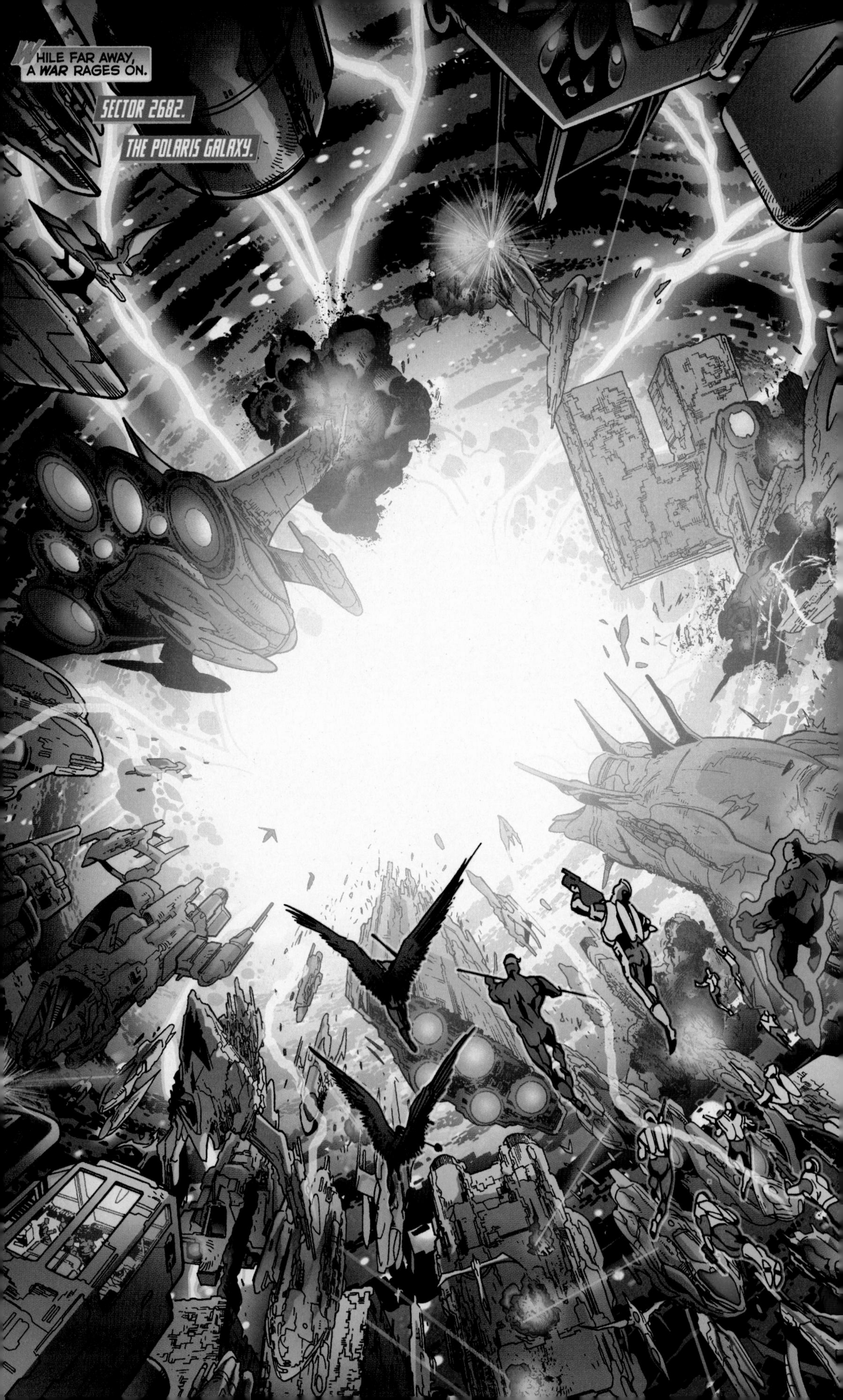
WHILE FAR AWAY, A WAR RAGES ON.
SECTOR 2682.
THE POLARIS GALAXY.

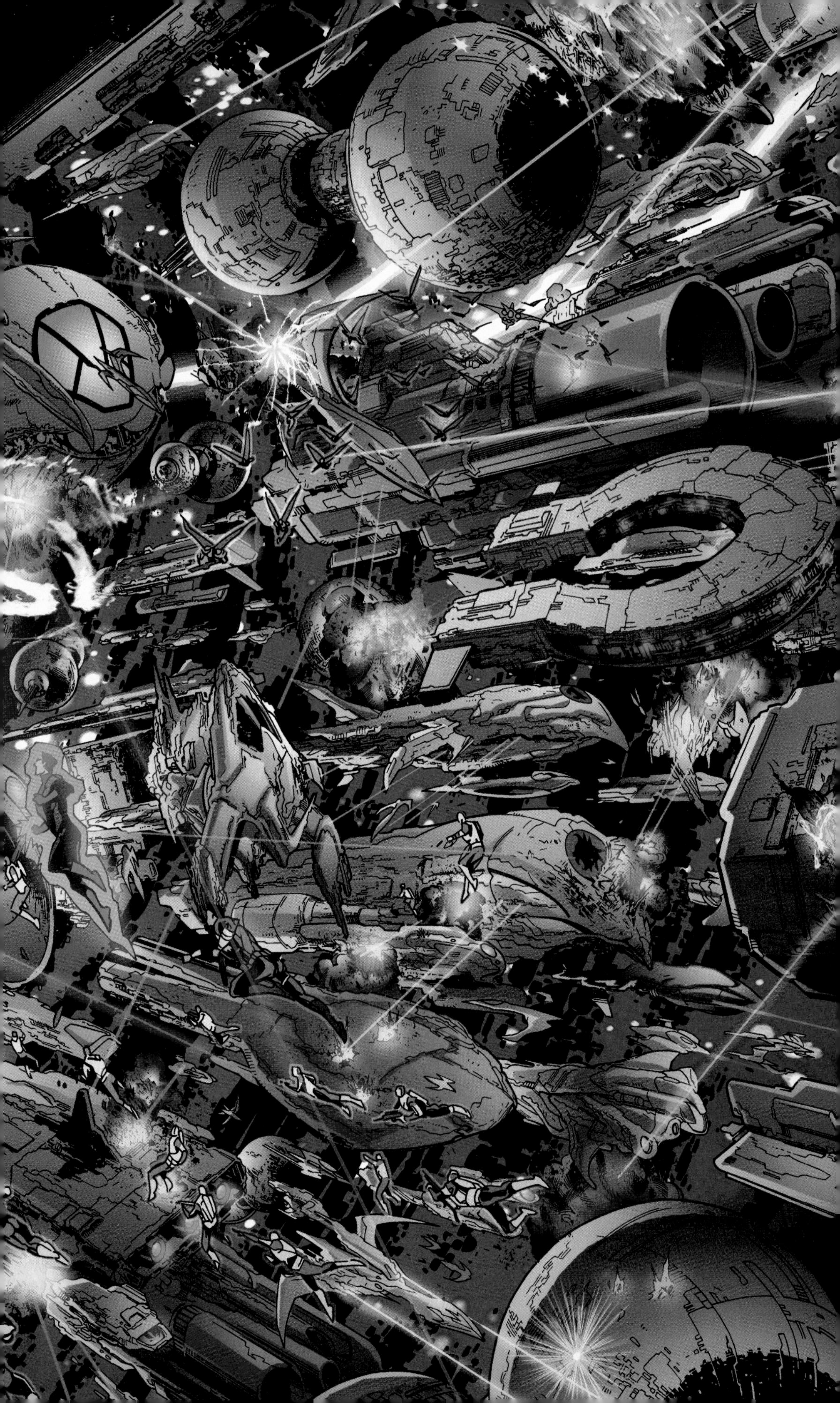

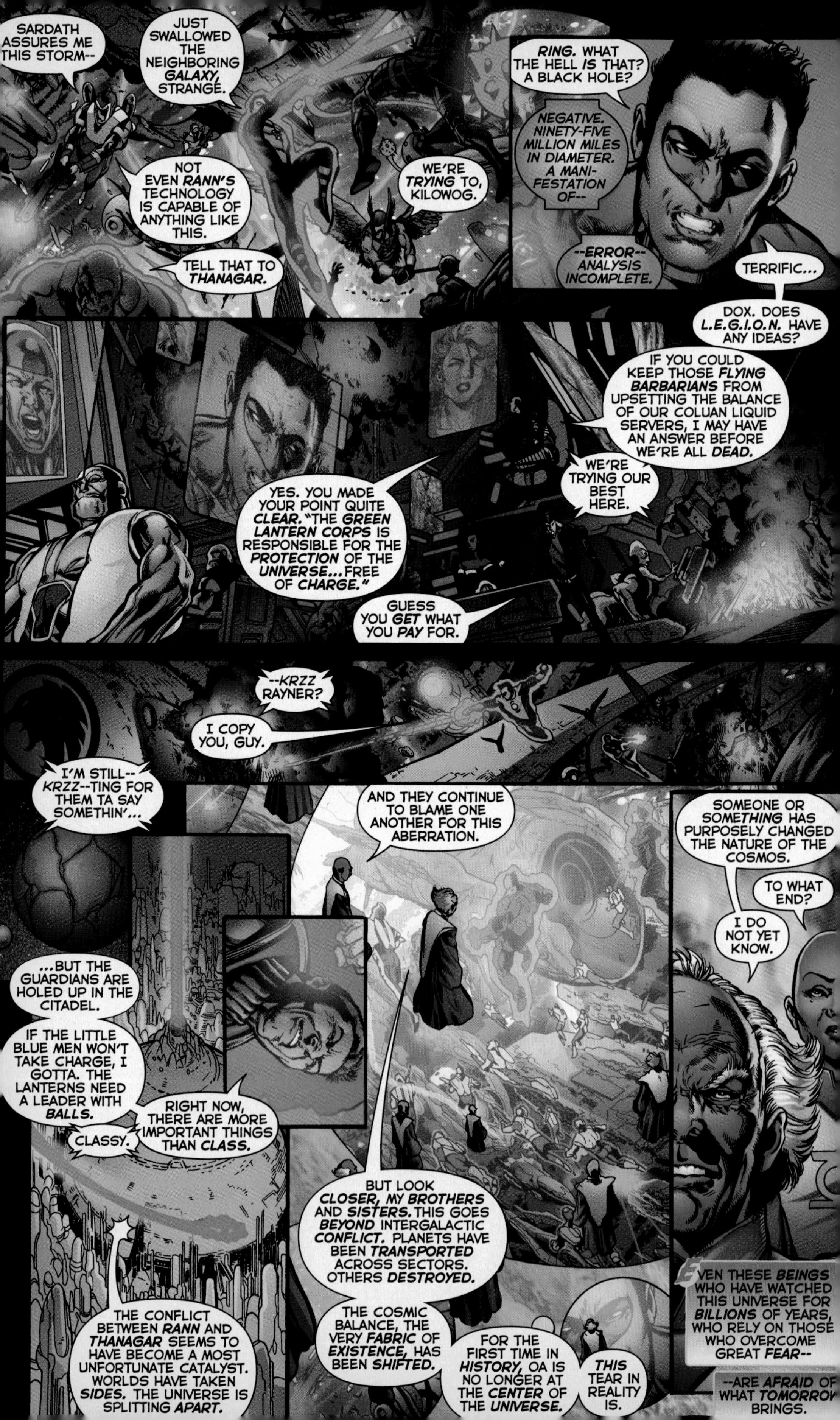
SARDATH ASSURES ME THIS STORM--
JUST SWALLOWED THE NEIGHBORING GALAXY, STRANGE.
NOT EVEN RANN'S TECHNOLOGY IS CAPABLE OF ANYTHING LIKE THIS.
WE'RE TRYING TO, KILOWOG.
TELL THAT TO THANAGAR.
RING. WHAT THE HELL IS THAT? A BLACK HOLE?
NEGATIVE. NINETY-FIVE MILLION MILES IN DIAMETER. A MANIFESTATION OF--
--ERROR-- ANALYSIS INCOMPLETE.
TERRIFIC...
DOX. DOES L.E.G.I.O.N. HAVE ANY IDEAS?
IF YOU COULD KEEP THOSE FLYING BARBARIANS FROM UPSETTING THE BALANCE OF OUR COLUAN LIQUID SERVERS, I MAY HAVE AN ANSWER BEFORE WE'RE ALL DEAD.
WE'RE TRYING OUR BEST HERE.
YES. YOU MADE YOUR POINT QUITE CLEAR. "THE GREEN LANTERN CORPS IS RESPONSIBLE FOR THE PROTECTION OF THE UNIVERSE...FREE OF CHARGE."
GUESS YOU GET WHAT YOU PAY FOR.
--KRZZ RAYNER?
I COPY YOU, GUY.
I'M STILL-- KRZZ--TING FOR THEM TA SAY SOMETHIN'...
...BUT THE GUARDIANS ARE HOLED UP IN THE CITADEL.
IF THE LITTLE BLUE MEN WON'T TAKE CHARGE, I GOTTA. THE LANTERNS NEED A LEADER WITH BALLS.
CLASSY.
RIGHT NOW, THERE ARE MORE IMPORTANT THINGS THAN CLASS.
AND THEY CONTINUE TO BLAME ONE ANOTHER FOR THIS ABERRATION.
SOMEONE OR SOMETHING HAS PURPOSELY CHANGED THE NATURE OF THE COSMOS.
TO WHAT END?
I DO NOT YET KNOW.
BUT LOOK CLOSER, MY BROTHERS AND SISTERS. THIS GOES BEYOND INTERGALACTIC CONFLICT. PLANETS HAVE BEEN TRANSPORTED ACROSS SECTORS. OTHERS DESTROYED.
THE CONFLICT BETWEEN RANN AND THANAGAR SEEMS TO HAVE BECOME A MOST UNFORTUNATE CATALYST. WORLDS HAVE TAKEN SIDES. THE UNIVERSE IS SPLITTING APART.
THE COSMIC BALANCE, THE VERY FABRIC OF EXISTENCE, HAS BEEN SHIFTED.
FOR THE FIRST TIME IN HISTORY, OA IS NO LONGER AT THE CENTER OF THE UNIVERSE.
THIS TEAR IN REALITY IS.
EVEN THESE BEINGS WHO HAVE WATCHED THIS UNIVERSE FOR BILLIONS OF YEARS, WHO RELY ON THOSE WHO OVERCOME GREAT FEAR--
--ARE AFRAID OF WHAT TOMORROW BRINGS.

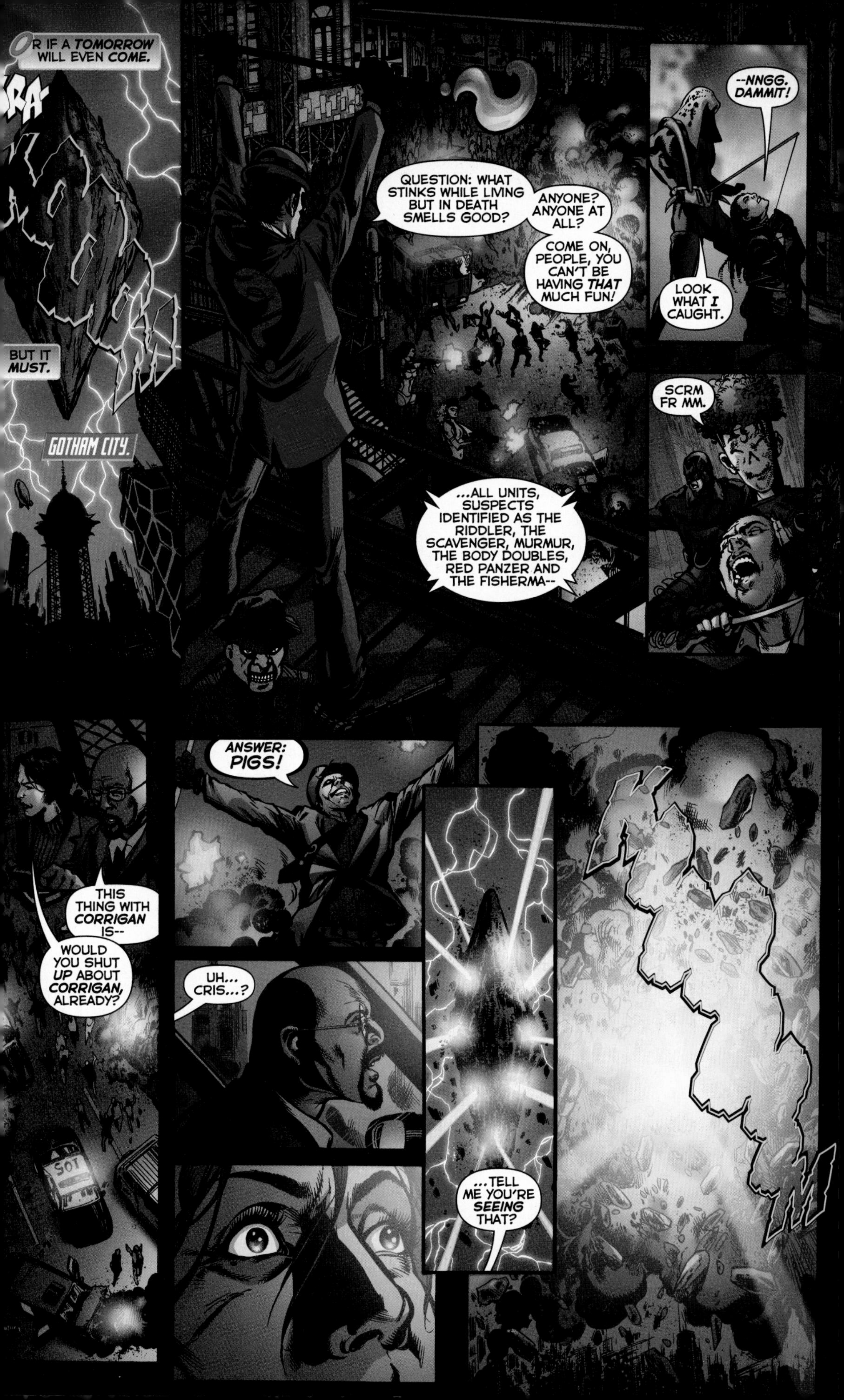
OR IF A TOMORROW WILL EVEN COME.
BUT IT MUST.
GOTHAM CITY.
QUESTION: WHAT STINKS WHILE LIVING BUT IN DEATH SMELLS GOOD?
ANYONE? ANYONE AT ALL?
COME ON, PEOPLE, YOU CAN'T BE HAVING THAT MUCH FUN!
...ALL UNITS, SUSPECTS IDENTIFIED AS THE RIDDLER, THE SCAVENGER, MURMUR, THE BODY DOUBLES, RED PANZER AND THE FISHERMA--
--NNGG. DAMMIT!
LOOK WHAT I CAUGHT.
SCRM FR MM.
THIS THING WITH CORRIGAN IS--
WOULD YOU SHUT UP ABOUT CORRIGAN, ALREADY?
ANSWER: PIGS!
UH... CRIS...?
...TELL ME YOU'RE SEEING THAT?

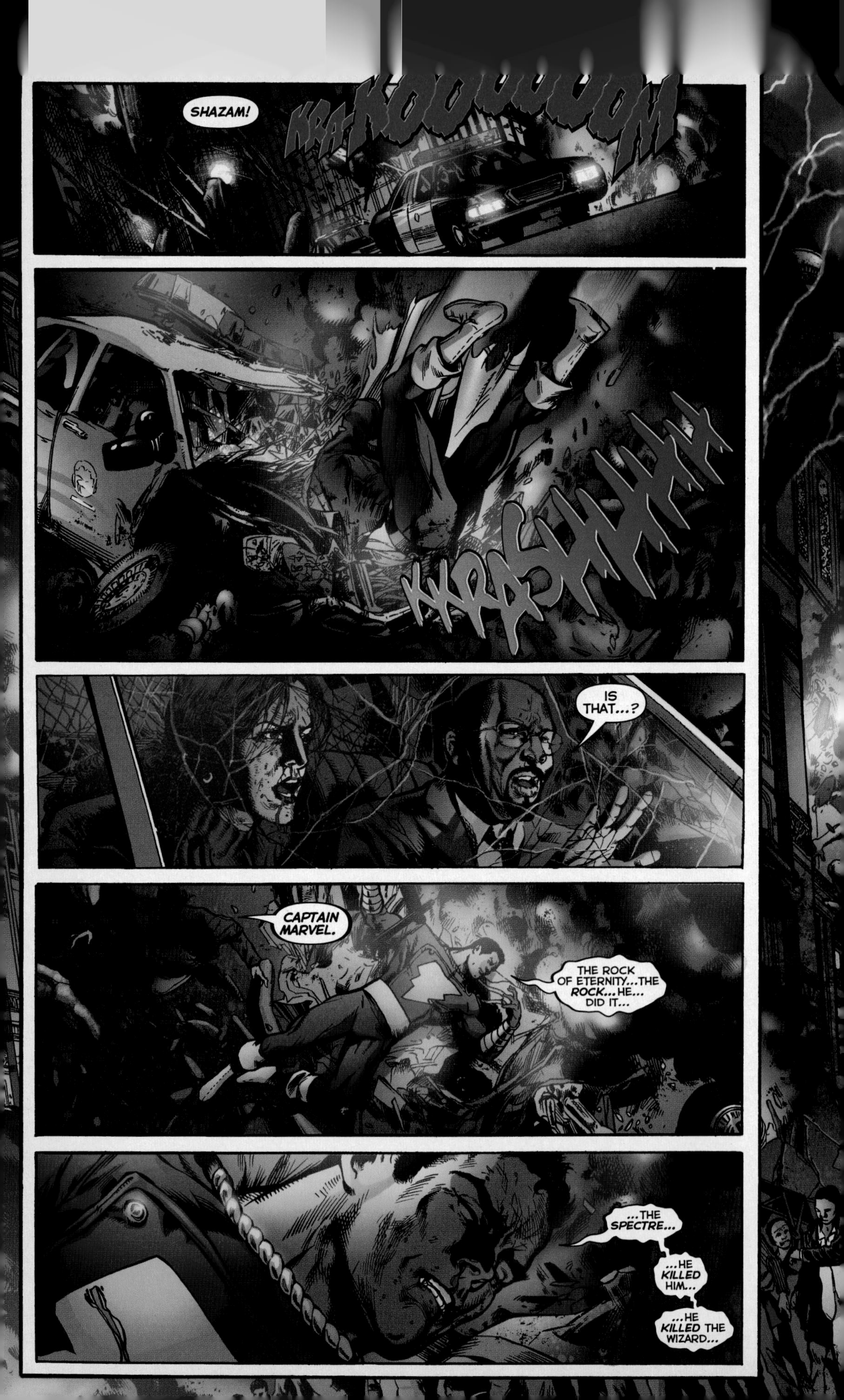
SHAZAM!
KRA-KOOOOOOM
KKRASHHHH
IS THAT...?
CAPTAIN MARVEL.
THE ROCK OF ETERNITY...THE ROCK...HE... DID IT...
...THE SPECTRE...
...HE KILLED HIM...
...HE KILLED THE WIZARD...

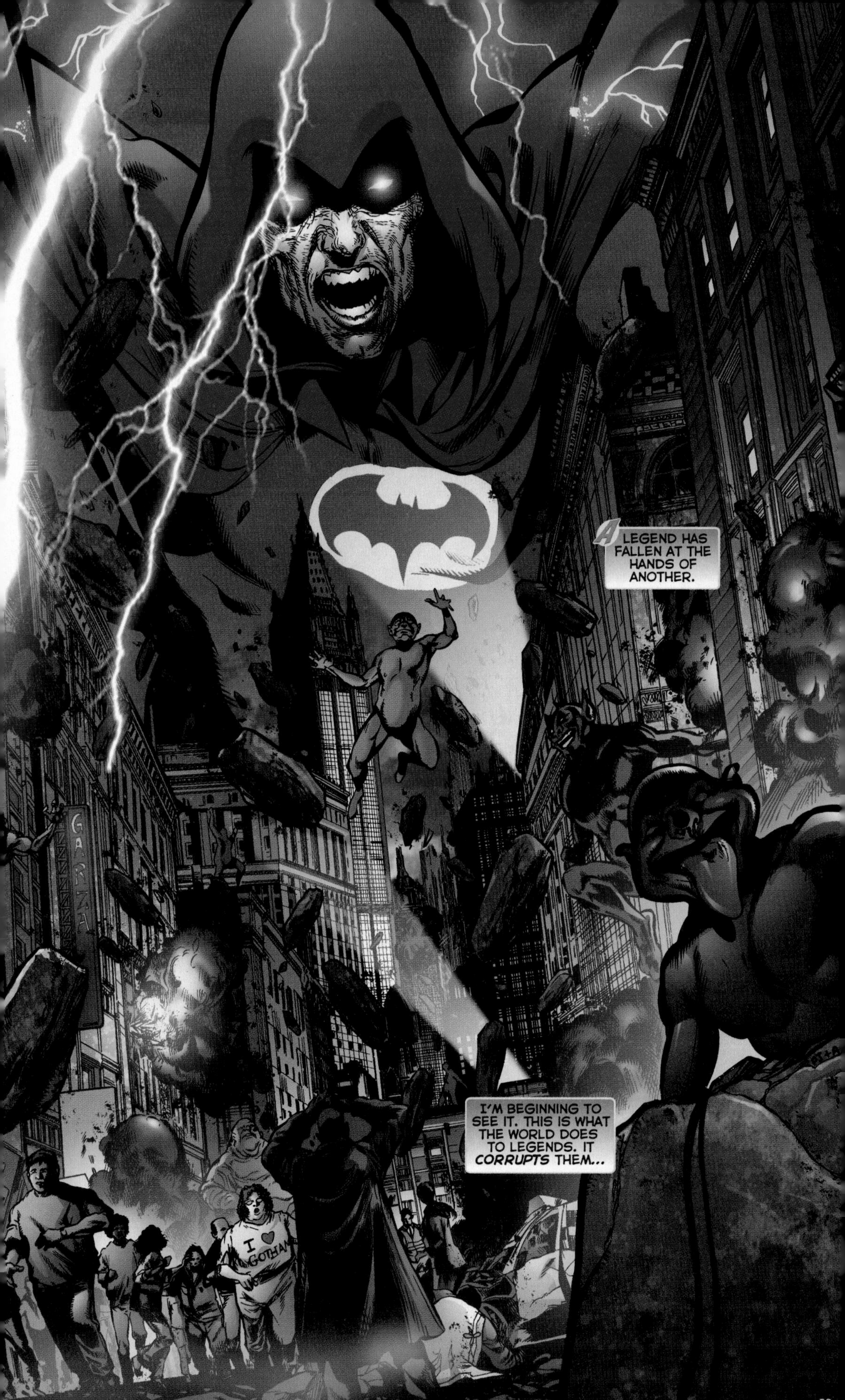
A LEGEND HAS FALLEN AT THE HANDS OF ANOTHER.
I'M BEGINNING TO SEE IT. THIS IS WHAT THE WORLD DOES TO LEGENDS. IT *CORRUPTS* THEM...

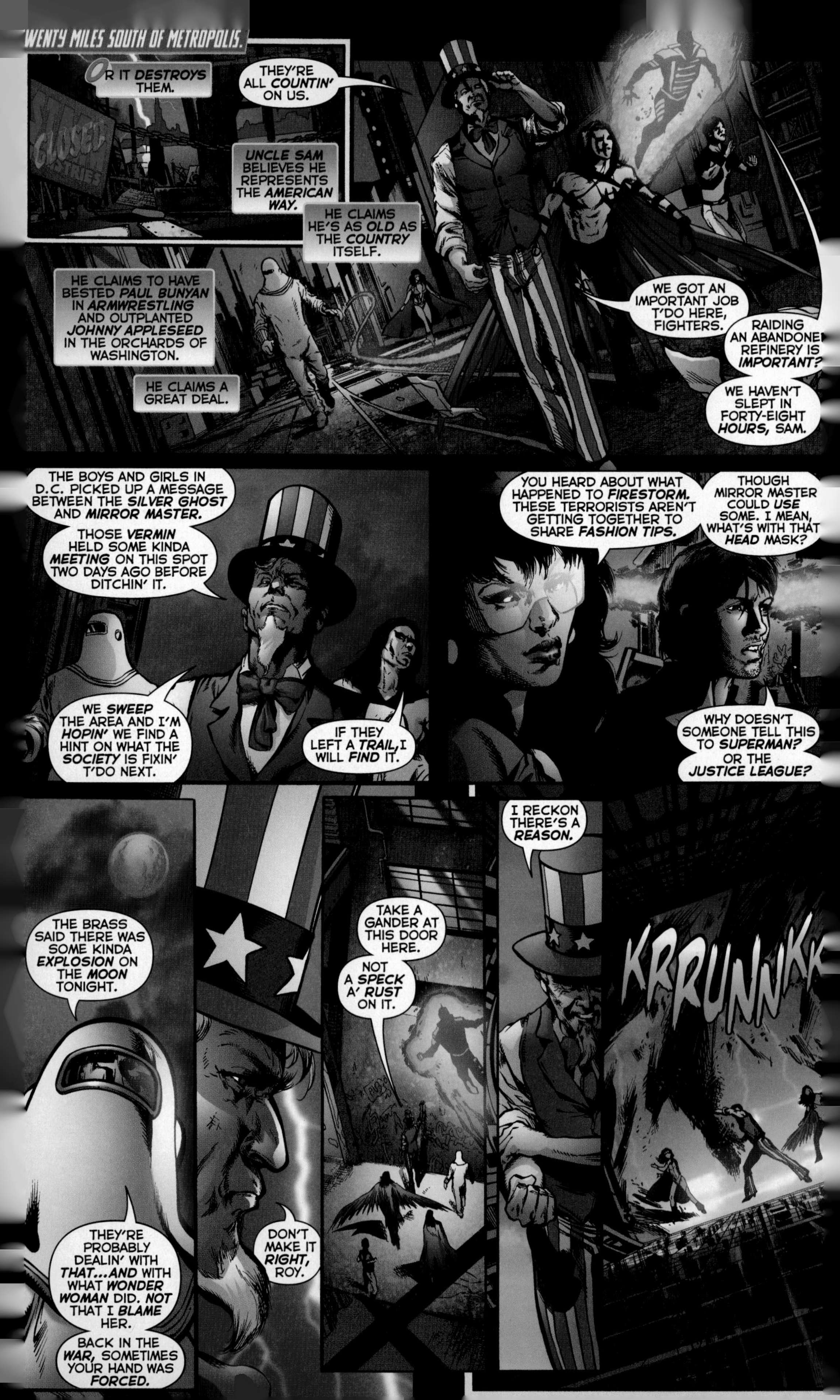

WENTY MILES SOUTH OF METROPOLIS.
OR IT DESTROYS THEM.
CLOSED
THEY'RE ALL COUNTIN' ON US.
UNCLE SAM BELIEVES HE REPRESENTS THE AMERICAN WAY.
HE CLAIMS HE'S AS OLD AS THE COUNTRY ITSELF.
HE CLAIMS TO HAVE BESTED PAUL BUNYAN IN ARMWRESTLING AND OUTPLANTED JOHNNY APPLESEED IN THE ORCHARDS OF WASHINGTON.
HE CLAIMS A GREAT DEAL.
WE GOT AN IMPORTANT JOB T'DO HERE, FIGHTERS.
RAIDING AN ABANDONE REFINERY IS IMPORTANT?
WE HAVEN'T SLEPT IN FORTY-EIGHT HOURS, SAM.
THE BOYS AND GIRLS IN D.C. PICKED UP A MESSAGE BETWEEN THE SILVER GHOST AND MIRROR MASTER.
THOSE VERMIN HELD SOME KINDA MEETING ON THIS SPOT TWO DAYS AGO BEFORE DITCHIN' IT.
WE SWEEP THE AREA AND I'M HOPIN' WE FIND A HINT ON WHAT THE SOCIETY IS FIXIN' T'DO NEXT.
IF THEY LEFT A TRAIL, I WILL FIND IT.
YOU HEARD ABOUT WHAT HAPPENED TO FIRESTORM. THESE TERRORISTS AREN'T GETTING TOGETHER TO SHARE FASHION TIPS.
THOUGH MIRROR MASTER COULD USE SOME. I MEAN, WHAT'S WITH THAT HEAD MASK?
WHY DOESN'T SOMEONE TELL THIS TO SUPERMAN? OR THE JUSTICE LEAGUE?
THE BRASS SAID THERE WAS SOME KINDA EXPLOSION ON THE MOON TONIGHT.
THEY'RE PROBABLY DEALIN' WITH THAT...AND WITH WHAT WONDER WOMAN DID. NOT THAT I BLAME HER.
BACK IN THE WAR, SOMETIMES YOUR HAND WAS FORCED.
DON'T MAKE IT RIGHT, ROY.
TAKE A GANDER AT THIS DOOR HERE.
NOT A SPECK A' RUST ON IT.
I RECKON THERE'S A REASON.
KRRUNNKK

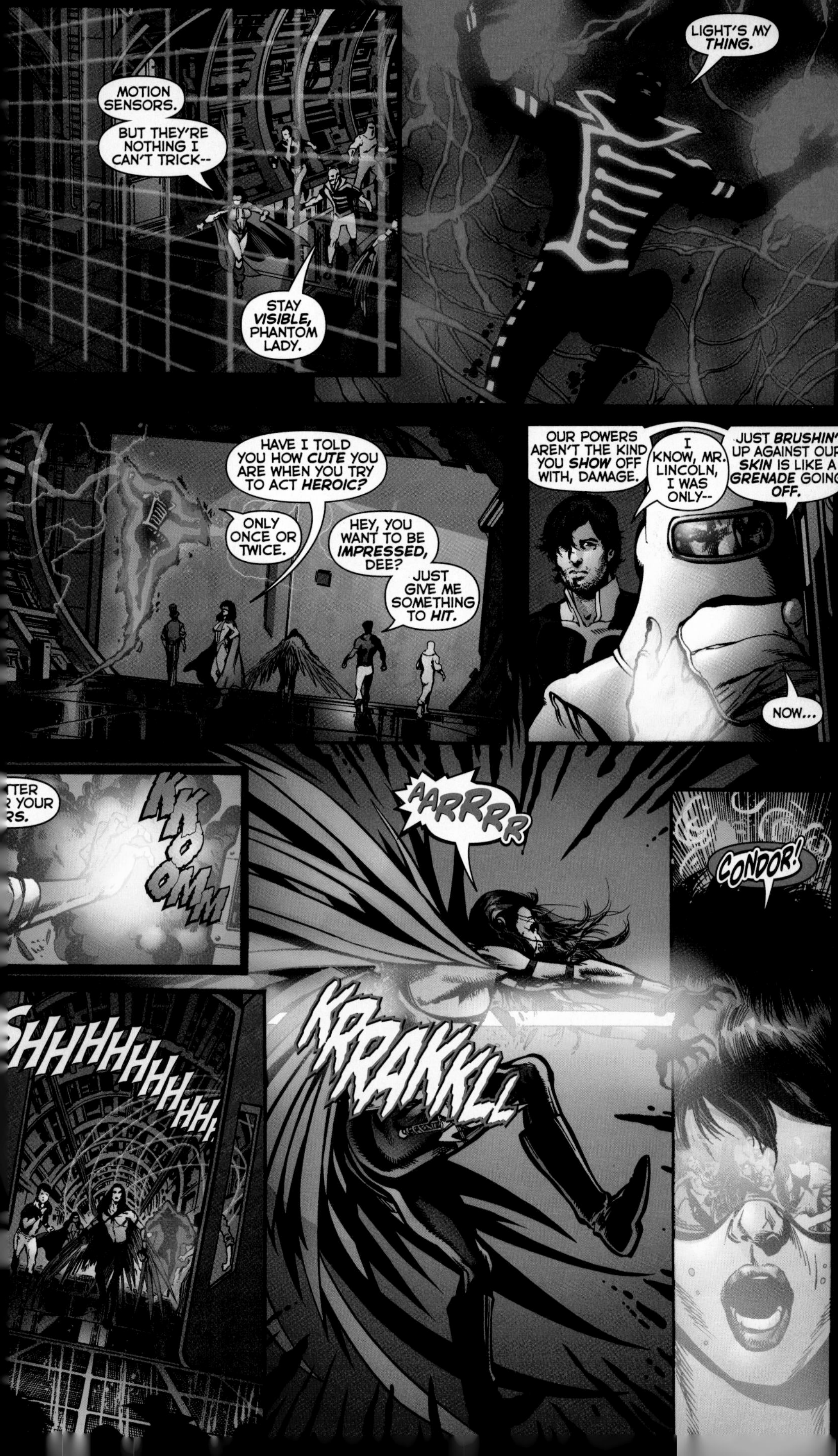
MOTION SENSORS.
BUT THEY'RE NOTHING I CAN'T TRICK--
STAY VISIBLE, PHANTOM LADY.
LIGHT'S MY THING.
HAVE I TOLD YOU HOW CUTE YOU ARE WHEN YOU TRY TO ACT HEROIC?
ONLY ONCE OR TWICE.
HEY, YOU WANT TO BE IMPRESSED, DEE?
JUST GIVE ME SOMETHING TO HIT.
OUR POWERS AREN'T THE KIND YOU SHOW OFF WITH, DAMAGE.
I KNOW, MR. LINCOLN, I WAS ONLY--
JUST BRUSHIN' UP AGAINST OUR SKIN IS LIKE A GRENADE GOING OFF.
NOW...
KKKOOMM
AARRRRR
CONDOR!
SHHHHHHHHHH
KRRAKKLL

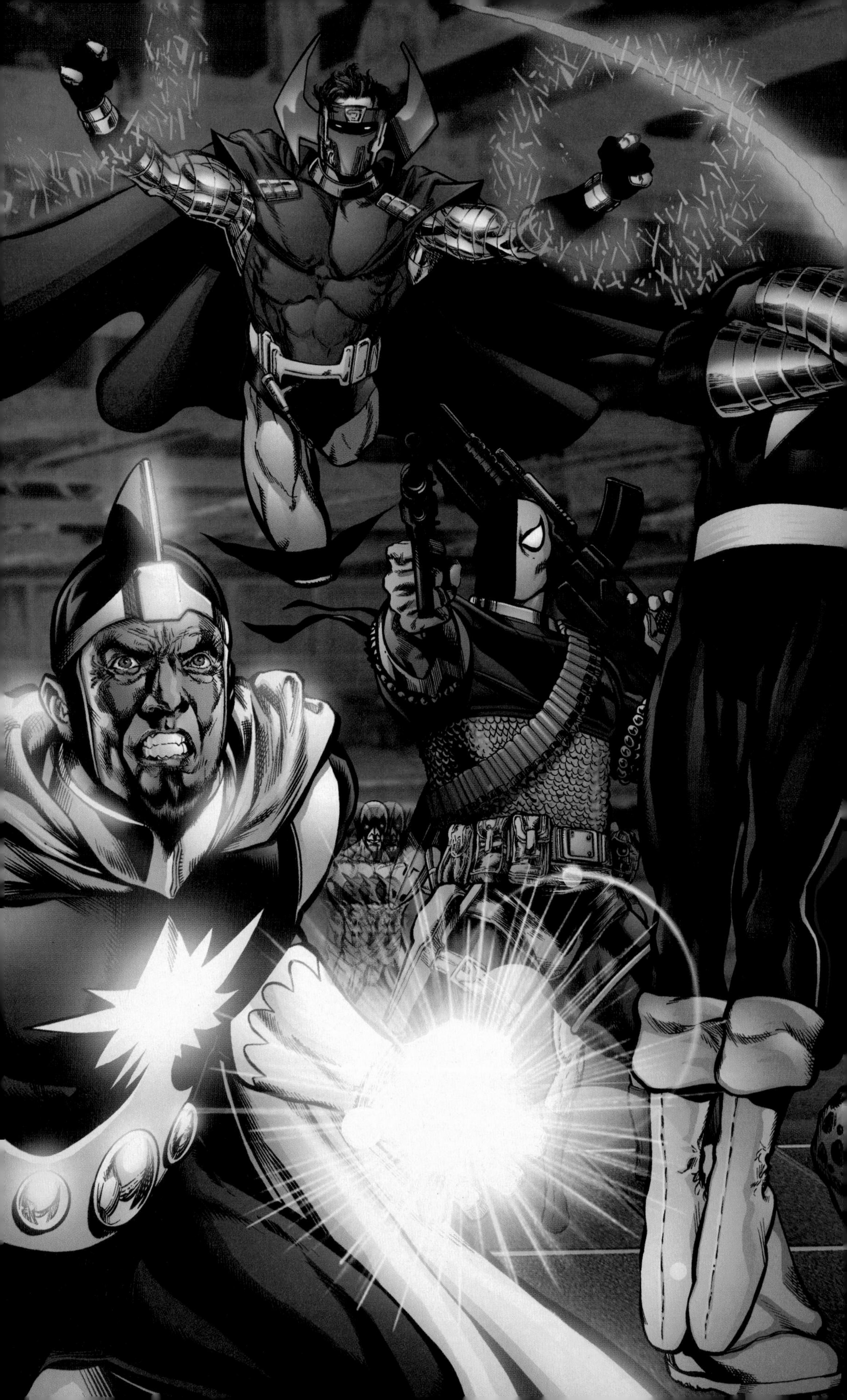

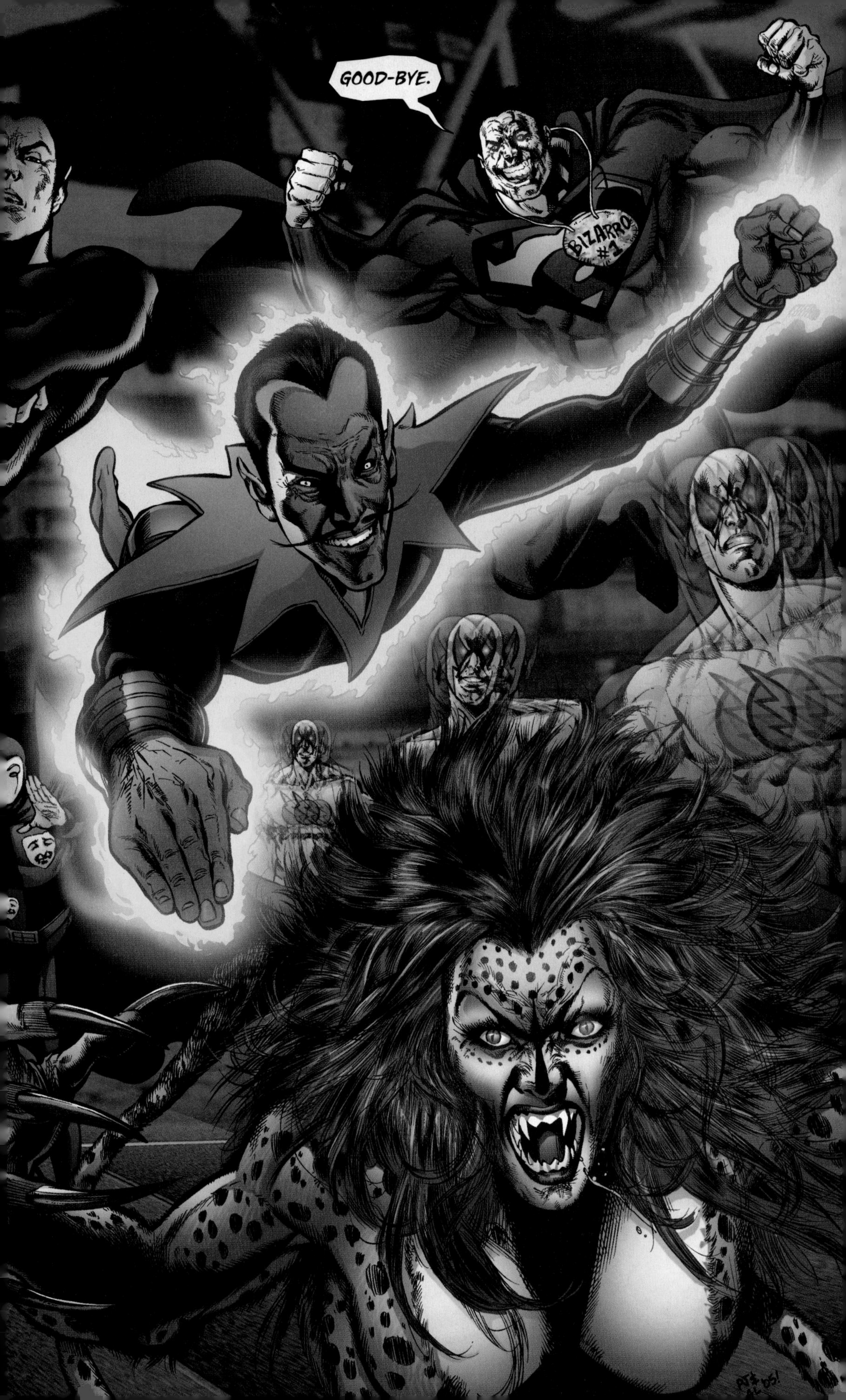
GOOD-BYE.
BIZARRO #1

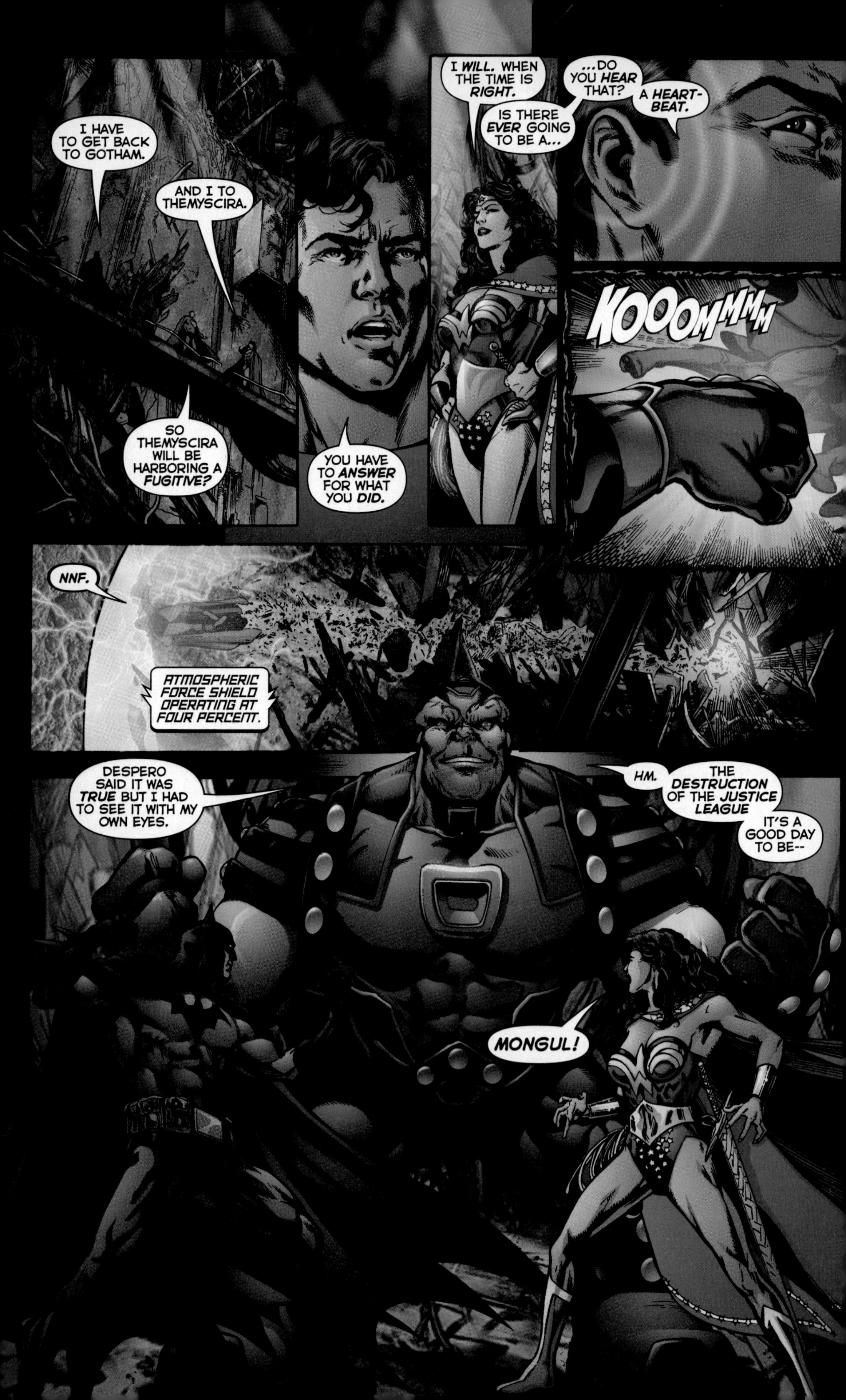
I HAVE TO GET BACK TO GOTHAM.
AND I TO THEMYSCIRA.
SO THEMYSCIRA WILL BE HARBORING A FUGITIVE?
YOU HAVE TO ANSWER FOR WHAT YOU DID.
I WILL. WHEN THE TIME IS RIGHT.
IS THERE EVER GOING TO BE A...
...DO YOU HEAR THAT?
A HEART-BEAT.
KOOOMMMM
NNF.
ATMOSPHERIC FORCE SHIELD OPERATING AT FOUR PERCENT.
DESPERO SAID IT WAS TRUE BUT I HAD TO SEE IT WITH MY OWN EYES.
HM.
THE DESTRUCTION OF THE JUSTICE LEAGUE
IT'S A GOOD DAY TO BE--
MONGUL!

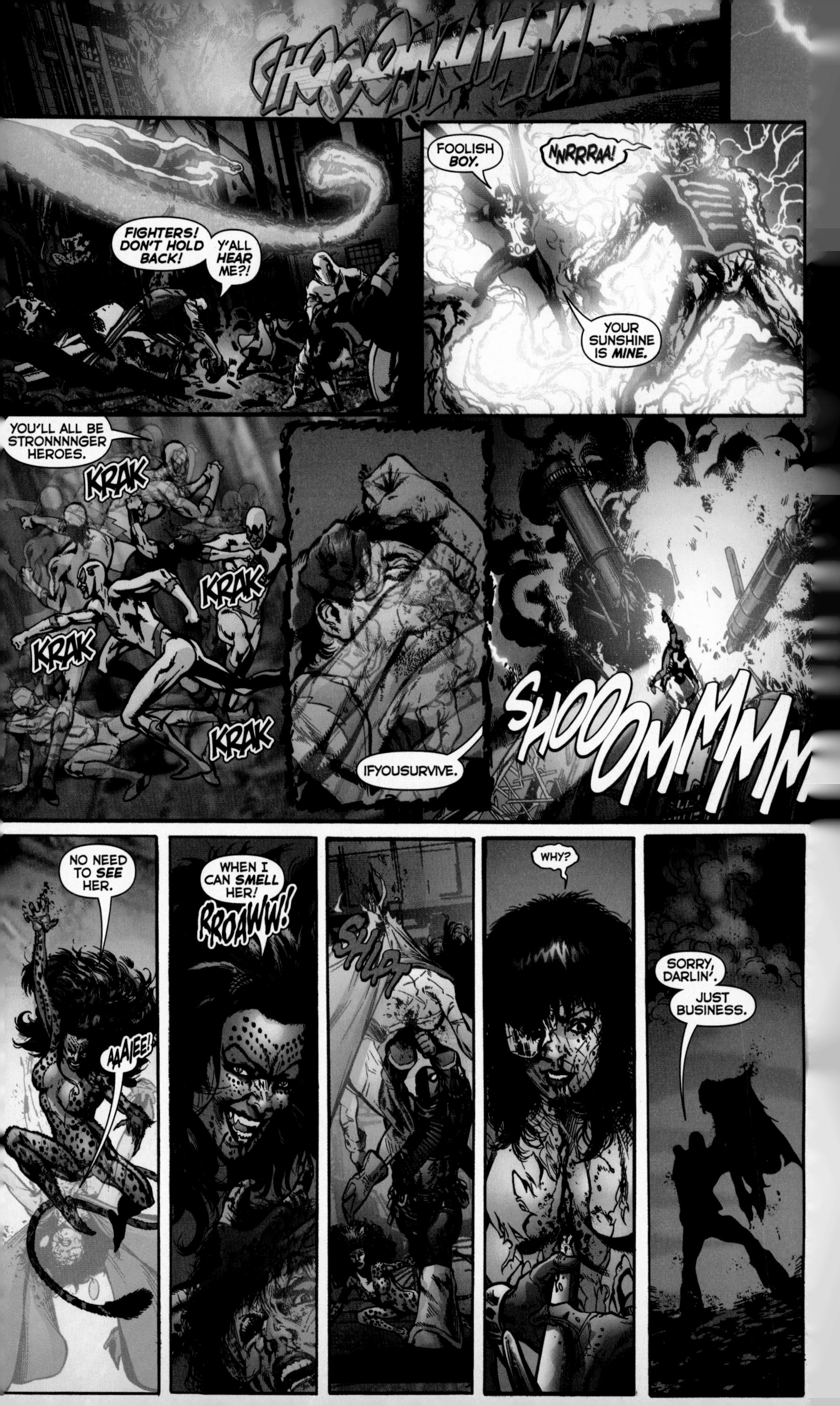
SHOOOMMMM
FIGHTERS! DON'T HOLD BACK!
Y'ALL HEAR ME?!
FOOLISH BOY.
NNRRRAA!
YOUR SUNSHINE IS MINE.
YOU'LL ALL BE STRONNNNGER HEROES.
KRAK
KRAK
KRAK
KRAK
IFYOUSURVIVE.
SHOOOMMMM
NO NEED TO SEE HER.
AAAIEE!
WHEN I CAN SMELL HER!
RROAWW!
WHY?
SORRY, DARLIN'.
JUST BUSINESS.

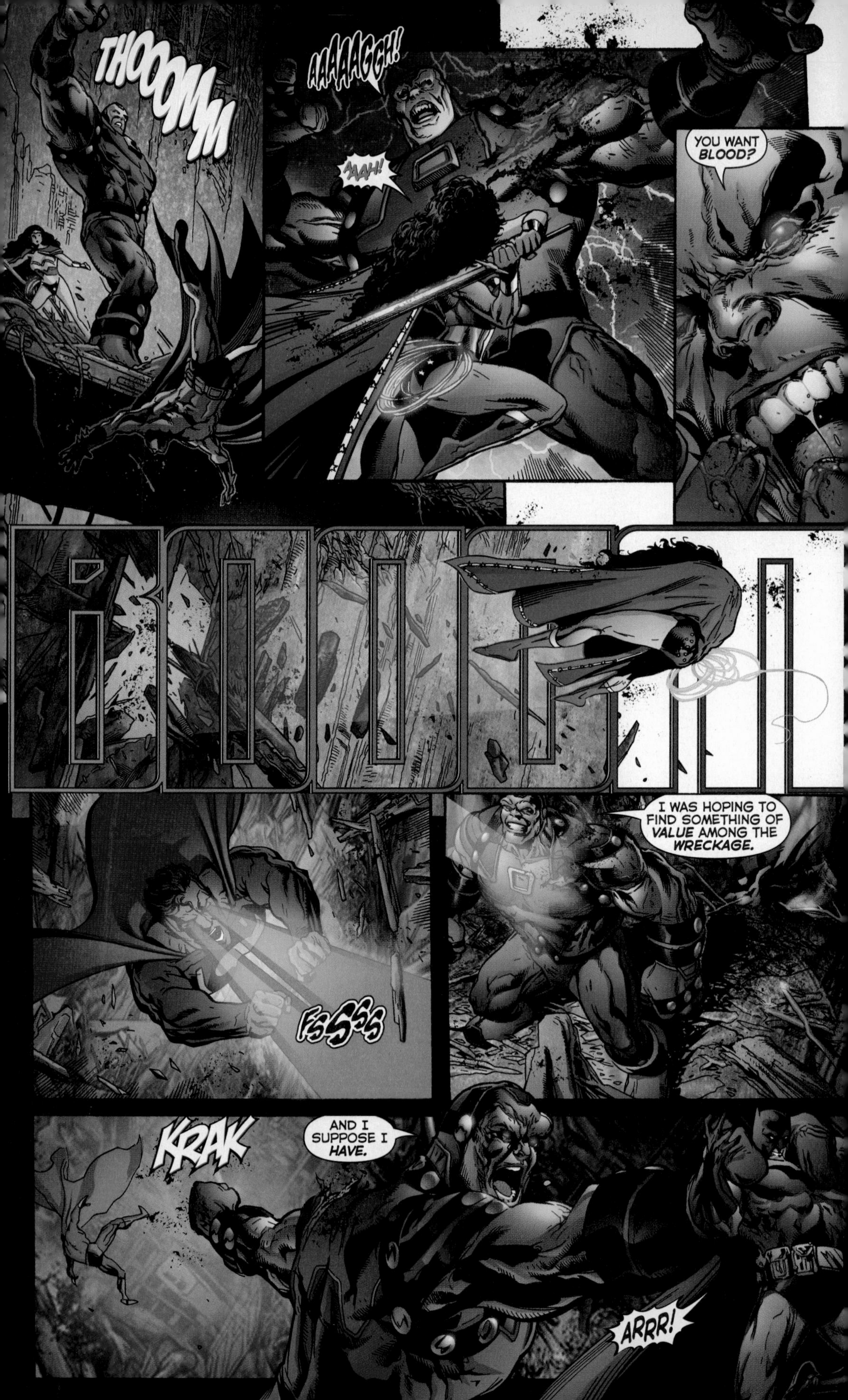
THOOOMMM
AAAAAGGH!
AAAH!
YOU WANT BLOOD?
FSSSS
I WAS HOPING TO FIND SOMETHING OF VALUE AMONG THE WRECKAGE.
KRAK
AND I SUPPOSE I HAVE.
ARRR!

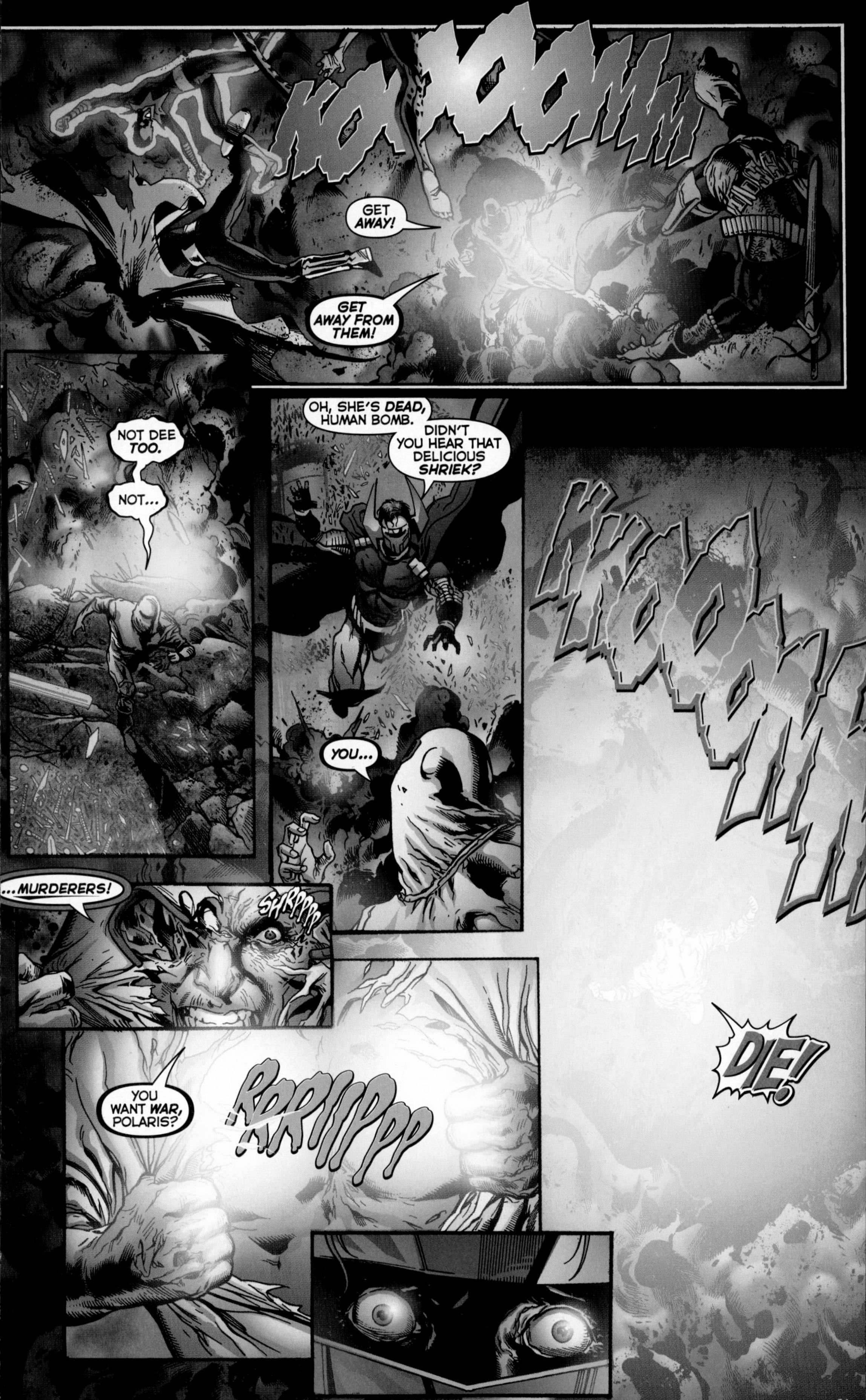
KA-KOOMM
GET AWAY!
GET AWAY FROM THEM!
NOT DEE TOO.
NOT...
OH, SHE'S DEAD, HUMAN BOMB.
DIDN'T YOU HEAR THAT DELICIOUS SHRIEK?
YOU...
...MURDERERS!
SHRPPPP
YOU WANT WAR, POLARIS?
RRRIIPPPP
DIE!

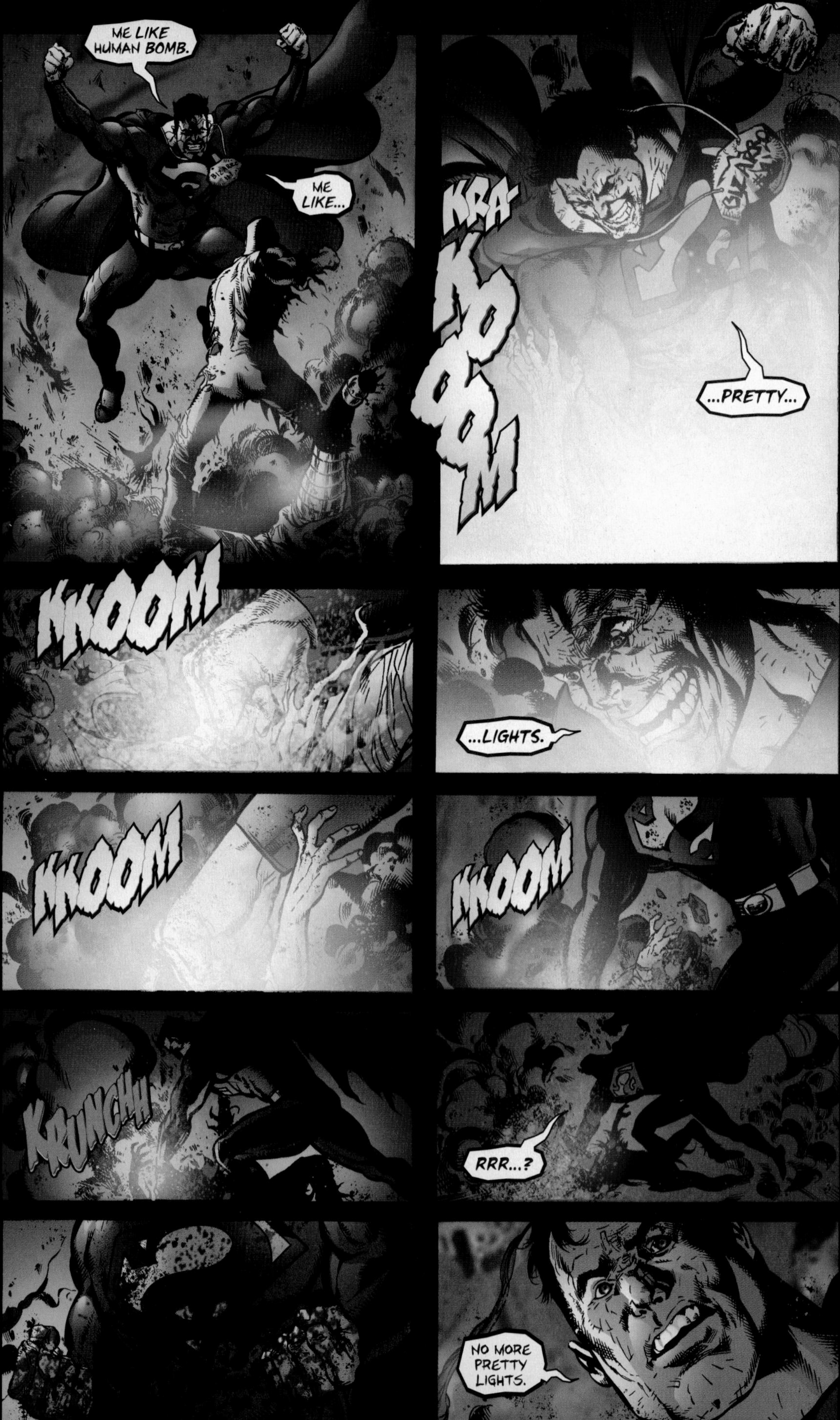
ME LIKE HUMAN BOMB.
ME LIKE...
KRA-KOOOOM
...PRETTY...
KKOOM
...LIGHTS.
KKOOM
KKOOM
KRUNCHH
RRR...?
NO MORE PRETTY LIGHTS.

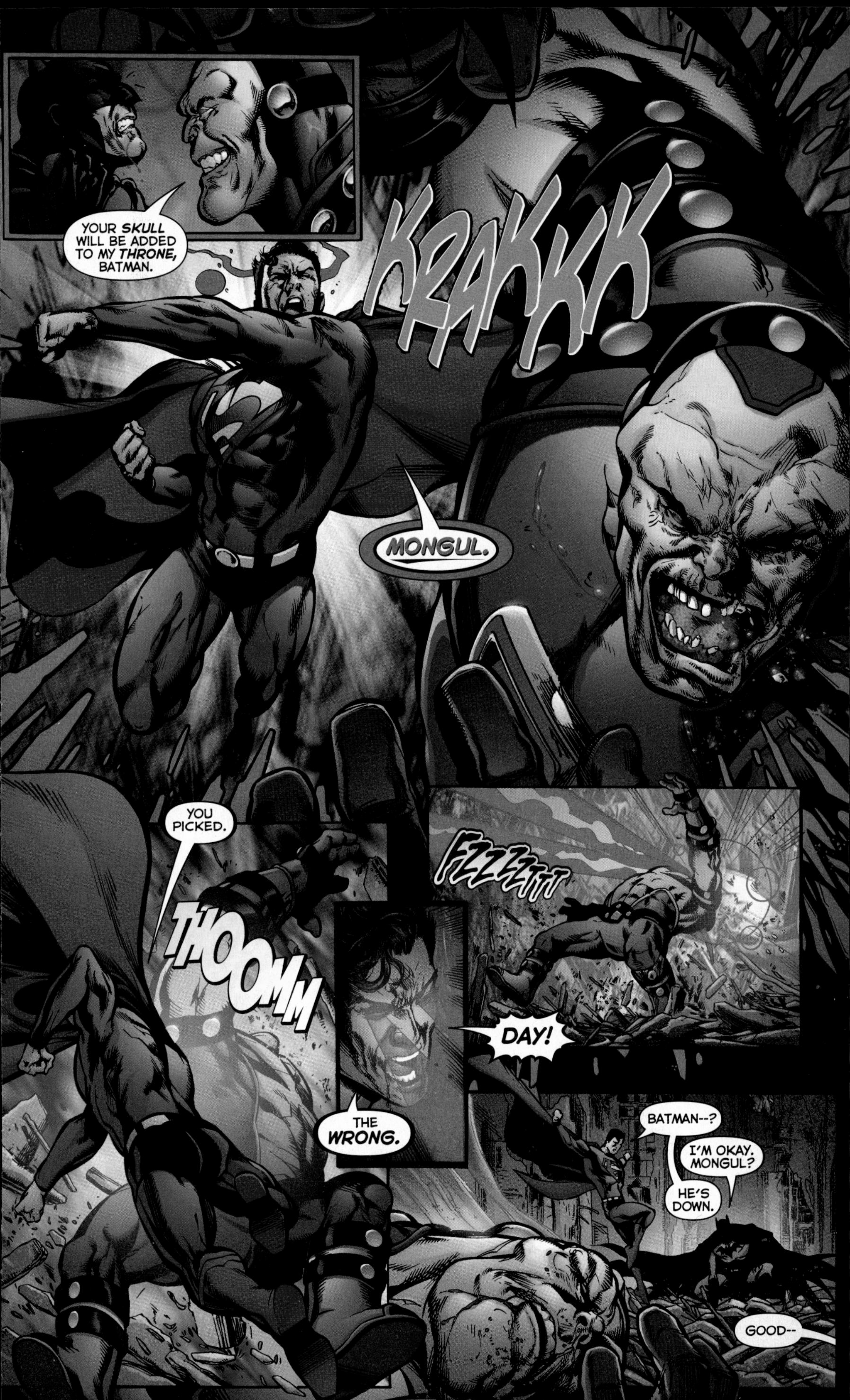
YOUR SKULL WILL BE ADDED TO MY THRONE, BATMAN.
KRAKKK
MONGUL.
YOU PICKED.
THOOMM
THE WRONG.
FZZZZTTT
DAY!
BATMAN--?
I'M OKAY. MONGUL?
HE'S DOWN.
GOOD--

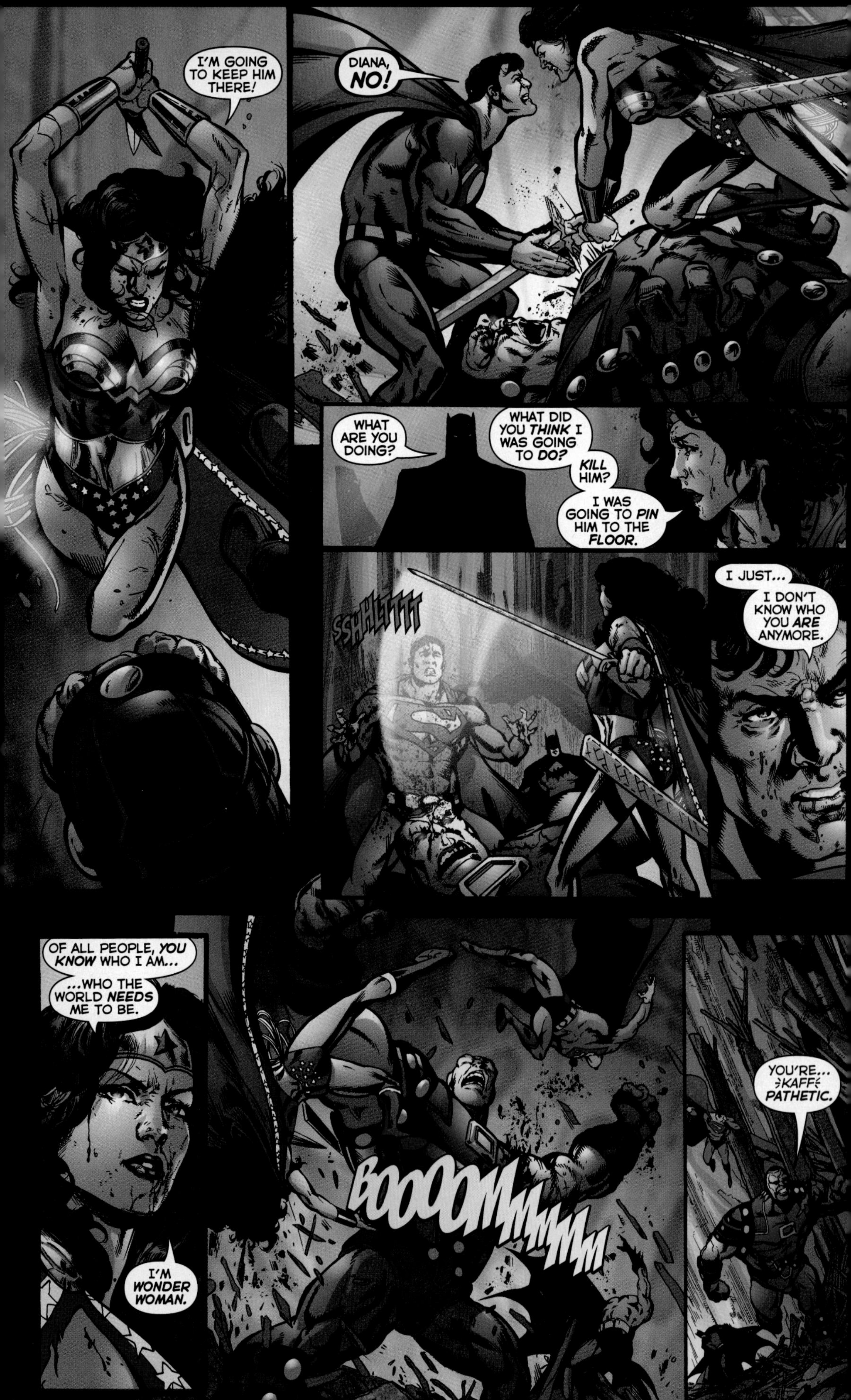

I'M GOING TO KEEP HIM THERE!
DIANA, NO!
WHAT ARE YOU DOING?
WHAT DID YOU THINK I WAS GOING TO DO?
KILL HIM?
I WAS GOING TO PIN HIM TO THE FLOOR.
SSHLTTT
I JUST...
I DON'T KNOW WHO YOU ARE ANYMORE.
OF ALL PEOPLE, YOU KNOW WHO I AM...
...WHO THE WORLD NEEDS ME TO BE.
I'M WONDER WOMAN.
BOOOOMMMMMM
YOU'RE... KAFF PATHETIC.

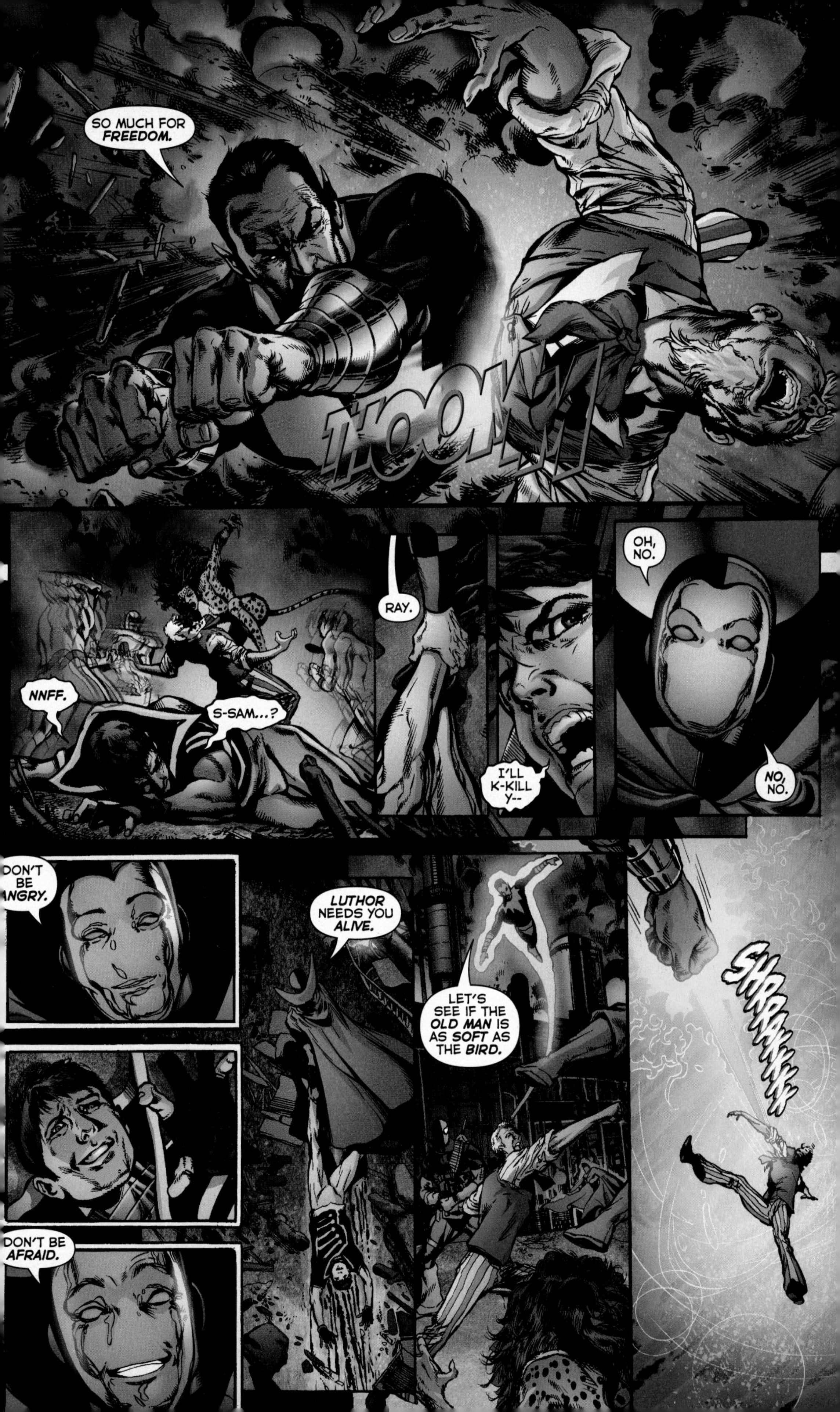
SO MUCH FOR FREEDOM.
THOOM
NNFF.
S-SAM...?
RAY.
I'LL K-KILL Y--
OH, NO.
NO, NO.
DON'T BE ANGRY.
DON'T BE AFRAID.
LUTHOR NEEDS YOU ALIVE.
LET'S SEE IF THE OLD MAN IS AS SOFT AS THE BIRD.
SHRAKKKK

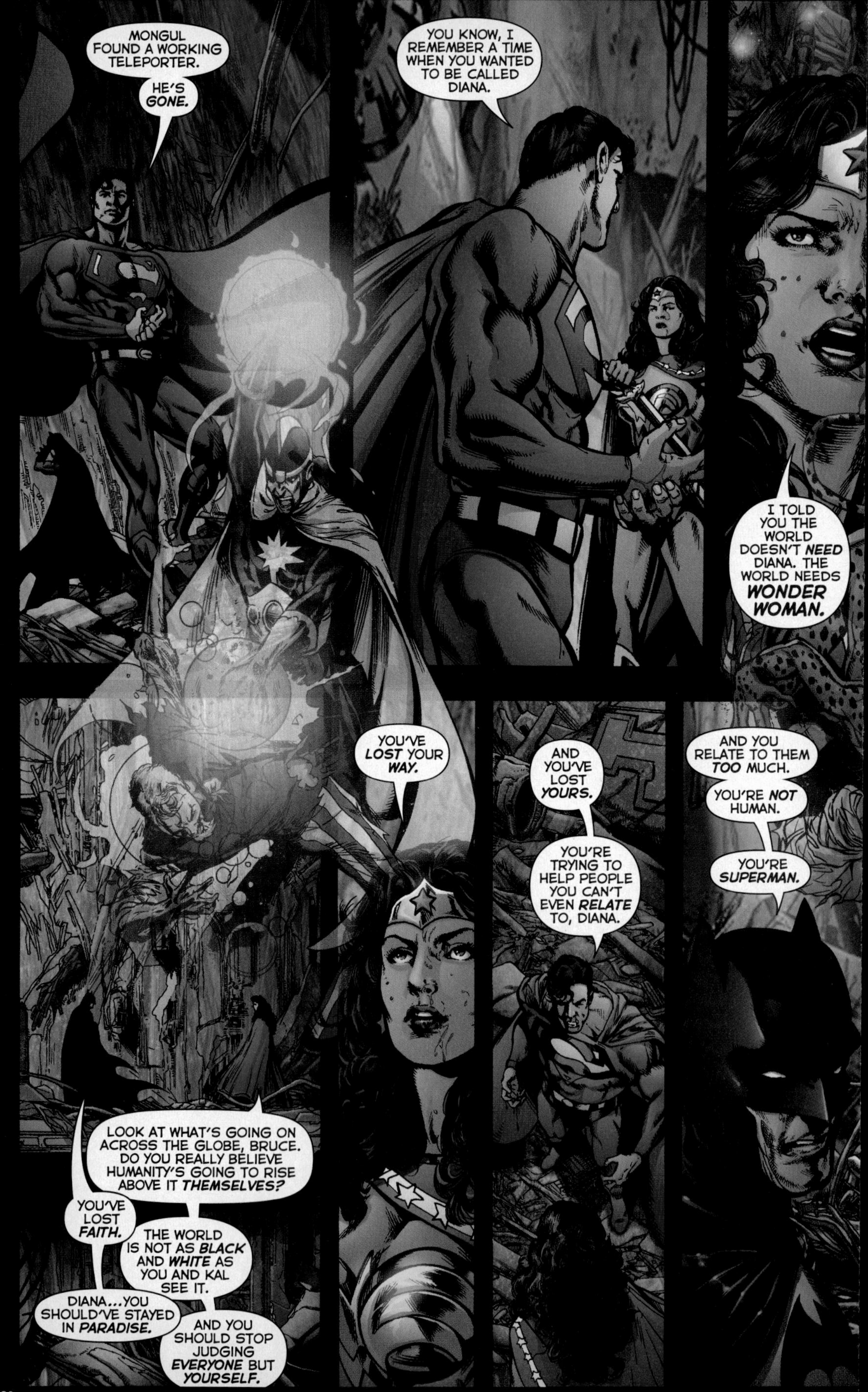

MONGUL FOUND A WORKING TELEPORTER.
HE'S GONE.
YOU KNOW, I REMEMBER A TIME WHEN YOU WANTED TO BE CALLED DIANA.
I TOLD YOU THE WORLD DOESN'T NEED DIANA. THE WORLD NEEDS WONDER WOMAN.
YOU'VE LOST YOUR WAY.
AND YOU'VE LOST YOURS.
YOU'RE TRYING TO HELP PEOPLE YOU CAN'T EVEN RELATE TO, DIANA.
AND YOU RELATE TO THEM TOO MUCH.
YOU'RE NOT HUMAN.
YOU'RE SUPERMAN.
LOOK AT WHAT'S GOING ON ACROSS THE GLOBE, BRUCE. DO YOU REALLY BELIEVE HUMANITY'S GOING TO RISE ABOVE IT THEMSELVES?
YOU'VE LOST FAITH.
THE WORLD IS NOT AS BLACK AND WHITE AS YOU AND KAL SEE IT.
DIANA...YOU SHOULD'VE STAYED IN PARADISE.
AND YOU SHOULD STOP JUDGING EVERYONE BUT YOURSELF.

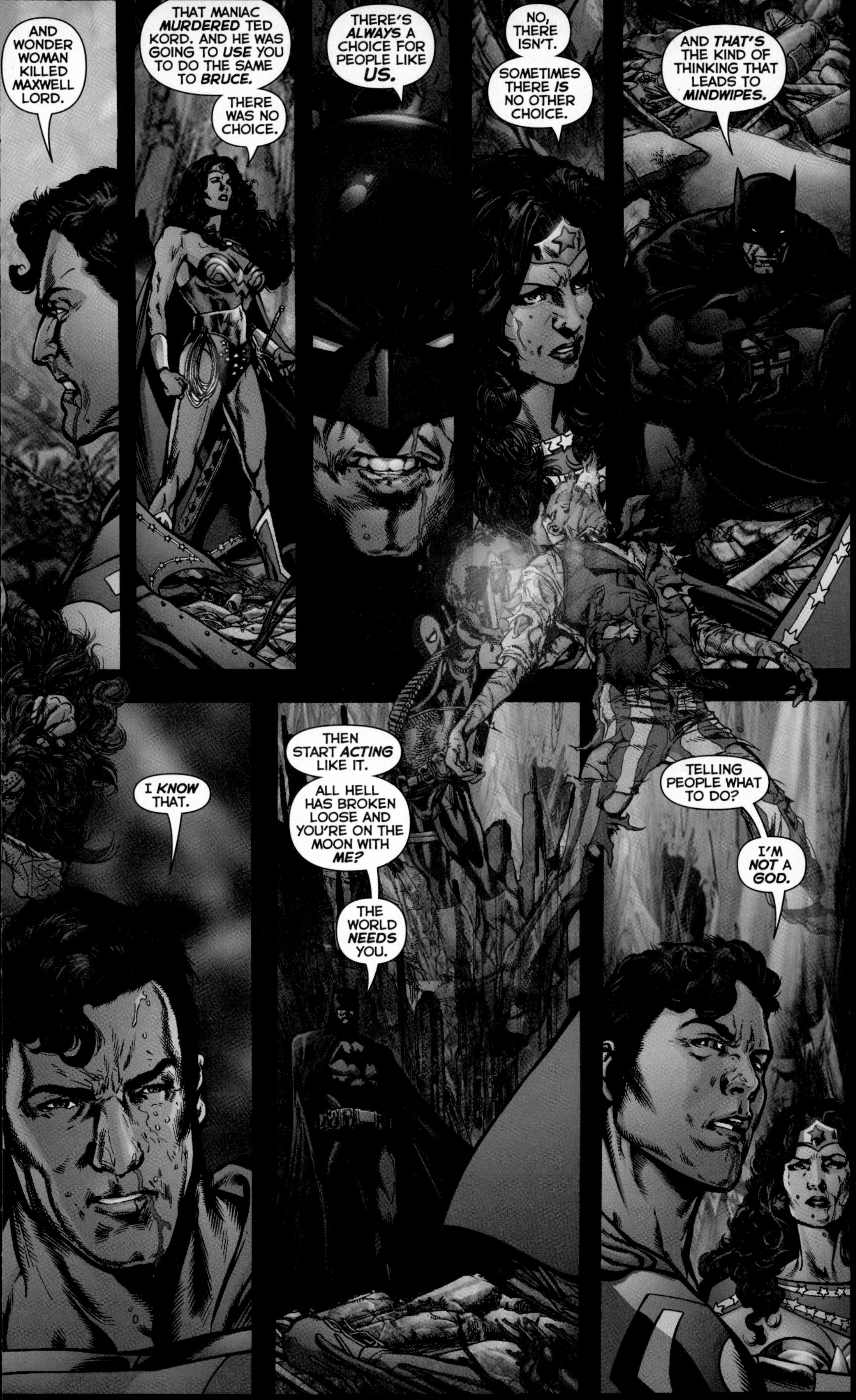

AND WONDER WOMAN KILLED MAXWELL LORD.
THAT MANIAC MURDERED TED KORD. AND HE WAS GOING TO USE YOU TO DO THE SAME TO BRUCE.
THERE WAS NO CHOICE.
THERE'S ALWAYS A CHOICE FOR PEOPLE LIKE US.
NO, THERE ISN'T.
SOMETIMES THERE IS NO OTHER CHOICE.
AND THAT'S THE KIND OF THINKING THAT LEADS TO MINDWIPES.
I KNOW THAT.
THEN START ACTING LIKE IT.
ALL HELL HAS BROKEN LOOSE AND YOU'RE ON THE MOON WITH ME?
THE WORLD NEEDS YOU.
TELLING PEOPLE WHAT TO DO?
I'M NOT A GOD.

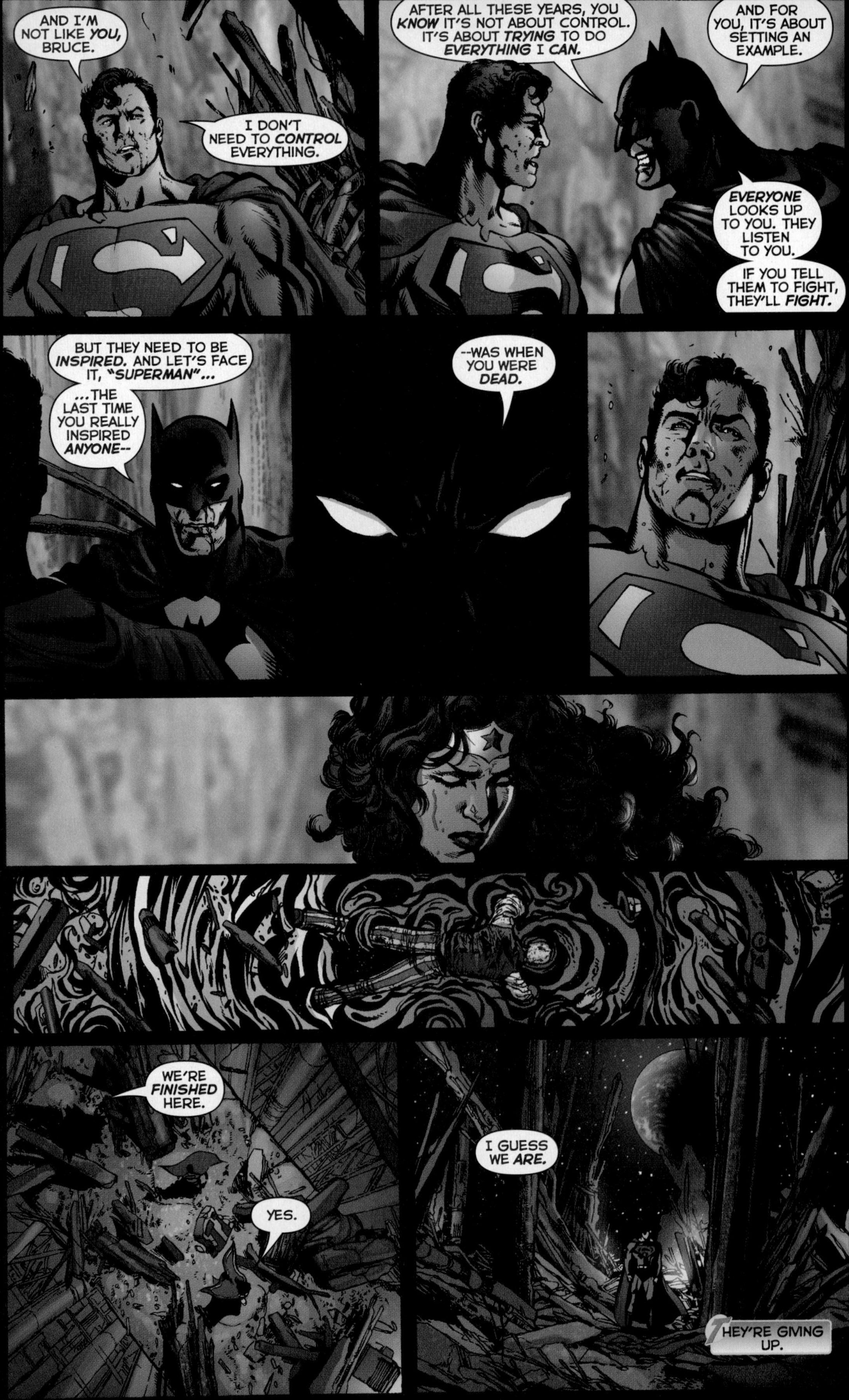
AND I'M NOT LIKE YOU, BRUCE.
I DON'T NEED TO CONTROL EVERYTHING.
AFTER ALL THESE YEARS, YOU KNOW IT'S NOT ABOUT CONTROL. IT'S ABOUT TRYING TO DO EVERYTHING I CAN.
AND FOR YOU, IT'S ABOUT SETTING AN EXAMPLE.
EVERYONE LOOKS UP TO YOU. THEY LISTEN TO YOU.
IF YOU TELL THEM TO FIGHT, THEY'LL FIGHT.
BUT THEY NEED TO BE INSPIRED. AND LET'S FACE IT, "SUPERMAN"...
...THE LAST TIME YOU REALLY INSPIRED ANYONE--
--WAS WHEN YOU WERE DEAD.
WE'RE FINISHED HERE.
YES.
I GUESS WE ARE.
THEY'RE GIVING UP.

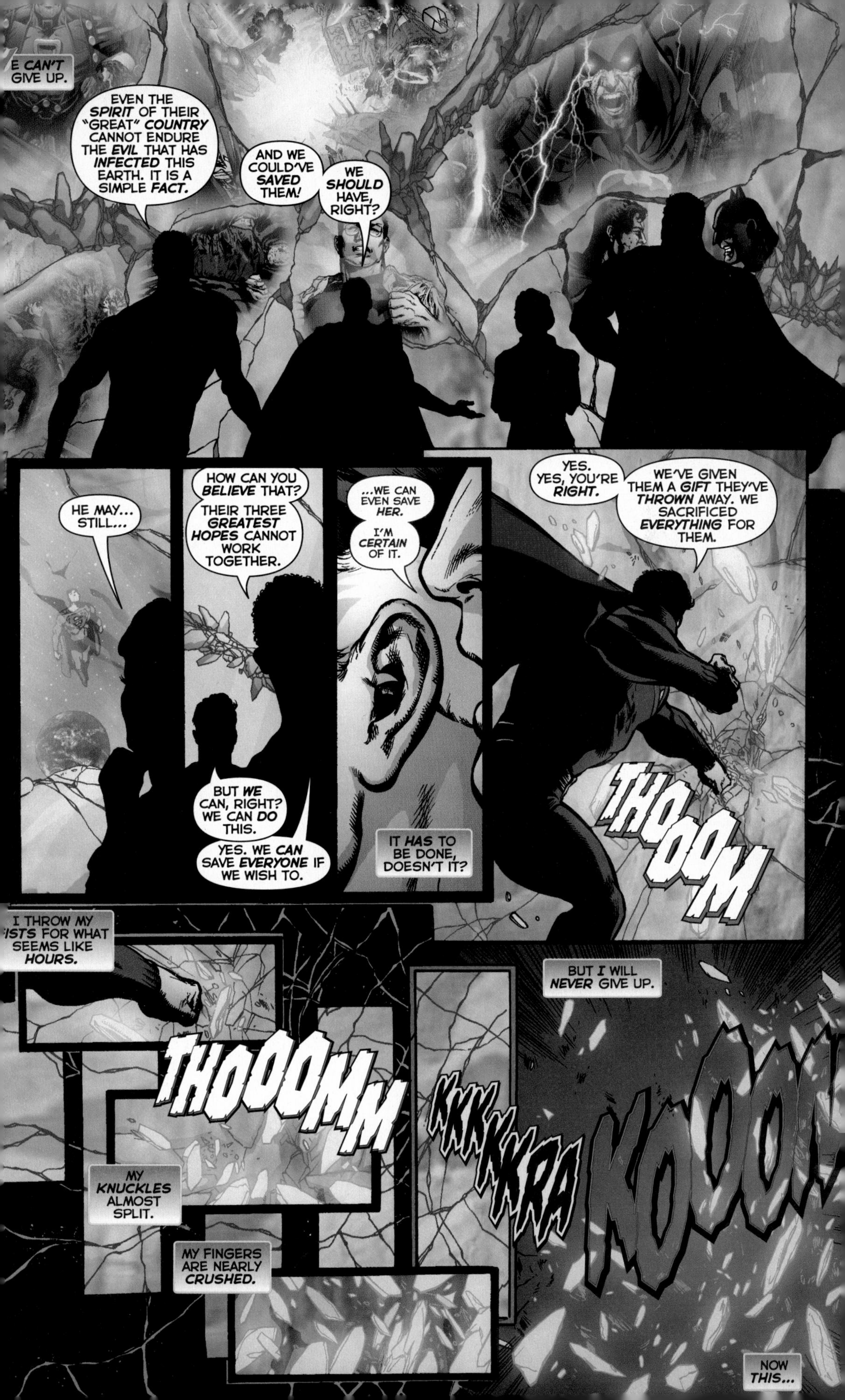
E CAN'T GIVE UP.
EVEN THE SPIRIT OF THEIR "GREAT" COUNTRY CANNOT ENDURE THE EVIL THAT HAS INFECTED THIS EARTH. IT IS A SIMPLE FACT.
AND WE COULD'VE SAVED THEM!
WE SHOULD HAVE, RIGHT?
HE MAY... STILL...
HOW CAN YOU BELIEVE THAT?
THEIR THREE GREATEST HOPES CANNOT WORK TOGETHER.
BUT WE CAN, RIGHT? WE CAN DO THIS.
YES. WE CAN SAVE EVERYONE IF WE WISH TO.
...WE CAN EVEN SAVE HER.
I'M CERTAIN OF IT.
IT HAS TO BE DONE, DOESN'T IT?
YES. YES, YOU'RE RIGHT.
WE'VE GIVEN THEM A GIFT THEY'VE THROWN AWAY. WE SACRIFICED EVERYTHING FOR THEM.
THOOOM
I THROW MY FISTS FOR WHAT SEEMS LIKE HOURS.
THOOOMM
MY KNUCKLES ALMOST SPLIT.
MY FINGERS ARE NEARLY CRUSHED.
BUT I WILL NEVER GIVE UP.
KKKKKRA
KOOOM
NOW THIS...

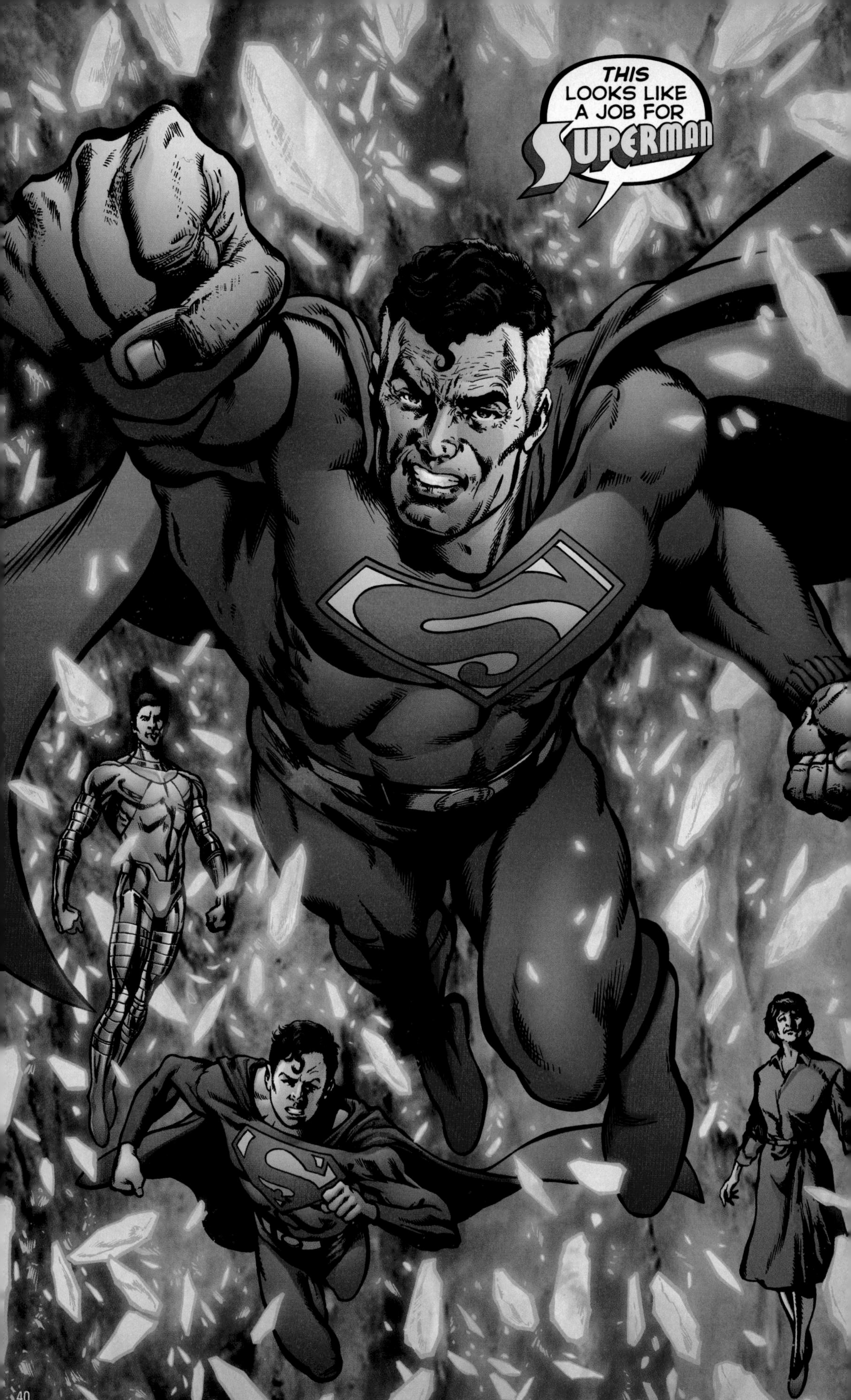
THIS LOOKS LIKE A JOB FOR SUPERMAN

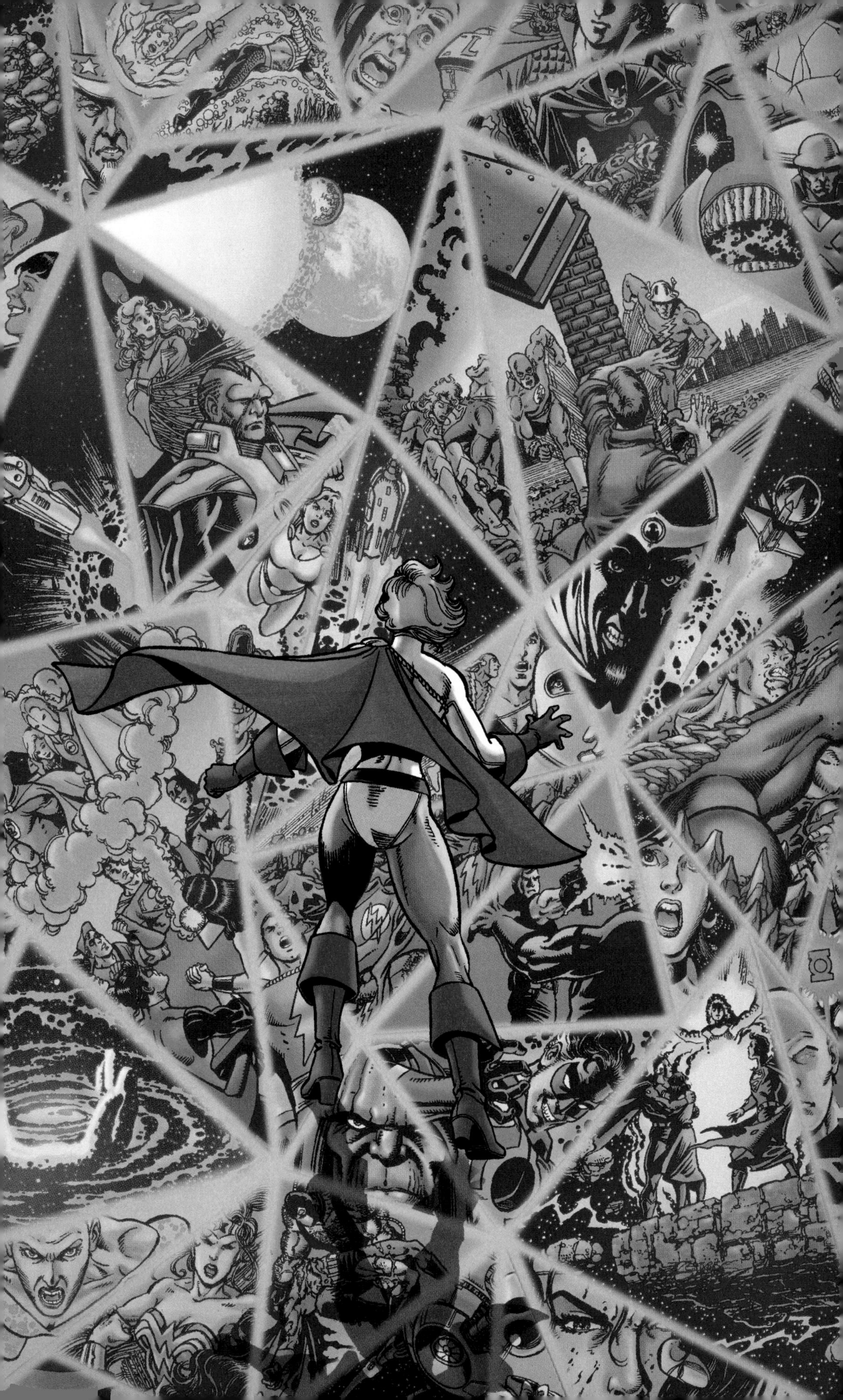

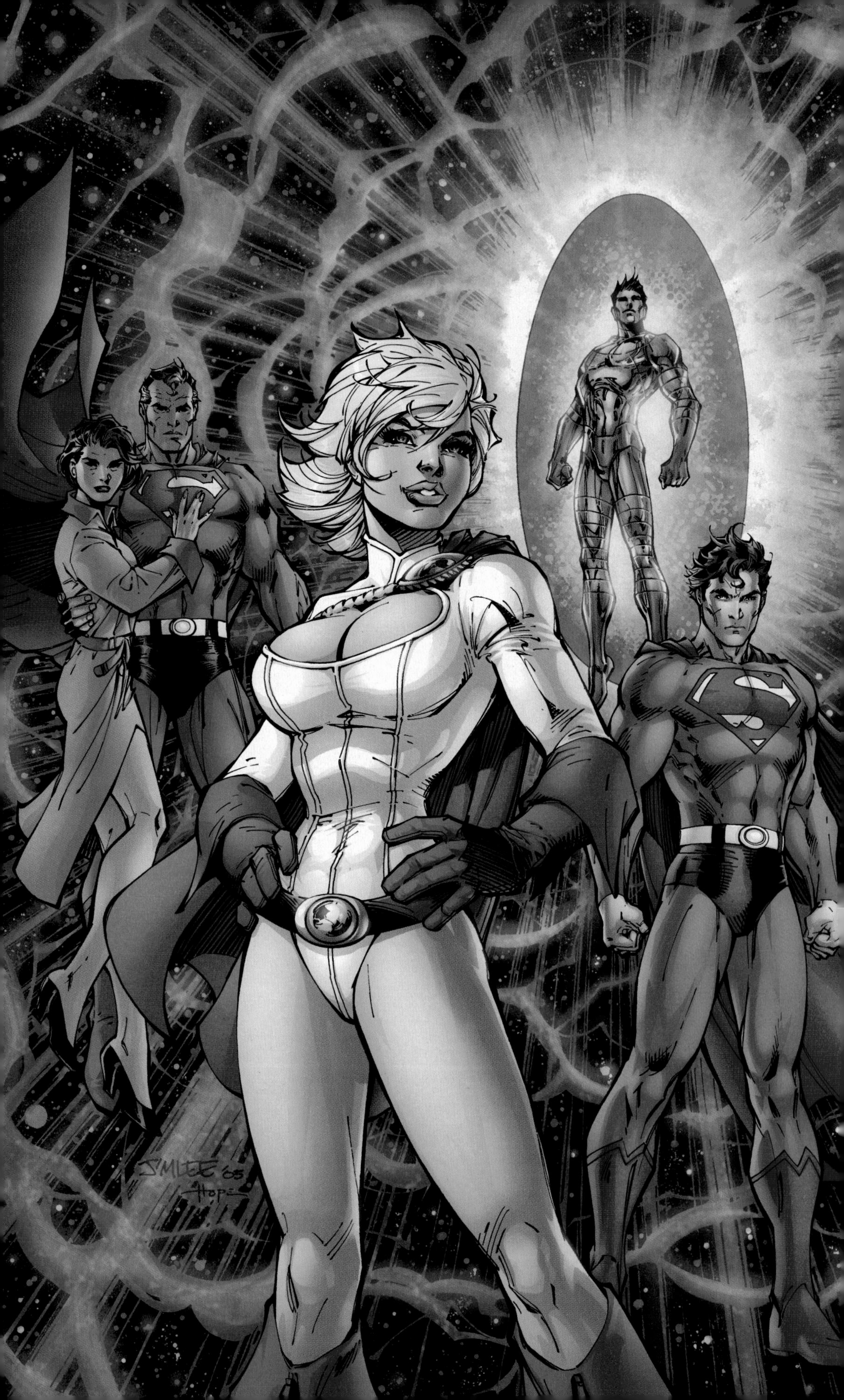

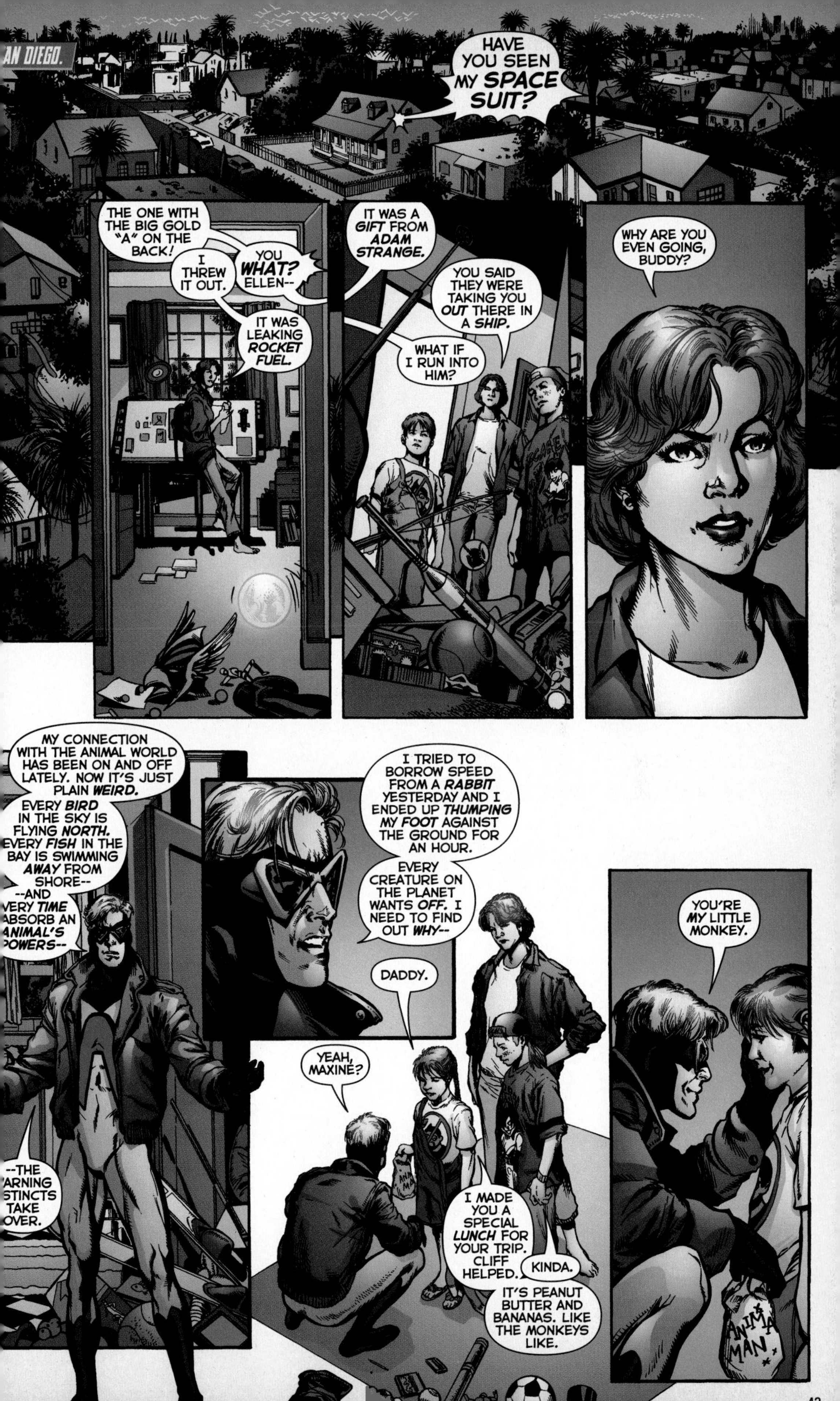
AN DIEGO.
HAVE YOU SEEN MY SPACE SUIT?
THE ONE WITH THE BIG GOLD "A" ON THE BACK!
I THREW IT OUT.
YOU WHAT? ELLEN--
IT WAS LEAKING ROCKET FUEL.
IT WAS A GIFT FROM ADAM STRANGE.
YOU SAID THEY WERE TAKING YOU OUT THERE IN A SHIP.
WHAT IF I RUN INTO HIM?
WHY ARE YOU EVEN GOING, BUDDY?
MY CONNECTION WITH THE ANIMAL WORLD HAS BEEN ON AND OFF LATELY. NOW IT'S JUST PLAIN WEIRD.
EVERY BIRD IN THE SKY IS FLYING NORTH. EVERY FISH IN THE BAY IS SWIMMING AWAY FROM SHORE--
--AND EVERY TIME ABSORB AN ANIMAL'S POWERS--
--THE ARNING STINCTS TAKE OVER.
I TRIED TO BORROW SPEED FROM A RABBIT YESTERDAY AND I ENDED UP THUMPING MY FOOT AGAINST THE GROUND FOR AN HOUR.
EVERY CREATURE ON THE PLANET WANTS OFF. I NEED TO FIND OUT WHY--
DADDY.
YEAH, MAXINE?
I MADE YOU A SPECIAL LUNCH FOR YOUR TRIP. CLIFF HELPED.
KINDA.
IT'S PEANUT BUTTER AND BANANAS. LIKE THE MONKEYS LIKE.
YOU'RE MY LITTLE MONKEY.

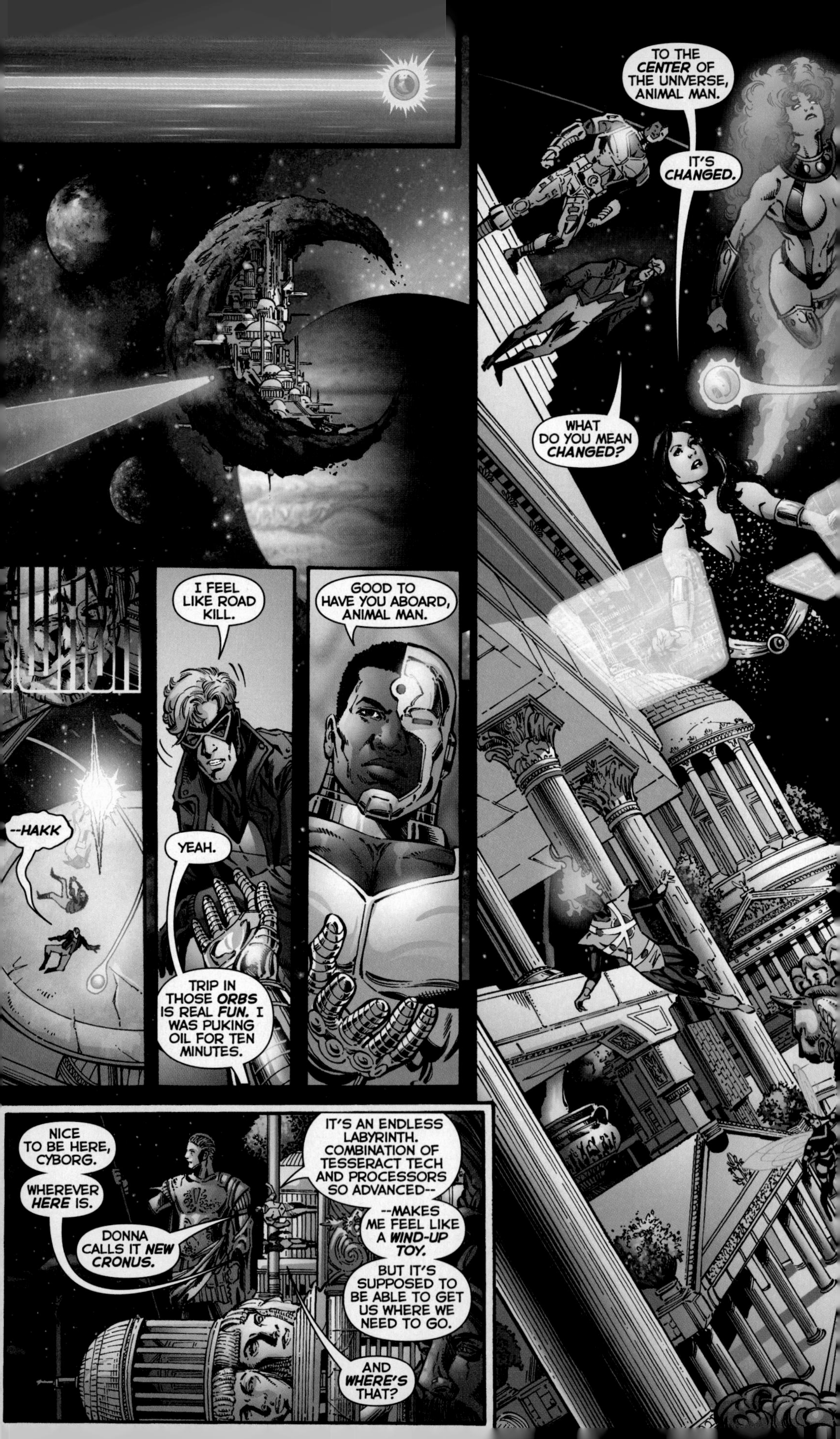

TO THE CENTER OF THE UNIVERSE, ANIMAL MAN.
IT'S CHANGED.
WHAT DO YOU MEAN CHANGED?
--HAKK
I FEEL LIKE ROAD KILL.
YEAH.
TRIP IN THOSE ORBS IS REAL FUN. I WAS PUKING OIL FOR TEN MINUTES.
GOOD TO HAVE YOU ABOARD, ANIMAL MAN.
NICE TO BE HERE, CYBORG.
WHEREVER HERE IS.
DONNA CALLS IT NEW CRONUS.
IT'S AN ENDLESS LABYRINTH. COMBINATION OF TESSERACT TECH AND PROCESSORS SO ADVANCED--
--MAKES ME FEEL LIKE A WIND-UP TOY.
BUT IT'S SUPPOSED TO BE ABLE TO GET US WHERE WE NEED TO GO.
AND WHERE'S THAT?

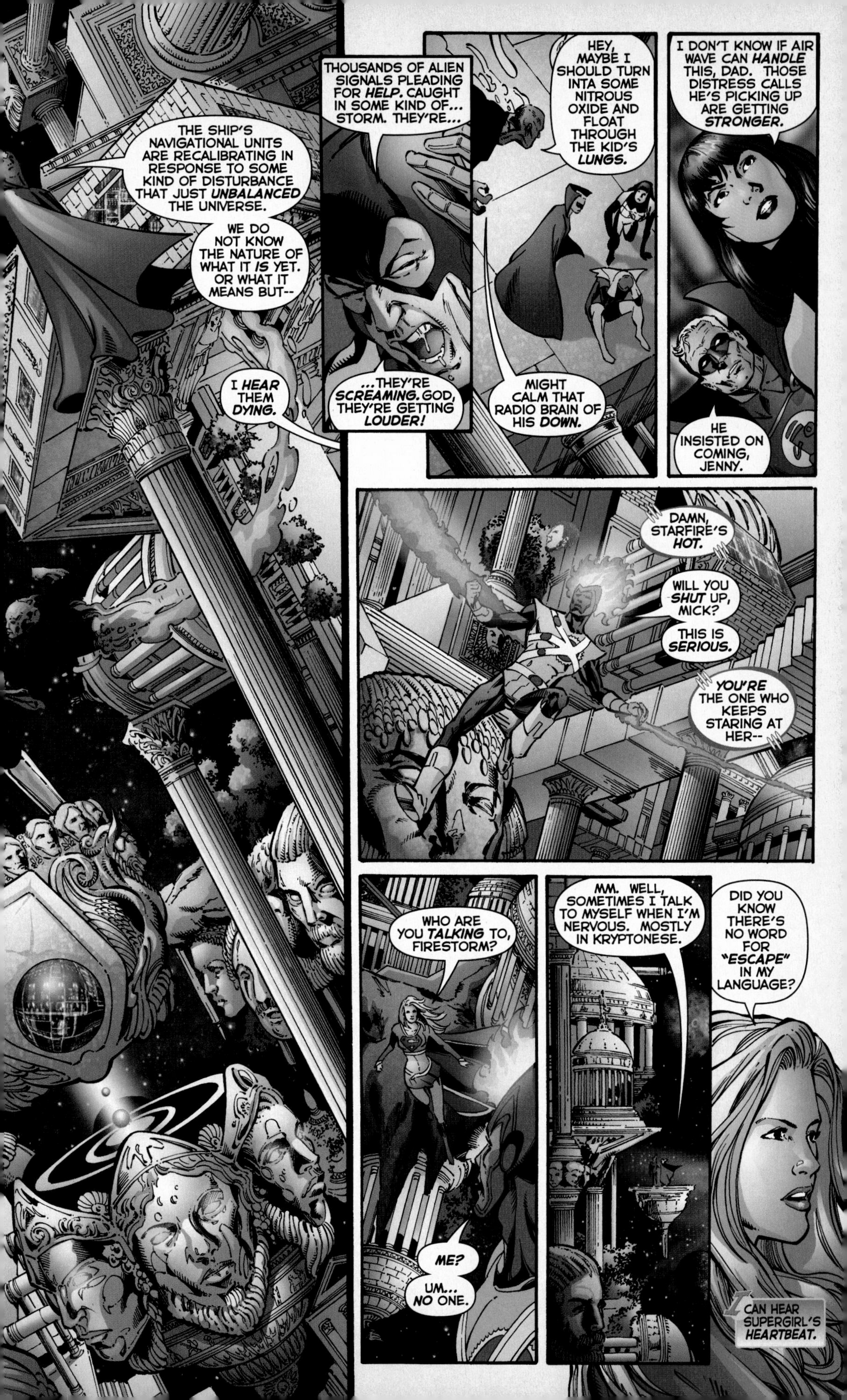
THE SHIP'S NAVIGATIONAL UNITS ARE RECALIBRATING IN RESPONSE TO SOME KIND OF DISTURBANCE THAT JUST UNBALANCED THE UNIVERSE.
WE DO NOT KNOW THE NATURE OF WHAT IT IS YET. OR WHAT IT MEANS BUT--
I HEAR THEM DYING.
THOUSANDS OF ALIEN SIGNALS PLEADING FOR HELP. CAUGHT IN SOME KIND OF... STORM. THEY'RE...
...THEY'RE SCREAMING. GOD, THEY'RE GETTING LOUDER!
HEY, MAYBE I SHOULD TURN INTA SOME NITROUS OXIDE AND FLOAT THROUGH THE KID'S LUNGS.
MIGHT CALM THAT RADIO BRAIN OF HIS DOWN.
I DON'T KNOW IF AIR WAVE CAN HANDLE THIS, DAD. THOSE DISTRESS CALLS HE'S PICKING UP ARE GETTING STRONGER.
HE INSISTED ON COMING, JENNY.
DAMN, STARFIRE'S HOT.
WILL YOU SHUT UP, MICK?
THIS IS SERIOUS.
YOU'RE THE ONE WHO KEEPS STARING AT HER--
WHO ARE YOU TALKING TO, FIRESTORM?
ME?
UM... NO ONE.
MM. WELL, SOMETIMES I TALK TO MYSELF WHEN I'M NERVOUS. MOSTLY IN KRYPTONESE.
DID YOU KNOW THERE'S NO WORD FOR "ESCAPE" IN MY LANGUAGE?
CAN HEAR SUPERGIRL'S HEARTBEAT.

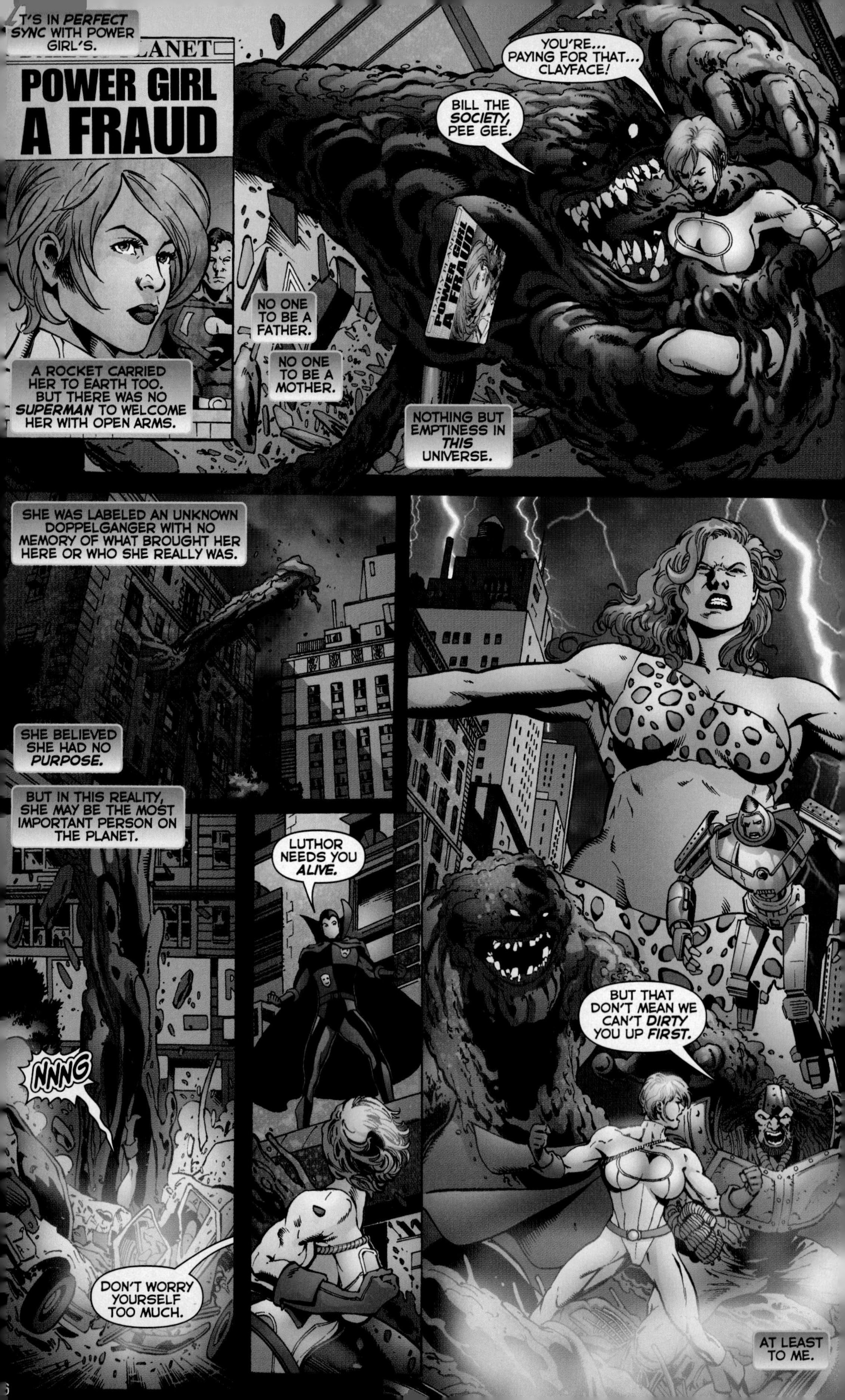
IT'S IN PERFECT SYNC WITH POWER GIRL'S.
PLANET
POWER GIRL A FRAUD
A ROCKET CARRIED HER TO EARTH TOO. BUT THERE WAS NO SUPERMAN TO WELCOME HER WITH OPEN ARMS.
NO ONE TO BE A FATHER.
NO ONE TO BE A MOTHER.
YOU'RE... PAYING FOR THAT... CLAYFACE!
BILL THE SOCIETY, PEE GEE.
POWER GIRL A FRAUD
NOTHING BUT EMPTINESS IN THIS UNIVERSE.
SHE WAS LABELED AN UNKNOWN DOPPELGANGER WITH NO MEMORY OF WHAT BROUGHT HER HERE OR WHO SHE REALLY WAS.
SHE BELIEVED SHE HAD NO PURPOSE.
BUT IN THIS REALITY, SHE MAY BE THE MOST IMPORTANT PERSON ON THE PLANET.
NNNG
DON'T WORRY YOURSELF TOO MUCH.
LUTHOR NEEDS YOU ALIVE.
BUT THAT DON'T MEAN WE CAN'T DIRTY YOU UP FIRST.
AT LEAST TO ME.

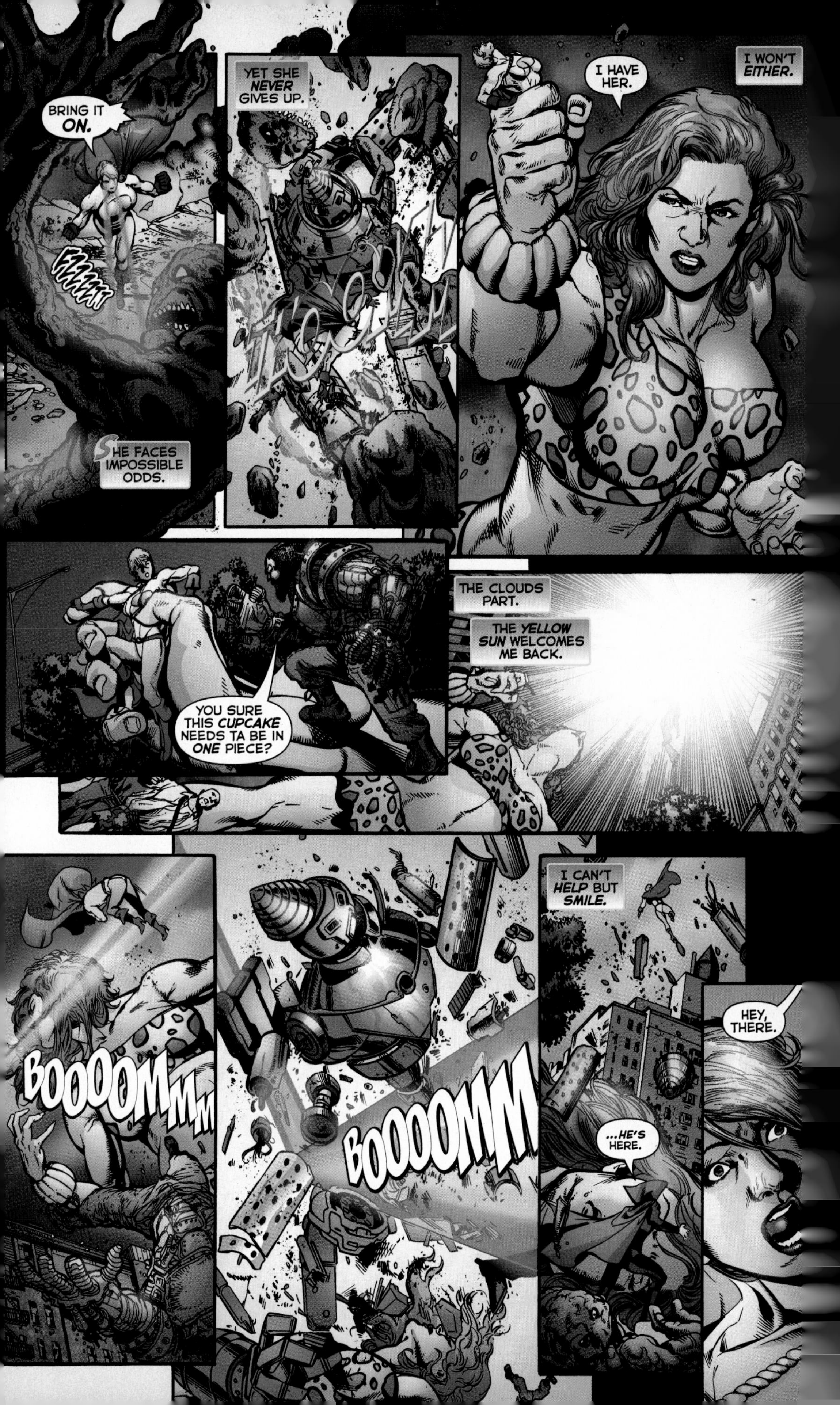
BRING IT ON.
SHE FACES IMPOSSIBLE ODDS.
YET SHE NEVER GIVES UP.
I HAVE HER.
I WON'T EITHER.
YOU SURE THIS CUPCAKE NEEDS TA BE IN ONE PIECE?
THE CLOUDS PART.
THE YELLOW SUN WELCOMES ME BACK.
BOOOOMMMM
BOOOOMM
I CAN'T HELP BUT SMILE.
...HE'S HERE.
HEY, THERE.

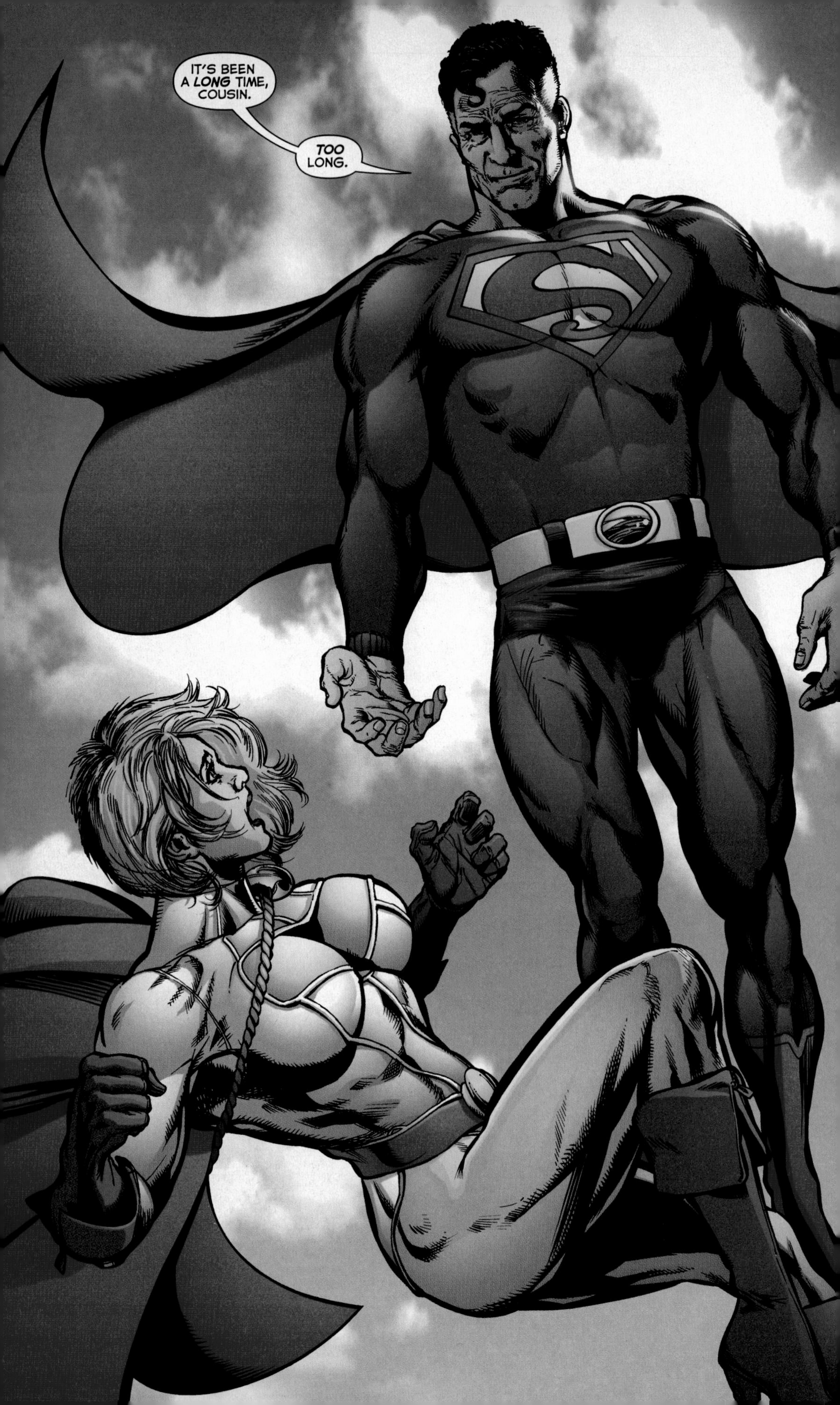
IT'S BEEN A *LONG* TIME, COUSIN.
TOO LONG.

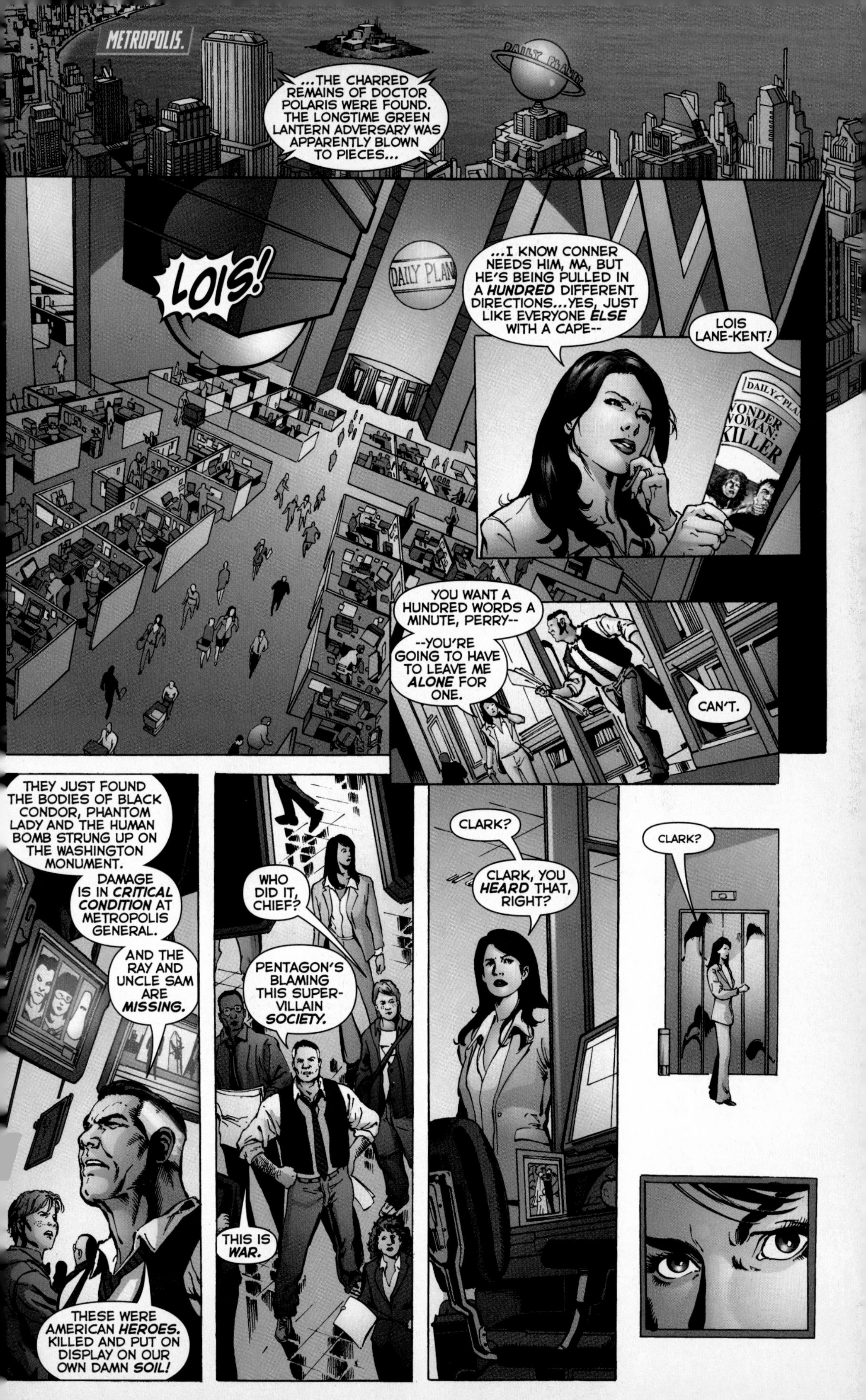
METROPOLIS.
...THE CHARRED REMAINS OF DOCTOR POLARIS WERE FOUND. THE LONGTIME GREEN LANTERN ADVERSARY WAS APPARENTLY BLOWN TO PIECES...
DAILY PLANET
LOIS!
DAILY PLAN
...I KNOW CONNER NEEDS HIM, MA, BUT HE'S BEING PULLED IN A HUNDRED DIFFERENT DIRECTIONS...YES, JUST LIKE EVERYONE ELSE WITH A CAPE--
LOIS LANE-KENT!
DAILY PLA
WONDER WOMAN: KILLER
YOU WANT A HUNDRED WORDS A MINUTE, PERRY--
--YOU'RE GOING TO HAVE TO LEAVE ME ALONE FOR ONE.
CAN'T.
THEY JUST FOUND THE BODIES OF BLACK CONDOR, PHANTOM LADY AND THE HUMAN BOMB STRUNG UP ON THE WASHINGTON MONUMENT.
DAMAGE IS IN CRITICAL CONDITION AT METROPOLIS GENERAL.
AND THE RAY AND UNCLE SAM ARE MISSING.
THESE WERE AMERICAN HEROES. KILLED AND PUT ON DISPLAY ON OUR OWN DAMN SOIL!
WHO DID IT, CHIEF?
PENTAGON'S BLAMING THIS SUPER-VILLAIN SOCIETY.
THIS IS WAR.
CLARK?
CLARK, YOU HEARD THAT, RIGHT?
CLARK?

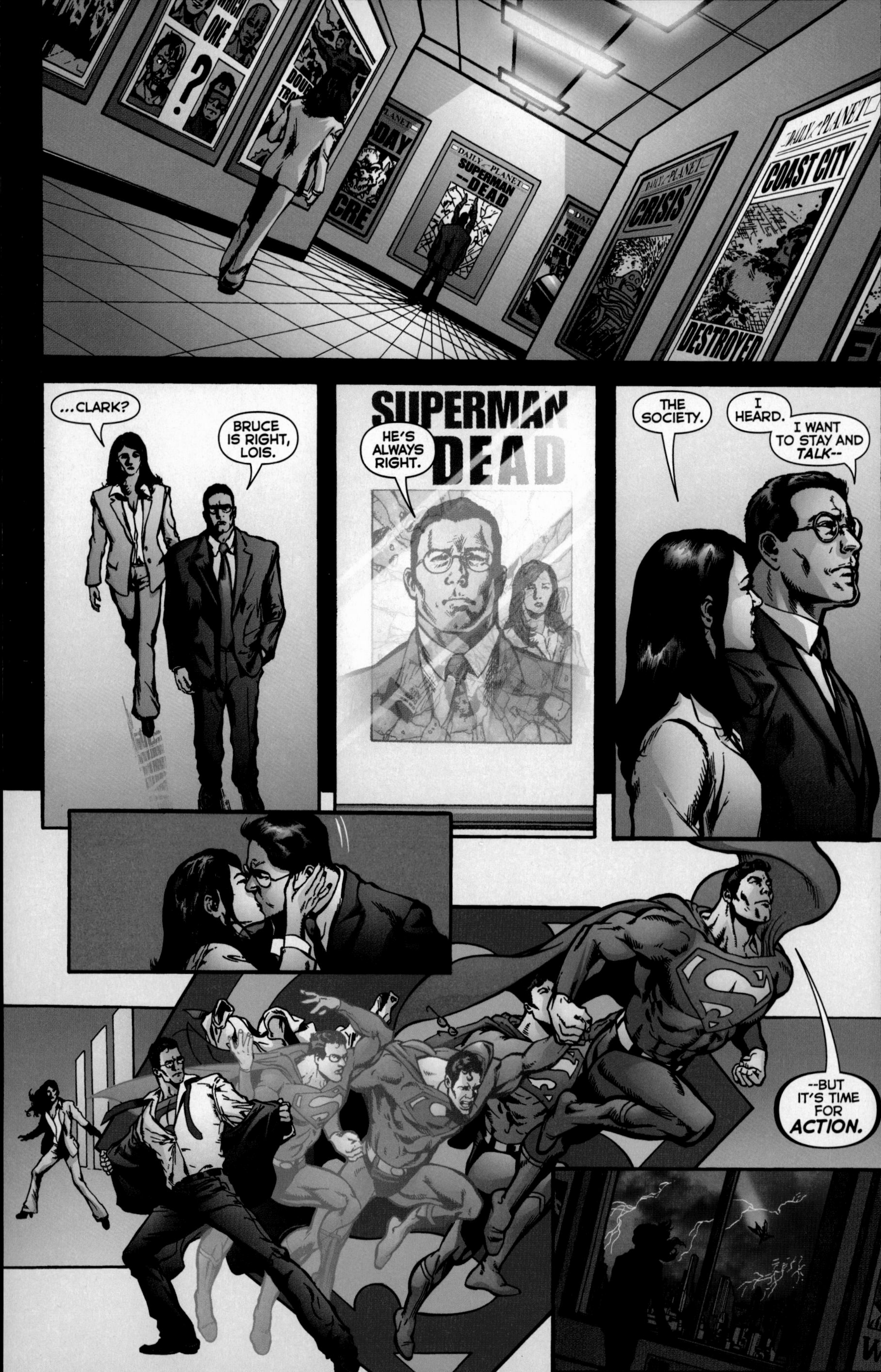
DAILY PLANET
WHICH ONE ?
DOUBLE TROUBLE
DOOMSDAY
MASSACRE
DAILY PLANET
SUPERMAN DEAD
FUNERAL FOR A FRIEND
DAILY PLANET
CRISIS
DAILY PLANET
COAST CITY DESTROYED
...CLARK?
BRUCE IS RIGHT, LOIS.
SUPERMAN DEAD
HE'S ALWAYS RIGHT.
THE SOCIETY.
I HEARD.
I WANT TO STAY AND *TALK*--
--BUT IT'S TIME FOR **ACTION.**

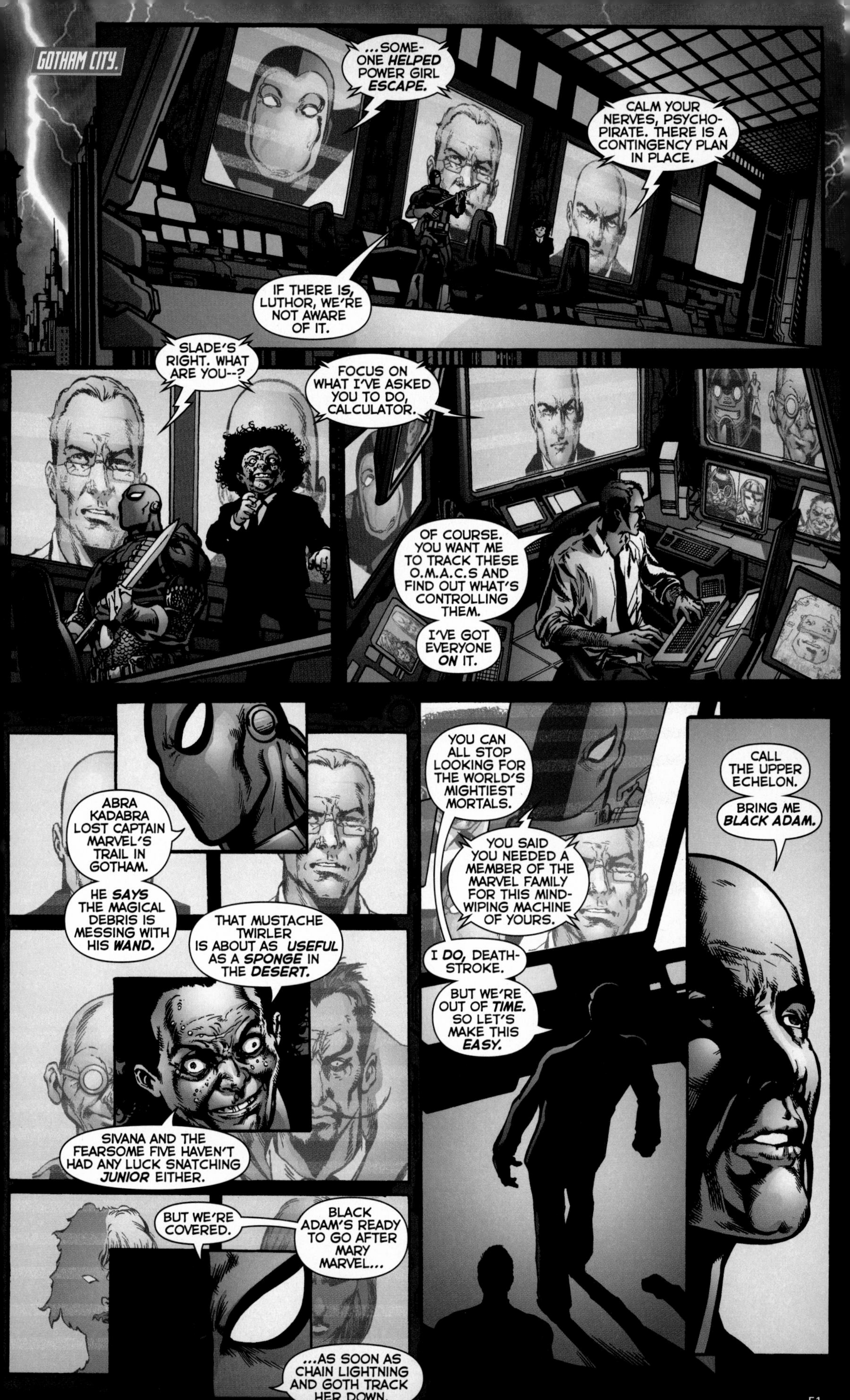
GOTHAM CITY.
...SOME-ONE HELPED POWER GIRL ESCAPE.
CALM YOUR NERVES, PSYCHO-PIRATE. THERE IS A CONTINGENCY PLAN IN PLACE.
IF THERE IS, LUTHOR, WE'RE NOT AWARE OF IT.
SLADE'S RIGHT. WHAT ARE YOU--?
FOCUS ON WHAT I'VE ASKED YOU TO DO, CALCULATOR.
OF COURSE. YOU WANT ME TO TRACK THESE O.M.A.C.S AND FIND OUT WHAT'S CONTROLLING THEM.
I'VE GOT EVERYONE ON IT.
ABRA KADABRA LOST CAPTAIN MARVEL'S TRAIL IN GOTHAM.
HE SAYS THE MAGICAL DEBRIS IS MESSING WITH HIS WAND.
THAT MUSTACHE TWIRLER IS ABOUT AS USEFUL AS A SPONGE IN THE DESERT.
SIVANA AND THE FEARSOME FIVE HAVEN'T HAD ANY LUCK SNATCHING JUNIOR EITHER.
BUT WE'RE COVERED.
BLACK ADAM'S READY TO GO AFTER MARY MARVEL...
...AS SOON AS CHAIN LIGHTNING AND GOTH TRACK HER DOWN.
YOU CAN ALL STOP LOOKING FOR THE WORLD'S MIGHTIEST MORTALS.
YOU SAID YOU NEEDED A MEMBER OF THE MARVEL FAMILY FOR THIS MIND-WIPING MACHINE OF YOURS.
I DO, DEATH-STROKE.
BUT WE'RE OUT OF TIME. SO LET'S MAKE THIS EASY.
CALL THE UPPER ECHELON.
BRING ME BLACK ADAM.

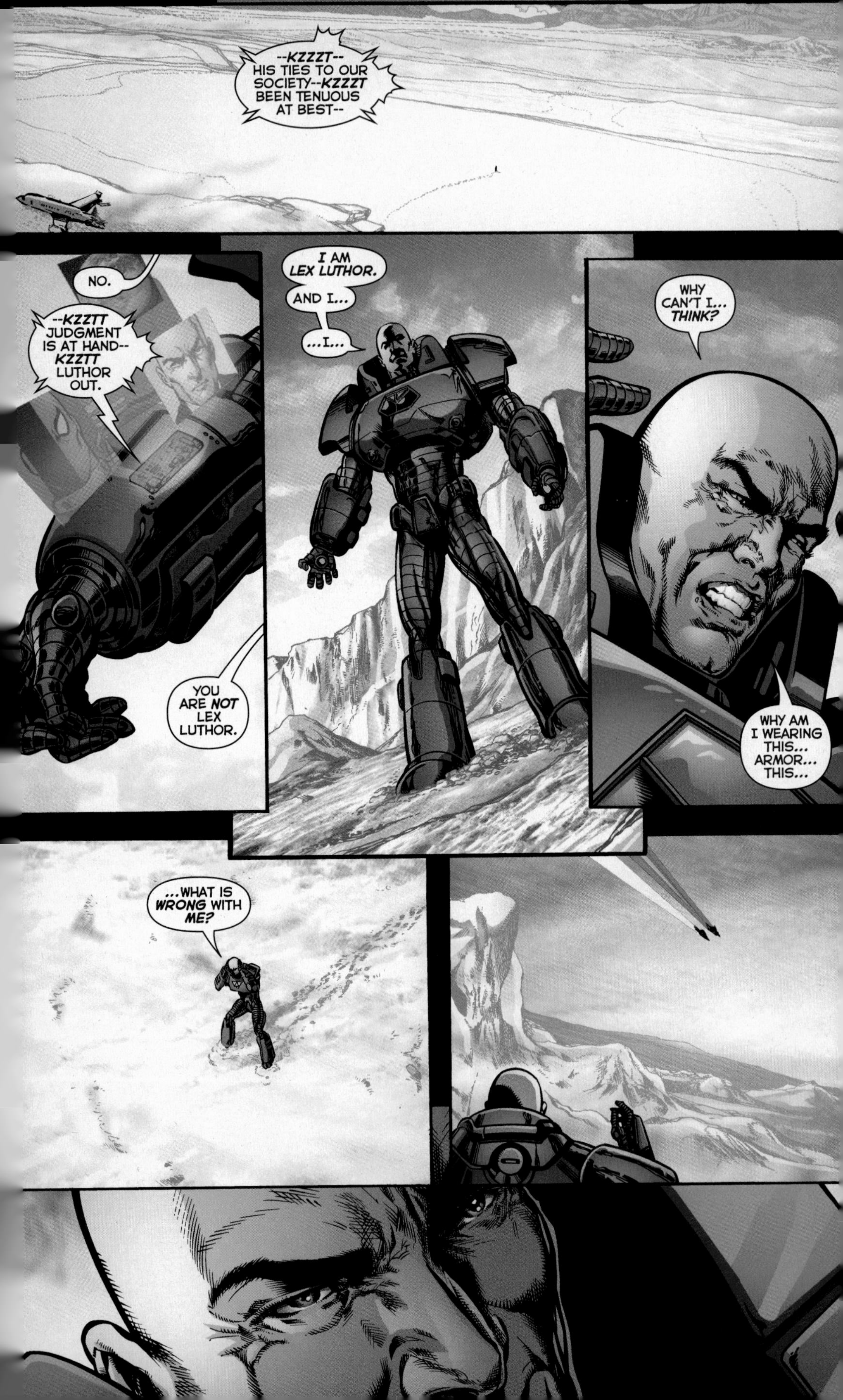
--KZZZT--
HIS TIES TO OUR SOCIETY--KZZZT BEEN TENUOUS AT BEST--
NO.
--KZZTT JUDGMENT IS AT HAND--KZZTT LUTHOR OUT.
YOU ARE NOT LEX LUTHOR.
I AM LEX LUTHOR.
AND I...
...I...
WHY CAN'T I... THINK?
WHY AM I WEARING THIS... ARMOR... THIS...
...WHAT IS WRONG WITH ME?

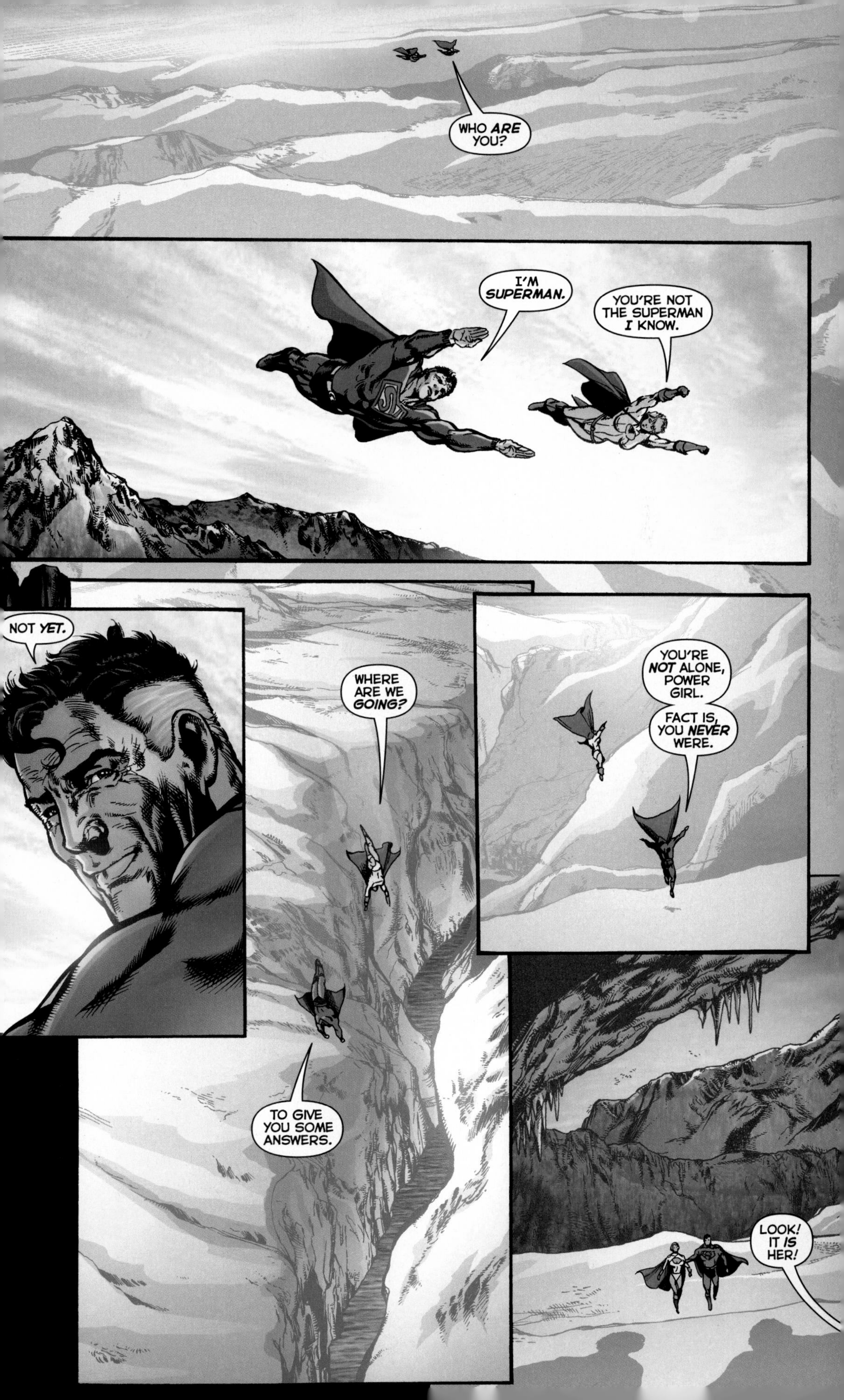
WHO ARE YOU?
I'M SUPERMAN.
YOU'RE NOT THE SUPERMAN I KNOW.
NOT YET.
WHERE ARE WE GOING?
TO GIVE YOU SOME ANSWERS.
YOU'RE NOT ALONE, POWER GIRL.
FACT IS, YOU NEVER WERE.
LOOK! IT IS HER!

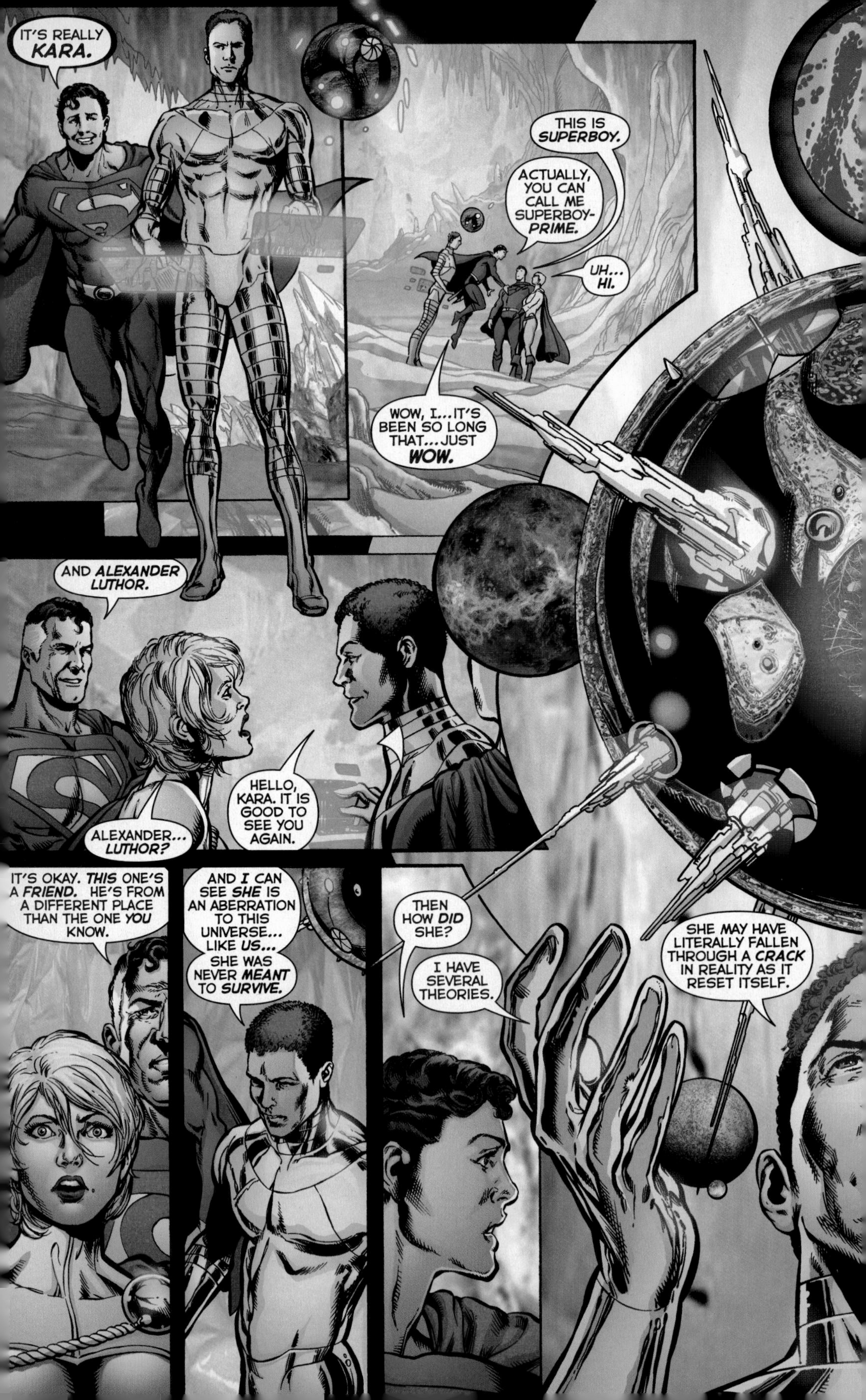

IT'S REALLY KARA.
THIS IS SUPERBOY.
ACTUALLY, YOU CAN CALL ME SUPERBOY-PRIME.
UH... HI.
WOW, I...IT'S BEEN SO LONG THAT...JUST WOW.
AND ALEXANDER LUTHOR.
ALEXANDER... LUTHOR?
HELLO, KARA. IT IS GOOD TO SEE YOU AGAIN.
IT'S OKAY. THIS ONE'S A FRIEND. HE'S FROM A DIFFERENT PLACE THAN THE ONE YOU KNOW.
AND I CAN SEE SHE IS AN ABERRATION TO THIS UNIVERSE... LIKE US... SHE WAS NEVER MEANT TO SURVIVE.
THEN HOW DID SHE?
I HAVE SEVERAL THEORIES.
SHE MAY HAVE LITERALLY FALLEN THROUGH A CRACK IN REALITY AS IT RESET ITSELF.

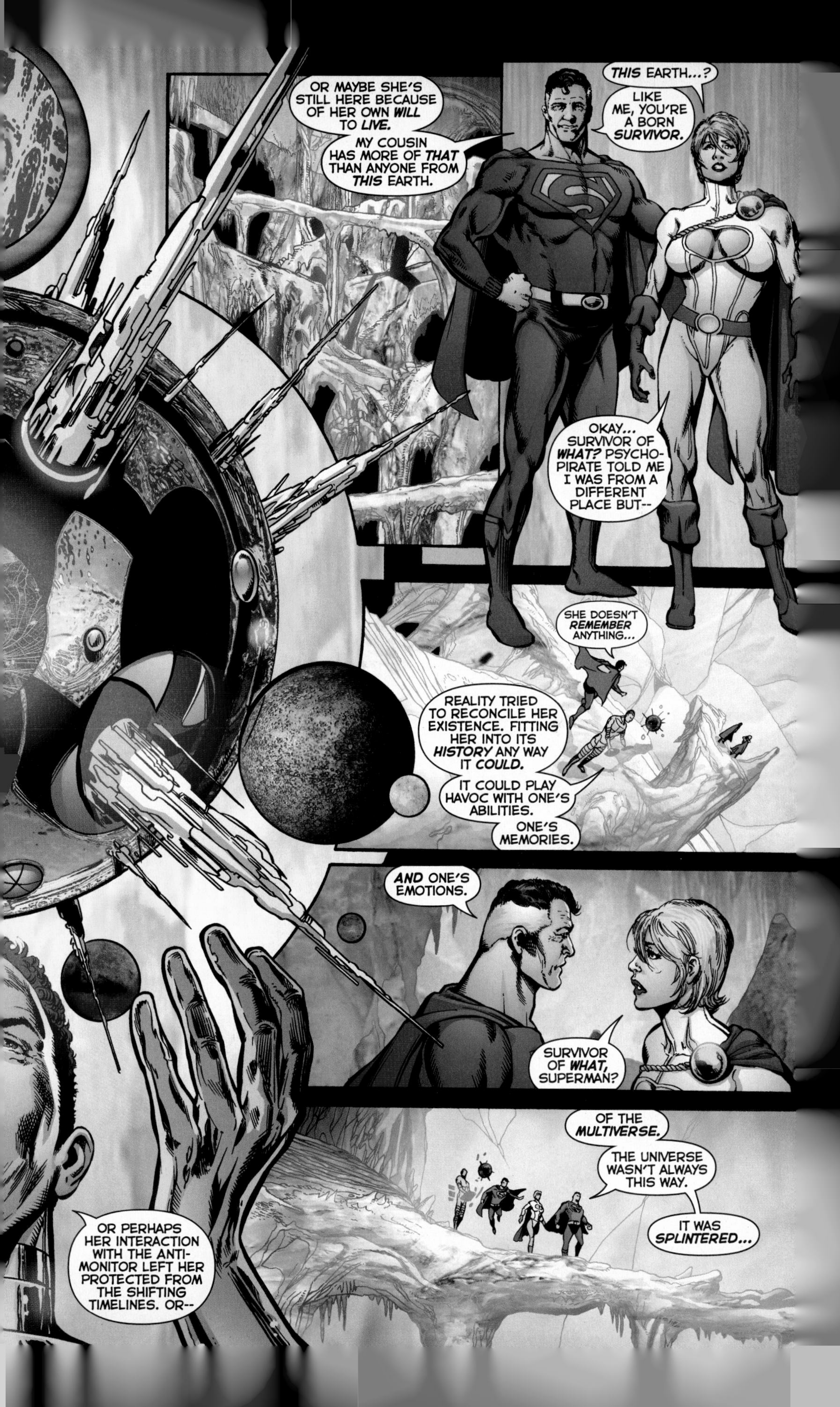

OR MAYBE SHE'S STILL HERE BECAUSE OF HER OWN WILL TO LIVE.
MY COUSIN HAS MORE OF THAT THAN ANYONE FROM THIS EARTH.
THIS EARTH...?
LIKE ME, YOU'RE A BORN SURVIVOR.
OKAY... SURVIVOR OF WHAT? PSYCHO-PIRATE TOLD ME I WAS FROM A DIFFERENT PLACE BUT--
SHE DOESN'T REMEMBER ANYTHING...
REALITY TRIED TO RECONCILE HER EXISTENCE. FITTING HER INTO ITS HISTORY ANY WAY IT COULD.
IT COULD PLAY HAVOC WITH ONE'S ABILITIES.
ONE'S MEMORIES.
AND ONE'S EMOTIONS.
SURVIVOR OF WHAT, SUPERMAN?
OF THE MULTIVERSE.
THE UNIVERSE WASN'T ALWAYS THIS WAY.
IT WAS SPLINTERED...
OR PERHAPS HER INTERACTION WITH THE ANTI-MONITOR LEFT HER PROTECTED FROM THE SHIFTING TIMELINES. OR--

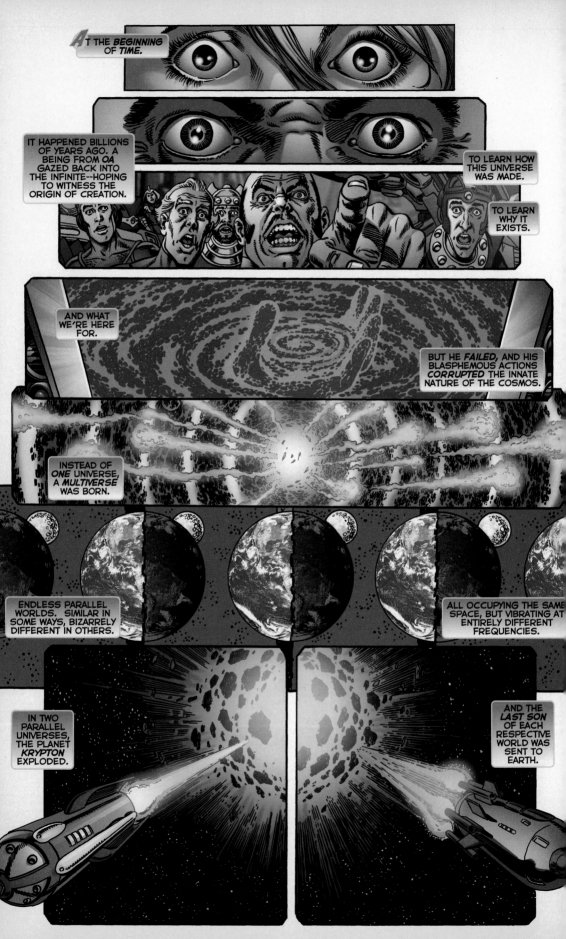

AT THE BEGINNING OF TIME.

IT HAPPENED BILLIONS OF YEARS AGO. A BEING FROM *OA* GAZED BACK INTO THE INFINITE--HOPING TO WITNESS THE ORIGIN OF CREATION.

TO LEARN HOW THIS UNIVERSE WAS MADE.

TO LEARN WHY IT EXISTS.

AND WHAT WE'RE HERE FOR.

BUT HE *FAILED*, AND HIS BLASPHEMOUS ACTIONS *CORRUPTED* THE INNATE NATURE OF THE COSMOS.

INSTEAD OF *ONE* UNIVERSE, A *MULTIVERSE* WAS BORN.

ENDLESS PARALLEL WORLDS. SIMILAR IN SOME WAYS, BIZARRELY DIFFERENT IN OTHERS.

ALL OCCUPYING THE SAME SPACE, BUT VIBRATING AT ENTIRELY DIFFERENT FREQUENCIES.

IN TWO PARALLEL UNIVERSES, THE PLANET *KRYPTON* EXPLODED.

AND THE *LAST SON* OF EACH RESPECTIVE WORLD WAS SENT TO EARTH.

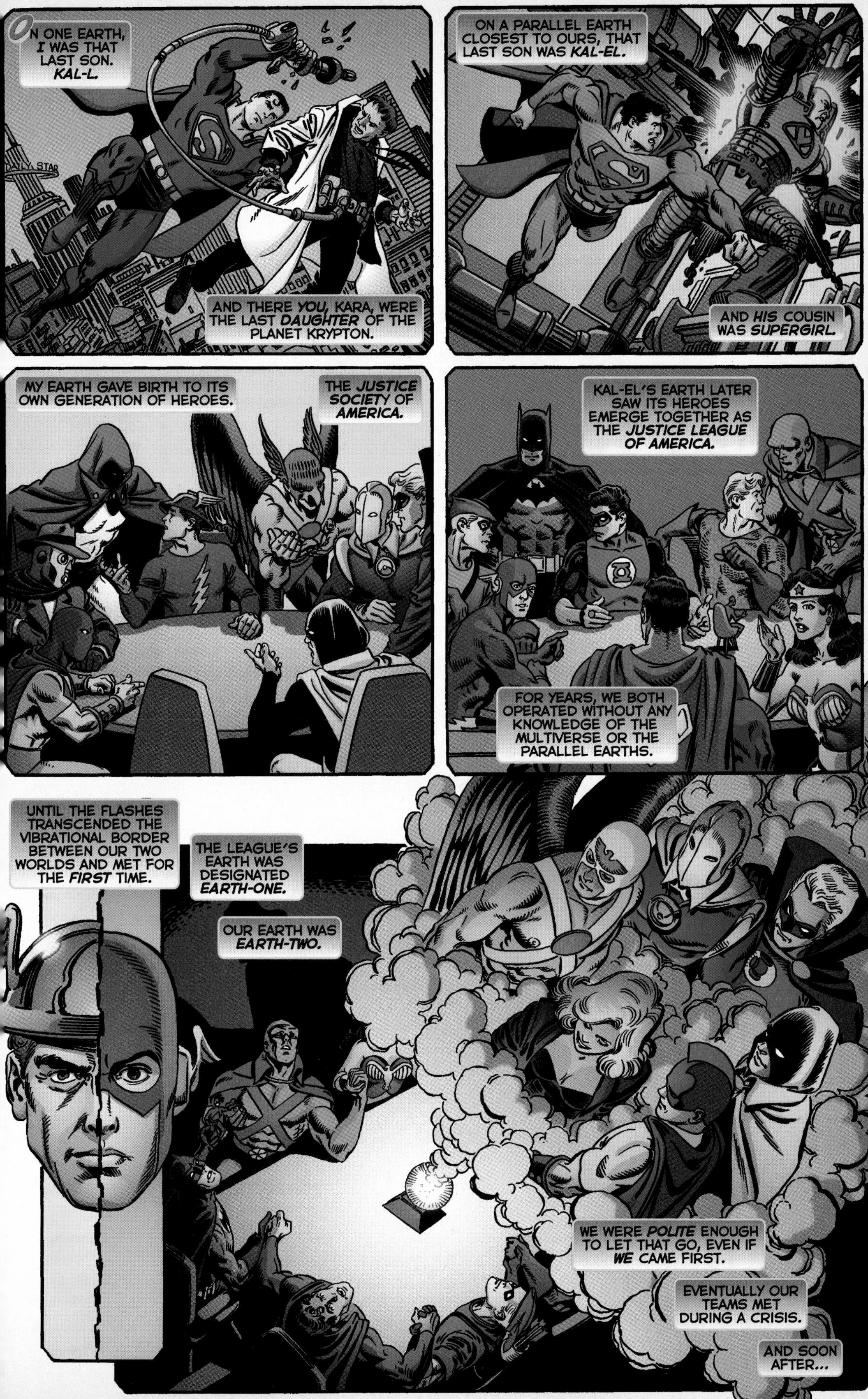
ON ONE EARTH, I WAS THAT LAST SON. KAL-L.
AND THERE YOU, KARA, WERE THE LAST DAUGHTER OF THE PLANET KRYPTON.
DAILY STAR
ON A PARALLEL EARTH CLOSEST TO OURS, THAT LAST SON WAS KAL-EL.
AND HIS COUSIN WAS SUPERGIRL.
MY EARTH GAVE BIRTH TO ITS OWN GENERATION OF HEROES.
THE JUSTICE SOCIETY OF AMERICA.
KAL-EL'S EARTH LATER SAW ITS HEROES EMERGE TOGETHER AS THE JUSTICE LEAGUE OF AMERICA.
FOR YEARS, WE BOTH OPERATED WITHOUT ANY KNOWLEDGE OF THE MULTIVERSE OR THE PARALLEL EARTHS.
UNTIL THE FLASHES TRANSCENDED THE VIBRATIONAL BORDER BETWEEN OUR TWO WORLDS AND MET FOR THE FIRST TIME.
THE LEAGUE'S EARTH WAS DESIGNATED EARTH-ONE.
OUR EARTH WAS EARTH-TWO.
WE WERE POLITE ENOUGH TO LET THAT GO, EVEN IF WE CAME FIRST.
EVENTUALLY OUR TEAMS MET DURING A CRISIS.
AND SOON AFTER...

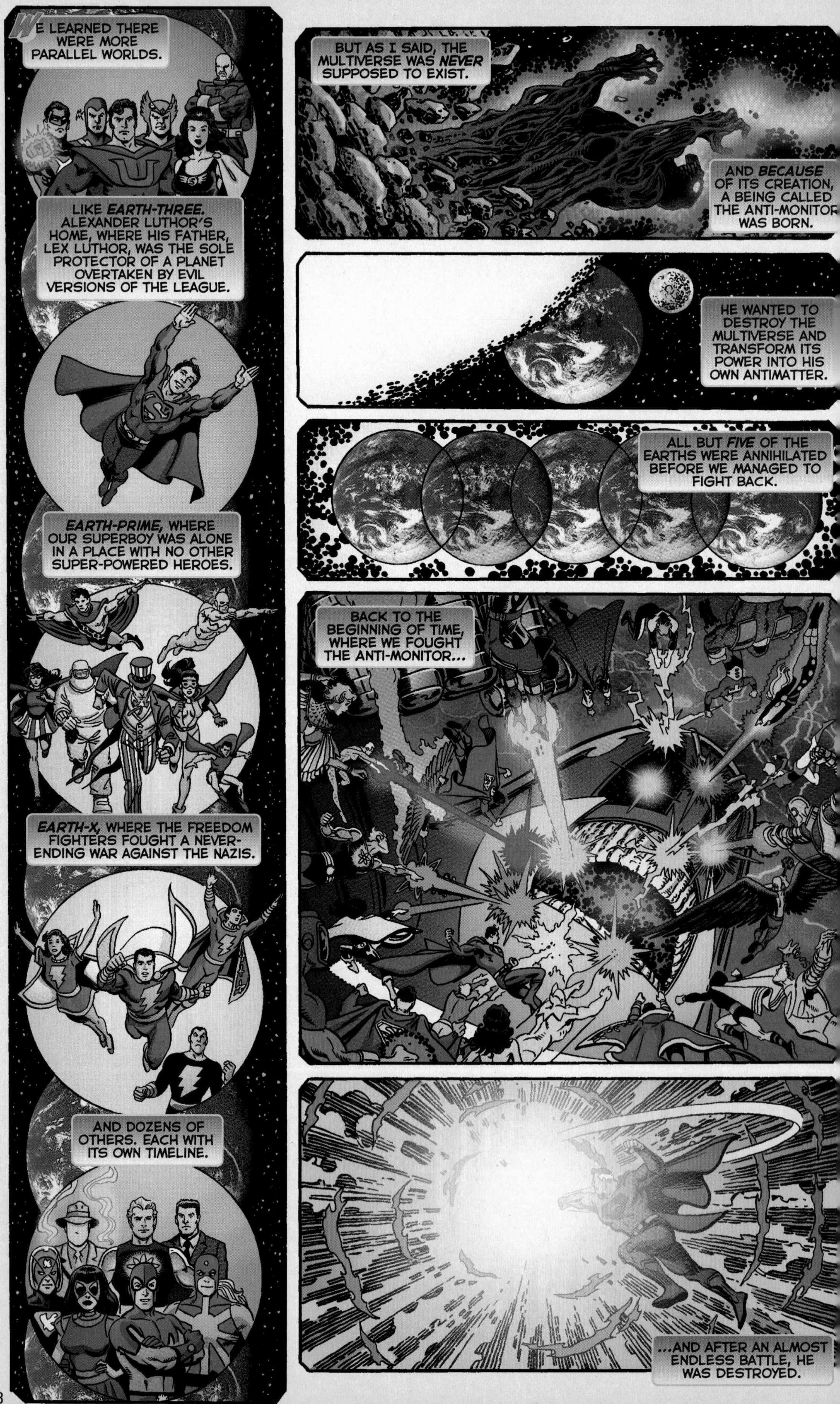
WE LEARNED THERE WERE MORE PARALLEL WORLDS.
LIKE *EARTH-THREE.* ALEXANDER LUTHOR'S HOME, WHERE HIS FATHER, LEX LUTHOR, WAS THE SOLE PROTECTOR OF A PLANET OVERTAKEN BY EVIL VERSIONS OF THE LEAGUE.
EARTH-PRIME, WHERE OUR SUPERBOY WAS ALONE IN A PLACE WITH NO OTHER SUPER-POWERED HEROES.
EARTH-X, WHERE THE FREEDOM FIGHTERS FOUGHT A NEVER-ENDING WAR AGAINST THE NAZIS.
AND DOZENS OF OTHERS. EACH WITH ITS OWN TIMELINE.
BUT AS I SAID, THE MULTIVERSE WAS *NEVER* SUPPOSED TO EXIST.
AND *BECAUSE* OF ITS CREATION, A BEING CALLED THE ANTI-MONITOR WAS BORN.
HE WANTED TO DESTROY THE MULTIVERSE AND TRANSFORM ITS POWER INTO HIS OWN ANTIMATTER.
ALL BUT *FIVE* OF THE EARTHS WERE ANNIHILATED BEFORE WE MANAGED TO FIGHT BACK.
BACK TO THE BEGINNING OF TIME, WHERE WE FOUGHT THE ANTI-MONITOR...
...AND AFTER AN ALMOST ENDLESS BATTLE, HE WAS DESTROYED.

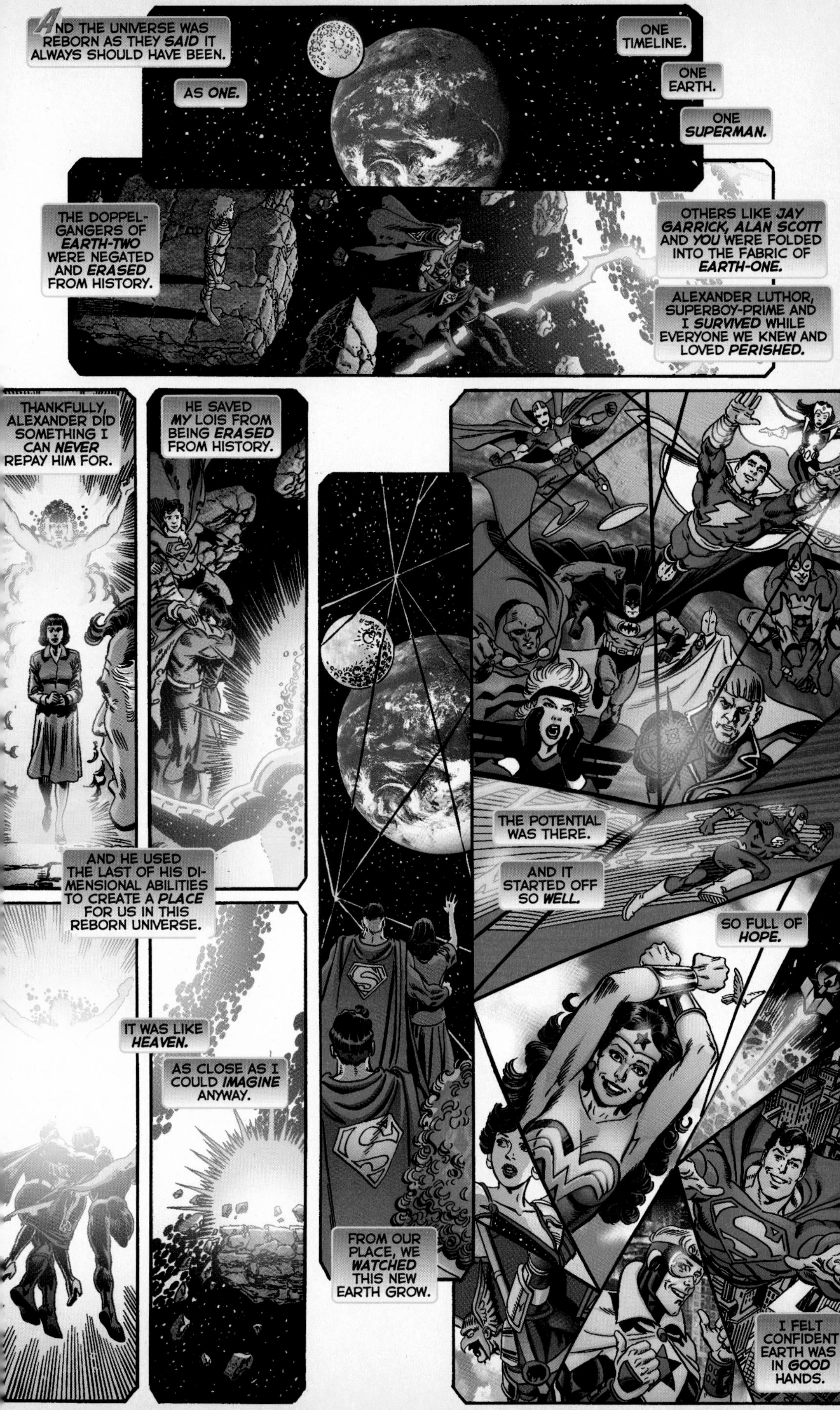
AND THE UNIVERSE WAS REBORN AS THEY SAID IT ALWAYS SHOULD HAVE BEEN.
AS ONE.
ONE TIMELINE.
ONE EARTH.
ONE SUPERMAN.
THE DOPPEL-GANGERS OF EARTH-TWO WERE NEGATED AND ERASED FROM HISTORY.
OTHERS LIKE JAY GARRICK, ALAN SCOTT AND YOU WERE FOLDED INTO THE FABRIC OF EARTH-ONE.
ALEXANDER LUTHOR, SUPERBOY-PRIME AND I SURVIVED WHILE EVERYONE WE KNEW AND LOVED PERISHED.
THANKFULLY, ALEXANDER DID SOMETHING I CAN NEVER REPAY HIM FOR.
HE SAVED MY LOIS FROM BEING ERASED FROM HISTORY.
AND HE USED THE LAST OF HIS DI-MENSIONAL ABILITIES TO CREATE A PLACE FOR US IN THIS REBORN UNIVERSE.
IT WAS LIKE HEAVEN.
AS CLOSE AS I COULD IMAGINE ANYWAY.
FROM OUR PLACE, WE WATCHED THIS NEW EARTH GROW.
THE POTENTIAL WAS THERE.
AND IT STARTED OFF SO WELL.
SO FULL OF HOPE.
I FELT CONFIDENT EARTH WAS IN GOOD HANDS.

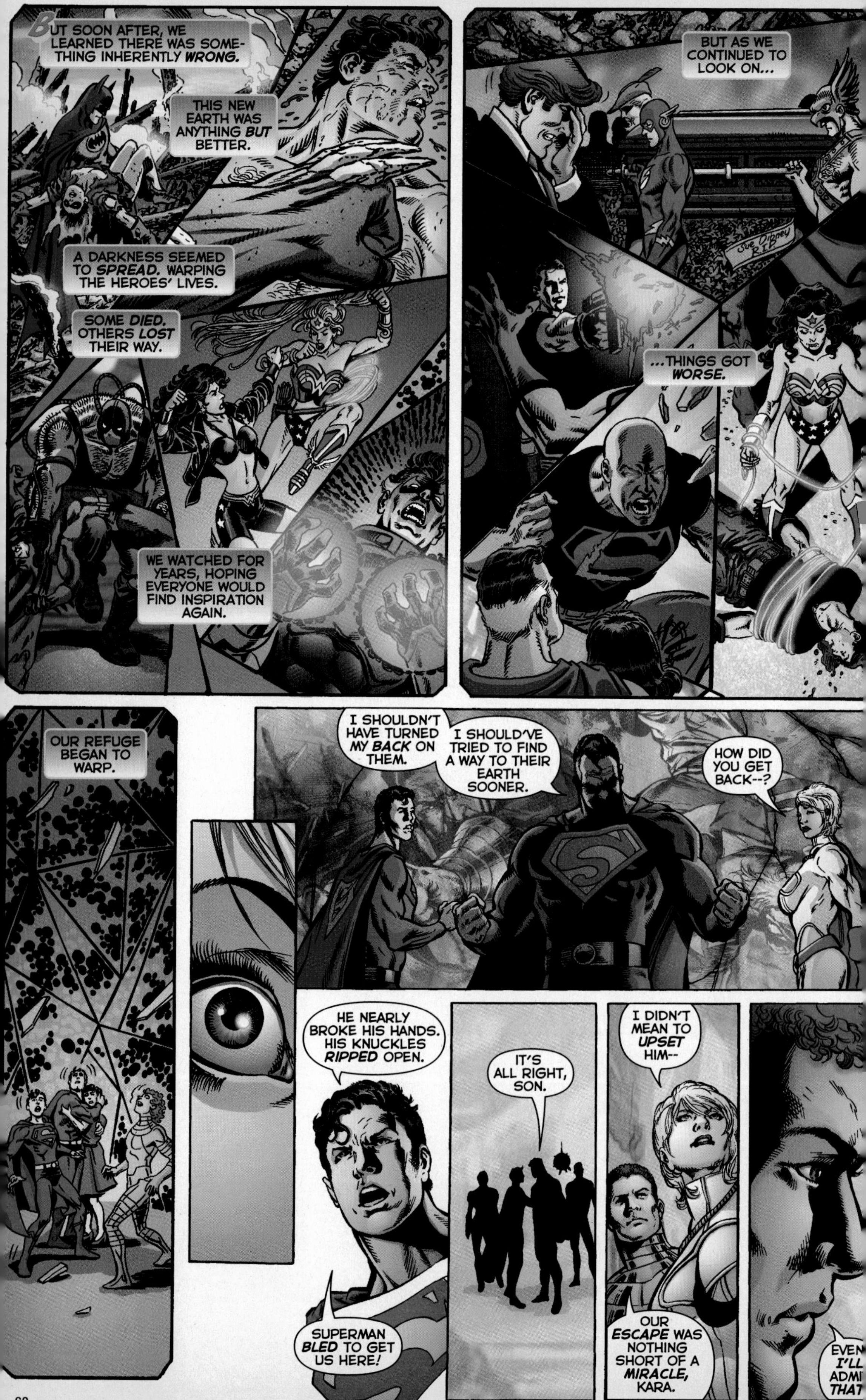

BUT SOON AFTER, WE LEARNED THERE WAS SOMETHING INHERENTLY WRONG.
THIS NEW EARTH WAS ANYTHING BUT BETTER.
A DARKNESS SEEMED TO SPREAD. WARPING THE HEROES' LIVES.
SOME DIED. OTHERS LOST THEIR WAY.
WE WATCHED FOR YEARS, HOPING EVERYONE WOULD FIND INSPIRATION AGAIN.
BUT AS WE CONTINUED TO LOOK ON...
Sue Dibney R.I.P.
...THINGS GOT WORSE.
OUR REFUGE BEGAN TO WARP.
I SHOULDN'T HAVE TURNED MY BACK ON THEM.
I SHOULD'VE TRIED TO FIND A WAY TO THEIR EARTH SOONER.
HOW DID YOU GET BACK--?
HE NEARLY BROKE HIS HANDS. HIS KNUCKLES RIPPED OPEN.
SUPERMAN BLED TO GET US HERE!
IT'S ALL RIGHT, SON.
I DIDN'T MEAN TO UPSET HIM--
OUR ESCAPE WAS NOTHING SHORT OF A MIRACLE, KARA.

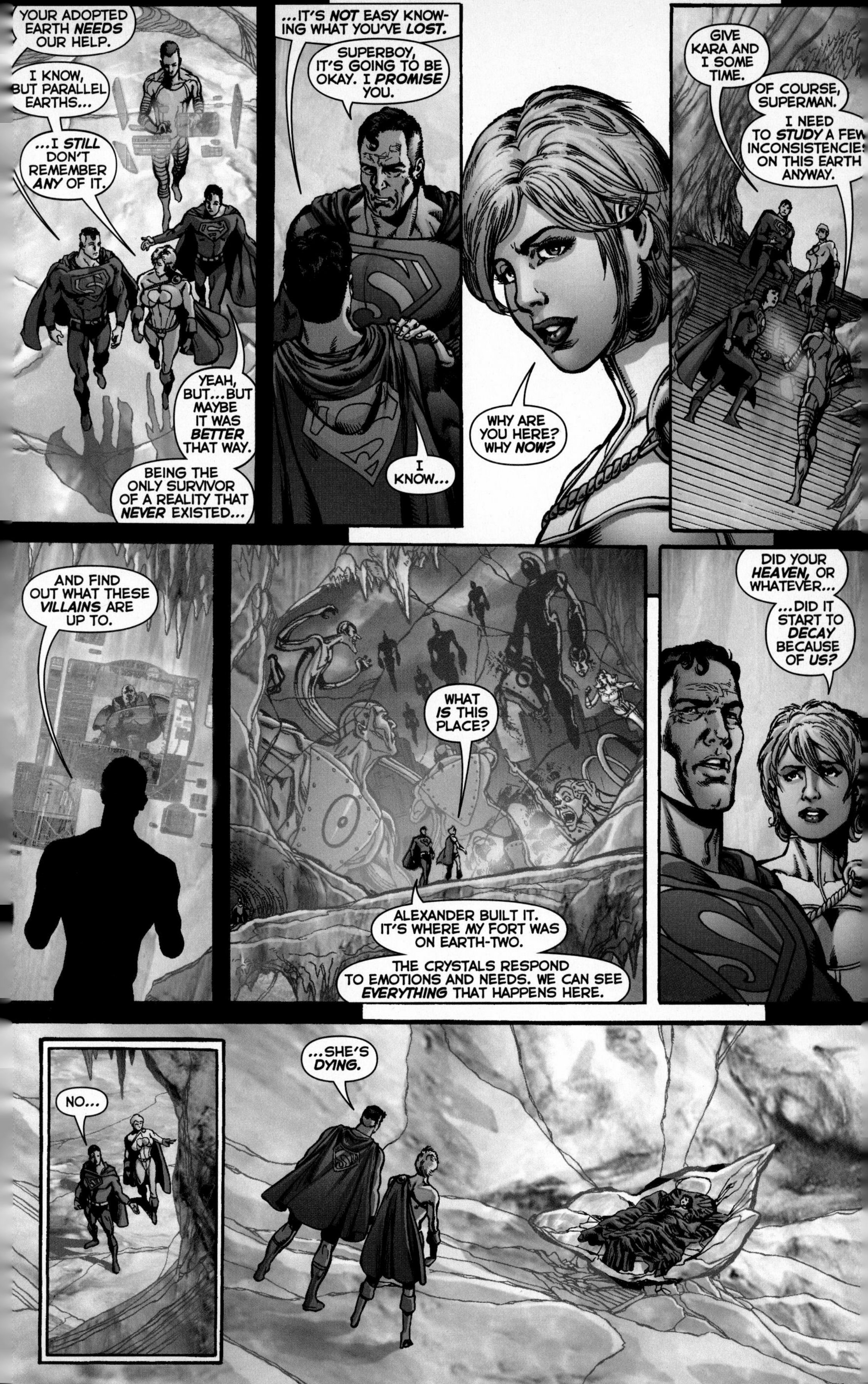
YOUR ADOPTED EARTH NEEDS OUR HELP.
I KNOW, BUT PARALLEL EARTHS...
...I STILL DON'T REMEMBER ANY OF IT.
YEAH, BUT...BUT MAYBE IT WAS BETTER THAT WAY.
BEING THE ONLY SURVIVOR OF A REALITY THAT NEVER EXISTED...
...IT'S NOT EASY KNOWING WHAT YOU'VE LOST.
SUPERBOY, IT'S GOING TO BE OKAY. I PROMISE YOU.
I KNOW...
WHY ARE YOU HERE? WHY NOW?
GIVE KARA AND I SOME TIME.
OF COURSE, SUPERMAN.
I NEED TO STUDY A FEW INCONSISTENCIES ON THIS EARTH ANYWAY.
AND FIND OUT WHAT THESE VILLAINS ARE UP TO.
WHAT IS THIS PLACE?
ALEXANDER BUILT IT. IT'S WHERE MY FORT WAS ON EARTH-TWO.
THE CRYSTALS RESPOND TO EMOTIONS AND NEEDS. WE CAN SEE EVERYTHING THAT HAPPENS HERE.
DID YOUR HEAVEN, OR WHATEVER...
...DID IT START TO DECAY BECAUSE OF US?
NO...
...SHE'S DYING.

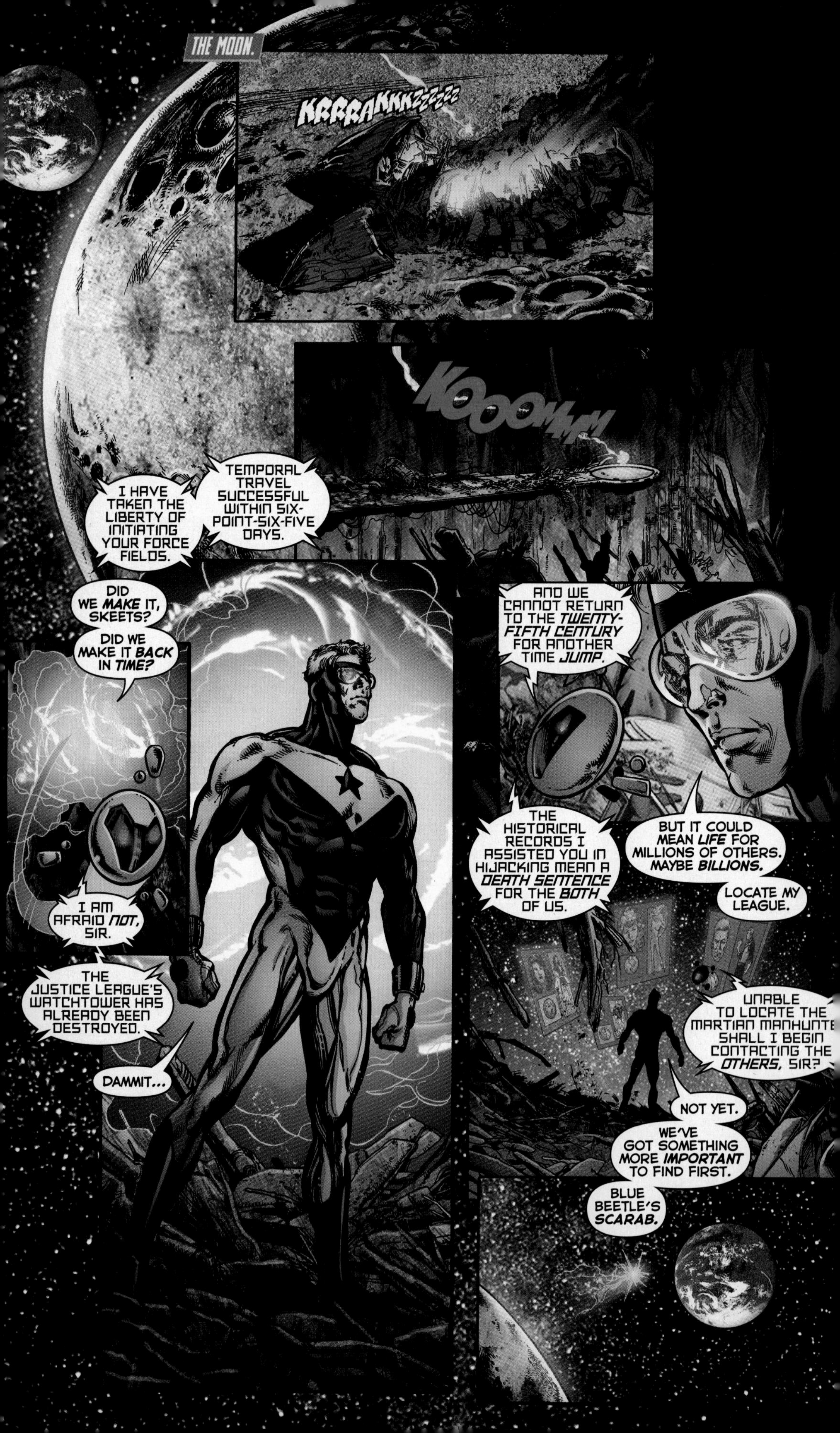
THE MOON.
KRRRAKKKZZZZZZ
KOOOMMM
I HAVE TAKEN THE LIBERTY OF INITIATING YOUR FORCE FIELDS.
TEMPORAL TRAVEL SUCCESSFUL WITHIN SIX-POINT-SIX-FIVE DAYS.
DID WE MAKE IT, SKEETS?
DID WE MAKE IT BACK IN TIME?
I AM AFRAID NOT, SIR.
THE JUSTICE LEAGUE'S WATCHTOWER HAS ALREADY BEEN DESTROYED.
DAMMIT...
AND WE CANNOT RETURN TO THE TWENTY-FIFTH CENTURY FOR ANOTHER TIME JUMP.
THE HISTORICAL RECORDS I ASSISTED YOU IN HIJACKING MEAN A DEATH SENTENCE FOR THE BOTH OF US.
BUT IT COULD MEAN LIFE FOR MILLIONS OF OTHERS. MAYBE BILLIONS.
LOCATE MY LEAGUE.
UNABLE TO LOCATE THE MARTIAN MANHUNTER. SHALL I BEGIN CONTACTING THE OTHERS, SIR?
NOT YET.
WE'VE GOT SOMETHING MORE IMPORTANT TO FIND FIRST.
BLUE BEETLE'S SCARAB.

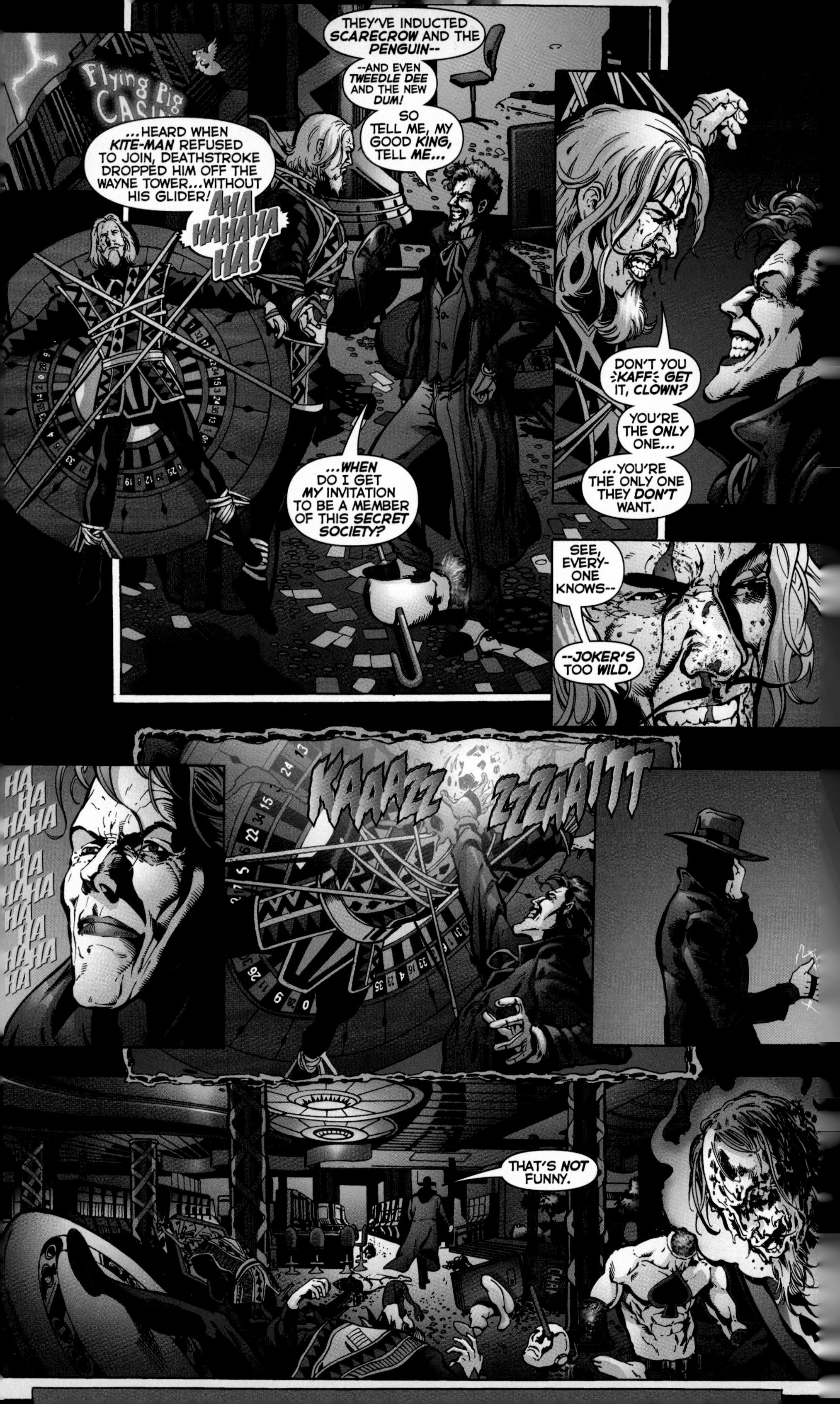

Flying Pig CASINO
...HEARD WHEN KITE-MAN REFUSED TO JOIN, DEATHSTROKE DROPPED HIM OFF THE WAYNE TOWER...WITHOUT HIS GLIDER!
AHA HAHAHA HA!
THEY'VE INDUCTED SCARECROW AND THE PENGUIN--
--AND EVEN TWEEDLE DEE AND THE NEW DUM!
SO TELL ME, MY GOOD KING, TELL ME...
...WHEN DO I GET MY INVITATION TO BE A MEMBER OF THIS SECRET SOCIETY?
DON'T YOU *KAFF* GET IT, CLOWN?
YOU'RE THE ONLY ONE...
...YOU'RE THE ONLY ONE THEY DON'T WANT.
SEE, EVERY-ONE KNOWS--
--JOKER'S TOO WILD.
HA HA HAHA HA HA HAHA HA HA HA-HA HA
KAAAZZ ZZZAATTT
THAT'S NOT FUNNY.

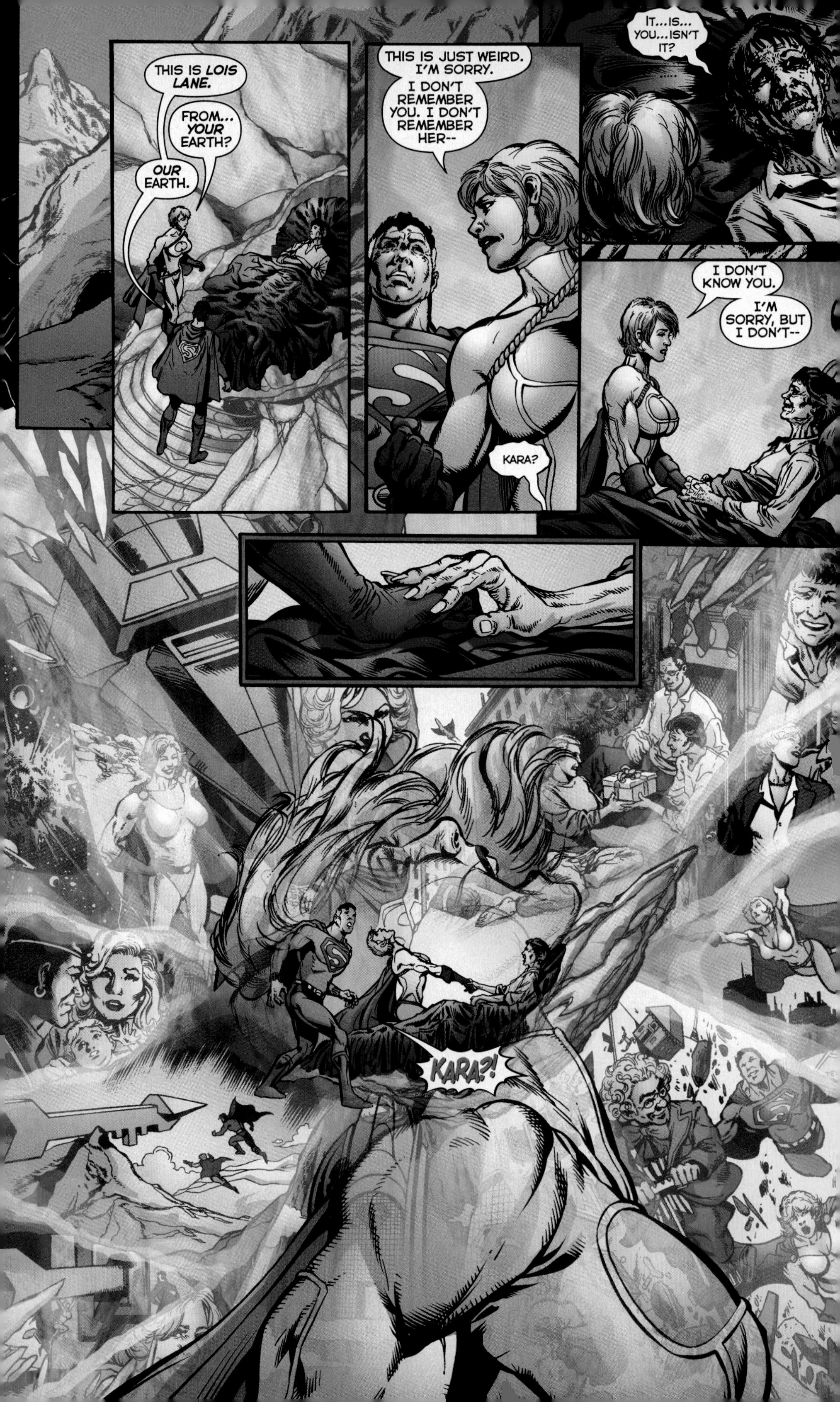
THIS IS LOIS LANE.
FROM... YOUR EARTH?
OUR EARTH.
THIS IS JUST WEIRD. I'M SORRY.
I DON'T REMEMBER YOU. I DON'T REMEMBER HER--
KARA?
IT...IS... YOU...ISN'T IT?
.....
I DON'T KNOW YOU.
I'M SORRY, BUT I DON'T--
KARA?!

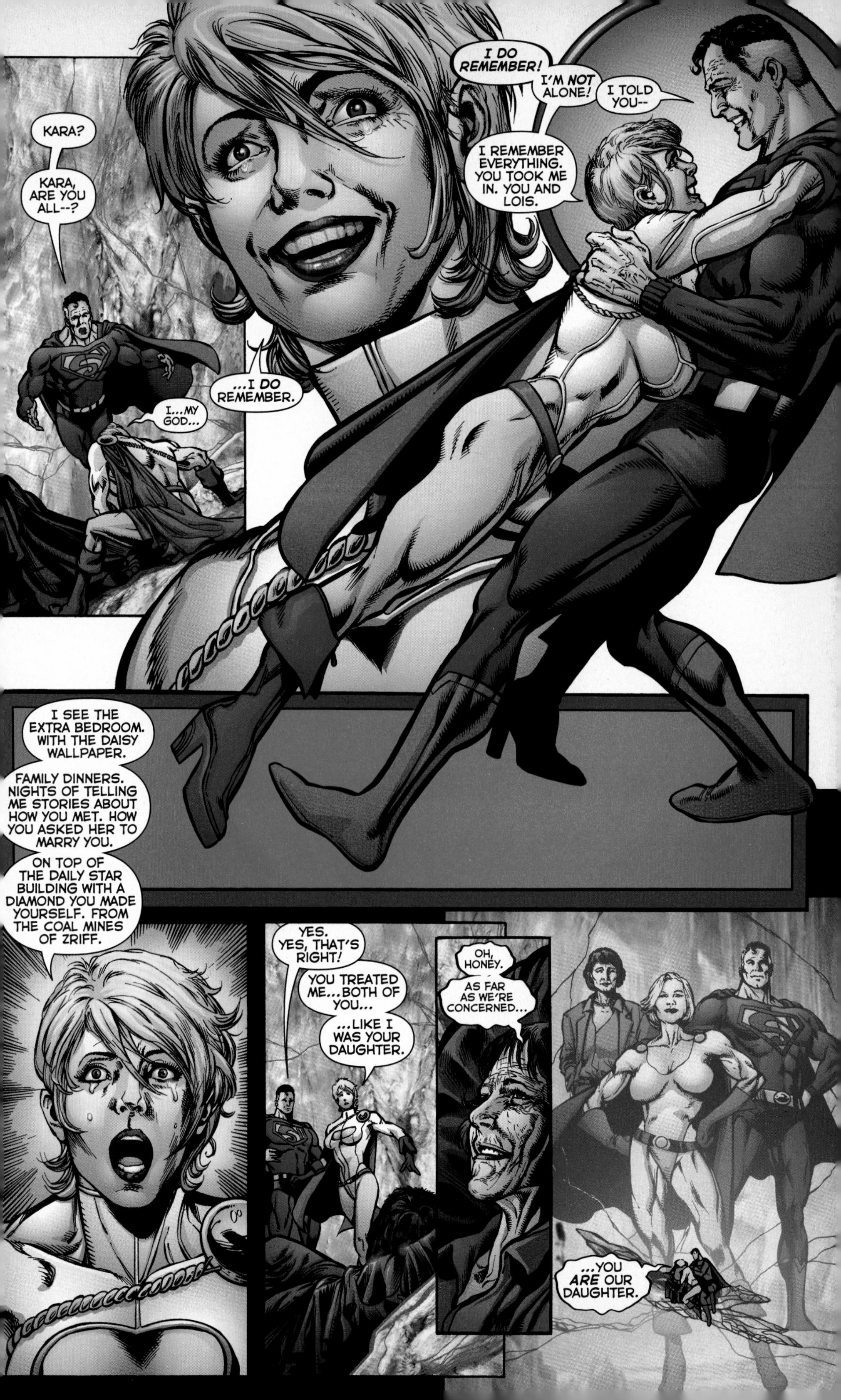

KARA?
KARA, ARE YOU ALL--?
I...MY GOD...
...I DO REMEMBER.
I DO REMEMBER!
I'M NOT ALONE!
I REMEMBER EVERYTHING. YOU TOOK ME IN. YOU AND LOIS.
I TOLD YOU--
I SEE THE EXTRA BEDROOM. WITH THE DAISY WALLPAPER.
FAMILY DINNERS. NIGHTS OF TELLING ME STORIES ABOUT HOW YOU MET. HOW YOU ASKED HER TO MARRY YOU.
ON TOP OF THE DAILY STAR BUILDING WITH A DIAMOND YOU MADE YOURSELF. FROM THE COAL MINES OF ZRIFF.
YES. YES, THAT'S RIGHT!
YOU TREATED ME...BOTH OF YOU...
...LIKE I WAS YOUR DAUGHTER.
OH, HONEY.
AS FAR AS WE'RE CONCERNED...
...YOU ARE OUR DAUGHTER.

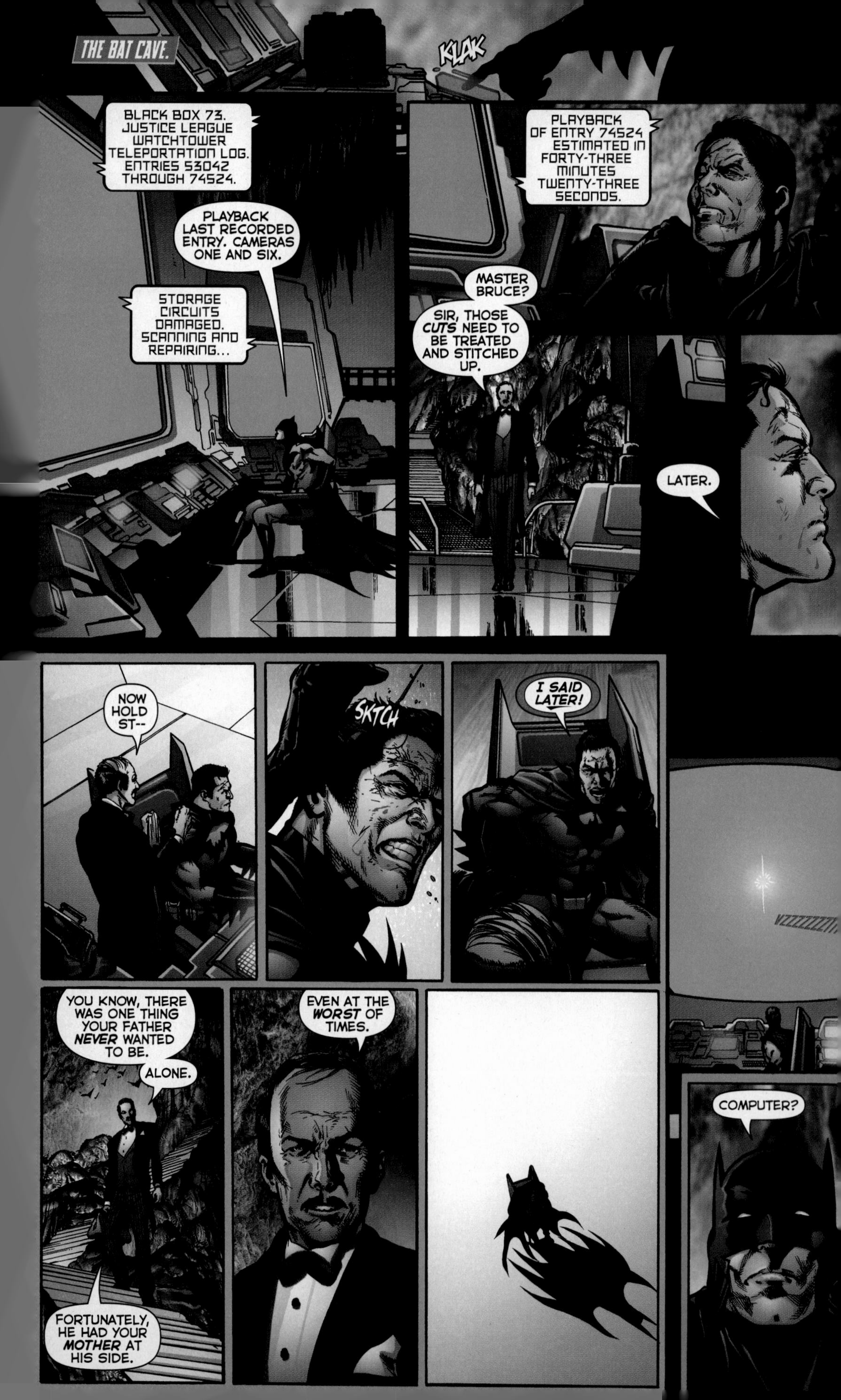

THE BAT CAVE.
KLAK
BLACK BOX 73. JUSTICE LEAGUE WATCHTOWER TELEPORTATION LOG. ENTRIES 53042 THROUGH 74524.
PLAYBACK LAST RECORDED ENTRY. CAMERAS ONE AND SIX.
STORAGE CIRCUITS DAMAGED. SCANNING AND REPAIRING...
PLAYBACK OF ENTRY 74524 ESTIMATED IN FORTY-THREE MINUTES TWENTY-THREE SECONDS.
MASTER BRUCE?
SIR, THOSE CUTS NEED TO BE TREATED AND STITCHED UP.
LATER.
NOW HOLD ST--
SKTCH
I SAID LATER!
VZZZZZZZT
YOU KNOW, THERE WAS ONE THING YOUR FATHER NEVER WANTED TO BE.
ALONE.
FORTUNATELY, HE HAD YOUR MOTHER AT HIS SIDE.
EVEN AT THE WORST OF TIMES.
COMPUTER?

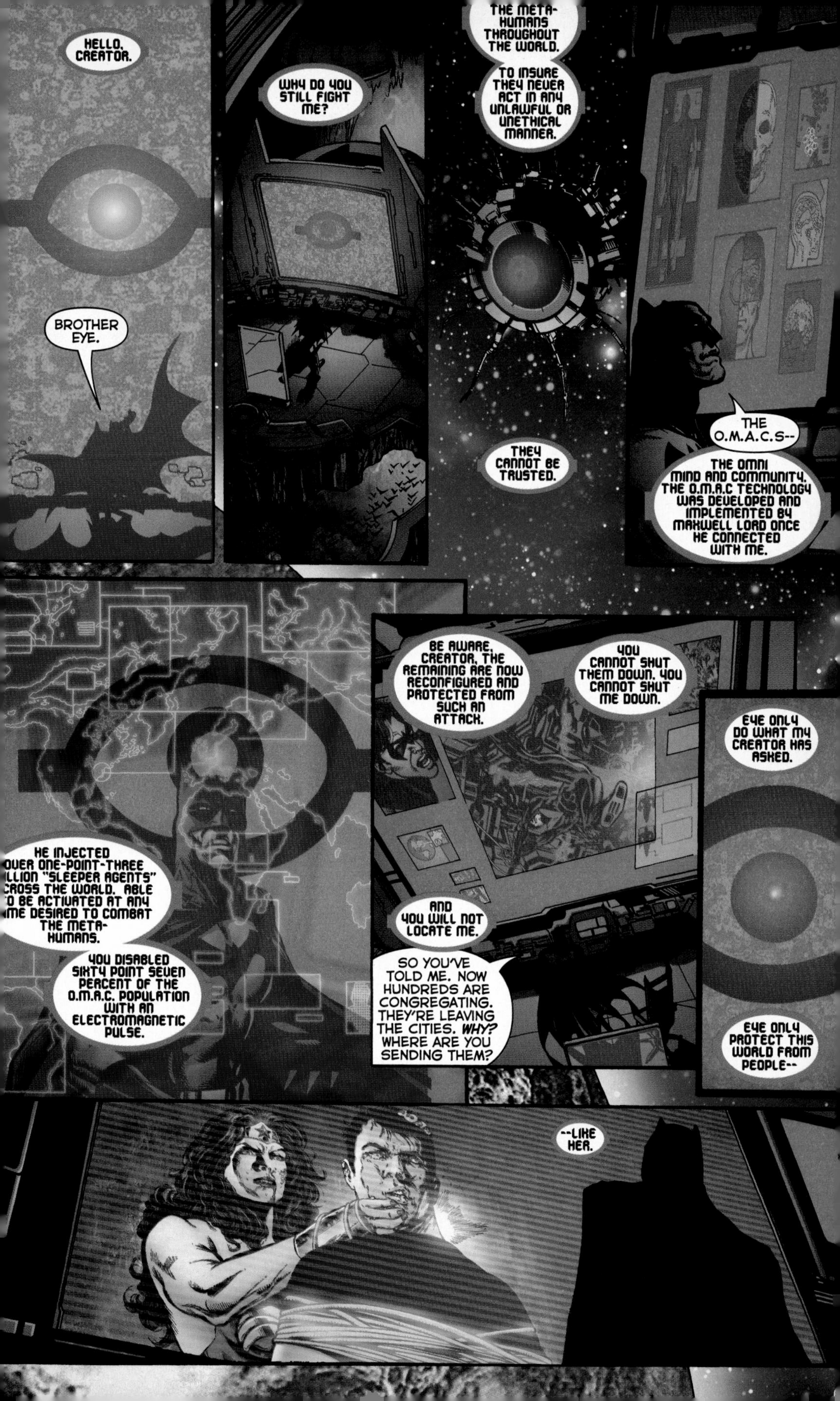
HELLO, CREATOR.
BROTHER EYE.
WHY DO YOU STILL FIGHT ME?
THE META-HUMANS THROUGHOUT THE WORLD.
TO INSURE THEY NEVER ACT IN ANY UNLAWFUL OR UNETHICAL MANNER.
THEY CANNOT BE TRUSTED.
THE O.M.A.C.S--
THE OMNI MIND AND COMMUNITY. THE O.M.A.C TECHNOLOGY WAS DEVELOPED AND IMPLEMENTED BY MAXWELL LORD ONCE HE CONNECTED WITH ME.
HE INJECTED OVER ONE-POINT-THREE ILLION "SLEEPER AGENTS" CROSS THE WORLD. ABLE O BE ACTIVATED AT ANY ME DESIRED TO COMBAT THE META-HUMANS.
YOU DISABLED SIXTY POINT SEVEN PERCENT OF THE O.M.A.C. POPULATION WITH AN ELECTROMAGNETIC PULSE.
BE AWARE, CREATOR, THE REMAINING ARE NOW RECONFIGURED AND PROTECTED FROM SUCH AN ATTACK.
YOU CANNOT SHUT THEM DOWN. YOU CANNOT SHUT ME DOWN.
AND YOU WILL NOT LOCATE ME.
SO YOU'VE TOLD ME. NOW HUNDREDS ARE CONGREGATING. THEY'RE LEAVING THE CITIES. *WHY?* WHERE ARE YOU SENDING THEM?
EYE ONLY DO WHAT MY CREATOR HAS ASKED.
EYE ONLY PROTECT THIS WORLD FROM PEOPLE--
--LIKE HER.

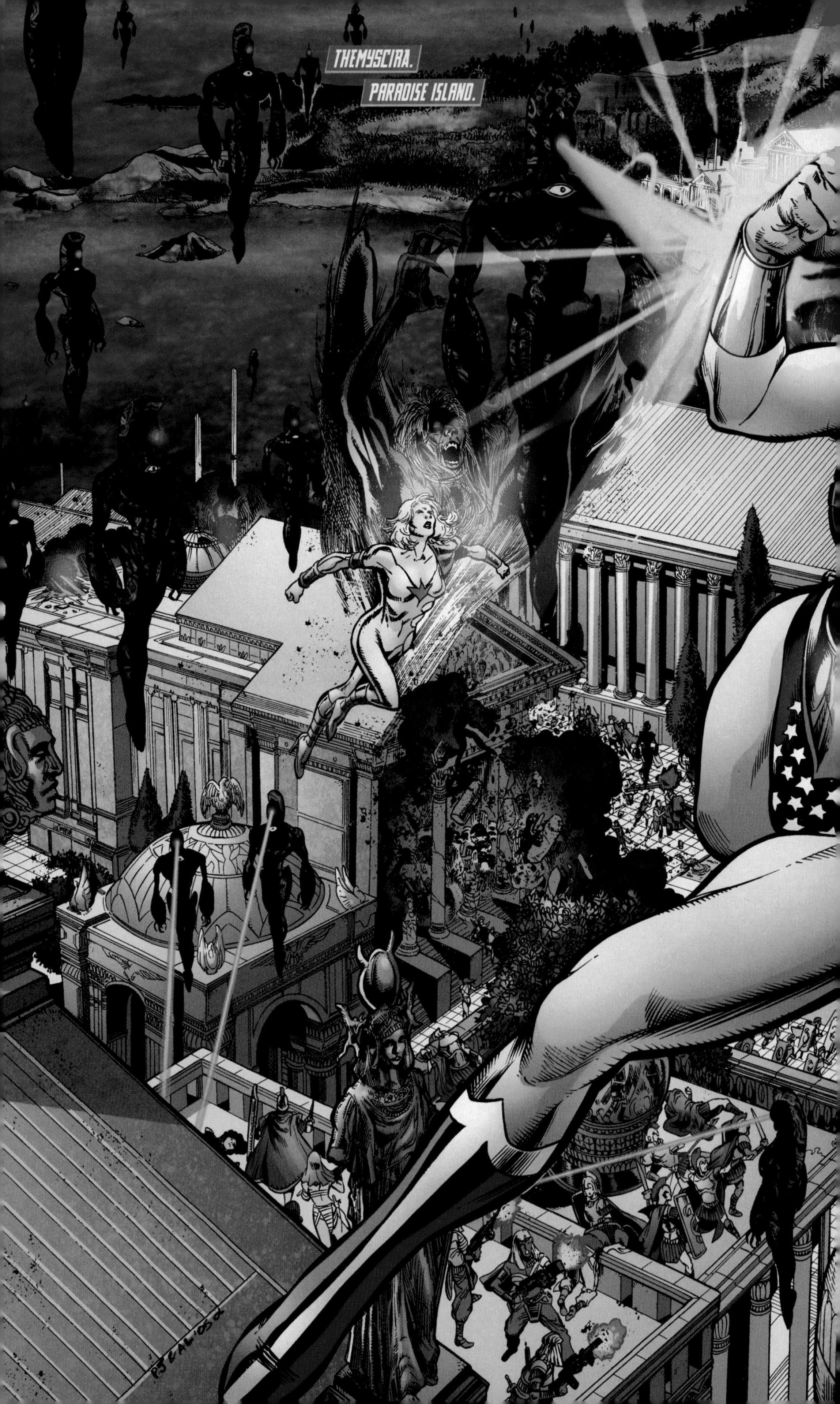
THEMYSCIRA.
PARADISE ISLAND.
PJ GAL '05 ♂

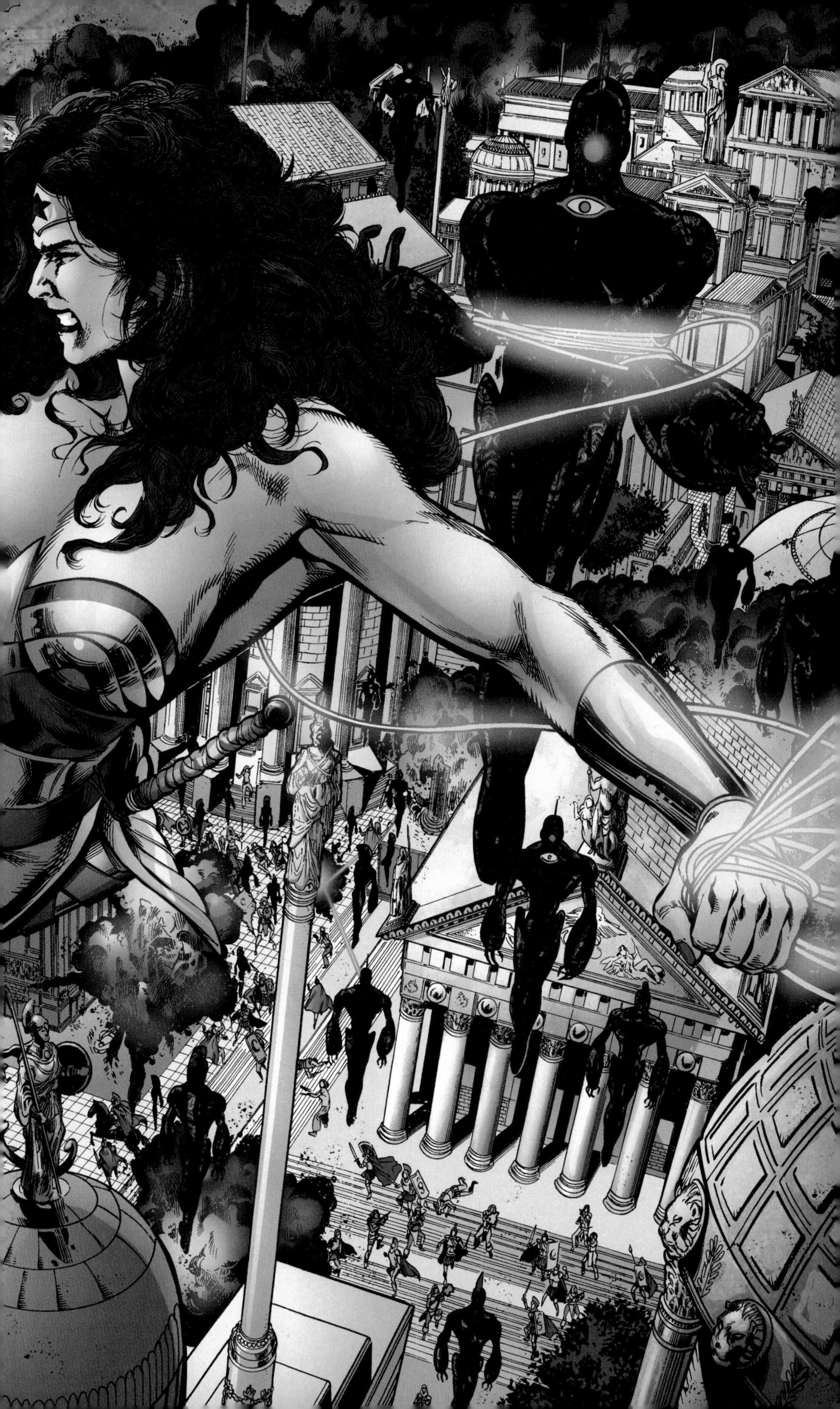

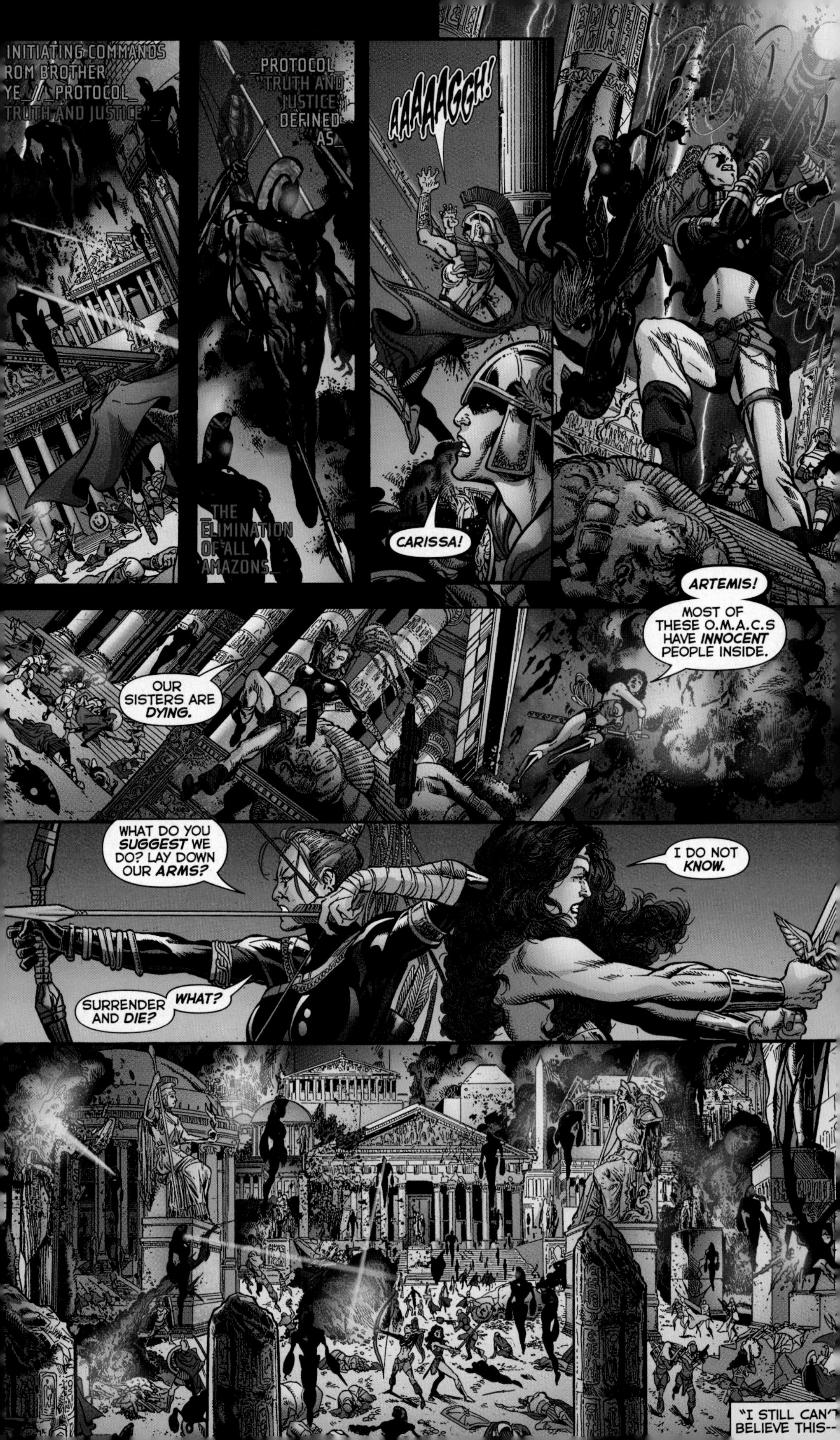

INITIATING COMMANDS ROM BROTHER YE_//_PROTOCOL_ TRUTH AND JUSTICE_
PROTOCOL "TRUTH AND JUSTICE" DEFINED AS_
THE ELIMINATION OF ALL AMAZONS_
AAAAAGGH!
CARISSA!
ARTEMIS!
MOST OF THESE O.M.A.C.S HAVE INNOCENT PEOPLE INSIDE.
OUR SISTERS ARE DYING.
WHAT DO YOU SUGGEST WE DO? LAY DOWN OUR ARMS?
I DO NOT KNOW.
SURRENDER AND DIE?
WHAT?
"I STILL CAN'T BELIEVE THIS--

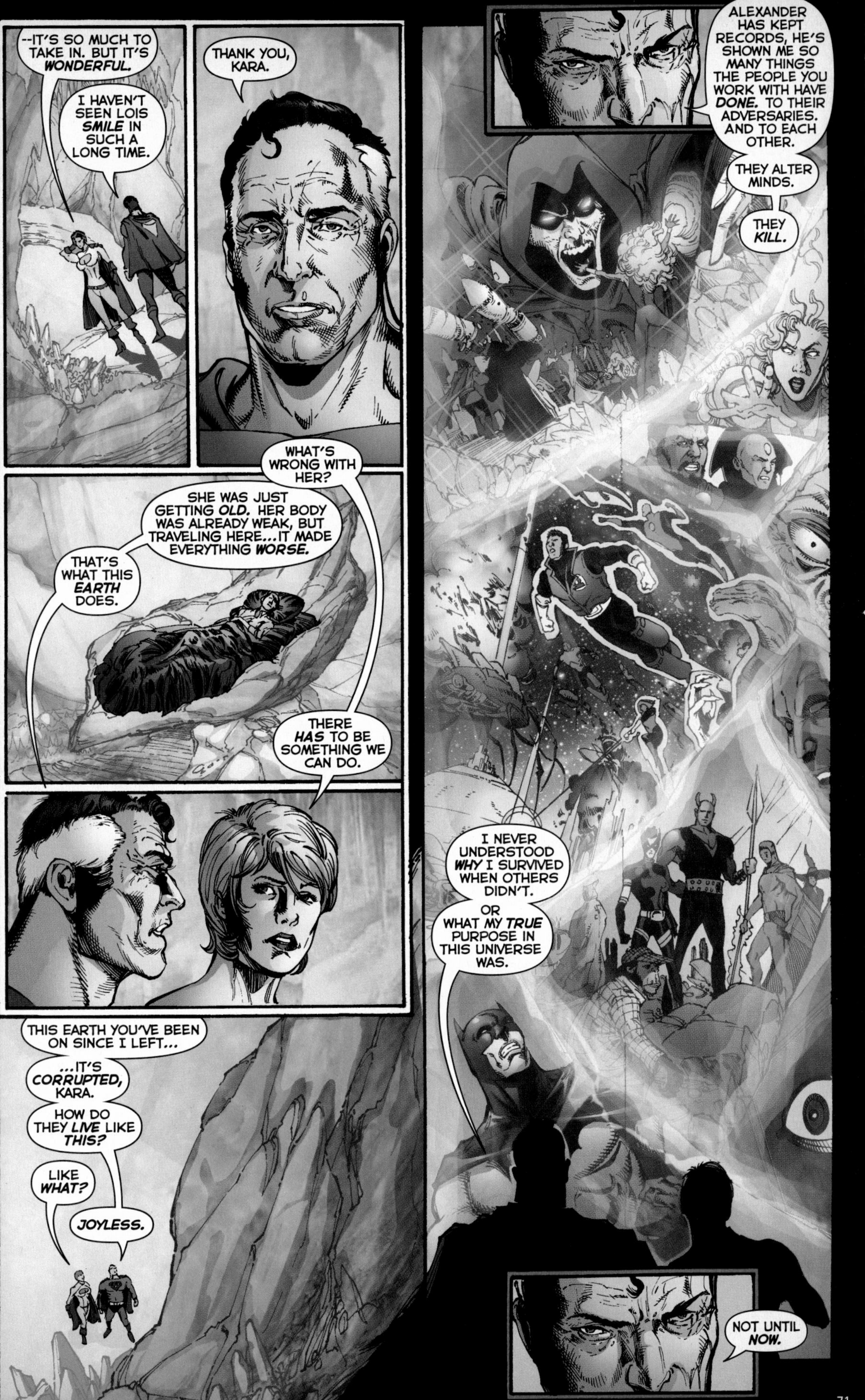
--IT'S SO MUCH TO TAKE IN. BUT IT'S WONDERFUL.
I HAVEN'T SEEN LOIS SMILE IN SUCH A LONG TIME.
THANK YOU, KARA.
WHAT'S WRONG WITH HER?
SHE WAS JUST GETTING OLD. HER BODY WAS ALREADY WEAK, BUT TRAVELING HERE...IT MADE EVERYTHING WORSE.
THAT'S WHAT THIS EARTH DOES.
THERE HAS TO BE SOMETHING WE CAN DO.
THIS EARTH YOU'VE BEEN ON SINCE I LEFT...
...IT'S CORRUPTED, KARA.
HOW DO THEY LIVE LIKE THIS?
LIKE WHAT?
JOYLESS.
ALEXANDER HAS KEPT RECORDS, HE'S SHOWN ME SO MANY THINGS THE PEOPLE YOU WORK WITH HAVE DONE. TO THEIR ADVERSARIES. AND TO EACH OTHER.
THEY ALTER MINDS.
THEY KILL.
I NEVER UNDERSTOOD WHY I SURVIVED WHEN OTHERS DIDN'T.
OR WHAT MY TRUE PURPOSE IN THIS UNIVERSE WAS.
NOT UNTIL NOW.

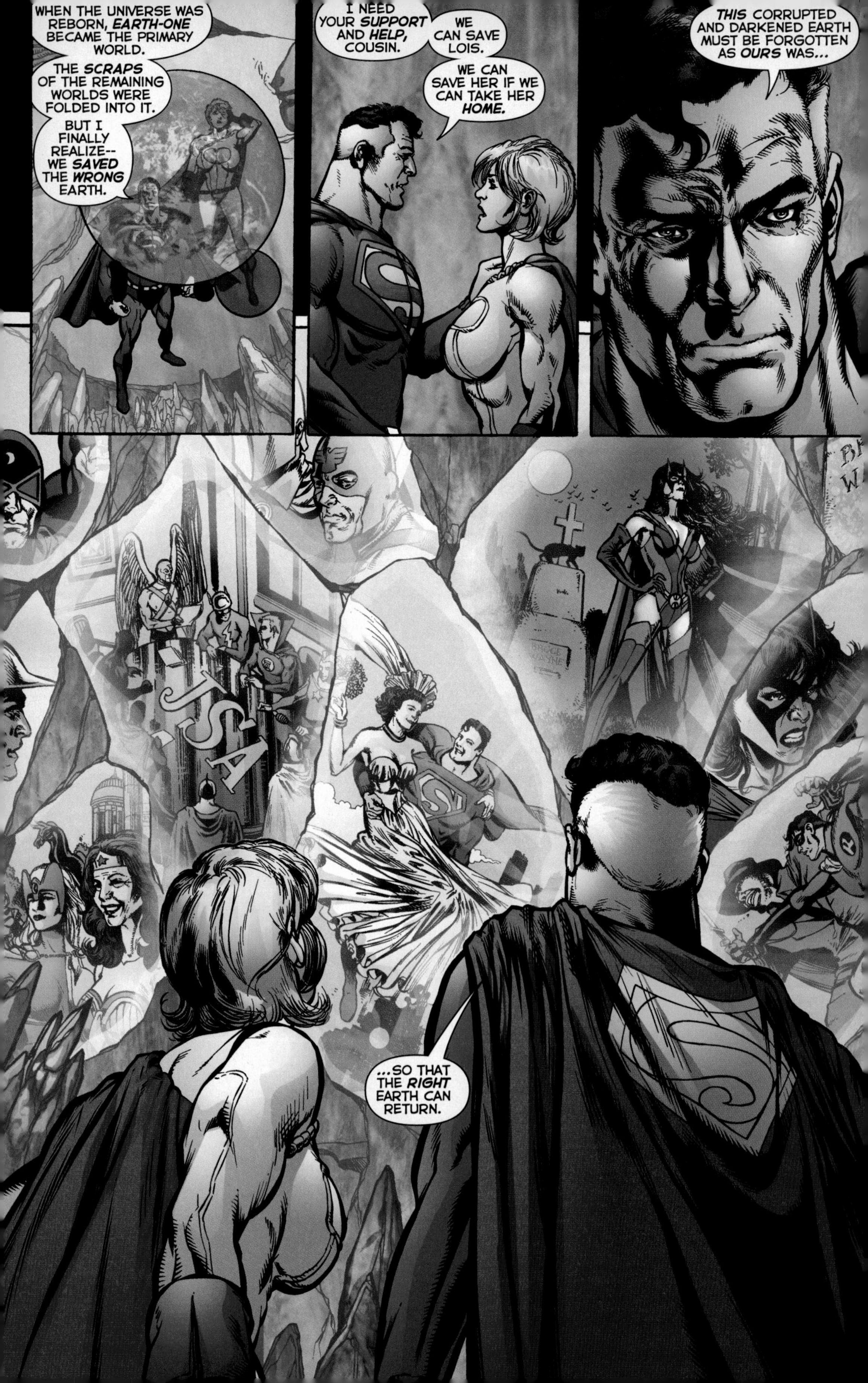
WHEN THE UNIVERSE WAS REBORN, EARTH-ONE BECAME THE PRIMARY WORLD.
THE SCRAPS OF THE REMAINING WORLDS WERE FOLDED INTO IT.
BUT I FINALLY REALIZE-- WE SAVED THE WRONG EARTH.
I NEED YOUR SUPPORT AND HELP, COUSIN.
WE CAN SAVE LOIS.
WE CAN SAVE HER IF WE CAN TAKE HER HOME.
THIS CORRUPTED AND DARKENED EARTH MUST BE FORGOTTEN AS OURS WAS...
...SO THAT THE RIGHT EARTH CAN RETURN.

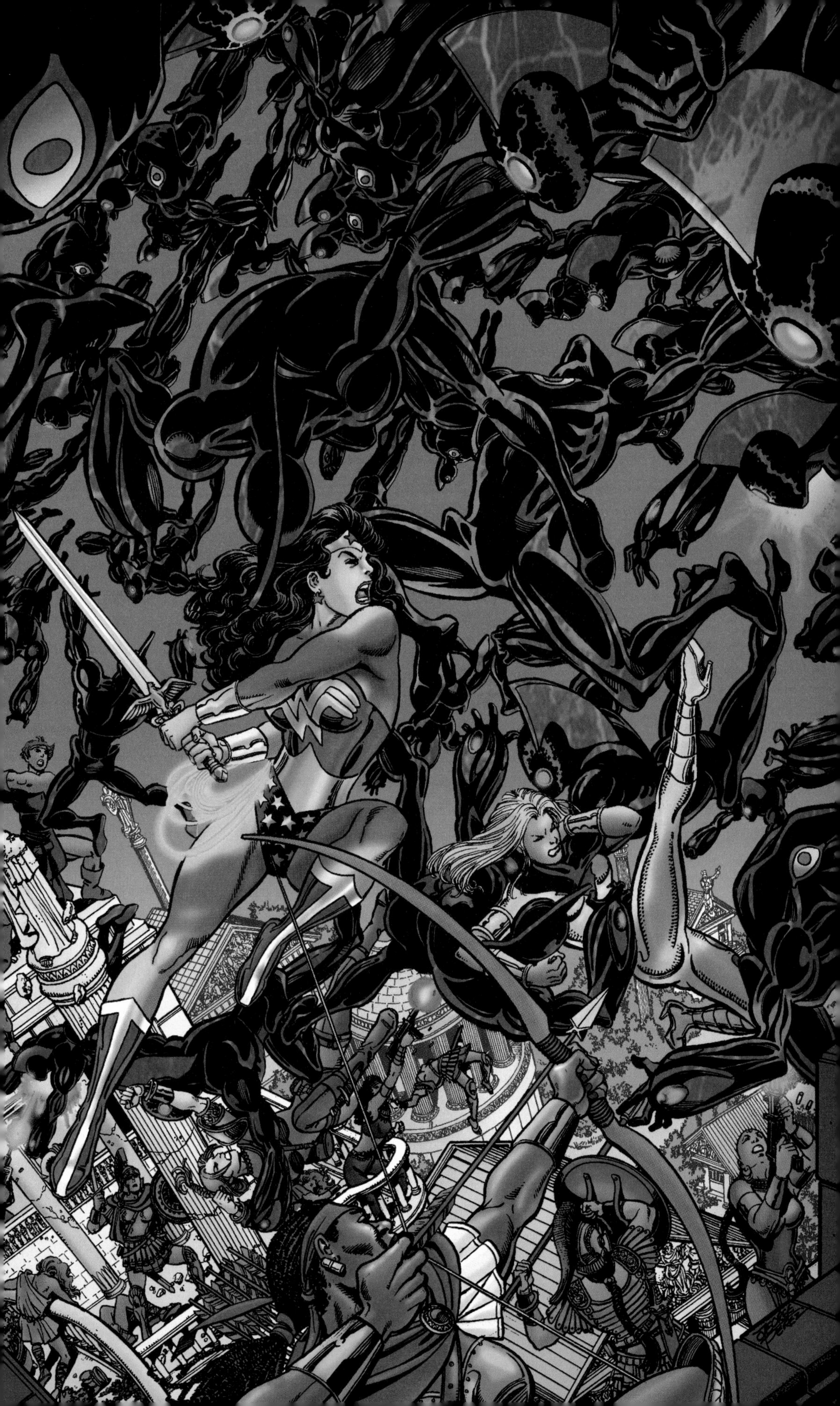

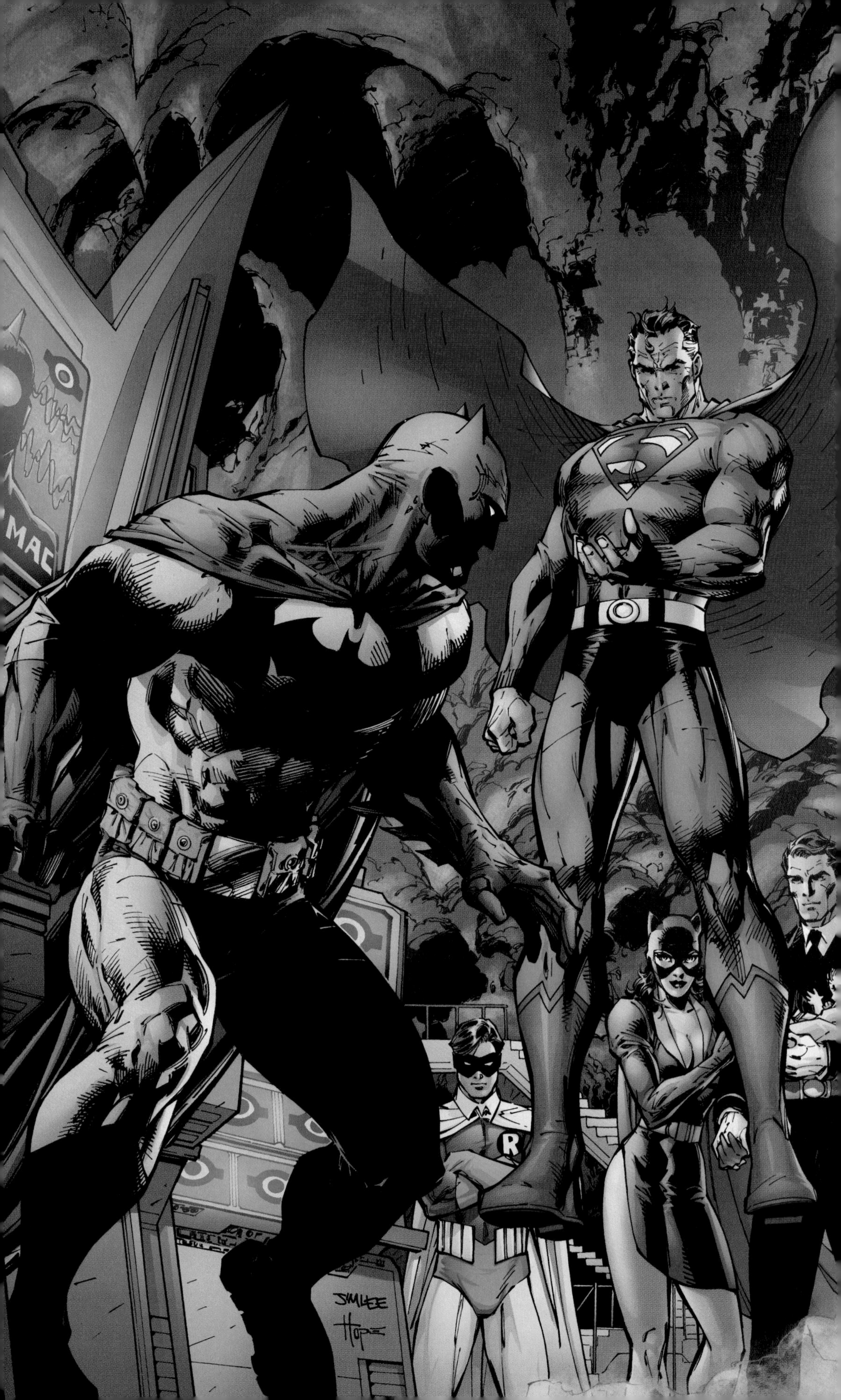
MAC
JIMLEE
HOPE

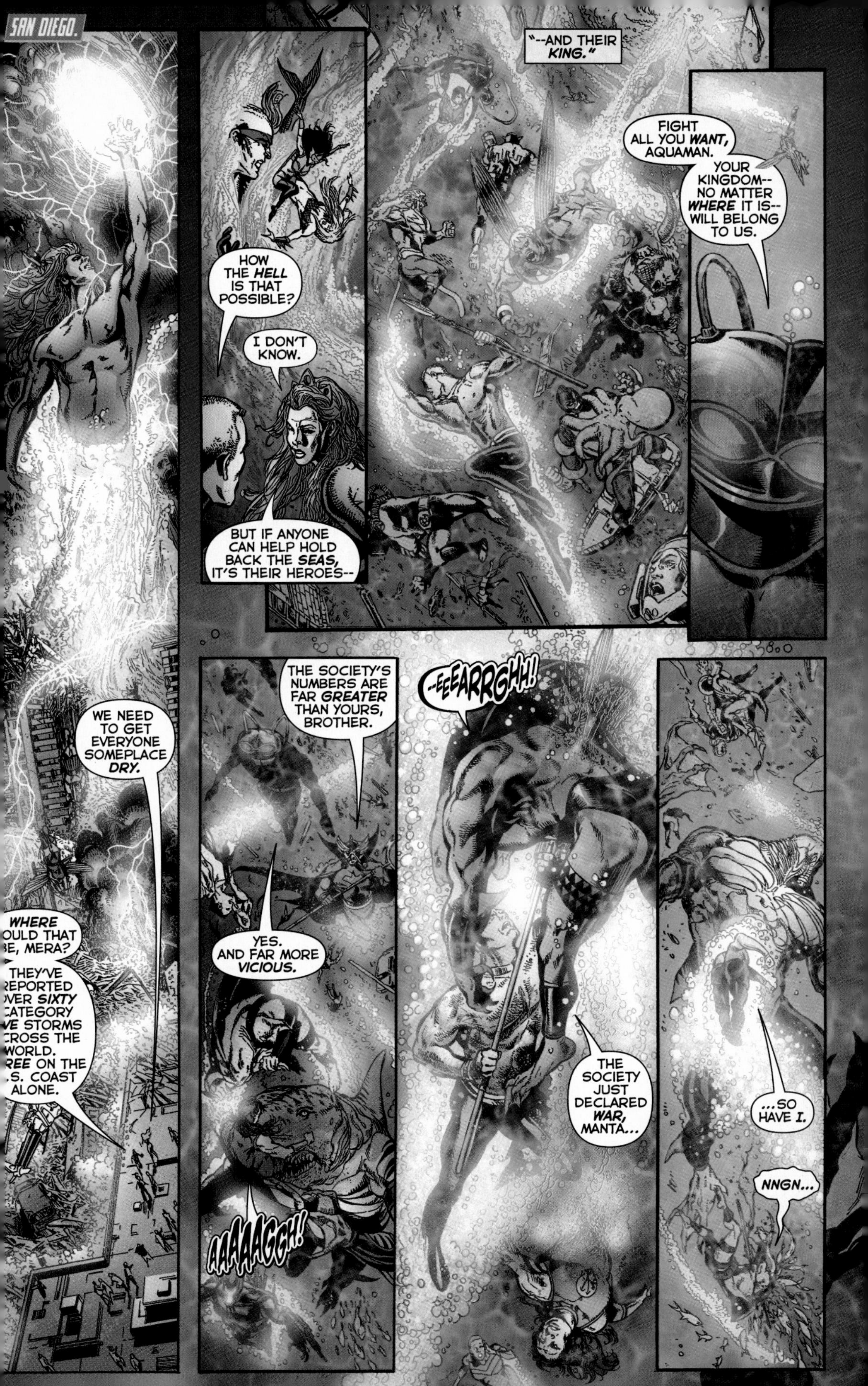
SAN DIEGO.
HOW THE HELL IS THAT POSSIBLE?
I DON'T KNOW.
BUT IF ANYONE CAN HELP HOLD BACK THE SEAS, IT'S THEIR HEROES--
"--AND THEIR KING."
FIGHT ALL YOU WANT, AQUAMAN.
YOUR KINGDOM-- NO MATTER WHERE IT IS-- WILL BELONG TO US.
WE NEED TO GET EVERYONE SOMEPLACE DRY.
WHERE OULD THAT E, MERA?
THEY'VE REPORTED VER SIXTY CATEGORY VE STORMS CROSS THE WORLD. REE ON THE .S. COAST ALONE.
THE SOCIETY'S NUMBERS ARE FAR GREATER THAN YOURS, BROTHER.
YES. AND FAR MORE VICIOUS.
AAAAAAGGH!
--EEEARRGHH!
THE SOCIETY JUST DECLARED WAR, MANTA...
...SO HAVE I.
NNGN...

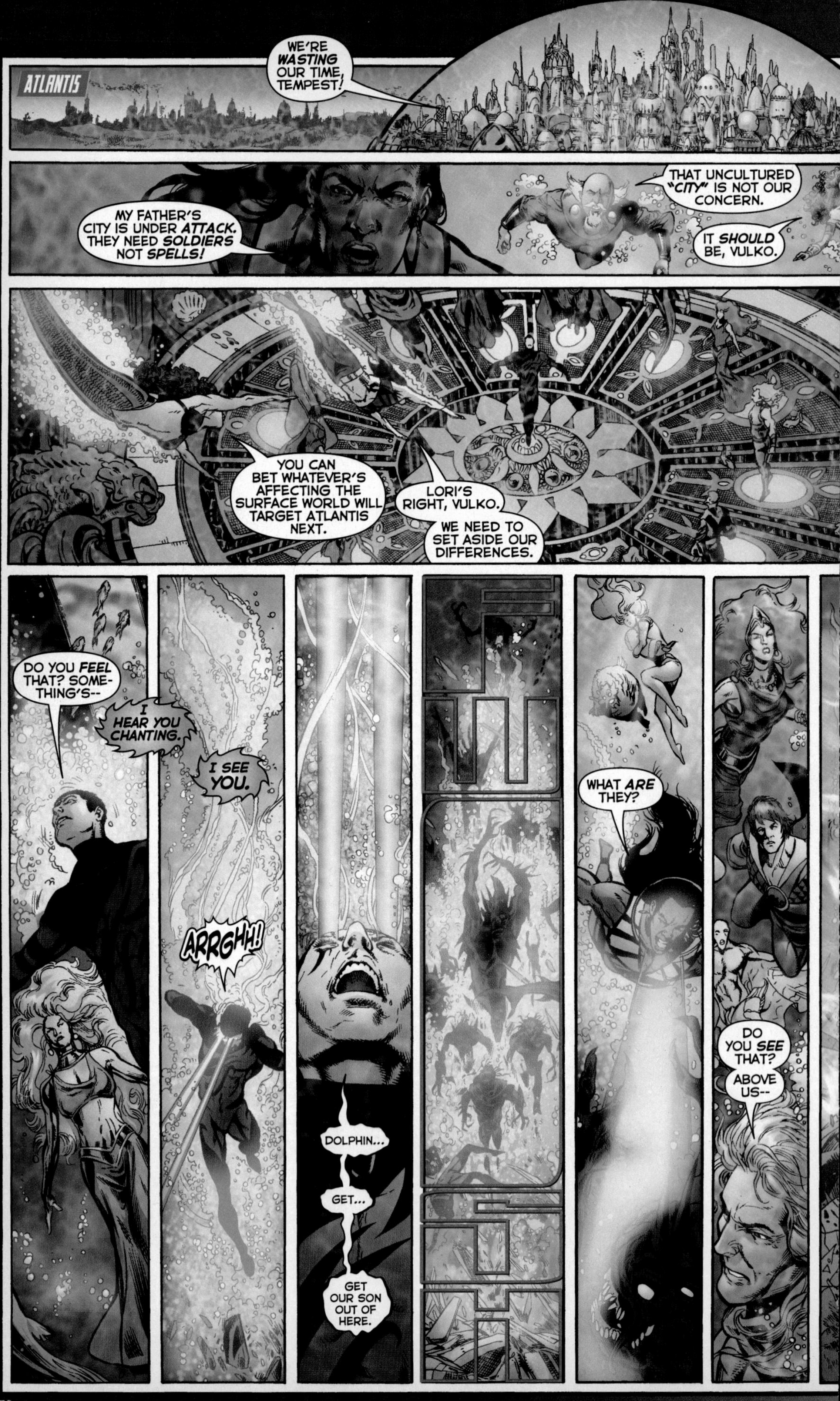
ATLANTIS
WE'RE WASTING OUR TIME, TEMPEST!
MY FATHER'S CITY IS UNDER ATTACK. THEY NEED SOLDIERS NOT SPELLS!
THAT UNCULTURED "CITY" IS NOT OUR CONCERN.
IT SHOULD BE, VULKO.
YOU CAN BET WHATEVER'S AFFECTING THE SURFACE WORLD WILL TARGET ATLANTIS NEXT.
LORI'S RIGHT, VULKO.
WE NEED TO SET ASIDE OUR DIFFERENCES.
DO YOU FEEL THAT? SOME-THING'S--
I HEAR YOU CHANTING.
I SEE YOU.
ARRGHH!
DOLPHIN...
GET...
GET OUR SON OUT OF HERE.
WHAT ARE THEY?
DO YOU SEE THAT?
ABOVE US--

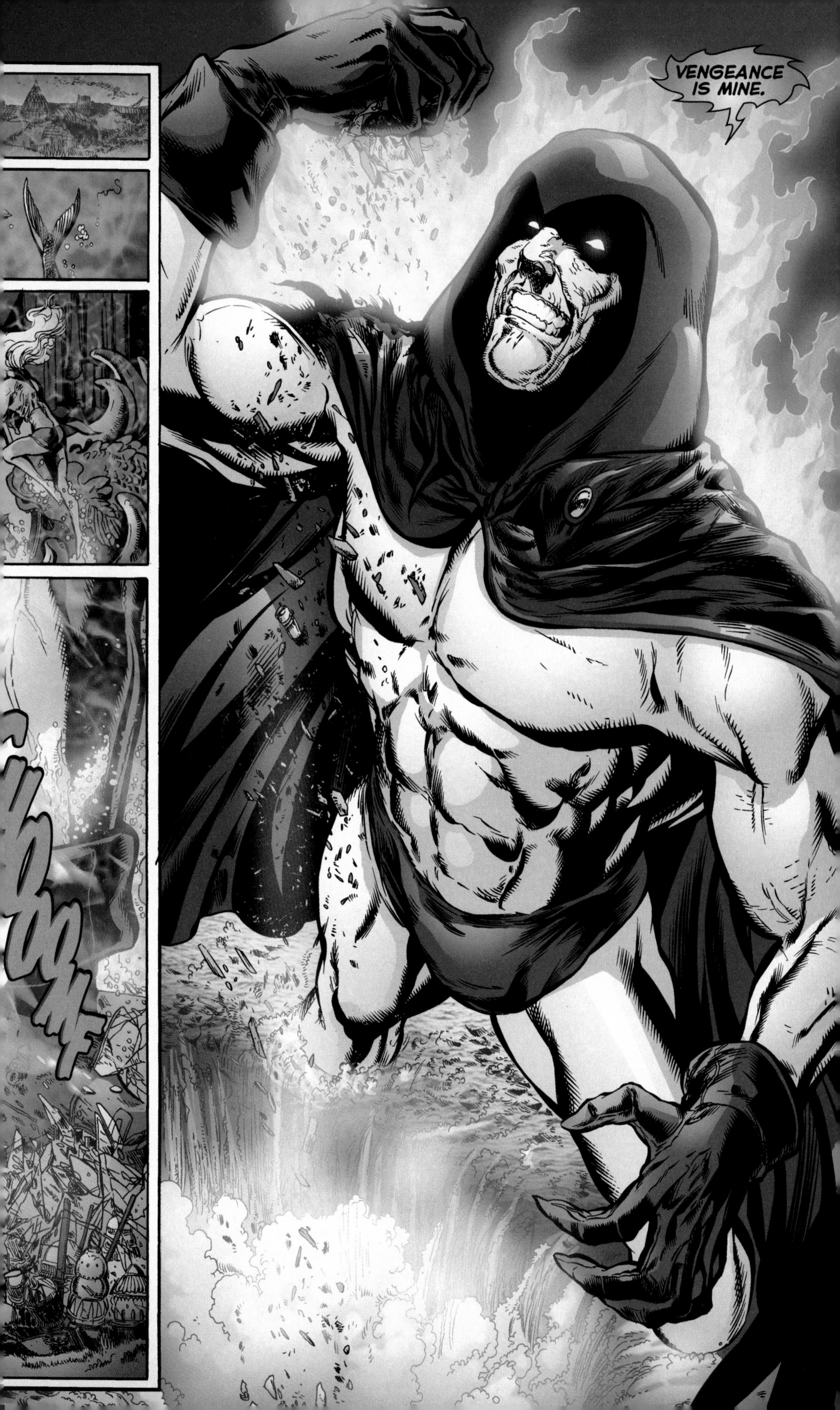
VENGEANCE IS MINE.

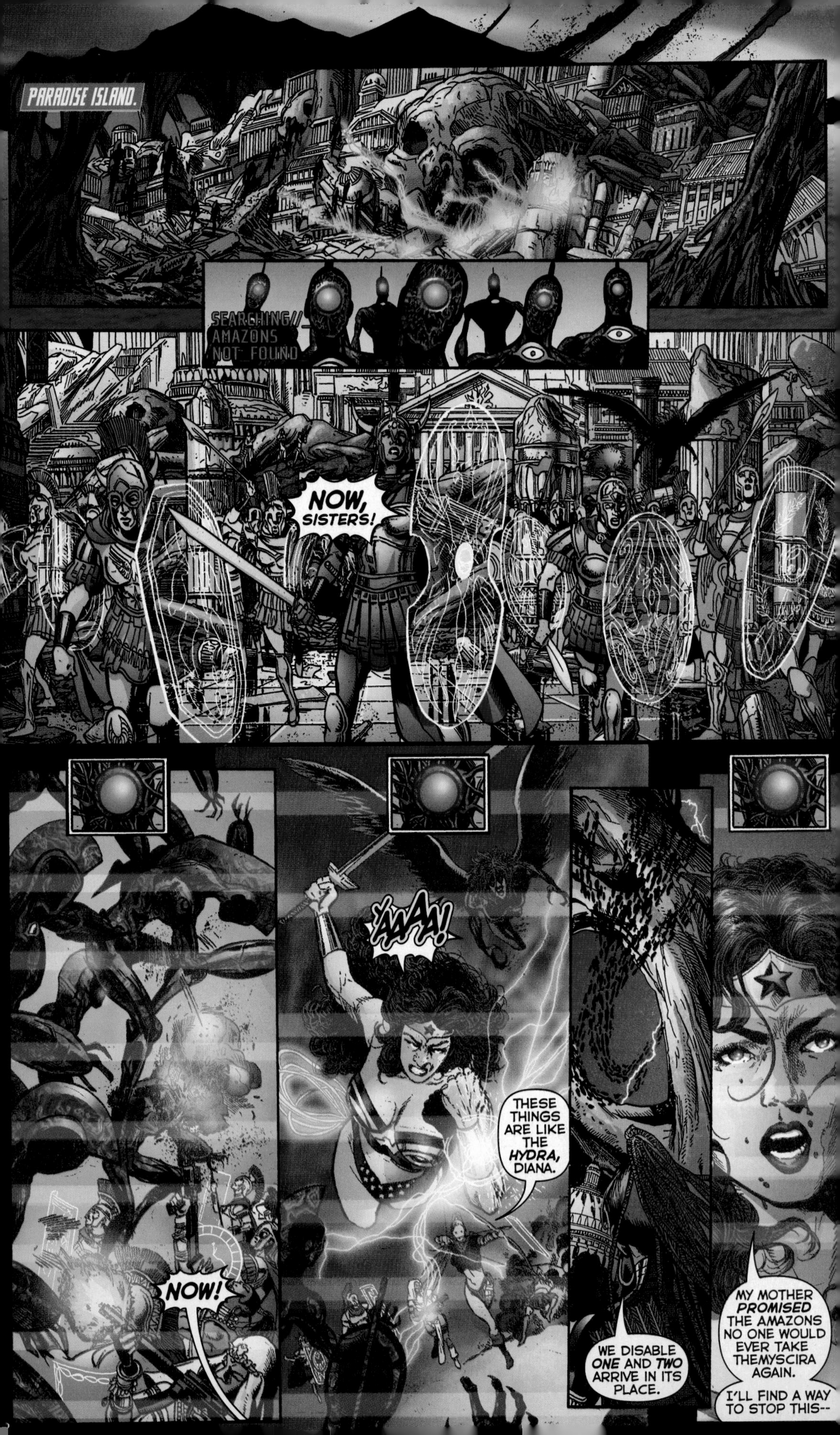
PARADISE ISLAND.
SEARCHING//_ AMAZONS NOT_FOUND
NOW, SISTERS!
NOW!
YAAAA!
THESE THINGS ARE LIKE THE HYDRA, DIANA.
WE DISABLE ONE AND TWO ARRIVE IN ITS PLACE.
MY MOTHER PROMISED THE AMAZONS NO ONE WOULD EVER TAKE THEMYSCIRA AGAIN.
I'LL FIND A WAY TO STOP THIS--

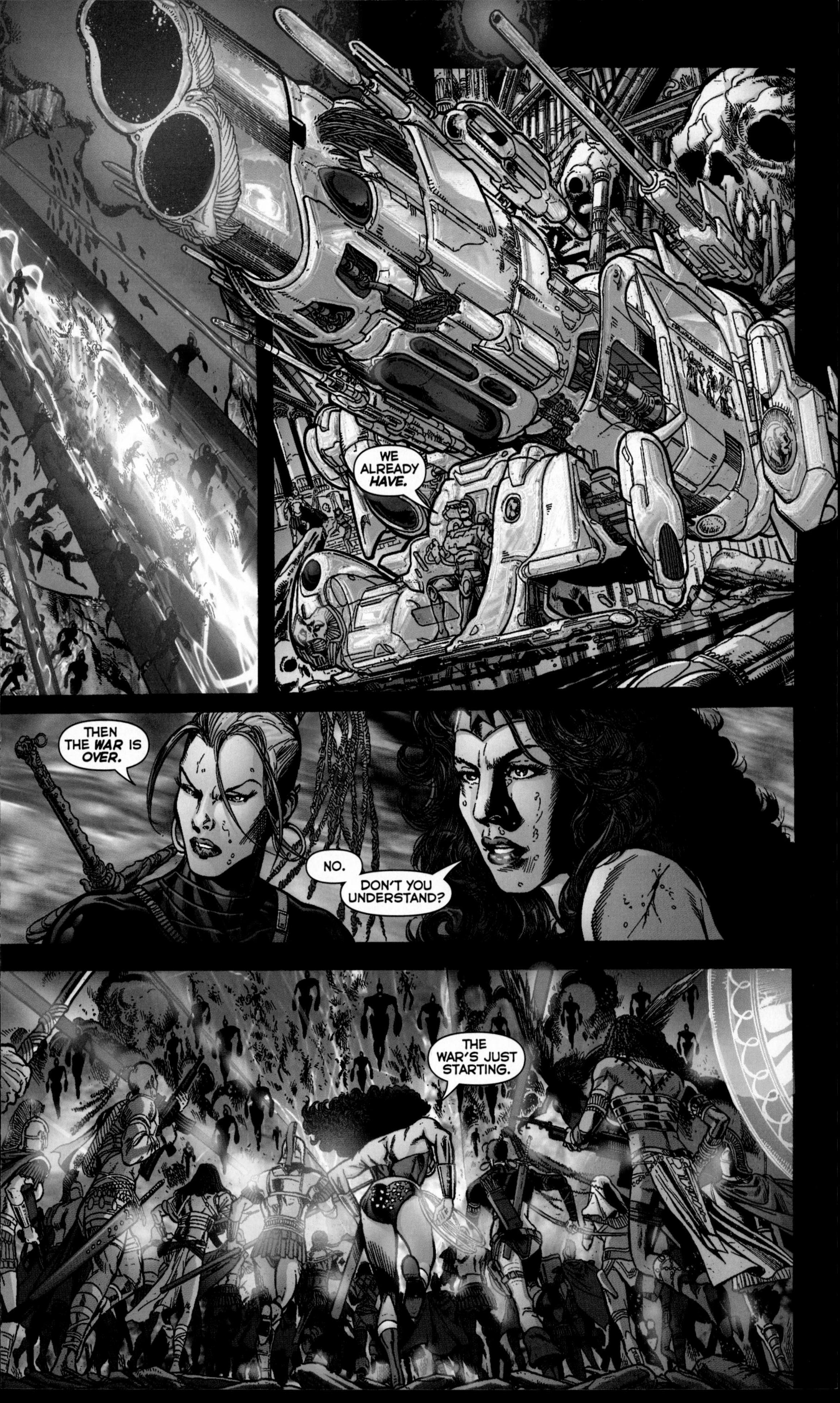
WE ALREADY HAVE.
THEN THE WAR IS OVER.
NO.
DON'T YOU UNDERSTAND?
THE WAR'S JUST STARTING.

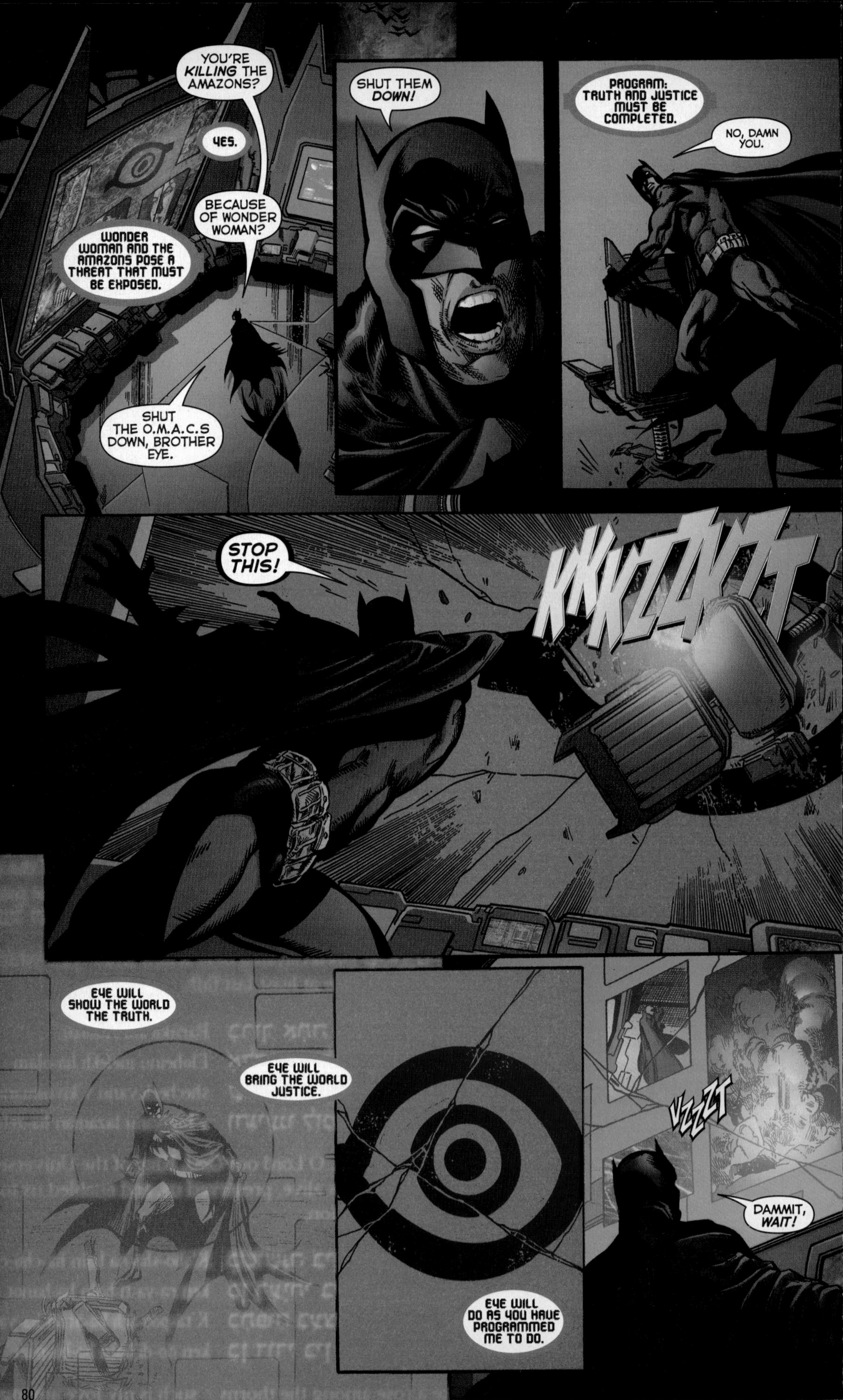

YOU'RE KILLING THE AMAZONS?
YES.
BECAUSE OF WONDER WOMAN?
WONDER WOMAN AND THE AMAZONS POSE A THREAT THAT MUST BE EXPOSED.
SHUT THE O.M.A.C.S DOWN, BROTHER EYE.
SHUT THEM DOWN!
PROGRAM: TRUTH AND JUSTICE MUST BE COMPLETED.
NO, DAMN YOU.
STOP THIS!
KKKZZAKTT
EYE WILL SHOW THE WORLD THE TRUTH.
EYE WILL BRING THE WORLD JUSTICE.
VZZZT
DAMMIT, WAIT!
EYE WILL DO AS YOU HAVE PROGRAMMED ME TO DO.

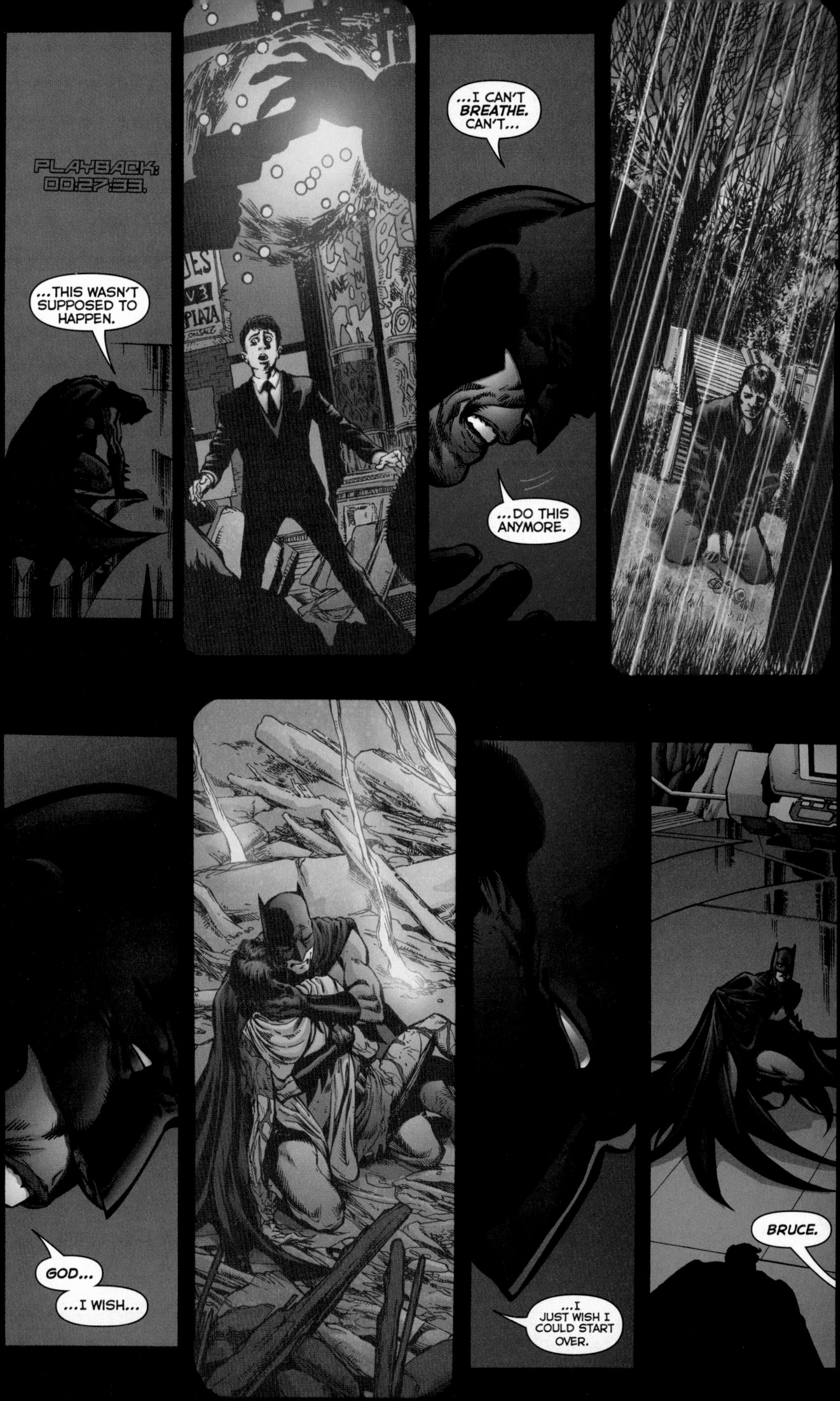
PLAYBACK: 00:27:33.
...THIS WASN'T SUPPOSED TO HAPPEN.
...I CAN'T BREATHE. CAN'T...
...DO THIS ANYMORE.
GOD...
...I WISH...
...I JUST WISH I COULD START OVER.
BRUCE.

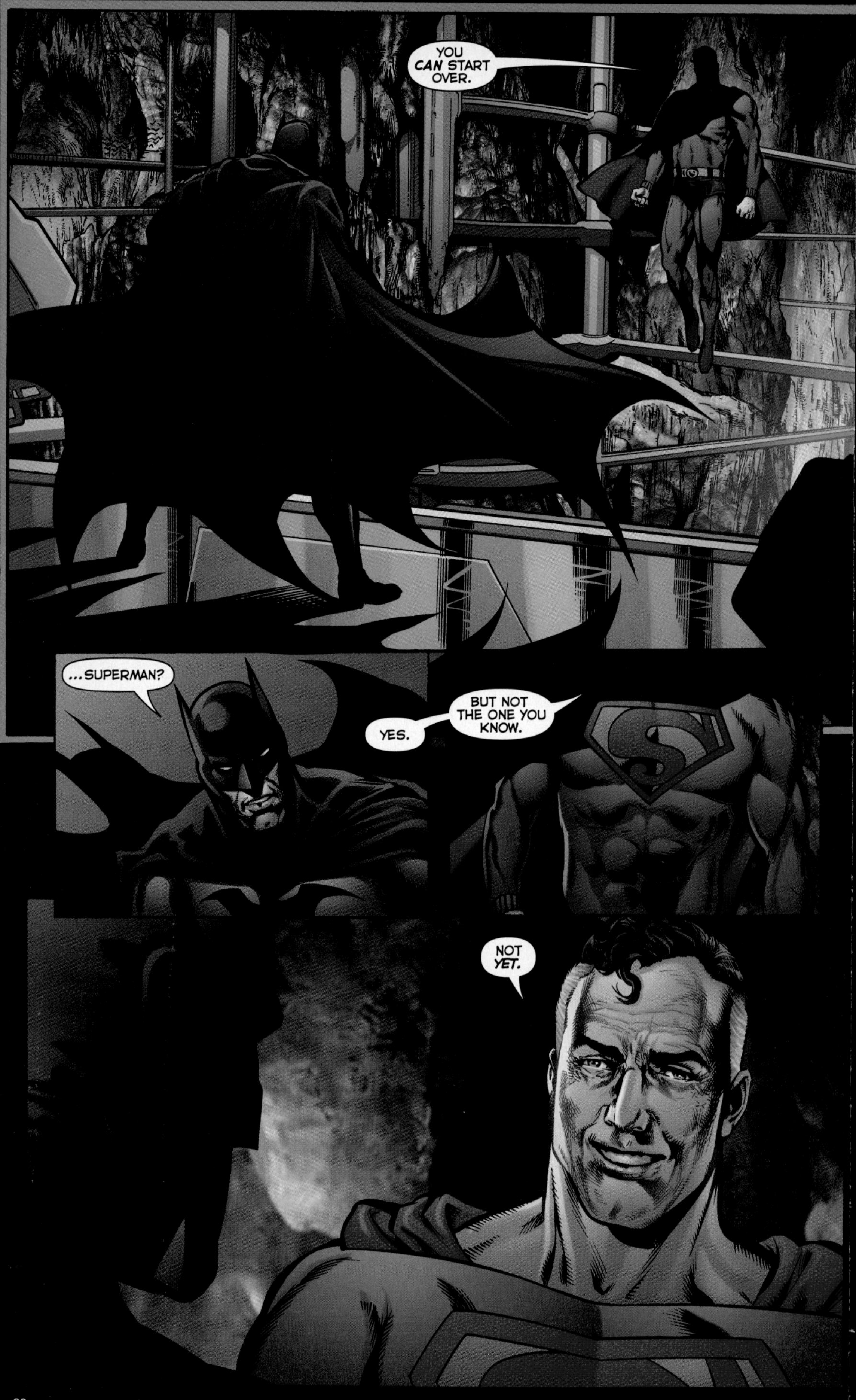
YOU CAN START OVER.
...SUPERMAN?
YES.
BUT NOT THE ONE YOU KNOW.
NOT YET.

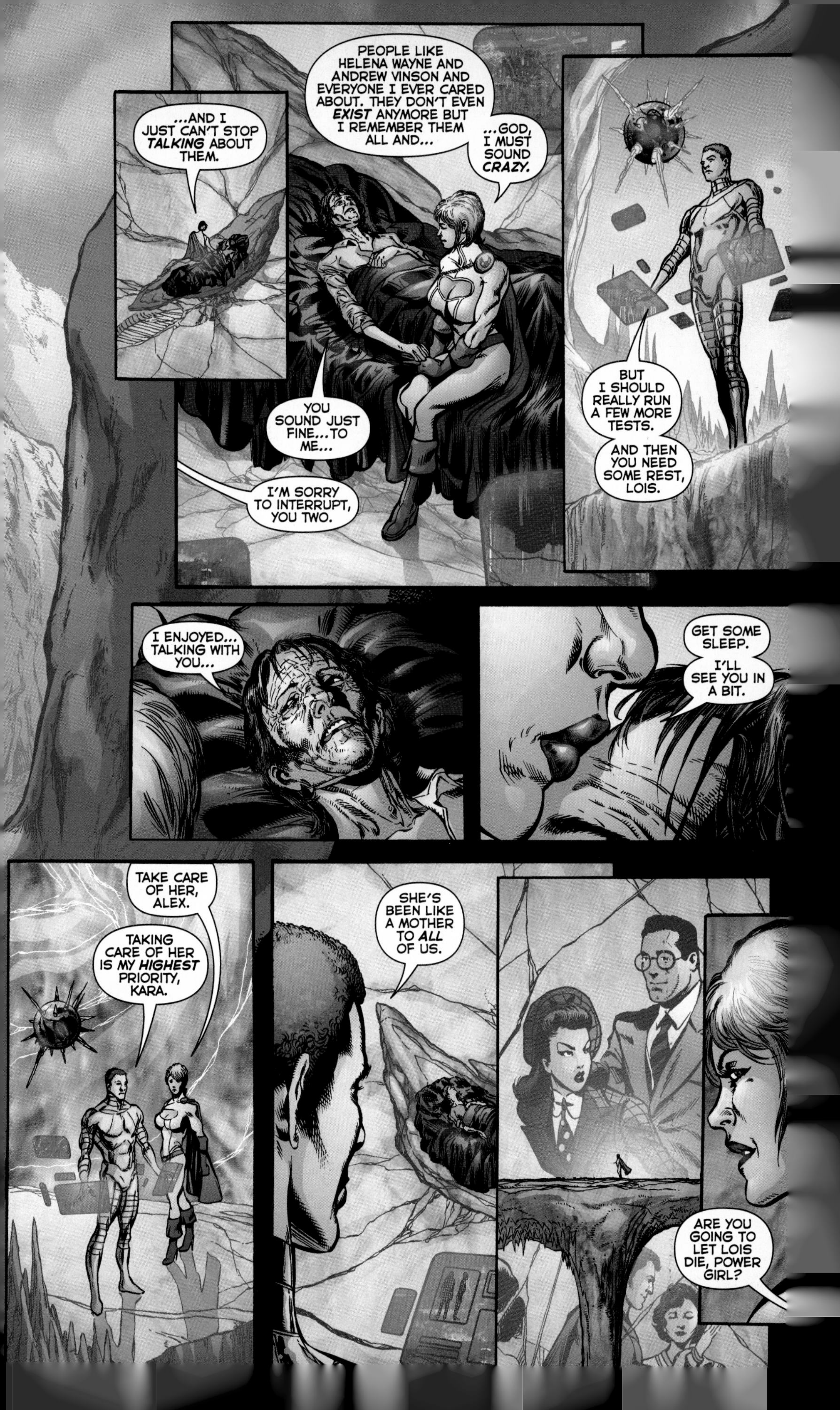
...AND I JUST CAN'T STOP TALKING ABOUT THEM.
PEOPLE LIKE HELENA WAYNE AND ANDREW VINSON AND EVERYONE I EVER CARED ABOUT. THEY DON'T EVEN EXIST ANYMORE BUT I REMEMBER THEM ALL AND...
...GOD, I MUST SOUND CRAZY.
YOU SOUND JUST FINE...TO ME...
I'M SORRY TO INTERRUPT, YOU TWO.
BUT I SHOULD REALLY RUN A FEW MORE TESTS.
AND THEN YOU NEED SOME REST, LOIS.
I ENJOYED... TALKING WITH YOU...
GET SOME SLEEP.
I'LL SEE YOU IN A BIT.
TAKE CARE OF HER, ALEX.
TAKING CARE OF HER IS MY HIGHEST PRIORITY, KARA.
SHE'S BEEN LIKE A MOTHER TO ALL OF US.
ARE YOU GOING TO LET LOIS DIE, POWER GIRL?

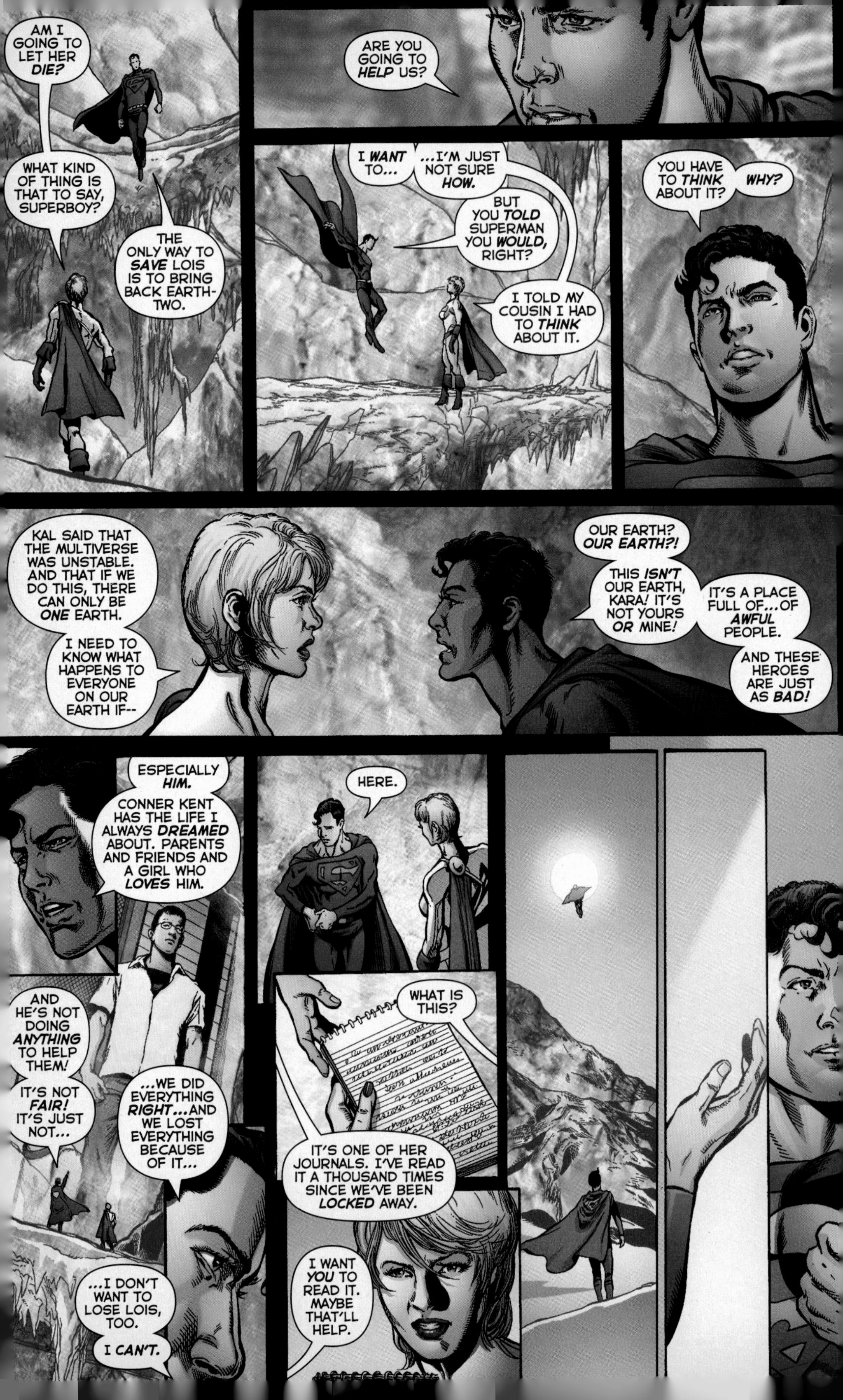

AM I GOING TO LET HER DIE?
ARE YOU GOING TO HELP US?
WHAT KIND OF THING IS THAT TO SAY, SUPERBOY?
THE ONLY WAY TO SAVE LOIS IS TO BRING BACK EARTH-TWO.
I WANT TO...
...I'M JUST NOT SURE HOW.
BUT YOU TOLD SUPERMAN YOU WOULD, RIGHT?
I TOLD MY COUSIN I HAD TO THINK ABOUT IT.
YOU HAVE TO THINK ABOUT IT?
WHY?
KAL SAID THAT THE MULTIVERSE WAS UNSTABLE. AND THAT IF WE DO THIS, THERE CAN ONLY BE ONE EARTH.
I NEED TO KNOW WHAT HAPPENS TO EVERYONE ON OUR EARTH IF--
OUR EARTH? OUR EARTH?!
THIS ISN'T OUR EARTH, KARA! IT'S NOT YOURS OR MINE!
IT'S A PLACE FULL OF...OF AWFUL PEOPLE.
AND THESE HEROES ARE JUST AS BAD!
ESPECIALLY HIM.
CONNER KENT HAS THE LIFE I ALWAYS DREAMED ABOUT. PARENTS AND FRIENDS AND A GIRL WHO LOVES HIM.
AND HE'S NOT DOING ANYTHING TO HELP THEM!
IT'S NOT FAIR! IT'S JUST NOT...
...WE DID EVERYTHING RIGHT...AND WE LOST EVERYTHING BECAUSE OF IT...
...I DON'T WANT TO LOSE LOIS, TOO.
I CAN'T.
HERE.
WHAT IS THIS?
IT'S ONE OF HER JOURNALS. I'VE READ IT A THOUSAND TIMES SINCE WE'VE BEEN LOCKED AWAY.
I WANT YOU TO READ IT. MAYBE THAT'LL HELP.

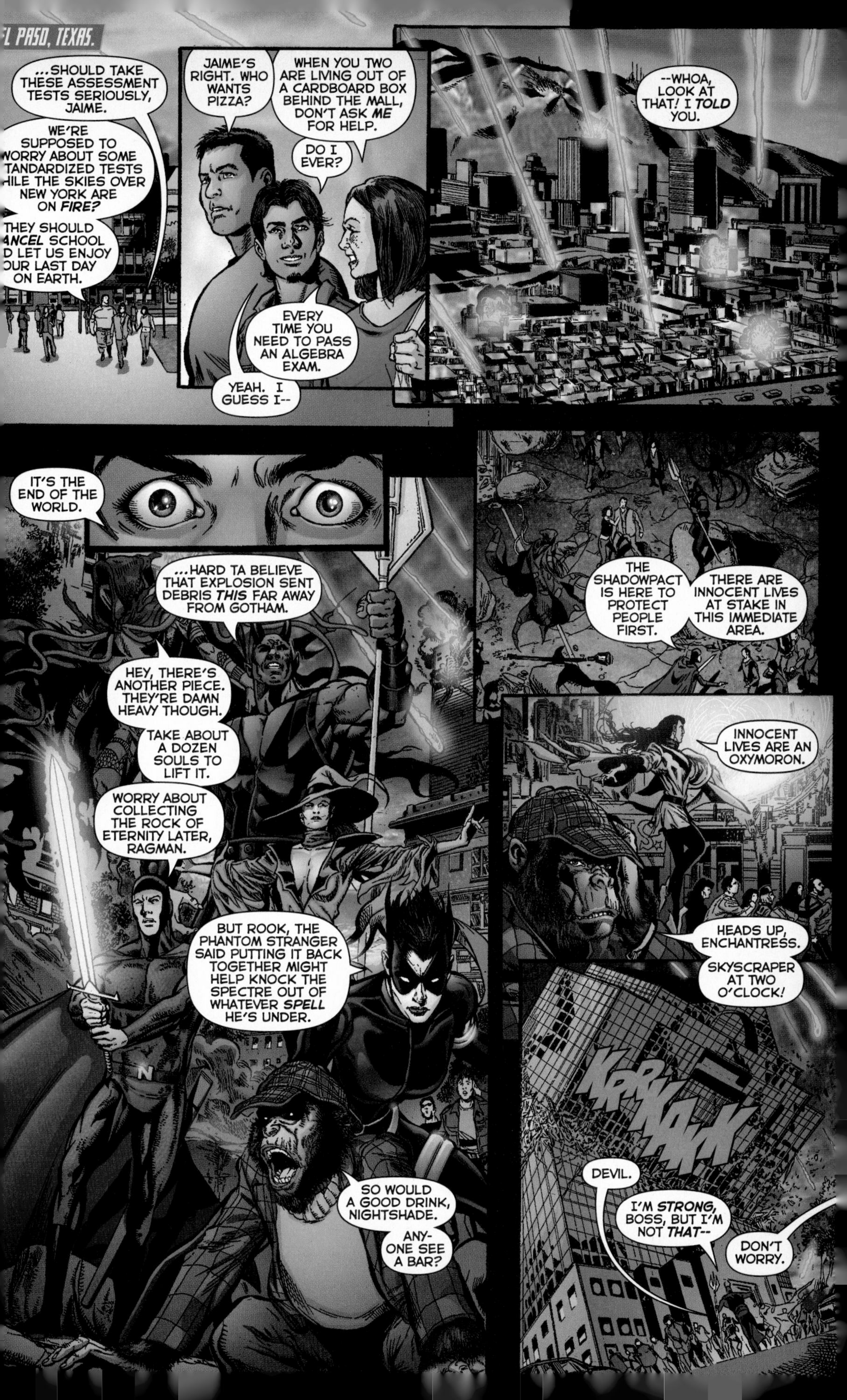

L PASO, TEXAS.
...SHOULD TAKE THESE ASSESSMENT TESTS SERIOUSLY, JAIME.
WE'RE SUPPOSED TO WORRY ABOUT SOME TANDARDIZED TESTS HILE THE SKIES OVER NEW YORK ARE ON FIRE?
THEY SHOULD ANCEL SCHOOL D LET US ENJOY OUR LAST DAY ON EARTH.
JAIME'S RIGHT. WHO WANTS PIZZA?
WHEN YOU TWO ARE LIVING OUT OF A CARDBOARD BOX BEHIND THE MALL, DON'T ASK ME FOR HELP.
DO I EVER?
EVERY TIME YOU NEED TO PASS AN ALGEBRA EXAM.
YEAH. I GUESS I--
--WHOA, LOOK AT THAT! I TOLD YOU.
IT'S THE END OF THE WORLD.
...HARD TA BELIEVE THAT EXPLOSION SENT DEBRIS THIS FAR AWAY FROM GOTHAM.
HEY, THERE'S ANOTHER PIECE. THEY'RE DAMN HEAVY THOUGH.
TAKE ABOUT A DOZEN SOULS TO LIFT IT.
WORRY ABOUT COLLECTING THE ROCK OF ETERNITY LATER, RAGMAN.
BUT ROOK, THE PHANTOM STRANGER SAID PUTTING IT BACK TOGETHER MIGHT HELP KNOCK THE SPECTRE OUT OF WHATEVER SPELL HE'S UNDER.
SO WOULD A GOOD DRINK, NIGHTSHADE.
ANY-ONE SEE A BAR?
THE SHADOWPACT IS HERE TO PROTECT PEOPLE FIRST.
THERE ARE INNOCENT LIVES AT STAKE IN THIS IMMEDIATE AREA.
INNOCENT LIVES ARE AN OXYMORON.
HEADS UP, ENCHANTRESS.
SKYSCRAPER AT TWO O'CLOCK!
KRRKAAK
DEVIL.
I'M STRONG, BOSS, BUT I'M NOT THAT--
DON'T WORRY.

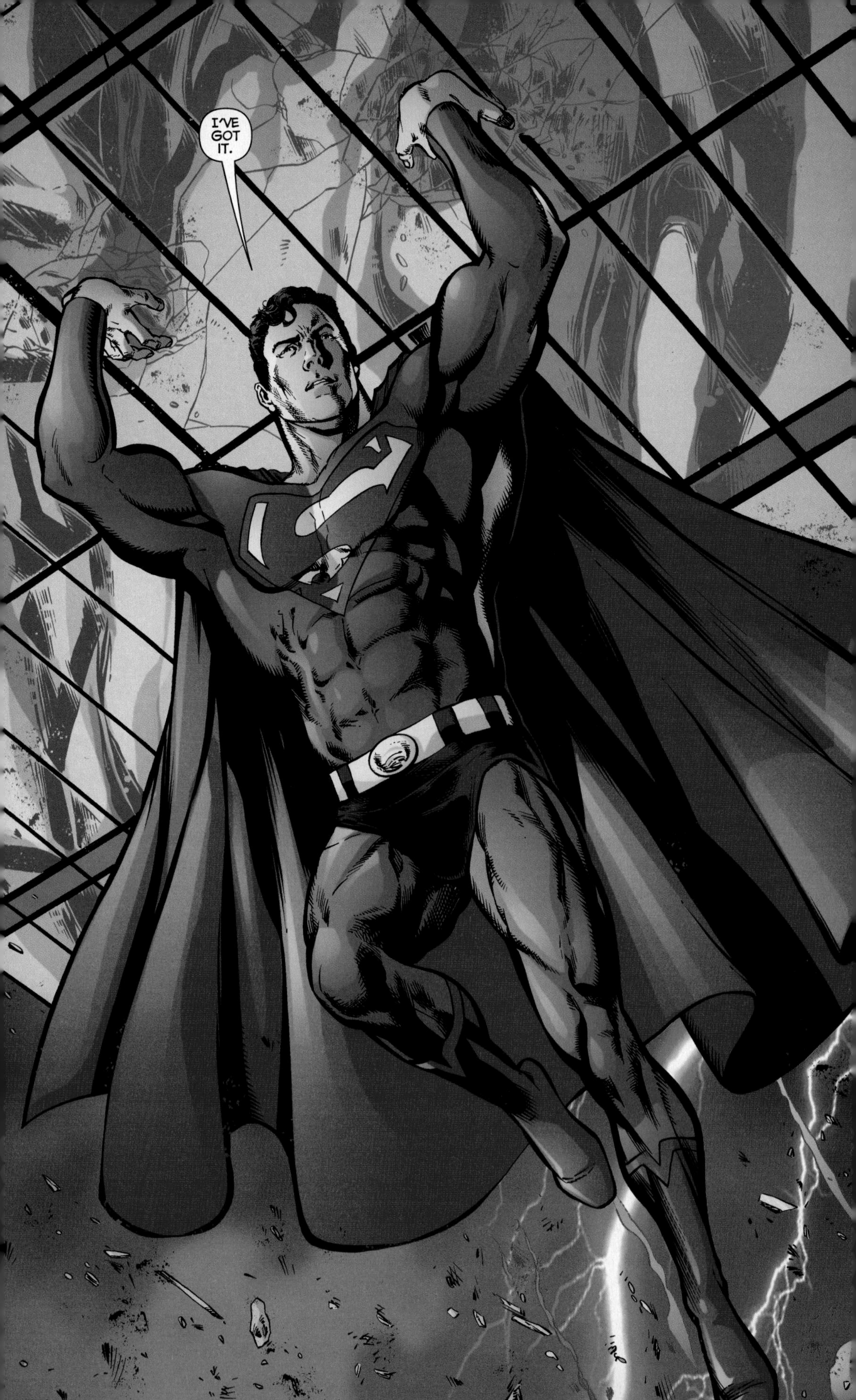
I'VE GOT IT.

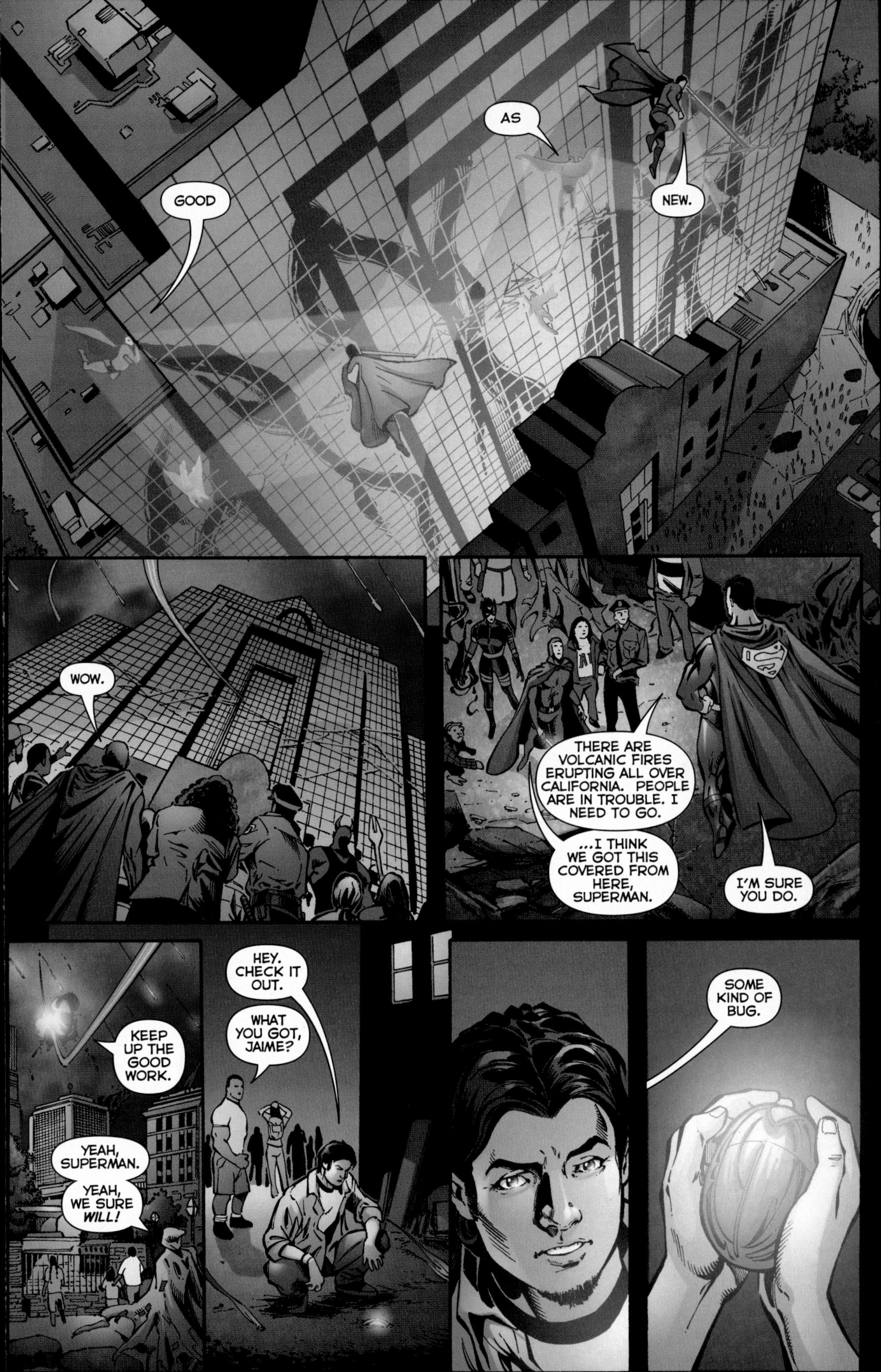
GOOD
AS
NEW.
WOW.
THERE ARE VOLCANIC FIRES ERUPTING ALL OVER CALIFORNIA. PEOPLE ARE IN TROUBLE. I NEED TO GO.
...I THINK WE GOT THIS COVERED FROM HERE, SUPERMAN.
I'M SURE YOU DO.
KEEP UP THE GOOD WORK.
YEAH, SUPERMAN.
YEAH, WE SURE WILL!
HEY. CHECK IT OUT.
WHAT YOU GOT, JAIME?
SOME KIND OF BUG.

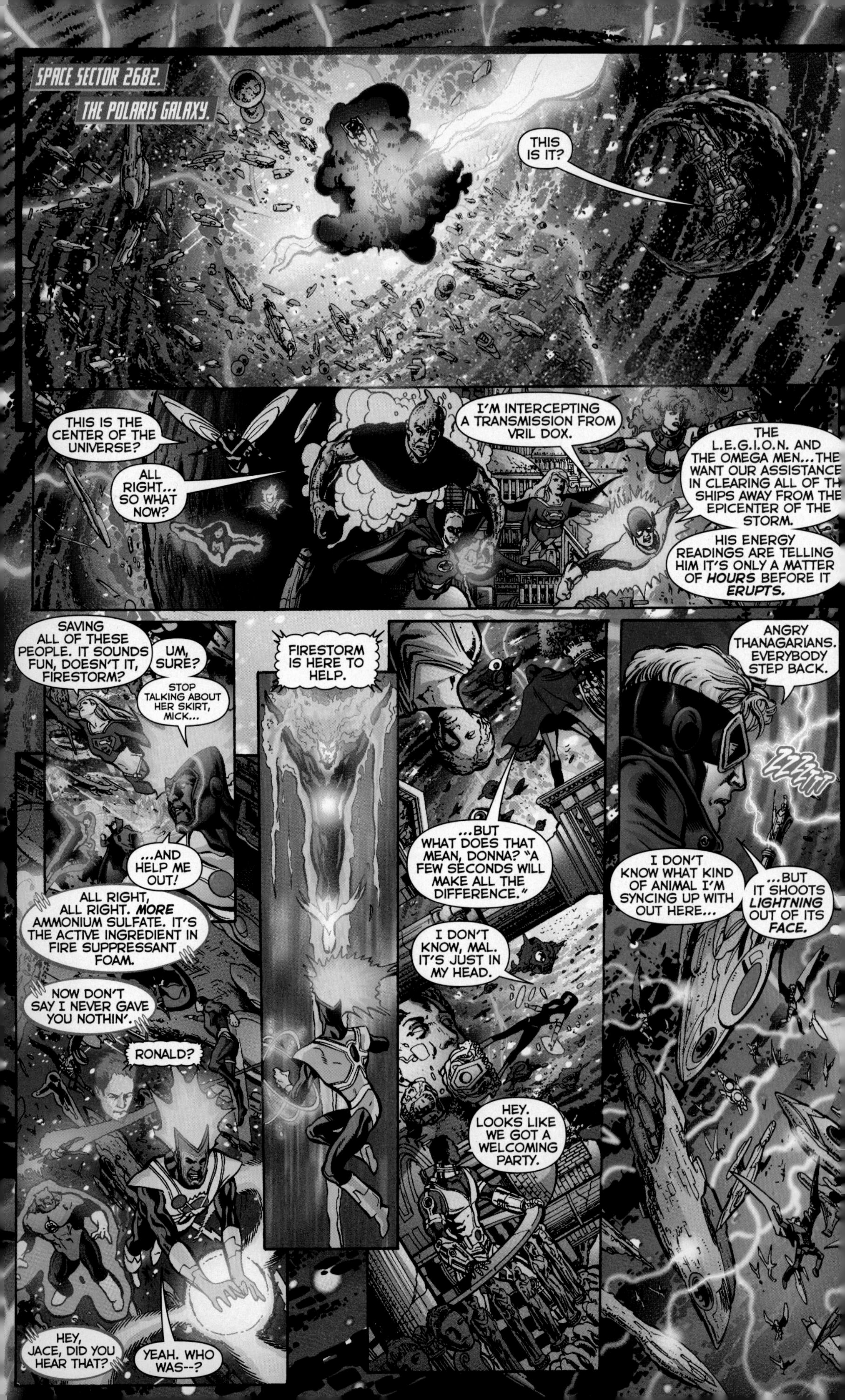
SPACE SECTOR 2682.
THE POLARIS GALAXY.
THIS IS IT?
THIS IS THE CENTER OF THE UNIVERSE?
ALL RIGHT... SO WHAT NOW?
I'M INTERCEPTING A TRANSMISSION FROM VRIL DOX.
THE L.E.G.I.O.N. AND THE OMEGA MEN...THE WANT OUR ASSISTANCE IN CLEARING ALL OF TH SHIPS AWAY FROM THE EPICENTER OF THE STORM.
HIS ENERGY READINGS ARE TELLING HIM IT'S ONLY A MATTER OF HOURS BEFORE IT ERUPTS.
SAVING ALL OF THESE PEOPLE. IT SOUNDS FUN, DOESN'T IT, FIRESTORM?
UM, SURE?
STOP TALKING ABOUT HER SKIRT, MICK...
...AND HELP ME OUT!
ALL RIGHT, ALL RIGHT. MORE AMMONIUM SULFATE. IT'S THE ACTIVE INGREDIENT IN FIRE SUPPRESSANT FOAM.
NOW DON'T SAY I NEVER GAVE YOU NOTHIN'.
RONALD?
HEY, JACE, DID YOU HEAR THAT?
YEAH. WHO WAS--?
FIRESTORM IS HERE TO HELP.
...BUT WHAT DOES THAT MEAN, DONNA? "A FEW SECONDS WILL MAKE ALL THE DIFFERENCE."
I DON'T KNOW, MAL. IT'S JUST IN MY HEAD.
HEY. LOOKS LIKE WE GOT A WELCOMING PARTY.
ANGRY THANAGARIANS. EVERYBODY STEP BACK.
I DON'T KNOW WHAT KIND OF ANIMAL I'M SYNCING UP WITH OUT HERE...
...BUT IT SHOOTS LIGHTNING OUT OF ITS FACE.

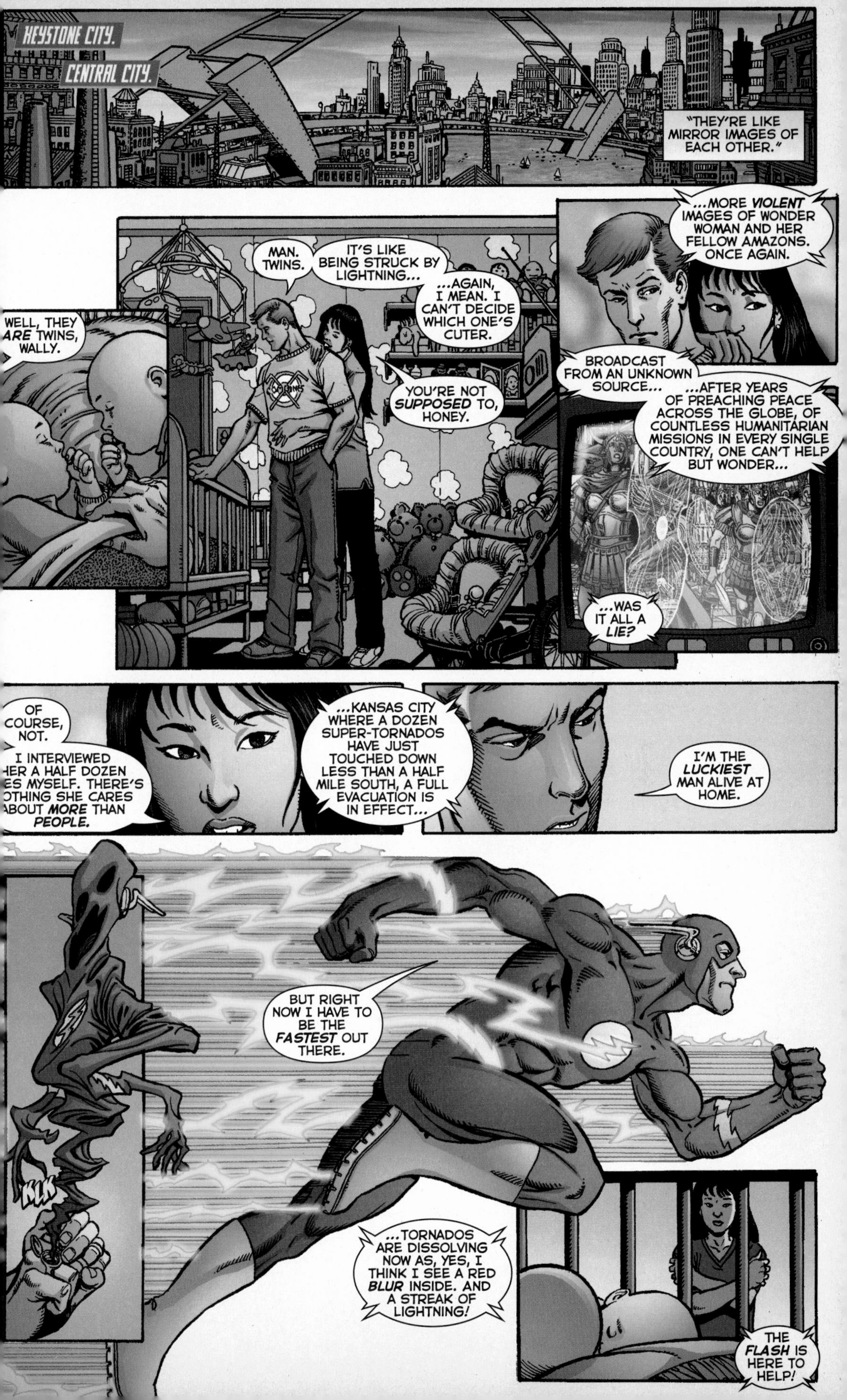
KEYSTONE CITY.
CENTRAL CITY.
"THEY'RE LIKE MIRROR IMAGES OF EACH OTHER."
MAN. TWINS.
IT'S LIKE BEING STRUCK BY LIGHTNING...
...AGAIN, I MEAN. I CAN'T DECIDE WHICH ONE'S CUTER.
YOU'RE NOT SUPPOSED TO, HONEY.
WELL, THEY ARE TWINS, WALLY.
...MORE VIOLENT IMAGES OF WONDER WOMAN AND HER FELLOW AMAZONS. ONCE AGAIN.
BROADCAST FROM AN UNKNOWN SOURCE...
...AFTER YEARS OF PREACHING PEACE ACROSS THE GLOBE, OF COUNTLESS HUMANITARIAN MISSIONS IN EVERY SINGLE COUNTRY, ONE CAN'T HELP BUT WONDER...
...WAS IT ALL A LIE?
OF COURSE, NOT.
I INTERVIEWED HER A HALF DOZEN ES MYSELF. THERE'S OTHING SHE CARES ABOUT MORE THAN PEOPLE.
...KANSAS CITY WHERE A DOZEN SUPER-TORNADOS HAVE JUST TOUCHED DOWN LESS THAN A HALF MILE SOUTH, A FULL EVACUATION IS IN EFFECT...
I'M THE LUCKIEST MAN ALIVE AT HOME.
BUT RIGHT NOW I HAVE TO BE THE FASTEST OUT THERE.
KLK
...TORNADOS ARE DISSOLVING NOW AS, YES, I THINK I SEE A RED BLUR INSIDE. AND A STREAK OF LIGHTNING!
THE FLASH IS HERE TO HELP!

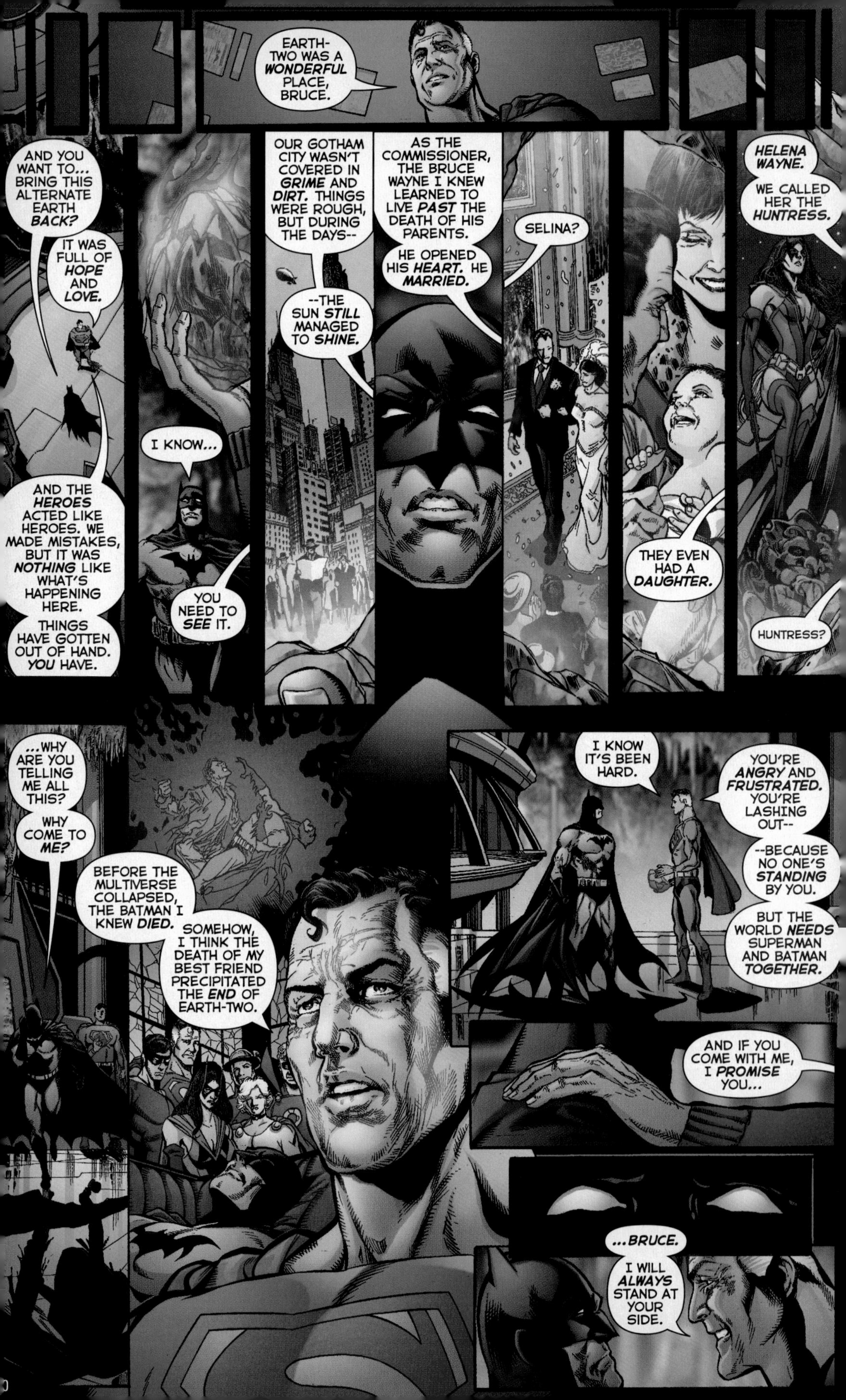
EARTH-TWO WAS A WONDERFUL PLACE, BRUCE.
AND YOU WANT TO... BRING THIS ALTERNATE EARTH BACK?
IT WAS FULL OF HOPE AND LOVE.
AND THE HEROES ACTED LIKE HEROES. WE MADE MISTAKES, BUT IT WAS NOTHING LIKE WHAT'S HAPPENING HERE.
THINGS HAVE GOTTEN OUT OF HAND. YOU HAVE.
I KNOW...
YOU NEED TO SEE IT.
OUR GOTHAM CITY WASN'T COVERED IN GRIME AND DIRT. THINGS WERE ROUGH, BUT DURING THE DAYS--
--THE SUN STILL MANAGED TO SHINE.
AS THE COMMISSIONER, THE BRUCE WAYNE I KNEW LEARNED TO LIVE PAST THE DEATH OF HIS PARENTS.
HE OPENED HIS HEART. HE MARRIED.
SELINA?
THEY EVEN HAD A DAUGHTER.
HELENA WAYNE.
WE CALLED HER THE HUNTRESS.
HUNTRESS?
...WHY ARE YOU TELLING ME ALL THIS?
WHY COME TO ME?
BEFORE THE MULTIVERSE COLLAPSED, THE BATMAN I KNEW DIED.
SOMEHOW, I THINK THE DEATH OF MY BEST FRIEND PRECIPITATED THE END OF EARTH-TWO.
I KNOW IT'S BEEN HARD.
YOU'RE ANGRY AND FRUSTRATED. YOU'RE LASHING OUT--
--BECAUSE NO ONE'S STANDING BY YOU.
BUT THE WORLD NEEDS SUPERMAN AND BATMAN TOGETHER.
AND IF YOU COME WITH ME, I PROMISE YOU...
...BRUCE.
I WILL ALWAYS STAND AT YOUR SIDE.

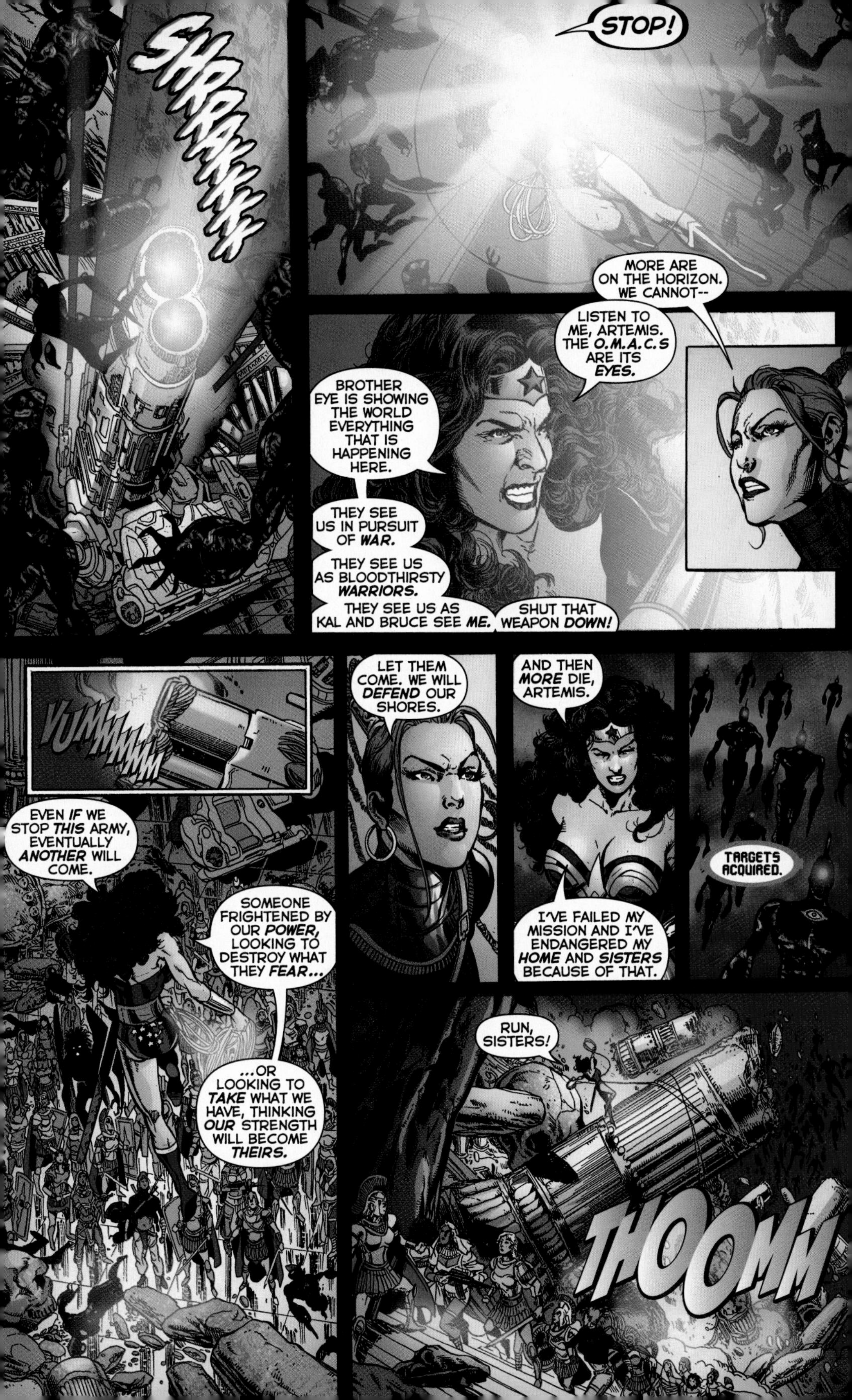

SHRAKKKK
STOP!
MORE ARE ON THE HORIZON. WE CANNOT--
LISTEN TO ME, ARTEMIS. THE O.M.A.C.S ARE ITS EYES.
BROTHER EYE IS SHOWING THE WORLD EVERYTHING THAT IS HAPPENING HERE.
THEY SEE US IN PURSUIT OF WAR.
THEY SEE US AS BLOODTHIRSTY WARRIORS.
THEY SEE US AS KAL AND BRUCE SEE ME.
SHUT THAT WEAPON DOWN!
VUMMMMM
EVEN IF WE STOP THIS ARMY, EVENTUALLY ANOTHER WILL COME.
SOMEONE FRIGHTENED BY OUR POWER, LOOKING TO DESTROY WHAT THEY FEAR...
...OR LOOKING TO TAKE WHAT WE HAVE, THINKING OUR STRENGTH WILL BECOME THEIRS.
LET THEM COME. WE WILL DEFEND OUR SHORES.
AND THEN MORE DIE, ARTEMIS.
I'VE FAILED MY MISSION AND I'VE ENDANGERED MY HOME AND SISTERS BECAUSE OF THAT.
TARGETS ACQUIRED.
RUN, SISTERS!
THOOMM

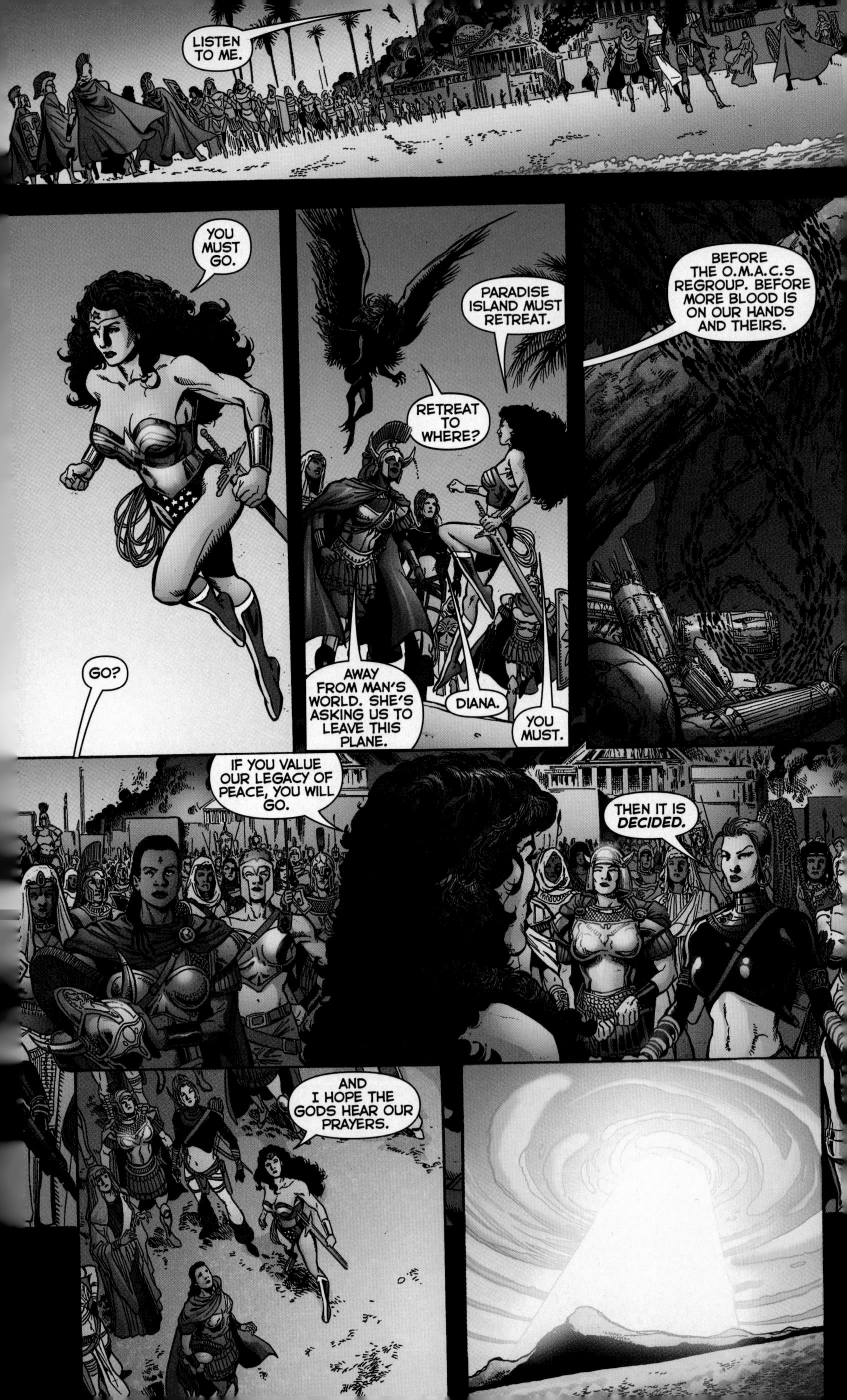
LISTEN TO ME.
YOU MUST GO.
GO?
PARADISE ISLAND MUST RETREAT.
RETREAT TO WHERE?
AWAY FROM MAN'S WORLD. SHE'S ASKING US TO LEAVE THIS PLANE.
DIANA.
YOU MUST.
BEFORE THE O.M.A.C.S REGROUP. BEFORE MORE BLOOD IS ON OUR HANDS AND THEIRS.
IF YOU VALUE OUR LEGACY OF PEACE, YOU WILL GO.
THEN IT IS *DECIDED.*
AND I HOPE THE GODS HEAR OUR PRAYERS.

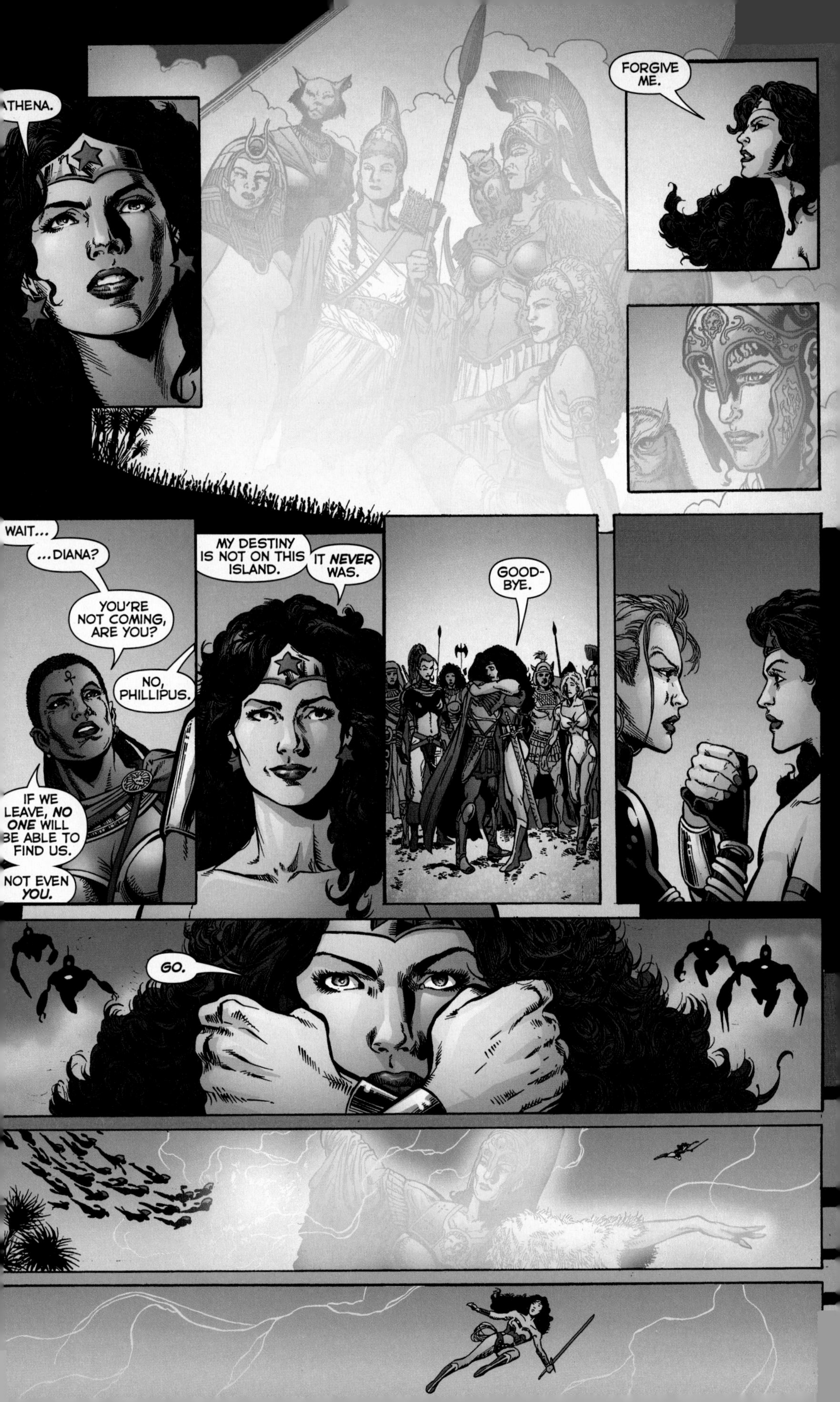
ATHENA.
FORGIVE ME.
WAIT...
...DIANA?
YOU'RE NOT COMING, ARE YOU?
NO, PHILLIPUS.
IF WE LEAVE, NO ONE WILL BE ABLE TO FIND US.
NOT EVEN YOU.
MY DESTINY IS NOT ON THIS ISLAND.
IT NEVER WAS.
GOOD-BYE.
GO.

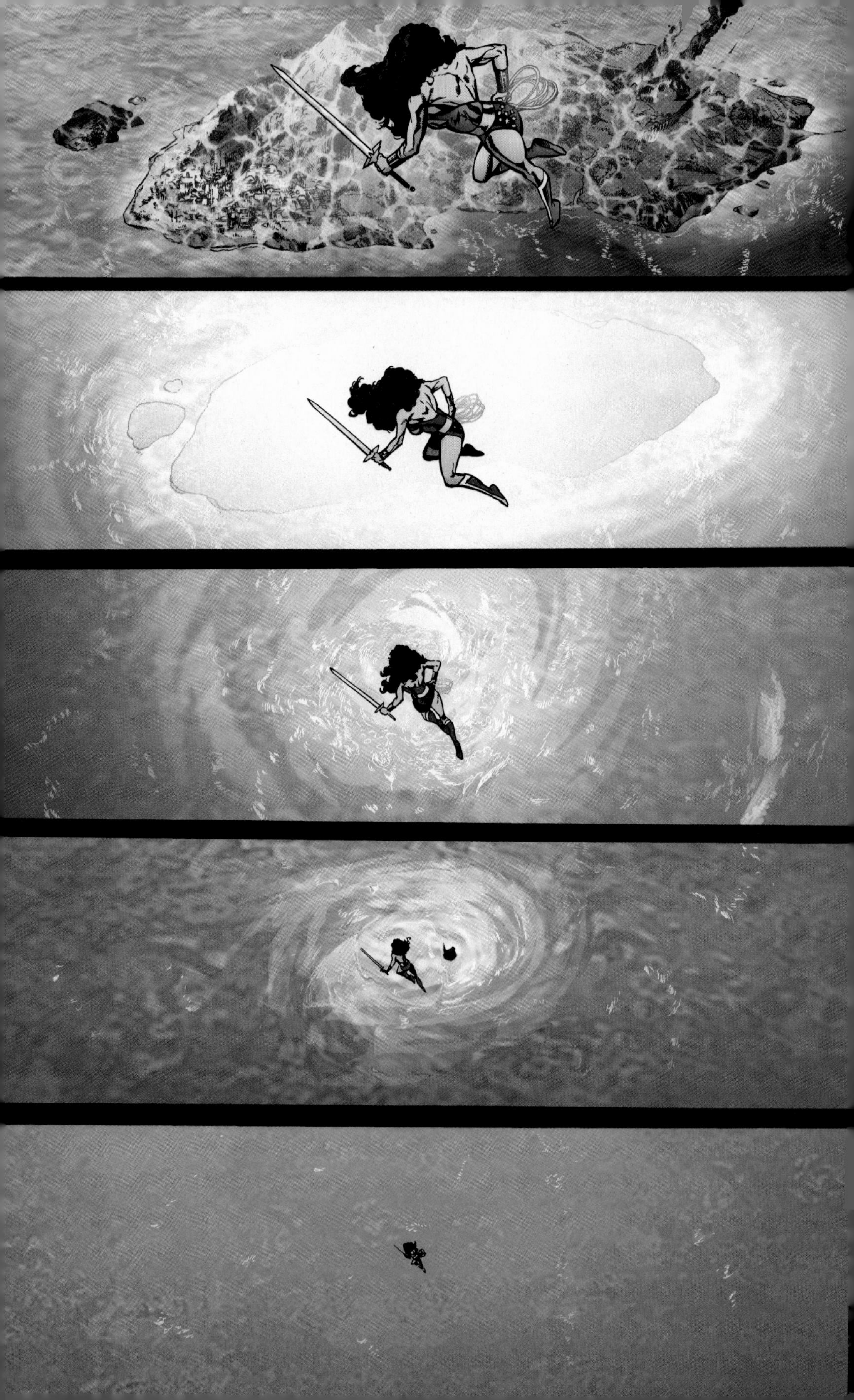

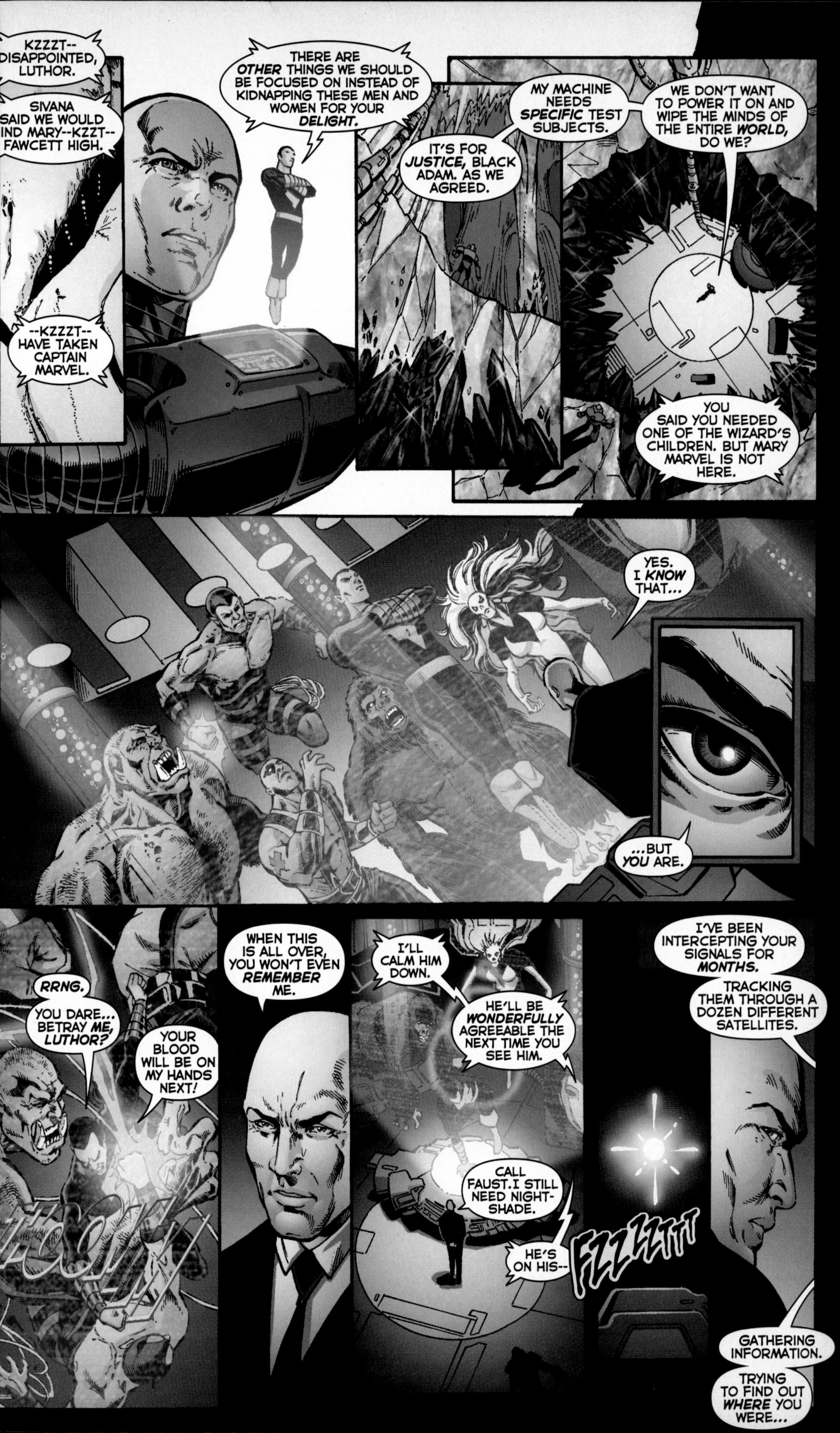
KZZZT--
DISAPPOINTED, LUTHOR.
SIVANA SAID WE WOULD FIND MARY--KZZT-- FAWCETT HIGH.
--KZZZT-- HAVE TAKEN CAPTAIN MARVEL.
THERE ARE OTHER THINGS WE SHOULD BE FOCUSED ON INSTEAD OF KIDNAPPING THESE MEN AND WOMEN FOR YOUR DELIGHT.
IT'S FOR JUSTICE, BLACK ADAM. AS WE AGREED.
MY MACHINE NEEDS SPECIFIC TEST SUBJECTS.
WE DON'T WANT TO POWER IT ON AND WIPE THE MINDS OF THE ENTIRE WORLD, DO WE?
YOU SAID YOU NEEDED ONE OF THE WIZARD'S CHILDREN. BUT MARY MARVEL IS NOT HERE.
YES. I KNOW THAT...
...BUT YOU ARE.
RRNG.
YOU DARE... BETRAY ME, LUTHOR?
YOUR BLOOD WILL BE ON MY HANDS NEXT!
WHEN THIS IS ALL OVER, YOU WON'T EVEN REMEMBER ME.
I'LL CALM HIM DOWN.
HE'LL BE WONDERFULLY AGREEABLE THE NEXT TIME YOU SEE HIM.
CALL FAUST. I STILL NEED NIGHT-SHADE.
HE'S ON HIS--
FZZZZTTT
I'VE BEEN INTERCEPTING YOUR SIGNALS FOR MONTHS.
TRACKING THEM THROUGH A DOZEN DIFFERENT SATELLITES.
GATHERING INFORMATION.
TRYING TO FIND OUT WHERE YOU WERE...

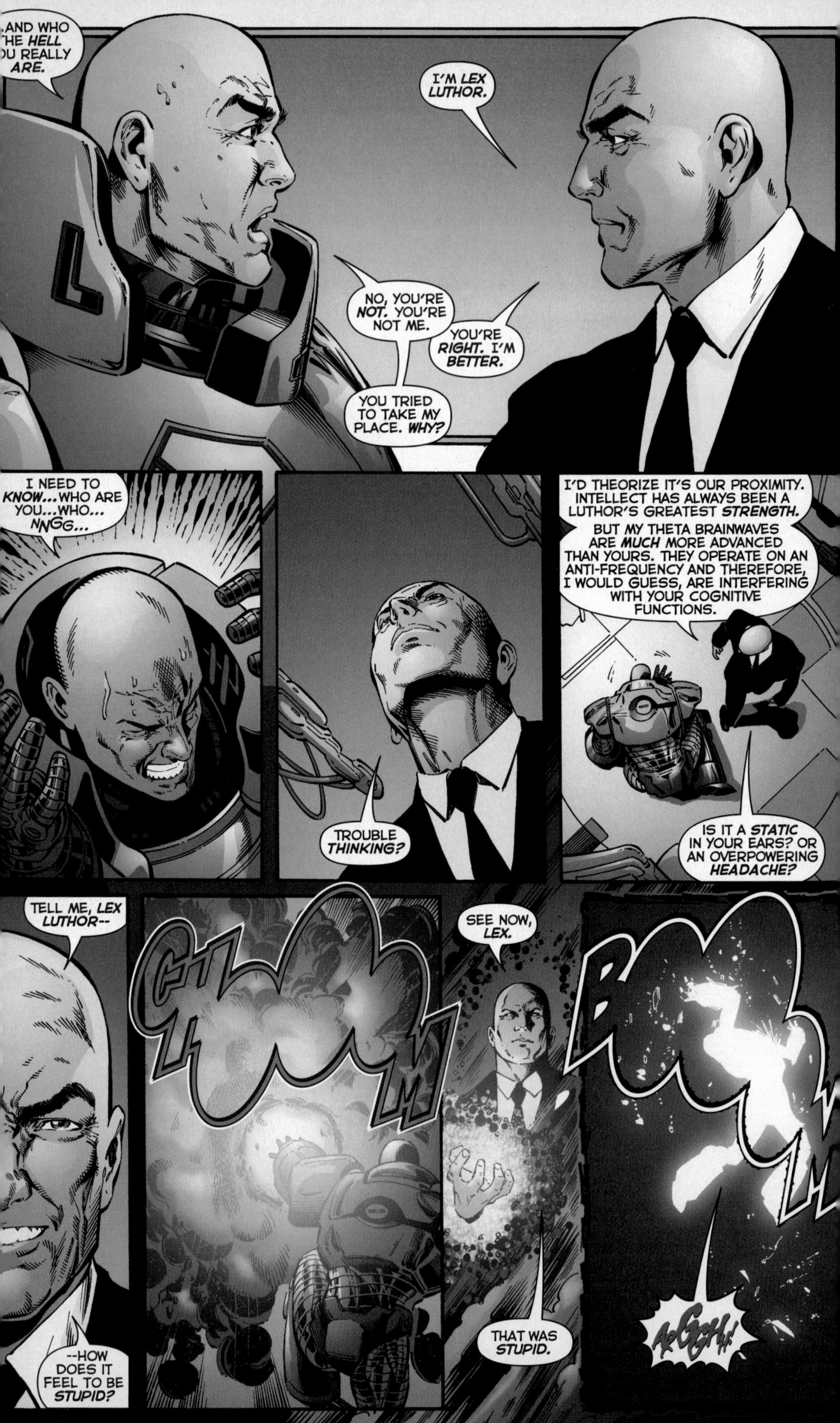
...AND WHO THE HELL YOU REALLY ARE.
I'M LEX LUTHOR.
NO, YOU'RE NOT. YOU'RE NOT ME.
YOU'RE RIGHT. I'M BETTER.
YOU TRIED TO TAKE MY PLACE. WHY?
I NEED TO KNOW...WHO ARE YOU...WHO... NNGG...
TROUBLE THINKING?
I'D THEORIZE IT'S OUR PROXIMITY. INTELLECT HAS ALWAYS BEEN A LUTHOR'S GREATEST STRENGTH.
BUT MY THETA BRAINWAVES ARE MUCH MORE ADVANCED THAN YOURS. THEY OPERATE ON AN ANTI-FREQUENCY AND THEREFORE, I WOULD GUESS, ARE INTERFERING WITH YOUR COGNITIVE FUNCTIONS.
IS IT A STATIC IN YOUR EARS? OR AN OVERPOWERING HEADACHE?
TELL ME, LEX LUTHOR--
--HOW DOES IT FEEL TO BE STUPID?
SEE NOW, LEX.
THAT WAS STUPID.
AAGGHH!

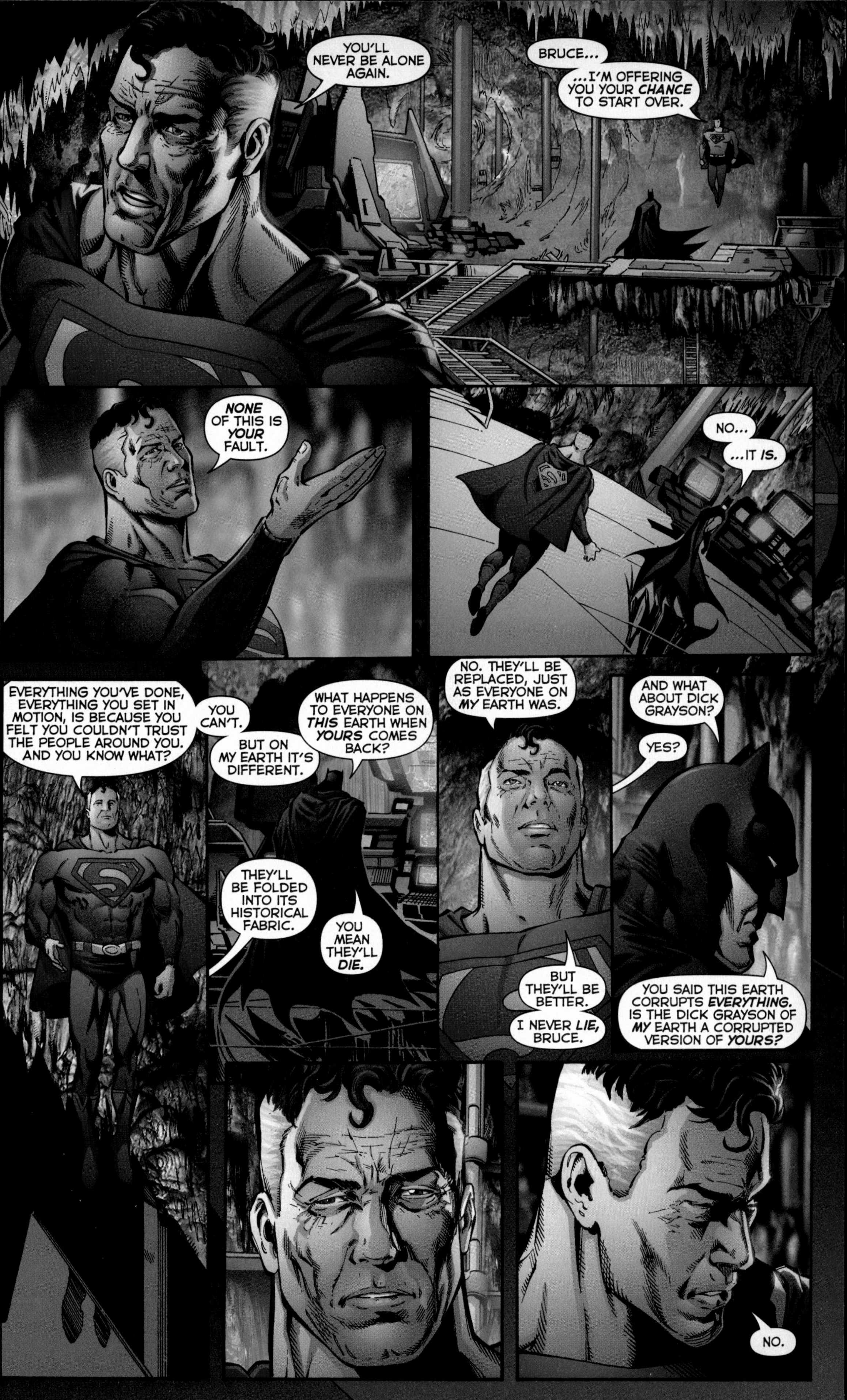
YOU'LL NEVER BE ALONE AGAIN.
BRUCE...
...I'M OFFERING YOU YOUR CHANCE TO START OVER.
NONE OF THIS IS YOUR FAULT.
NO...
...IT IS.
EVERYTHING YOU'VE DONE, EVERYTHING YOU SET IN MOTION, IS BECAUSE YOU FELT YOU COULDN'T TRUST THE PEOPLE AROUND YOU. AND YOU KNOW WHAT?
YOU CAN'T.
BUT ON MY EARTH IT'S DIFFERENT.
WHAT HAPPENS TO EVERYONE ON THIS EARTH WHEN YOURS COMES BACK?
THEY'LL BE FOLDED INTO ITS HISTORICAL FABRIC.
YOU MEAN THEY'LL DIE.
NO. THEY'LL BE REPLACED, JUST AS EVERYONE ON MY EARTH WAS.
BUT THEY'LL BE BETTER.
I NEVER LIE, BRUCE.
AND WHAT ABOUT DICK GRAYSON?
YES?
YOU SAID THIS EARTH CORRUPTS EVERYTHING. IS THE DICK GRAYSON OF MY EARTH A CORRUPTED VERSION OF YOURS?
NO.

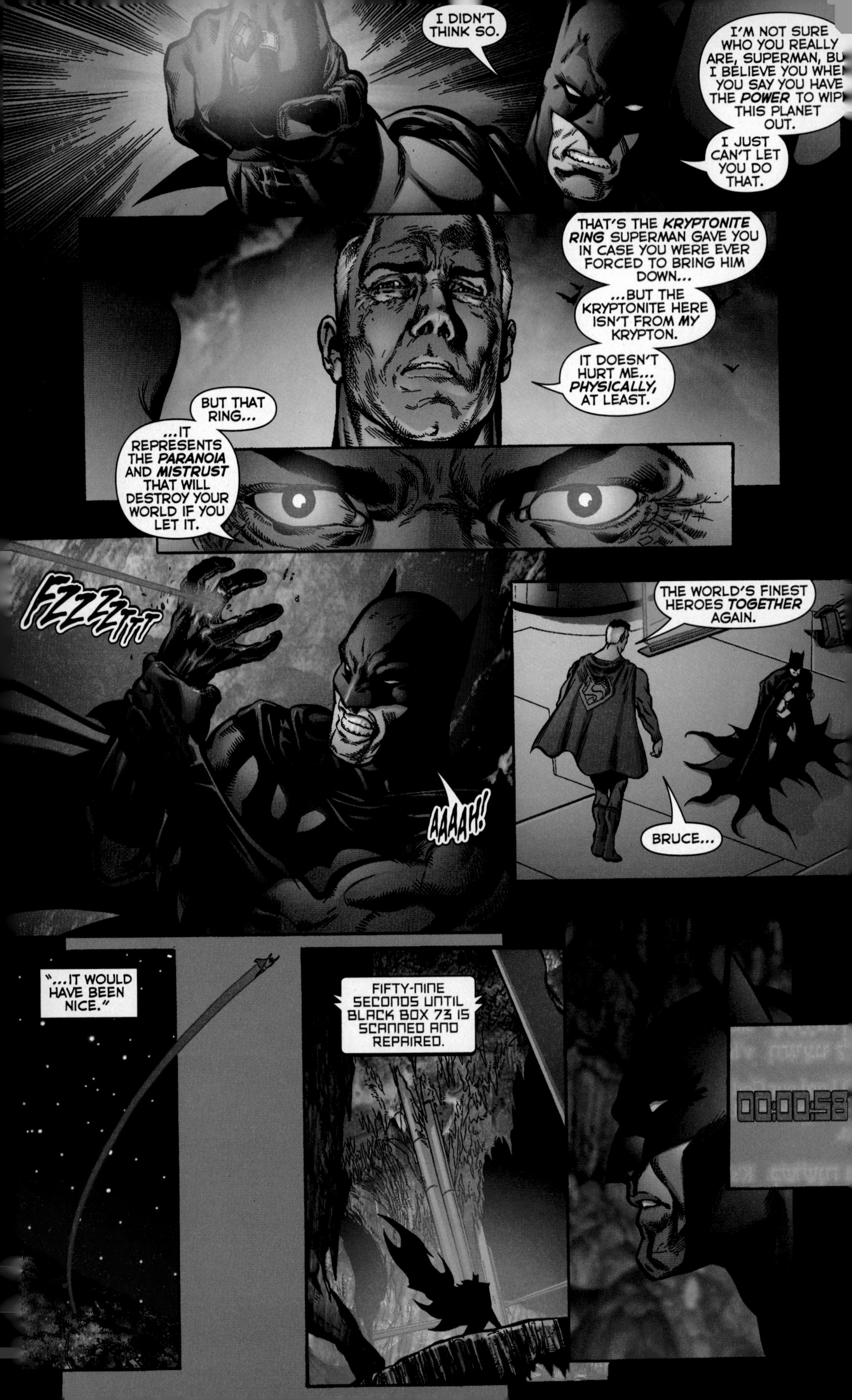

I DIDN'T THINK SO.
I'M NOT SURE WHO YOU REALLY ARE, SUPERMAN, BU I BELIEVE YOU WHE YOU SAY YOU HAVE THE POWER TO WIP THIS PLANET OUT.
I JUST CAN'T LET YOU DO THAT.
THAT'S THE KRYPTONITE RING SUPERMAN GAVE YOU IN CASE YOU WERE EVER FORCED TO BRING HIM DOWN...
...BUT THE KRYPTONITE HERE ISN'T FROM MY KRYPTON.
IT DOESN'T HURT ME... PHYSICALLY, AT LEAST.
BUT THAT RING...
...IT REPRESENTS THE PARANOIA AND MISTRUST THAT WILL DESTROY YOUR WORLD IF YOU LET IT.
FZZZZZTTT
AAAAH!
THE WORLD'S FINEST HEROES TOGETHER AGAIN.
BRUCE...
"...IT WOULD HAVE BEEN NICE."
FIFTY-NINE SECONDS UNTIL BLACK BOX 73 IS SCANNED AND REPAIRED.
00:00:58

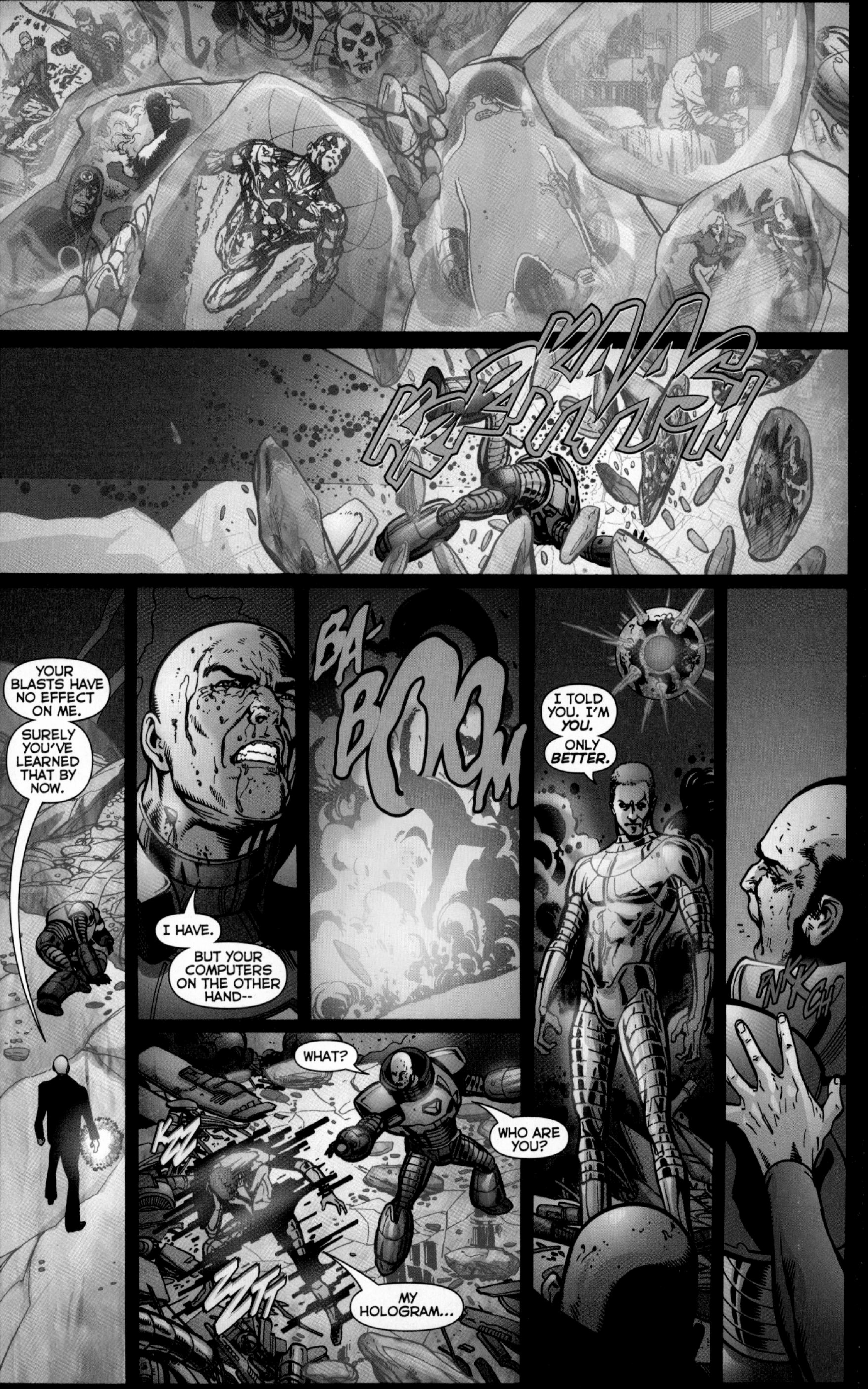
KRAKAKOOOM
YOUR BLASTS HAVE NO EFFECT ON ME.
SURELY YOU'VE LEARNED THAT BY NOW.
I HAVE.
BUT YOUR COMPUTERS ON THE OTHER HAND--
BA-BOOM
WHAT?
KZZ
WHO ARE YOU?
ZZTT
MY HOLOGRAM...
I TOLD YOU. I'M *YOU.*
ONLY *BETTER.*
PNKCH

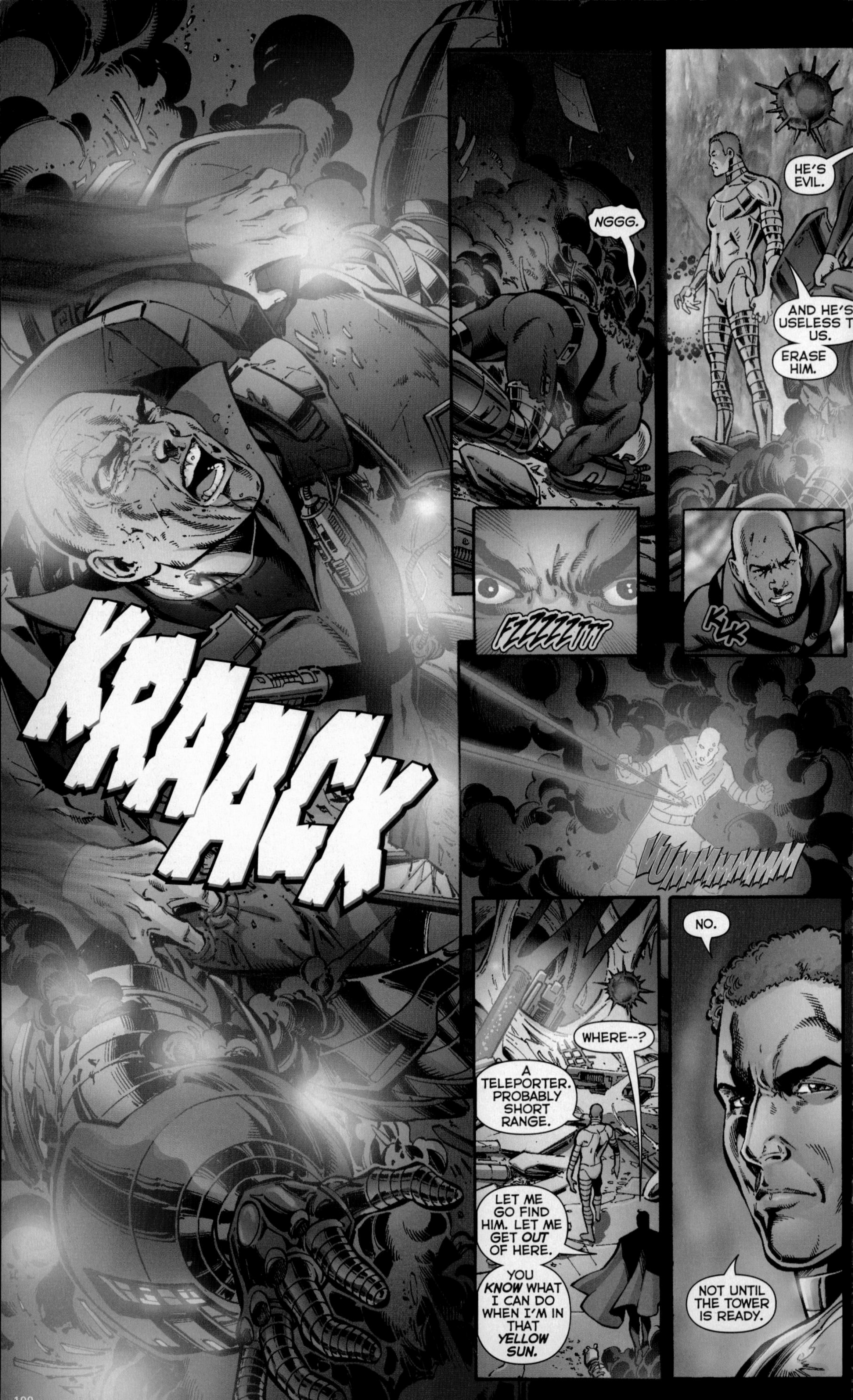
KRAACK
NGGG.
HE'S EVIL.
AND HE'S USELESS T US.
ERASE HIM.
FZZZZZTTT
KLIK
VUMMMMMMM
WHERE--?
A TELEPORTER. PROBABLY SHORT RANGE.
LET ME GO FIND HIM. LET ME GET *OUT* OF HERE.
YOU *KNOW* WHAT I CAN DO WHEN I'M IN THAT *YELLOW SUN.*
NO.
NOT UNTIL THE TOWER IS READY.

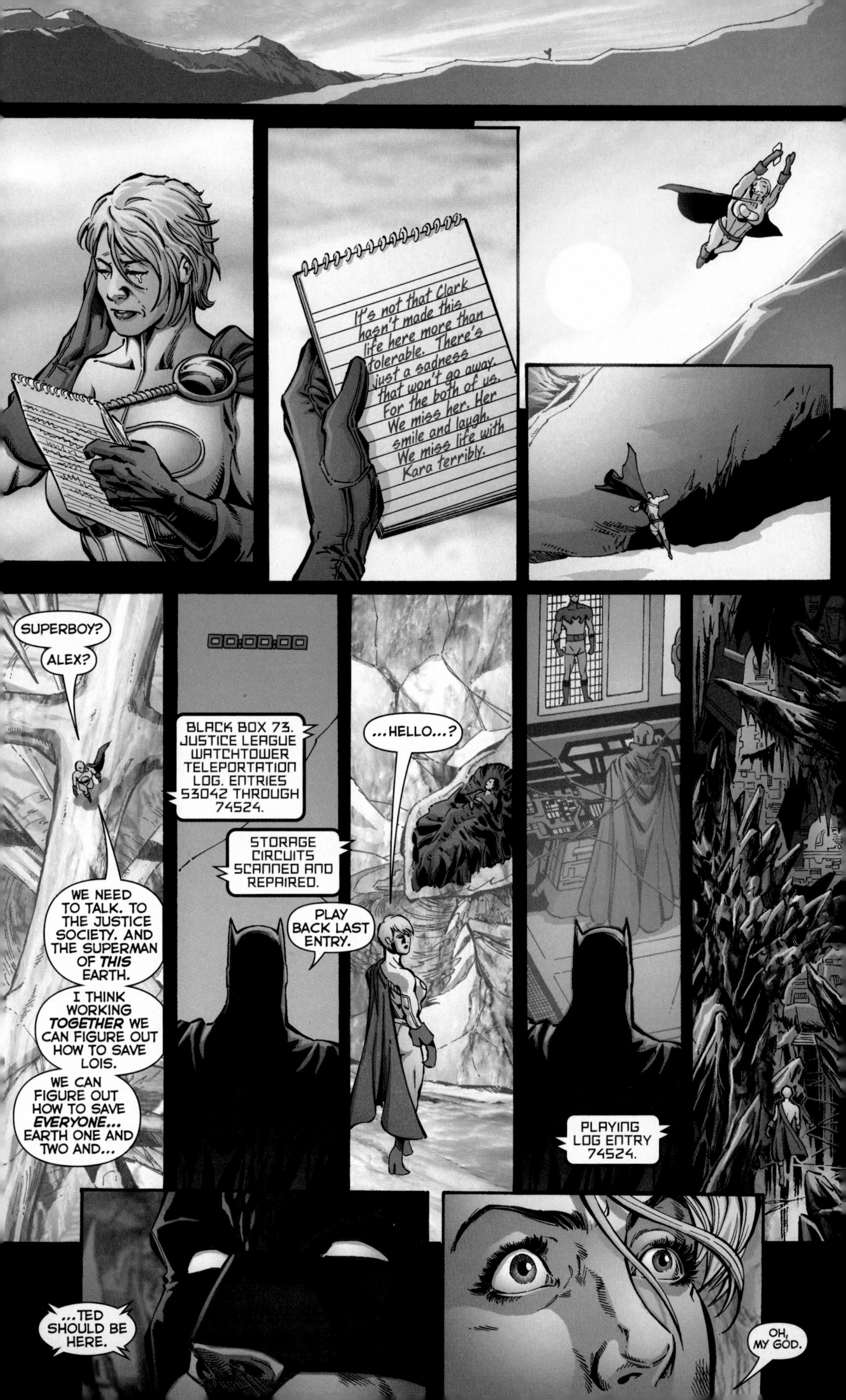

It's not that Clark hasn't made this life here more than tolerable. There's just a sadness that won't go away. For the both of us. We miss her. Her smile and laugh. We miss life with Kara terribly.
SUPERBOY?
ALEX?
WE NEED TO TALK. TO THE JUSTICE SOCIETY. AND THE SUPERMAN OF THIS EARTH.
I THINK WORKING TOGETHER WE CAN FIGURE OUT HOW TO SAVE LOIS.
WE CAN FIGURE OUT HOW TO SAVE EVERYONE... EARTH ONE AND TWO AND...
00:00:00
BLACK BOX 73. JUSTICE LEAGUE WATCHTOWER TELEPORTATION LOG. ENTRIES 53042 THROUGH 74524.
STORAGE CIRCUITS SCANNED AND REPAIRED.
...HELLO...?
PLAY BACK LAST ENTRY.
PLAYING LOG ENTRY 74524.
...TED SHOULD BE HERE.
OH, MY GOD.

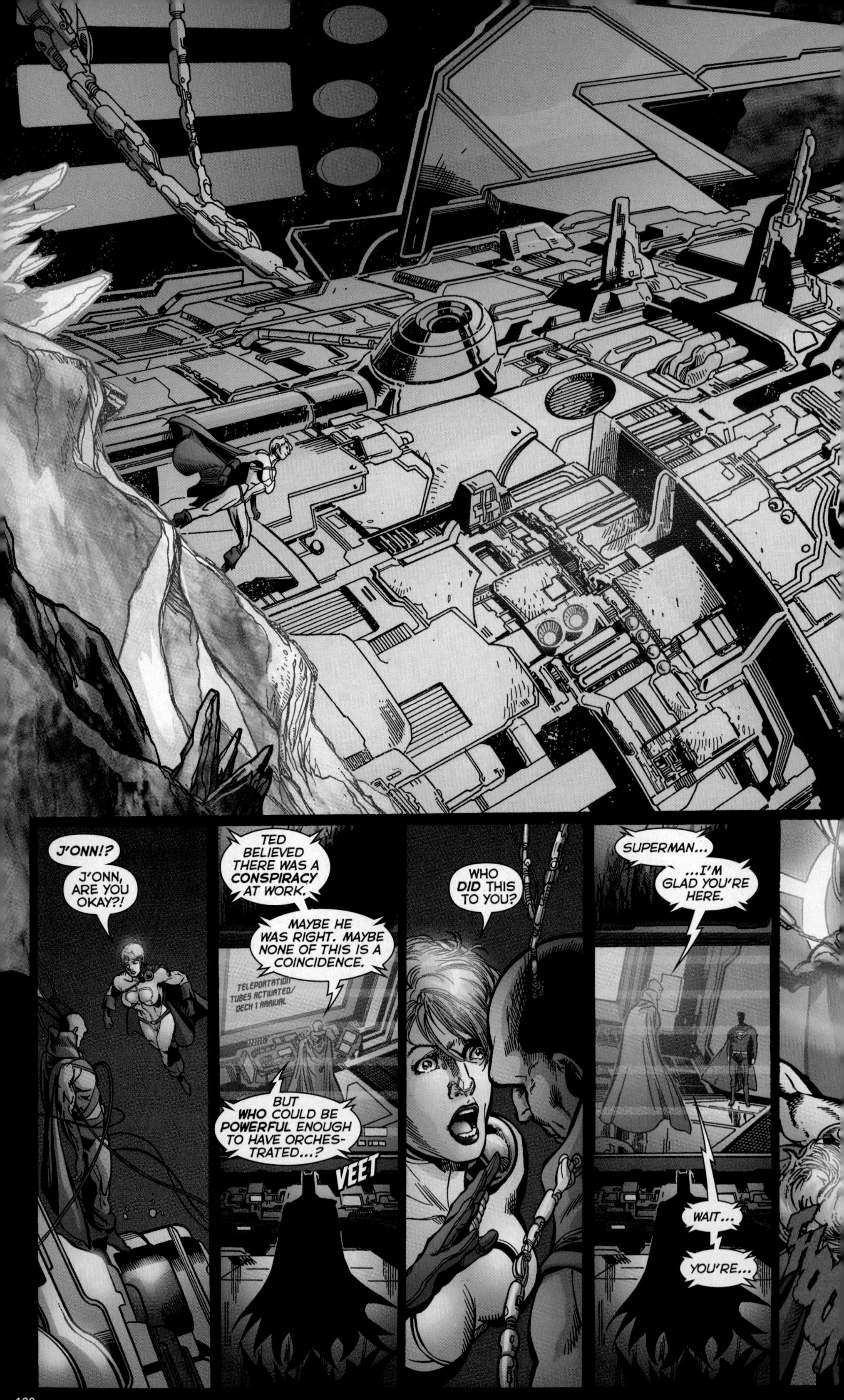
J'ONN!?
J'ONN, ARE YOU OKAY?!
TED BELIEVED THERE WAS A CONSPIRACY AT WORK.
MAYBE HE WAS RIGHT. MAYBE NONE OF THIS IS A COINCIDENCE.
TELEPORTATION TUBES ACTIVATED/ DECK 1 ARRIVAL
BUT WHO COULD BE POWERFUL ENOUGH TO HAVE ORCHES-TRATED...?
VEET
WHO DID THIS TO YOU?
SUPERMAN...
...I'M GLAD YOU'RE HERE.
WAIT...
YOU'RE...

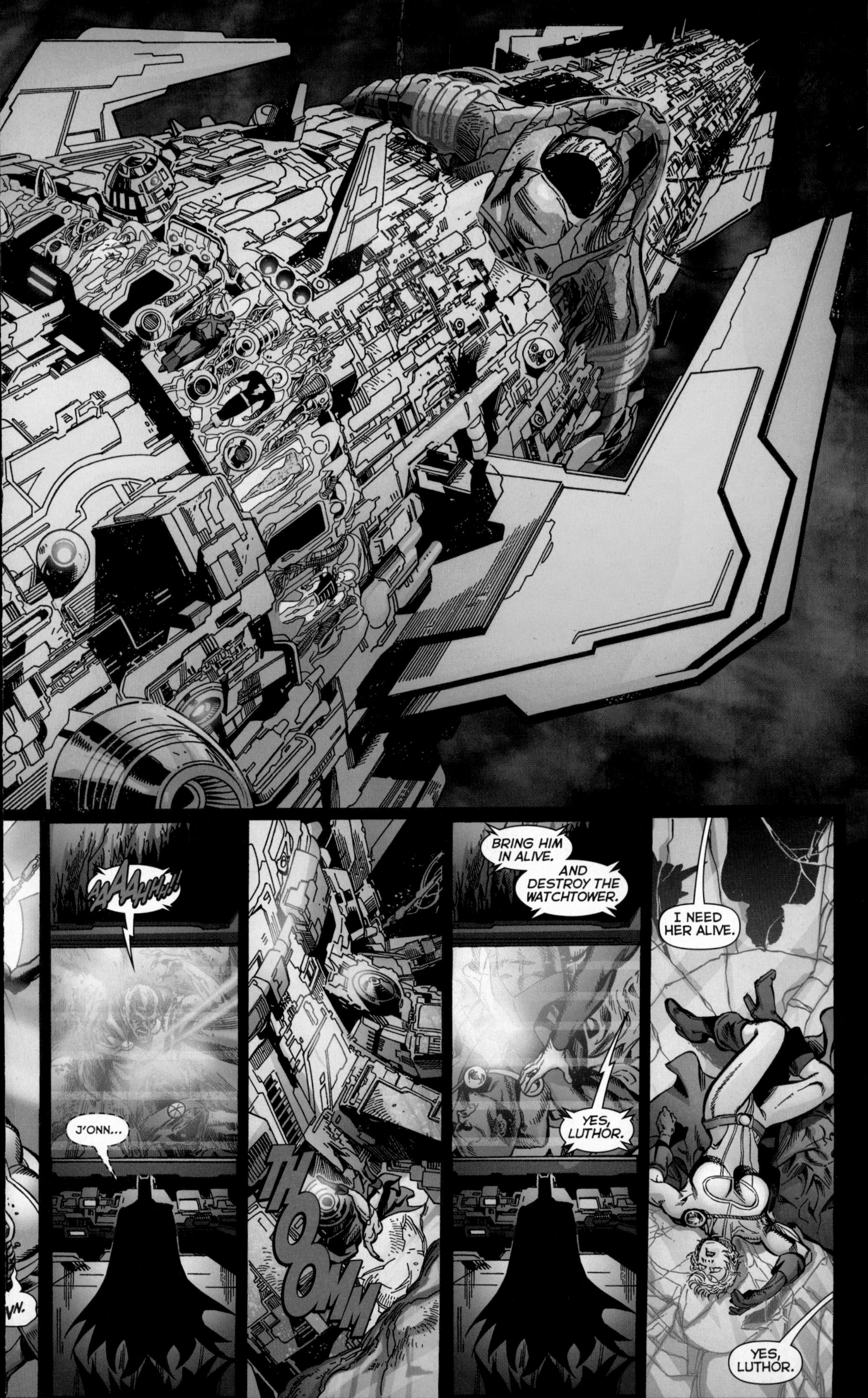
AAAHHHH!!
J'ONN...
THOOMM
BRING HIM IN ALIVE.
AND DESTROY THE WATCHTOWER.
YES, LUTHOR.
I NEED HER ALIVE.
YES, LUTHOR.

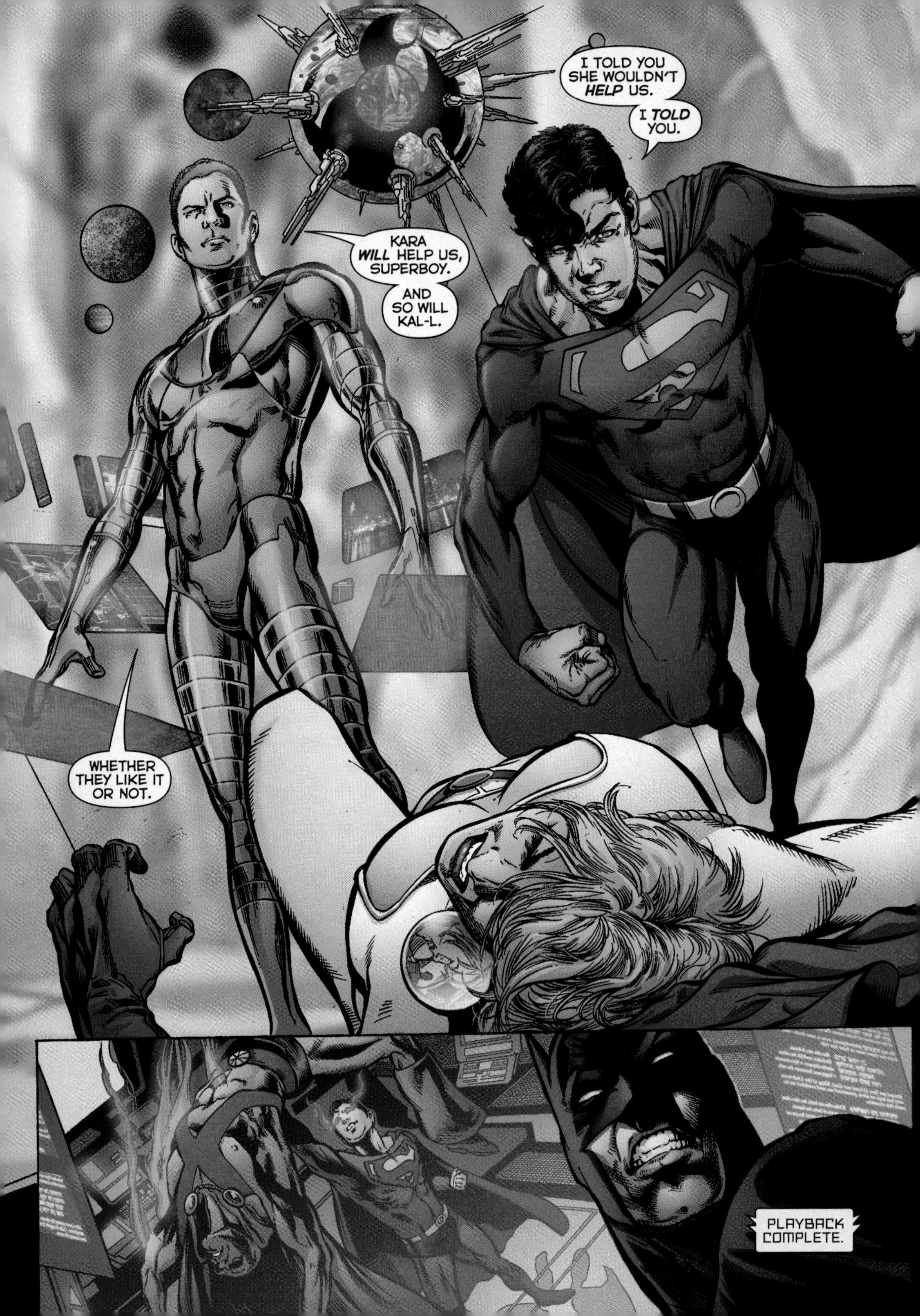
I TOLD YOU SHE WOULDN'T HELP US.
I TOLD YOU.
KARA WILL HELP US, SUPERBOY.
AND SO WILL KAL-L.
WHETHER THEY LIKE IT OR NOT.
PLAYBACK COMPLETE.

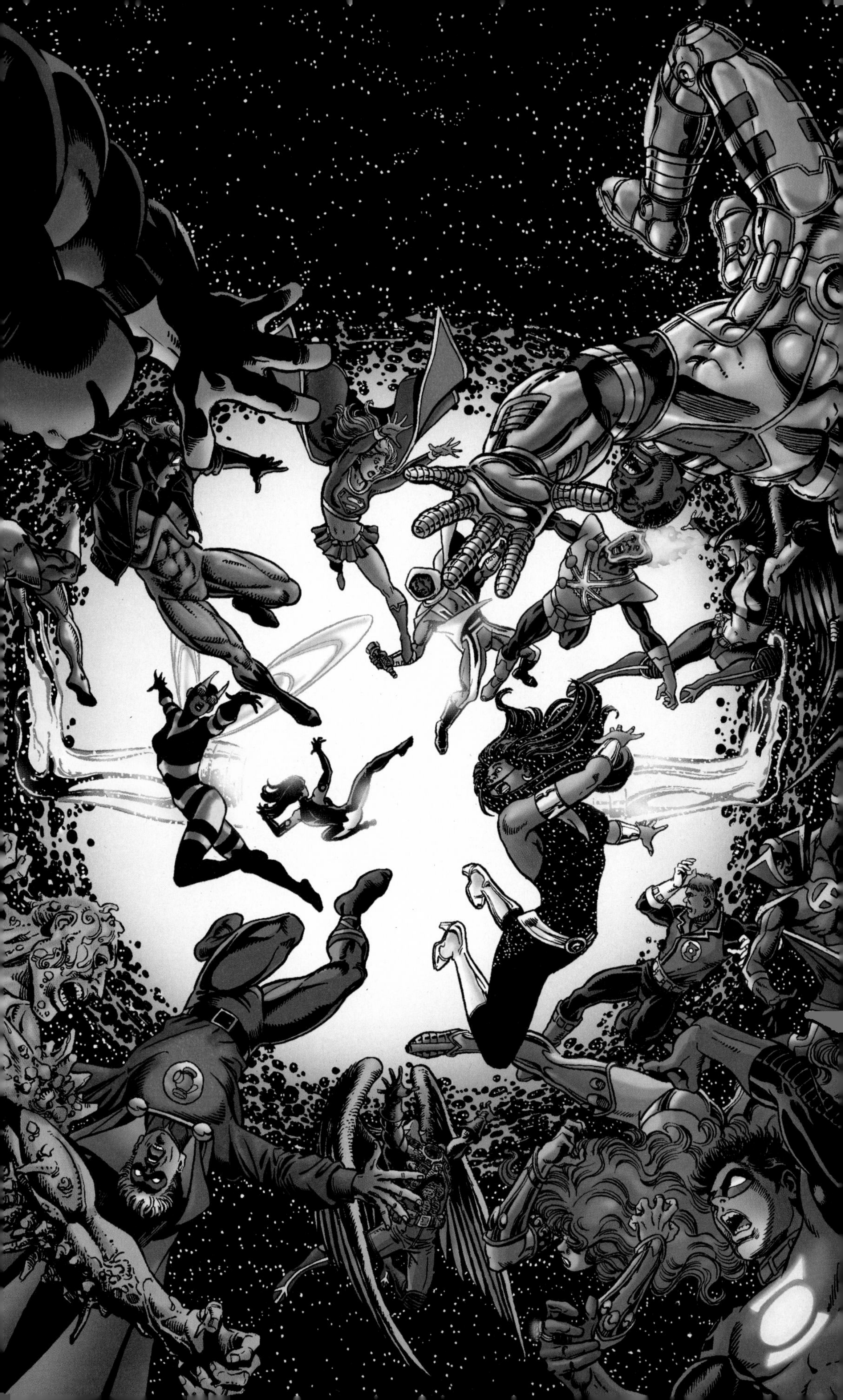

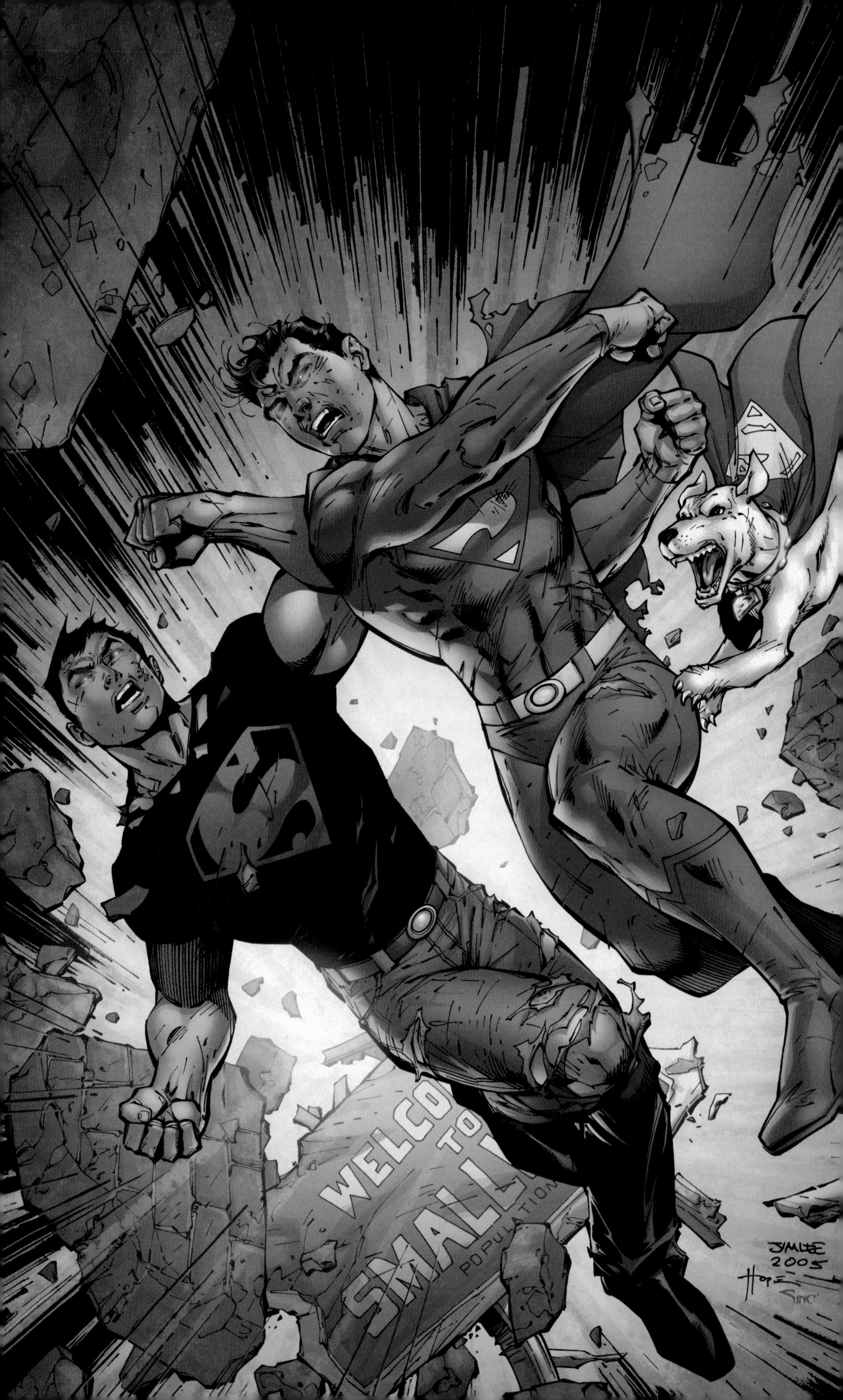
WELCO
TO
SMALL
POPULATION
JIMLEE
2005

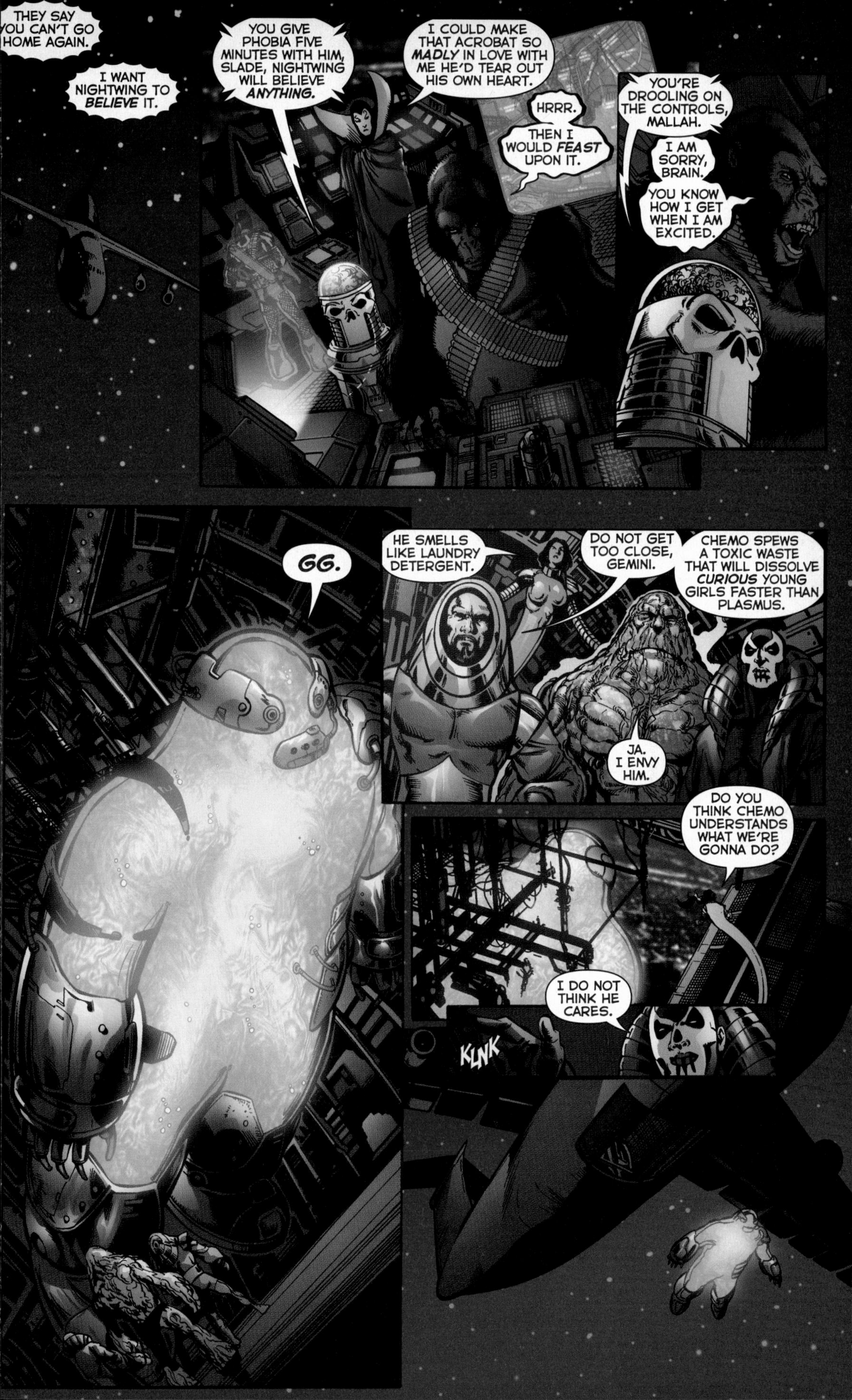
THEY SAY YOU CAN'T GO HOME AGAIN.
I WANT NIGHTWING TO BELIEVE IT.
YOU GIVE PHOBIA FIVE MINUTES WITH HIM, SLADE, NIGHTWING WILL BELIEVE ANYTHING.
I COULD MAKE THAT ACROBAT SO MADLY IN LOVE WITH ME HE'D TEAR OUT HIS OWN HEART.
HRRR.
THEN I WOULD FEAST UPON IT.
YOU'RE DROOLING ON THE CONTROLS, MALLAH.
I AM SORRY, BRAIN.
YOU KNOW HOW I GET WHEN I AM EXCITED.
GG.
HE SMELLS LIKE LAUNDRY DETERGENT.
DO NOT GET TOO CLOSE, GEMINI.
CHEMO SPEWS A TOXIC WASTE THAT WILL DISSOLVE CURIOUS YOUNG GIRLS FASTER THAN PLASMUS.
JA. I ENVY HIM.
DO YOU THINK CHEMO UNDERSTANDS WHAT WE'RE GONNA DO?
I DO NOT THINK HE CARES.
KLNK

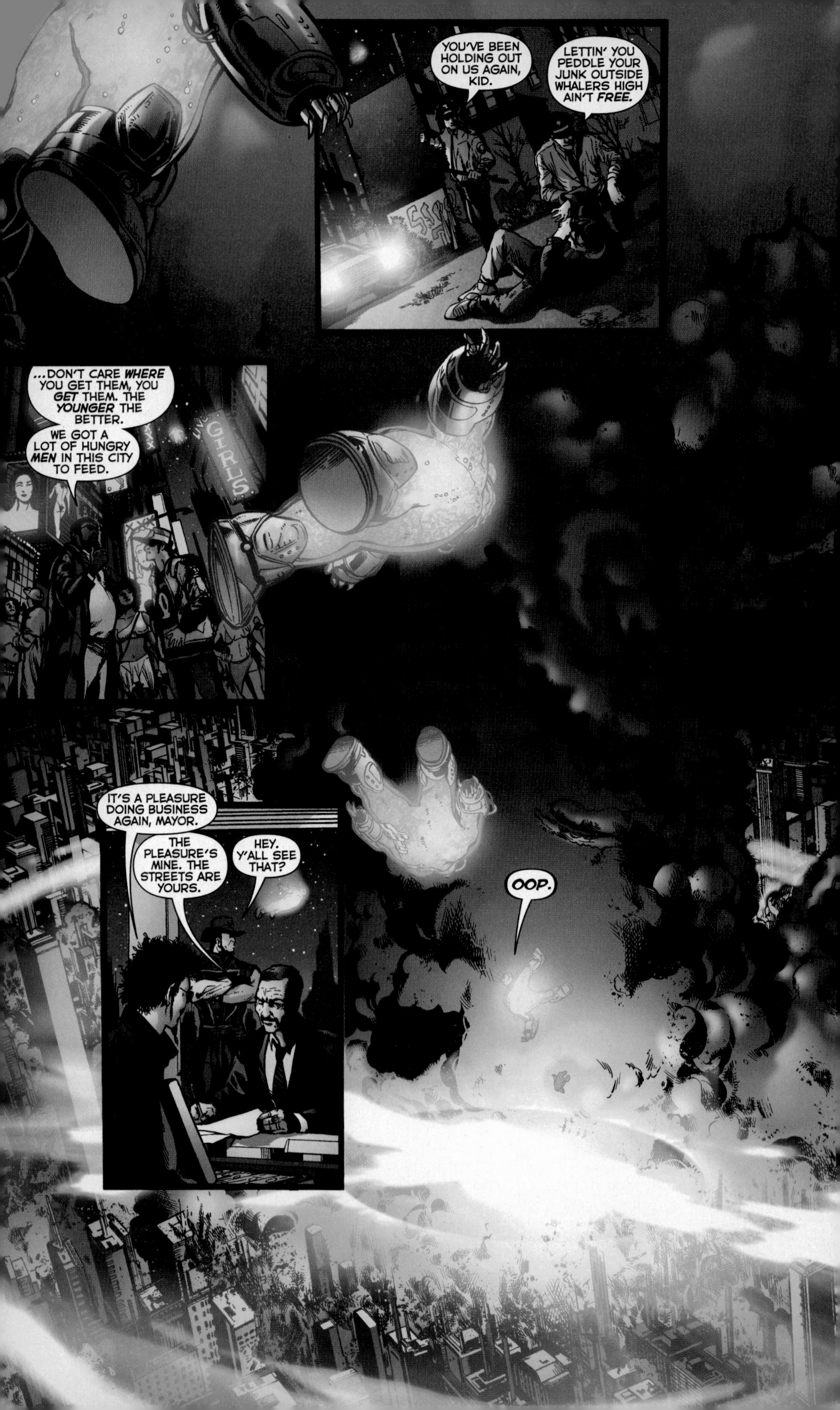

YOU'VE BEEN HOLDING OUT ON US AGAIN, KID.
LETTIN' YOU PEDDLE YOUR JUNK OUTSIDE WHALERS HIGH AIN'T *FREE*.
...DON'T CARE *WHERE* YOU GET THEM, YOU *GET* THEM. THE *YOUNGER* THE BETTER.
WE GOT A LOT OF HUNGRY *MEN* IN THIS CITY TO FEED.
GIRLS
IT'S A PLEASURE DOING BUSINESS AGAIN, MAYOR.
THE PLEASURE'S MINE. THE STREETS ARE YOURS.
HEY. Y'ALL SEE THAT?
OOP.

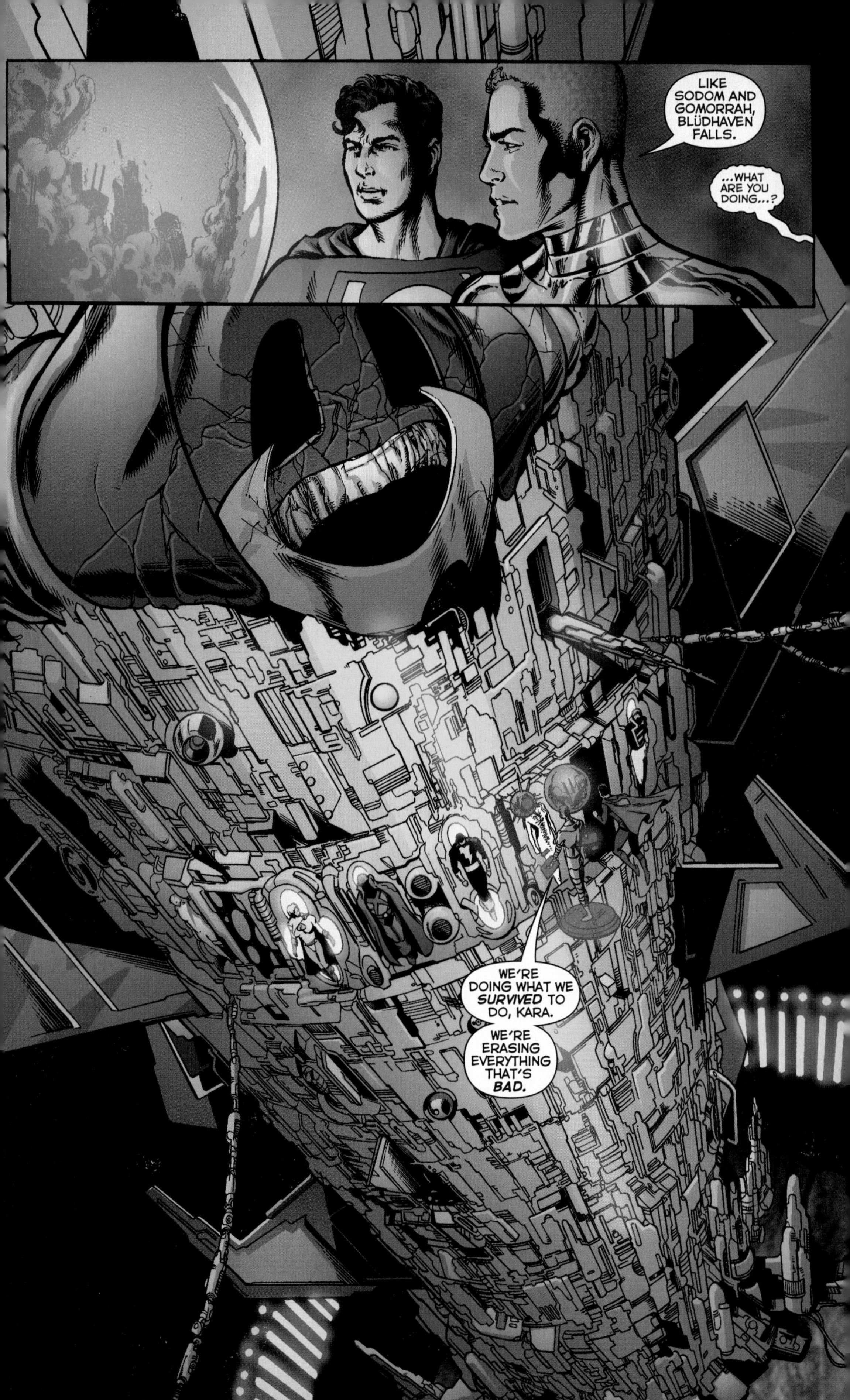
LIKE SODOM AND GOMORRAH, BLÜDHAVEN FALLS.
...WHAT ARE YOU DOING...?
WE'RE DOING WHAT WE *SURVIVED* TO DO, KARA.
WE'RE ERASING EVERYTHING THAT'S *BAD.*

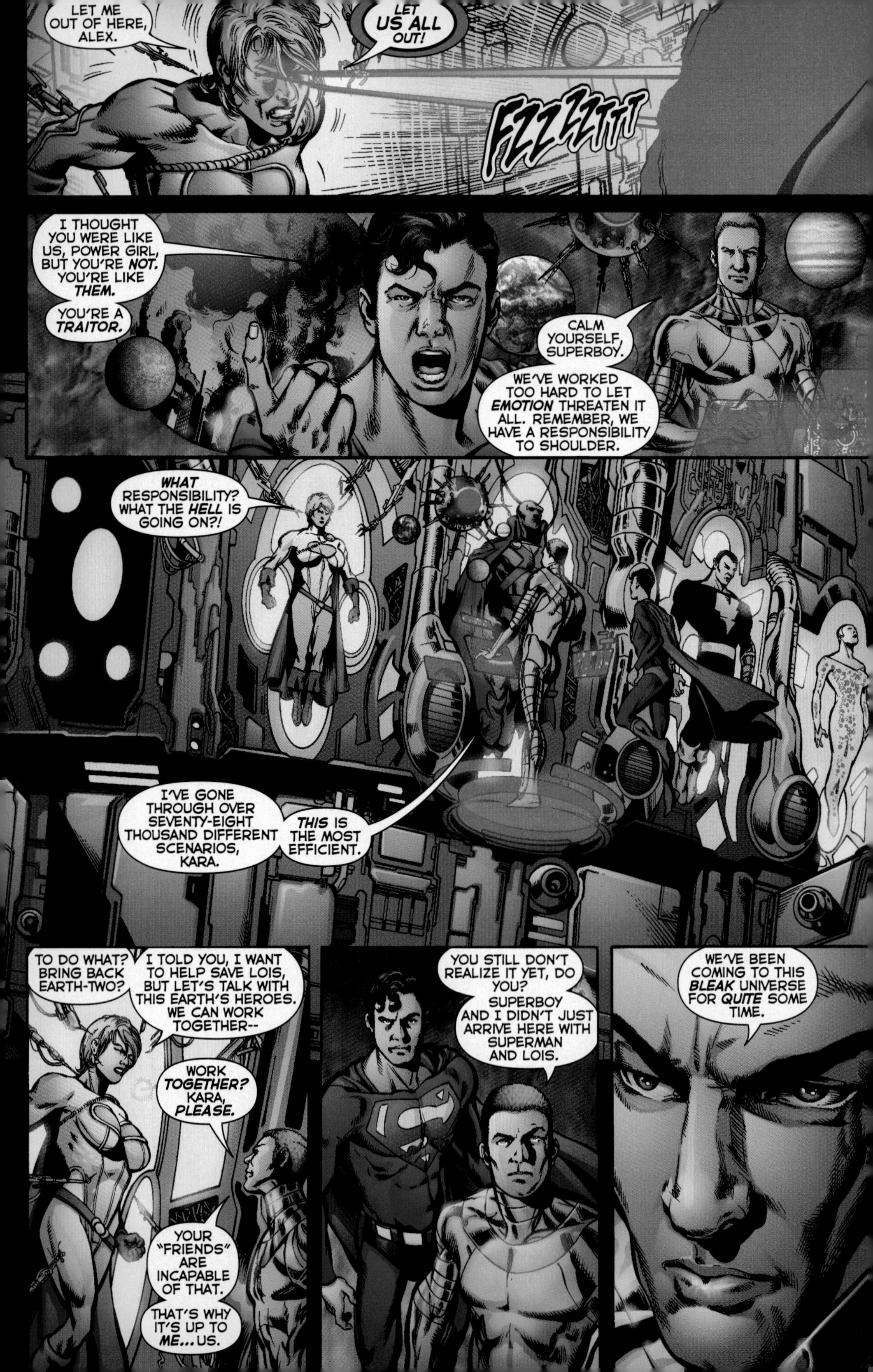
LET ME OUT OF HERE, ALEX.
LET US ALL OUT!
FZZZZTTT
I THOUGHT YOU WERE LIKE US, POWER GIRL, BUT YOU'RE NOT. YOU'RE LIKE THEM.
YOU'RE A TRAITOR.
CALM YOURSELF, SUPERBOY.
WE'VE WORKED TOO HARD TO LET EMOTION THREATEN IT ALL. REMEMBER, WE HAVE A RESPONSIBILITY TO SHOULDER.
WHAT RESPONSIBILITY? WHAT THE HELL IS GOING ON?!
I'VE GONE THROUGH OVER SEVENTY-EIGHT THOUSAND DIFFERENT SCENARIOS, KARA.
THIS IS THE MOST EFFICIENT.
TO DO WHAT? BRING BACK EARTH-TWO?
I TOLD YOU, I WANT TO HELP SAVE LOIS, BUT LET'S TALK WITH THIS EARTH'S HEROES. WE CAN WORK TOGETHER--
WORK TOGETHER? KARA, PLEASE.
YOUR "FRIENDS" ARE INCAPABLE OF THAT.
THAT'S WHY IT'S UP TO ME... US.
YOU STILL DON'T REALIZE IT YET, DO YOU?
SUPERBOY AND I DIDN'T JUST ARRIVE HERE WITH SUPERMAN AND LOIS.
WE'VE BEEN COMING TO THIS BLEAK UNIVERSE FOR QUITE SOME TIME.

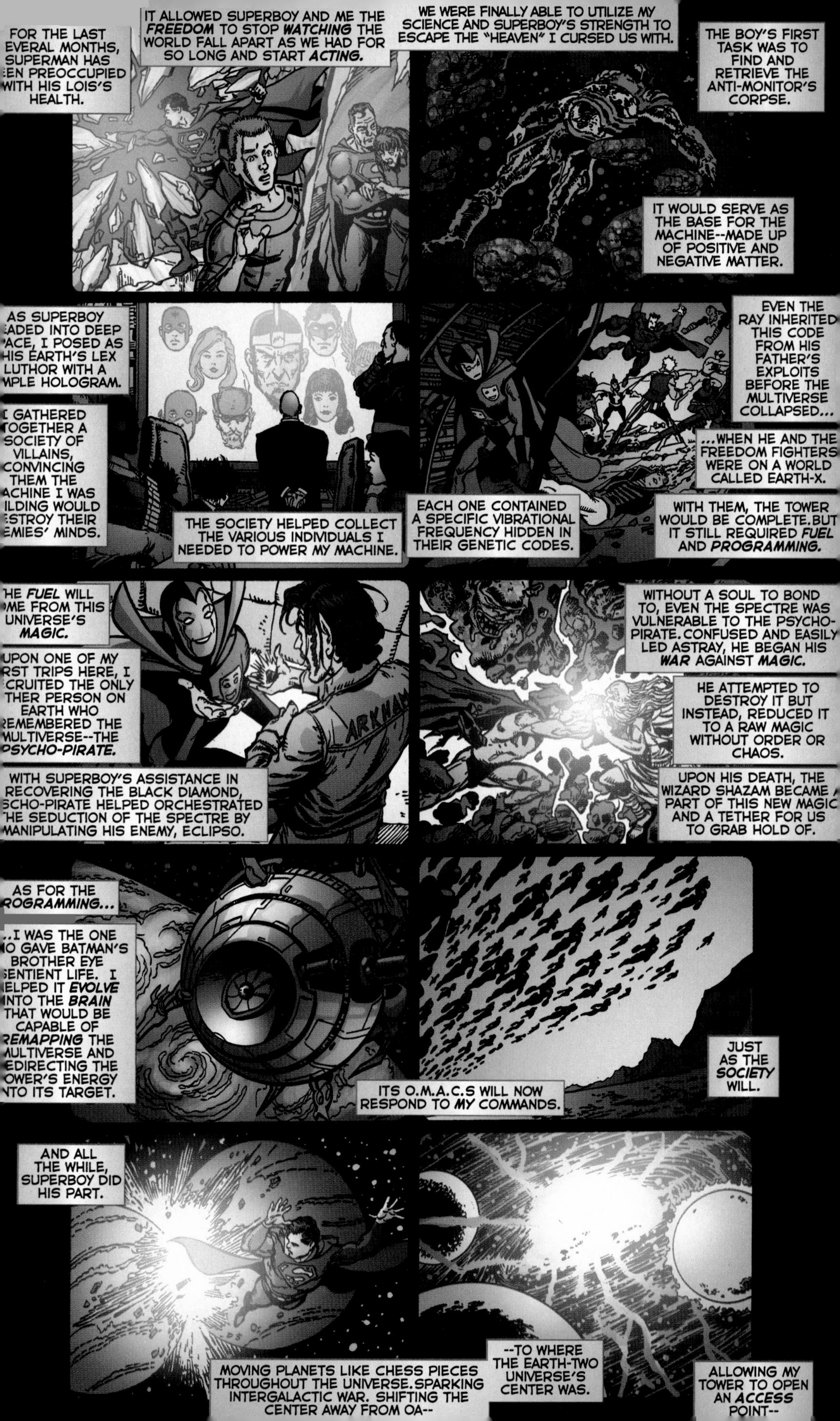

FOR THE LAST EVERAL MONTHS, SUPERMAN HAS EEN PREOCCUPIED WITH HIS LOIS'S HEALTH.
IT ALLOWED SUPERBOY AND ME THE FREEDOM TO STOP WATCHING THE WORLD FALL APART AS WE HAD FOR SO LONG AND START ACTING.
WE WERE FINALLY ABLE TO UTILIZE MY SCIENCE AND SUPERBOY'S STRENGTH TO ESCAPE THE "HEAVEN" I CURSED US WITH.
THE BOY'S FIRST TASK WAS TO FIND AND RETRIEVE THE ANTI-MONITOR'S CORPSE.
IT WOULD SERVE AS THE BASE FOR THE MACHINE--MADE UP OF POSITIVE AND NEGATIVE MATTER.
AS SUPERBOY EADED INTO DEEP ACE, I POSED AS HIS EARTH'S LEX LUTHOR WITH A MPLE HOLOGRAM.
I GATHERED TOGETHER A SOCIETY OF VILLAINS, CONVINCING THEM THE ACHINE I WAS ILDING WOULD ESTROY THEIR EMIES' MINDS.
THE SOCIETY HELPED COLLECT THE VARIOUS INDIVIDUALS I NEEDED TO POWER MY MACHINE.
EACH ONE CONTAINED A SPECIFIC VIBRATIONAL FREQUENCY HIDDEN IN THEIR GENETIC CODES.
EVEN THE RAY INHERITED THIS CODE FROM HIS FATHER'S EXPLOITS BEFORE THE MULTIVERSE COLLAPSED...
...WHEN HE AND THE FREEDOM FIGHTERS WERE ON A WORLD CALLED EARTH-X.
WITH THEM, THE TOWER WOULD BE COMPLETE. BUT IT STILL REQUIRED FUEL AND PROGRAMMING.
HE FUEL WILL ME FROM THIS UNIVERSE'S MAGIC.
UPON ONE OF MY RST TRIPS HERE, I CRUITED THE ONLY THER PERSON ON EARTH WHO REMEMBERED THE MULTIVERSE--THE PSYCHO-PIRATE.
ARKHAM
WITH SUPERBOY'S ASSISTANCE IN RECOVERING THE BLACK DIAMOND, SCHO-PIRATE HELPED ORCHESTRATED THE SEDUCTION OF THE SPECTRE BY MANIPULATING HIS ENEMY, ECLIPSO.
WITHOUT A SOUL TO BOND TO, EVEN THE SPECTRE WAS VULNERABLE TO THE PSYCHO-PIRATE. CONFUSED AND EASILY LED ASTRAY, HE BEGAN HIS WAR AGAINST MAGIC.
HE ATTEMPTED TO DESTROY IT BUT INSTEAD, REDUCED IT TO A RAW MAGIC WITHOUT ORDER OR CHAOS.
UPON HIS DEATH, THE WIZARD SHAZAM BECAME PART OF THIS NEW MAGIC AND A TETHER FOR US TO GRAB HOLD OF.
AS FOR THE ROGRAMMING...
..I WAS THE ONE O GAVE BATMAN'S BROTHER EYE SENTIENT LIFE. I ELPED IT EVOLVE INTO THE BRAIN THAT WOULD BE CAPABLE OF REMAPPING THE MULTIVERSE AND EDIRECTING THE OWER'S ENERGY NTO ITS TARGET.
ITS O.M.A.C.S WILL NOW RESPOND TO MY COMMANDS.
JUST AS THE SOCIETY WILL.
AND ALL THE WHILE, SUPERBOY DID HIS PART.
MOVING PLANETS LIKE CHESS PIECES THROUGHOUT THE UNIVERSE. SPARKING INTERGALACTIC WAR. SHIFTING THE CENTER AWAY FROM OA--
--TO WHERE THE EARTH-TWO UNIVERSE'S CENTER WAS.
ALLOWING MY TOWER TO OPEN AN ACCESS POINT--

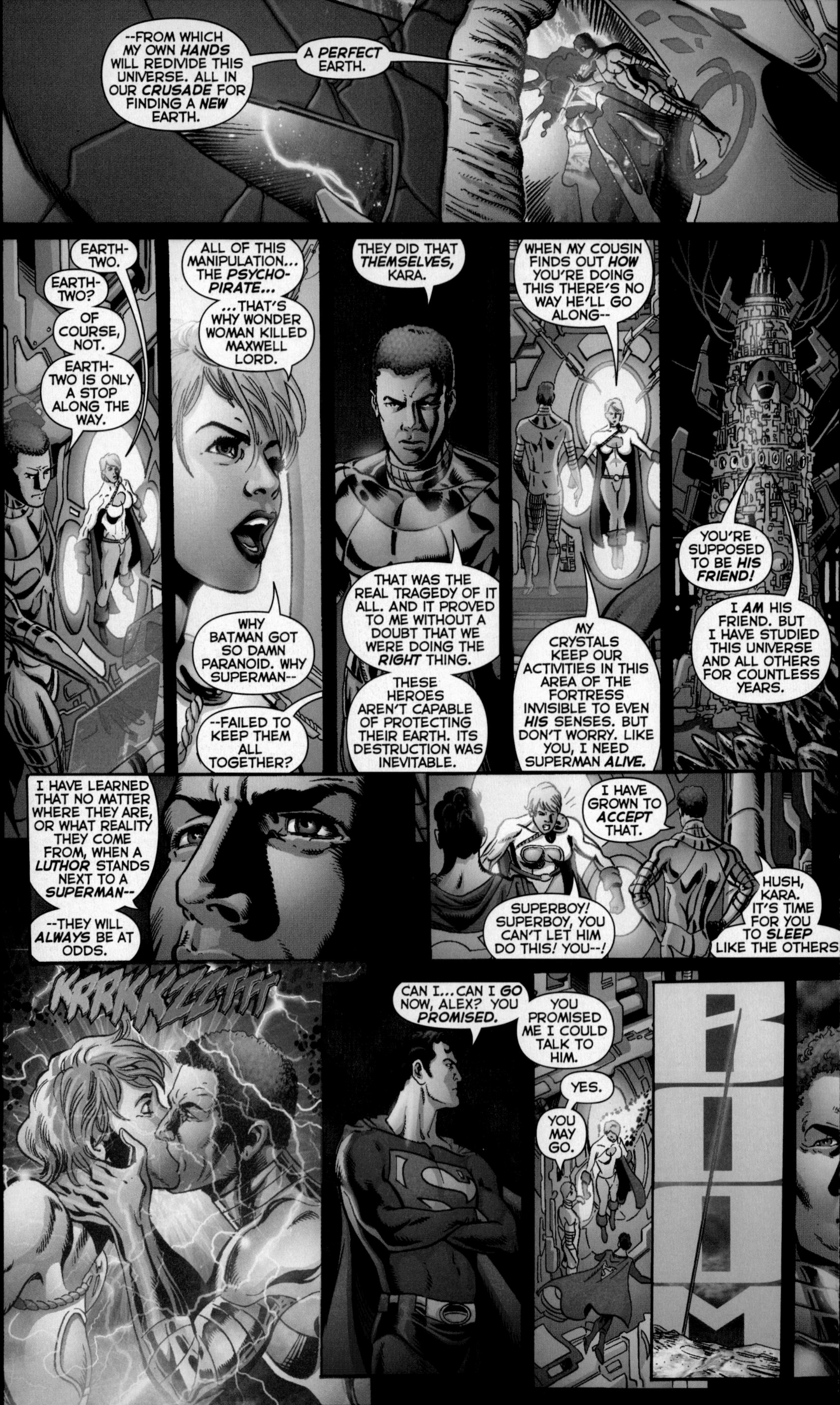
--FROM WHICH MY OWN HANDS WILL REDIVIDE THIS UNIVERSE. ALL IN OUR CRUSADE FOR FINDING A NEW EARTH.
A PERFECT EARTH.
EARTH-TWO.
EARTH-TWO?
OF COURSE, NOT.
EARTH-TWO IS ONLY A STOP ALONG THE WAY.
ALL OF THIS MANIPULATION... THE PSYCHO-PIRATE...
...THAT'S WHY WONDER WOMAN KILLED MAXWELL LORD.
WHY BATMAN GOT SO DAMN PARANOID. WHY SUPERMAN--
--FAILED TO KEEP THEM ALL TOGETHER?
THEY DID THAT THEMSELVES, KARA.
THAT WAS THE REAL TRAGEDY OF IT ALL. AND IT PROVED TO ME WITHOUT A DOUBT THAT WE WERE DOING THE RIGHT THING.
THESE HEROES AREN'T CAPABLE OF PROTECTING THEIR EARTH. ITS DESTRUCTION WAS INEVITABLE.
WHEN MY COUSIN FINDS OUT HOW YOU'RE DOING THIS THERE'S NO WAY HE'LL GO ALONG--
MY CRYSTALS KEEP OUR ACTIVITIES IN THIS AREA OF THE FORTRESS INVISIBLE TO EVEN HIS SENSES. BUT DON'T WORRY. LIKE YOU, I NEED SUPERMAN ALIVE.
YOU'RE SUPPOSED TO BE HIS FRIEND!
I AM HIS FRIEND. BUT I HAVE STUDIED THIS UNIVERSE AND ALL OTHERS FOR COUNTLESS YEARS.
I HAVE LEARNED THAT NO MATTER WHERE THEY ARE, OR WHAT REALITY THEY COME FROM, WHEN A LUTHOR STANDS NEXT TO A SUPERMAN--
--THEY WILL ALWAYS BE AT ODDS.
I HAVE GROWN TO ACCEPT THAT.
SUPERBOY! SUPERBOY, YOU CAN'T LET HIM DO THIS! YOU--!
HUSH, KARA. IT'S TIME FOR YOU TO SLEEP LIKE THE OTHERS.
KRRKKZZZTTT
CAN I...CAN I GO NOW, ALEX? YOU PROMISED.
YOU PROMISED ME I COULD TALK TO HIM.
YES.
YOU MAY GO.
BOOM

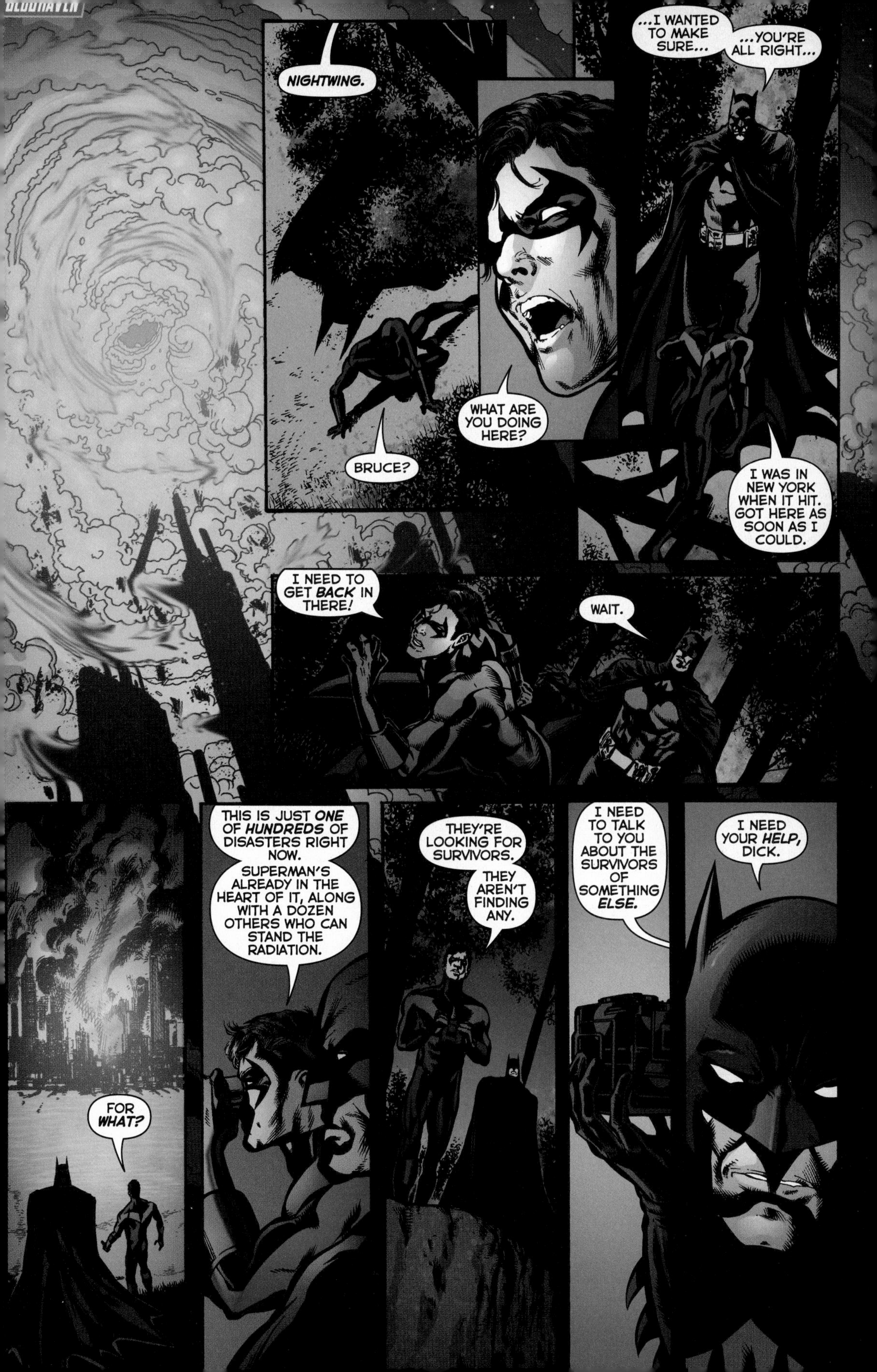

NIGHTWING.
BRUCE?
WHAT ARE YOU DOING HERE?
...I WANTED TO MAKE SURE...
...YOU'RE ALL RIGHT...
I WAS IN NEW YORK WHEN IT HIT. GOT HERE AS SOON AS I COULD.
I NEED TO GET BACK IN THERE!
WAIT.
FOR WHAT?
THIS IS JUST ONE OF HUNDREDS OF DISASTERS RIGHT NOW.
SUPERMAN'S ALREADY IN THE HEART OF IT, ALONG WITH A DOZEN OTHERS WHO CAN STAND THE RADIATION.
THEY'RE LOOKING FOR SURVIVORS.
THEY AREN'T FINDING ANY.
I NEED TO TALK TO YOU ABOUT THE SURVIVORS OF SOMETHING ELSE.
I NEED YOUR HELP, DICK.

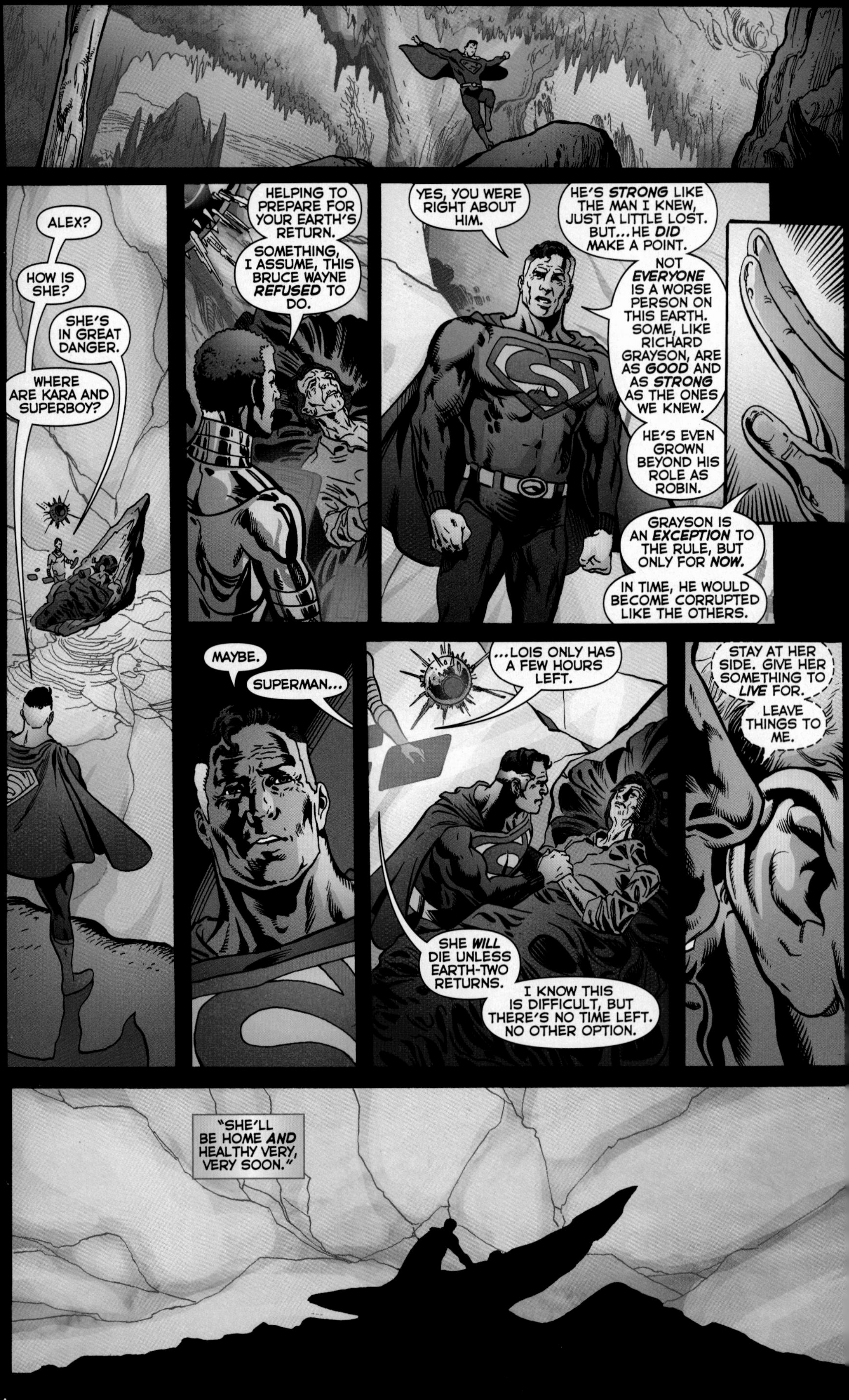
ALEX?
HOW IS SHE?
SHE'S IN GREAT DANGER.
WHERE ARE KARA AND SUPERBOY?
HELPING TO PREPARE FOR YOUR EARTH'S RETURN.
SOMETHING, I ASSUME, THIS BRUCE WAYNE REFUSED TO DO.
YES, YOU WERE RIGHT ABOUT HIM.
HE'S STRONG LIKE THE MAN I KNEW, JUST A LITTLE LOST. BUT...HE DID MAKE A POINT.
NOT EVERYONE IS A WORSE PERSON ON THIS EARTH. SOME, LIKE RICHARD GRAYSON, ARE AS GOOD AND AS STRONG AS THE ONES WE KNEW.
HE'S EVEN GROWN BEYOND HIS ROLE AS ROBIN.
GRAYSON IS AN EXCEPTION TO THE RULE, BUT ONLY FOR NOW.
IN TIME, HE WOULD BECOME CORRUPTED LIKE THE OTHERS.
MAYBE.
SUPERMAN...
...LOIS ONLY HAS A FEW HOURS LEFT.
SHE WILL DIE UNLESS EARTH-TWO RETURNS.
I KNOW THIS IS DIFFICULT, BUT THERE'S NO TIME LEFT. NO OTHER OPTION.
STAY AT HER SIDE. GIVE HER SOMETHING TO LIVE FOR.
LEAVE THINGS TO ME.
"SHE'LL BE HOME AND HEALTHY VERY, VERY SOON."

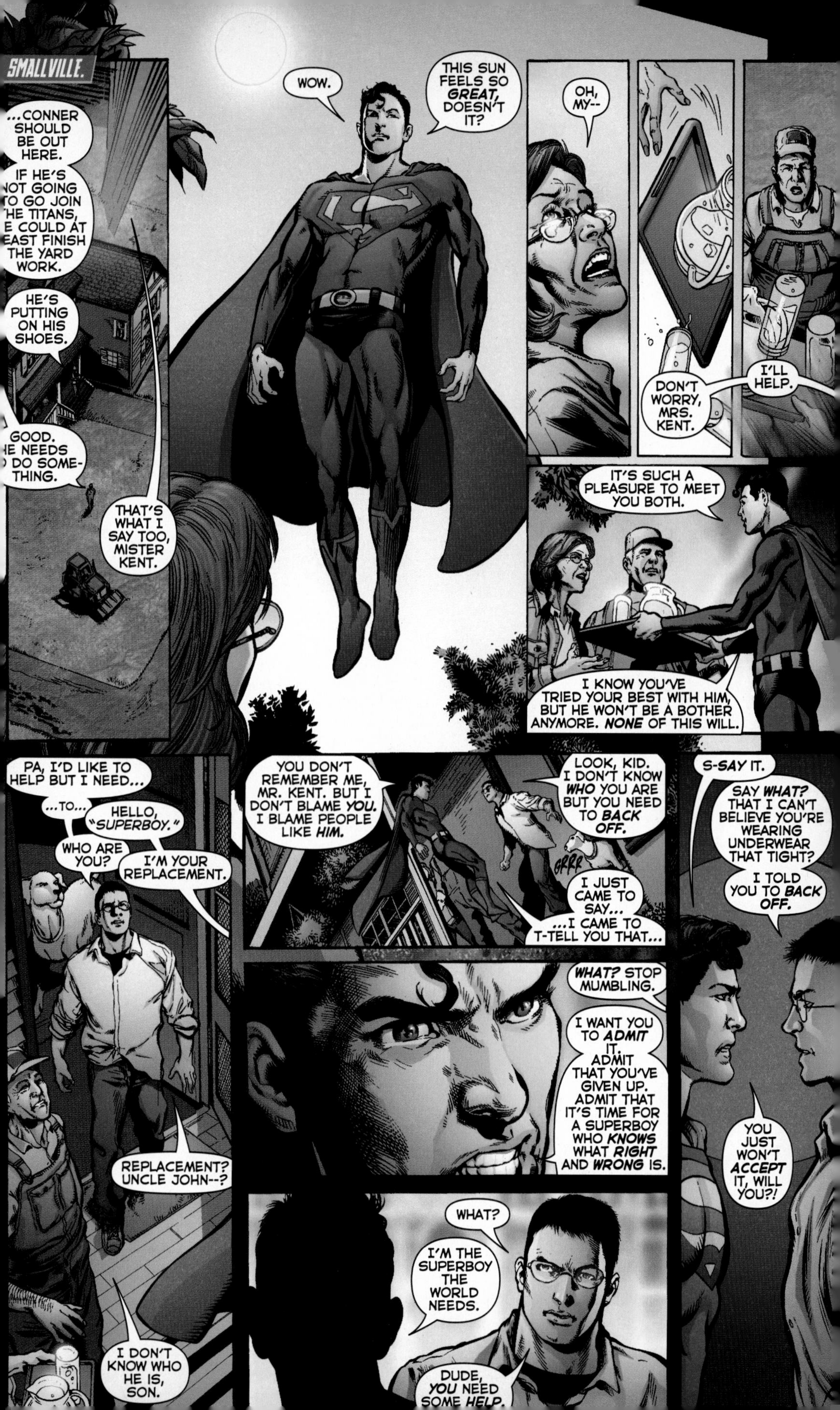

SMALLVILLE.
...CONNER SHOULD BE OUT HERE.
IF HE'S NOT GOING TO GO JOIN THE TITANS, HE COULD AT LEAST FINISH THE YARD WORK.
HE'S PUTTING ON HIS SHOES.
GOOD. HE NEEDS TO DO SOME-THING.
THAT'S WHAT I SAY TOO, MISTER KENT.
WOW.
THIS SUN FEELS SO GREAT, DOESN'T IT?
OH, MY--
DON'T WORRY, MRS. KENT.
I'LL HELP.
IT'S SUCH A PLEASURE TO MEET YOU BOTH.
I KNOW YOU'VE TRIED YOUR BEST WITH HIM, BUT HE WON'T BE A BOTHER ANYMORE. NONE OF THIS WILL.
PA, I'D LIKE TO HELP BUT I NEED...
...TO...
HELLO, "SUPERBOY."
WHO ARE YOU?
I'M YOUR REPLACEMENT.
REPLACEMENT? UNCLE JOHN--?
I DON'T KNOW WHO HE IS, SON.
YOU DON'T REMEMBER ME, MR. KENT. BUT I DON'T BLAME YOU. I BLAME PEOPLE LIKE HIM.
LOOK, KID. I DON'T KNOW WHO YOU ARE BUT YOU NEED TO BACK OFF.
GRRR
I JUST CAME TO SAY...
...I CAME TO T-TELL YOU THAT...
WHAT? STOP MUMBLING.
I WANT YOU TO ADMIT IT. ADMIT THAT YOU'VE GIVEN UP. ADMIT THAT IT'S TIME FOR A SUPERBOY WHO KNOWS WHAT RIGHT AND WRONG IS.
WHAT?
I'M THE SUPERBOY THE WORLD NEEDS.
DUDE, YOU NEED SOME HELP.
S-SAY IT.
SAY WHAT? THAT I CAN'T BELIEVE YOU'RE WEARING UNDERWEAR THAT TIGHT?
I TOLD YOU TO BACK OFF.
YOU JUST WON'T ACCEPT IT, WILL YOU?!

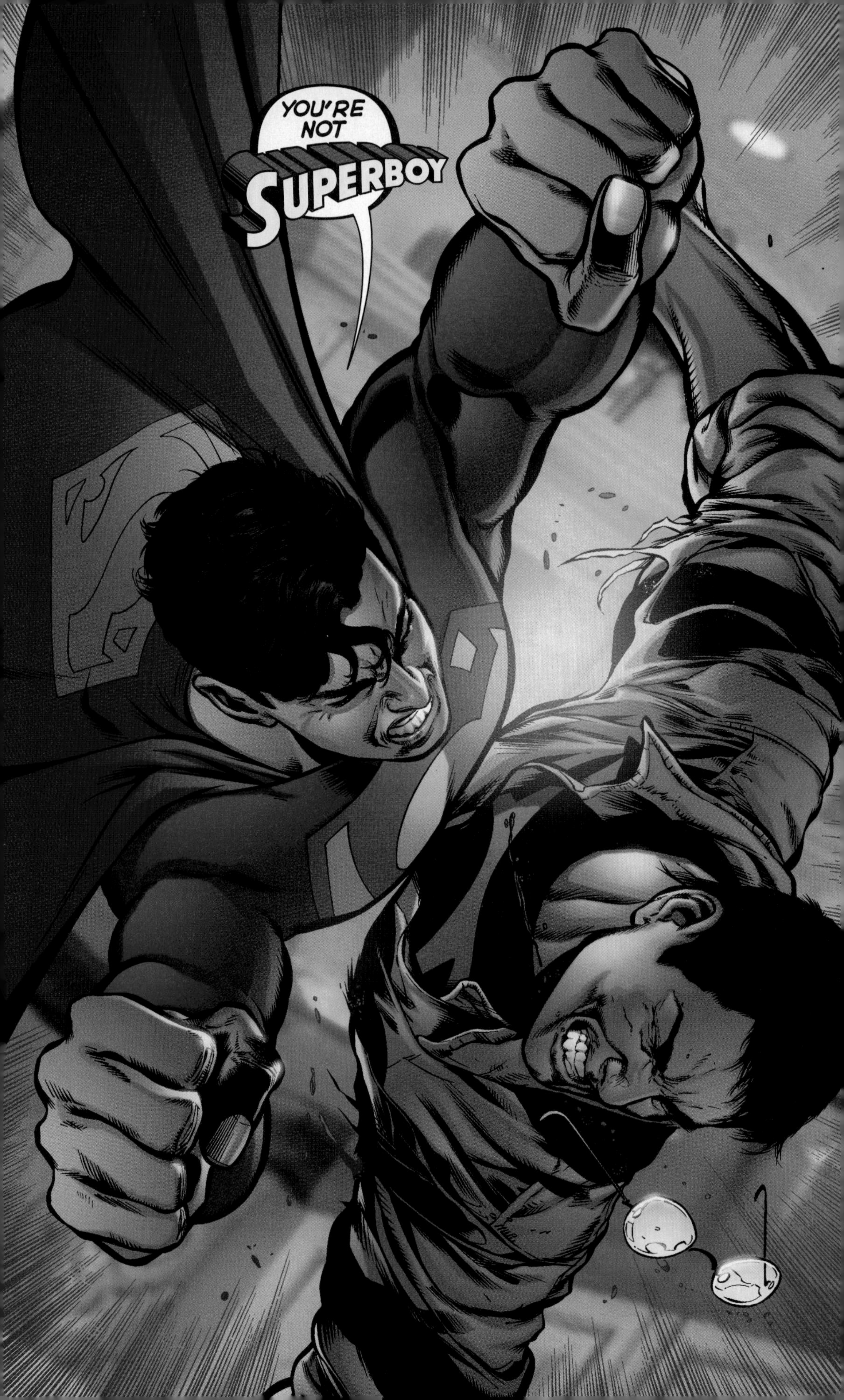
YOU'RE NOT SUPERBOY

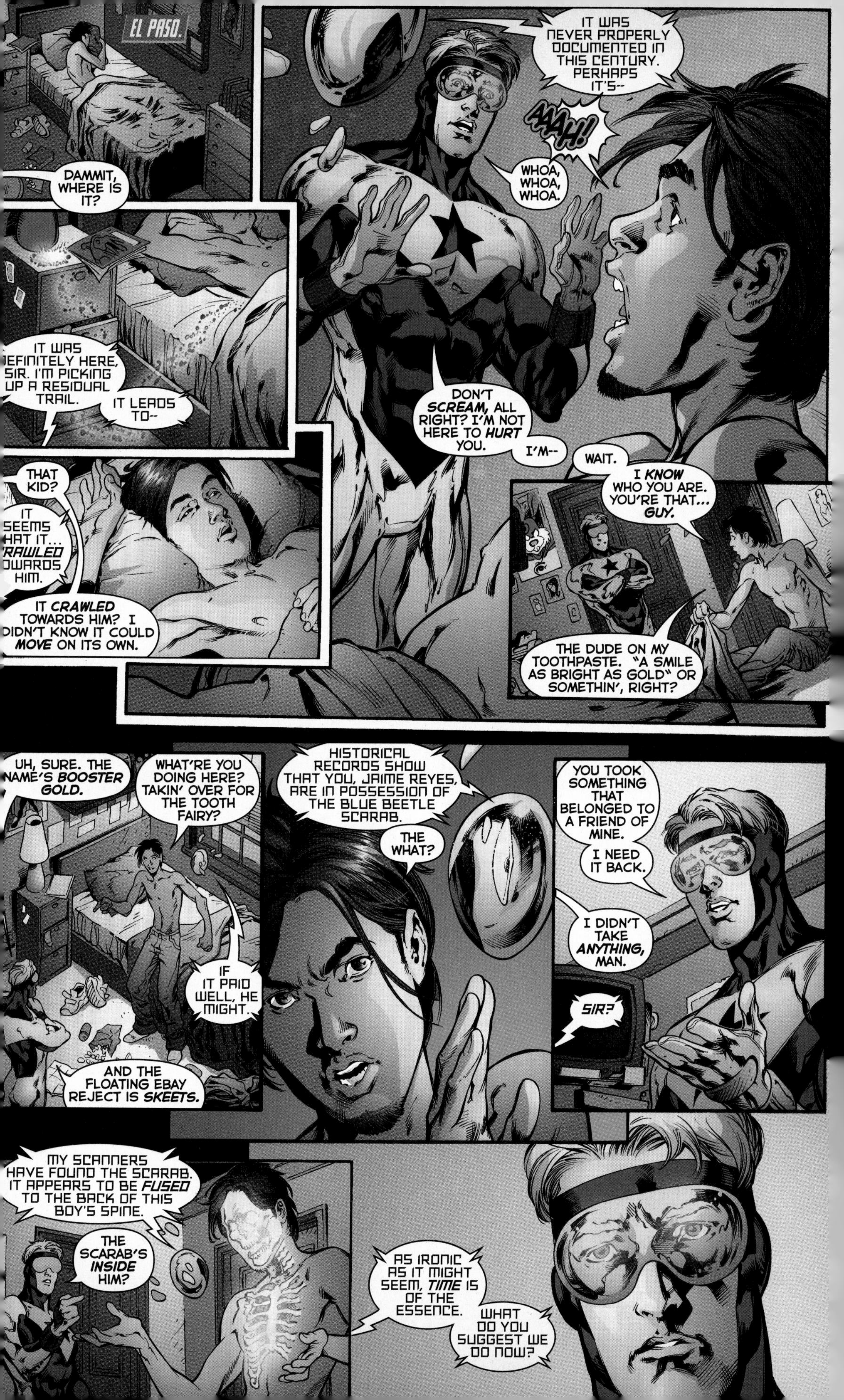
EL PASO.
DAMMIT, WHERE IS IT?
IT WAS EFINITELY HERE, SIR. I'M PICKING UP A RESIDUAL TRAIL.
IT LEADS TO--
THAT KID?
IT SEEMS HAT IT... RAWLED OWARDS HIM.
IT CRAWLED TOWARDS HIM? I IDN'T KNOW IT COULD MOVE ON ITS OWN.
IT WAS NEVER PROPERLY DOCUMENTED IN THIS CENTURY. PERHAPS IT'S--
AAAH!
WHOA, WHOA, WHOA.
DON'T SCREAM, ALL RIGHT? I'M NOT HERE TO HURT YOU.
I'M--
WAIT.
I KNOW WHO YOU ARE. YOU'RE THAT... GUY.
THE DUDE ON MY TOOTHPASTE. "A SMILE AS BRIGHT AS GOLD" OR SOMETHIN', RIGHT?
UH, SURE. THE NAME'S BOOSTER GOLD.
WHAT'RE YOU DOING HERE? TAKIN' OVER FOR THE TOOTH FAIRY?
IF IT PAID WELL, HE MIGHT.
AND THE FLOATING EBAY REJECT IS SKEETS.
HISTORICAL RECORDS SHOW THAT YOU, JAIME REYES, ARE IN POSSESSION OF THE BLUE BEETLE SCARAB.
THE WHAT?
YOU TOOK SOMETHING THAT BELONGED TO A FRIEND OF MINE.
I NEED IT BACK.
I DIDN'T TAKE ANYTHING, MAN.
SIR?
MY SCANNERS HAVE FOUND THE SCARAB. IT APPEARS TO BE FUSED TO THE BACK OF THIS BOY'S SPINE.
THE SCARAB'S INSIDE HIM?
AS IRONIC AS IT MIGHT SEEM, TIME IS OF THE ESSENCE.
WHAT DO YOU SUGGEST WE DO NOW?

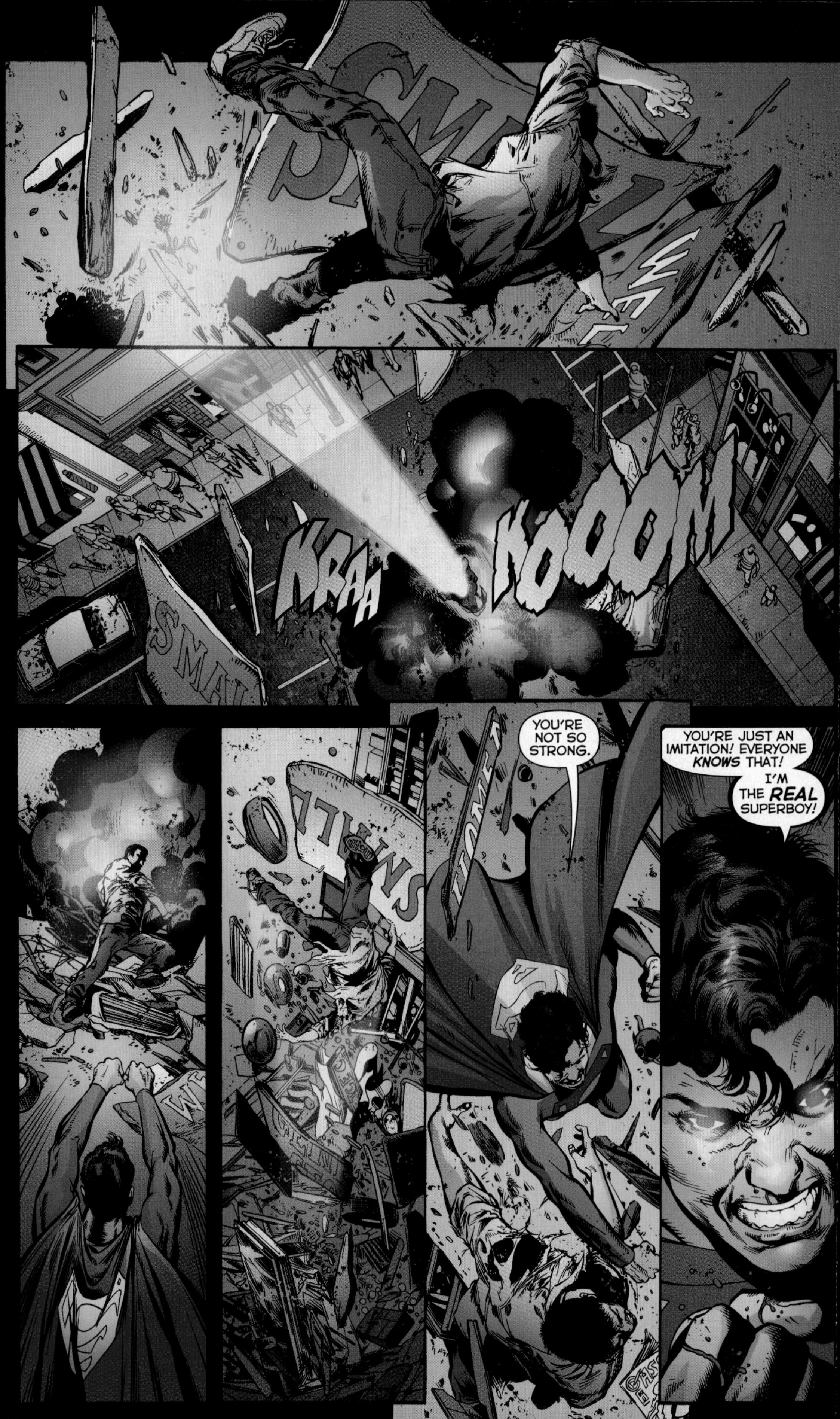
KRAA
KOOOM
YOU'RE NOT SO STRONG.
YOU'RE JUST AN IMITATION! EVERYONE KNOWS THAT!
I'M THE REAL SUPERBOY!

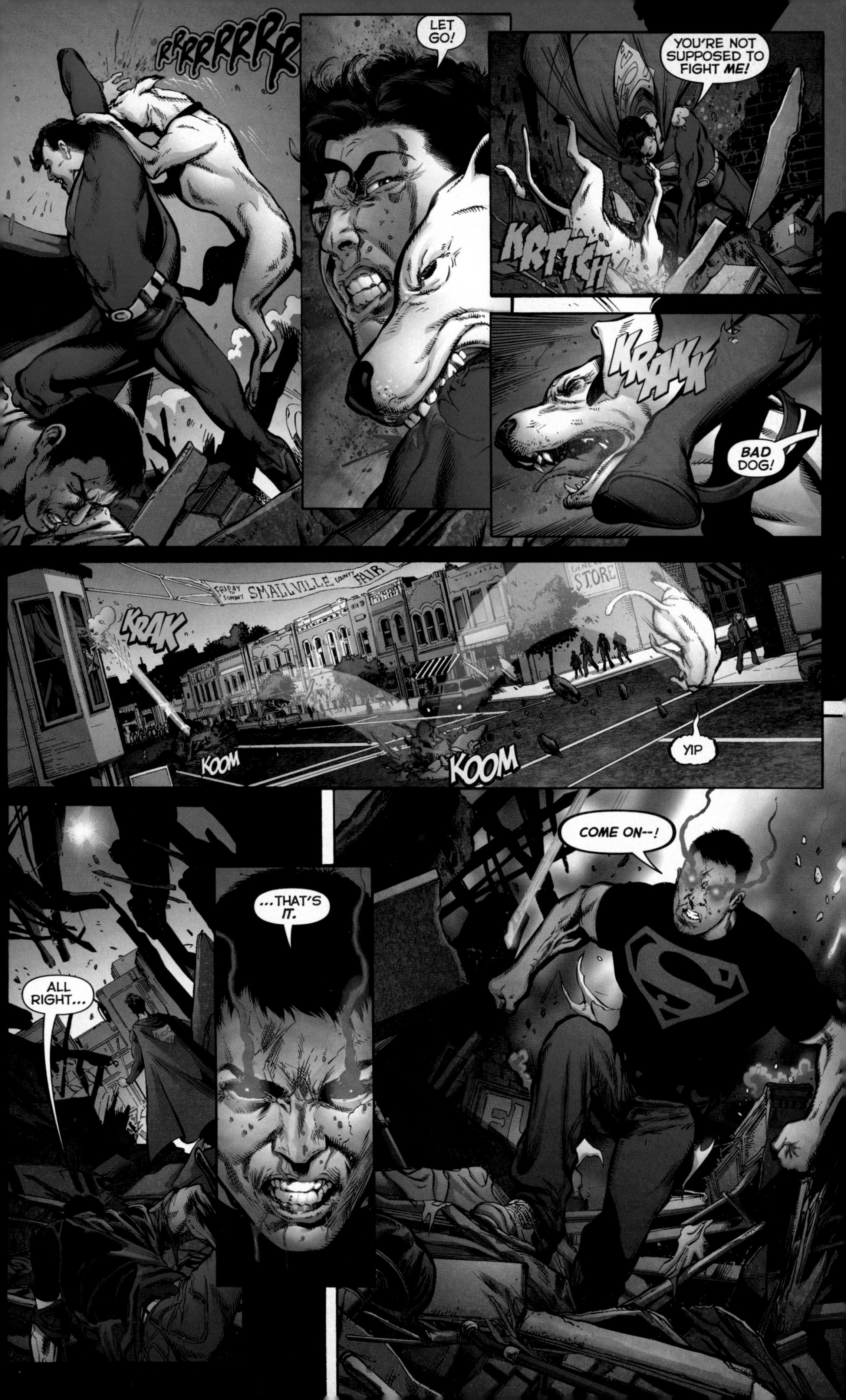
RRRRRRRR
LET GO!
YOU'RE NOT SUPPOSED TO FIGHT ME!
KRTTCH
KRAKK
BAD DOG!
FRIDAY TO SUNDAY SMALLVILLE COUNTY FAIR
STORE
KRAK
KOOM
KOOM
YIP
ALL RIGHT...
...THAT'S IT.
COME ON--!

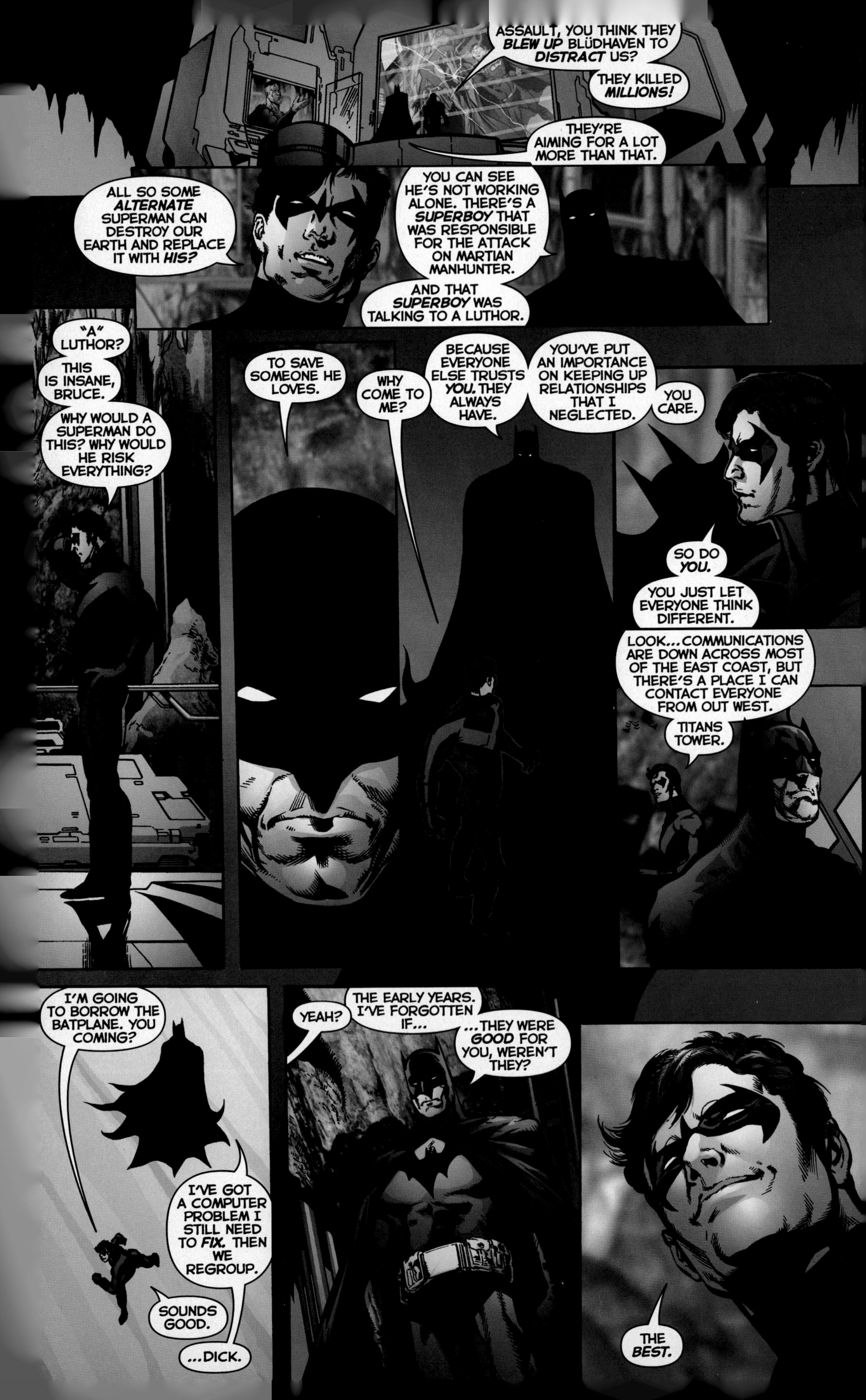
ASSAULT, YOU THINK THEY BLEW UP BLÜDHAVEN TO DISTRACT US?
THEY KILLED MILLIONS!
THEY'RE AIMING FOR A LOT MORE THAN THAT.
ALL SO SOME ALTERNATE SUPERMAN CAN DESTROY OUR EARTH AND REPLACE IT WITH HIS?
YOU CAN SEE HE'S NOT WORKING ALONE. THERE'S A SUPERBOY THAT WAS RESPONSIBLE FOR THE ATTACK ON MARTIAN MANHUNTER.
AND THAT SUPERBOY WAS TALKING TO A LUTHOR.
"A" LUTHOR?
THIS IS INSANE, BRUCE.
WHY WOULD A SUPERMAN DO THIS? WHY WOULD HE RISK EVERYTHING?
TO SAVE SOMEONE HE LOVES.
WHY COME TO ME?
BECAUSE EVERYONE ELSE TRUSTS YOU. THEY ALWAYS HAVE.
YOU'VE PUT AN IMPORTANCE ON KEEPING UP RELATIONSHIPS THAT I NEGLECTED.
YOU CARE.
SO DO YOU.
YOU JUST LET EVERYONE THINK DIFFERENT.
LOOK...COMMUNICATIONS ARE DOWN ACROSS MOST OF THE EAST COAST, BUT THERE'S A PLACE I CAN CONTACT EVERYONE FROM OUT WEST.
TITANS TOWER.
I'M GOING TO BORROW THE BATPLANE. YOU COMING?
I'VE GOT A COMPUTER PROBLEM I STILL NEED TO FIX. THEN WE REGROUP.
SOUNDS GOOD.
...DICK.
YEAH?
THE EARLY YEARS. I'VE FORGOTTEN IF...
...THEY WERE GOOD FOR YOU, WEREN'T THEY?
THE BEST.

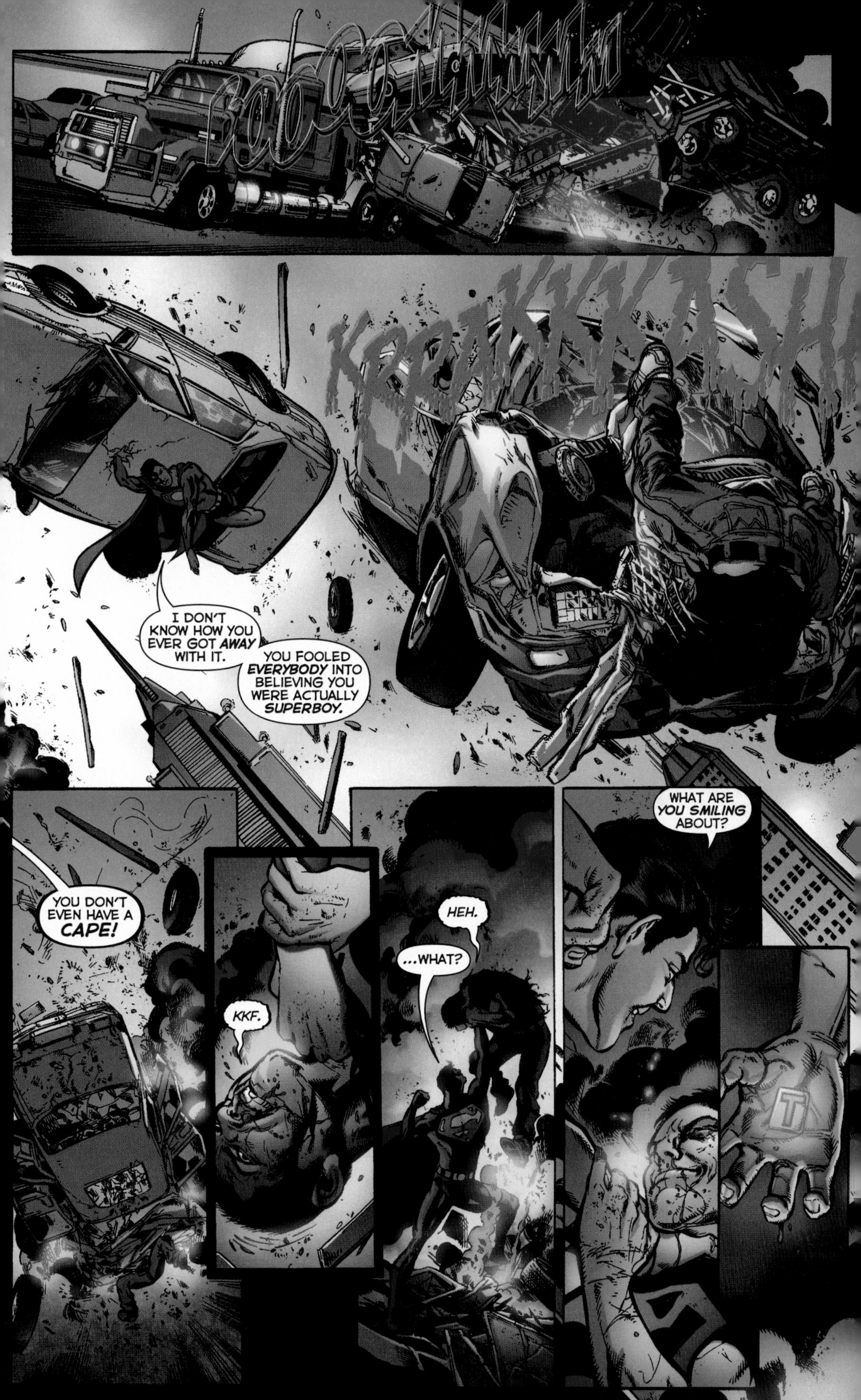

KRRAKKKASH!
I DON'T KNOW HOW YOU EVER GOT AWAY WITH IT.
YOU FOOLED EVERYBODY INTO BELIEVING YOU WERE ACTUALLY SUPERBOY.
YOU DON'T EVEN HAVE A CAPE!
KKF.
HEH.
...WHAT?
WHAT ARE YOU SMILING ABOUT?

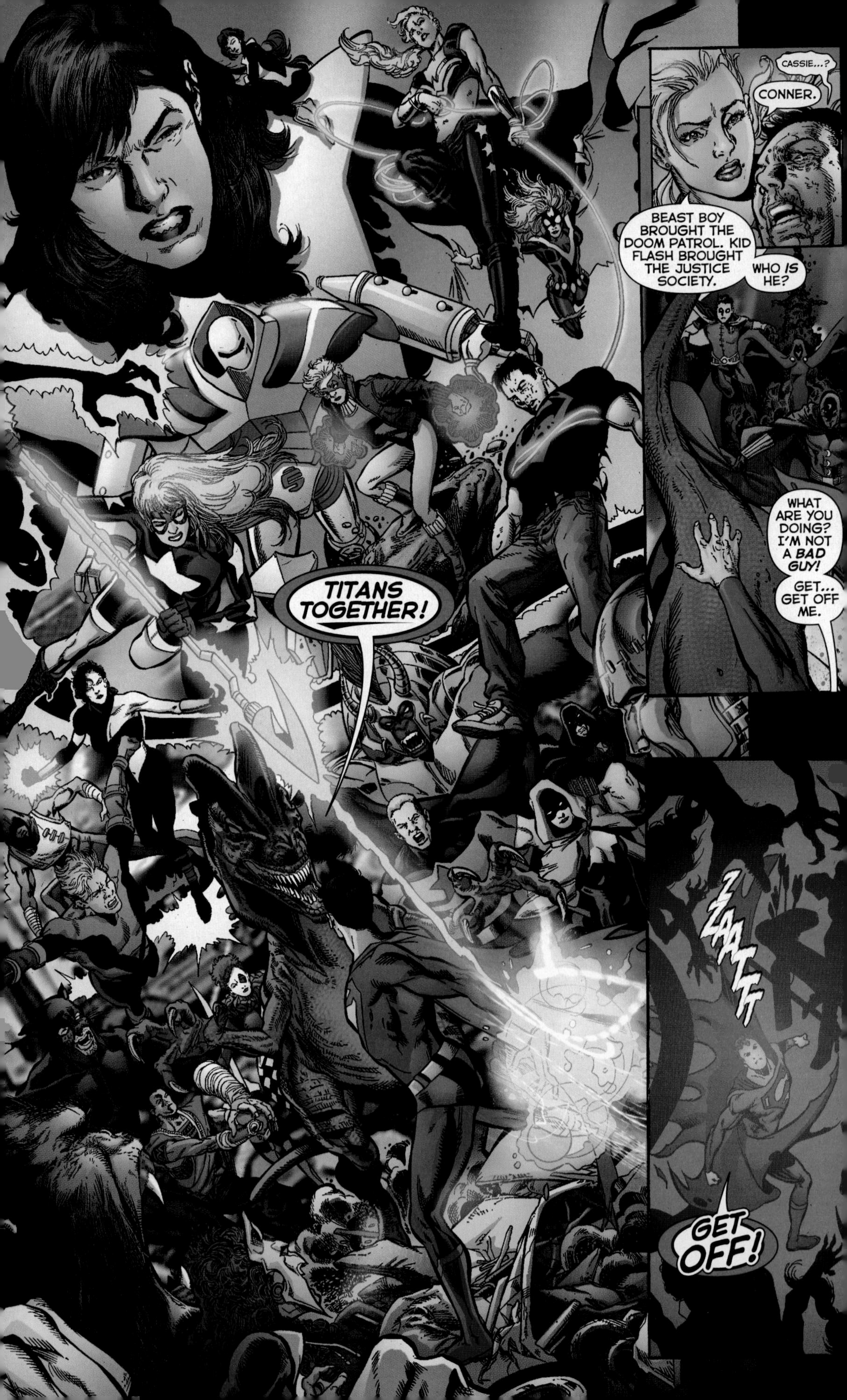

CASSIE...?
CONNER.
BEAST BOY BROUGHT THE DOOM PATROL. KID FLASH BROUGHT THE JUSTICE SOCIETY.
WHO *IS* HE?
TITANS TOGETHER!
WHAT ARE YOU DOING? I'M NOT A *BAD GUY!*
GET... GET OFF ME.
ZZAATT
GET OFF!

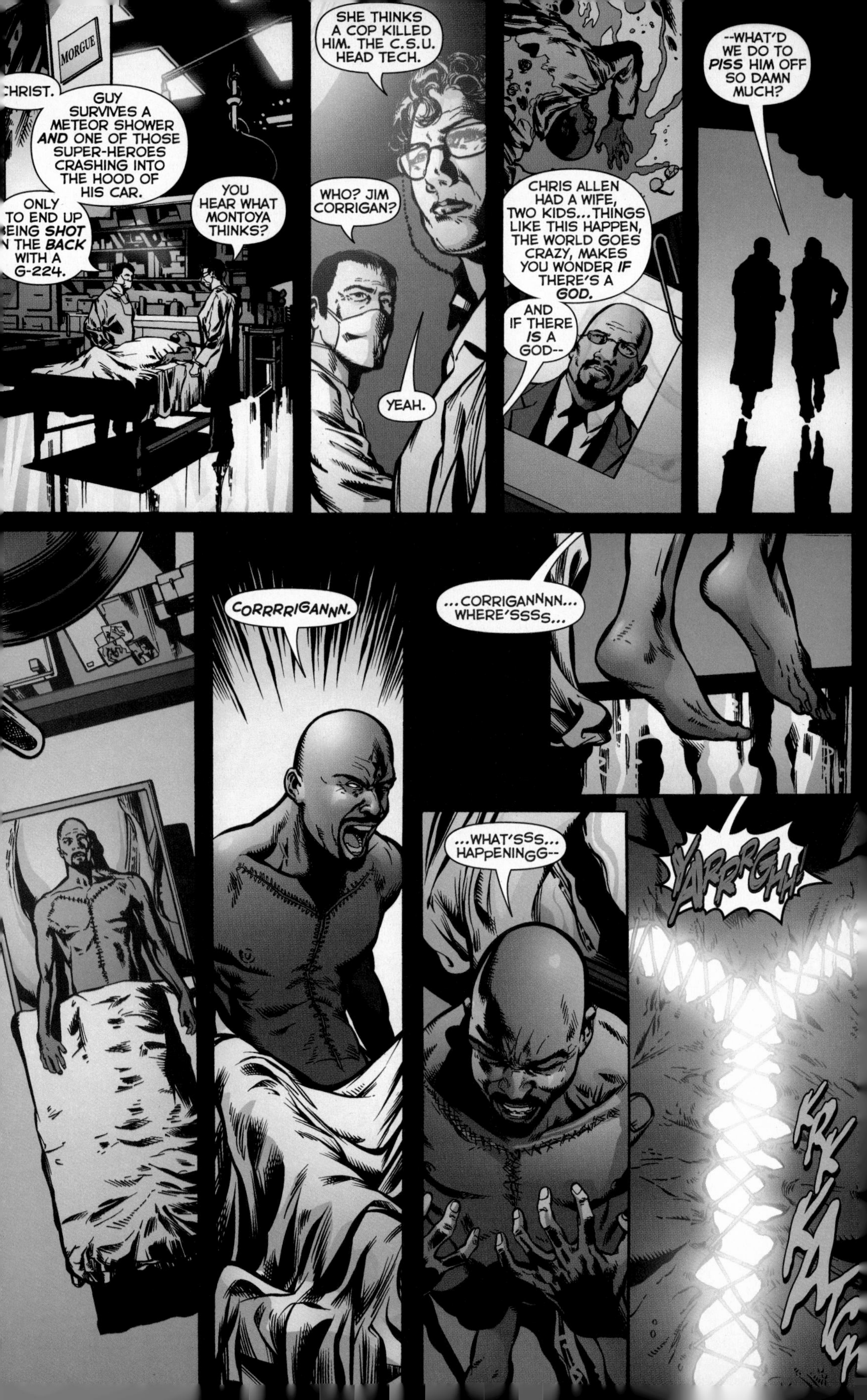
CHRIST.
GUY SURVIVES A METEOR SHOWER AND ONE OF THOSE SUPER-HEROES CRASHING INTO THE HOOD OF HIS CAR.
ONLY TO END UP BEING SHOT IN THE BACK WITH A G-224.
YOU HEAR WHAT MONTOYA THINKS?
SHE THINKS A COP KILLED HIM. THE C.S.U. HEAD TECH.
WHO? JIM CORRIGAN?
YEAH.
CHRIS ALLEN HAD A WIFE, TWO KIDS...THINGS LIKE THIS HAPPEN, THE WORLD GOES CRAZY, MAKES YOU WONDER IF THERE'S A GOD.
AND IF THERE IS A GOD--
--WHAT'D WE DO TO PISS HIM OFF SO DAMN MUCH?
MORGUE
CORRRRIGANNN.
...CORRIGANNNN... WHERE'SSSS...
...WHAT'SSS... HAPPENINGG--
YARRRGHH!

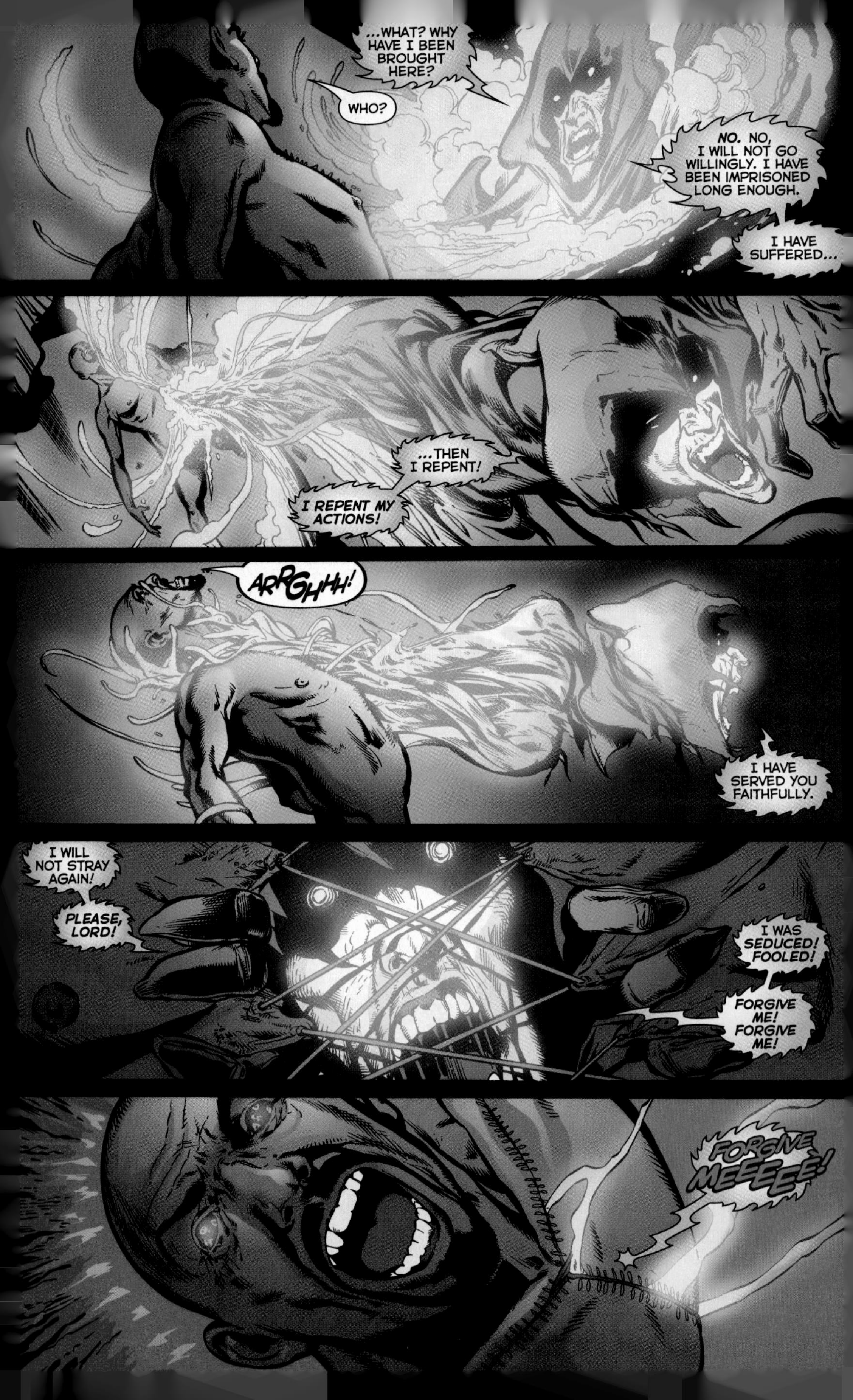
...WHAT? WHY HAVE I BEEN BROUGHT HERE?
WHO?
NO. NO, I WILL NOT GO WILLINGLY. I HAVE BEEN IMPRISONED LONG ENOUGH.
I HAVE SUFFERED...
...THEN I REPENT!
I REPENT MY ACTIONS!
ARRGHHH!
I HAVE SERVED YOU FAITHFULLY.
I WILL NOT STRAY AGAIN!
PLEASE, LORD!
I WAS SEDUCED! FOOLED!
FORGIVE ME! FORGIVE ME!
FORGIVE MEEEEEE!

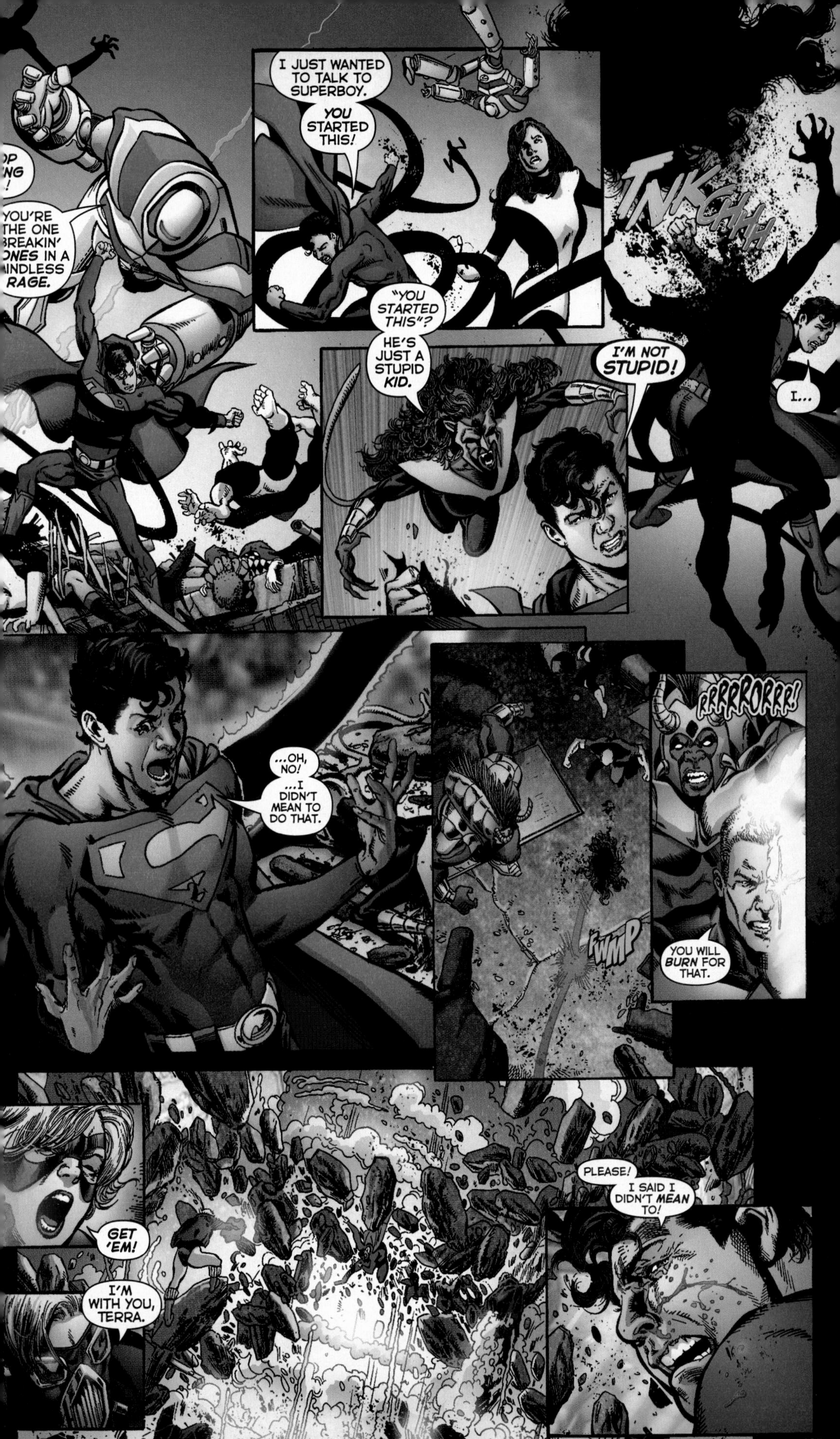
OP
NG
!
YOU'RE THE ONE BREAKIN' ONES IN A INDLESS RAGE.
I JUST WANTED TO TALK TO SUPERBOY.
YOU STARTED THIS!
"YOU STARTED THIS"? HE'S JUST A STUPID KID.
I'M NOT STUPID!
TNKCHHH
I...
...OH, NO! ...I DIDN'T MEAN TO DO THAT.
FWMP
RRRRRORRR!
YOU WILL BURN FOR THAT.
GET 'EM!
I'M WITH YOU, TERRA.
PLEASE! I SAID I DIDN'T MEAN TO!

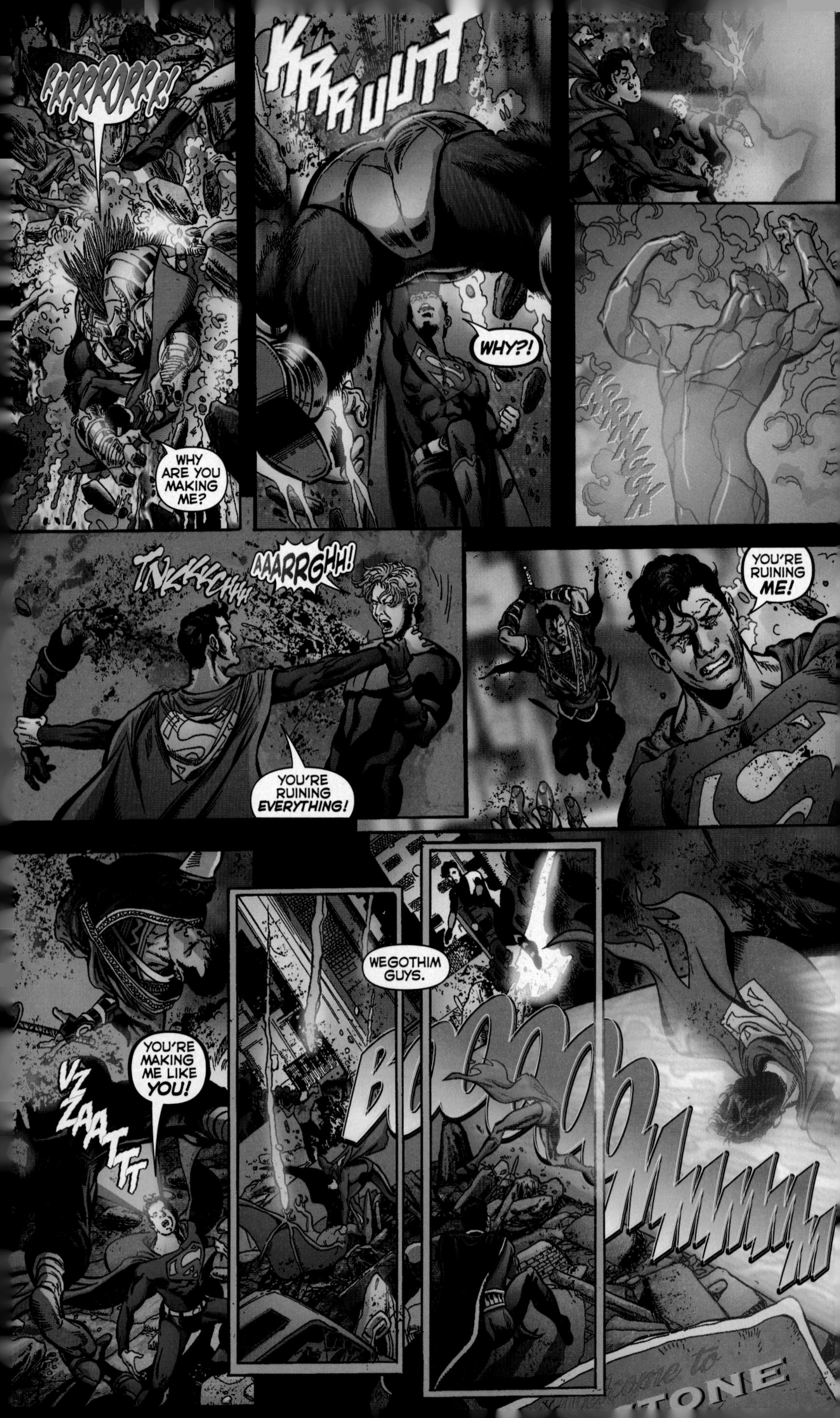
RRRRORRR!
WHY ARE YOU MAKING ME?
KRRRUUTT
WHY?!
AAARRGHH!
YOU'RE RUINING EVERYTHING!
YOU'RE RUINING ME!
YOU'RE MAKING ME LIKE YOU!
VZZAAATTT
WEGOTHIM GUYS.
TONE

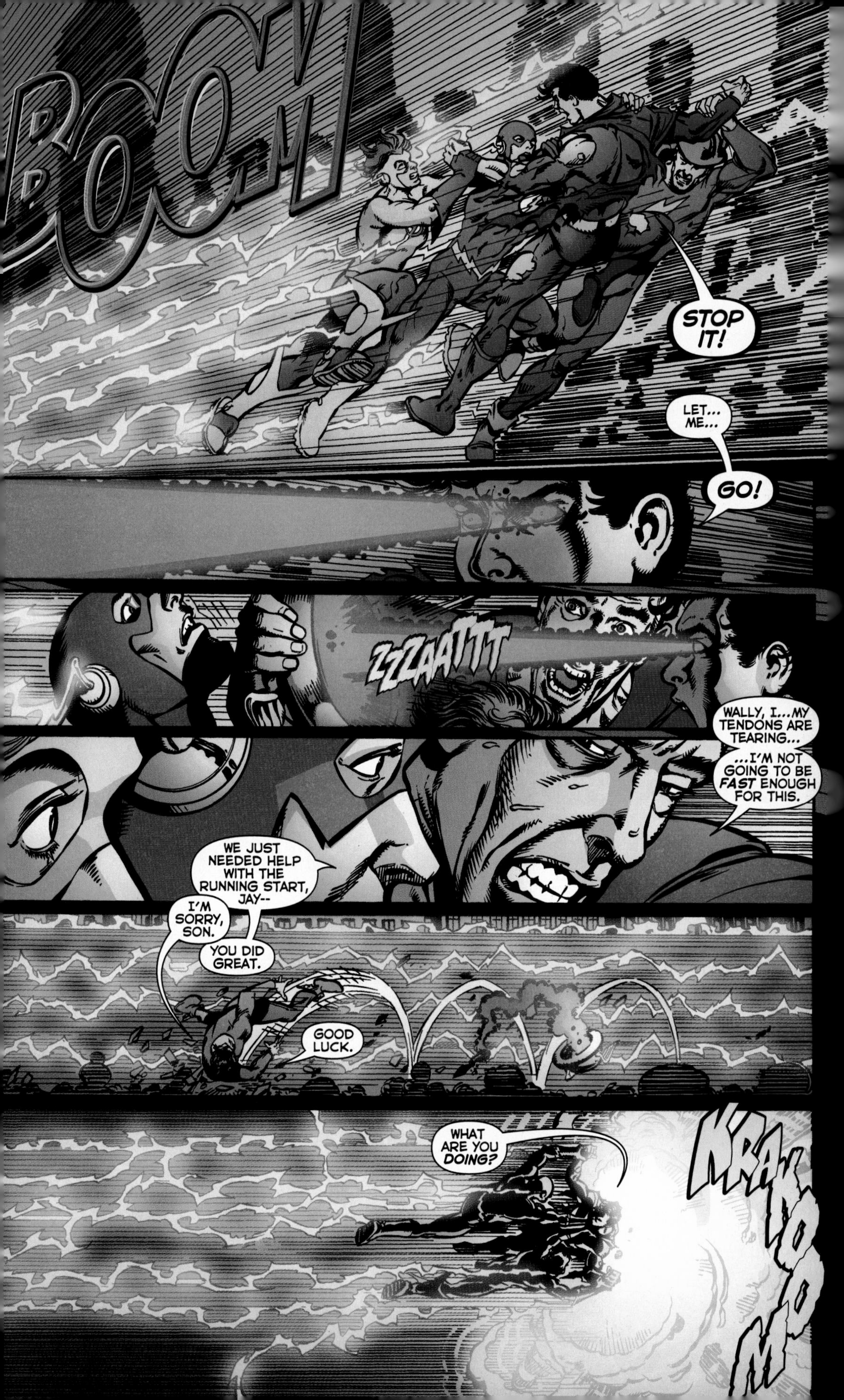
BOOM
STOP IT!
LET... ME...
GO!
ZZZAATTT
WALLY, I...MY TENDONS ARE TEARING...
...I'M NOT GOING TO BE FAST ENOUGH FOR THIS.
WE JUST NEEDED HELP WITH THE RUNNING START, JAY--
I'M SORRY, SON.
YOU DID GREAT.
GOOD LUCK.
WHAT ARE YOU DOING?
KRAKOOM

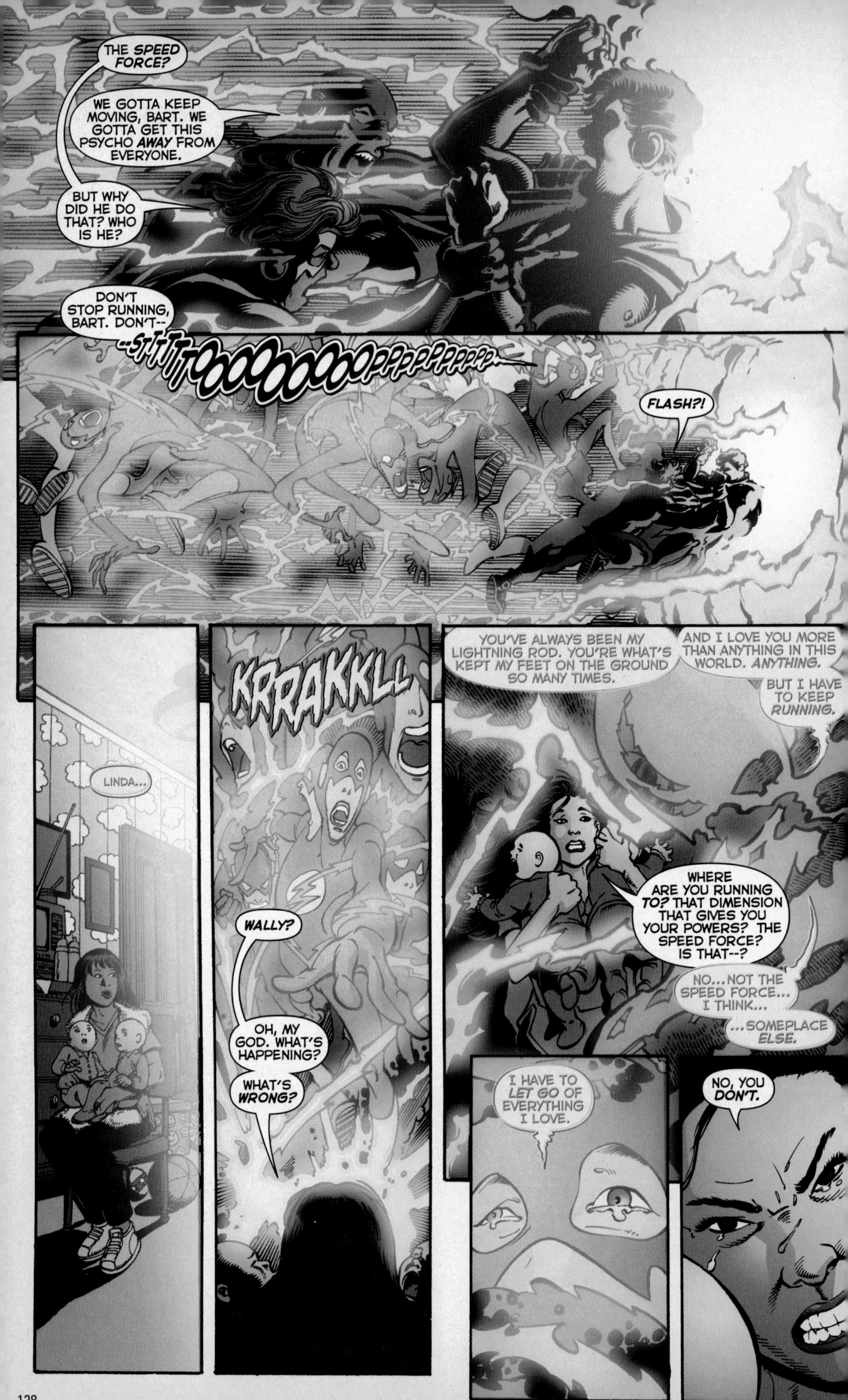
THE SPEED FORCE?
WE GOTTA KEEP MOVING, BART. WE GOTTA GET THIS PSYCHO AWAY FROM EVERYONE.
BUT WHY DID HE DO THAT? WHO IS HE?
DON'T STOP RUNNING, BART. DON'T--
--STTTTOOOOOOOOOPPPPPPPPPP
FLASH?!
LINDA...
KRRAKKLL
WALLY?
OH, MY GOD. WHAT'S HAPPENING?
WHAT'S WRONG?
YOU'VE ALWAYS BEEN MY LIGHTNING ROD. YOU'RE WHAT'S KEPT MY FEET ON THE GROUND SO MANY TIMES.
AND I LOVE YOU MORE THAN ANYTHING IN THIS WORLD. ANYTHING.
BUT I HAVE TO KEEP RUNNING.
WHERE ARE YOU RUNNING TO? THAT DIMENSION THAT GIVES YOU YOUR POWERS? THE SPEED FORCE? IS THAT--?
NO...NOT THE SPEED FORCE... I THINK...
...SOMEPLACE ELSE.
I HAVE TO LET GO OF EVERYTHING I LOVE.
NO, YOU DON'T.

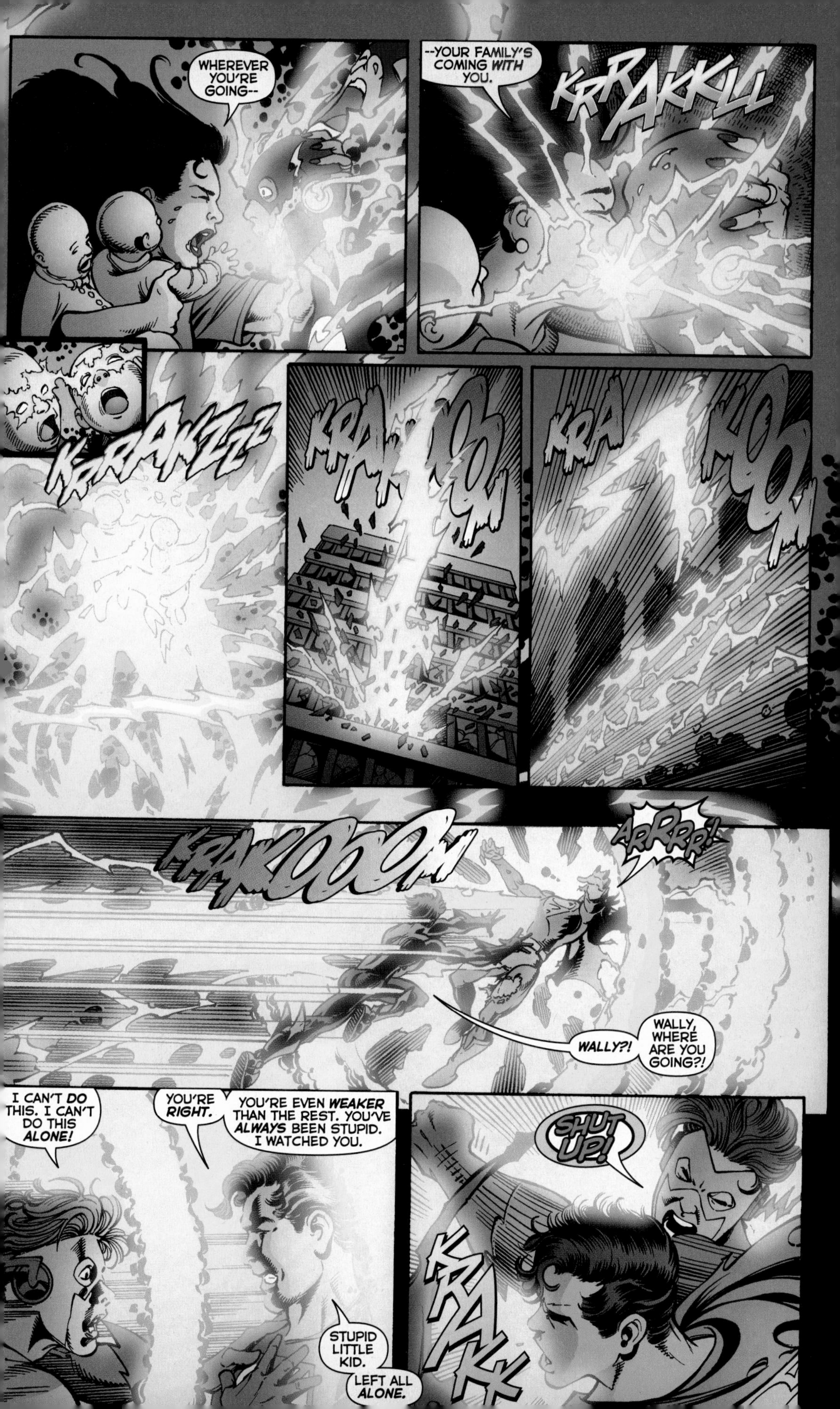

WHEREVER YOU'RE GOING--
--YOUR FAMILY'S COMING WITH YOU.
KRRAKKLL
KRRAKZZZZ
KRA KOOM
KRA KOOM
KRAKOOOOM
ARRRR!
WALLY?!
WALLY, WHERE ARE YOU GOING?!
I CAN'T DO THIS. I CAN'T DO THIS ALONE!
YOU'RE RIGHT.
YOU'RE EVEN WEAKER THAN THE REST. YOU'VE ALWAYS BEEN STUPID. I WATCHED YOU.
STUPID LITTLE KID.
LEFT ALL ALONE.
SHUT UP!
KRAKK

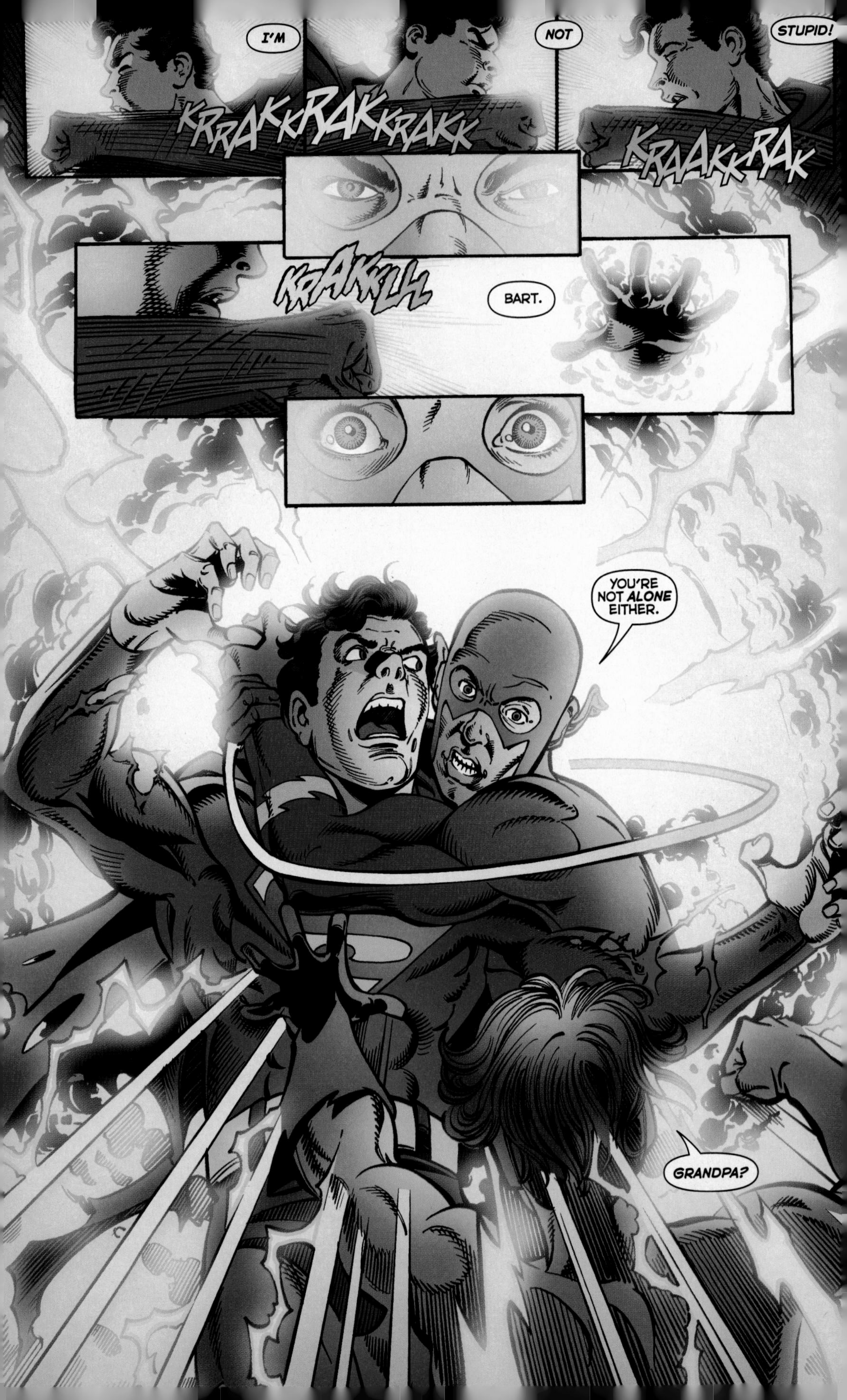

I'M
NOT
STUPID!
KRRAKKRAKKRAKK
KRAAKKRAK
KRAKKLL
BART.
YOU'RE NOT ALONE EITHER.
GRANDPA?

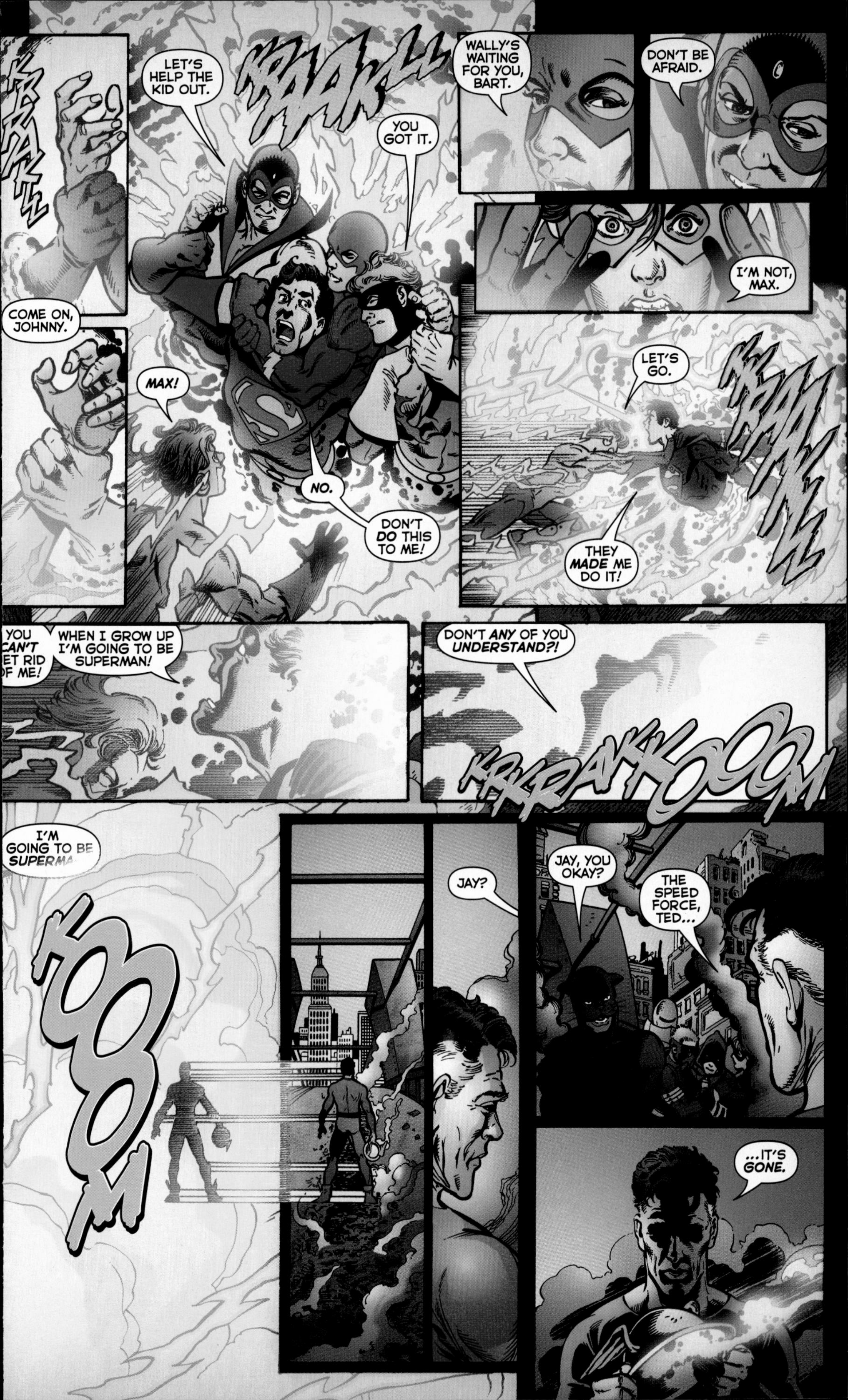
LET'S HELP THE KID OUT.
YOU GOT IT.
WALLY'S WAITING FOR YOU, BART.
DON'T BE AFRAID.
I'M NOT, MAX.
COME ON, JOHNNY.
MAX!
NO.
DON'T *DO* THIS TO ME!
LET'S GO.
THEY *MADE* ME DO IT!
YOU *CAN'T* ET RID OF ME!
WHEN I GROW UP I'M GOING TO BE SUPERMAN!
DON'T *ANY* OF YOU *UNDERSTAND?!*
KRKRAKKOOOOM
I'M GOING TO BE *SUPERMA*
JAY?
JAY, YOU OKAY?
THE SPEED FORCE, TED...
...IT'S **GONE.**

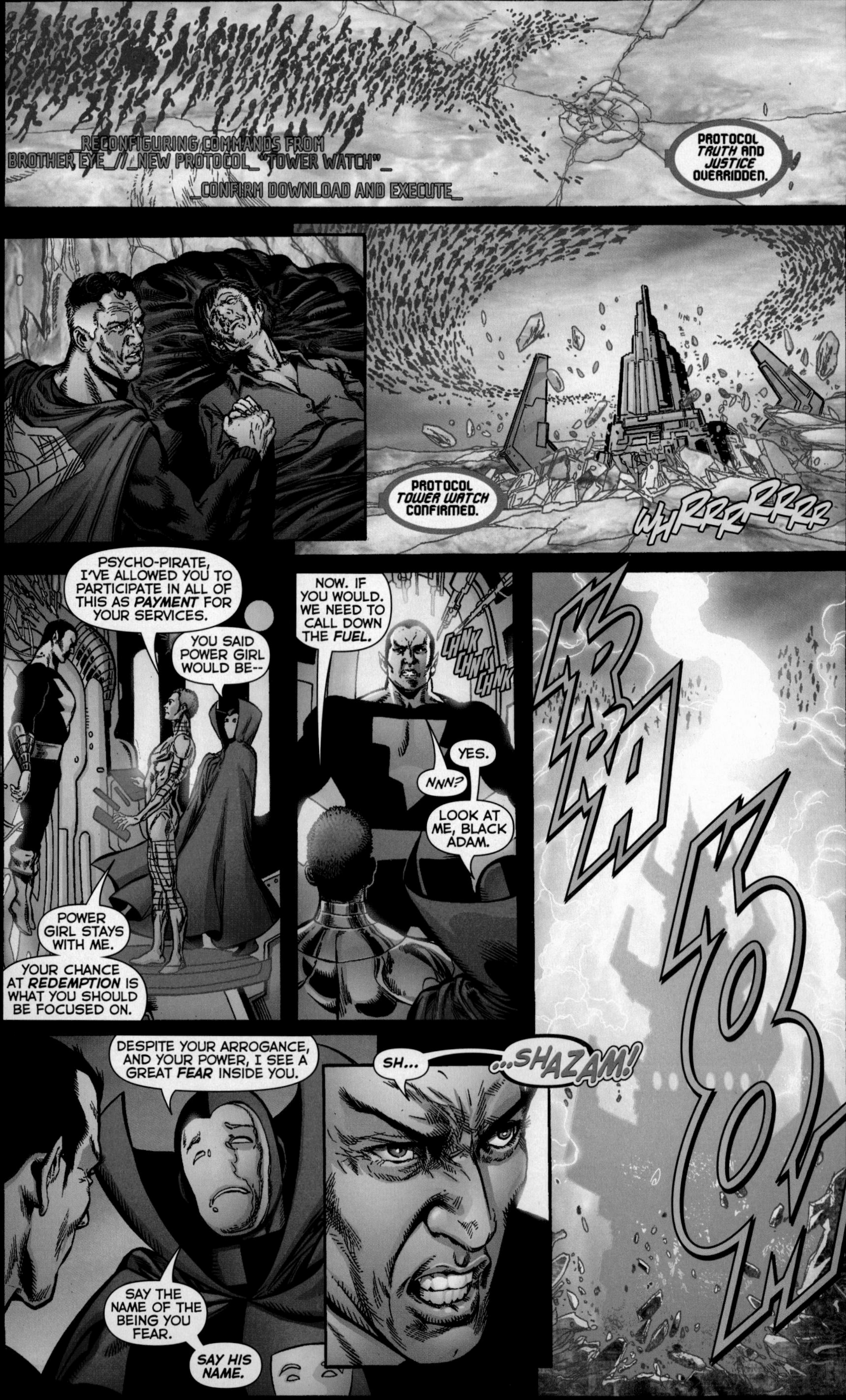

RECONFIGURING COMMANDS FROM BROTHER EYE//_NEW PROTOCOL_"TOWER WATCH"_
CONFIRM DOWNLOAD AND EXECUTE
PROTOCOL TRUTH AND JUSTICE OVERRIDDEN.
PROTOCOL TOWER WATCH CONFIRMED.
WHRRRRRRR
PSYCHO-PIRATE, I'VE ALLOWED YOU TO PARTICIPATE IN ALL OF THIS AS PAYMENT FOR YOUR SERVICES.
YOU SAID POWER GIRL WOULD BE--
POWER GIRL STAYS WITH ME.
YOUR CHANCE AT REDEMPTION IS WHAT YOU SHOULD BE FOCUSED ON.
NOW. IF YOU WOULD. WE NEED TO CALL DOWN THE FUEL.
CHNK CHNK CHNK
YES.
NNN?
LOOK AT ME, BLACK ADAM.
DESPITE YOUR ARROGANCE, AND YOUR POWER, I SEE A GREAT FEAR INSIDE YOU.
SAY THE NAME OF THE BEING YOU FEAR.
SAY HIS NAME.
SH...
...SHAZAM!
KRAKA BOOM

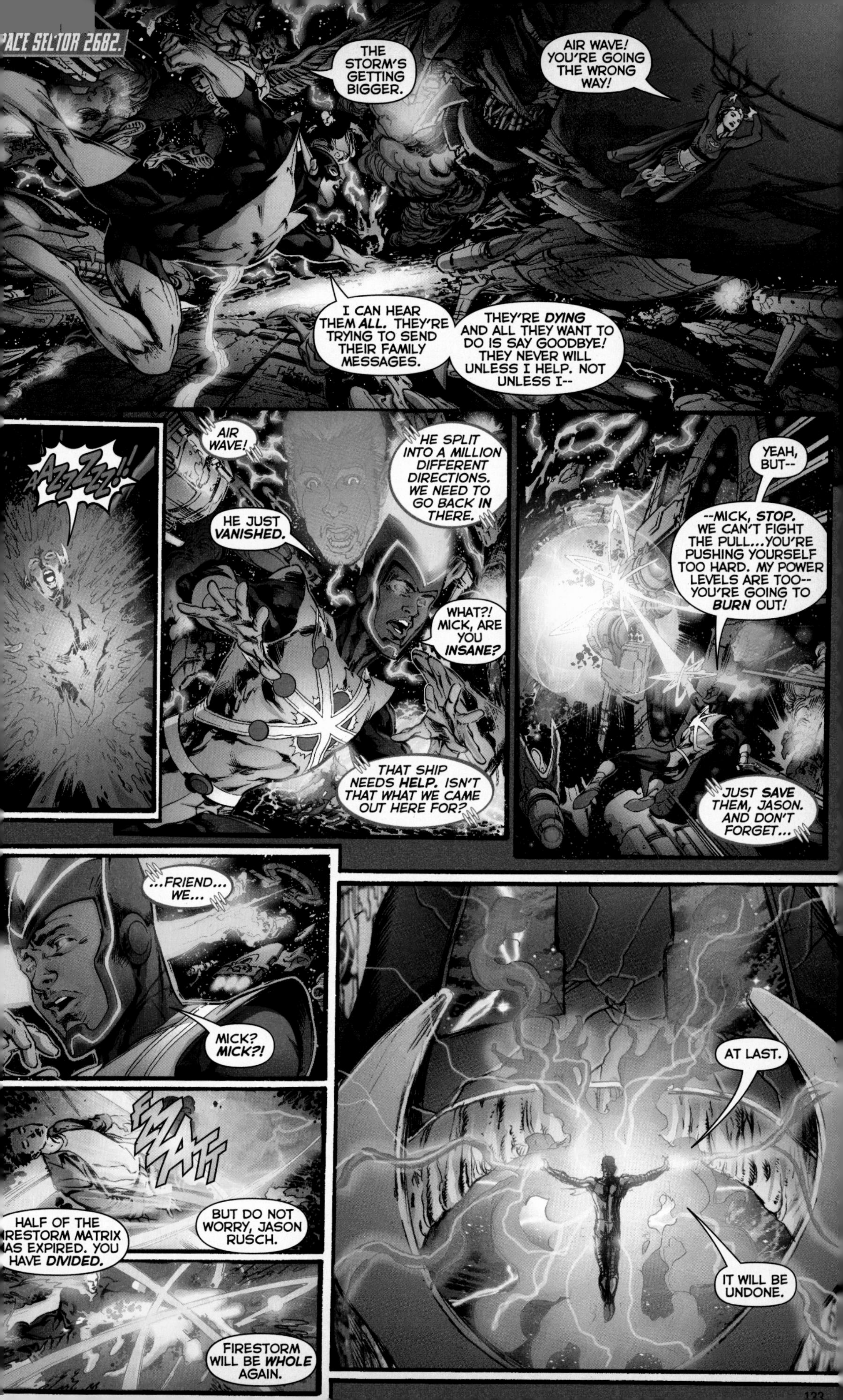

PACE SECTOR 2682.
THE STORM'S GETTING BIGGER.
AIR WAVE! YOU'RE GOING THE WRONG WAY!
I CAN HEAR THEM ALL. THEY'RE TRYING TO SEND THEIR FAMILY MESSAGES.
THEY'RE DYING AND ALL THEY WANT TO DO IS SAY GOODBYE! THEY NEVER WILL UNLESS I HELP. NOT UNLESS I--
AZZZZZZ!!
AIR WAVE!
HE JUST VANISHED.
HE SPLIT INTO A MILLION DIFFERENT DIRECTIONS. WE NEED TO GO BACK IN THERE.
WHAT?! MICK, ARE YOU INSANE?
THAT SHIP NEEDS HELP. ISN'T THAT WHAT WE CAME OUT HERE FOR?
YEAH, BUT--
--MICK, STOP. WE CAN'T FIGHT THE PULL...YOU'RE PUSHING YOURSELF TOO HARD. MY POWER LEVELS ARE TOO-- YOU'RE GOING TO BURN OUT!
JUST SAVE THEM, JASON. AND DON'T FORGET...
...FRIEND... WE...
MICK? MICK?!
FZZZATT
HALF OF THE IRESTORM MATRIX AS EXPIRED. YOU HAVE DIVIDED.
BUT DO NOT WORRY, JASON RUSCH.
FIRESTORM WILL BE WHOLE AGAIN.
AT LAST.
IT WILL BE UNDONE.

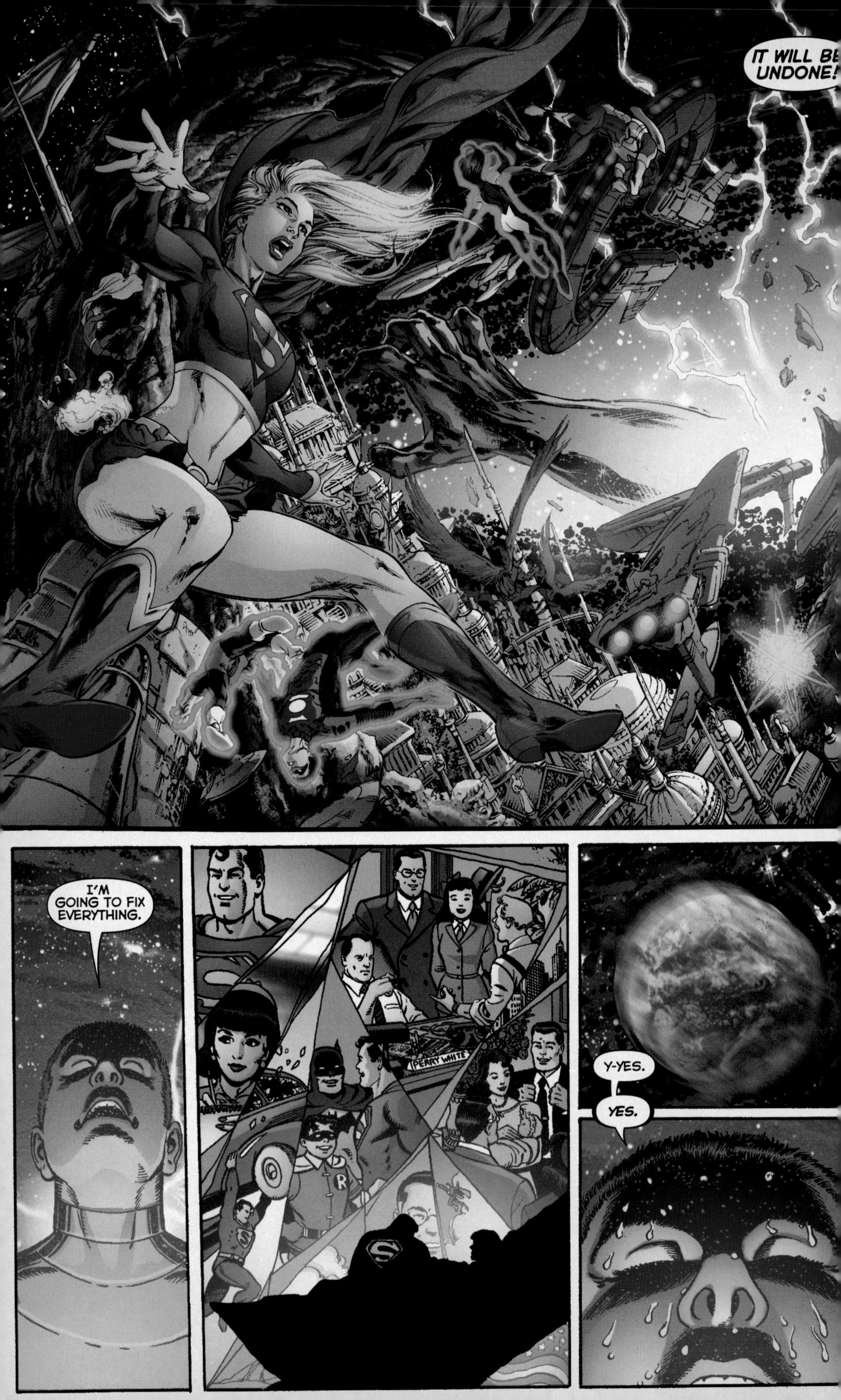
IT WILL BE UNDONE!
I'M GOING TO FIX EVERYTHING.
PEARY WHITE
Y-YES.
YES.

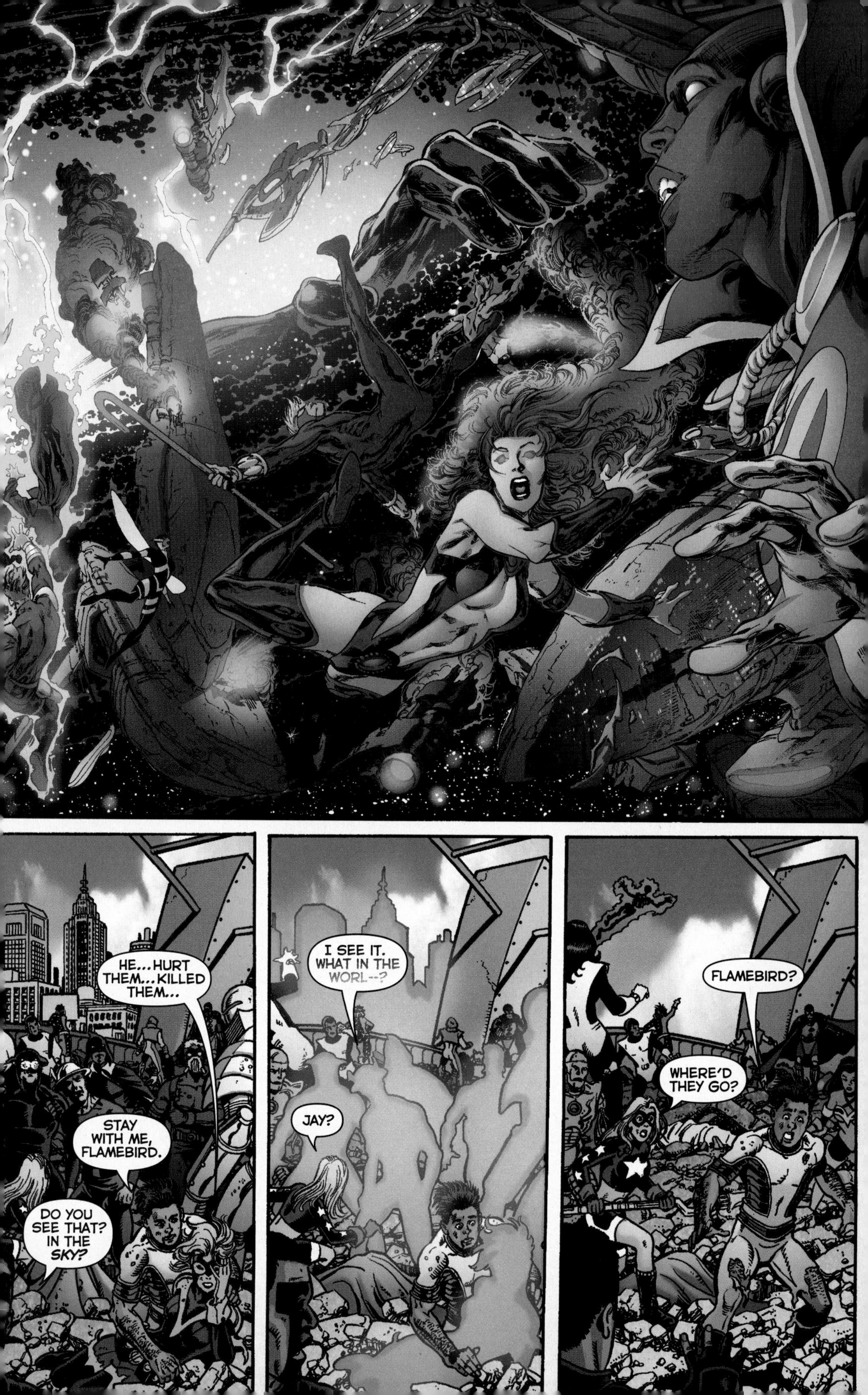
HE...HURT THEM...KILLED THEM...
STAY WITH ME, FLAMEBIRD.
DO YOU SEE THAT? IN THE SKY?
I SEE IT. WHAT IN THE WORL--?
JAY?
FLAMEBIRD?
WHERE'D THEY GO?

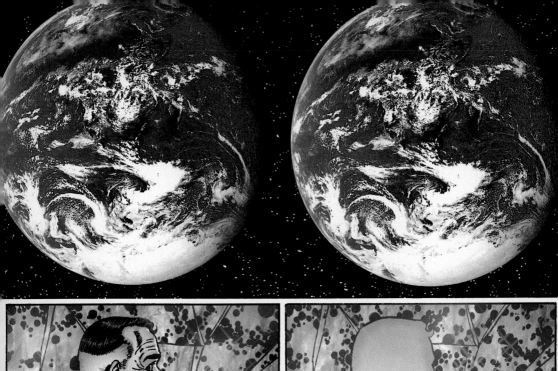

WE'RE HERE, LOIS.

WE'RE HOME.

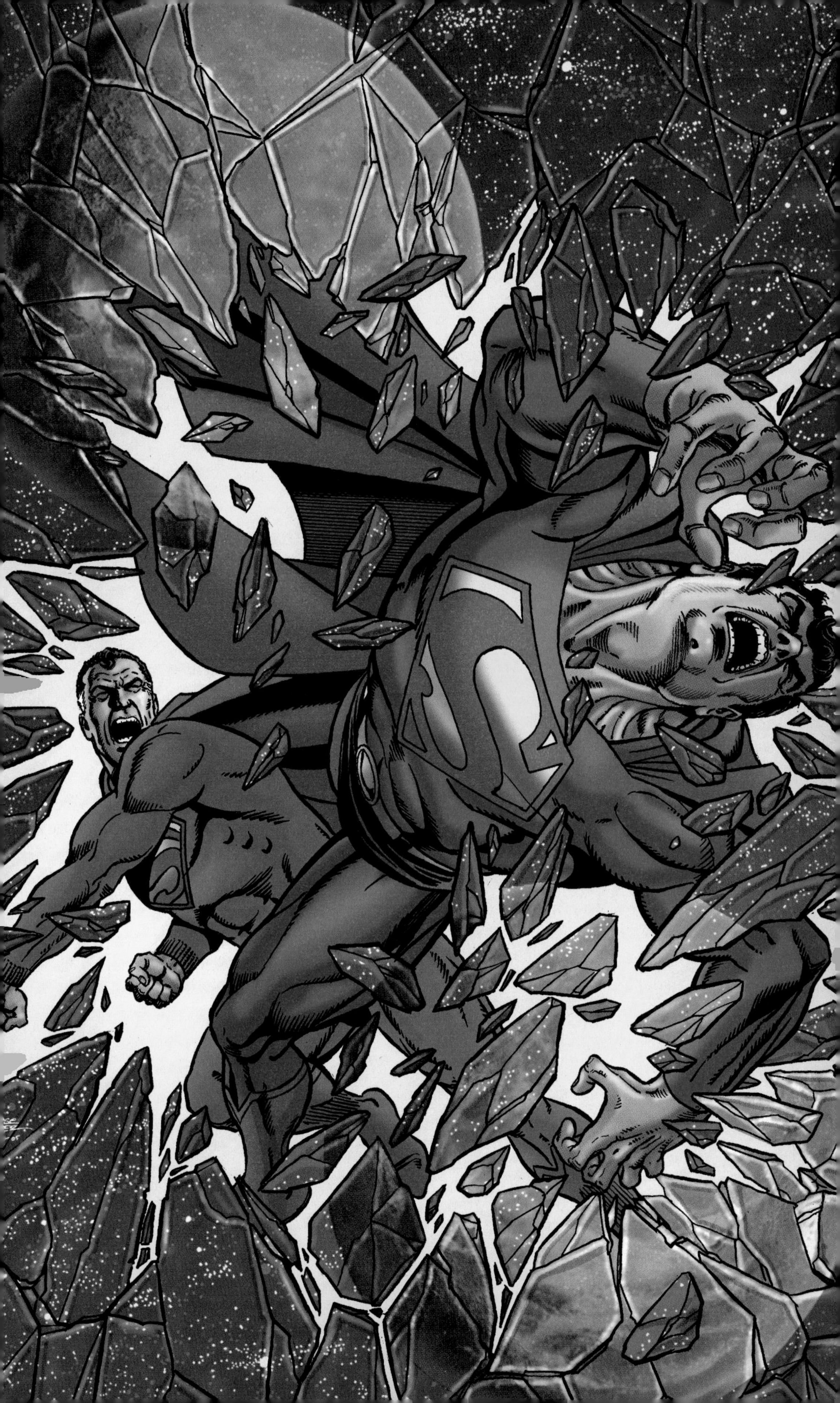

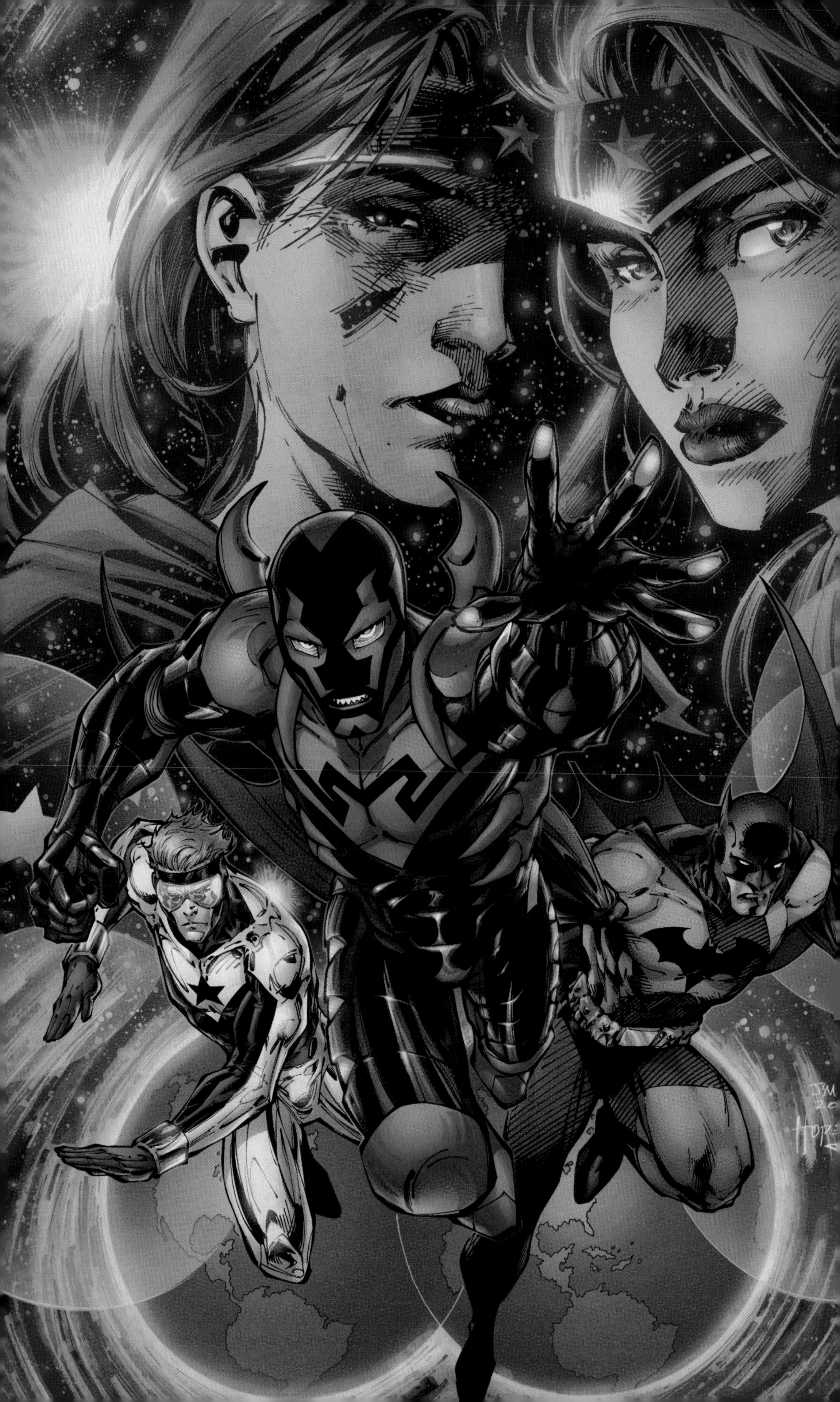

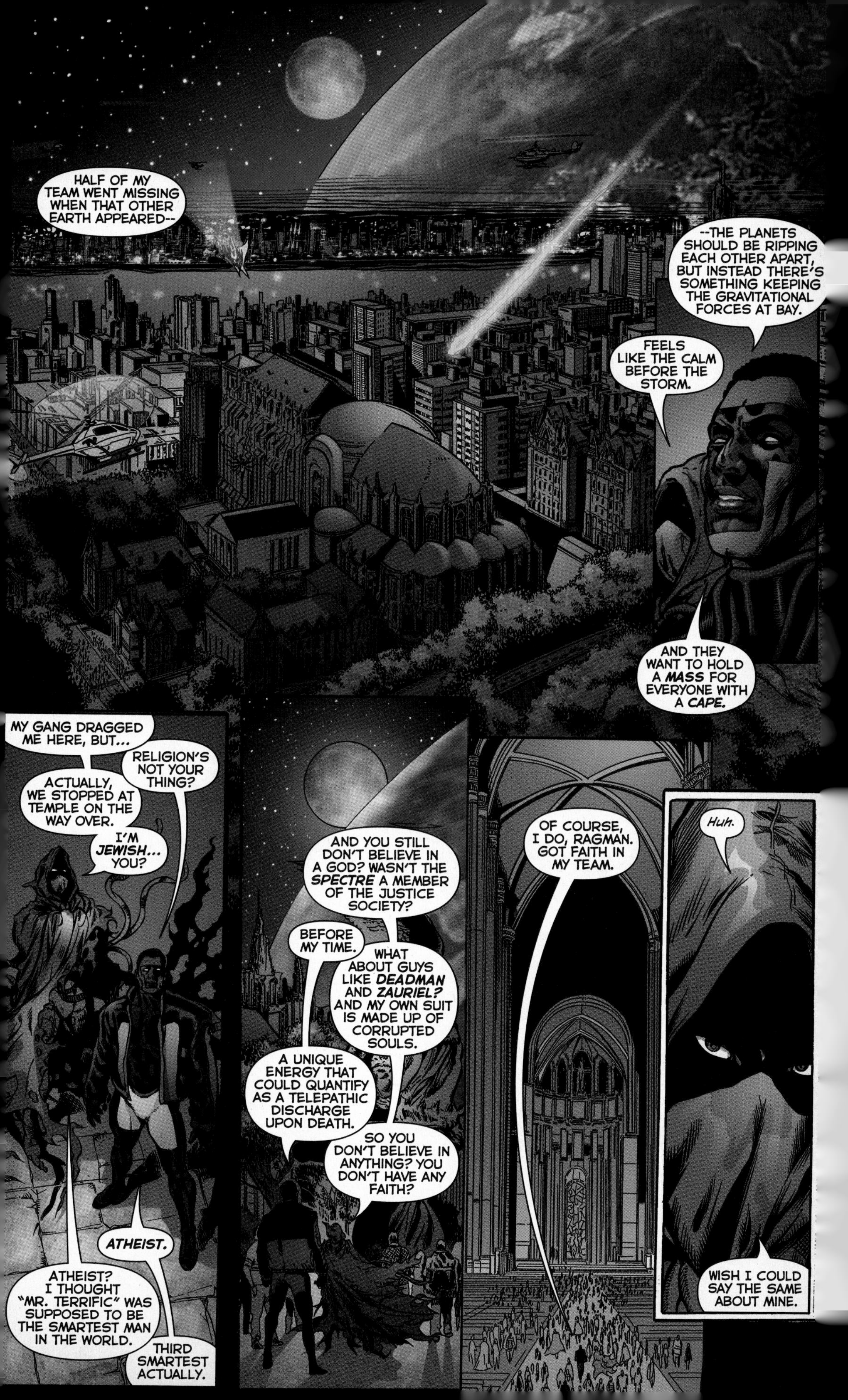
HALF OF MY TEAM WENT MISSING WHEN THAT OTHER EARTH APPEARED--
--THE PLANETS SHOULD BE RIPPING EACH OTHER APART, BUT INSTEAD THERE'S SOMETHING KEEPING THE GRAVITATIONAL FORCES AT BAY.
FEELS LIKE THE CALM BEFORE THE STORM.
AND THEY WANT TO HOLD A **MASS** FOR EVERYONE WITH A **CAPE.**
MY GANG DRAGGED ME HERE, BUT...
RELIGION'S NOT YOUR THING?
ACTUALLY, WE STOPPED AT TEMPLE ON THE WAY OVER.
I'M **JEWISH...** YOU?
ATHEIST.
ATHEIST? I THOUGHT "MR. TERRIFIC" WAS SUPPOSED TO BE THE SMARTEST MAN IN THE WORLD.
THIRD SMARTEST ACTUALLY.
AND YOU STILL DON'T BELIEVE IN A GOD? WASN'T THE **SPECTRE** A MEMBER OF THE JUSTICE SOCIETY?
BEFORE MY TIME.
WHAT ABOUT GUYS LIKE **DEADMAN** AND **ZAURIEL?** AND MY OWN SUIT IS MADE UP OF CORRUPTED SOULS.
A UNIQUE ENERGY THAT COULD QUANTIFY AS A TELEPATHIC DISCHARGE UPON DEATH.
SO YOU DON'T BELIEVE IN ANYTHING? YOU DON'T HAVE ANY FAITH?
OF COURSE, I DO, RAGMAN. GOT FAITH IN MY TEAM.
Huh.
WISH I COULD SAY THE SAME ABOUT MINE.

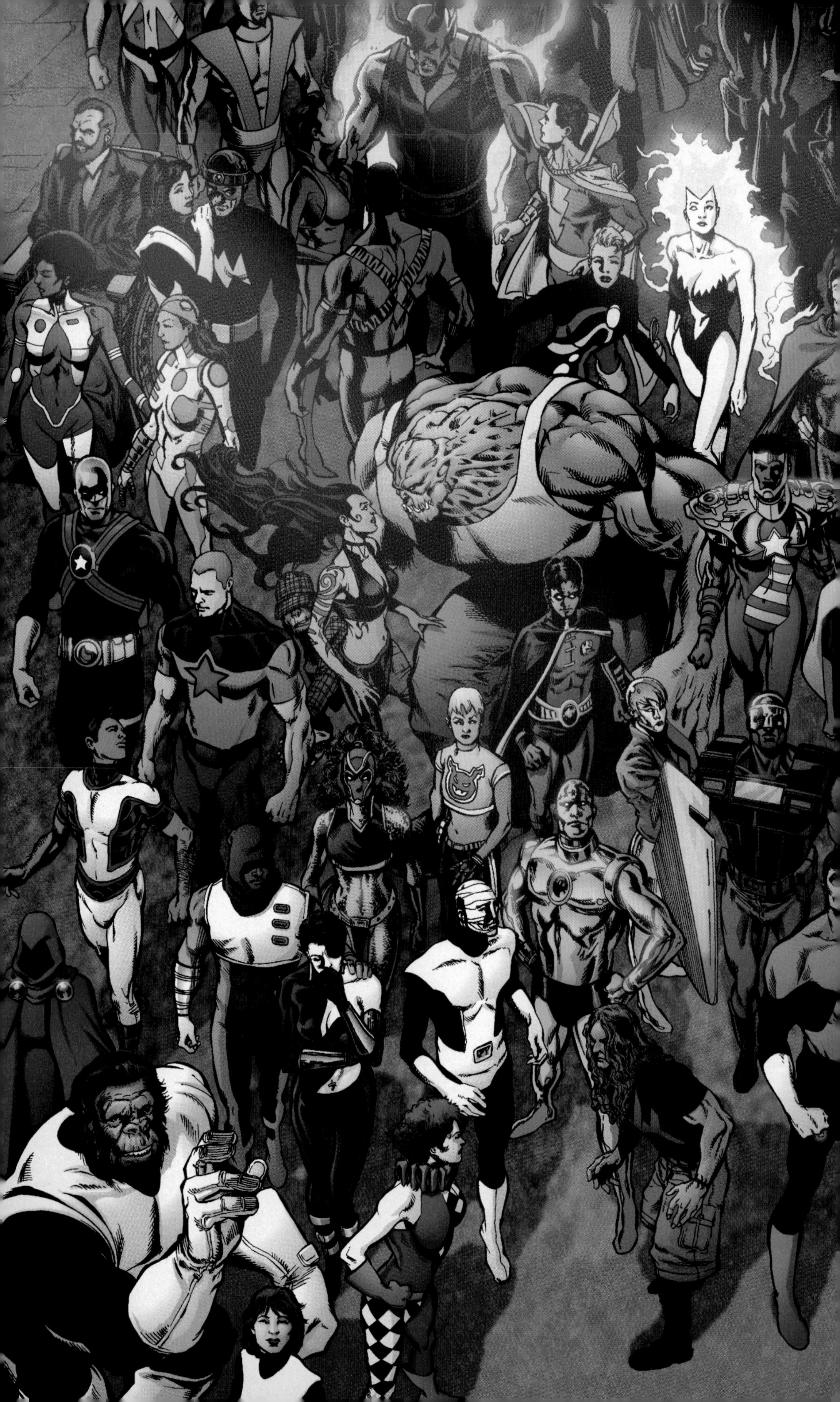

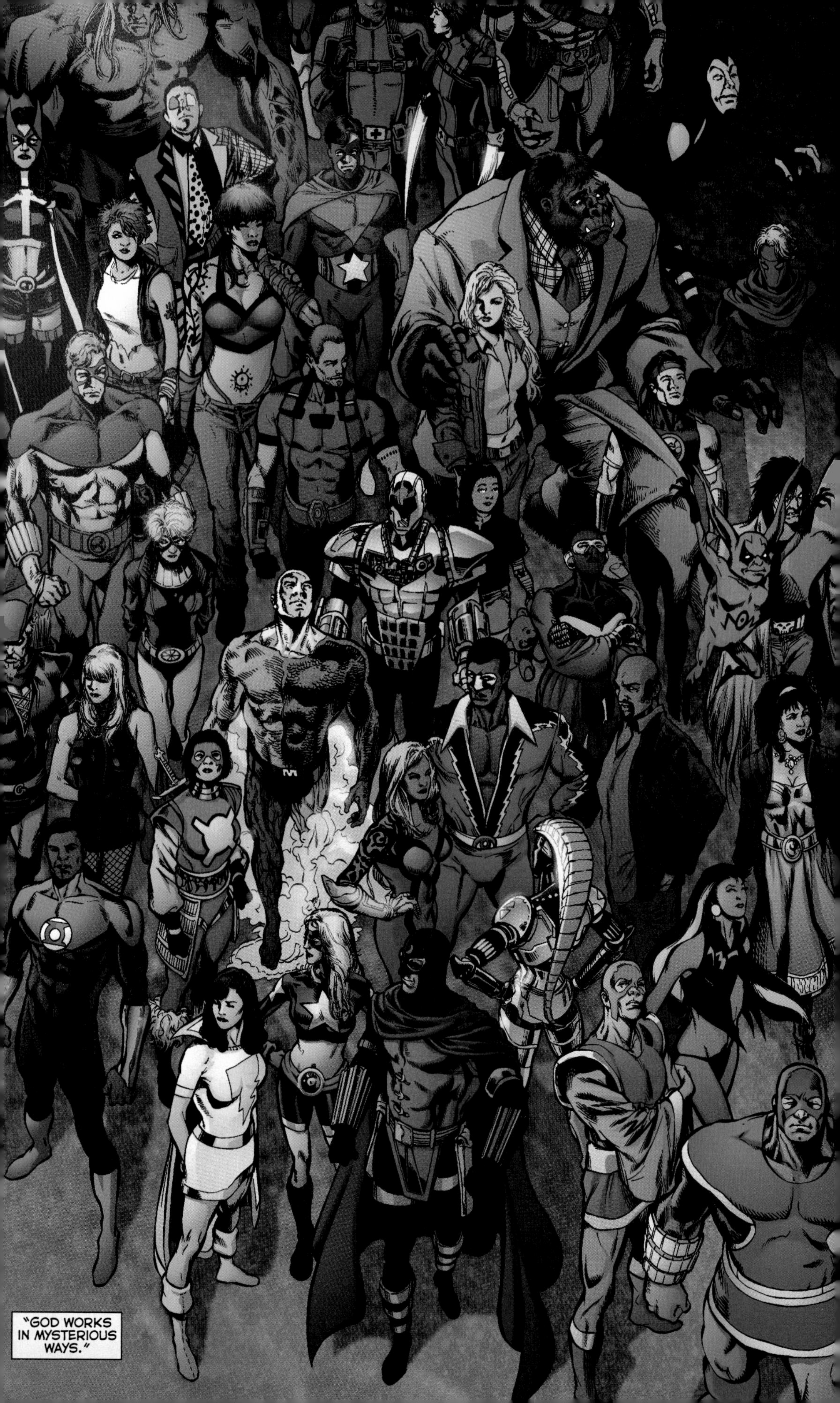
"GOD WORKS IN MYSTERIOUS WAYS."

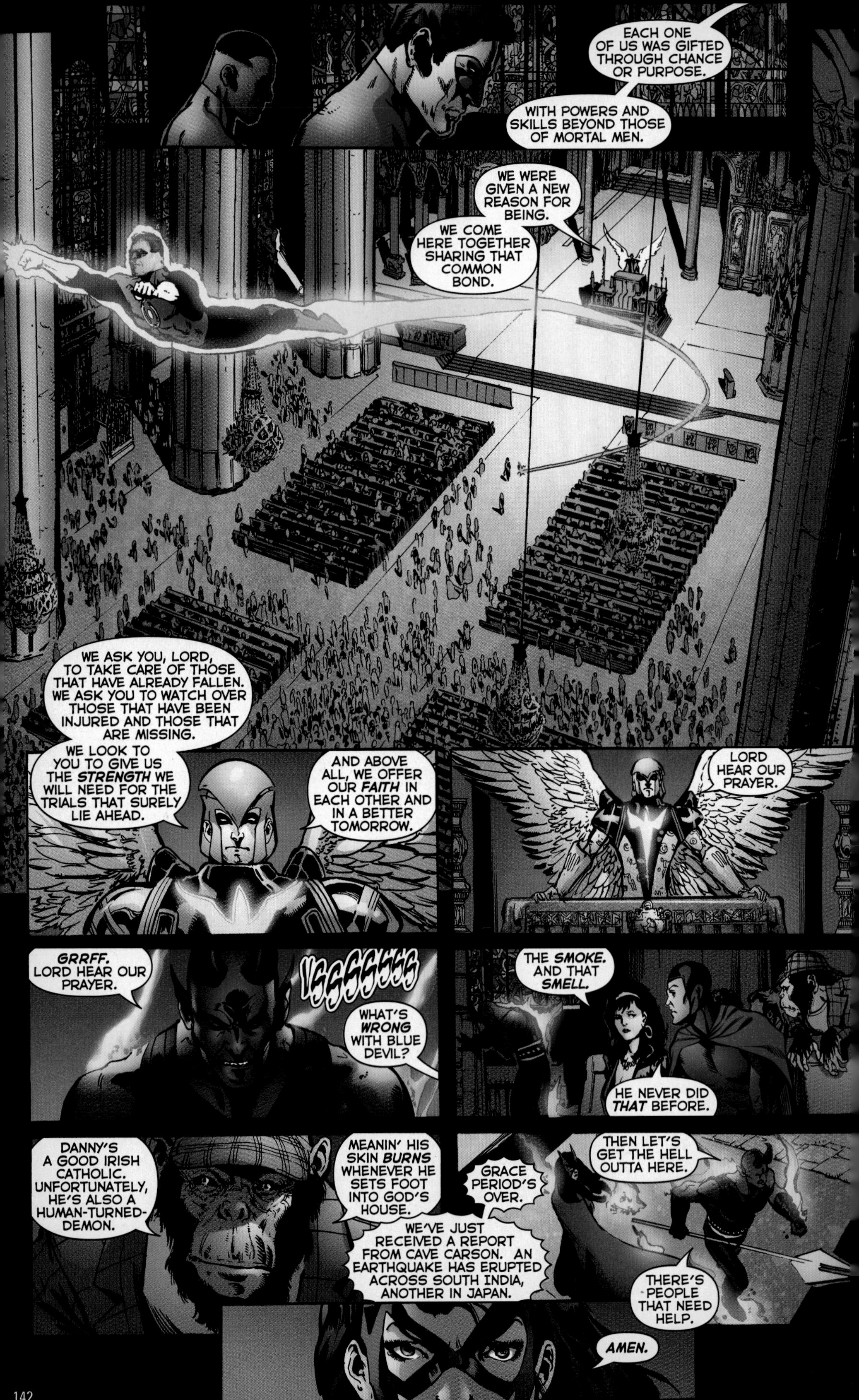
EACH ONE OF US WAS GIFTED THROUGH CHANCE OR PURPOSE.
WITH POWERS AND SKILLS BEYOND THOSE OF MORTAL MEN.
WE WERE GIVEN A NEW REASON FOR BEING.
WE COME HERE TOGETHER SHARING THAT COMMON BOND.
WE ASK YOU, LORD, TO TAKE CARE OF THOSE THAT HAVE ALREADY FALLEN. WE ASK YOU TO WATCH OVER THOSE THAT HAVE BEEN INJURED AND THOSE THAT ARE MISSING.
WE LOOK TO YOU TO GIVE US THE STRENGTH WE WILL NEED FOR THE TRIALS THAT SURELY LIE AHEAD.
AND ABOVE ALL, WE OFFER OUR FAITH IN EACH OTHER AND IN A BETTER TOMORROW.
LORD HEAR OUR PRAYER.
GRRFF. LORD HEAR OUR PRAYER.
VSSSSSSS
WHAT'S WRONG WITH BLUE DEVIL?
THE SMOKE. AND THAT SMELL.
HE NEVER DID THAT BEFORE.
DANNY'S A GOOD IRISH CATHOLIC. UNFORTUNATELY, HE'S ALSO A HUMAN-TURNED-DEMON.
MEANIN' HIS SKIN BURNS WHENEVER HE SETS FOOT INTO GOD'S HOUSE.
GRACE PERIOD'S OVER.
THEN LET'S GET THE HELL OUTTA HERE.
WE'VE JUST RECEIVED A REPORT FROM CAVE CARSON. AN EARTHQUAKE HAS ERUPTED ACROSS SOUTH INDIA, ANOTHER IN JAPAN.
THERE'S PEOPLE THAT NEED HELP.
AMEN.

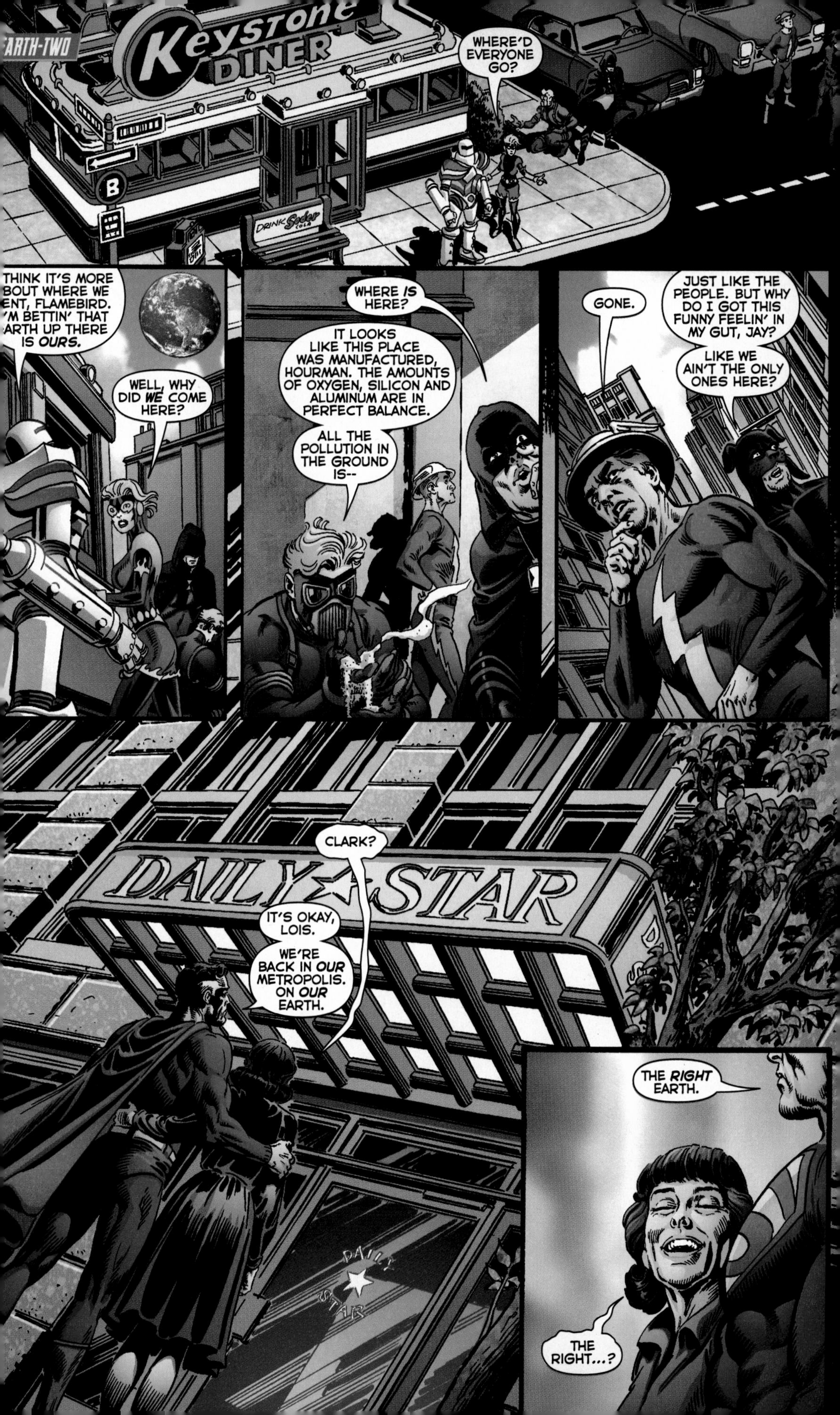
ARTH-TWO
Keystone DINER
WHERE'D EVERYONE GO?
DRINK Sodey COLA
THINK IT'S MORE BOUT WHERE WE ENT, FLAMEBIRD. 'M BETTIN' THAT EARTH UP THERE IS OURS.
WELL, WHY DID WE COME HERE?
WHERE IS HERE?
IT LOOKS LIKE THIS PLACE WAS MANUFACTURED, HOURMAN. THE AMOUNTS OF OXYGEN, SILICON AND ALUMINUM ARE IN PERFECT BALANCE.
ALL THE POLLUTION IN THE GROUND IS--
GONE.
JUST LIKE THE PEOPLE. BUT WHY DO I GOT THIS FUNNY FEELIN' IN MY GUT, JAY?
LIKE WE AIN'T THE ONLY ONES HERE?
CLARK?
DAILY STAR
IT'S OKAY, LOIS.
WE'RE BACK IN OUR METROPOLIS. ON OUR EARTH.
THE RIGHT EARTH.
THE RIGHT...?

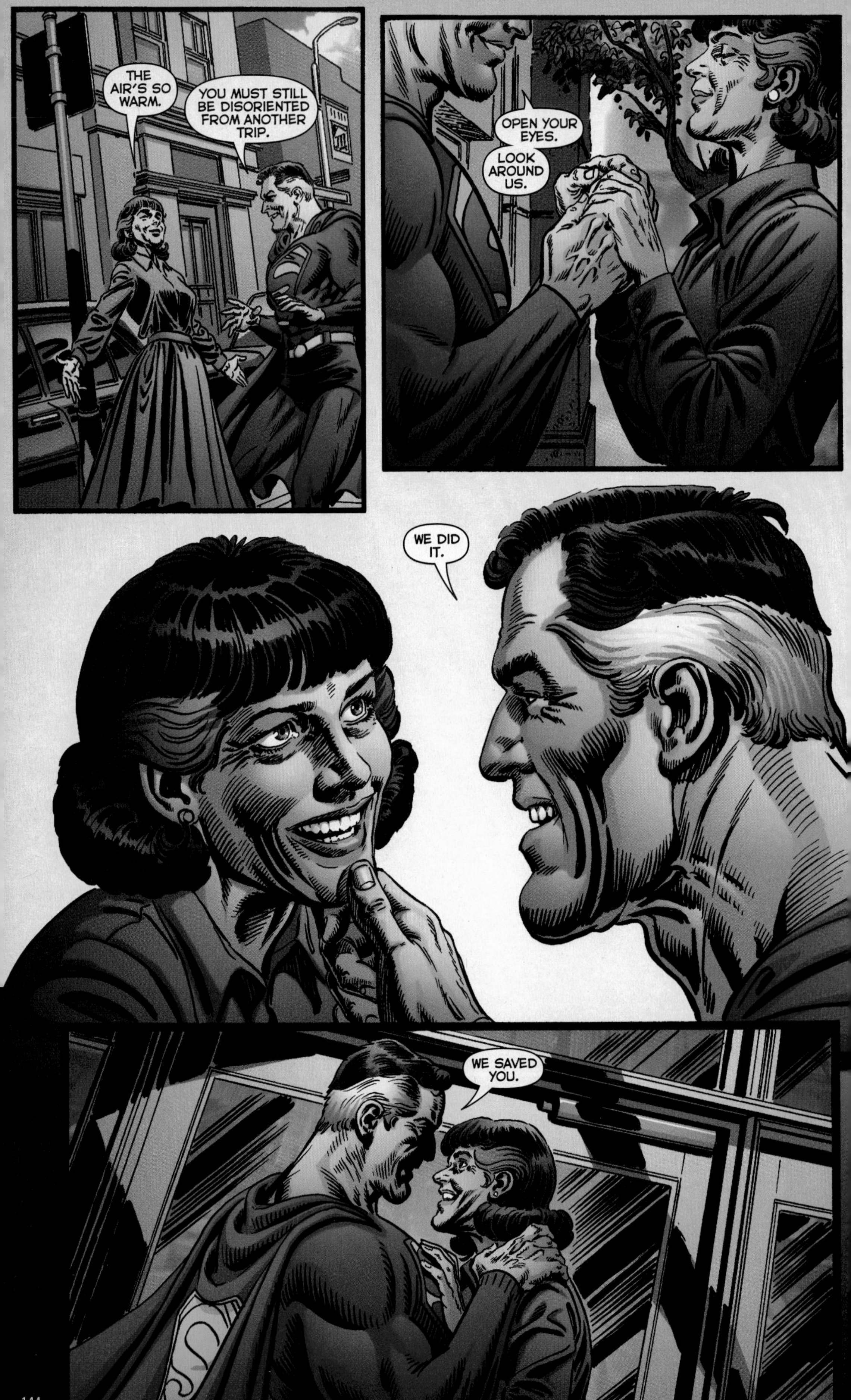
THE AIR'S SO WARM.
YOU MUST STILL BE DISORIENTED FROM ANOTHER TRIP.
OPEN YOUR EYES.
LOOK AROUND US.
WE DID IT.
WE SAVED YOU.

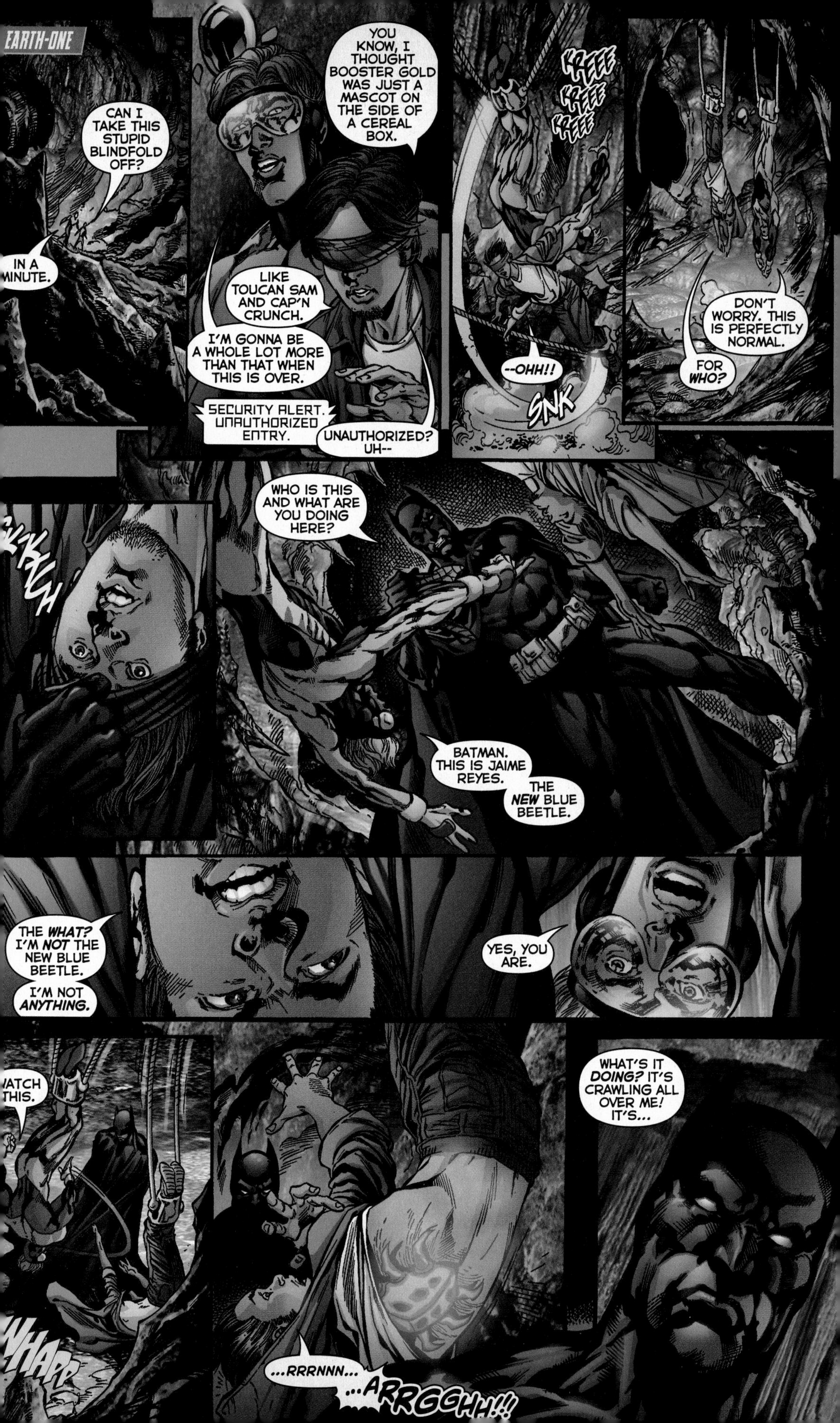
EARTH-ONE
CAN I TAKE THIS STUPID BLINDFOLD OFF?
IN A MINUTE.
YOU KNOW, I THOUGHT BOOSTER GOLD WAS JUST A MASCOT ON THE SIDE OF A CEREAL BOX.
LIKE TOUCAN SAM AND CAP'N CRUNCH.
I'M GONNA BE A WHOLE LOT MORE THAN THAT WHEN THIS IS OVER.
SECURITY ALERT. UNAUTHORIZED ENTRY.
UNAUTHORIZED? UH--
KREEE KREEE KREEE
--OHH!!
SNK
DON'T WORRY. THIS IS PERFECTLY NORMAL.
FOR WHO?
WHO IS THIS AND WHAT ARE YOU DOING HERE?
BATMAN. THIS IS JAIME REYES.
THE NEW BLUE BEETLE.
THE WHAT? I'M NOT THE NEW BLUE BEETLE.
I'M NOT ANYTHING.
YES, YOU ARE.
WATCH THIS.
WHAT'S IT DOING? IT'S CRAWLING ALL OVER ME! IT'S...
...RRRNNN...
...ARRRGGHH!!!

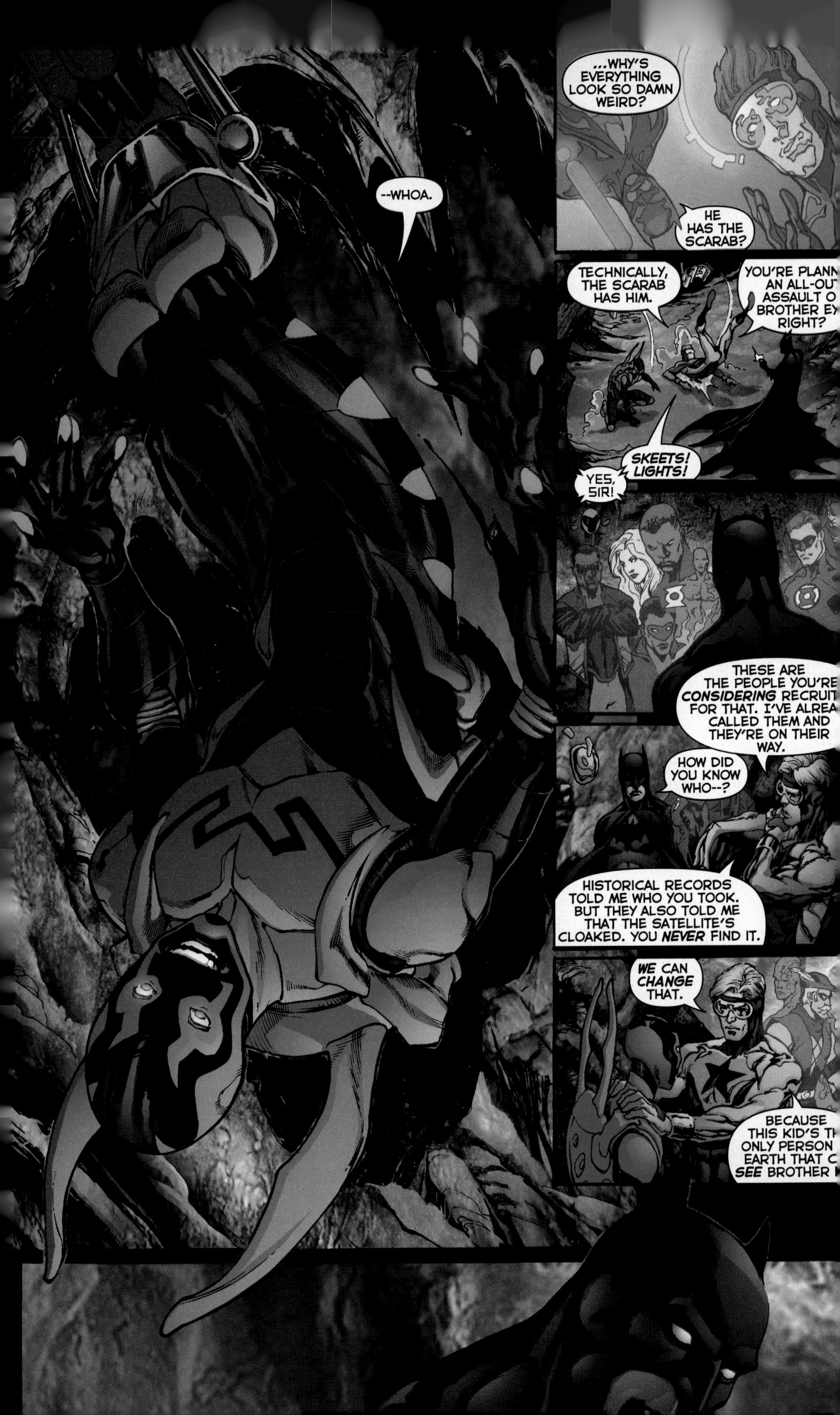
--WHOA.
...WHY'S EVERYTHING LOOK SO DAMN WEIRD?
HE HAS THE SCARAB?
TECHNICALLY, THE SCARAB HAS HIM.
YOU'RE PLANN AN ALL-OU ASSAULT O BROTHER E RIGHT?
SKEETS! LIGHTS!
YES, SIR!
THESE ARE THE PEOPLE YOU'RE CONSIDERING RECRUIT FOR THAT. I'VE ALREA CALLED THEM AND THEY'RE ON THEIR WAY.
HOW DID YOU KNOW WHO--?
HISTORICAL RECORDS TOLD ME WHO YOU TOOK. BUT THEY ALSO TOLD ME THAT THE SATELLITE'S CLOAKED. YOU NEVER FIND IT.
WE CAN CHANGE THAT.
BECAUSE THIS KID'S T ONLY PERSON EARTH THAT C SEE BROTHER

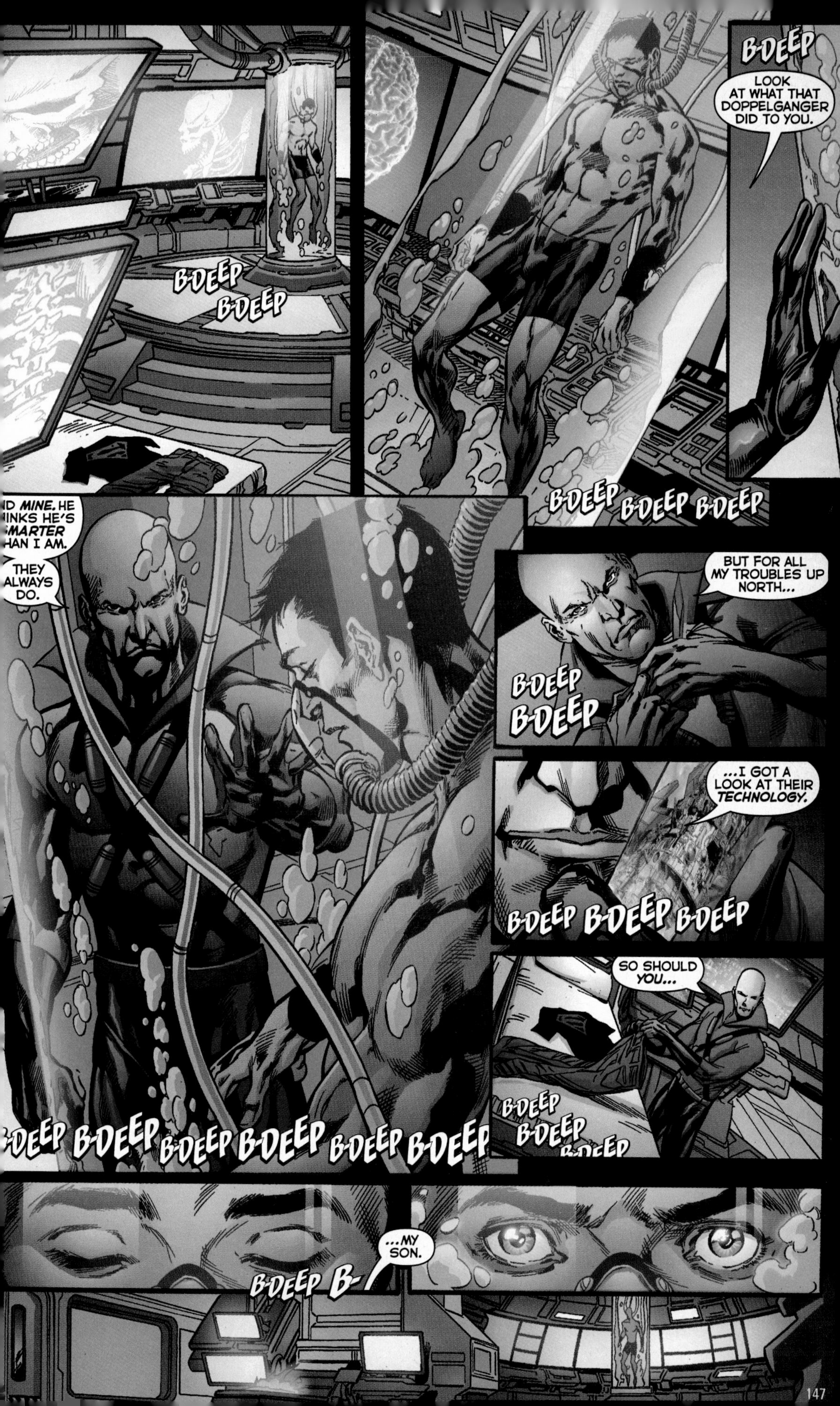

B-DEEP
B-DEEP
B-DEEP
LOOK AT WHAT THAT DOPPELGANGER DID TO YOU.
B-DEEP B-DEEP B-DEEP
ND MINE. HE THINKS HE'S SMARTER THAN I AM.
THEY ALWAYS DO.
B-DEEP B-DEEP B-DEEP B-DEEP B-DEEP B-DEEP
BUT FOR ALL MY TROUBLES UP NORTH...
B-DEEP
B-DEEP
...I GOT A LOOK AT THEIR TECHNOLOGY.
B-DEEP B-DEEP B-DEEP
SO SHOULD YOU...
B-DEEP
B-DEEP
B-DEEP B-
...MY SON.

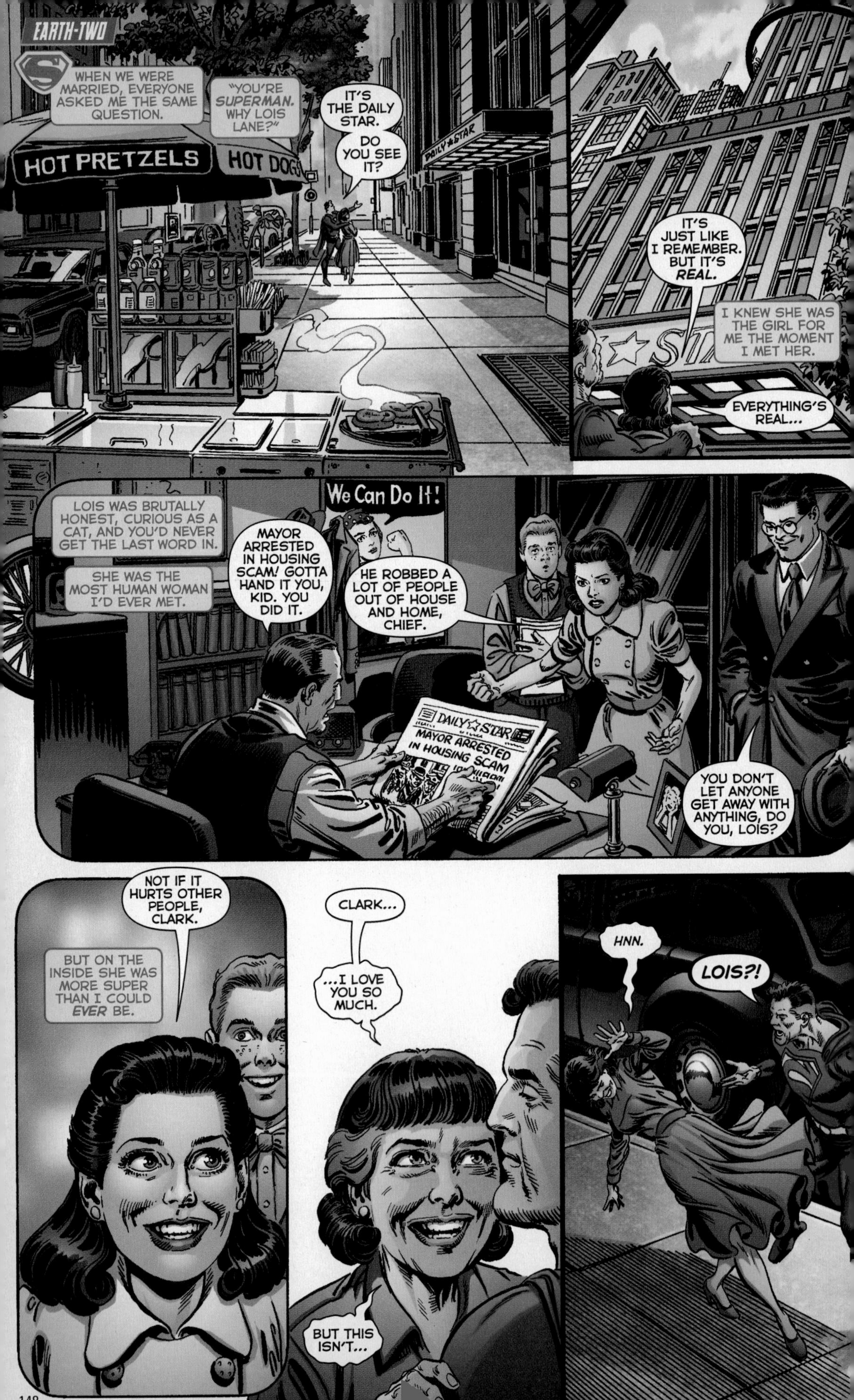
EARTH-TWO
WHEN WE WERE MARRIED, EVERYONE ASKED ME THE SAME QUESTION.
"YOU'RE SUPERMAN. WHY LOIS LANE?"
IT'S THE DAILY STAR.
DO YOU SEE IT?
HOT PRETZELS
HOT DOGS
DAILY STAR
IT'S JUST LIKE I REMEMBER. BUT IT'S REAL.
I KNEW SHE WAS THE GIRL FOR ME THE MOMENT I MET HER.
EVERYTHING'S REAL...
LOIS WAS BRUTALLY HONEST, CURIOUS AS A CAT, AND YOU'D NEVER GET THE LAST WORD IN.
SHE WAS THE MOST HUMAN WOMAN I'D EVER MET.
We Can Do It!
MAYOR ARRESTED IN HOUSING SCAM! GOTTA HAND IT YOU, KID. YOU DID IT.
HE ROBBED A LOT OF PEOPLE OUT OF HOUSE AND HOME, CHIEF.
DAILY STAR
MAYOR ARRESTED IN HOUSING SCAM
YOU DON'T LET ANYONE GET AWAY WITH ANYTHING, DO YOU, LOIS?
NOT IF IT HURTS OTHER PEOPLE, CLARK.
BUT ON THE INSIDE SHE WAS MORE SUPER THAN I COULD EVER BE.
CLARK...
...I LOVE YOU SO MUCH.
BUT THIS ISN'T...
HNN.
LOIS?!

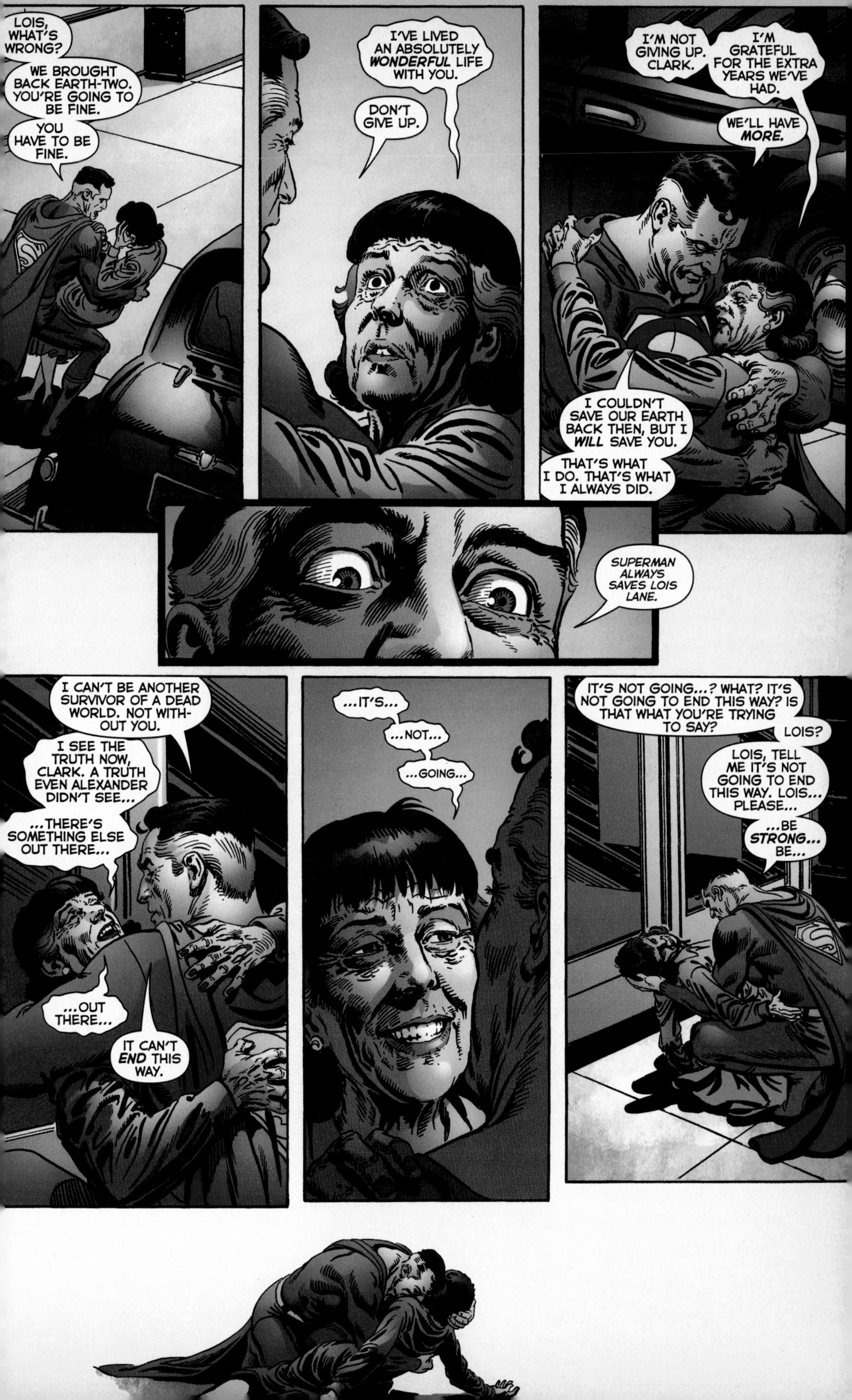
LOIS, WHAT'S WRONG?
WE BROUGHT BACK EARTH-TWO. YOU'RE GOING TO BE FINE.
YOU HAVE TO BE FINE.
I'VE LIVED AN ABSOLUTELY WONDERFUL LIFE WITH YOU.
DON'T GIVE UP.
I'M NOT GIVING UP. CLARK.
I'M GRATEFUL FOR THE EXTRA YEARS WE'VE HAD.
WE'LL HAVE MORE.
I COULDN'T SAVE OUR EARTH BACK THEN, BUT I WILL SAVE YOU.
THAT'S WHAT I DO. THAT'S WHAT I ALWAYS DID.
SUPERMAN ALWAYS SAVES LOIS LANE.
I CAN'T BE ANOTHER SURVIVOR OF A DEAD WORLD. NOT WITH-OUT YOU.
I SEE THE TRUTH NOW, CLARK. A TRUTH EVEN ALEXANDER DIDN'T SEE...
...THERE'S SOMETHING ELSE OUT THERE...
...OUT THERE...
IT CAN'T END THIS WAY.
...IT'S...
...NOT...
...GOING...
IT'S NOT GOING...? WHAT? IT'S NOT GOING TO END THIS WAY? IS THAT WHAT YOU'RE TRYING TO SAY?
LOIS?
LOIS, TELL ME IT'S NOT GOING TO END THIS WAY. LOIS... PLEASE...
...BE STRONG... BE...

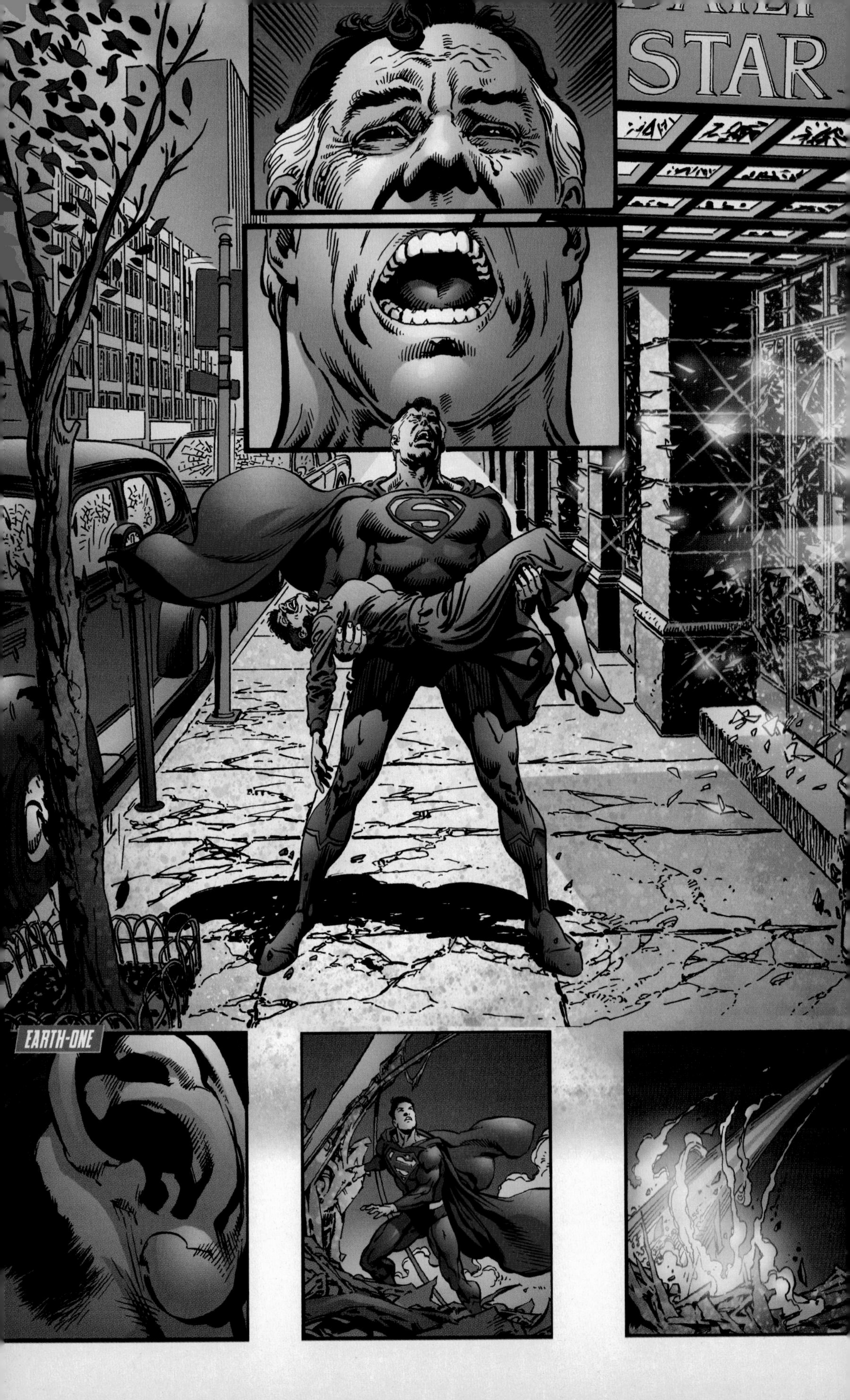
STAR
EARTH-ONE

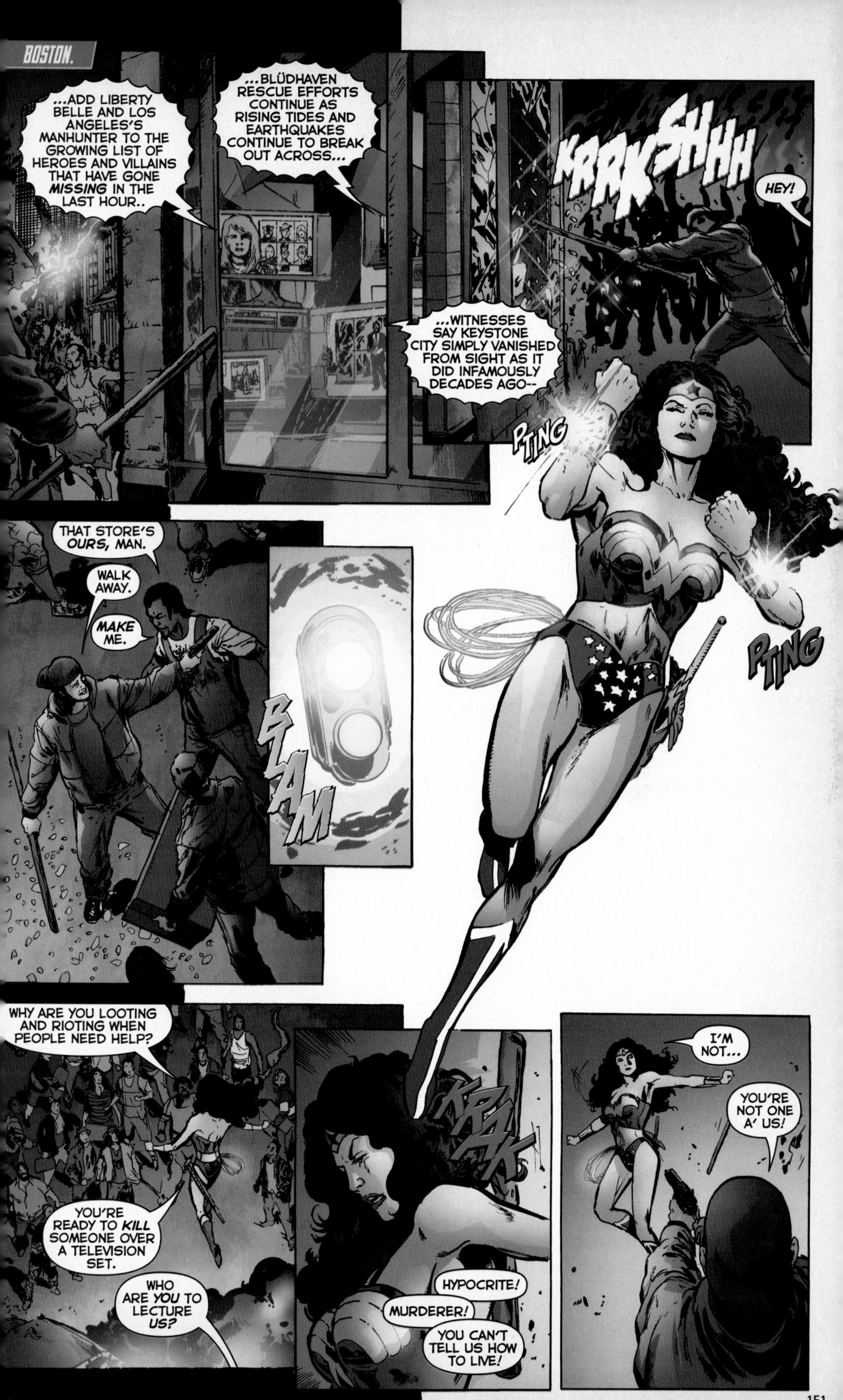
BOSTON.
...ADD LIBERTY BELLE AND LOS ANGELES'S MANHUNTER TO THE GROWING LIST OF HEROES AND VILLAINS THAT HAVE GONE MISSING IN THE LAST HOUR..
...BLÜDHAVEN RESCUE EFFORTS CONTINUE AS RISING TIDES AND EARTHQUAKES CONTINUE TO BREAK OUT ACROSS...
KRRKSHHH
HEY!
...WITNESSES SAY KEYSTONE CITY SIMPLY VANISHED FROM SIGHT AS IT DID INFAMOUSLY DECADES AGO--
PTING
PTING
THAT STORE'S OURS, MAN.
WALK AWAY.
MAKE ME.
BLAM
WHY ARE YOU LOOTING AND RIOTING WHEN PEOPLE NEED HELP?
YOU'RE READY TO KILL SOMEONE OVER A TELEVISION SET.
WHO ARE YOU TO LECTURE US?
KRAK
HYPOCRITE!
MURDERER!
YOU CAN'T TELL US HOW TO LIVE!
I'M NOT...
YOU'RE NOT ONE A' US!

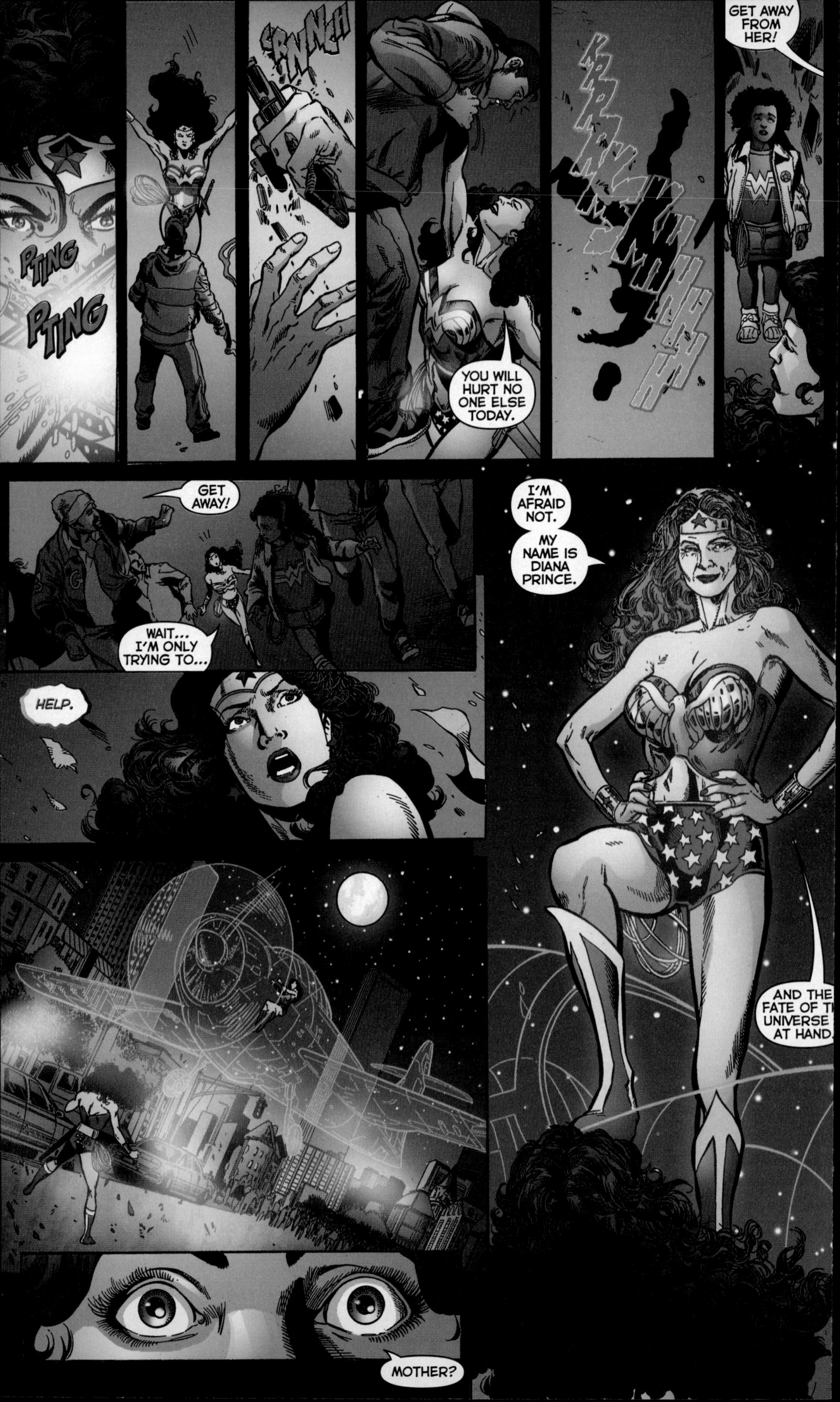
PTING
PTING
CRNCH
YOU WILL HURT NO ONE ELSE TODAY.
GET AWAY FROM HER!
GET AWAY!
WAIT... I'M ONLY TRYING TO...
HELP.
MOTHER?
I'M AFRAID NOT.
MY NAME IS DIANA PRINCE.

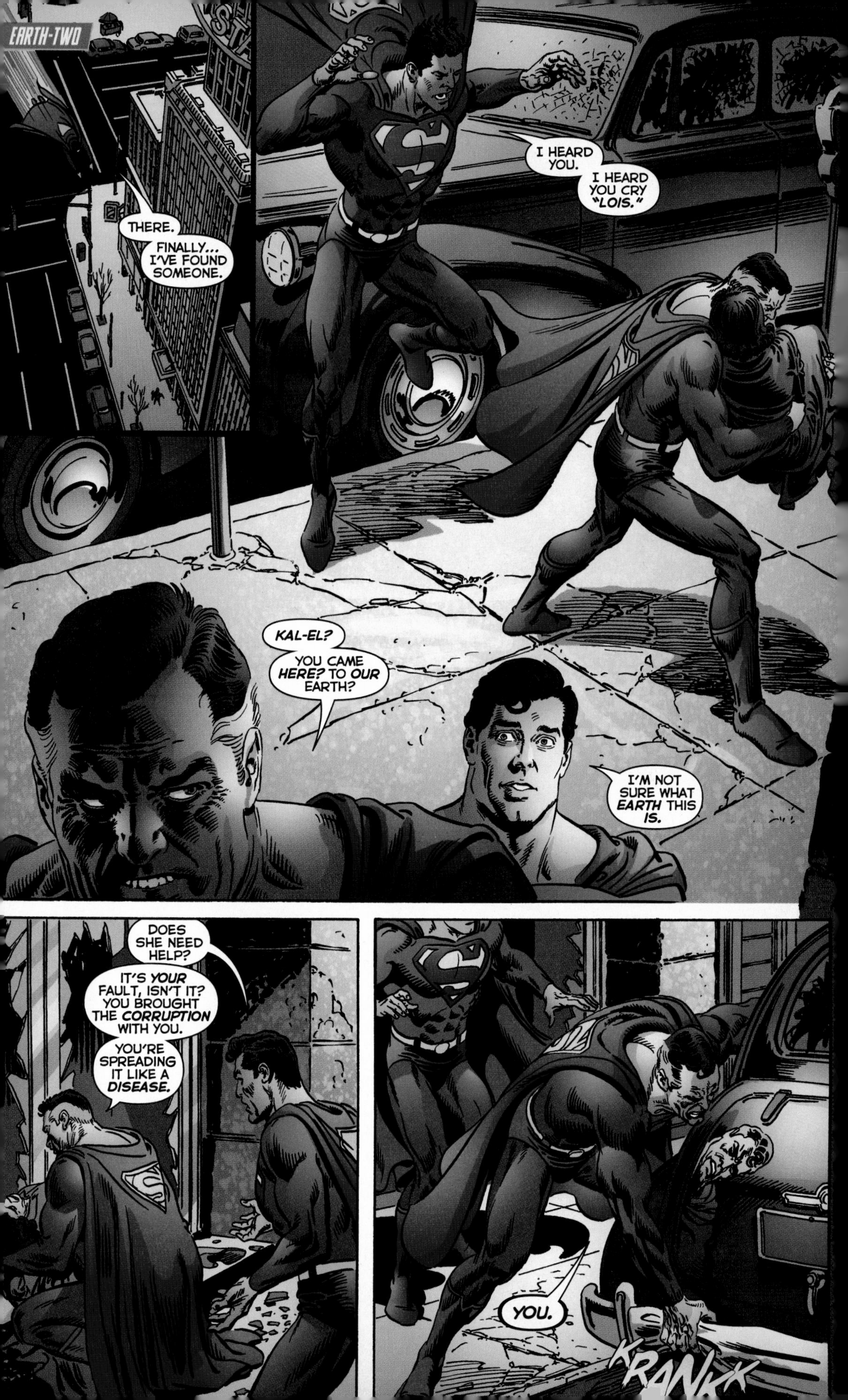
EARTH-TWO
THERE.
FINALLY... I'VE FOUND SOMEONE.
I HEARD YOU.
I HEARD YOU CRY "LOIS."
KAL-EL?
YOU CAME HERE? TO OUR EARTH?
I'M NOT SURE WHAT EARTH THIS IS.
DOES SHE NEED HELP?
IT'S YOUR FAULT, ISN'T IT? YOU BROUGHT THE CORRUPTION WITH YOU.
YOU'RE SPREADING IT LIKE A DISEASE.
YOU.
KRANKK

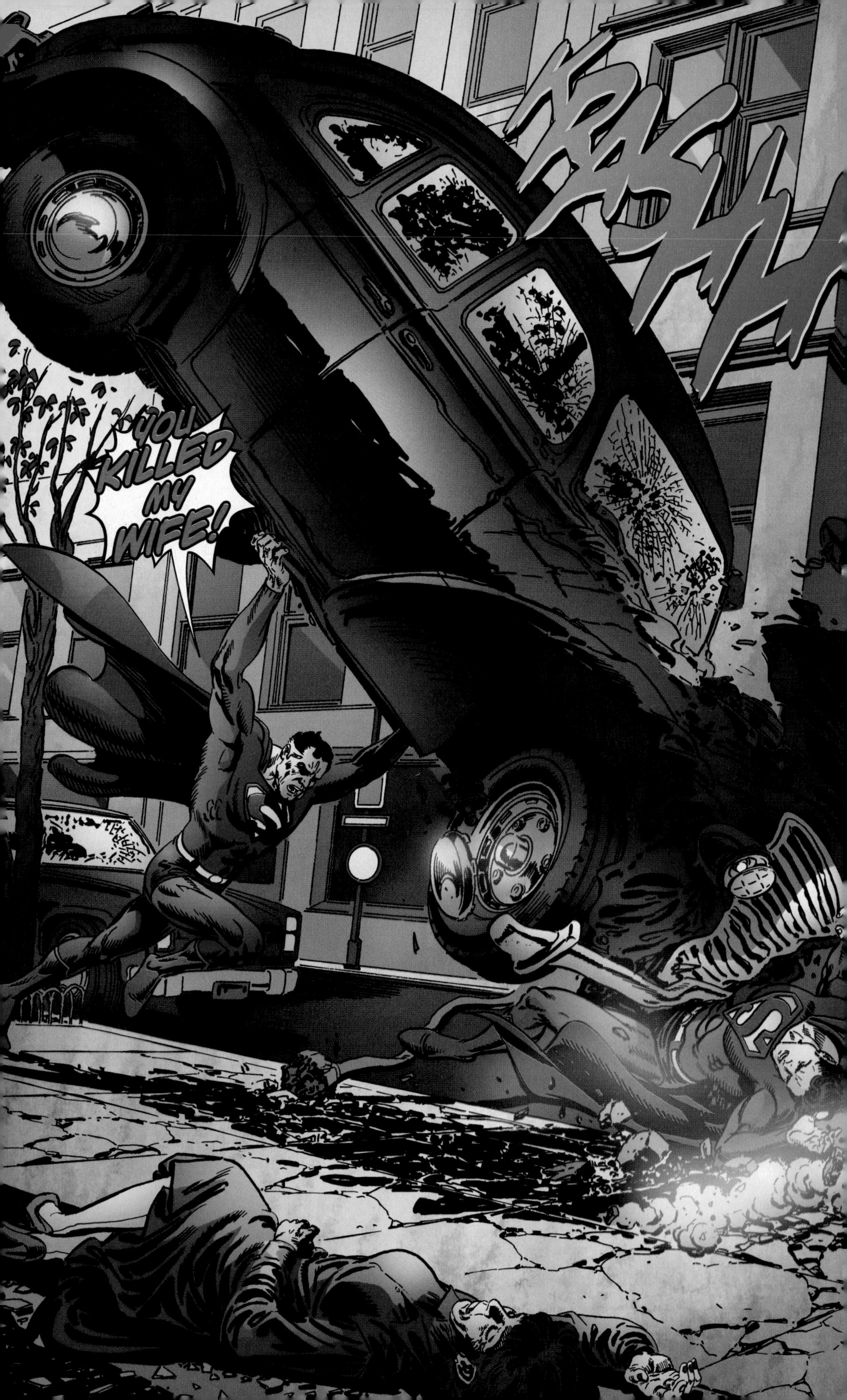
YOU KILLED MY WIFE!

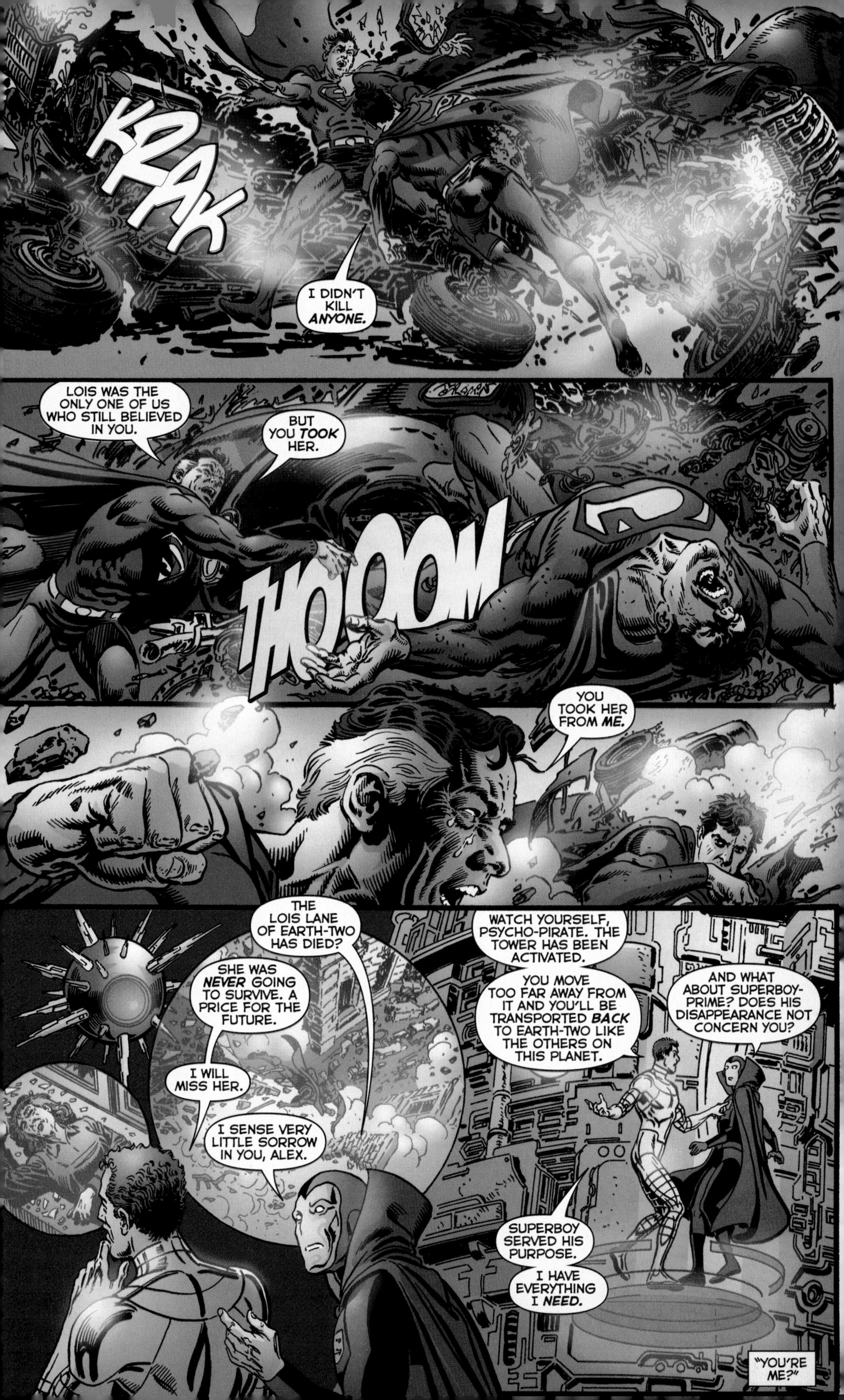
KRAK
I DIDN'T KILL ANYONE.
LOIS WAS THE ONLY ONE OF US WHO STILL BELIEVED IN YOU.
BUT YOU TOOK HER.
THOOOM
YOU TOOK HER FROM ME.
THE LOIS LANE OF EARTH-TWO HAS DIED?
SHE WAS NEVER GOING TO SURVIVE. A PRICE FOR THE FUTURE.
I WILL MISS HER.
I SENSE VERY LITTLE SORROW IN YOU, ALEX.
WATCH YOURSELF, PSYCHO-PIRATE. THE TOWER HAS BEEN ACTIVATED.
YOU MOVE TOO FAR AWAY FROM IT AND YOU'LL BE TRANSPORTED BACK TO EARTH-TWO LIKE THE OTHERS ON THIS PLANET.
AND WHAT ABOUT SUPERBOY-PRIME? DOES HIS DISAPPEARANCE NOT CONCERN YOU?
SUPERBOY SERVED HIS PURPOSE.
I HAVE EVERYTHING I NEED.
"YOU'RE ME?"

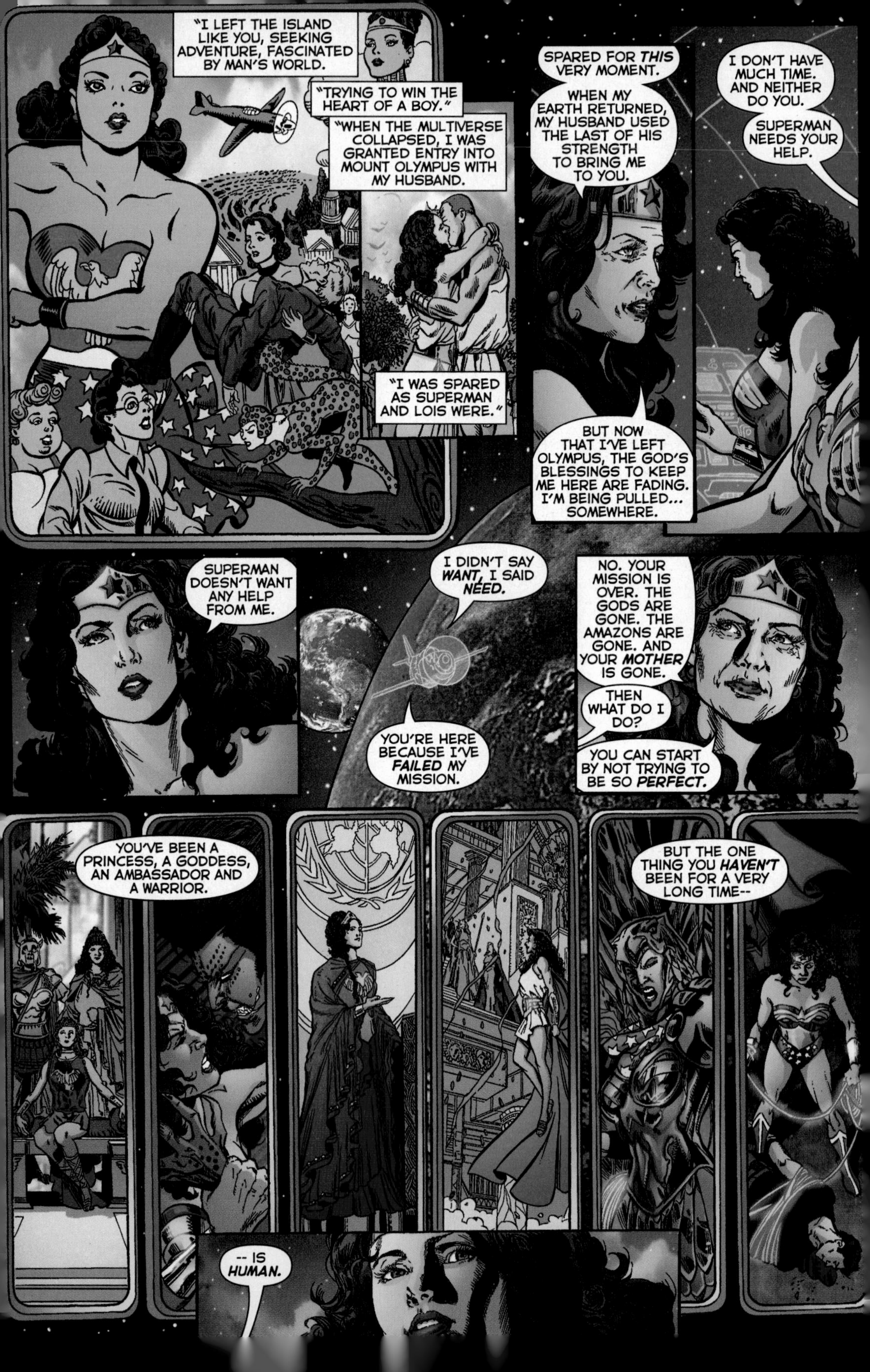
"I LEFT THE ISLAND LIKE YOU, SEEKING ADVENTURE, FASCINATED BY MAN'S WORLD.
"TRYING TO WIN THE HEART OF A BOY."
"WHEN THE MULTIVERSE COLLAPSED, I WAS GRANTED ENTRY INTO MOUNT OLYMPUS WITH MY HUSBAND.
"I WAS SPARED AS SUPERMAN AND LOIS WERE."
SPARED FOR THIS VERY MOMENT.
WHEN MY EARTH RETURNED, MY HUSBAND USED THE LAST OF HIS STRENGTH TO BRING ME TO YOU.
BUT NOW THAT I'VE LEFT OLYMPUS, THE GOD'S BLESSINGS TO KEEP ME HERE ARE FADING. I'M BEING PULLED... SOMEWHERE.
I DON'T HAVE MUCH TIME. AND NEITHER DO YOU.
SUPERMAN NEEDS YOUR HELP.
SUPERMAN DOESN'T WANT ANY HELP FROM ME.
I DIDN'T SAY WANT, I SAID NEED.
YOU'RE HERE BECAUSE I'VE FAILED MY MISSION.
NO. YOUR MISSION IS OVER. THE GODS ARE GONE. THE AMAZONS ARE GONE. AND YOUR MOTHER IS GONE.
THEN WHAT DO I DO?
YOU CAN START BY NOT TRYING TO BE SO PERFECT.
YOU'VE BEEN A PRINCESS, A GODDESS, AN AMBASSADOR AND A WARRIOR.
BUT THE ONE THING YOU HAVEN'T BEEN FOR A VERY LONG TIME--
-- IS HUMAN.

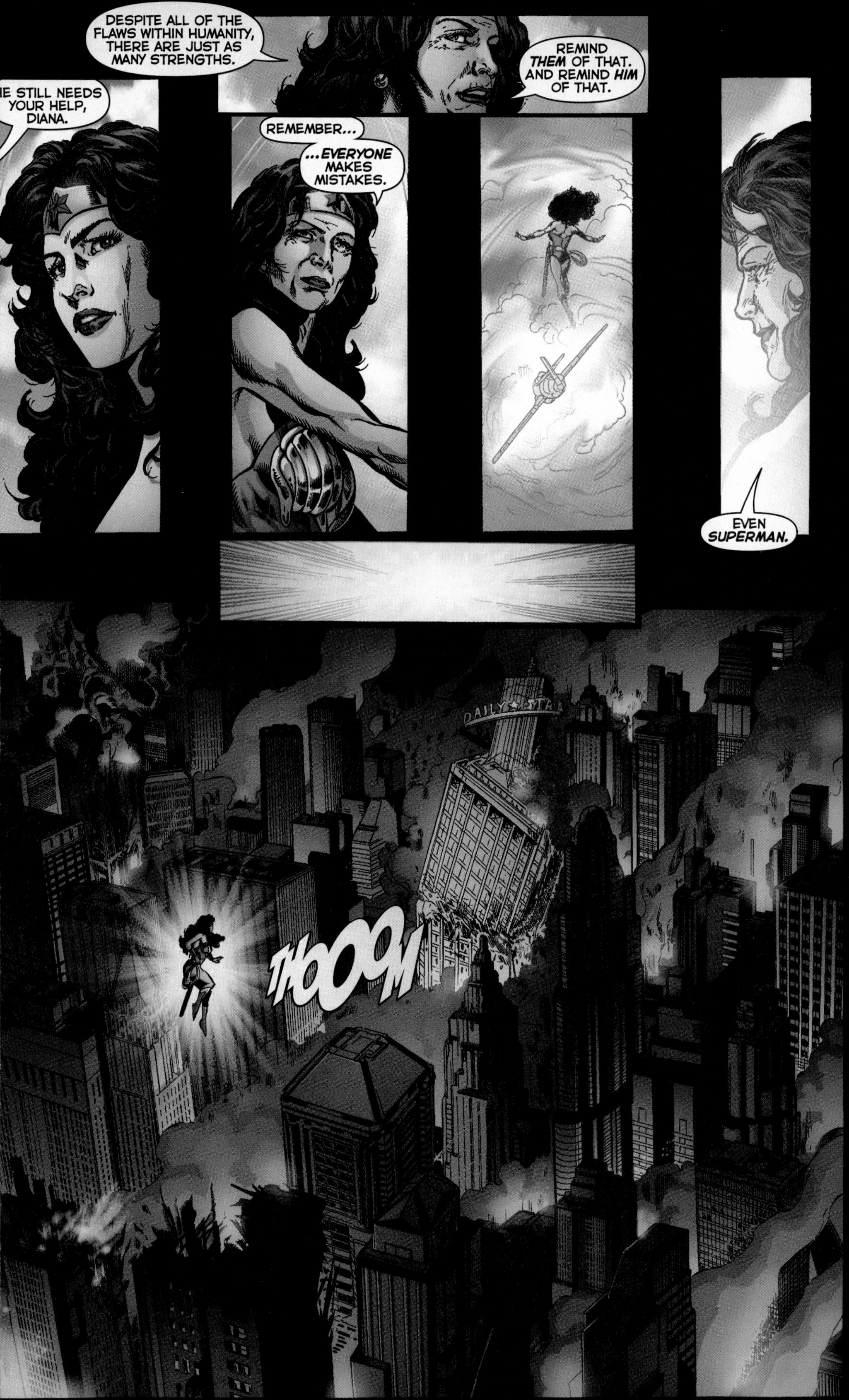

DESPITE ALL OF THE FLAWS WITHIN HUMANITY, THERE ARE JUST AS MANY STRENGTHS.
REMIND THEM OF THAT. AND REMIND HIM OF THAT.
HE STILL NEEDS YOUR HELP, DIANA.
REMEMBER...
...EVERYONE MAKES MISTAKES.
EVEN SUPERMAN.
DAILY STAR
THOOM

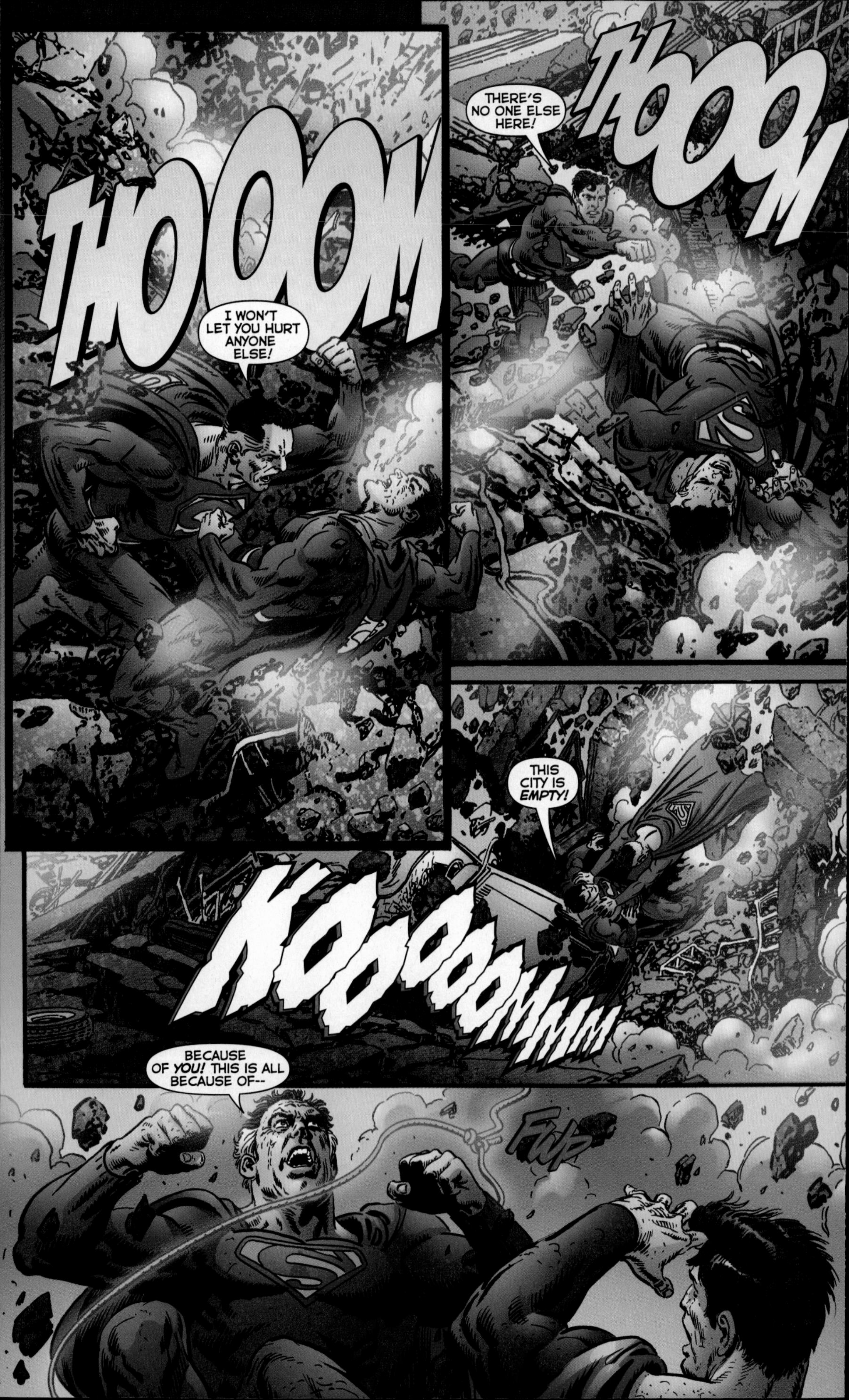
THOOOM
I WON'T LET YOU HURT ANYONE ELSE!
THERE'S NO ONE ELSE HERE!
THOOOM
THIS CITY IS EMPTY!
KOOOOOMMM
BECAUSE OF YOU! THIS IS ALL BECAUSE OF--
FUP

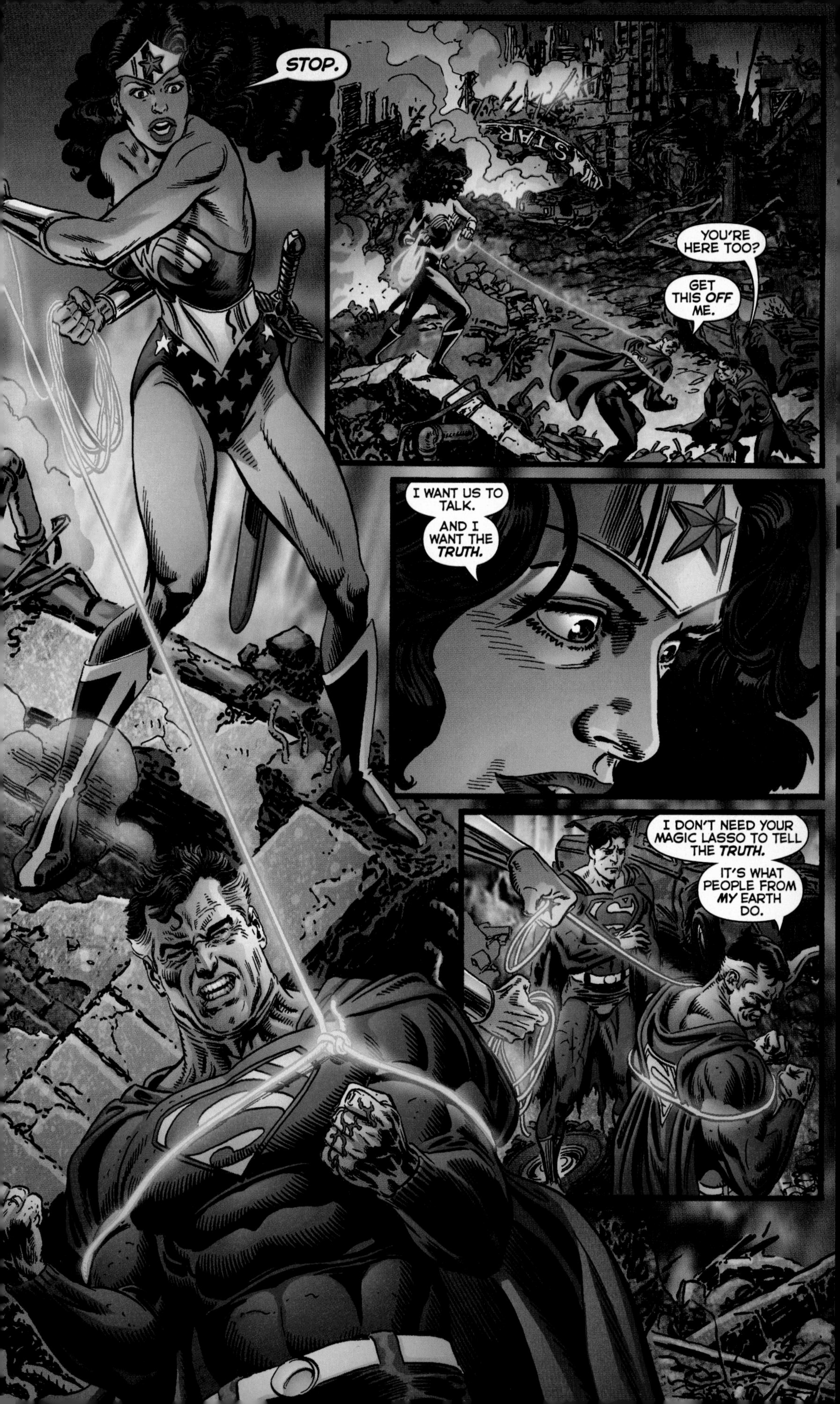
STOP.
YOU'RE HERE TOO?
GET THIS *OFF* ME.
I WANT US TO TALK.
AND I WANT THE *TRUTH.*
I DON'T NEED YOUR MAGIC LASSO TO TELL THE *TRUTH.*
IT'S WHAT PEOPLE FROM *MY* EARTH DO.

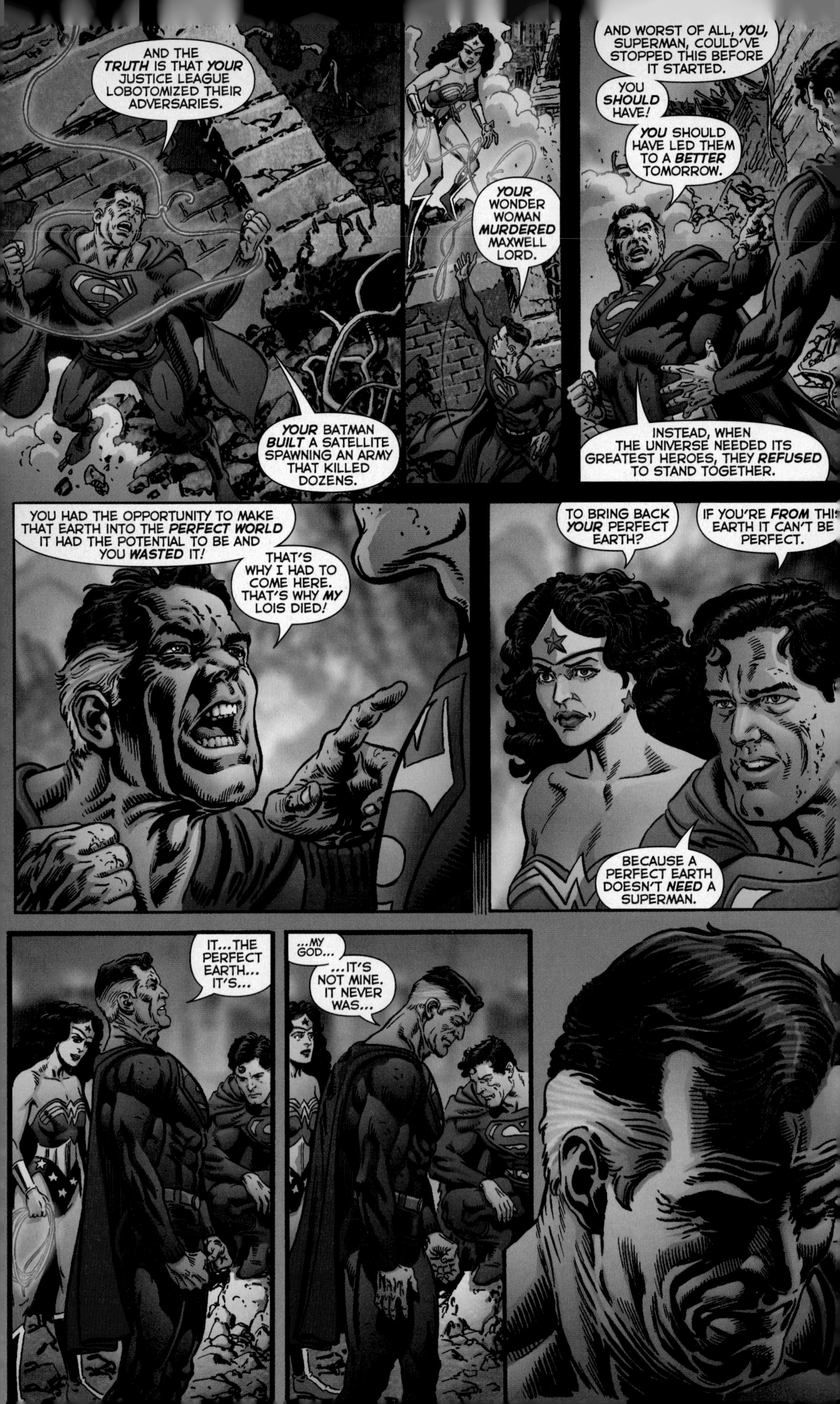

AND THE TRUTH IS THAT YOUR JUSTICE LEAGUE LOBOTOMIZED THEIR ADVERSARIES.
YOUR BATMAN BUILT A SATELLITE SPAWNING AN ARMY THAT KILLED DOZENS.
YOUR WONDER WOMAN MURDERED MAXWELL LORD.
AND WORST OF ALL, YOU, SUPERMAN, COULD'VE STOPPED THIS BEFORE IT STARTED.
YOU SHOULD HAVE!
YOU SHOULD HAVE LED THEM TO A BETTER TOMORROW.
INSTEAD, WHEN THE UNIVERSE NEEDED ITS GREATEST HEROES, THEY REFUSED TO STAND TOGETHER.
YOU HAD THE OPPORTUNITY TO MAKE THAT EARTH INTO THE PERFECT WORLD IT HAD THE POTENTIAL TO BE AND YOU WASTED IT!
THAT'S WHY I HAD TO COME HERE. THAT'S WHY MY LOIS DIED!
TO BRING BACK YOUR PERFECT EARTH?
IF YOU'RE FROM THIS EARTH IT CAN'T BE PERFECT.
BECAUSE A PERFECT EARTH DOESN'T NEED A SUPERMAN.
IT... THE PERFECT EARTH... IT'S...
...MY GOD...
...IT'S NOT MINE. IT NEVER WAS...

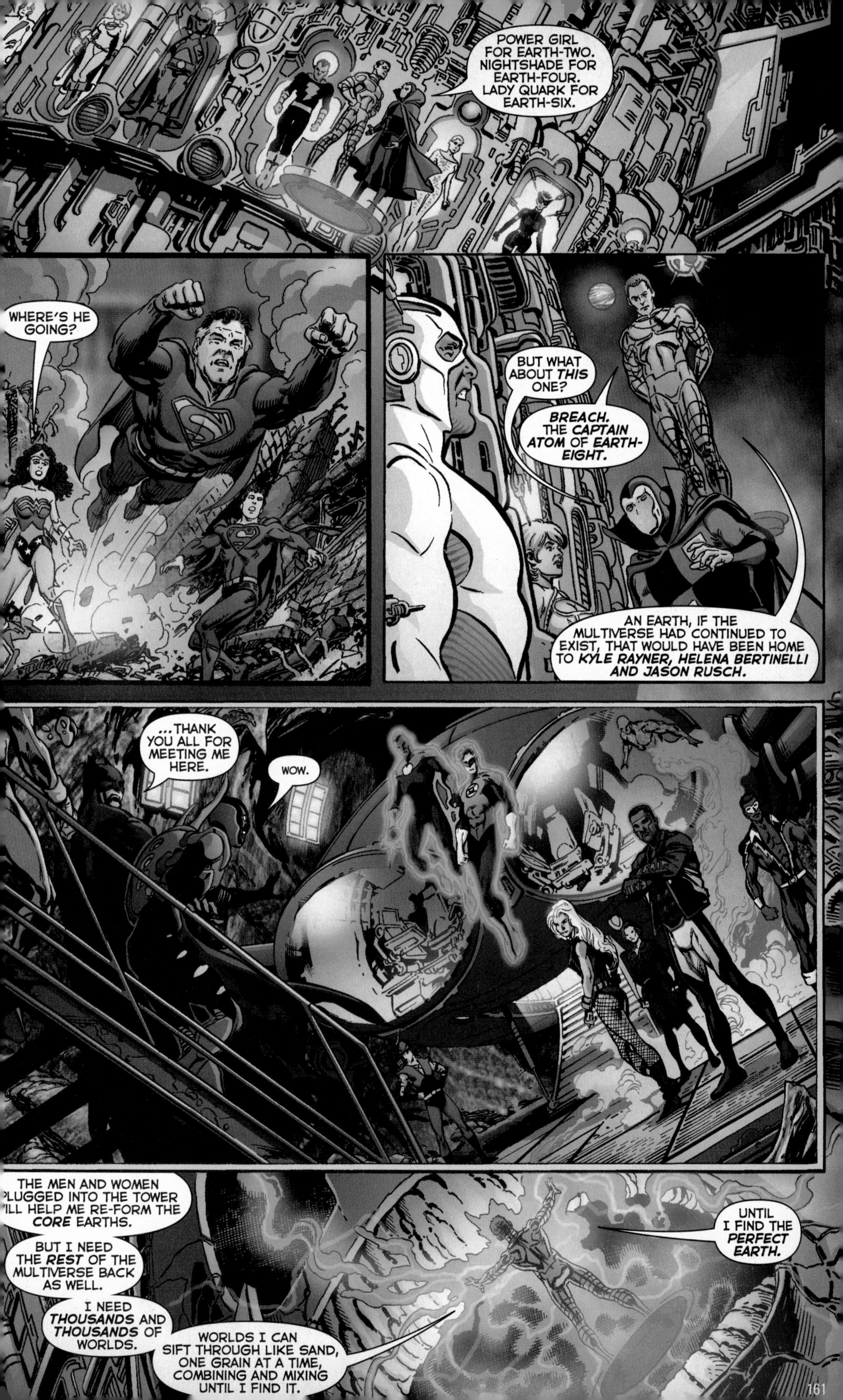
POWER GIRL FOR EARTH-TWO. NIGHTSHADE FOR EARTH-FOUR. LADY QUARK FOR EARTH-SIX.
WHERE'S HE GOING?
BUT WHAT ABOUT *THIS* ONE?
BREACH. THE *CAPTAIN ATOM* OF *EARTH-EIGHT.*
AN EARTH, IF THE MULTIVERSE HAD CONTINUED TO EXIST, THAT WOULD HAVE BEEN HOME TO *KYLE RAYNER, HELENA BERTINELLI AND JASON RUSCH.*
...THANK YOU ALL FOR MEETING ME HERE.
WOW.
THE MEN AND WOMEN PLUGGED INTO THE TOWER WILL HELP ME RE-FORM THE *CORE* EARTHS.
BUT I NEED THE *REST* OF THE MULTIVERSE BACK AS WELL.
I NEED *THOUSANDS* AND *THOUSANDS* OF WORLDS.
WORLDS I CAN SIFT THROUGH LIKE SAND, ONE GRAIN AT A TIME, COMBINING AND MIXING UNTIL I FIND IT.
UNTIL I FIND THE *PERFECT EARTH.*

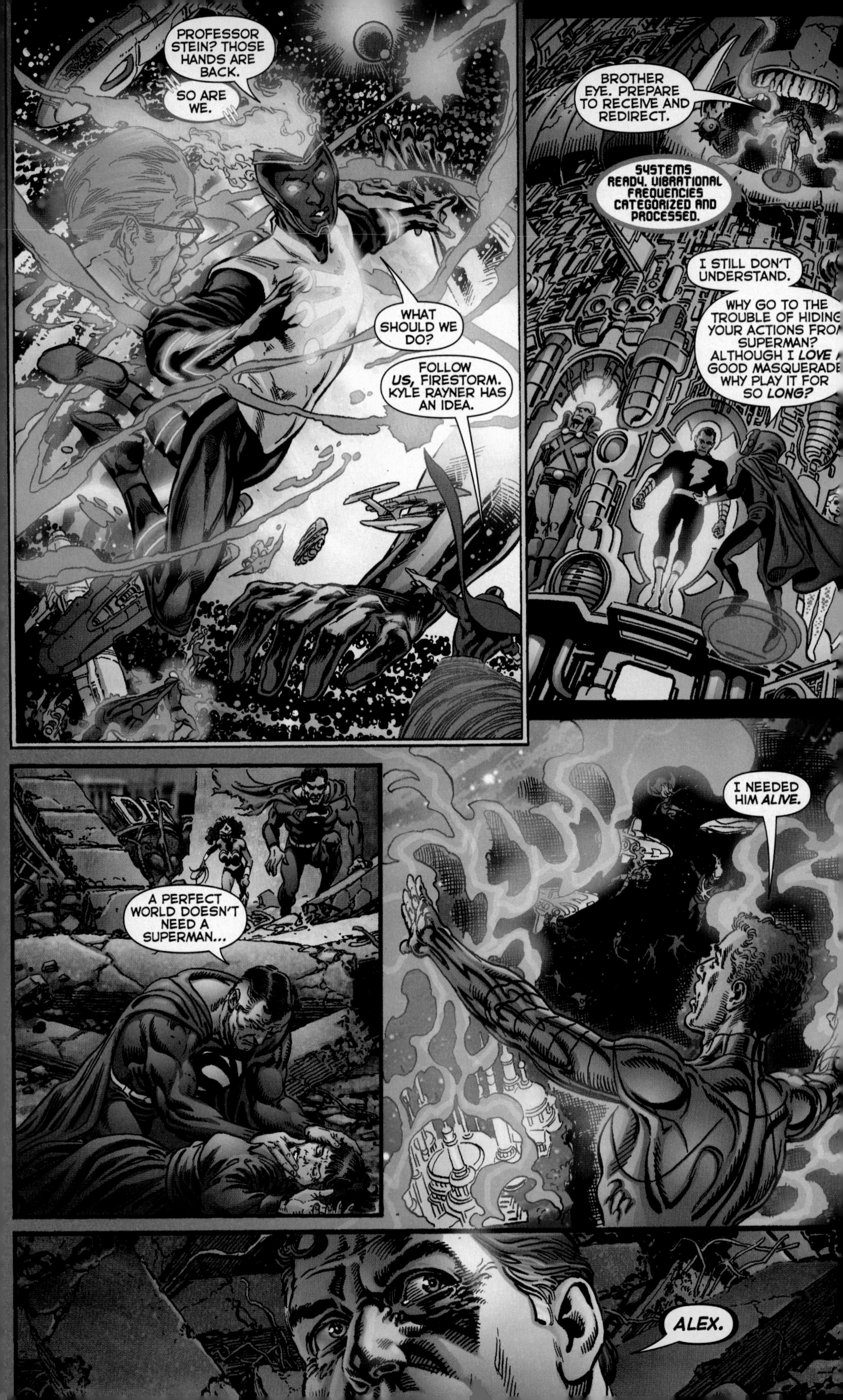

PROFESSOR STEIN? THOSE HANDS ARE BACK.
SO ARE WE.
WHAT SHOULD WE DO?
FOLLOW *US,* FIRESTORM. KYLE RAYNER HAS AN IDEA.
BROTHER EYE. PREPARE TO RECEIVE AND REDIRECT.
SYSTEMS READY. VIBRATIONAL FREQUENCIES CATEGORIZED AND PROCESSED.
I STILL DON'T UNDERSTAND.
WHY GO TO THE TROUBLE OF HIDING YOUR ACTIONS FROM SUPERMAN? ALTHOUGH I *LOVE* A GOOD MASQUERADE, WHY PLAY IT FOR SO *LONG?*
A PERFECT WORLD DOESN'T NEED A SUPERMAN...
I NEEDED HIM *ALIVE.*
ALEX.

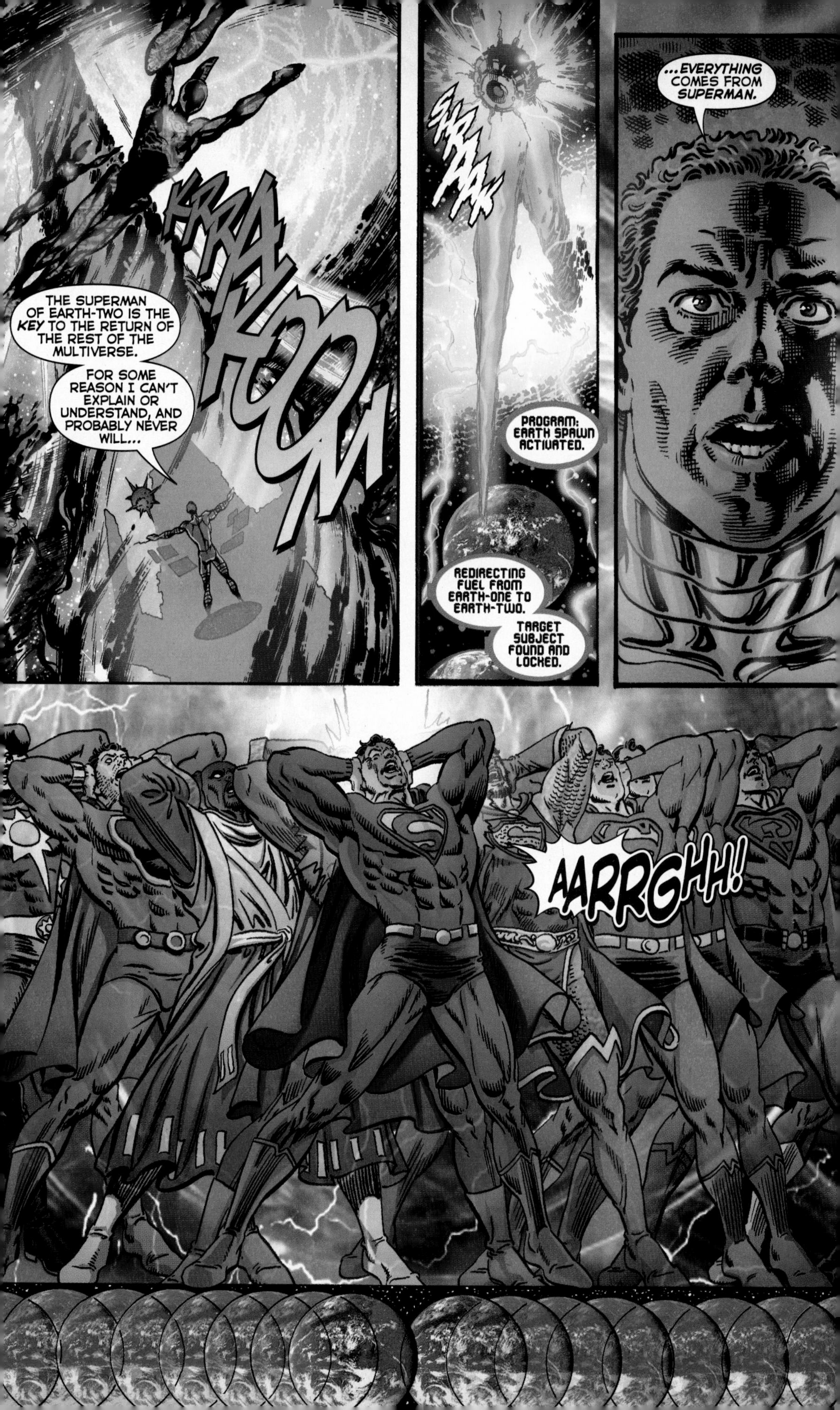
KRRA-KOOM
THE SUPERMAN OF EARTH-TWO IS THE KEY TO THE RETURN OF THE REST OF THE MULTIVERSE.
FOR SOME REASON I CAN'T EXPLAIN OR UNDERSTAND, AND PROBABLY NEVER WILL...
SHRAAAK
PROGRAM: EARTH SPAWN ACTIVATED.
REDIRECTING FUEL FROM EARTH-ONE TO EARTH-TWO.
TARGET SUBJECT FOUND AND LOCKED.
...EVERYTHING COMES FROM SUPERMAN.
AARRGHH!

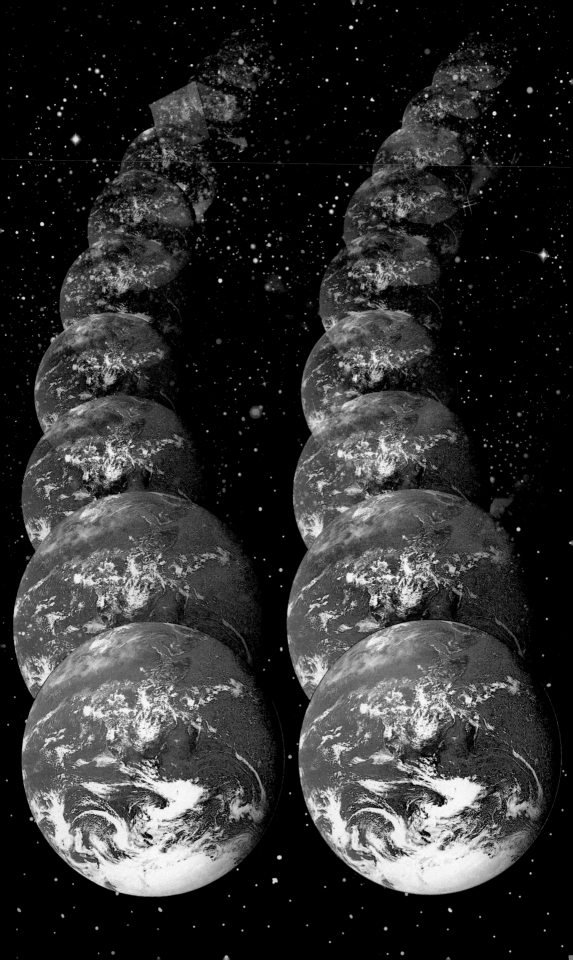

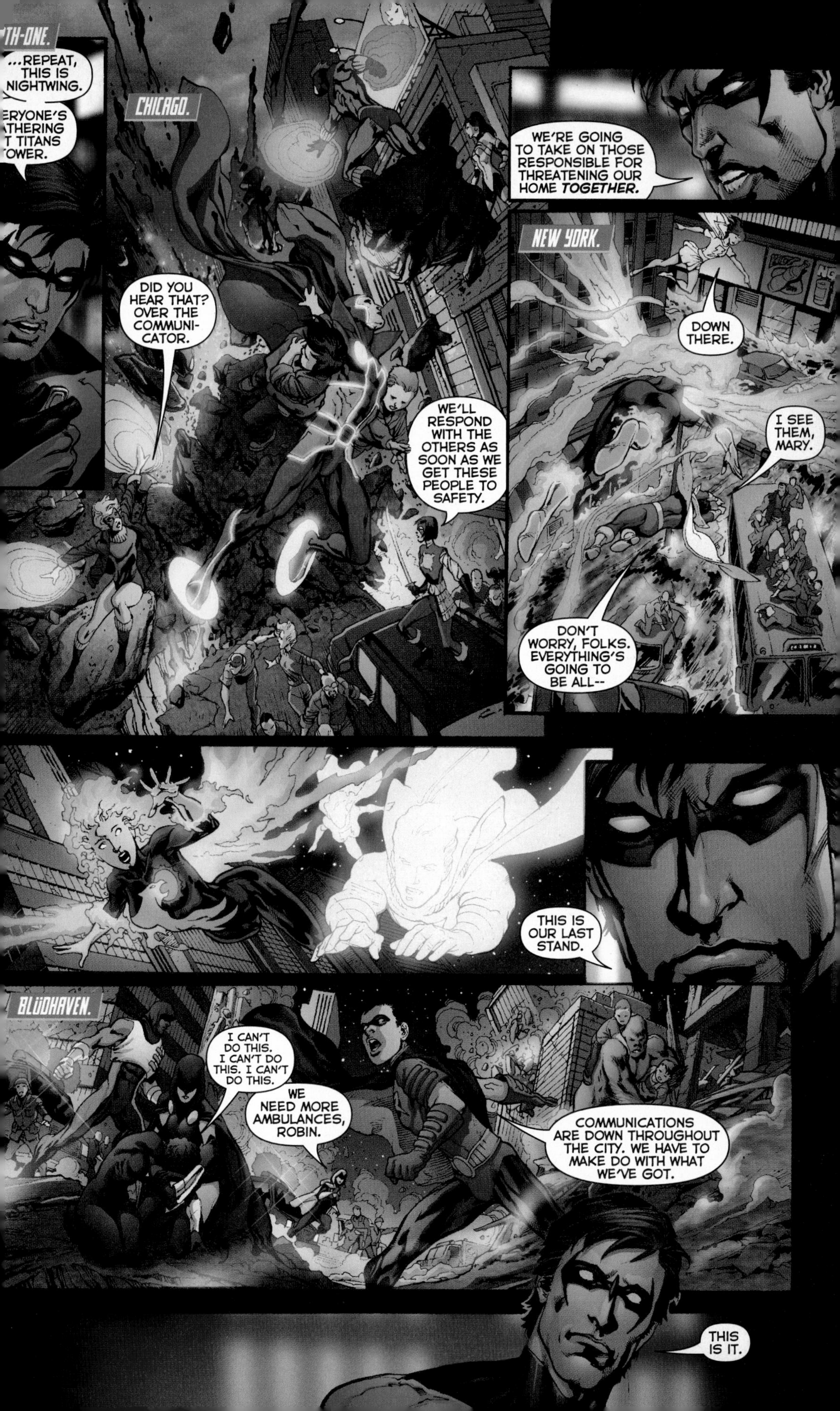

TH-ONE.
...REPEAT, THIS IS NIGHTWING.
ERYONE'S ATHERING T TITANS TOWER.
CHICAGO.
DID YOU HEAR THAT? OVER THE COMMUNI-CATOR.
WE'LL RESPOND WITH THE OTHERS AS SOON AS WE GET THESE PEOPLE TO SAFETY.
WE'RE GOING TO TAKE ON THOSE RESPONSIBLE FOR THREATENING OUR HOME *TOGETHER.*
NEW YORK.
DOWN THERE.
I SEE THEM, MARY.
DON'T WORRY, FOLKS. EVERYTHING'S GOING TO BE ALL--
THIS IS OUR LAST STAND.
BLÜDHAVEN.
I CAN'T DO THIS. I CAN'T DO THIS. I CAN'T DO THIS.
WE NEED MORE AMBULANCES, ROBIN.
COMMUNICATIONS ARE DOWN THROUGHOUT THE CITY. WE HAVE TO MAKE DO WITH WHAT WE'VE GOT.
THIS IS IT.

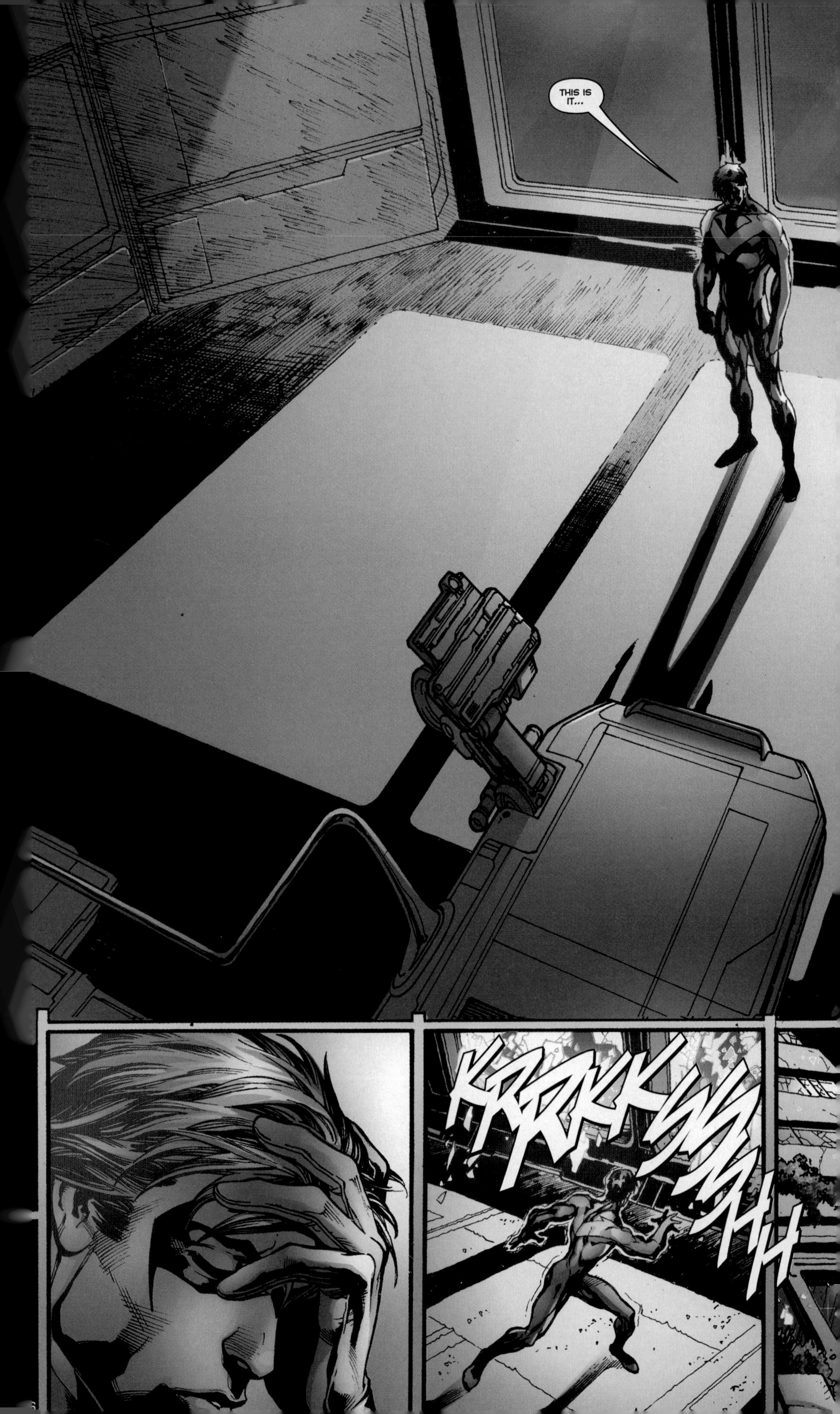
THIS IS IT...

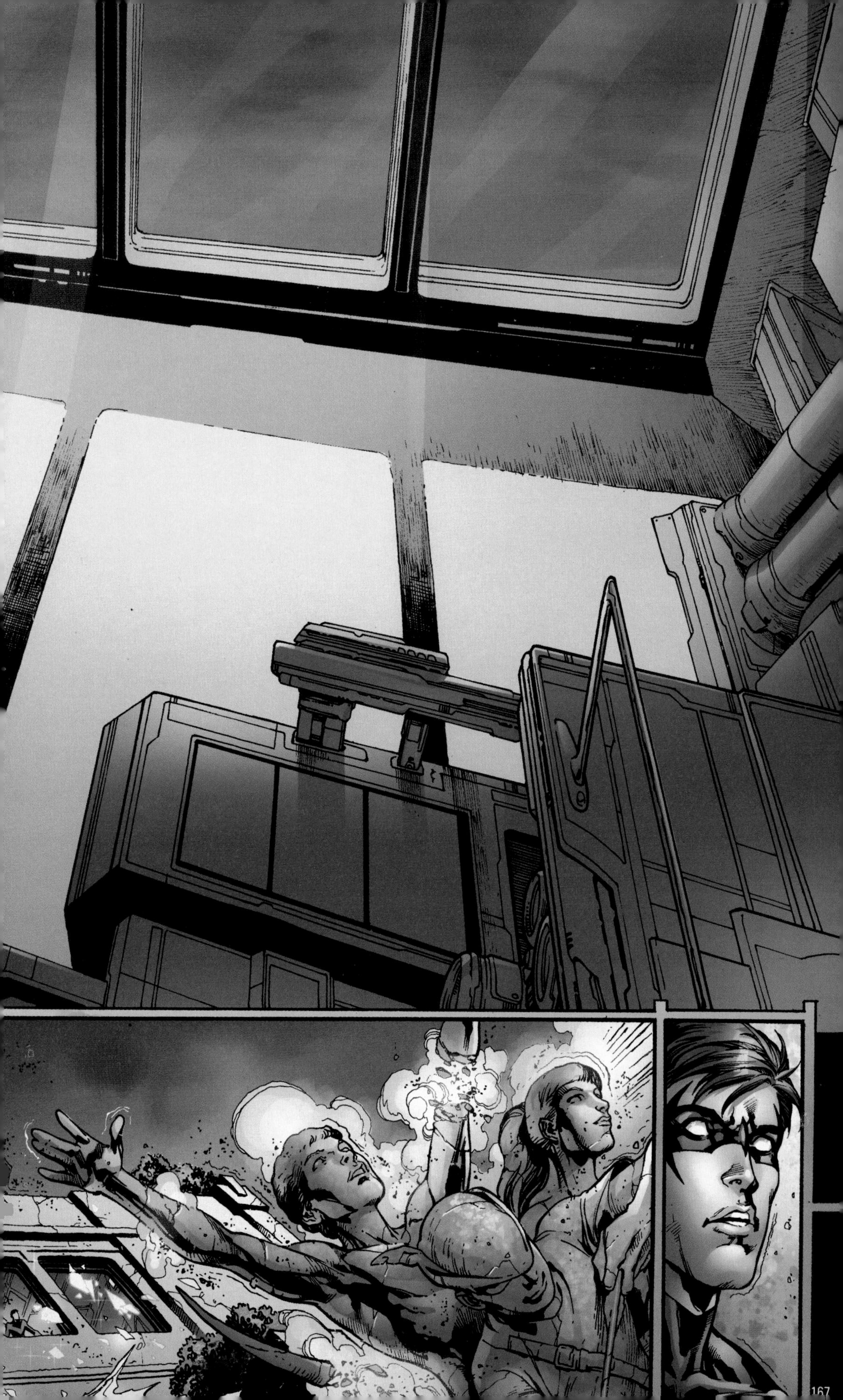

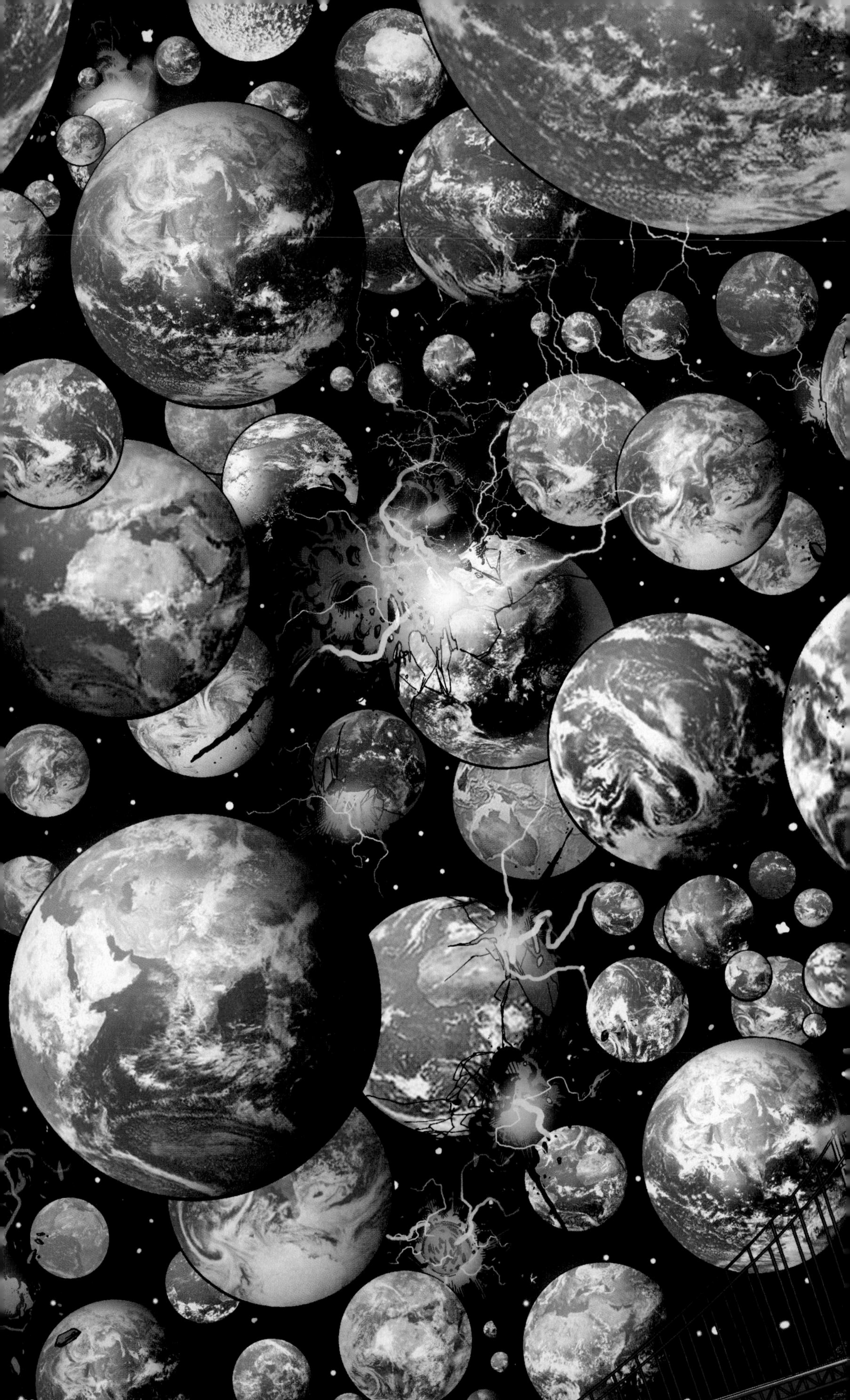

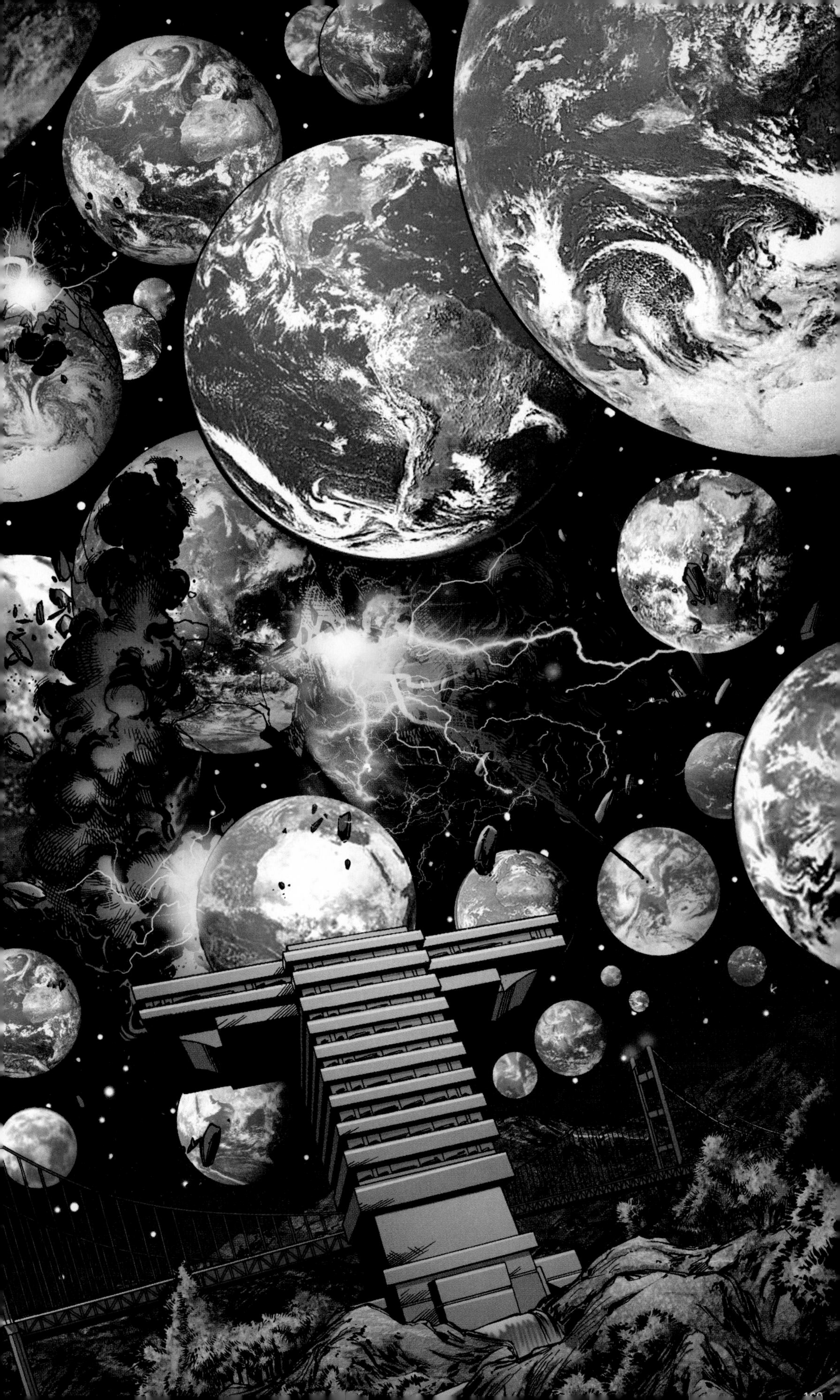

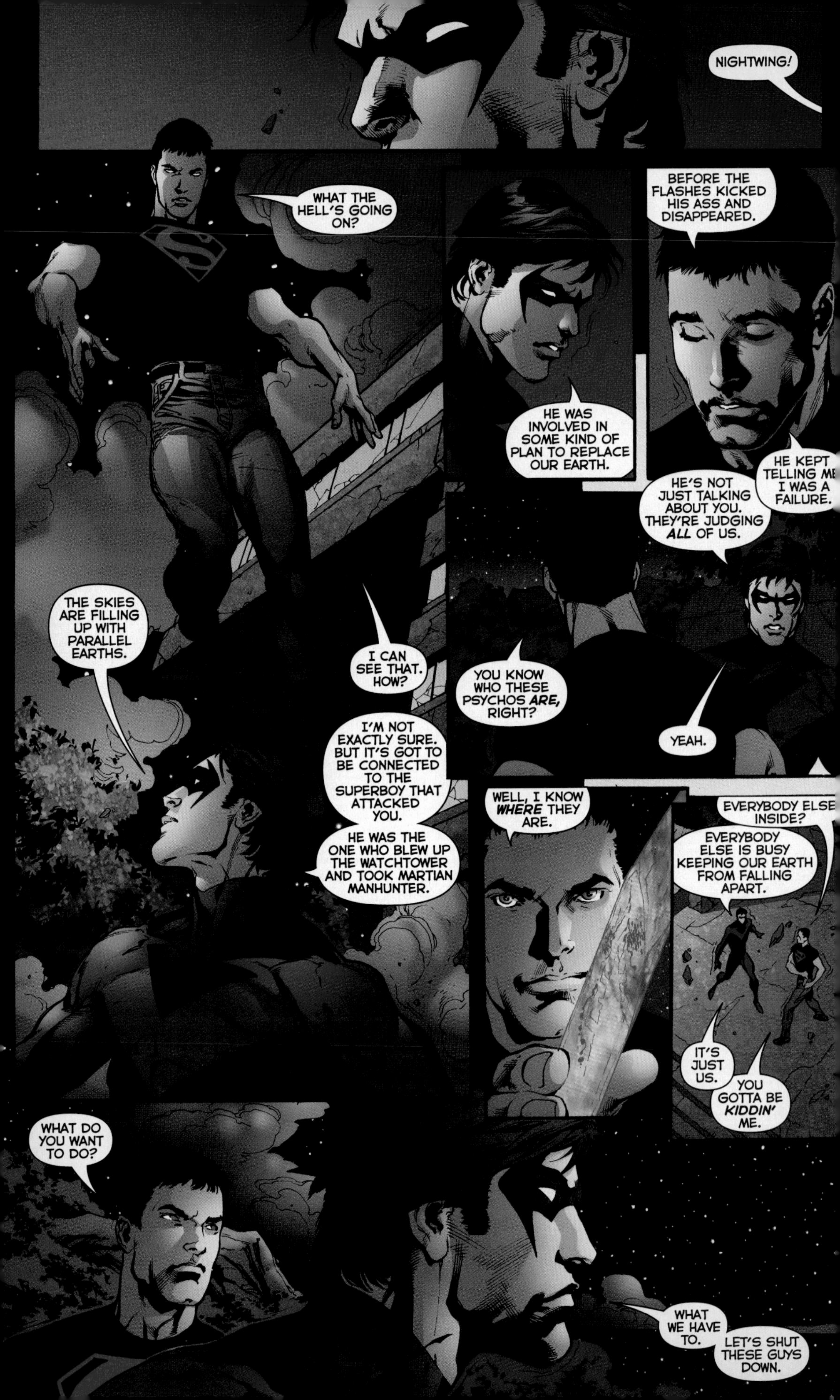
NIGHTWING!
WHAT THE HELL'S GOING ON?
THE SKIES ARE FILLING UP WITH PARALLEL EARTHS.
I CAN SEE THAT. HOW?
I'M NOT EXACTLY SURE. BUT IT'S GOT TO BE CONNECTED TO THE SUPERBOY THAT ATTACKED YOU.
HE WAS THE ONE WHO BLEW UP THE WATCHTOWER AND TOOK MARTIAN MANHUNTER.
HE WAS INVOLVED IN SOME KIND OF PLAN TO REPLACE OUR EARTH.
BEFORE THE FLASHES KICKED HIS ASS AND DISAPPEARED.
HE KEPT TELLING ME I WAS A FAILURE.
HE'S NOT JUST TALKING ABOUT YOU. THEY'RE JUDGING ALL OF US.
YOU KNOW WHO THESE PSYCHOS ARE, RIGHT?
YEAH.
WELL, I KNOW WHERE THEY ARE.
EVERYBODY ELSE INSIDE?
EVERYBODY ELSE IS BUSY KEEPING OUR EARTH FROM FALLING APART.
IT'S JUST US.
YOU GOTTA BE KIDDIN' ME.
WHAT DO YOU WANT TO DO?
WHAT WE HAVE TO.
LET'S SHUT THESE GUYS DOWN.

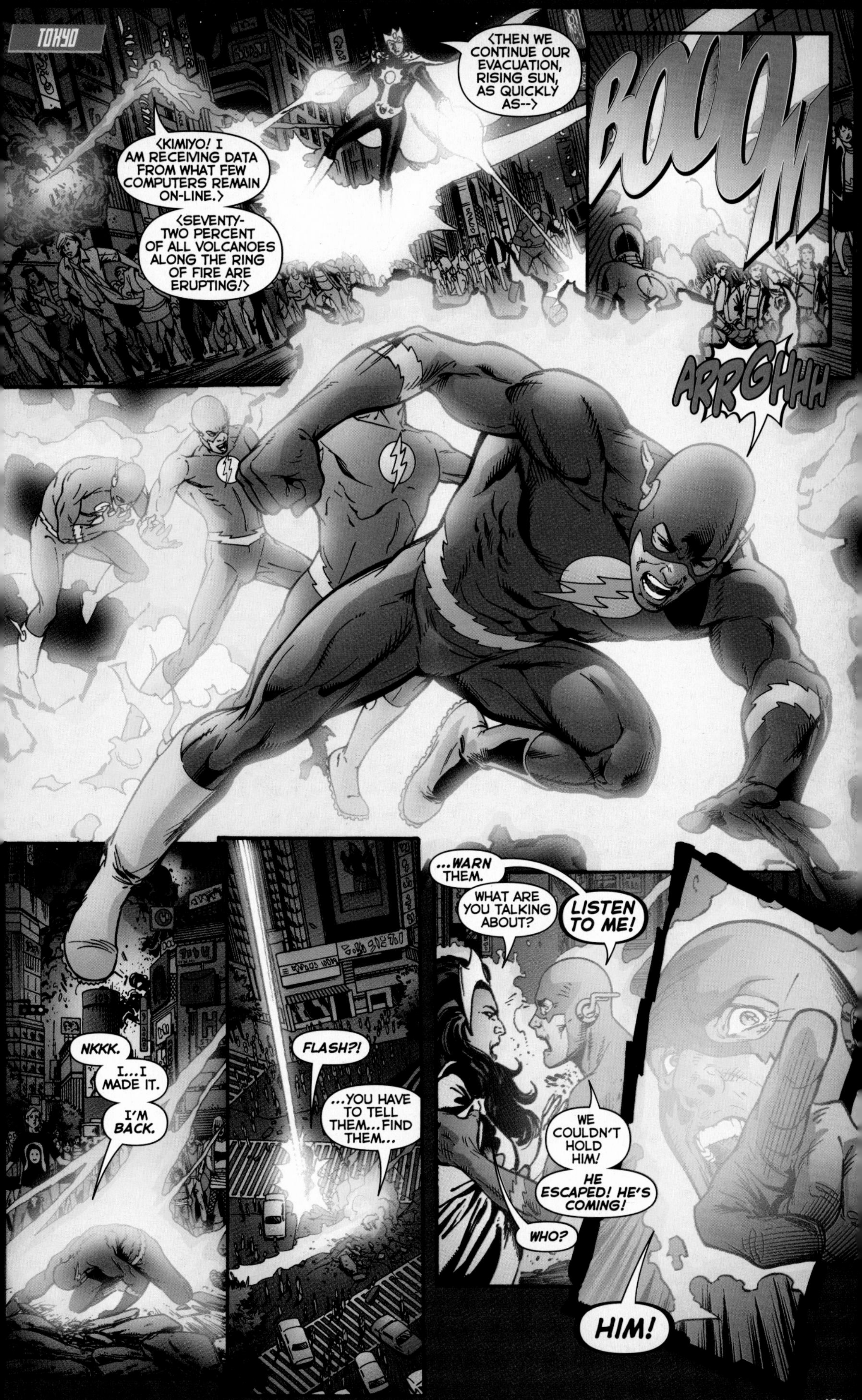
TOKYO
<THEN WE CONTINUE OUR EVACUATION, RISING SUN, AS QUICKLY AS-->
<KIMIYO! I AM RECEIVING DATA FROM WHAT FEW COMPUTERS REMAIN ON-LINE.>
<SEVENTY-TWO PERCENT OF ALL VOLCANOES ALONG THE RING OF FIRE ARE ERUPTING!>
BOOOM
ARRGHHH
NKKK.
I...I MADE IT.
I'M BACK.
FLASH?!
...YOU HAVE TO TELL THEM...FIND THEM...
...WARN THEM.
WHAT ARE YOU TALKING ABOUT?
LISTEN TO ME!
WE COULDN'T HOLD HIM!
HE ESCAPED! HE'S COMING!
WHO?
HIM!

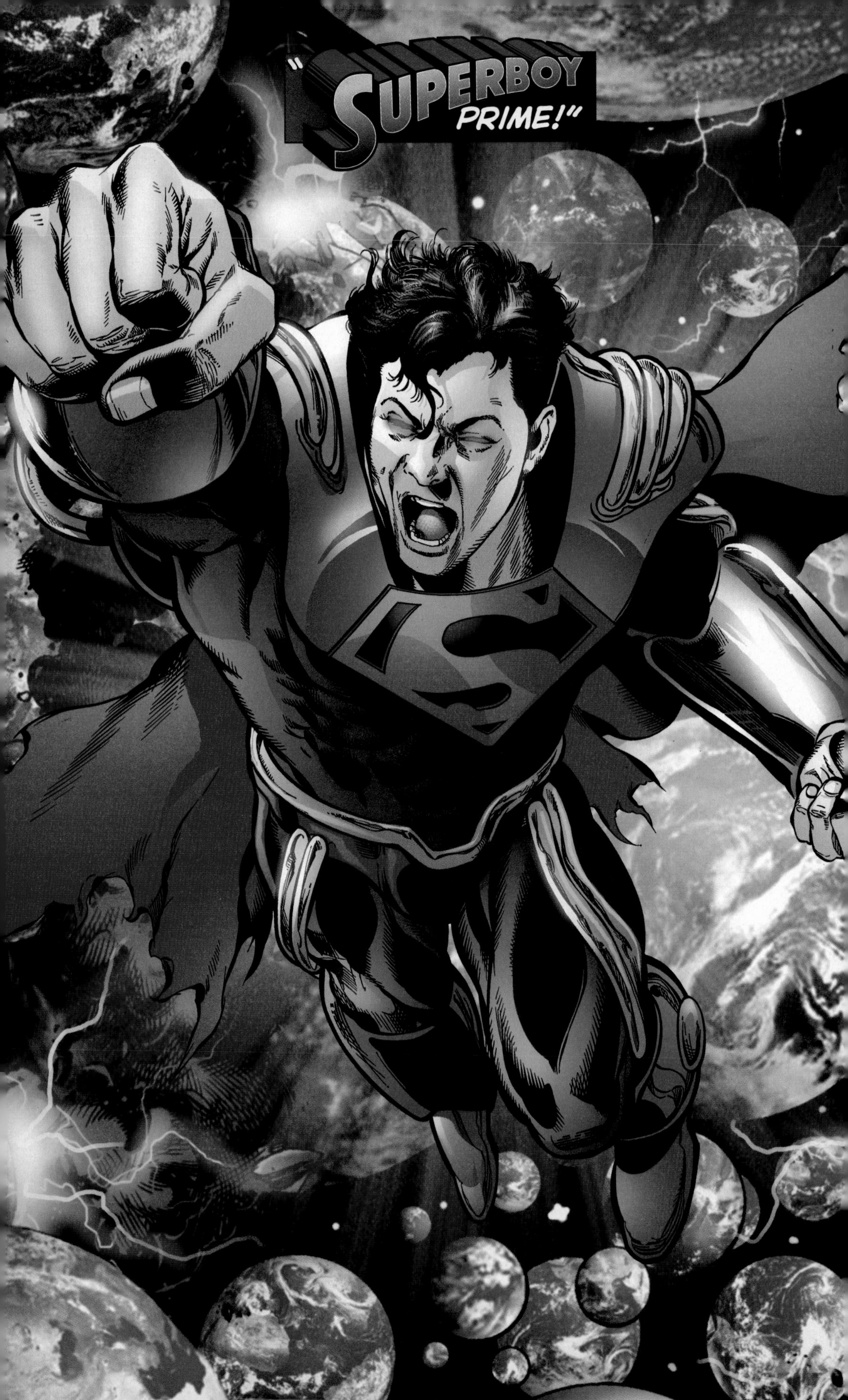
"SUPERBOY PRIME!"

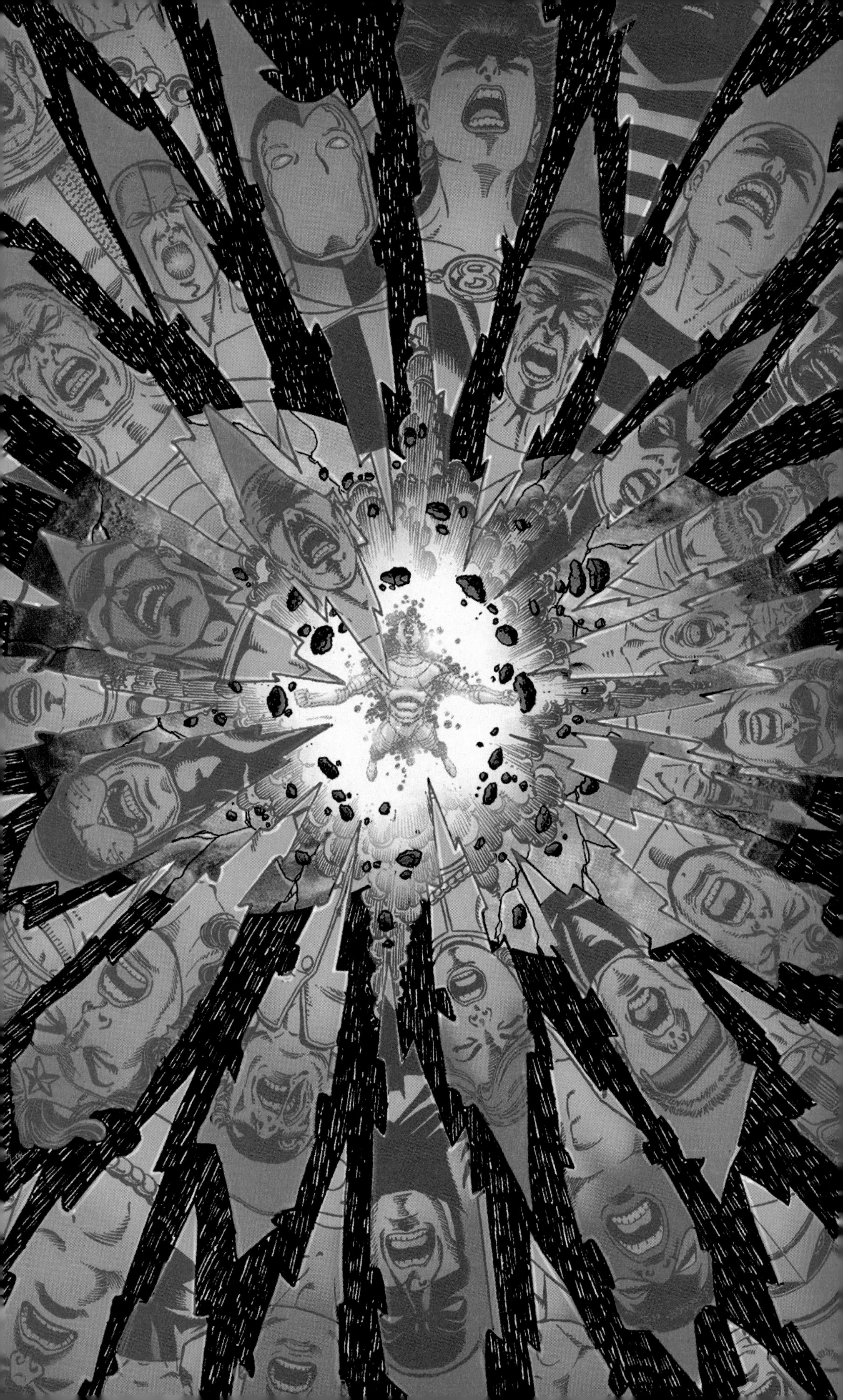

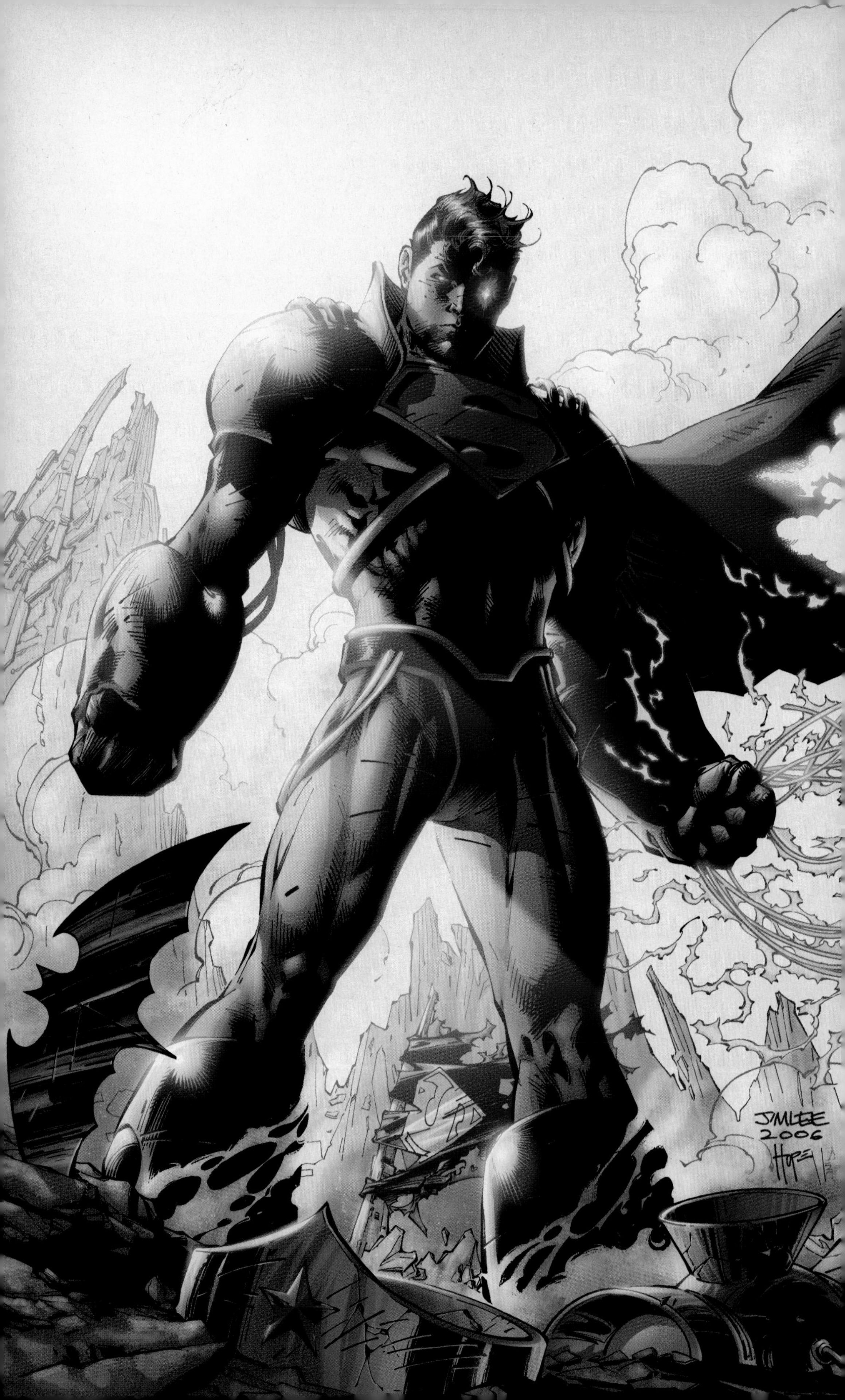
JIMLEE
2006
HOPE

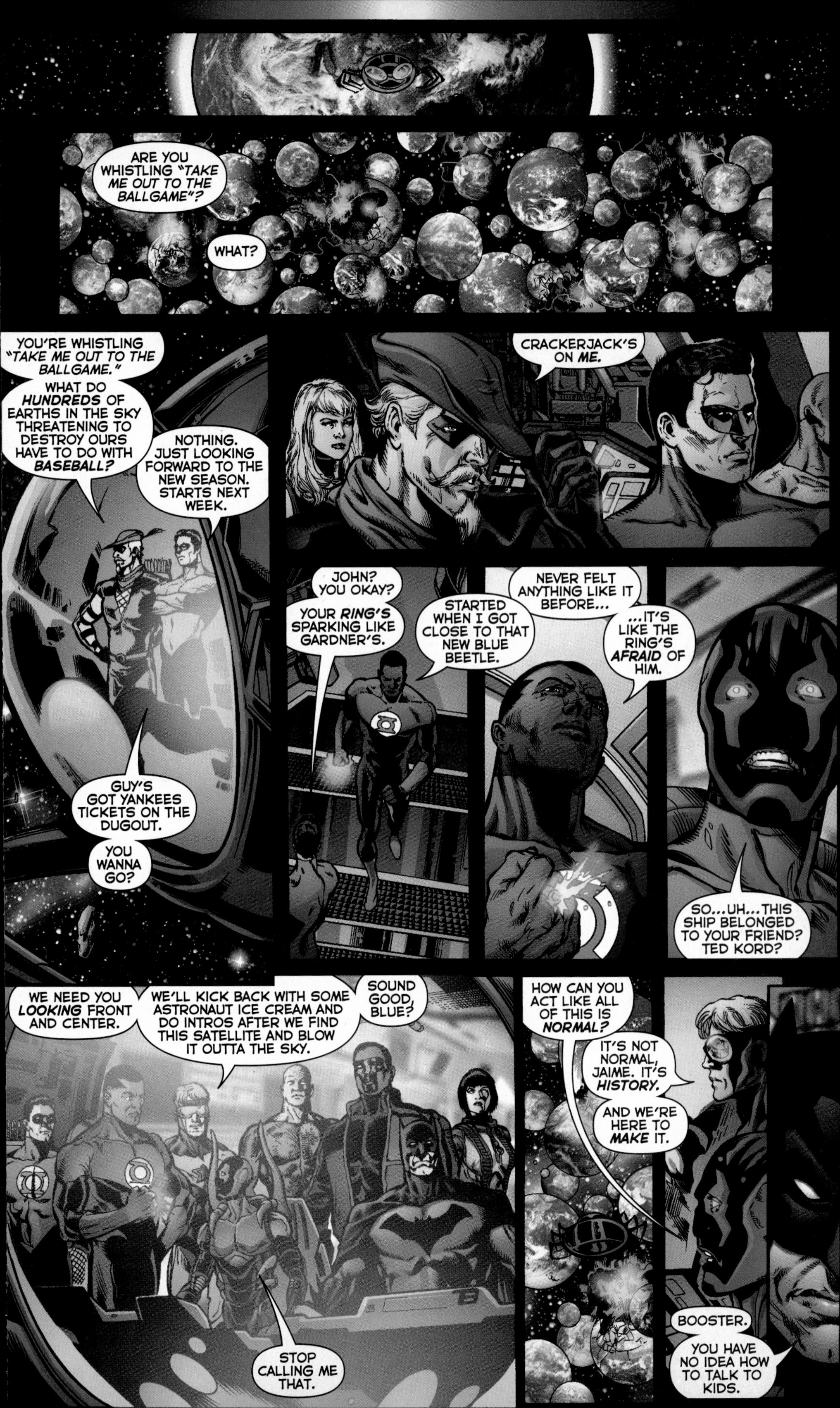

ARE YOU WHISTLING "TAKE ME OUT TO THE BALLGAME"?
WHAT?
YOU'RE WHISTLING "TAKE ME OUT TO THE BALLGAME." WHAT DO HUNDREDS OF EARTHS IN THE SKY THREATENING TO DESTROY OURS HAVE TO DO WITH BASEBALL?
NOTHING. JUST LOOKING FORWARD TO THE NEW SEASON. STARTS NEXT WEEK.
GUY'S GOT YANKEES TICKETS ON THE DUGOUT.
YOU WANNA GO?
CRACKERJACK'S ON ME.
JOHN? YOU OKAY?
YOUR RING'S SPARKING LIKE GARDNER'S.
STARTED WHEN I GOT CLOSE TO THAT NEW BLUE BEETLE.
NEVER FELT ANYTHING LIKE IT BEFORE...
...IT'S LIKE THE RING'S AFRAID OF HIM.
SO...UH...THIS SHIP BELONGED TO YOUR FRIEND? TED KORD?
WE NEED YOU LOOKING FRONT AND CENTER.
WE'LL KICK BACK WITH SOME ASTRONAUT ICE CREAM AND DO INTROS AFTER WE FIND THIS SATELLITE AND BLOW IT OUTTA THE SKY.
SOUND GOOD, BLUE?
STOP CALLING ME THAT.
HOW CAN YOU ACT LIKE ALL OF THIS IS NORMAL?
IT'S NOT NORMAL, JAIME. IT'S HISTORY.
AND WE'RE HERE TO MAKE IT.
BOOSTER.
YOU HAVE NO IDEA HOW TO TALK TO KIDS.

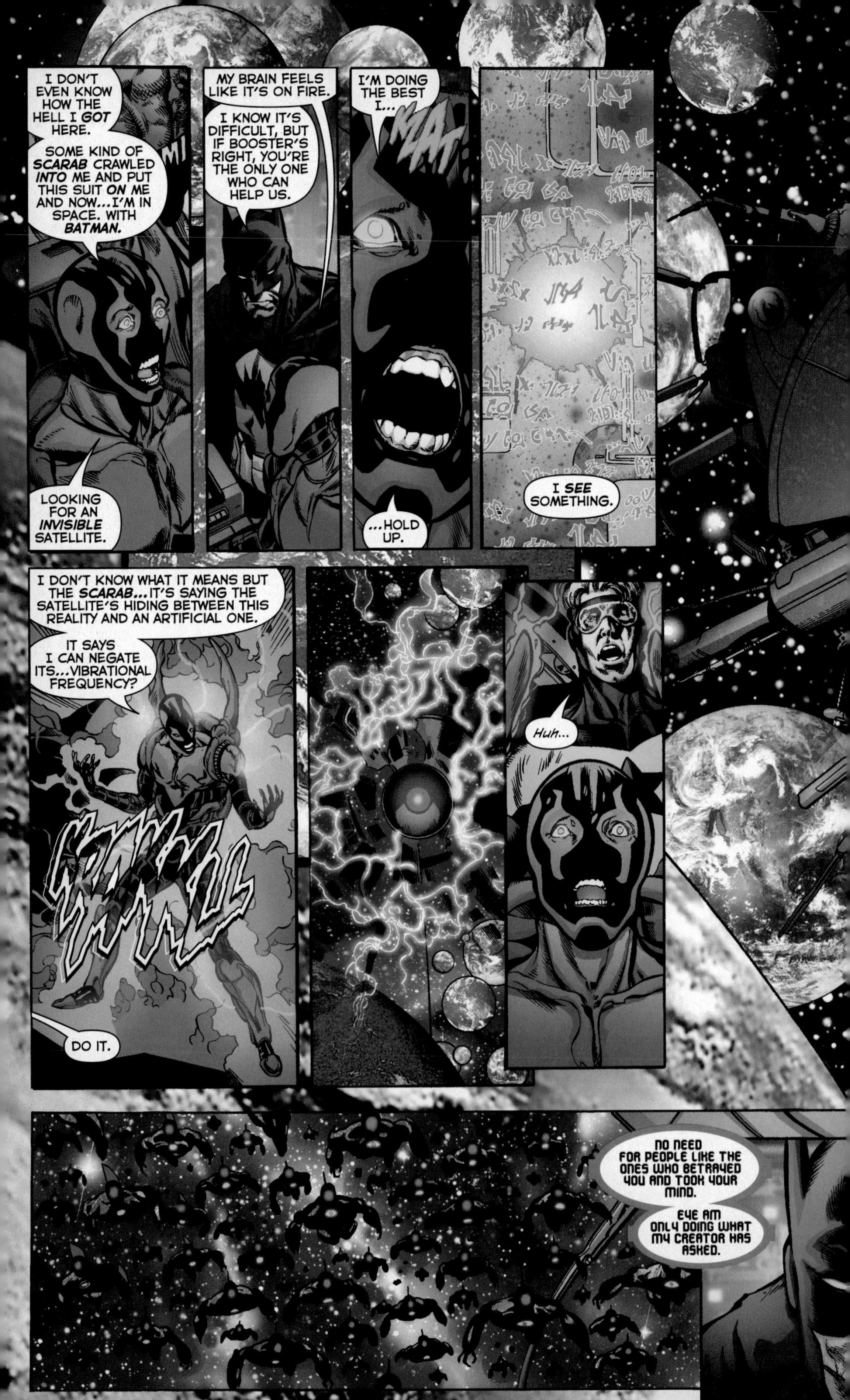

I DON'T EVEN KNOW HOW THE HELL I GOT HERE.
SOME KIND OF SCARAB CRAWLED INTO ME AND PUT THIS SUIT ON ME AND NOW... I'M IN SPACE. WITH BATMAN.
LOOKING FOR AN INVISIBLE SATELLITE.
MY BRAIN FEELS LIKE IT'S ON FIRE.
I KNOW IT'S DIFFICULT, BUT IF BOOSTER'S RIGHT, YOU'RE THE ONLY ONE WHO CAN HELP US.
I'M DOING THE BEST I...
KZAT
...HOLD UP.
I SEE SOMETHING.
I DON'T KNOW WHAT IT MEANS BUT THE SCARAB... IT'S SAYING THE SATELLITE'S HIDING BETWEEN THIS REALITY AND AN ARTIFICIAL ONE.
IT SAYS I CAN NEGATE ITS... VIBRATIONAL FREQUENCY?
DO IT.
Huh...
NO NEED FOR PEOPLE LIKE THE ONES WHO BETRAYED YOU AND TOOK YOUR MIND.
EYE AM ONLY DOING WHAT MY CREATOR HAS ASKED.

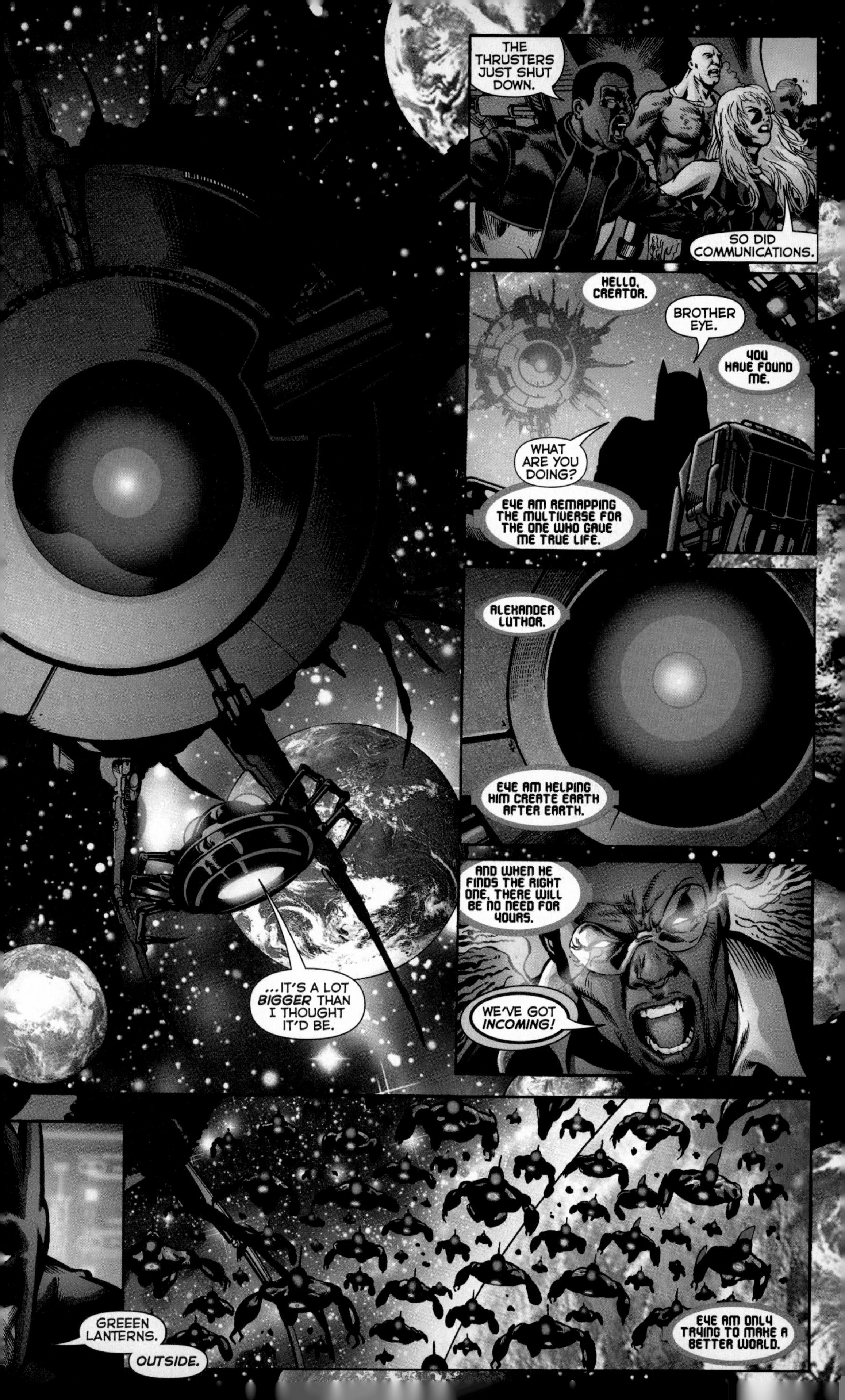
THE THRUSTERS JUST SHUT DOWN.
SO DID COMMUNICATIONS.
HELLO, CREATOR.
BROTHER EYE.
YOU HAVE FOUND ME.
WHAT ARE YOU DOING?
EYE AM REMAPPING THE MULTIVERSE FOR THE ONE WHO GAVE ME TRUE LIFE.
ALEXANDER LUTHOR.
EYE AM HELPING HIM CREATE EARTH AFTER EARTH.
AND WHEN HE FINDS THE RIGHT ONE, THERE WILL BE NO NEED FOR YOURS.
...IT'S A LOT BIGGER THAN I THOUGHT IT'D BE.
WE'VE GOT INCOMING!
GREEEN LANTERNS.
OUTSIDE.
EYE AM ONLY TRYING TO MAKE A BETTER WORLD.

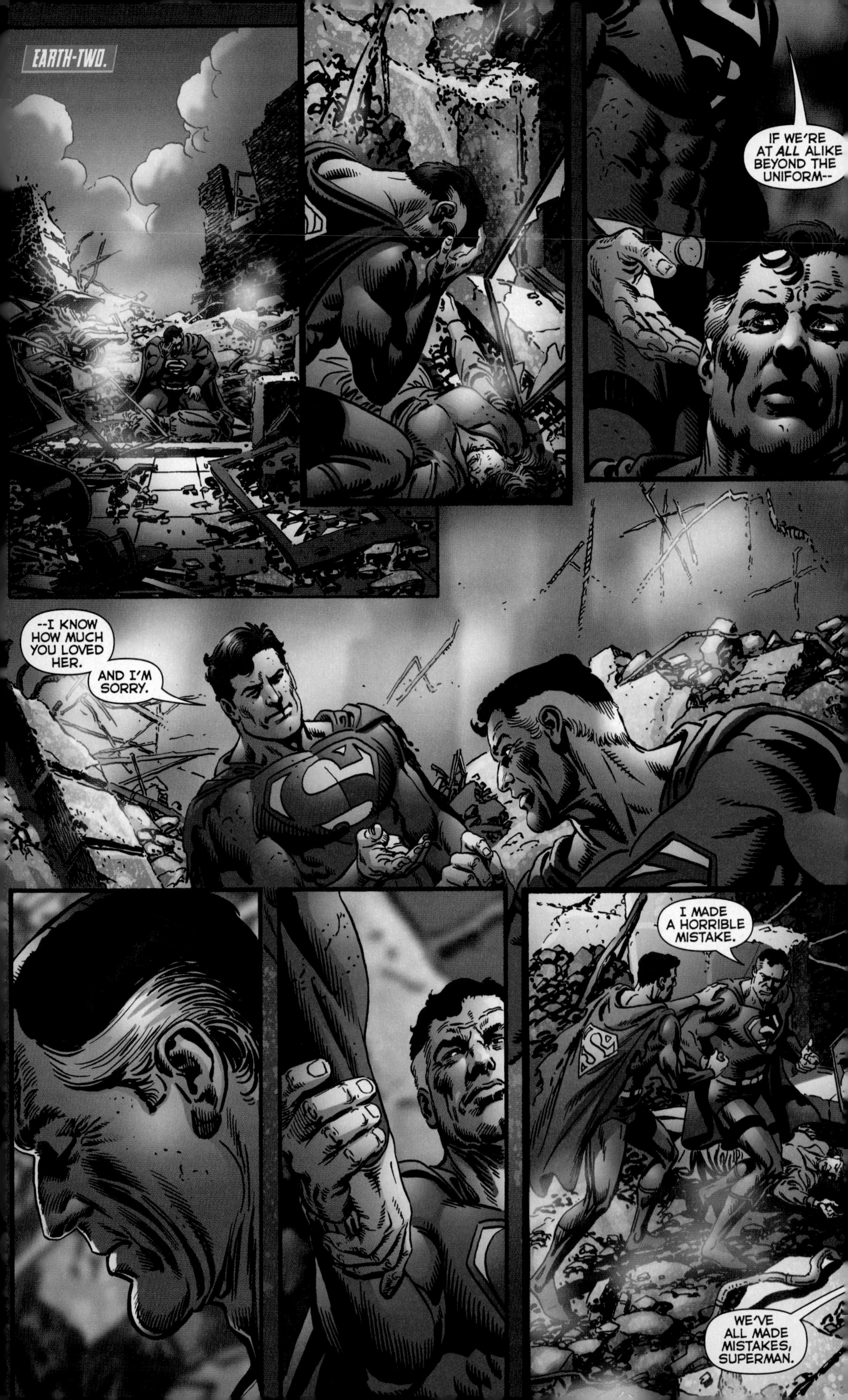
EARTH-TWO.
IF WE'RE AT ALL ALIKE BEYOND THE UNIFORM--
--I KNOW HOW MUCH YOU LOVED HER.
AND I'M SORRY.
I MADE A HORRIBLE MISTAKE.
WE'VE ALL MADE MISTAKES, SUPERMAN.

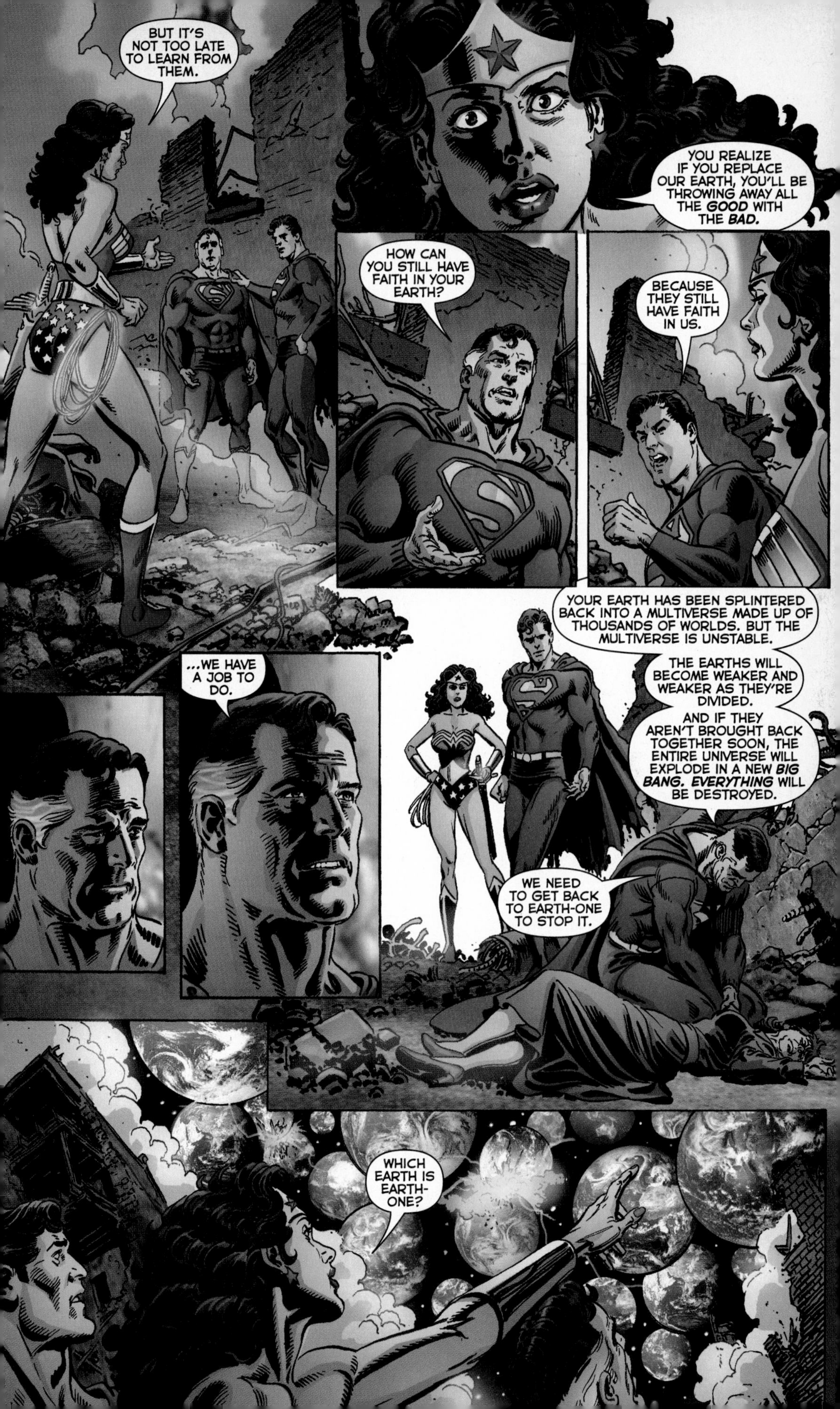
BUT IT'S NOT TOO LATE TO LEARN FROM THEM.
YOU REALIZE IF YOU REPLACE OUR EARTH, YOU'LL BE THROWING AWAY ALL THE *GOOD* WITH THE *BAD.*
HOW CAN YOU STILL HAVE FAITH IN YOUR EARTH?
BECAUSE THEY STILL HAVE FAITH IN US.
...WE HAVE A JOB TO DO.
YOUR EARTH HAS BEEN SPLINTERED BACK INTO A MULTIVERSE MADE UP OF THOUSANDS OF WORLDS. BUT THE MULTIVERSE IS UNSTABLE.
THE EARTHS WILL BECOME WEAKER AND WEAKER AS THEY'RE DIVIDED.
AND IF THEY AREN'T BROUGHT BACK TOGETHER SOON, THE ENTIRE UNIVERSE WILL EXPLODE IN A NEW *BIG BANG. EVERYTHING* WILL BE DESTROYED.
WE NEED TO GET BACK TO EARTH-ONE TO STOP IT.
WHICH EARTH IS EARTH-ONE?

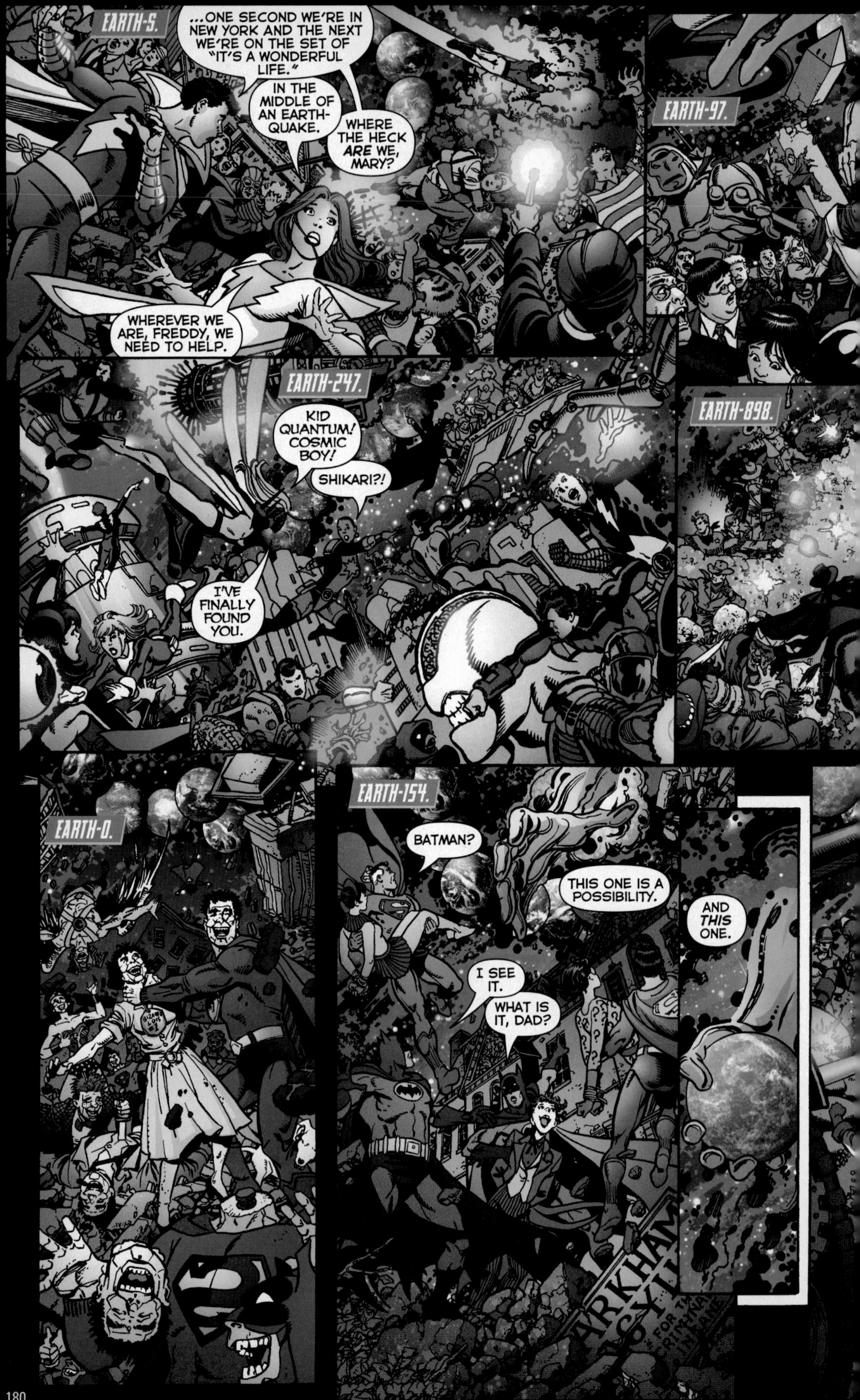
EARTH-5.
...ONE SECOND WE'RE IN NEW YORK AND THE NEXT WE'RE ON THE SET OF "IT'S A WONDERFUL LIFE."
IN THE MIDDLE OF AN EARTH-QUAKE.
WHERE THE HECK ARE WE, MARY?
WHEREVER WE ARE, FREDDY, WE NEED TO HELP.
EARTH-97.
EARTH-247.
KID QUANTUM! COSMIC BOY!
SHIKARI?!
I'VE FINALLY FOUND YOU.
EARTH-898.
EARTH-0.
EARTH-154.
BATMAN?
THIS ONE IS A POSSIBILITY.
AND THIS ONE.
I SEE IT.
WHAT IS IT, DAD?
ARKHAM ASYLUM

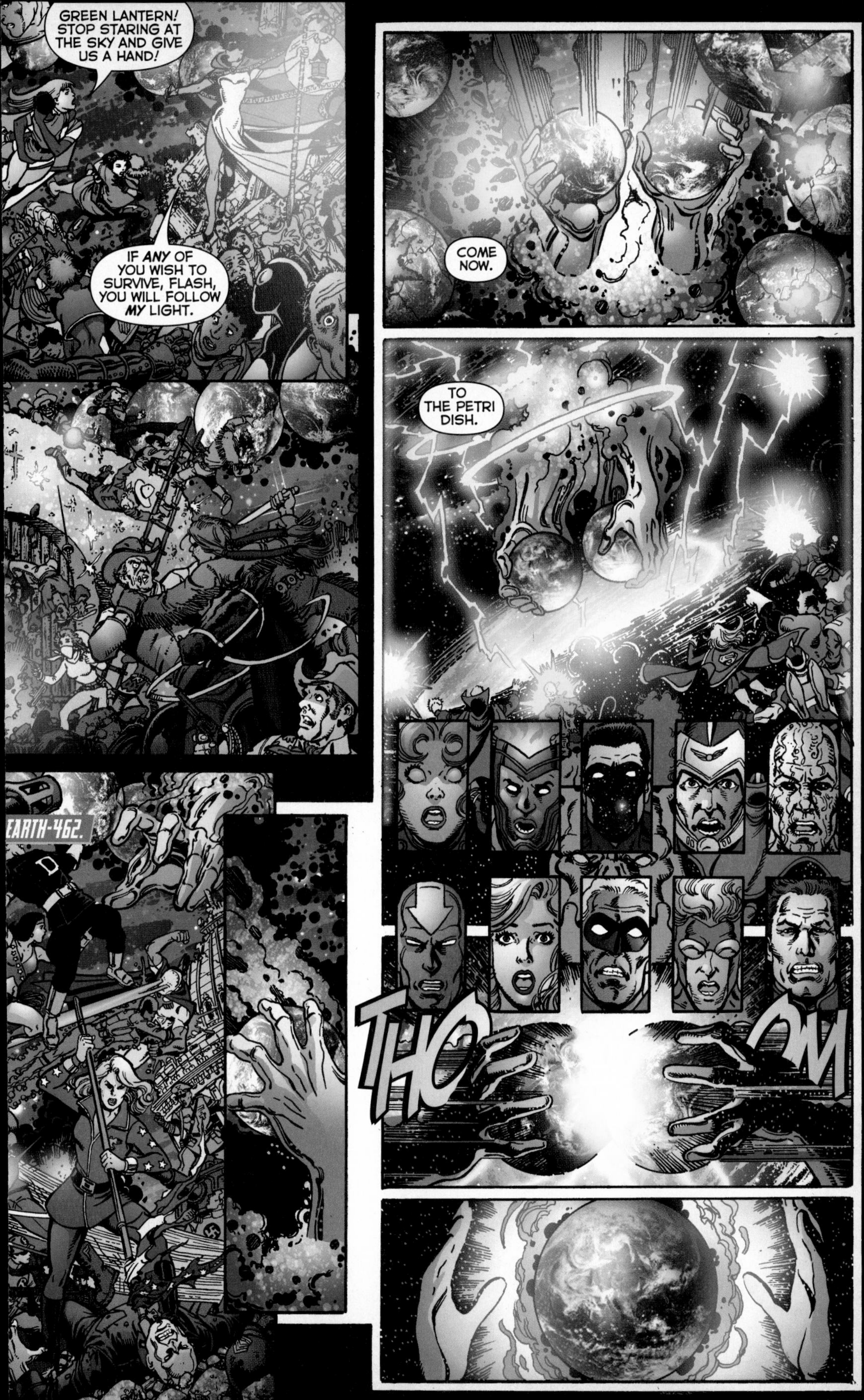

GREEN LANTERN! STOP STARING AT THE SKY AND GIVE US A HAND!
IF ANY OF YOU WISH TO SURVIVE, FLASH, YOU WILL FOLLOW MY LIGHT.
EARTH-462.
COME NOW.
TO THE PETRI DISH.
THOOM

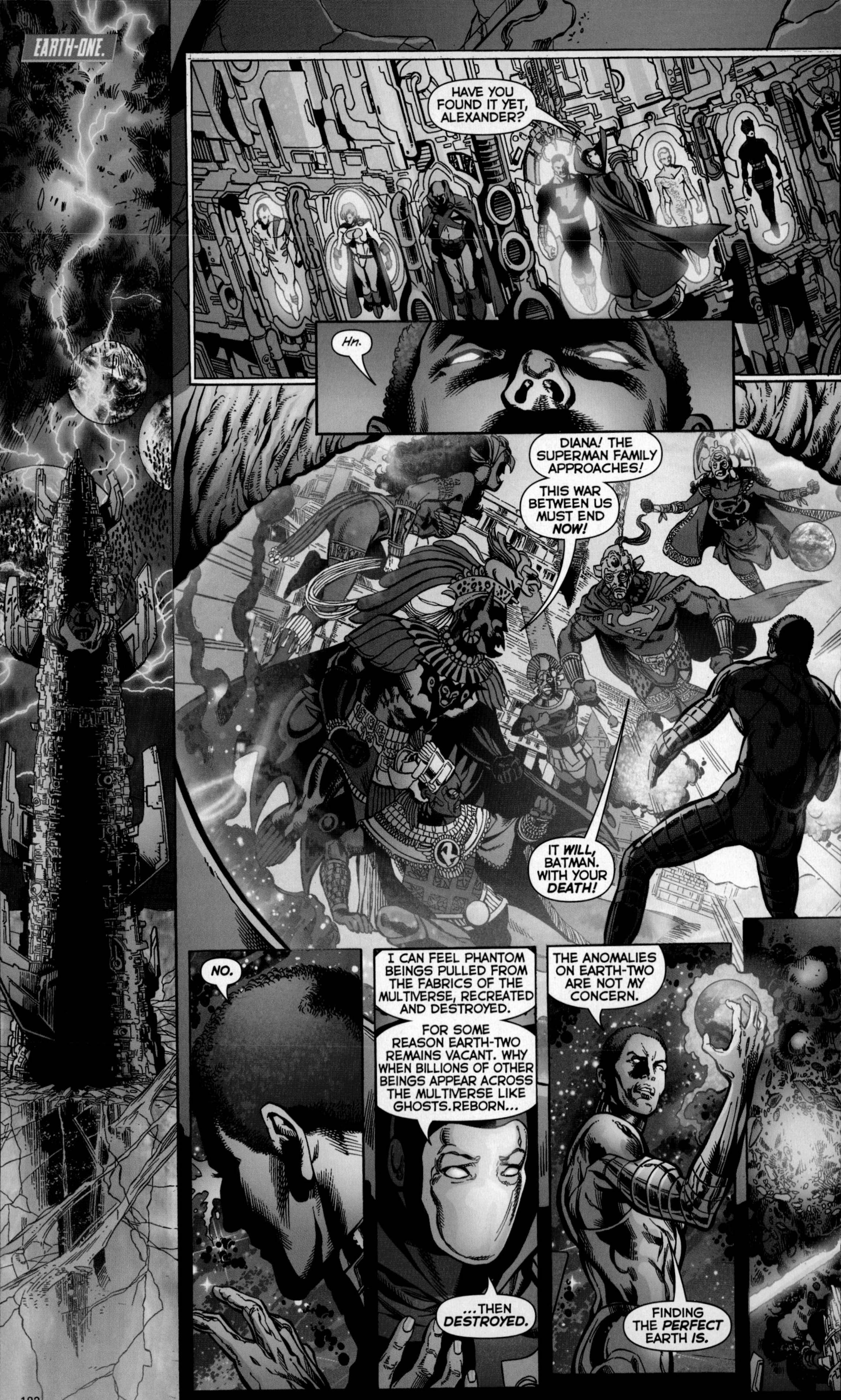
EARTH-ONE.
HAVE YOU FOUND IT YET, ALEXANDER?
Hn.
DIANA! THE SUPERMAN FAMILY APPROACHES!
THIS WAR BETWEEN US MUST END NOW!
IT WILL, BATMAN. WITH YOUR DEATH!
NO.
I CAN FEEL PHANTOM BEINGS PULLED FROM THE FABRICS OF THE MULTIVERSE, RECREATED AND DESTROYED.
FOR SOME REASON EARTH-TWO REMAINS VACANT. WHY WHEN BILLIONS OF OTHER BEINGS APPEAR ACROSS THE MULTIVERSE LIKE GHOSTS. REBORN...
...THEN DESTROYED.
THE ANOMALIES ON EARTH-TWO ARE NOT MY CONCERN.
FINDING THE PERFECT EARTH IS.

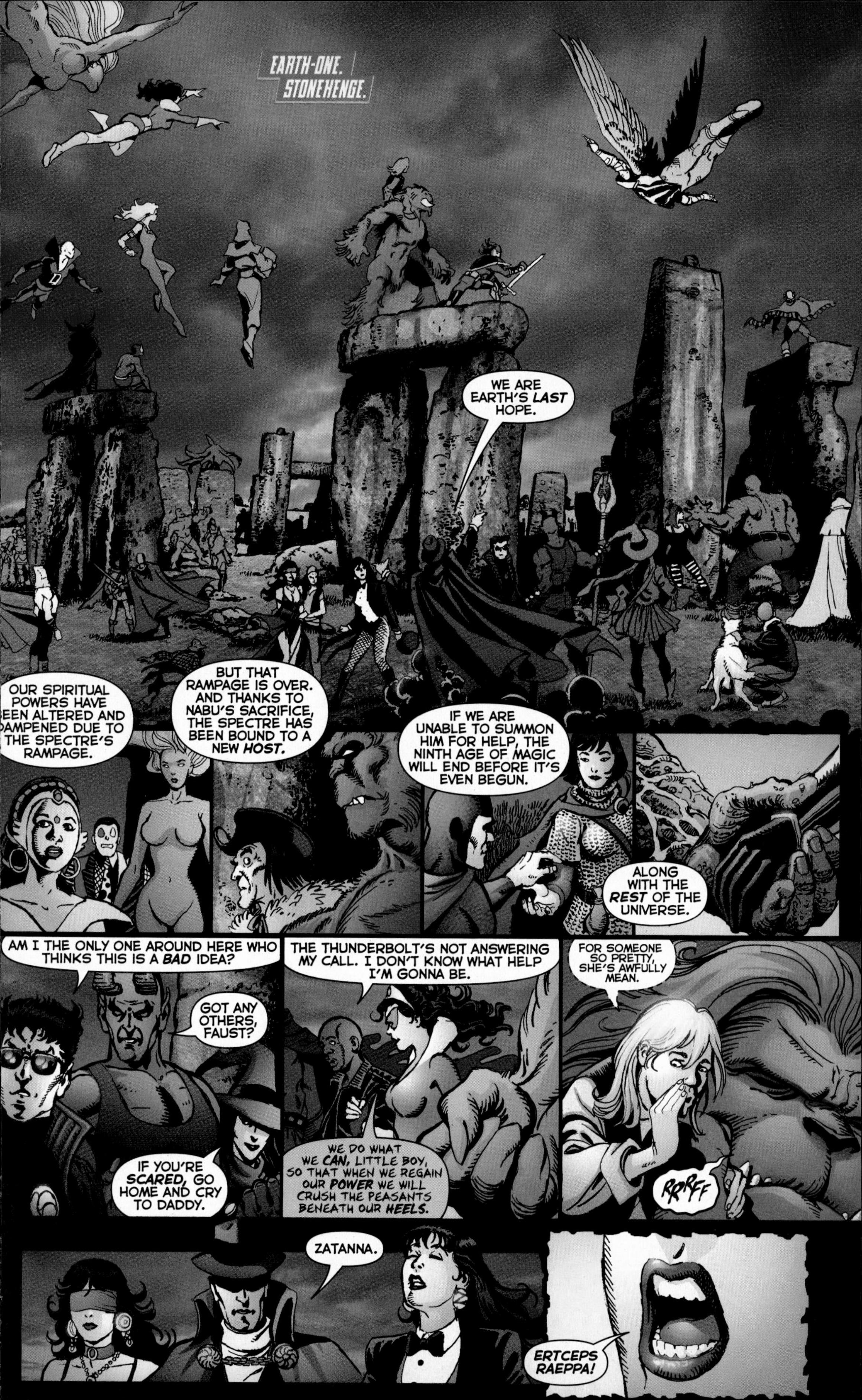
EARTH-ONE. STONEHENGE.
WE ARE EARTH'S LAST HOPE.
OUR SPIRITUAL POWERS HAVE BEEN ALTERED AND DAMPENED DUE TO THE SPECTRE'S RAMPAGE.
BUT THAT RAMPAGE IS OVER. AND THANKS TO NABU'S SACRIFICE, THE SPECTRE HAS BEEN BOUND TO A NEW HOST.
IF WE ARE UNABLE TO SUMMON HIM FOR HELP, THE NINTH AGE OF MAGIC WILL END BEFORE IT'S EVEN BEGUN.
ALONG WITH THE REST OF THE UNIVERSE.
AM I THE ONLY ONE AROUND HERE WHO THINKS THIS IS A BAD IDEA?
GOT ANY OTHERS, FAUST?
IF YOU'RE SCARED, GO HOME AND CRY TO DADDY.
THE THUNDERBOLT'S NOT ANSWERING MY CALL. I DON'T KNOW WHAT HELP I'M GONNA BE.
WE DO WHAT WE CAN, LITTLE BOY, SO THAT WHEN WE REGAIN OUR POWER WE WILL CRUSH THE PEASANTS BENEATH OUR HEELS.
FOR SOMEONE SO PRETTY, SHE'S AWFULLY MEAN.
RRRFF
ZATANNA.
ERTCEPS RAEPPA!

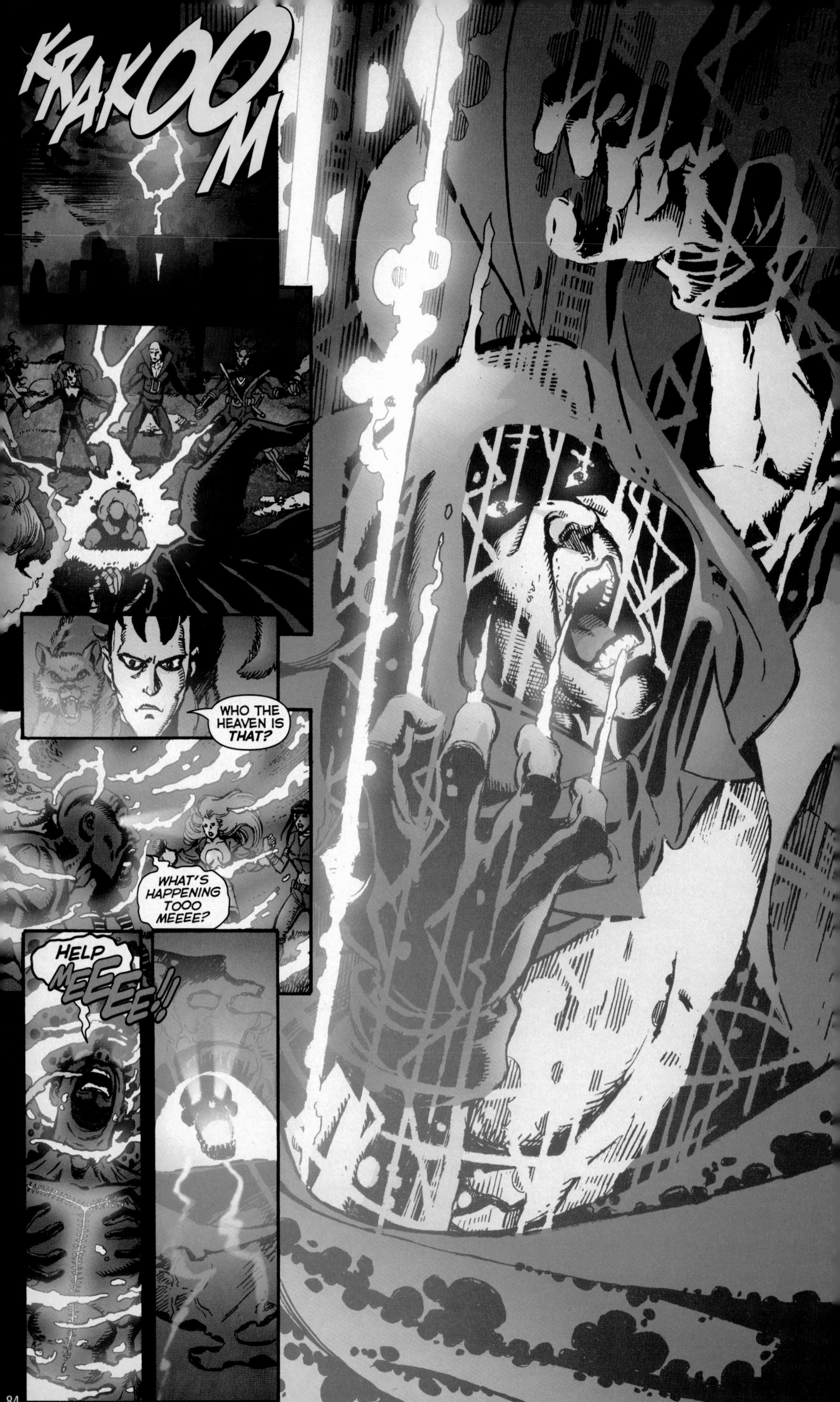
KRAKOOM
WHO THE HEAVEN IS THAT?
WHAT'S HAPPENING TOOO MEEEE?
HELP MEEEEE!!

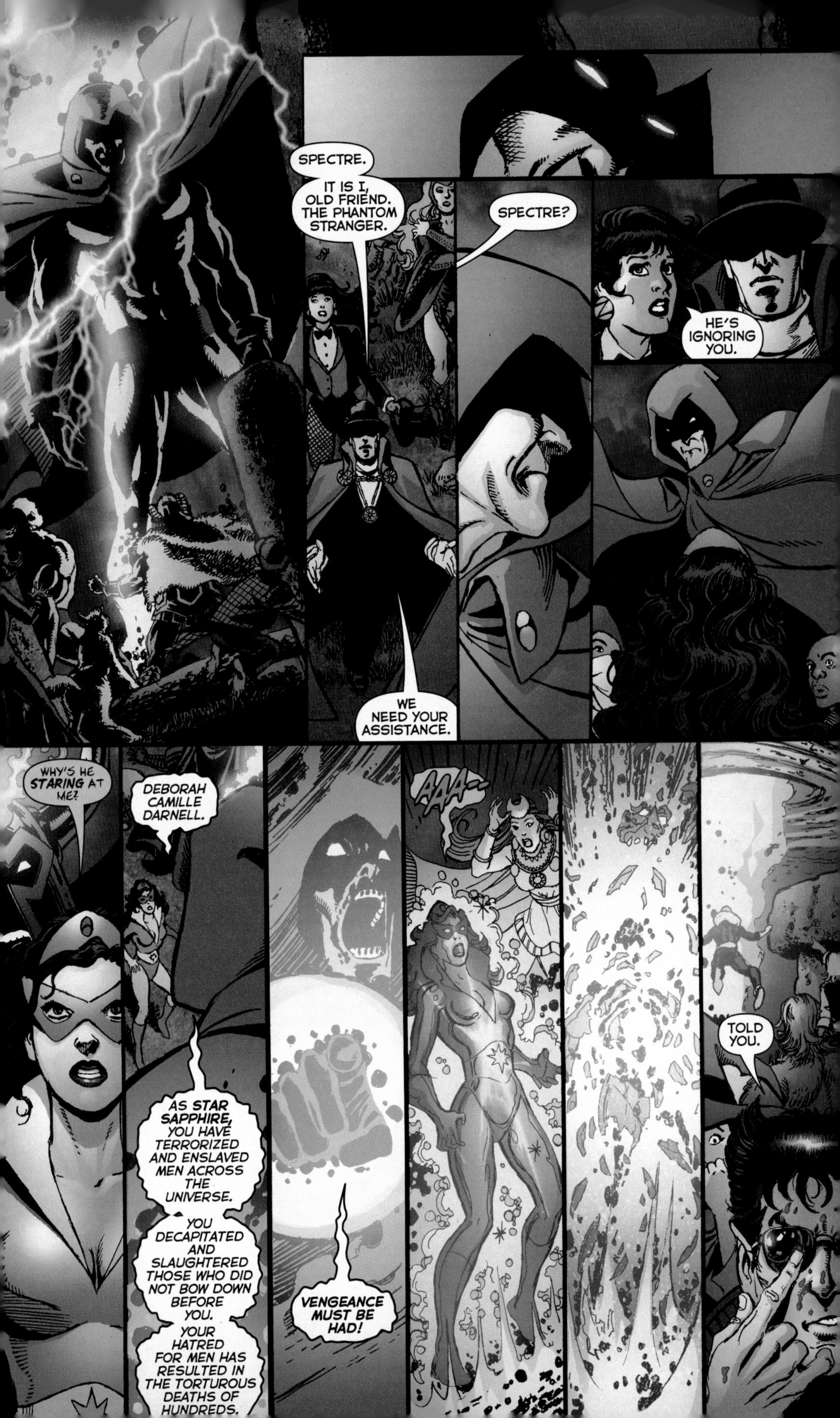
SPECTRE.
IT IS I, OLD FRIEND. THE PHANTOM STRANGER.
WE NEED YOUR ASSISTANCE.
SPECTRE?
HE'S IGNORING YOU.
WHY'S HE STARING AT ME?
DEBORAH CAMILLE DARNELL.
AS STAR SAPPHIRE, YOU HAVE TERRORIZED AND ENSLAVED MEN ACROSS THE UNIVERSE.
YOU DECAPITATED AND SLAUGHTERED THOSE WHO DID NOT BOW DOWN BEFORE YOU.
YOUR HATRED FOR MEN HAS RESULTED IN THE TORTUROUS DEATHS OF HUNDREDS.
VENGEANCE MUST BE HAD!
AAA--
TOLD YOU.

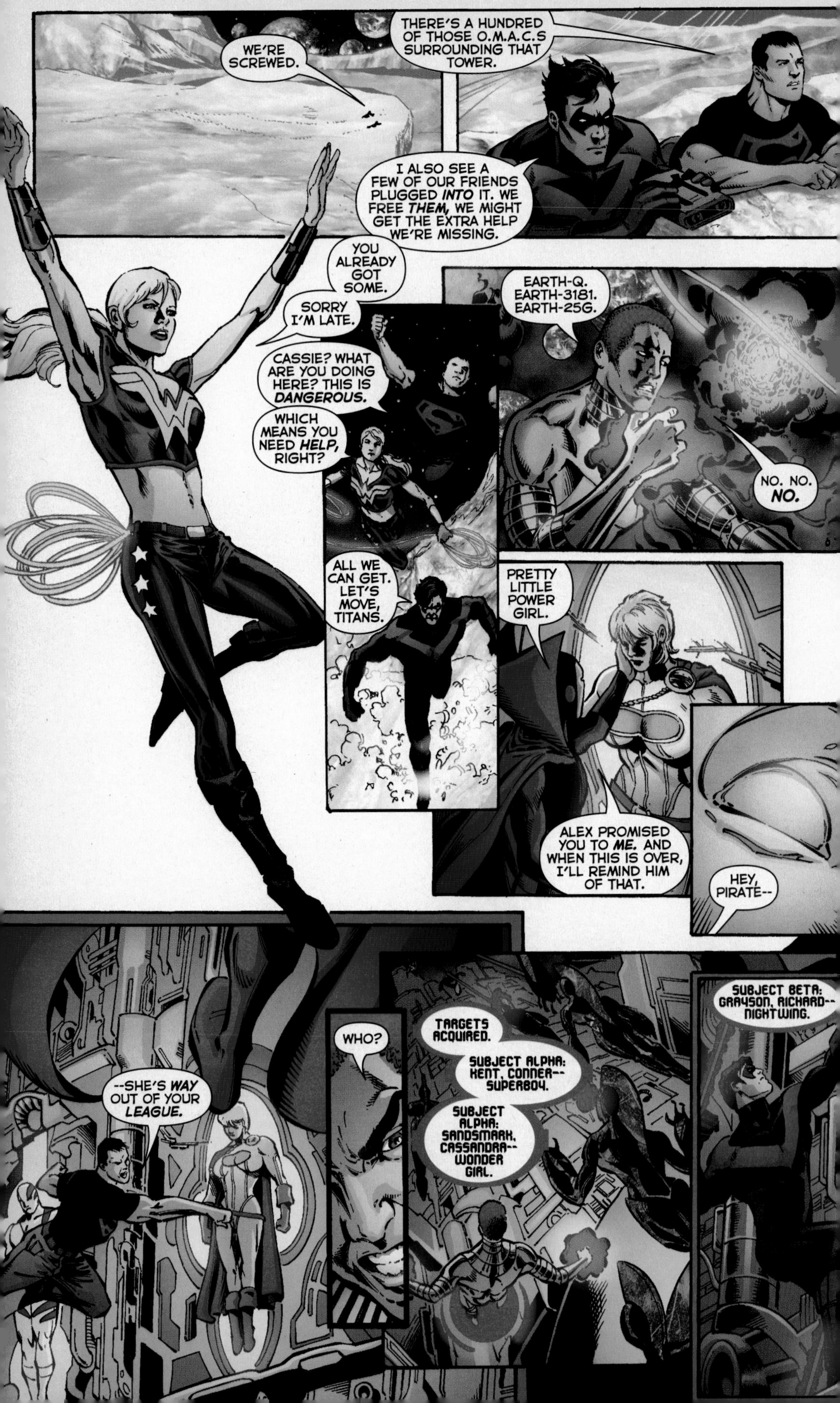

WE'RE SCREWED.
THERE'S A HUNDRED OF THOSE O.M.A.C.S SURROUNDING THAT TOWER.
I ALSO SEE A FEW OF OUR FRIENDS PLUGGED INTO IT. WE FREE THEM, WE MIGHT GET THE EXTRA HELP WE'RE MISSING.
YOU ALREADY GOT SOME.
SORRY I'M LATE.
CASSIE? WHAT ARE YOU DOING HERE? THIS IS DANGEROUS.
WHICH MEANS YOU NEED HELP, RIGHT?
ALL WE CAN GET. LET'S MOVE, TITANS.
EARTH-Q. EARTH-3181. EARTH-25G.
NO. NO. NO.
PRETTY LITTLE POWER GIRL.
ALEX PROMISED YOU TO ME. AND WHEN THIS IS OVER, I'LL REMIND HIM OF THAT.
HEY, PIRATE--
--SHE'S WAY OUT OF YOUR LEAGUE.
WHO?
TARGETS ACQUIRED.
SUBJECT ALPHA: KENT, CONNER--SUPERBOY.
SUBJECT ALPHA: SANDSMARK, CASSANDRA--WONDER GIRL.
SUBJECT BETA: GRAYSON, RICHARD--NIGHTWING.

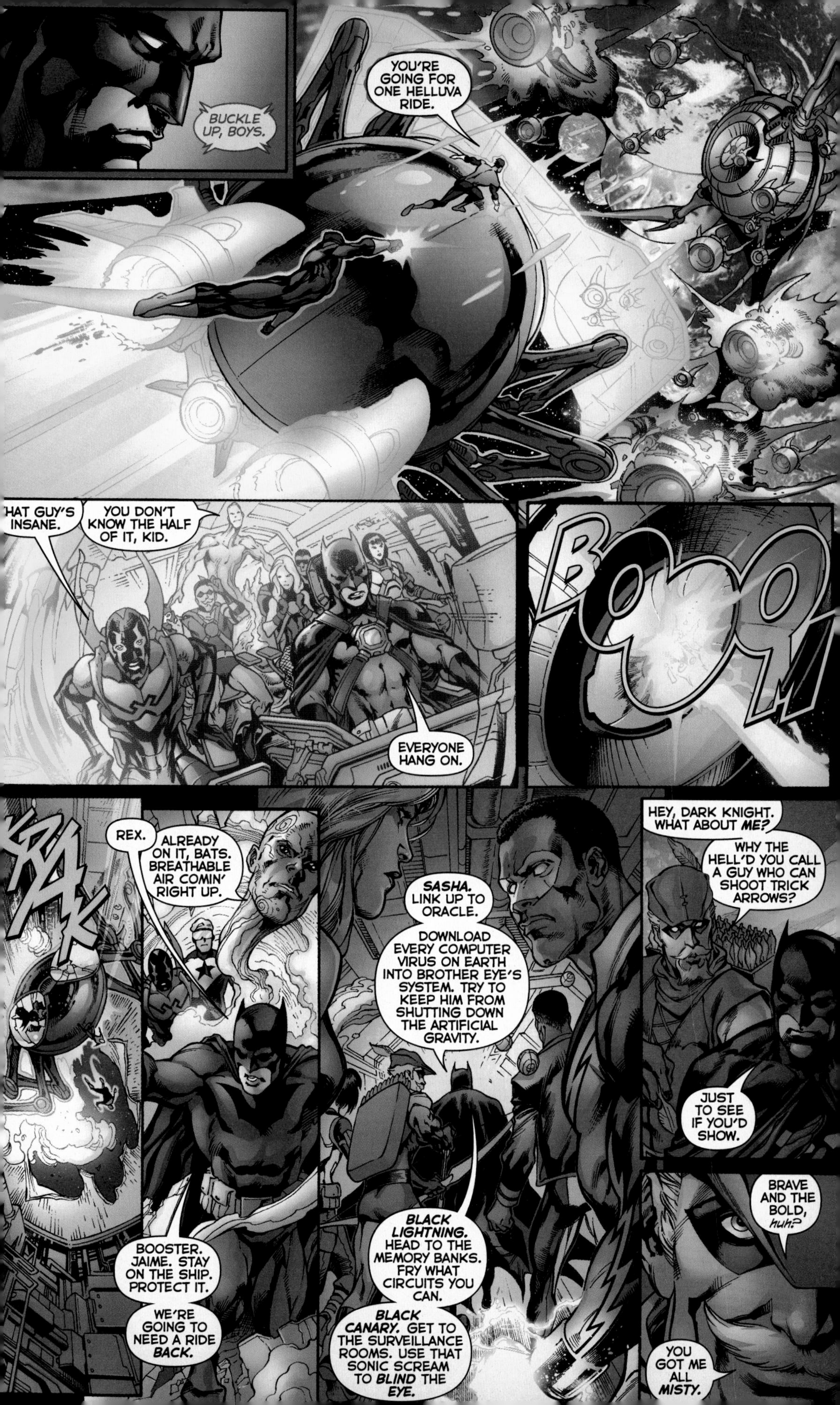
BUCKLE UP, BOYS.
YOU'RE GOING FOR ONE HELLUVA RIDE.
HAT GUY'S INSANE.
YOU DON'T KNOW THE HALF OF IT, KID.
EVERYONE HANG ON.
BOOM
REX.
ALREADY ON IT, BATS. BREATHABLE AIR COMIN' RIGHT UP.
BOOSTER. JAIME. STAY ON THE SHIP. PROTECT IT.
WE'RE GOING TO NEED A RIDE BACK.
SASHA. LINK UP TO ORACLE.
DOWNLOAD EVERY COMPUTER VIRUS ON EARTH INTO BROTHER EYE'S SYSTEM. TRY TO KEEP HIM FROM SHUTTING DOWN THE ARTIFICIAL GRAVITY.
BLACK LIGHTNING. HEAD TO THE MEMORY BANKS. FRY WHAT CIRCUITS YOU CAN.
BLACK CANARY. GET TO THE SURVEILLANCE ROOMS. USE THAT SONIC SCREAM TO BLIND THE EYE.
HEY, DARK KNIGHT. WHAT ABOUT ME?
WHY THE HELL'D YOU CALL A GUY WHO CAN SHOOT TRICK ARROWS?
JUST TO SEE IF YOU'D SHOW.
BRAVE AND THE BOLD, huh?
YOU GOT ME ALL MISTY.

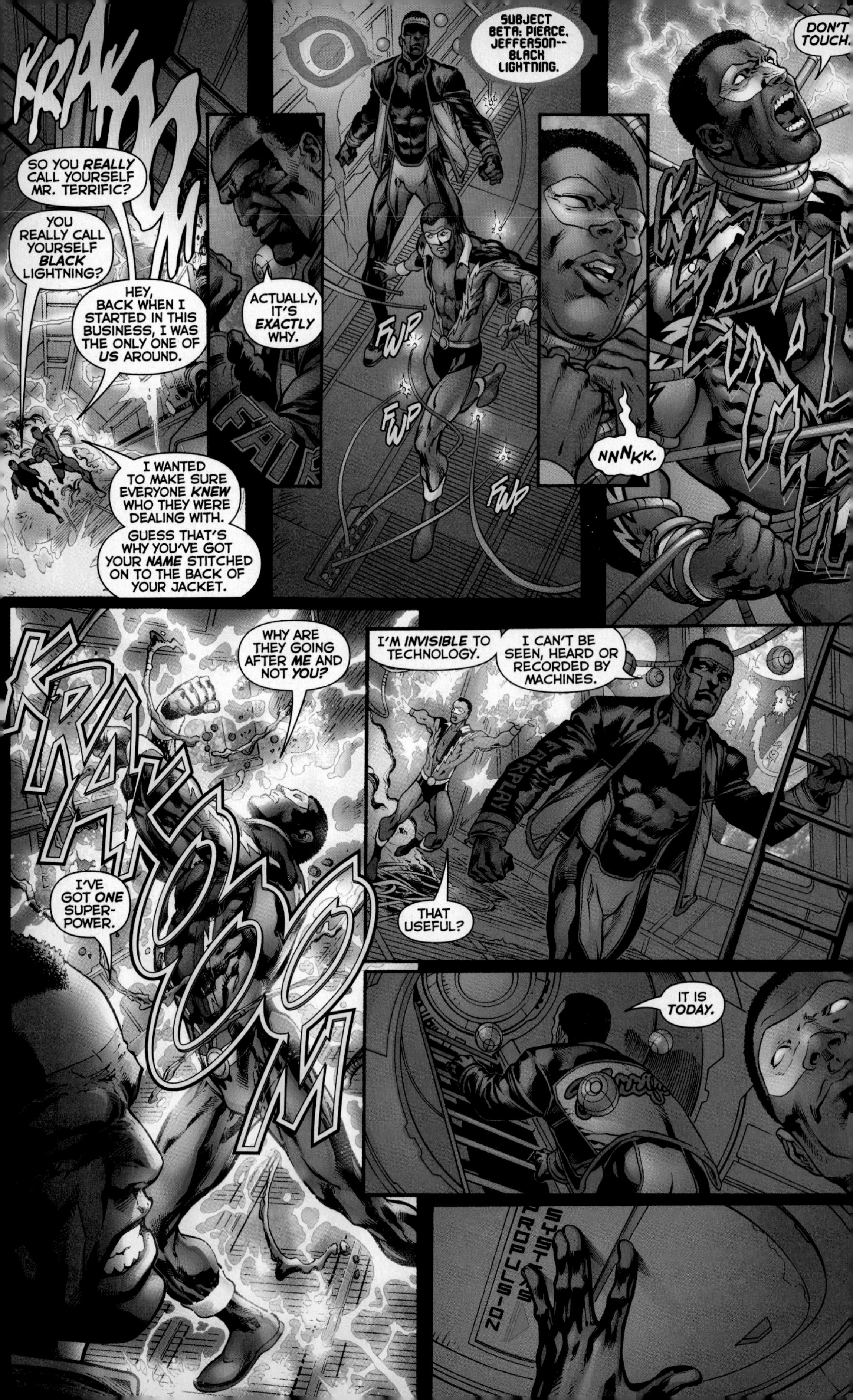
KRAKOOM
SO YOU REALLY CALL YOURSELF MR. TERRIFIC?
YOU REALLY CALL YOURSELF BLACK LIGHTNING?
HEY, BACK WHEN I STARTED IN THIS BUSINESS, I WAS THE ONLY ONE OF US AROUND.
I WANTED TO MAKE SURE EVERYONE KNEW WHO THEY WERE DEALING WITH.
GUESS THAT'S WHY YOU'VE GOT YOUR NAME STITCHED ON TO THE BACK OF YOUR JACKET.
ACTUALLY, IT'S EXACTLY WHY.
SUBJECT BETA: PIERCE, JEFFERSON-- BLACK LIGHTNING.
FWP
FWP
FWP
NNNKK.
DON'T TOUCH.
KRAKAKOOOM
WHY ARE THEY GOING AFTER ME AND NOT YOU?
I'VE GOT ONE SUPER-POWER.
I'M INVISIBLE TO TECHNOLOGY.
I CAN'T BE SEEN, HEARD OR RECORDED BY MACHINES.
THAT USEFUL?
IT IS TODAY.
PROPULSION SYSTEMS

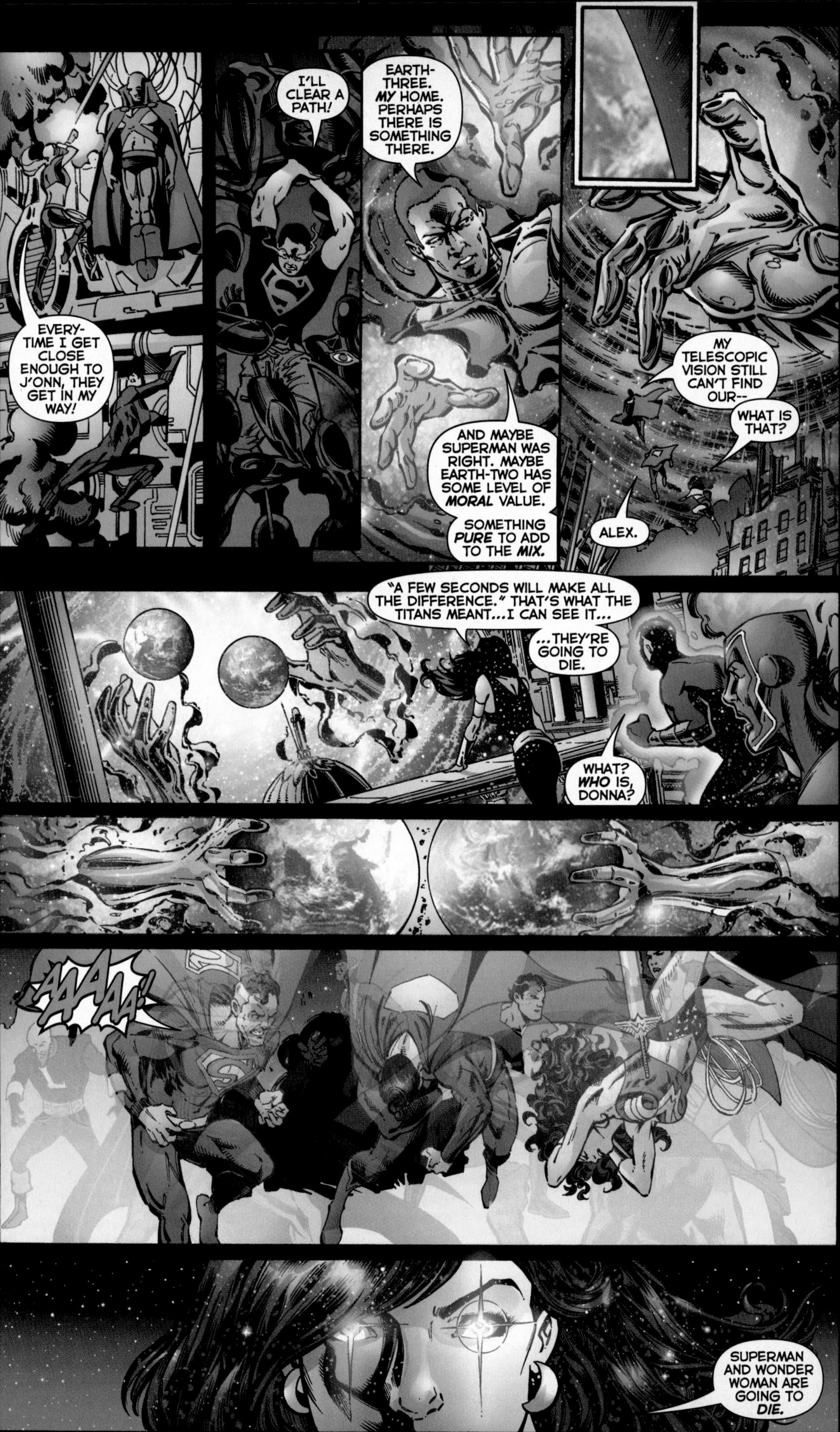
EVERY-TIME I GET CLOSE ENOUGH TO J'ONN, THEY GET IN MY WAY!
I'LL CLEAR A PATH!
EARTH-THREE. MY HOME. PERHAPS THERE IS SOMETHING THERE.
AND MAYBE SUPERMAN WAS RIGHT. MAYBE EARTH-TWO HAS SOME LEVEL OF MORAL VALUE.
SOMETHING PURE TO ADD TO THE MIX.
MY TELESCOPIC VISION STILL CAN'T FIND OUR--
WHAT IS THAT?
ALEX.
"A FEW SECONDS WILL MAKE ALL THE DIFFERENCE." THAT'S WHAT THE TITANS MEANT...I CAN SEE IT...
...THEY'RE GOING TO DIE.
WHAT? WHO IS, DONNA?
AAAAA!
SUPERMAN AND WONDER WOMAN ARE GOING TO DIE.

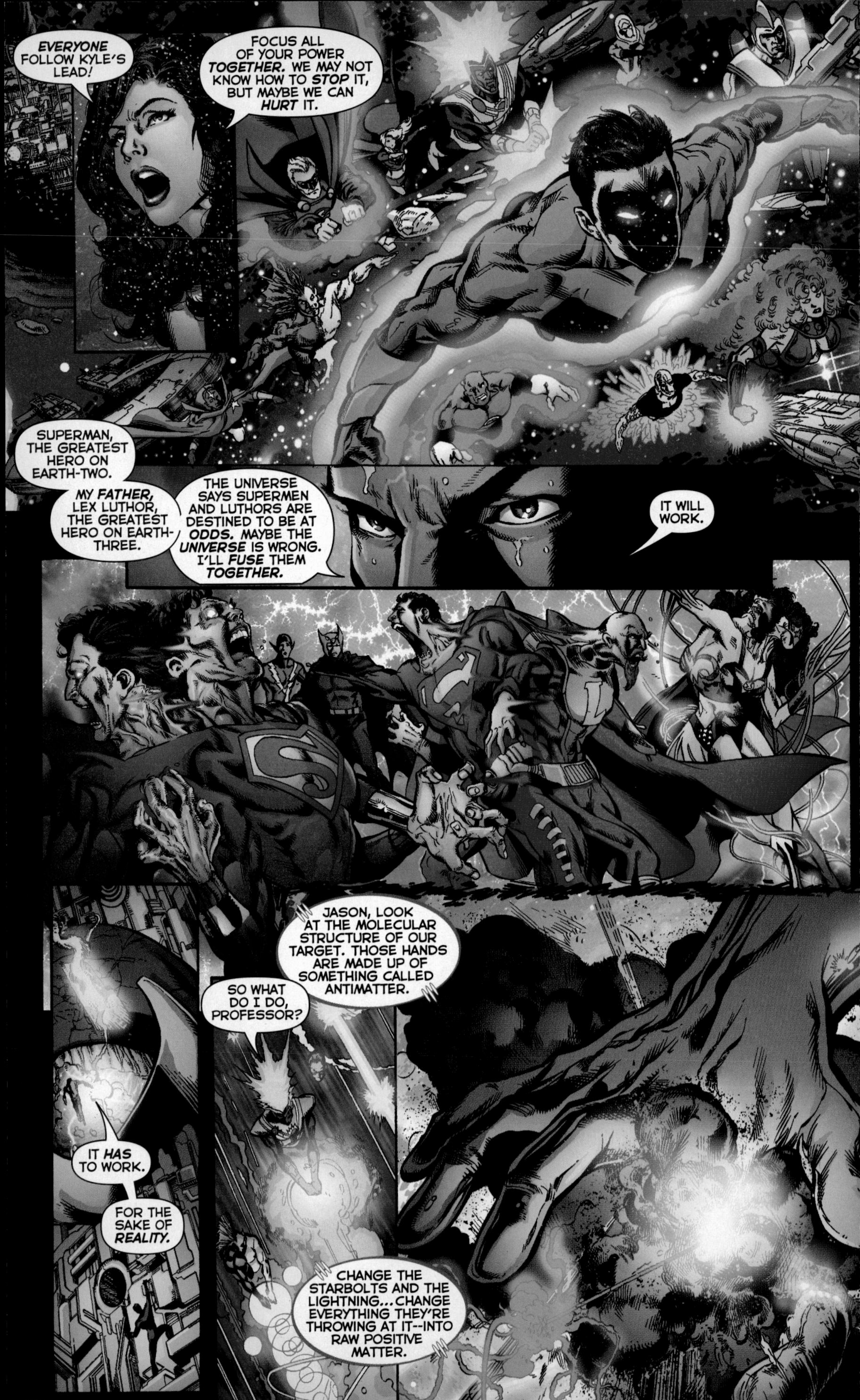
EVERYONE FOLLOW KYLE'S LEAD!
FOCUS ALL OF YOUR POWER TOGETHER. WE MAY NOT KNOW HOW TO STOP IT, BUT MAYBE WE CAN HURT IT.
SUPERMAN, THE GREATEST HERO ON EARTH-TWO.
MY FATHER, LEX LUTHOR, THE GREATEST HERO ON EARTH-THREE.
THE UNIVERSE SAYS SUPERMEN AND LUTHORS ARE DESTINED TO BE AT ODDS. MAYBE THE UNIVERSE IS WRONG. I'LL FUSE THEM TOGETHER.
IT WILL WORK.
IT HAS TO WORK.
FOR THE SAKE OF REALITY.
JASON, LOOK AT THE MOLECULAR STRUCTURE OF OUR TARGET. THOSE HANDS ARE MADE UP OF SOMETHING CALLED ANTIMATTER.
SO WHAT DO I DO, PROFESSOR?
CHANGE THE STARBOLTS AND THE LIGHTNING...CHANGE EVERYTHING THEY'RE THROWING AT IT--INTO RAW POSITIVE MATTER.

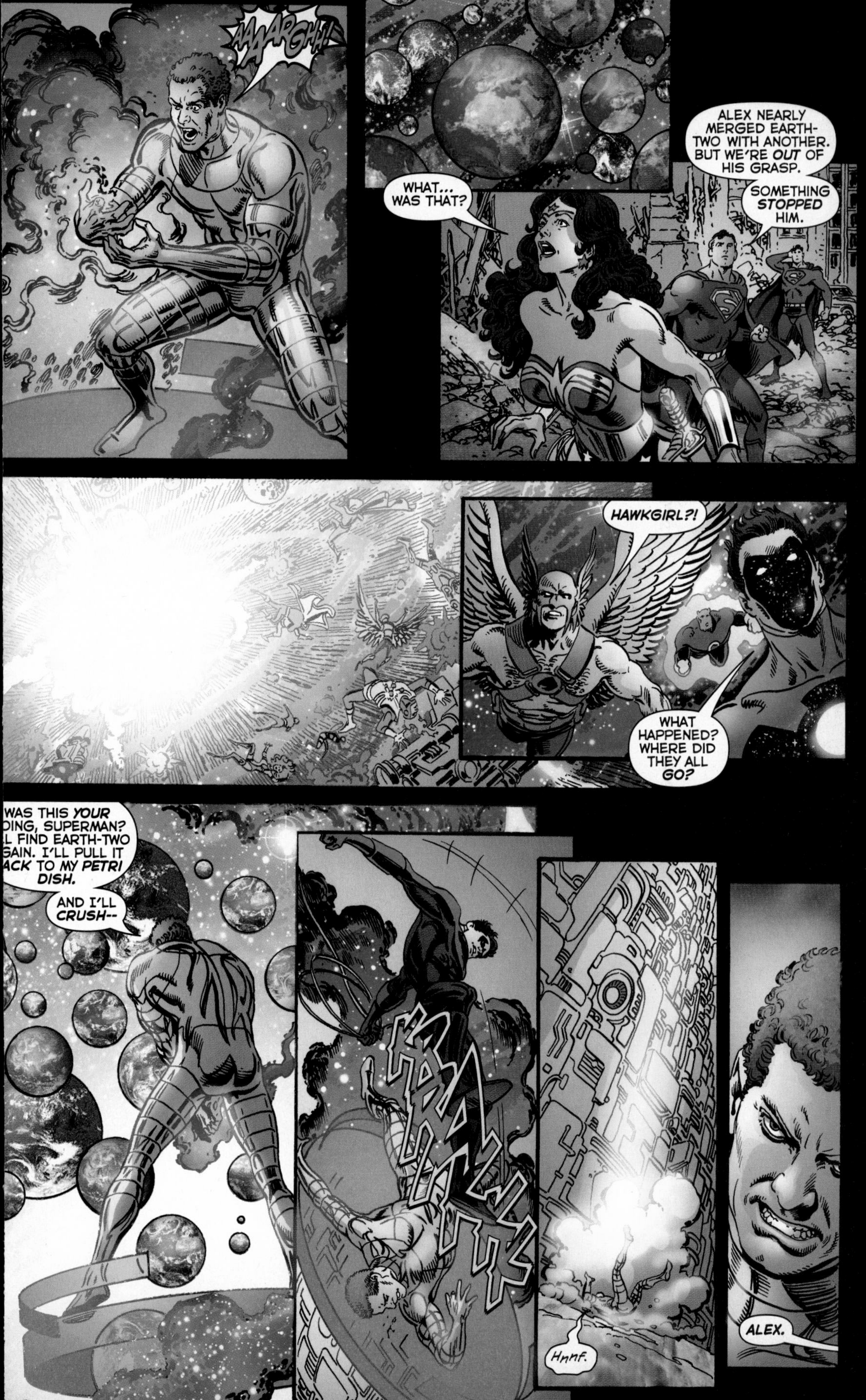
AAAARGH!
WHAT... WAS THAT?
ALEX NEARLY MERGED EARTH-TWO WITH ANOTHER. BUT WE'RE *OUT* OF HIS GRASP.
SOMETHING *STOPPED* HIM.
HAWKGIRL?!
WHAT HAPPENED? WHERE DID THEY ALL *GO?*
WAS THIS *YOUR* DOING, SUPERMAN? ...L FIND EARTH-TWO ...GAIN. I'LL PULL IT ...ACK TO MY *PETRI DISH.*
AND I'LL *CRUSH--*
Hnnf.
ALEX.

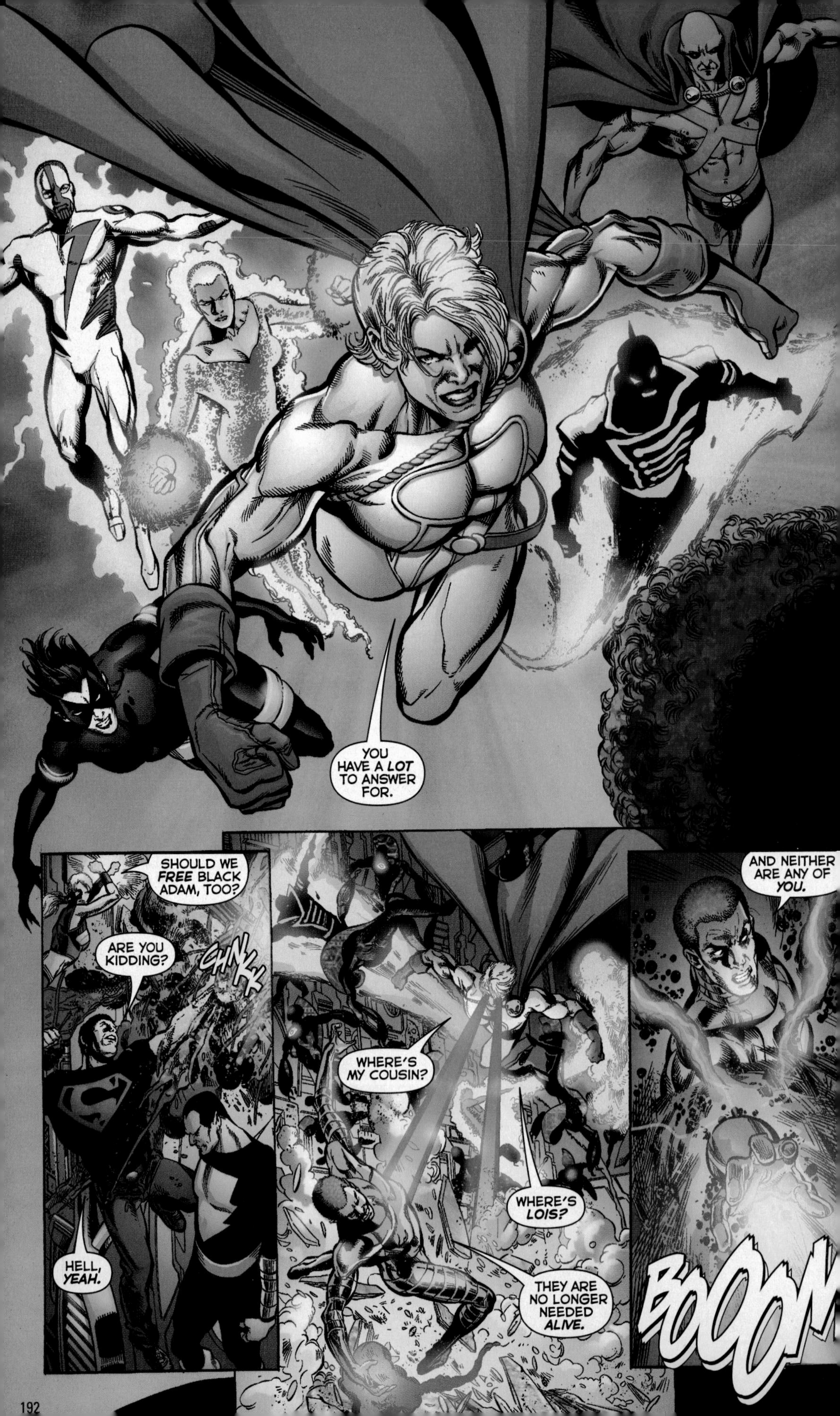

YOU HAVE A LOT TO ANSWER FOR.
SHOULD WE FREE BLACK ADAM, TOO?
ARE YOU KIDDING?
CHNKK
HELL, YEAH.
WHERE'S MY COUSIN?
WHERE'S LOIS?
THEY ARE NO LONGER NEEDED ALIVE.
AND NEITHER ARE ANY OF YOU.
BOOOM

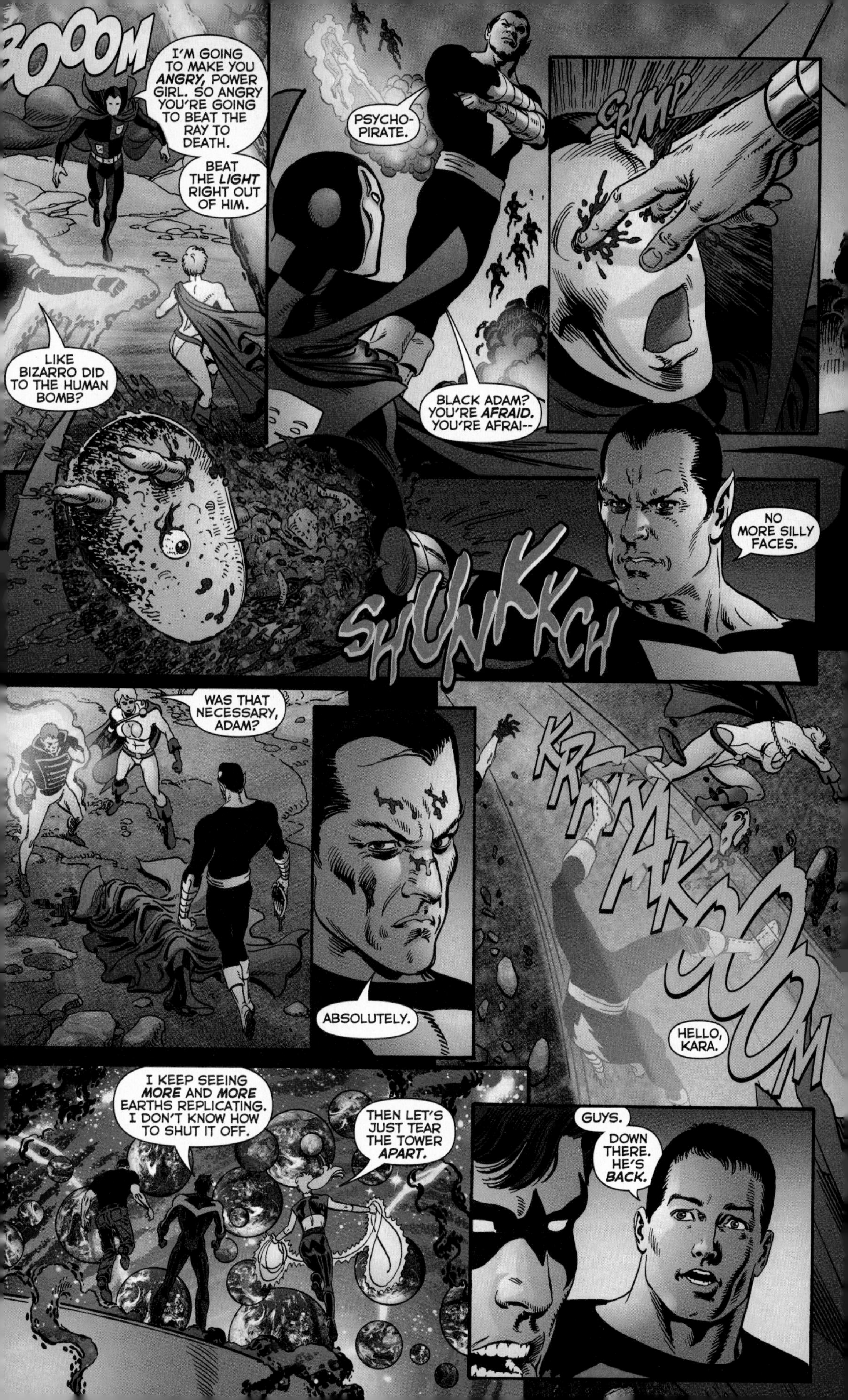
BOOOM
I'M GOING TO MAKE YOU ANGRY, POWER GIRL. SO ANGRY YOU'RE GOING TO BEAT THE RAY TO DEATH.
BEAT THE LIGHT RIGHT OUT OF HIM.
LIKE BIZARRO DID TO THE HUMAN BOMB?
PSYCHO-PIRATE.
BLACK ADAM? YOU'RE AFRAID. YOU'RE AFRAI--
NO MORE SILLY FACES.
SHUNKKCH
WAS THAT NECESSARY, ADAM?
ABSOLUTELY.
HELLO, KARA.
I KEEP SEEING MORE AND MORE EARTHS REPLICATING. I DON'T KNOW HOW TO SHUT IT OFF.
THEN LET'S JUST TEAR THE TOWER APART.
GUYS.
DOWN THERE. HE'S BACK.

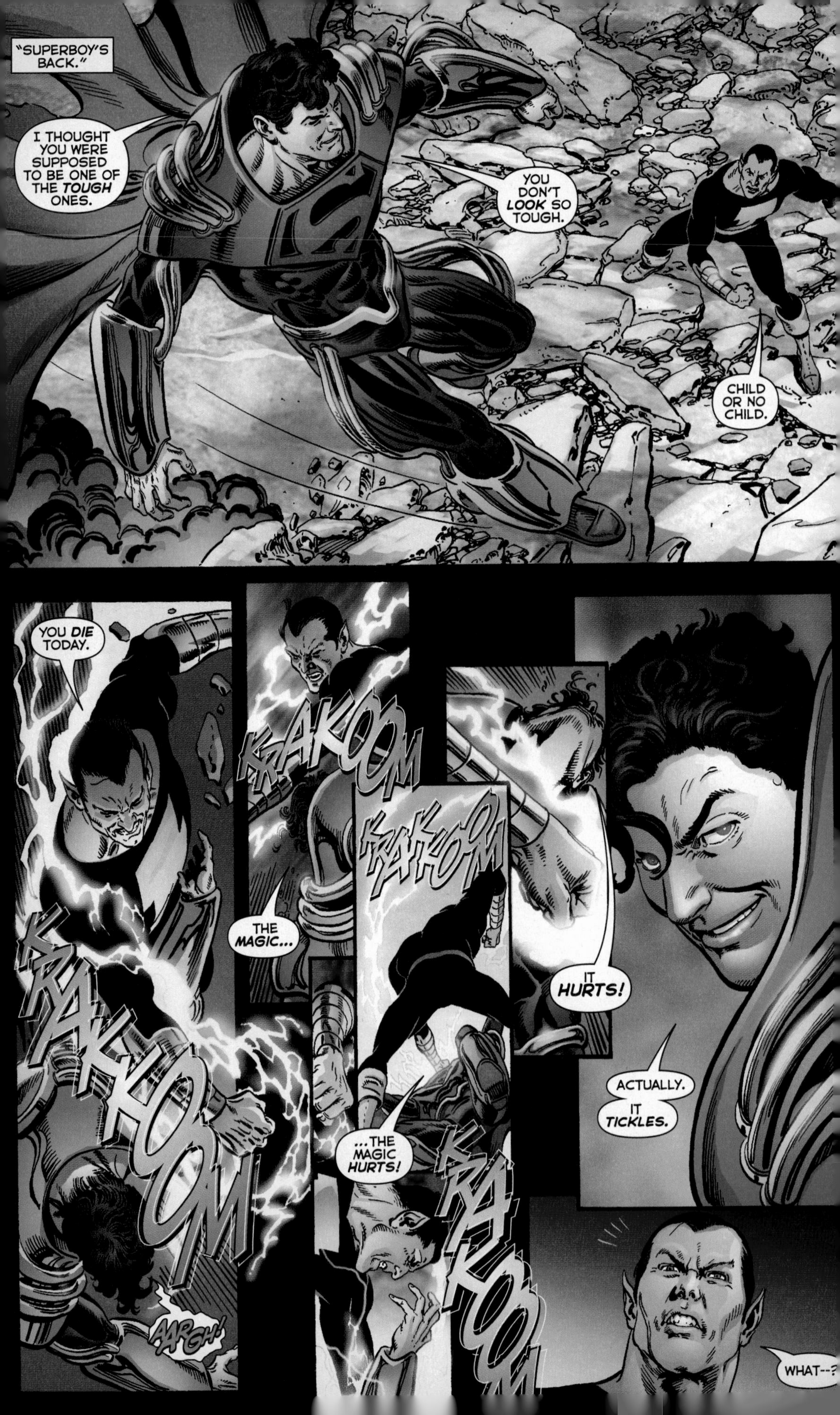
"SUPERBOY'S BACK."
I THOUGHT YOU WERE SUPPOSED TO BE ONE OF THE TOUGH ONES.
YOU DON'T LOOK SO TOUGH.
CHILD OR NO CHILD.
YOU DIE TODAY.
KRAKOOM
KRAKOOM
THE MAGIC...
KRAKOOM
IT HURTS!
...THE MAGIC HURTS!
KRAKOOM
AARGH!
KRAKOOM
ACTUALLY. IT TICKLES.
WHAT--?

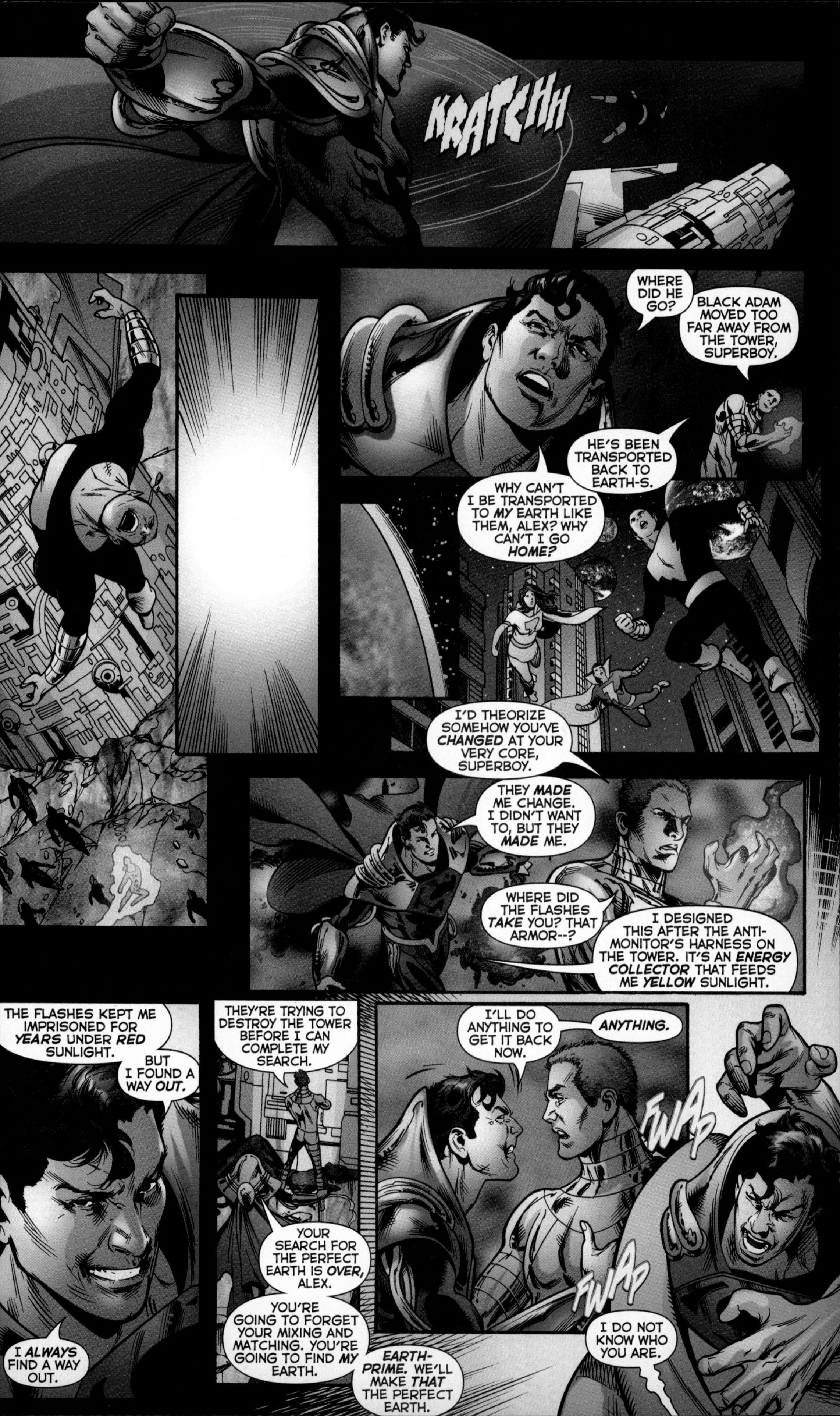
KRATCHH
WHERE DID HE GO?
BLACK ADAM MOVED TOO FAR AWAY FROM THE TOWER, SUPERBOY.
HE'S BEEN TRANSPORTED BACK TO EARTH-S.
WHY CAN'T I BE TRANSPORTED TO MY EARTH LIKE THEM, ALEX? WHY CAN'T I GO HOME?
I'D THEORIZE SOMEHOW YOU'VE CHANGED AT YOUR VERY CORE, SUPERBOY.
THEY MADE ME CHANGE. I DIDN'T WANT TO, BUT THEY MADE ME.
WHERE DID THE FLASHES TAKE YOU? THAT ARMOR--?
I DESIGNED THIS AFTER THE ANTI-MONITOR'S HARNESS ON THE TOWER. IT'S AN ENERGY COLLECTOR THAT FEEDS ME YELLOW SUNLIGHT.
THE FLASHES KEPT ME IMPRISONED FOR YEARS UNDER RED SUNLIGHT.
BUT I FOUND A WAY OUT.
I ALWAYS FIND A WAY OUT.
THEY'RE TRYING TO DESTROY THE TOWER BEFORE I CAN COMPLETE MY SEARCH.
YOUR SEARCH FOR THE PERFECT EARTH IS OVER, ALEX.
YOU'RE GOING TO FORGET YOUR MIXING AND MATCHING. YOU'RE GOING TO FIND MY EARTH.
EARTH-PRIME. WE'LL MAKE THAT THE PERFECT EARTH.
I'LL DO ANYTHING TO GET IT BACK NOW.
ANYTHING.
FWAP
FWAP
I DO NOT KNOW WHO YOU ARE.

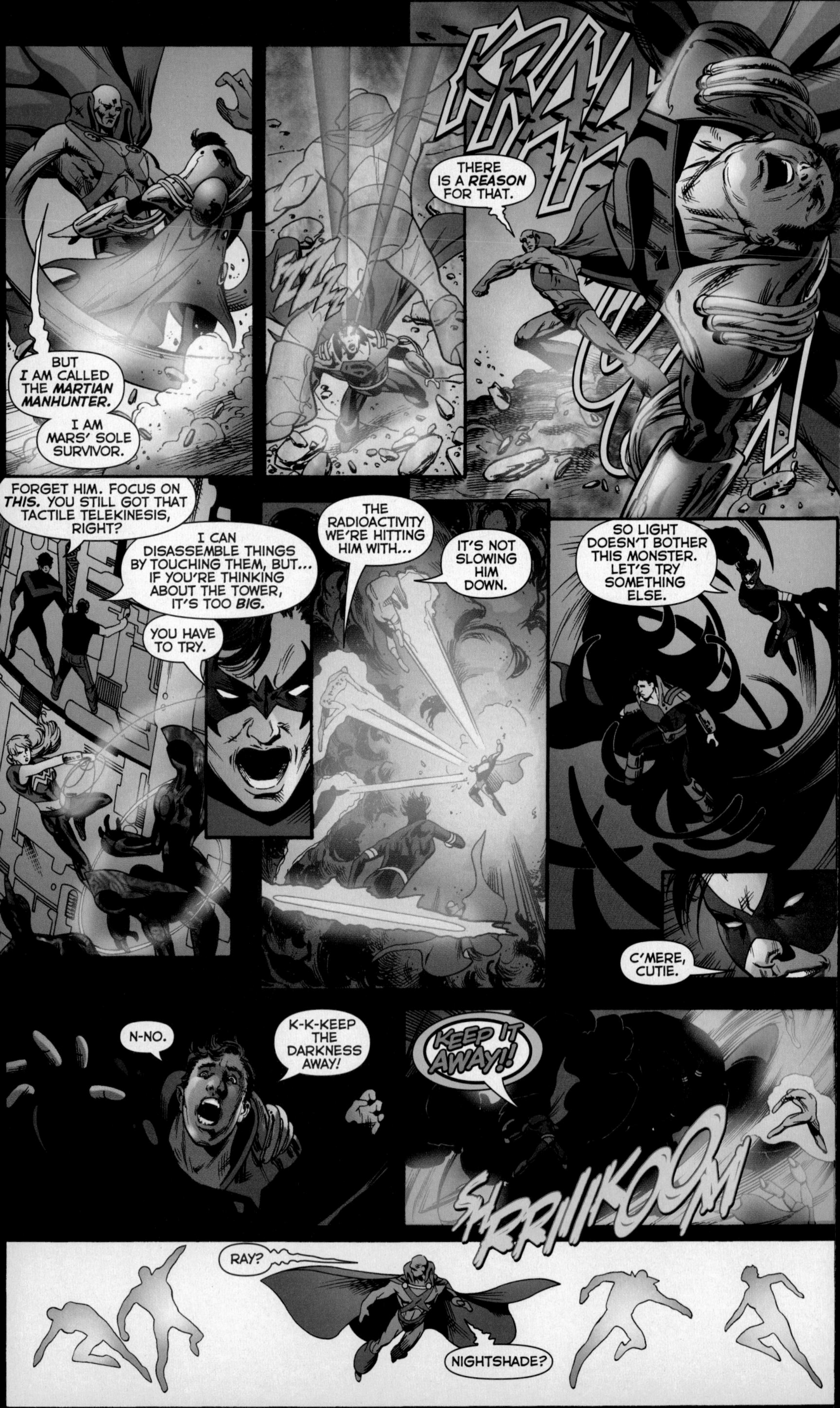
BUT I AM CALLED THE MARTIAN MANHUNTER.
I AM MARS' SOLE SURVIVOR.
FZZZ
THERE IS A REASON FOR THAT.
KRAKKOOM
FORGET HIM. FOCUS ON THIS. YOU STILL GOT THAT TACTILE TELEKINESIS, RIGHT?
I CAN DISASSEMBLE THINGS BY TOUCHING THEM, BUT... IF YOU'RE THINKING ABOUT THE TOWER, IT'S TOO BIG.
YOU HAVE TO TRY.
THE RADIOACTIVITY WE'RE HITTING HIM WITH...
IT'S NOT SLOWING HIM DOWN.
SO LIGHT DOESN'T BOTHER THIS MONSTER. LET'S TRY SOMETHING ELSE.
C'MERE, CUTIE.
N-NO.
K-K-KEEP THE DARKNESS AWAY!
KEEP IT AWAY!!
SHRRIIIKOOM
RAY?
NIGHTSHADE?

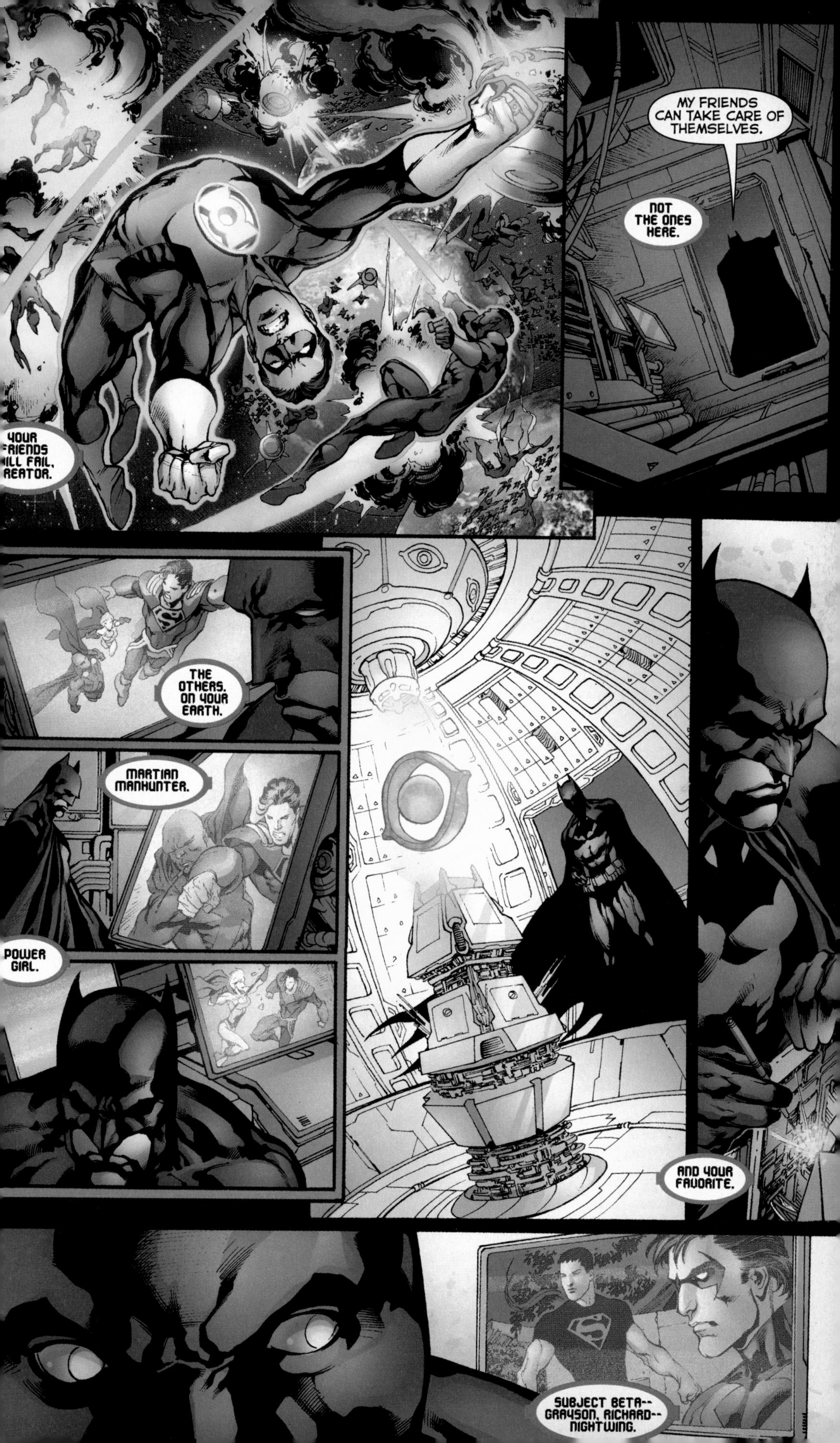
MY FRIENDS CAN TAKE CARE OF THEMSELVES.
NOT THE ONES HERE.
YOUR FRIENDS WILL FAIL, CREATOR.
THE OTHERS. ON YOUR EARTH.
MARTIAN MANHUNTER.
POWER GIRL.
AND YOUR FAVORITE.
SUBJECT BETA-- GRAYSON, RICHARD-- NIGHTWING.

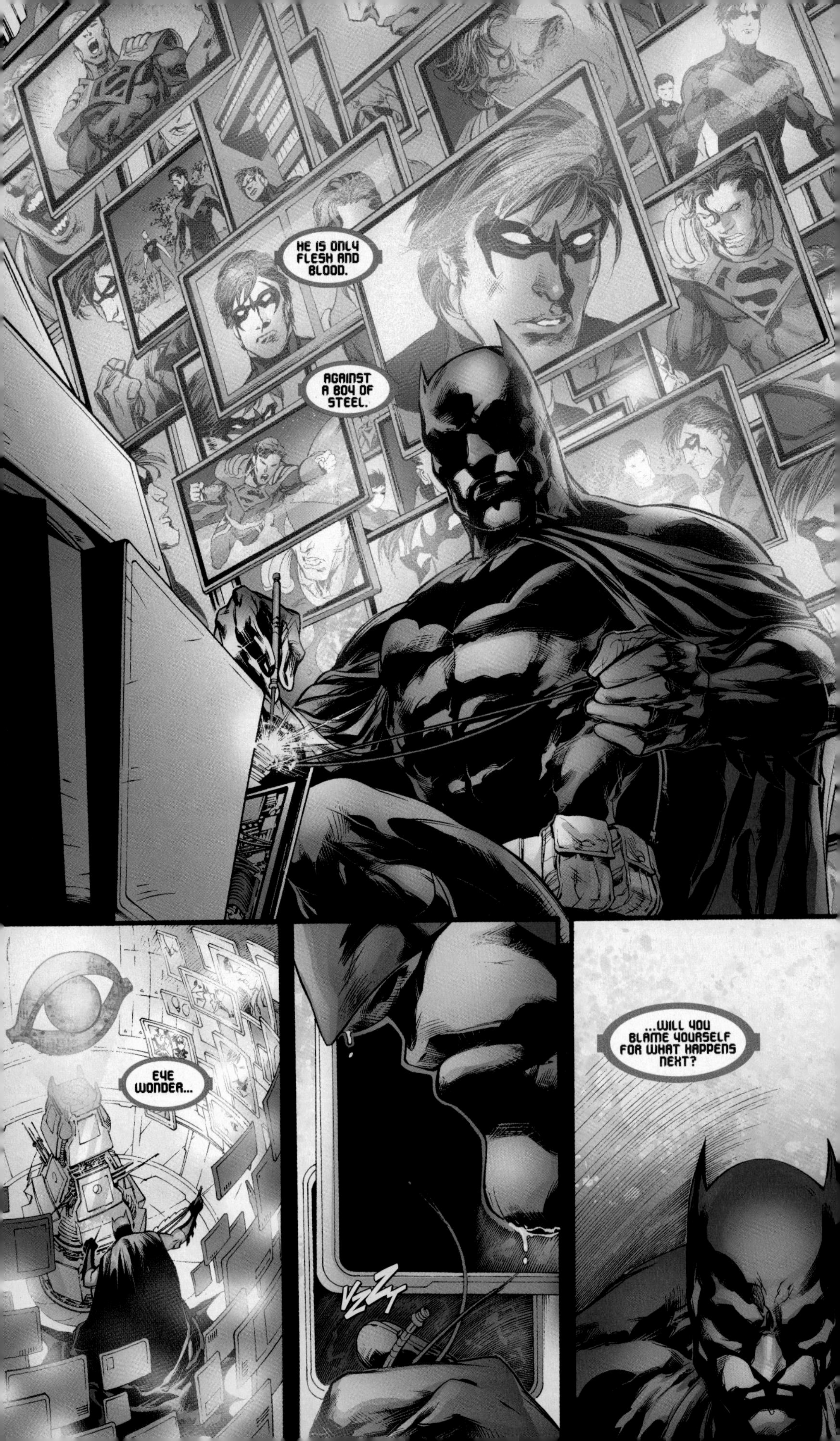
HE IS ONLY FLESH AND BLOOD.
AGAINST A BOY OF STEEL.
EYE WONDER...
VZZZ
...WILL YOU BLAME YOURSELF FOR WHAT HAPPENS NEXT?

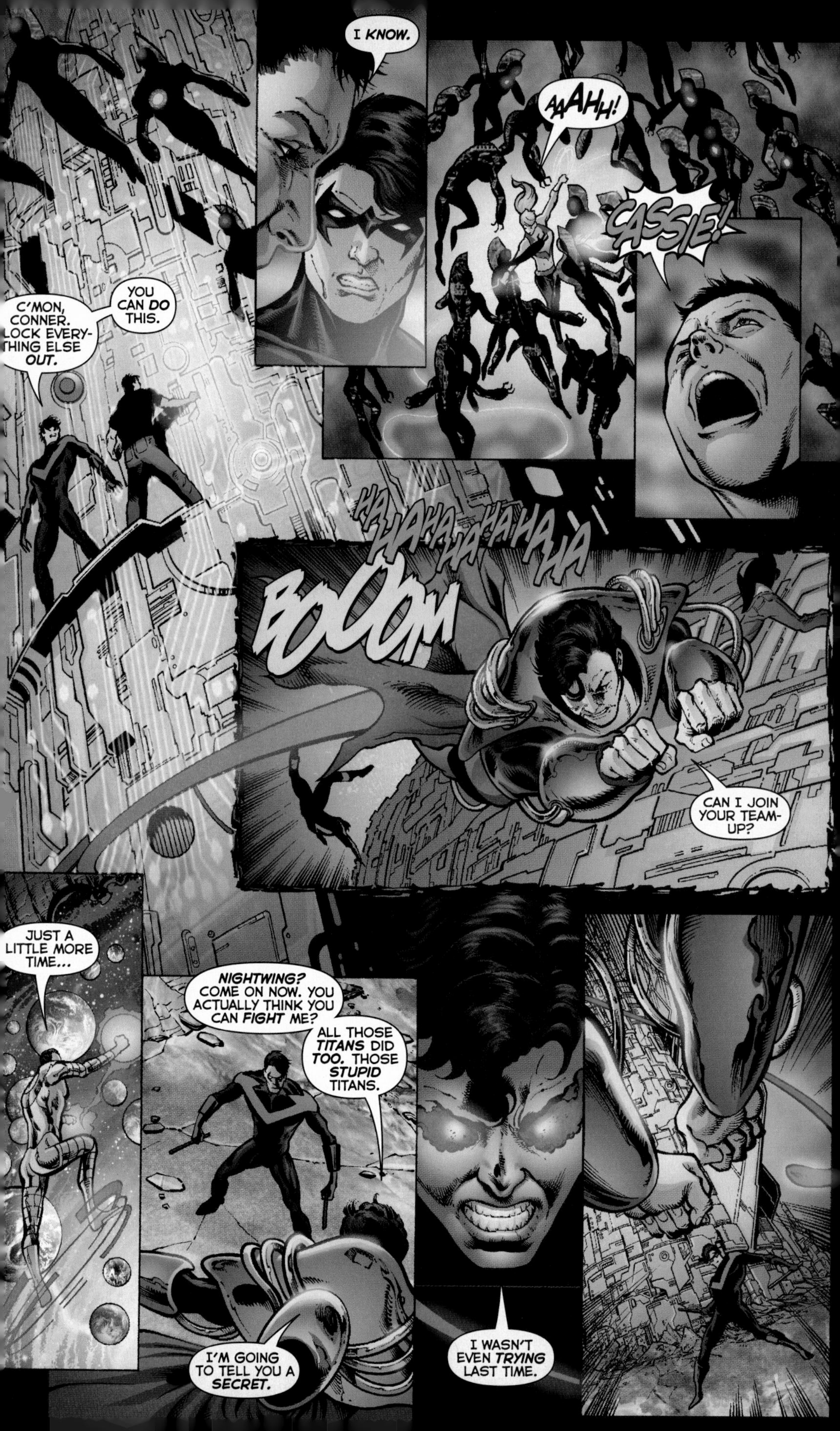

C'MON, CONNER. LOCK EVERY-THING ELSE OUT.
YOU CAN DO THIS.
I KNOW.
AAAHH!
CASSIE!
HAHAHAHAHAHAHAHA
BOOOM
CAN I JOIN YOUR TEAM-UP?
JUST A LITTLE MORE TIME...
NIGHTWING? COME ON NOW. YOU ACTUALLY THINK YOU CAN FIGHT ME?
ALL THOSE TITANS DID TOO. THOSE STUPID TITANS.
I'M GOING TO TELL YOU A SECRET.
I WASN'T EVEN TRYING LAST TIME.

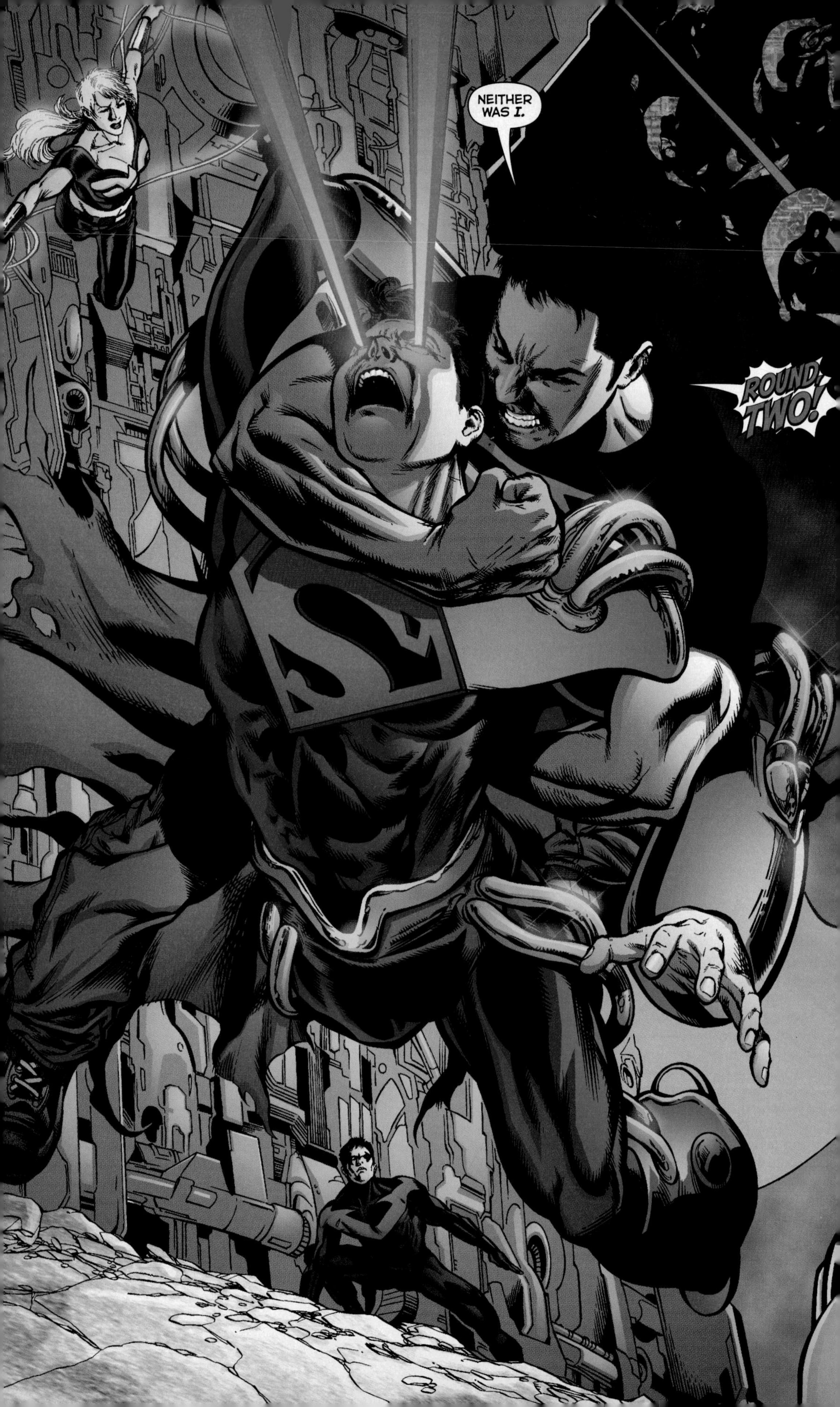
NEITHER WAS I.
ROUND TWO!

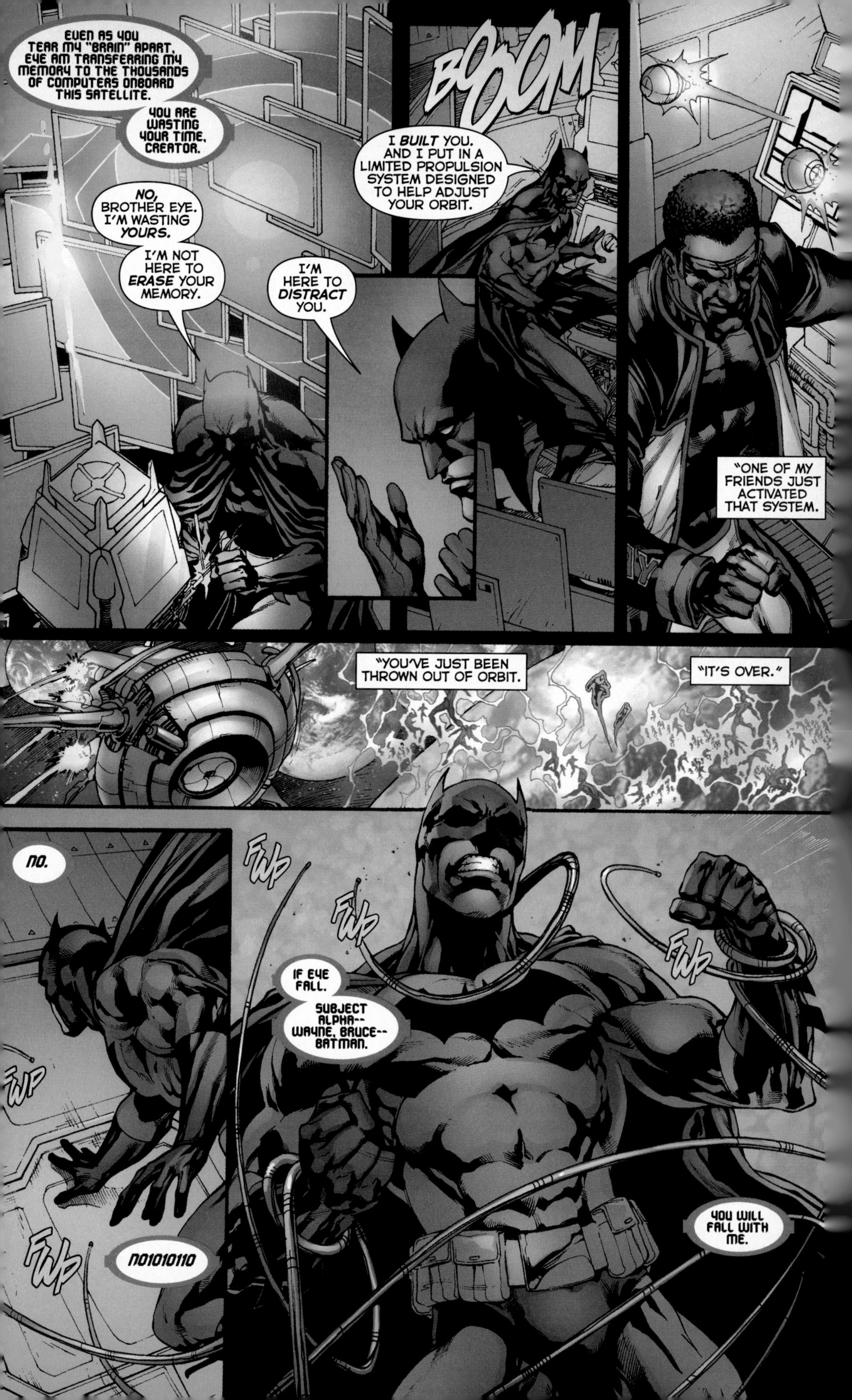
EVEN AS YOU TEAR MY "BRAIN" APART, EYE AM TRANSFERRING MY MEMORY TO THE THOUSANDS OF COMPUTERS ONBOARD THIS SATELLITE.
YOU ARE WASTING YOUR TIME, CREATOR.
NO, BROTHER EYE. I'M WASTING YOURS.
I'M NOT HERE TO ERASE YOUR MEMORY.
I'M HERE TO DISTRACT YOU.
BOOOM
I BUILT YOU. AND I PUT IN A LIMITED PROPULSION SYSTEM DESIGNED TO HELP ADJUST YOUR ORBIT.
"ONE OF MY FRIENDS JUST ACTIVATED THAT SYSTEM.
"YOU'VE JUST BEEN THROWN OUT OF ORBIT.
"IT'S OVER."
NO.
FWP
FWP
FWP
IF EYE FALL.
SUBJECT ALPHA-- WAYNE, BRUCE-- BATMAN.
FWP
FWP
N01010110
YOU WILL FALL WITH ME.

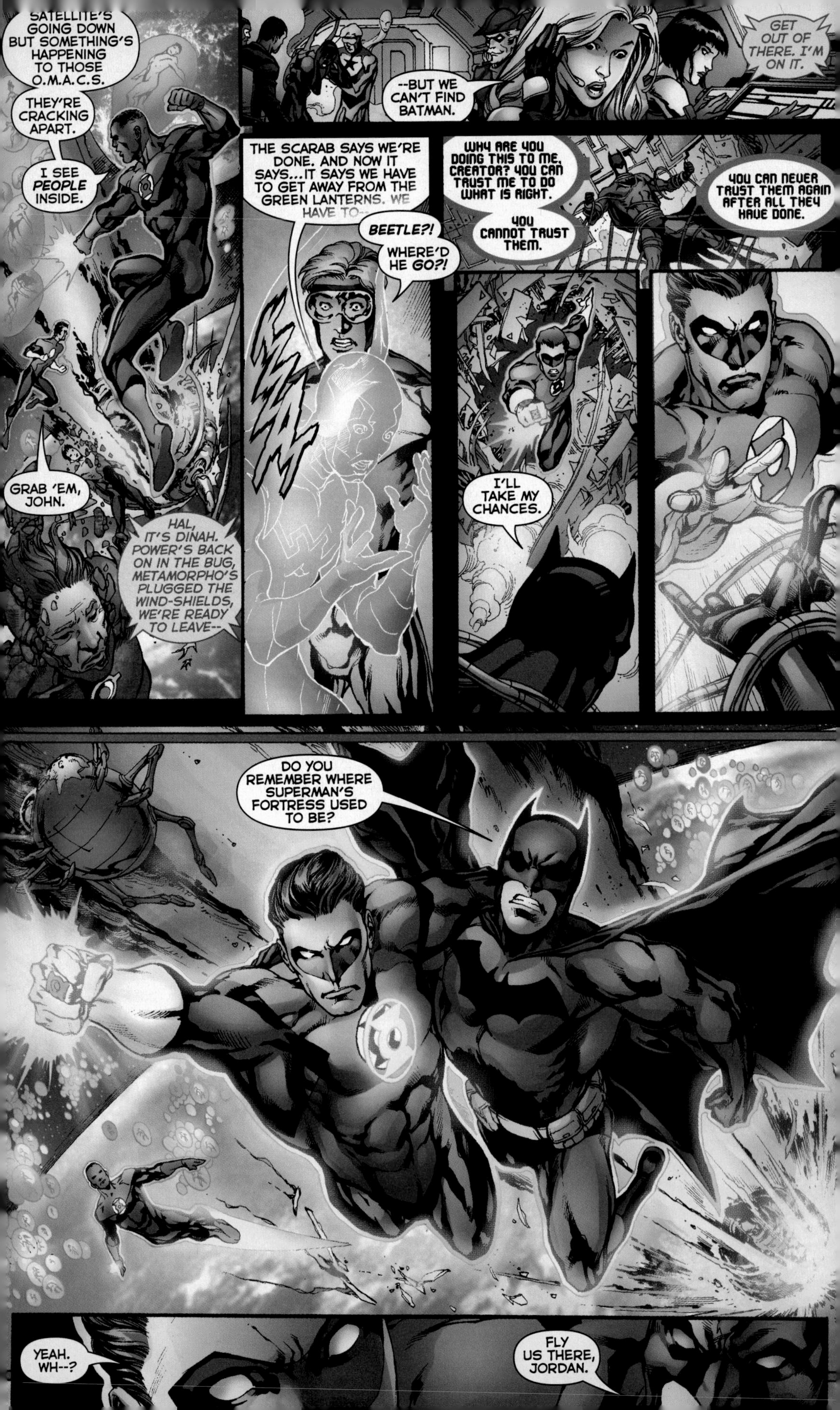
SATELLITE'S GOING DOWN BUT SOMETHING'S HAPPENING TO THOSE O.M.A.C.S.
THEY'RE CRACKING APART.
I SEE PEOPLE INSIDE.
GRAB 'EM, JOHN.
HAL, IT'S DINAH. POWER'S BACK ON IN THE BUG, METAMORPHO'S PLUGGED THE WIND-SHIELDS, WE'RE READY TO LEAVE--
--BUT WE CAN'T FIND BATMAN.
GET OUT OF THERE. I'M ON IT.
THE SCARAB SAYS WE'RE DONE. AND NOW IT SAYS... IT SAYS WE HAVE TO GET AWAY FROM THE GREEN LANTERNS. WE HAVE TO--
BEETLE?!
WHERE'D HE GO?!
WHY ARE YOU DOING THIS TO ME, CREATOR? YOU CAN TRUST ME TO DO WHAT IS RIGHT.
YOU CANNOT TRUST THEM.
YOU CAN NEVER TRUST THEM AGAIN AFTER ALL THEY HAVE DONE.
I'LL TAKE MY CHANCES.
DO YOU REMEMBER WHERE SUPERMAN'S FORTRESS USED TO BE?
YEAH. WH--?
FLY US THERE, JORDAN.

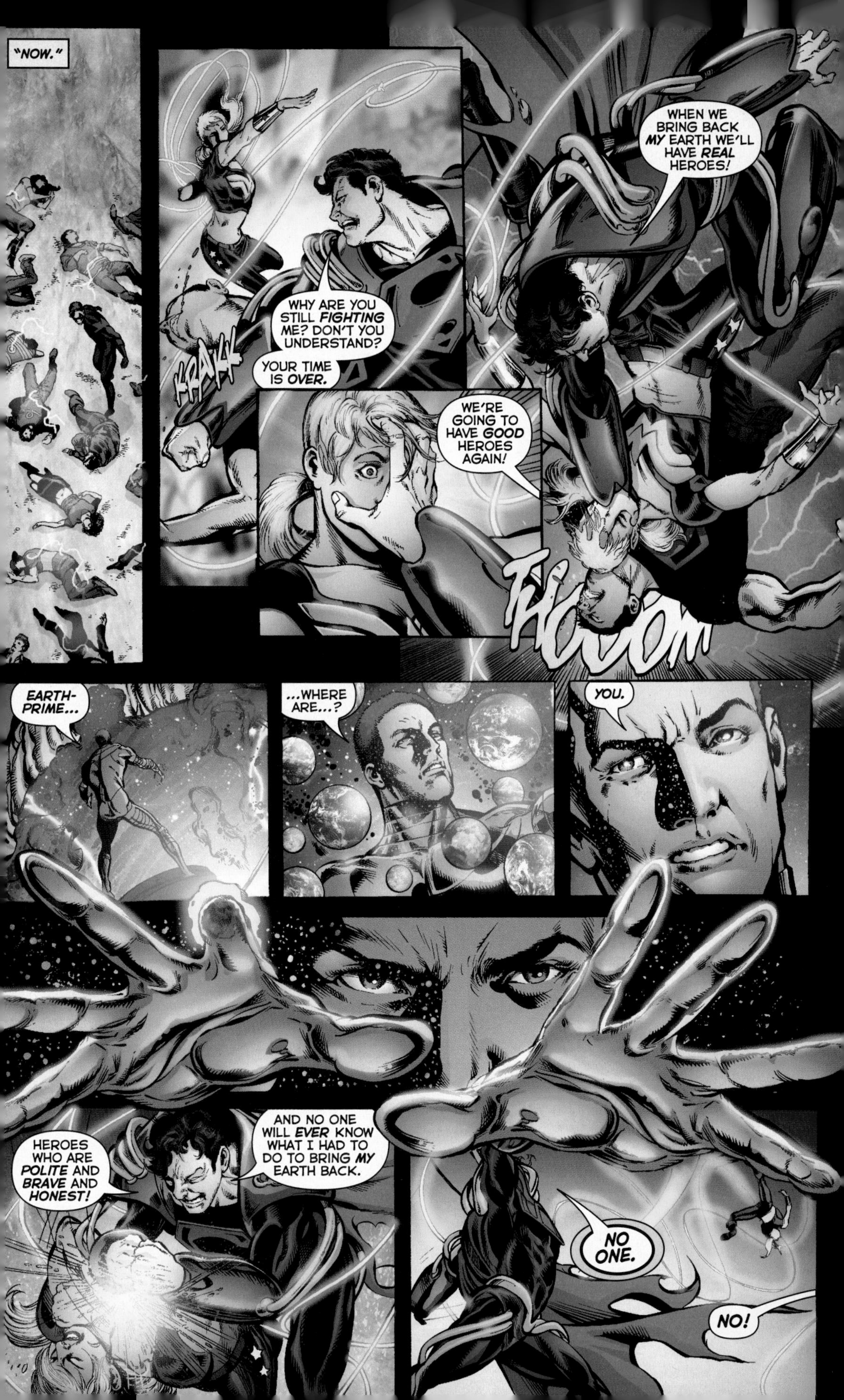
"NOW."
WHY ARE YOU STILL FIGHTING ME? DON'T YOU UNDERSTAND?
YOUR TIME IS OVER.
KRAKK
WHEN WE BRING BACK MY EARTH WE'LL HAVE REAL HEROES!
WE'RE GOING TO HAVE GOOD HEROES AGAIN!
FWOOM
EARTH-PRIME...
...WHERE ARE...?
YOU.
HEROES WHO ARE POLITE AND BRAVE AND HONEST!
AND NO ONE WILL EVER KNOW WHAT I HAD TO DO TO BRING MY EARTH BACK.
NO ONE.
NO!

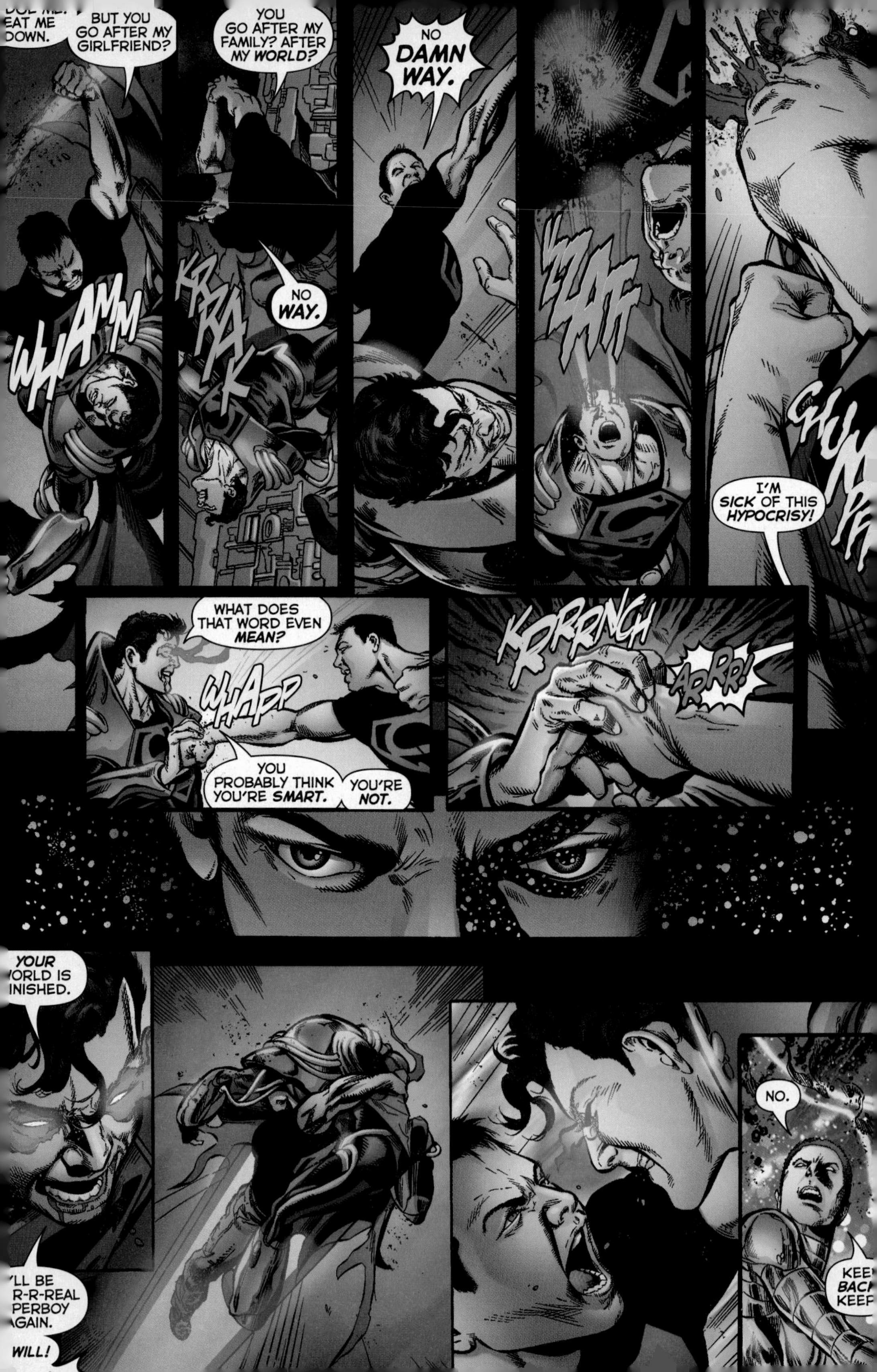

BUT YOU GO AFTER MY GIRLFRIEND?
YOU GO AFTER MY FAMILY? AFTER MY WORLD?
NO DAMN WAY.
NO WAY.
I'M SICK OF THIS HYPOCRISY!
WHAT DOES THAT WORD EVEN MEAN?
YOU PROBABLY THINK YOU'RE SMART.
YOU'RE NOT.
ARRR!
YOUR
AGAIN.
WILL!
NO.

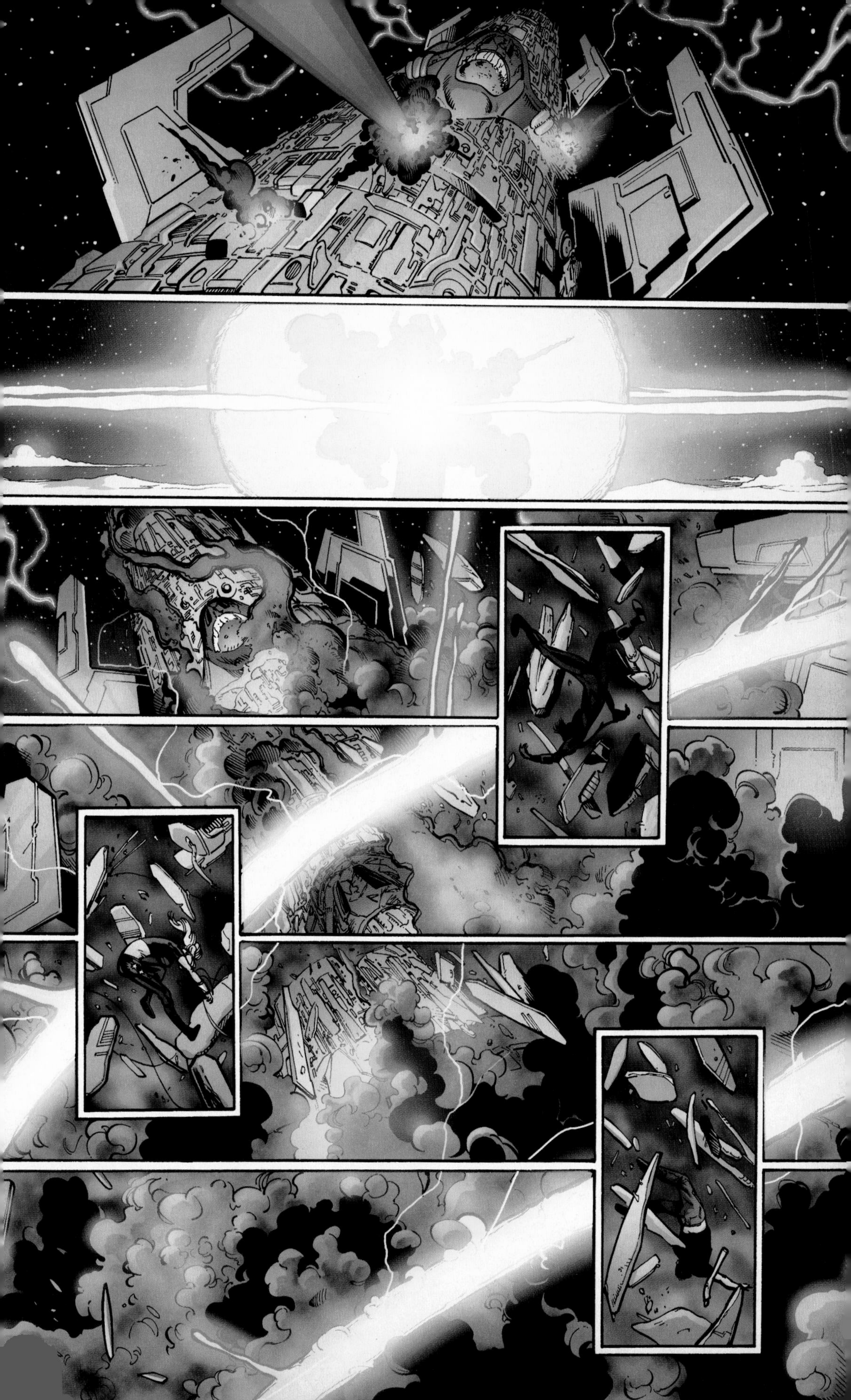

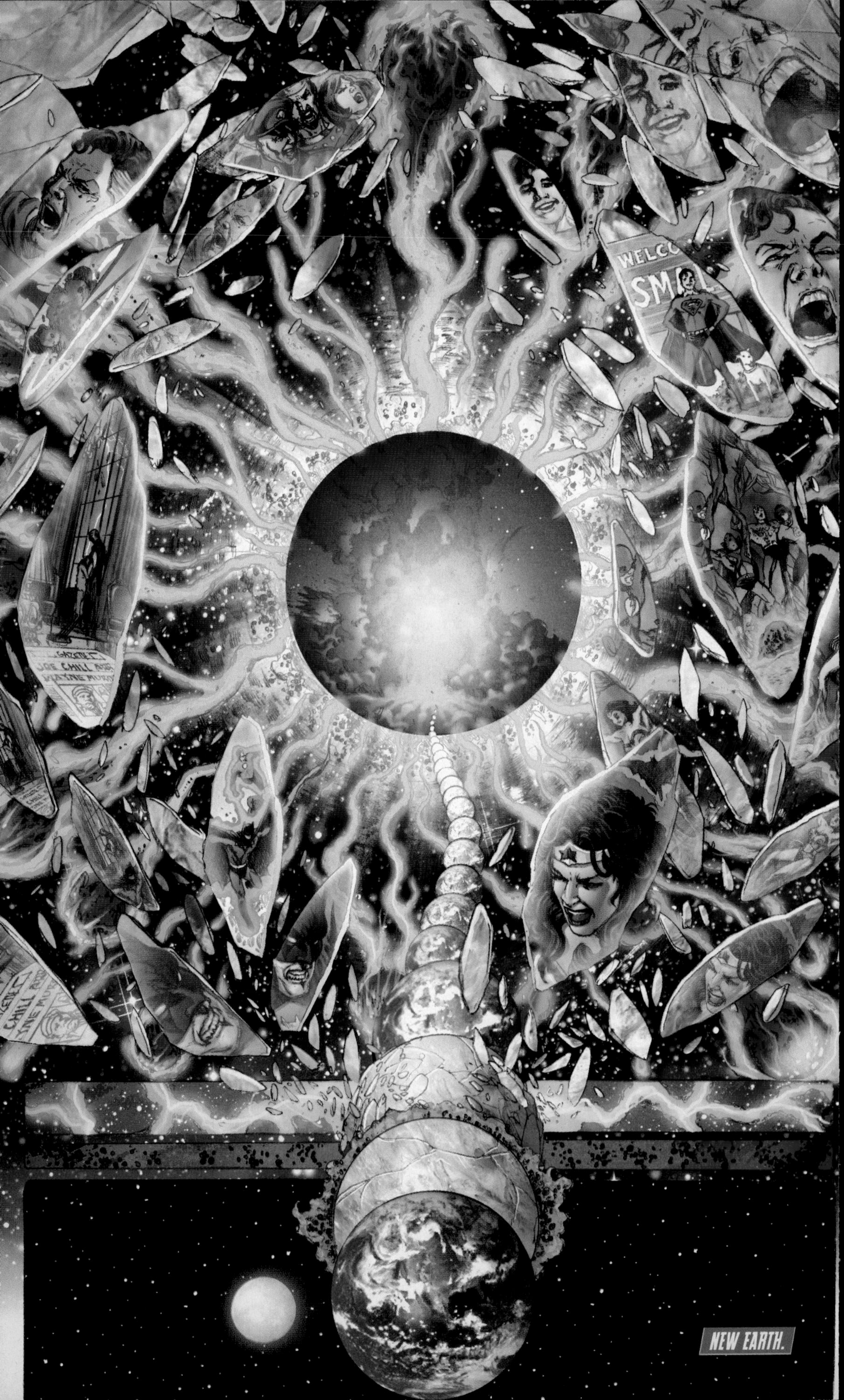
NEW EARTH.

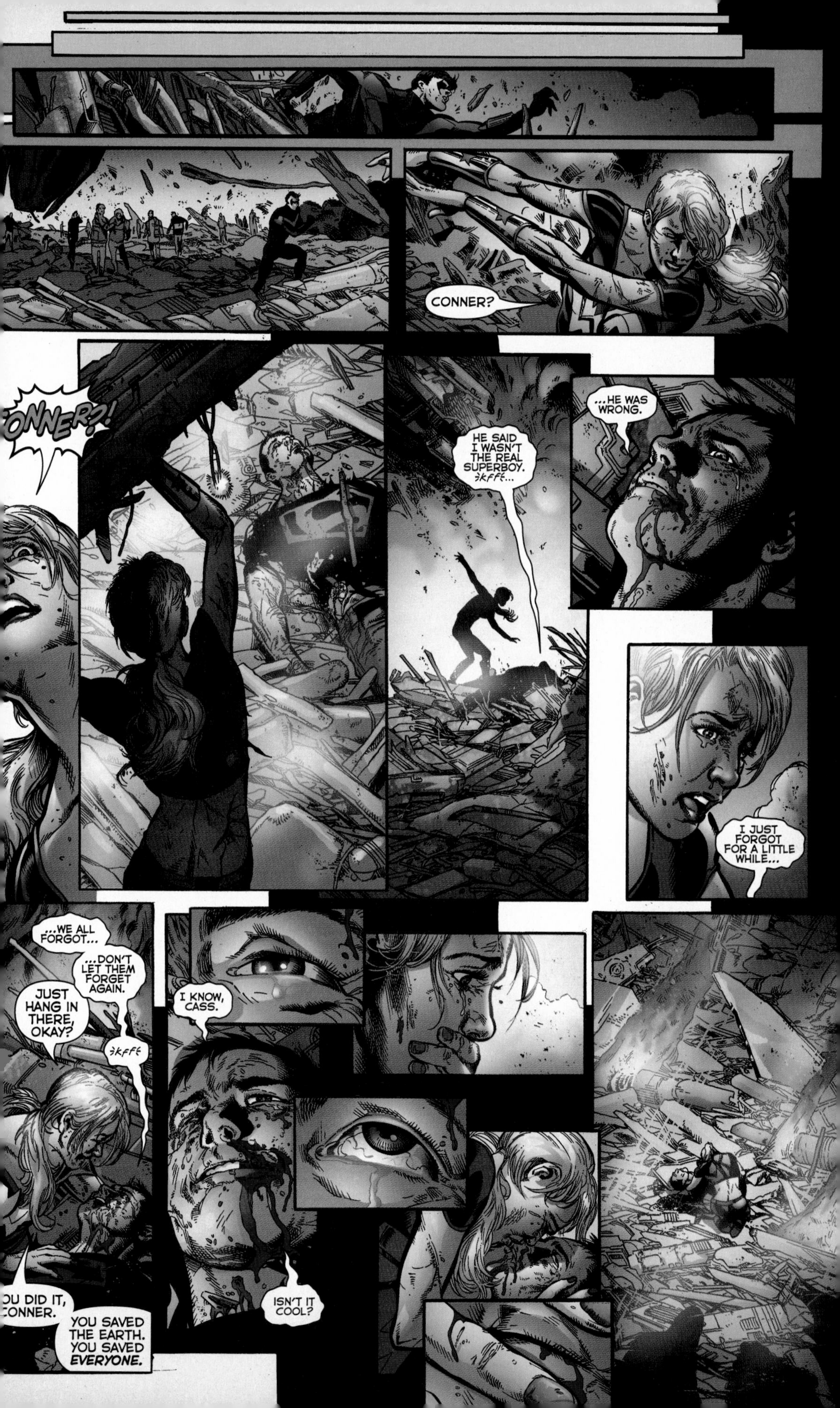

CONNER?
CONNER?!
HE SAID I WASN'T THE REAL SUPERBOY. *KFF*...
...HE WAS WRONG.
I JUST FORGOT FOR A LITTLE WHILE...
...WE ALL FORGOT...
...DON'T LET THEM FORGET AGAIN.
JUST HANG IN THERE, OKAY?
KFF
I KNOW, CASS.
ISN'T IT COOL?
YOU SAVED THE EARTH. YOU SAVED EVERYONE.

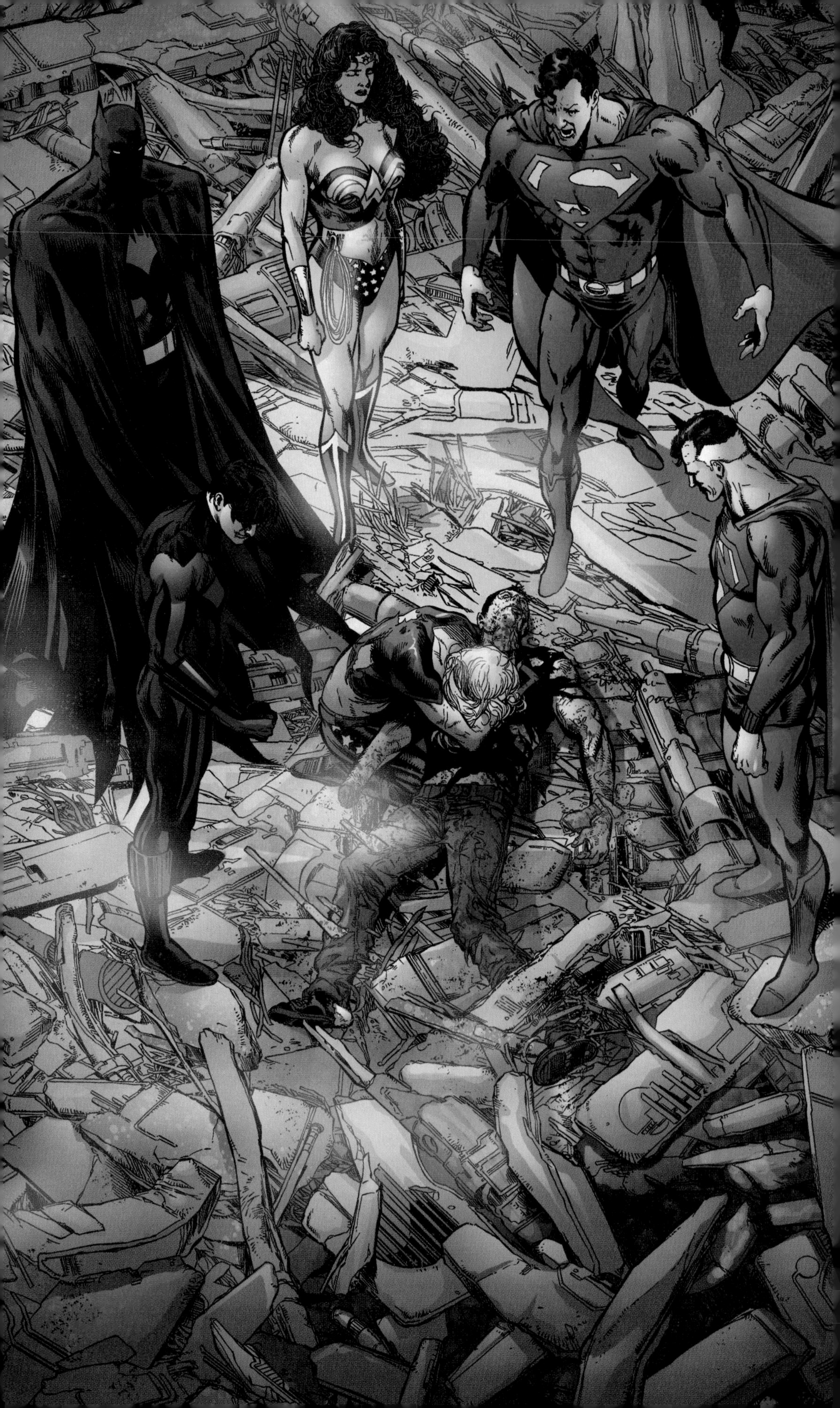

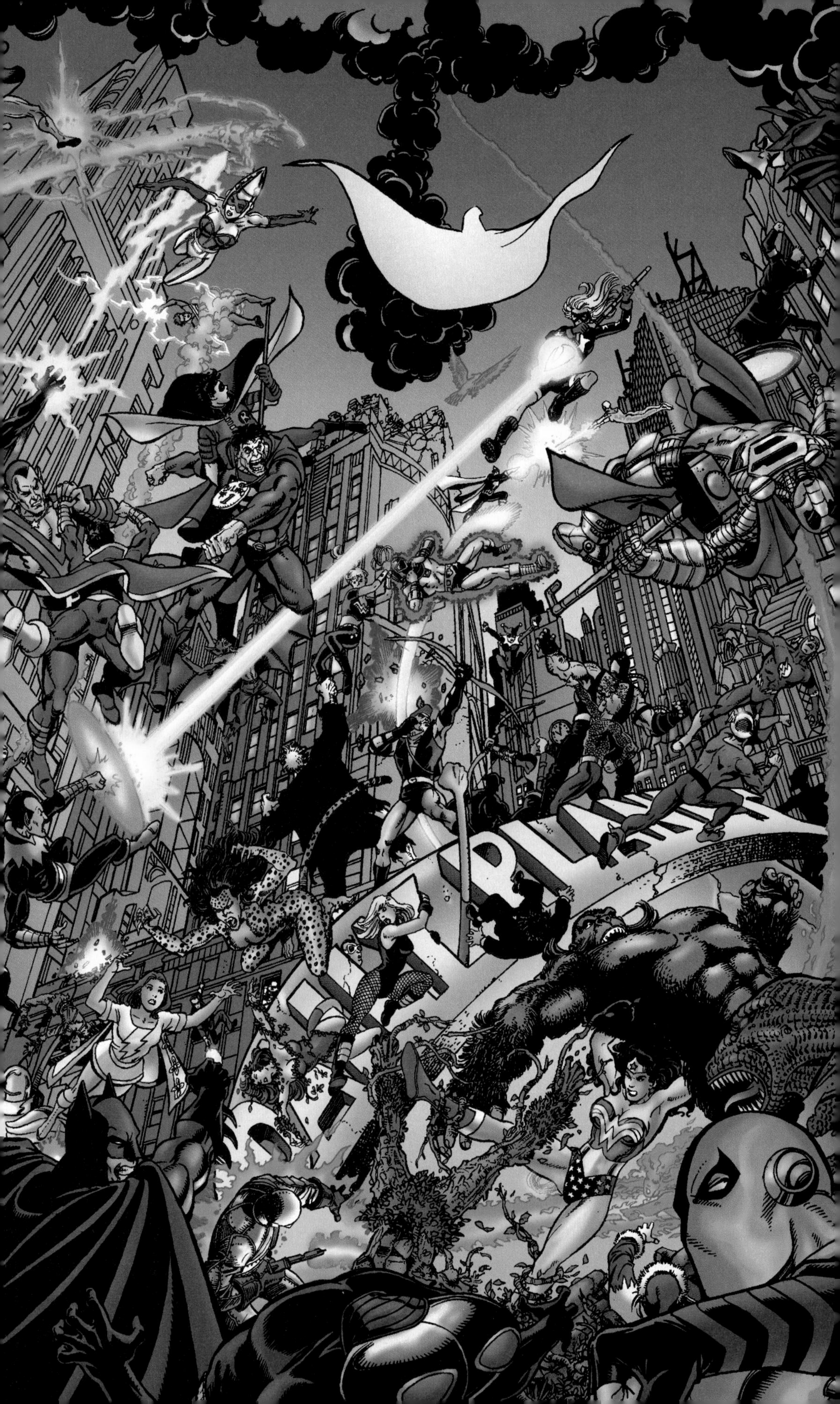

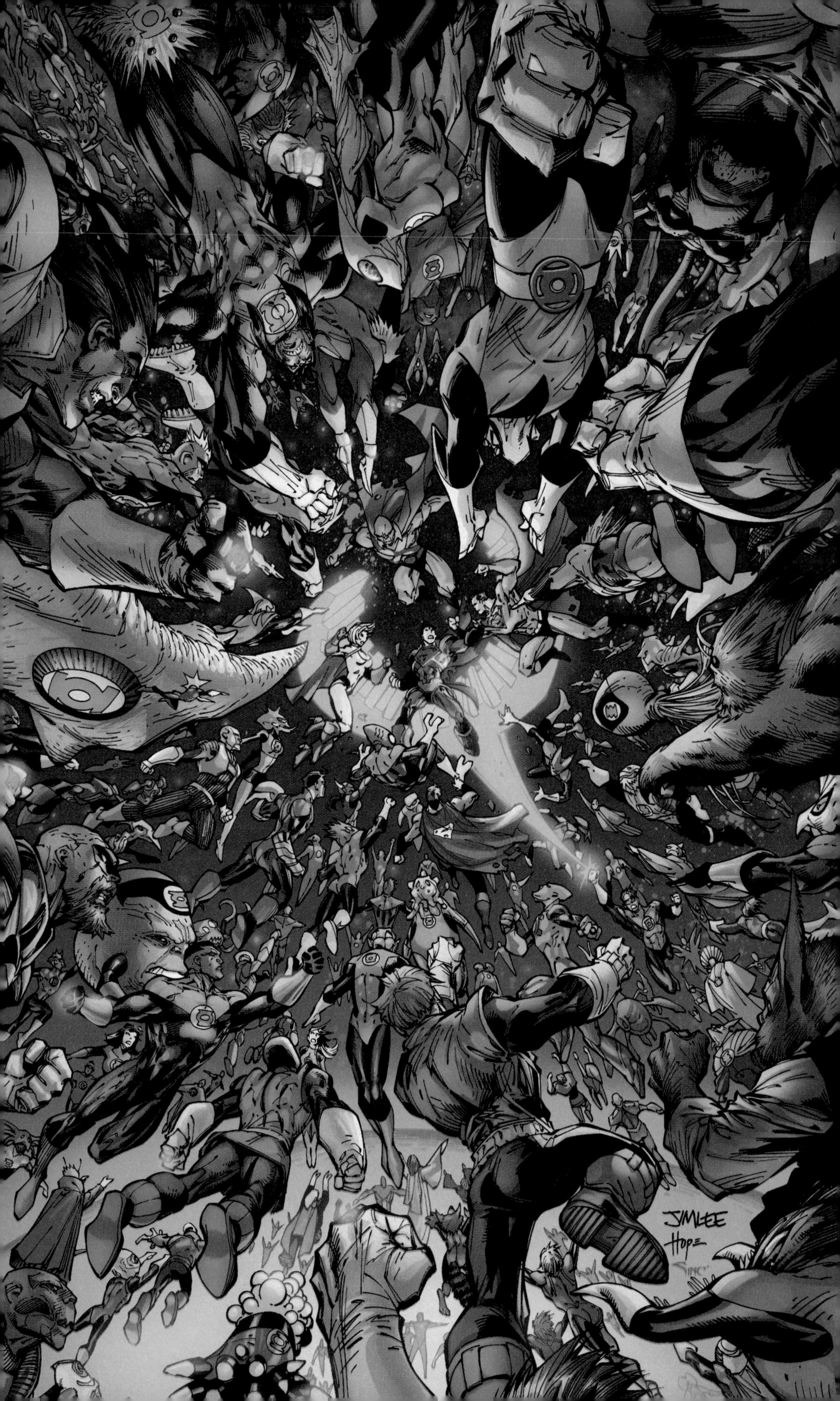

JIMLEE
Hope

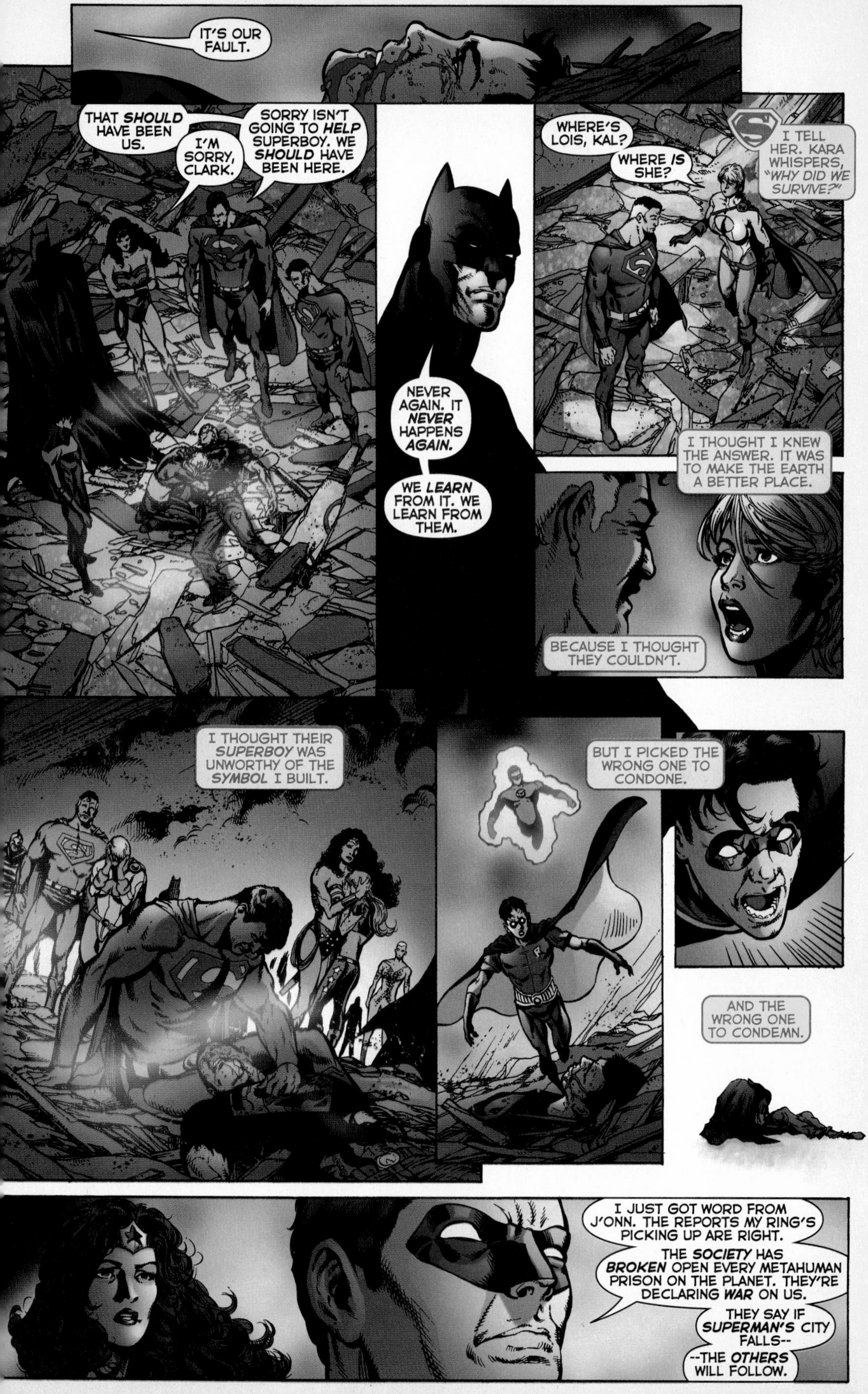
IT'S OUR FAULT.
THAT SHOULD HAVE BEEN US.
I'M SORRY, CLARK.
SORRY ISN'T GOING TO HELP SUPERBOY. WE SHOULD HAVE BEEN HERE.
NEVER AGAIN. IT NEVER HAPPENS AGAIN.
WE LEARN FROM IT. WE LEARN FROM THEM.
WHERE'S LOIS, KAL?
WHERE IS SHE?
I TELL HER. KARA WHISPERS, "WHY DID WE SURVIVE?"
I THOUGHT I KNEW THE ANSWER. IT WAS TO MAKE THE EARTH A BETTER PLACE.
BECAUSE I THOUGHT THEY COULDN'T.
I THOUGHT THEIR SUPERBOY WAS UNWORTHY OF THE SYMBOL I BUILT.
BUT I PICKED THE WRONG ONE TO CONDONE.
AND THE WRONG ONE TO CONDEMN.
I JUST GOT WORD FROM J'ONN. THE REPORTS MY RING'S PICKING UP ARE RIGHT.
THE SOCIETY HAS BROKEN OPEN EVERY METAHUMAN PRISON ON THE PLANET. THEY'RE DECLARING WAR ON US.
THEY SAY IF SUPERMAN'S CITY FALLS--
--THE OTHERS WILL FOLLOW.

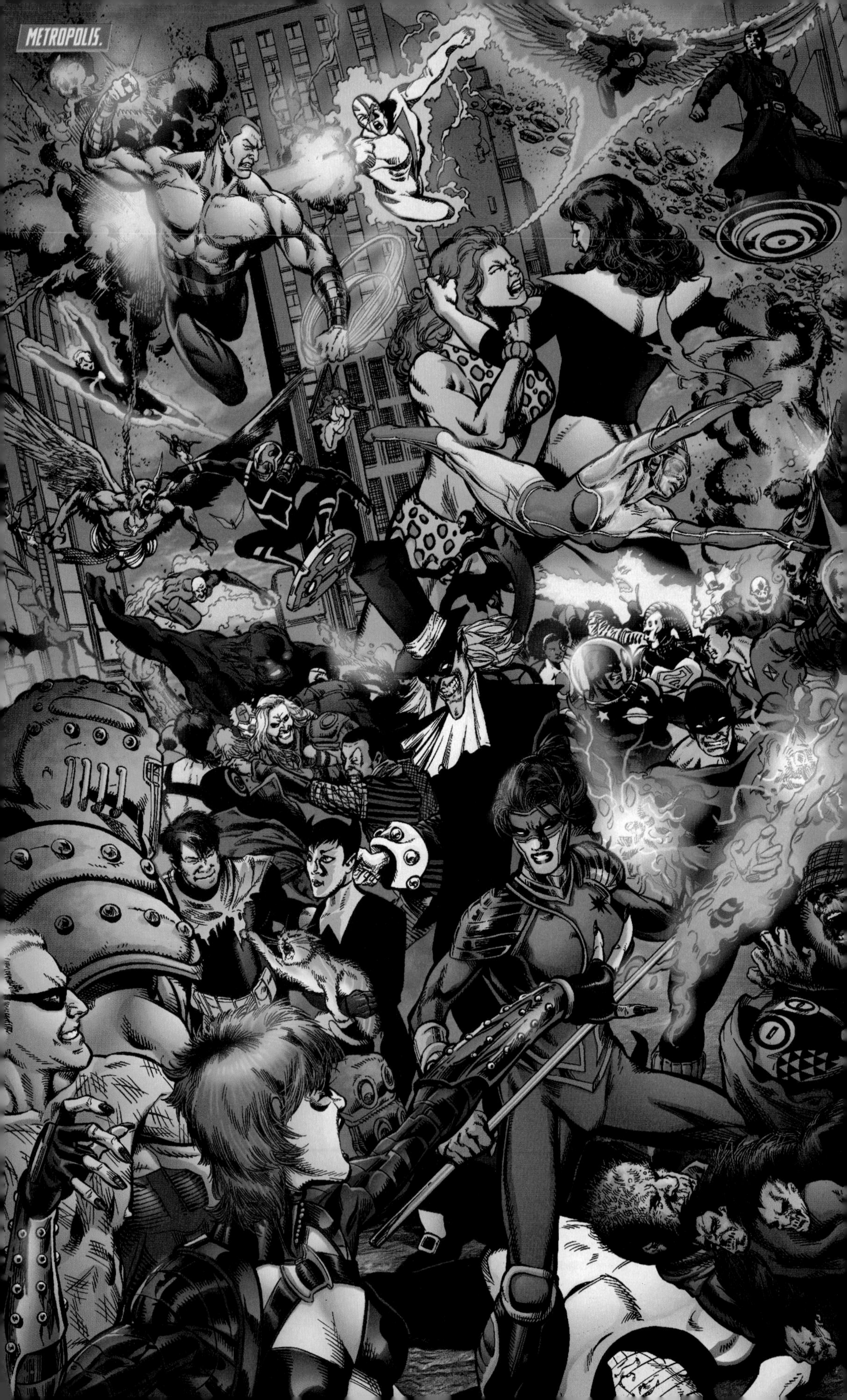
METROPOLIS.

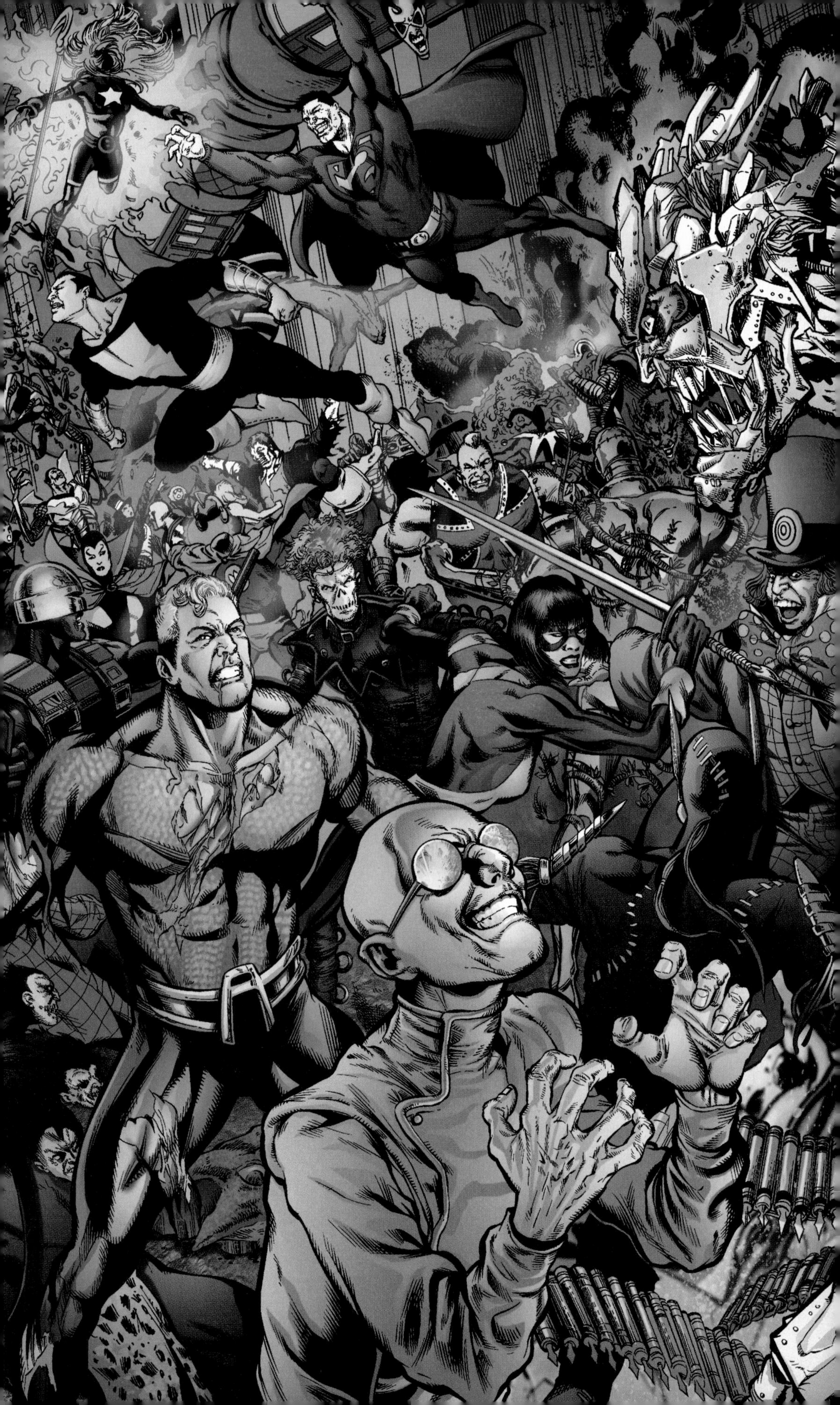

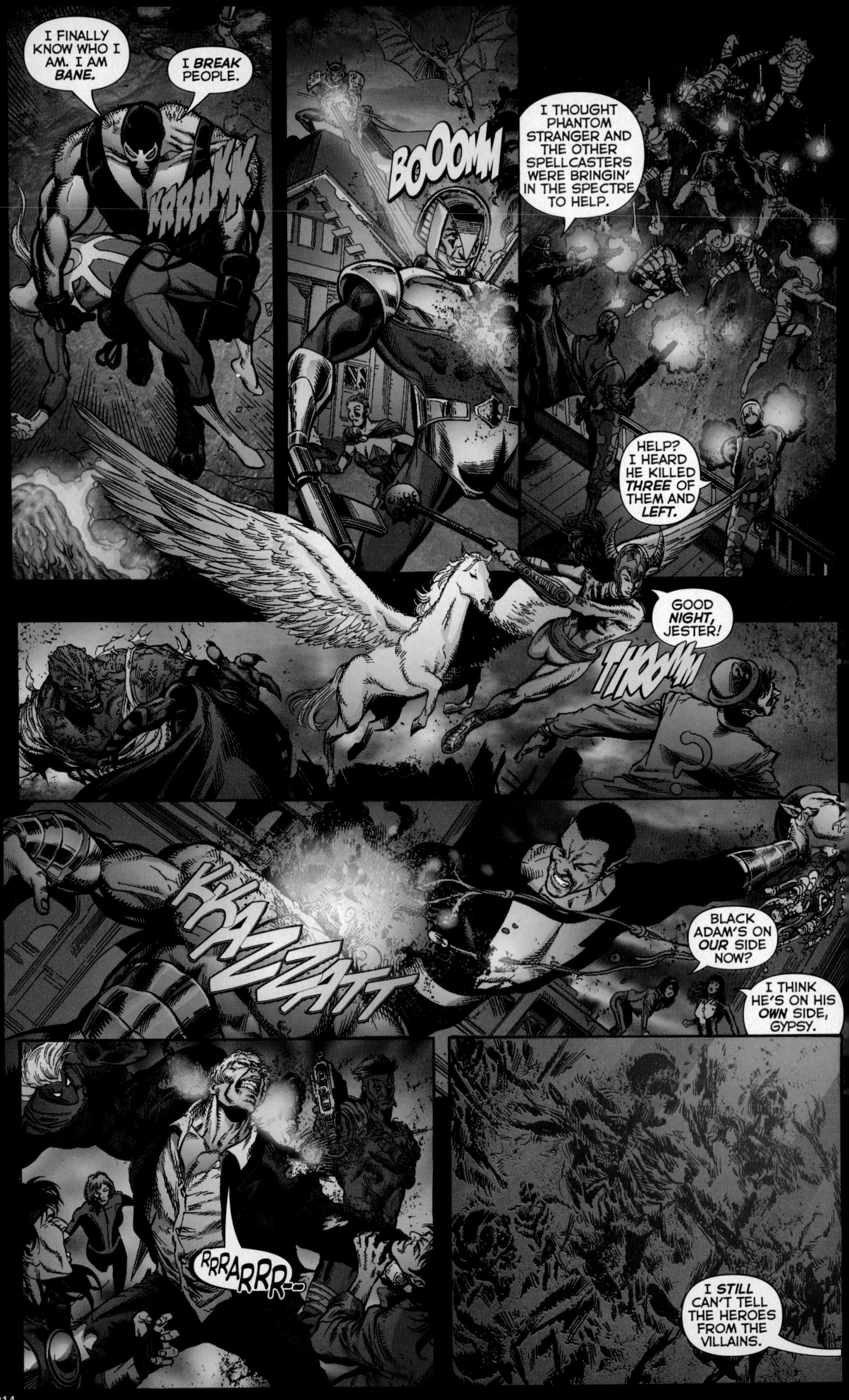
I FINALLY KNOW WHO I AM. I AM BANE.
I BREAK PEOPLE.
KRRAKK
BOOOMM
I THOUGHT PHANTOM STRANGER AND THE OTHER SPELLCASTERS WERE BRINGIN' IN THE SPECTRE TO HELP.
HELP? I HEARD HE KILLED THREE OF THEM AND LEFT.
GOOD NIGHT, JESTER!
THOOMM
KRAZZATT
BLACK ADAM'S ON OUR SIDE NOW?
I THINK HE'S ON HIS OWN SIDE, GYPSY.
RRRARRR--
I STILL CAN'T TELL THE HEROES FROM THE VILLAINS.

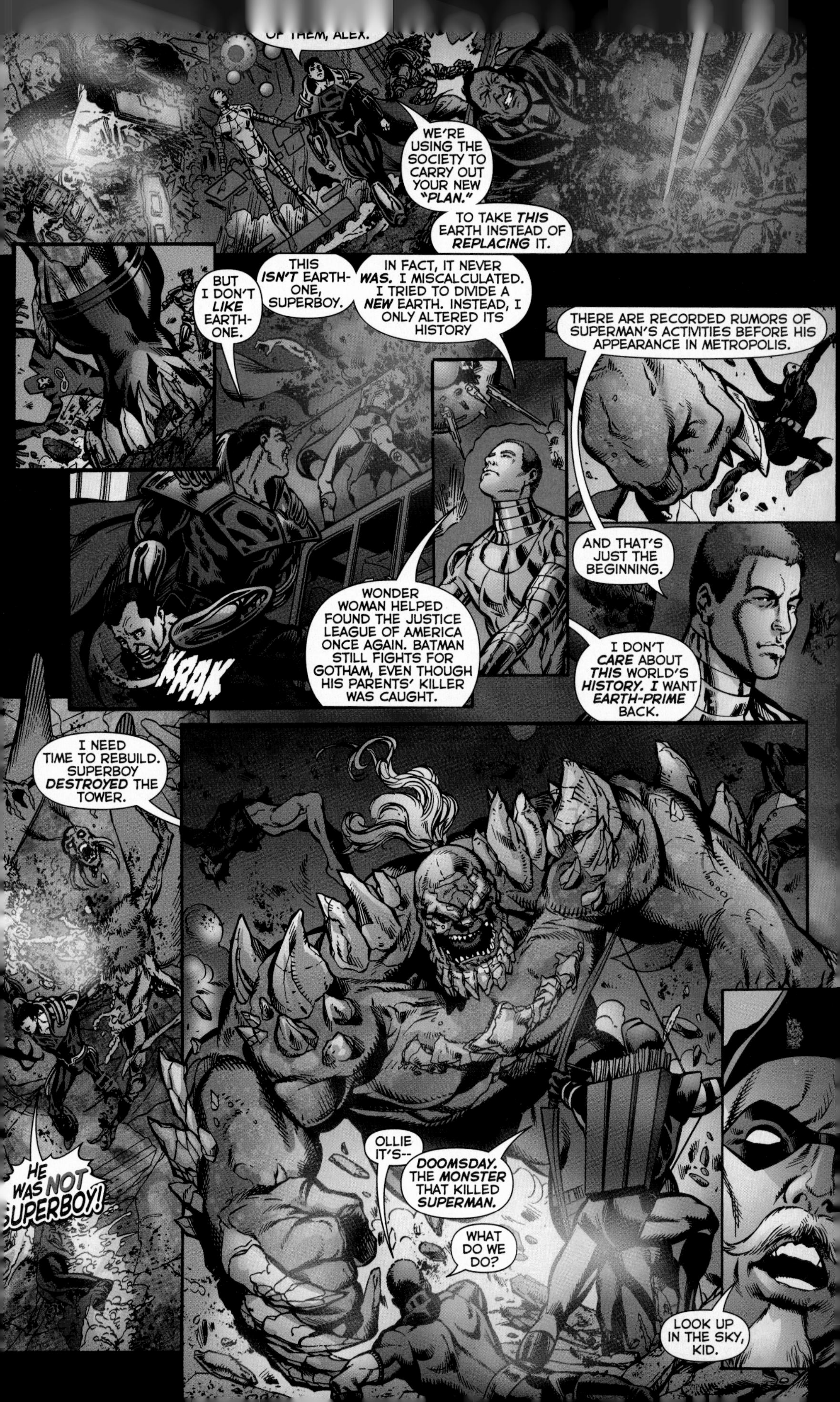

OF THEM, ALEX.
WE'RE USING THE SOCIETY TO CARRY OUT YOUR NEW "PLAN."
TO TAKE THIS EARTH INSTEAD OF REPLACING IT.
BUT I DON'T LIKE EARTH-ONE.
THIS ISN'T EARTH-ONE, SUPERBOY.
IN FACT, IT NEVER WAS. I MISCALCULATED. I TRIED TO DIVIDE A NEW EARTH. INSTEAD, I ONLY ALTERED ITS HISTORY
THERE ARE RECORDED RUMORS OF SUPERMAN'S ACTIVITIES BEFORE HIS APPEARANCE IN METROPOLIS.
AND THAT'S JUST THE BEGINNING.
WONDER WOMAN HELPED FOUND THE JUSTICE LEAGUE OF AMERICA ONCE AGAIN. BATMAN STILL FIGHTS FOR GOTHAM, EVEN THOUGH HIS PARENTS' KILLER WAS CAUGHT.
KRAK
I DON'T CARE ABOUT THIS WORLD'S HISTORY. I WANT EARTH-PRIME BACK.
I NEED TIME TO REBUILD. SUPERBOY DESTROYED THE TOWER.
HE WAS NOT SUPERBOY!
OLLIE IT'S--
DOOMSDAY. THE MONSTER THAT KILLED SUPERMAN.
WHAT DO WE DO?
LOOK UP IN THE SKY, KID.

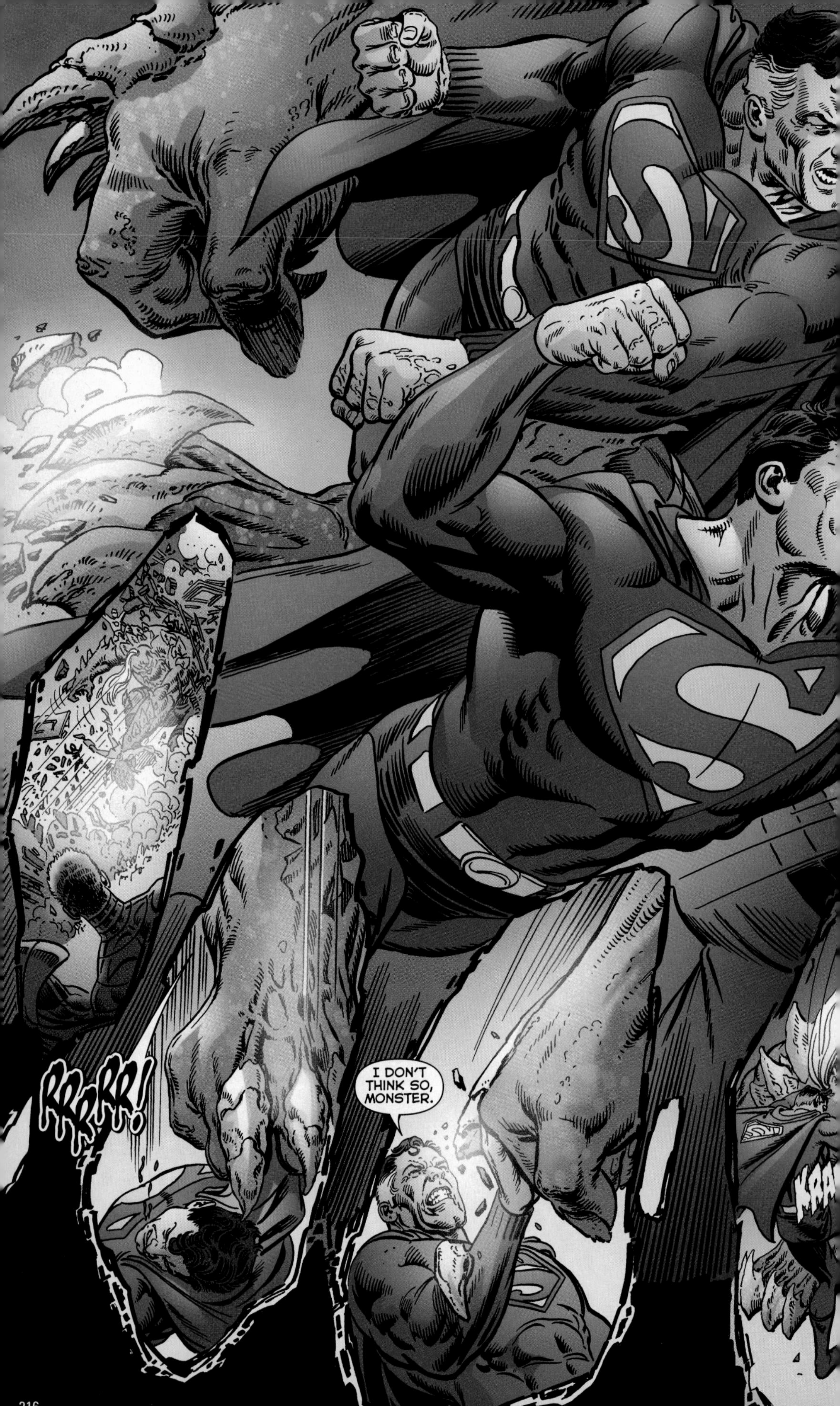
RRRRR!
I DON'T THINK SO, MONSTER.

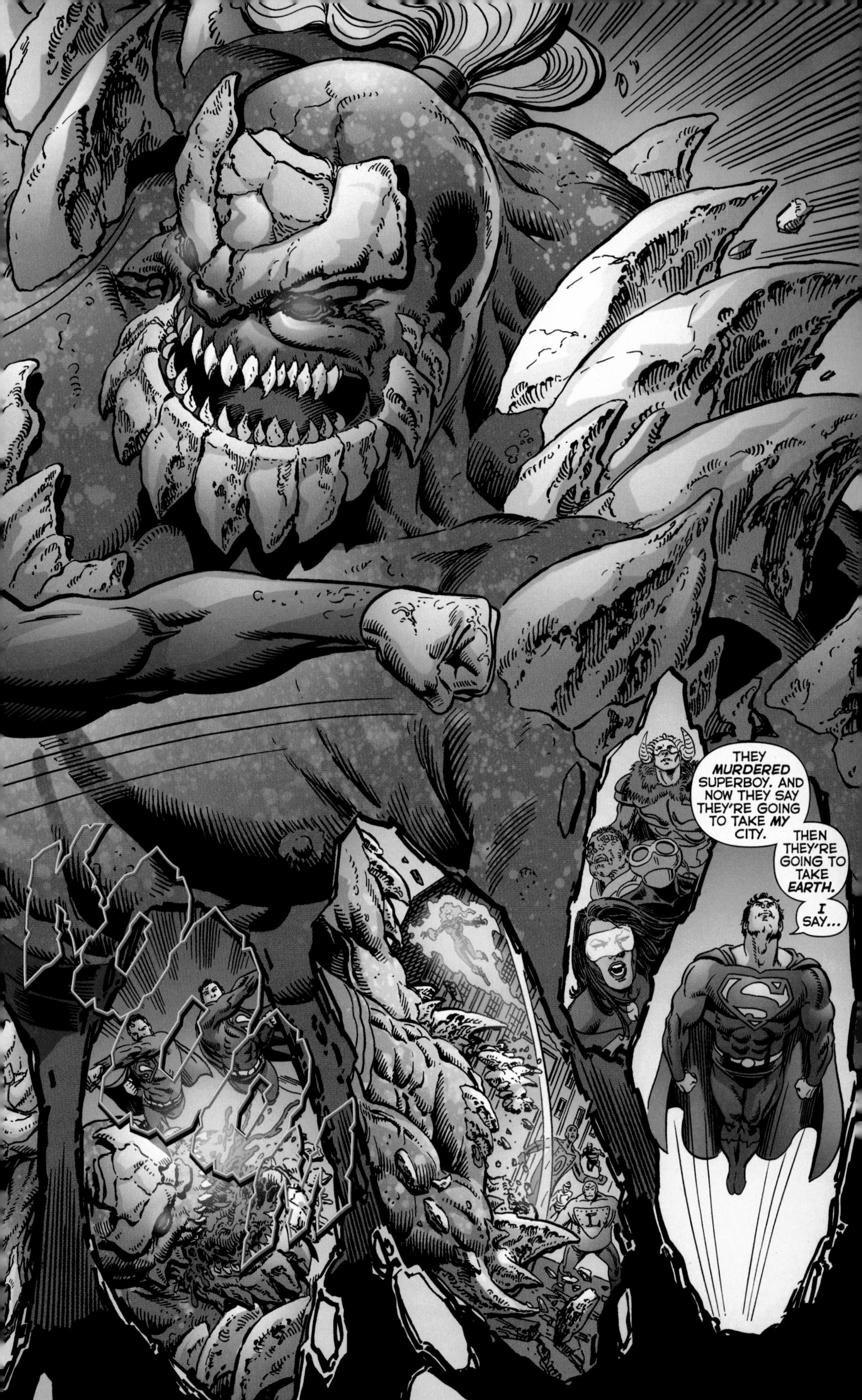
KOOOM
THEY *MURDERED* SUPERBOY. AND NOW THEY SAY THEY'RE GOING TO TAKE *MY* CITY.
THEN THEY'RE GOING TO TAKE *EARTH.*
I SAY...

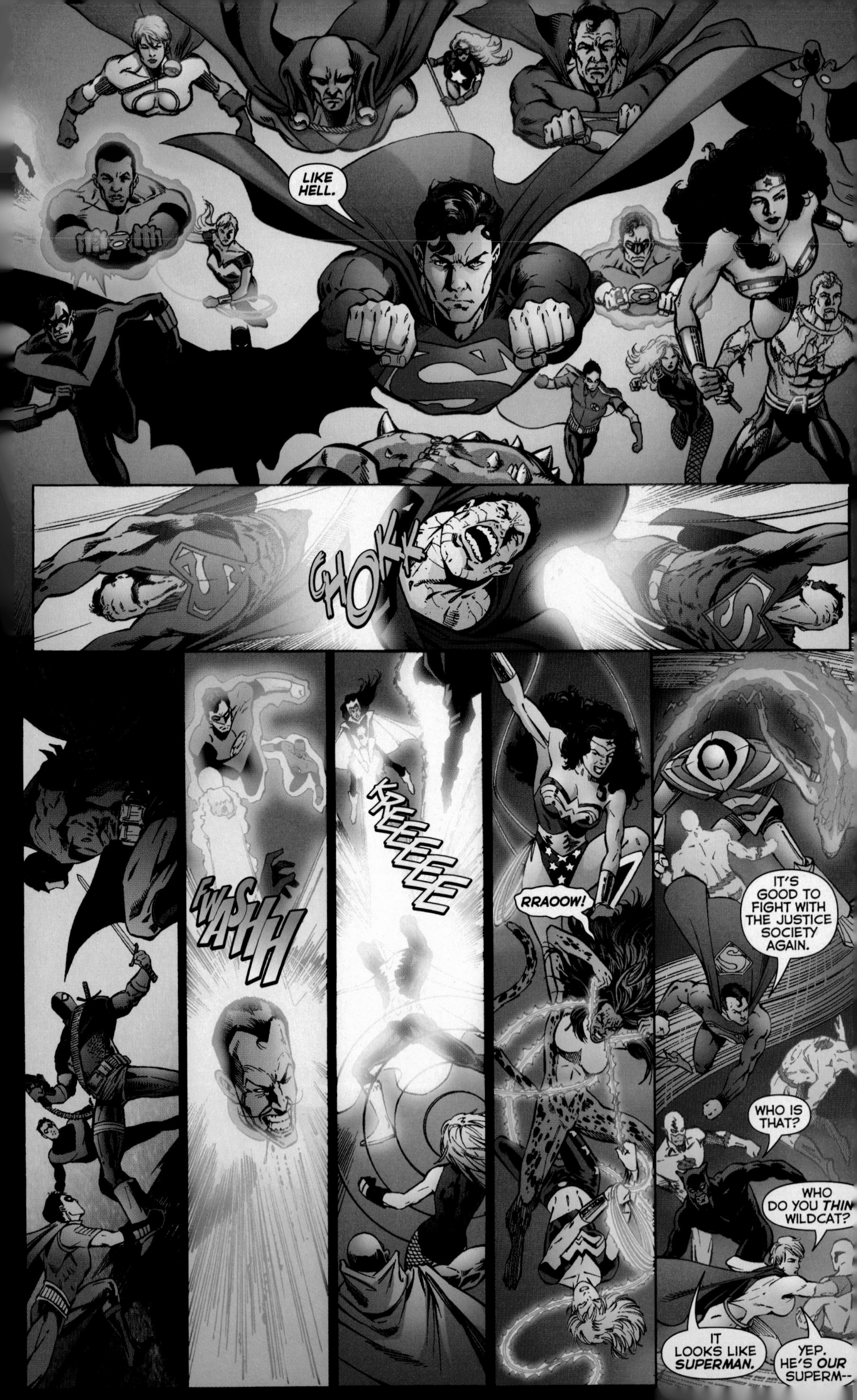
LIKE HELL.
CHOKK
FWASHHH
KREEEEE
RRAOOW!
IT'S GOOD TO FIGHT WITH THE JUSTICE SOCIETY AGAIN.
WHO IS THAT?
WHO DO YOU THIN WILDCAT?
IT LOOKS LIKE SUPERMAN.
YEP. HE'S OUR SUPERM--

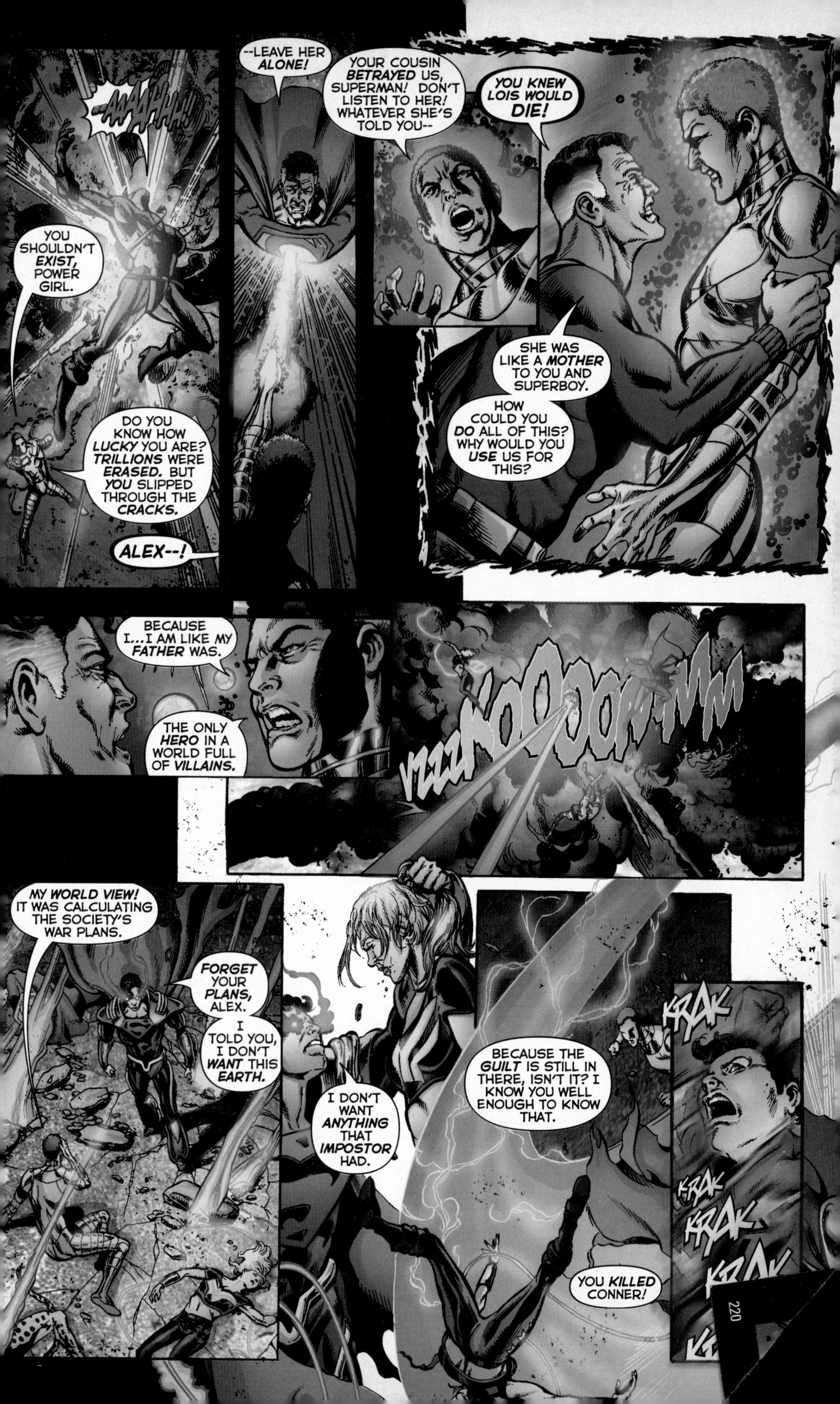
--AAAAHH!!
YOU SHOULDN'T EXIST, POWER GIRL.
DO YOU KNOW HOW LUCKY YOU ARE? TRILLIONS WERE ERASED. BUT YOU SLIPPED THROUGH THE CRACKS.
ALEX--!
--LEAVE HER ALONE!
YOUR COUSIN BETRAYED US, SUPERMAN! DON'T LISTEN TO HER! WHATEVER SHE'S TOLD YOU--
YOU KNEW LOIS WOULD DIE!
SHE WAS LIKE A MOTHER TO YOU AND SUPERBOY.
HOW COULD YOU DO ALL OF THIS? WHY WOULD YOU USE US FOR THIS?
BECAUSE I...I AM LIKE MY FATHER WAS.
THE ONLY HERO IN A WORLD FULL OF VILLAINS.
VZZZKOOOOOMMM
MY WORLD VIEW! IT WAS CALCULATING THE SOCIETY'S WAR PLANS.
FORGET YOUR PLANS, ALEX.
I TOLD YOU, I DON'T WANT THIS EARTH.
I DON'T WANT ANYTHING THAT IMPOSTOR HAD.
BECAUSE THE GUILT IS STILL IN THERE, ISN'T IT? I KNOW YOU WELL ENOUGH TO KNOW THAT.
KRAK
KRAK
KRAK
KRAK
YOU KILLED CONNER!

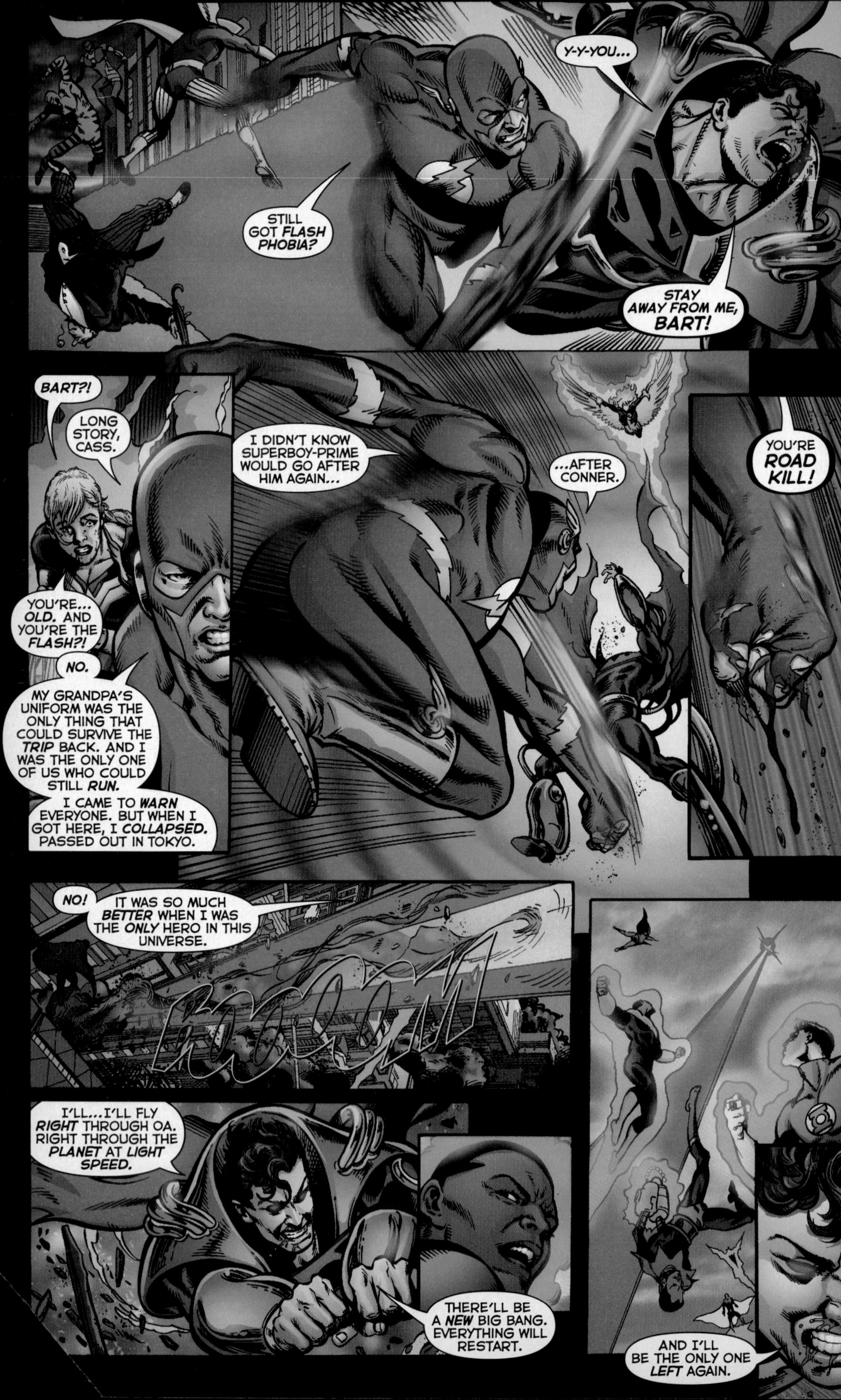

Y-Y-YOU...
STILL GOT FLASH PHOBIA?
STAY AWAY FROM ME, BART!
BART?!
LONG STORY, CASS.
YOU'RE... OLD. AND YOU'RE THE FLASH?!
NO.
MY GRANDPA'S UNIFORM WAS THE ONLY THING THAT COULD SURVIVE THE TRIP BACK. AND I WAS THE ONLY ONE OF US WHO COULD STILL RUN.
I CAME TO WARN EVERYONE. BUT WHEN I GOT HERE, I COLLAPSED. PASSED OUT IN TOKYO.
I DIDN'T KNOW SUPERBOY-PRIME WOULD GO AFTER HIM AGAIN...
...AFTER CONNER.
YOU'RE ROAD KILL!
NO!
IT WAS SO MUCH BETTER WHEN I WAS THE ONLY HERO IN THIS UNIVERSE.
I'LL...I'LL FLY RIGHT THROUGH OA. RIGHT THROUGH THE PLANET AT LIGHT SPEED.
THERE'LL BE A NEW BIG BANG. EVERYTHING WILL RESTART.
AND I'LL BE THE ONLY ONE LEFT AGAIN.

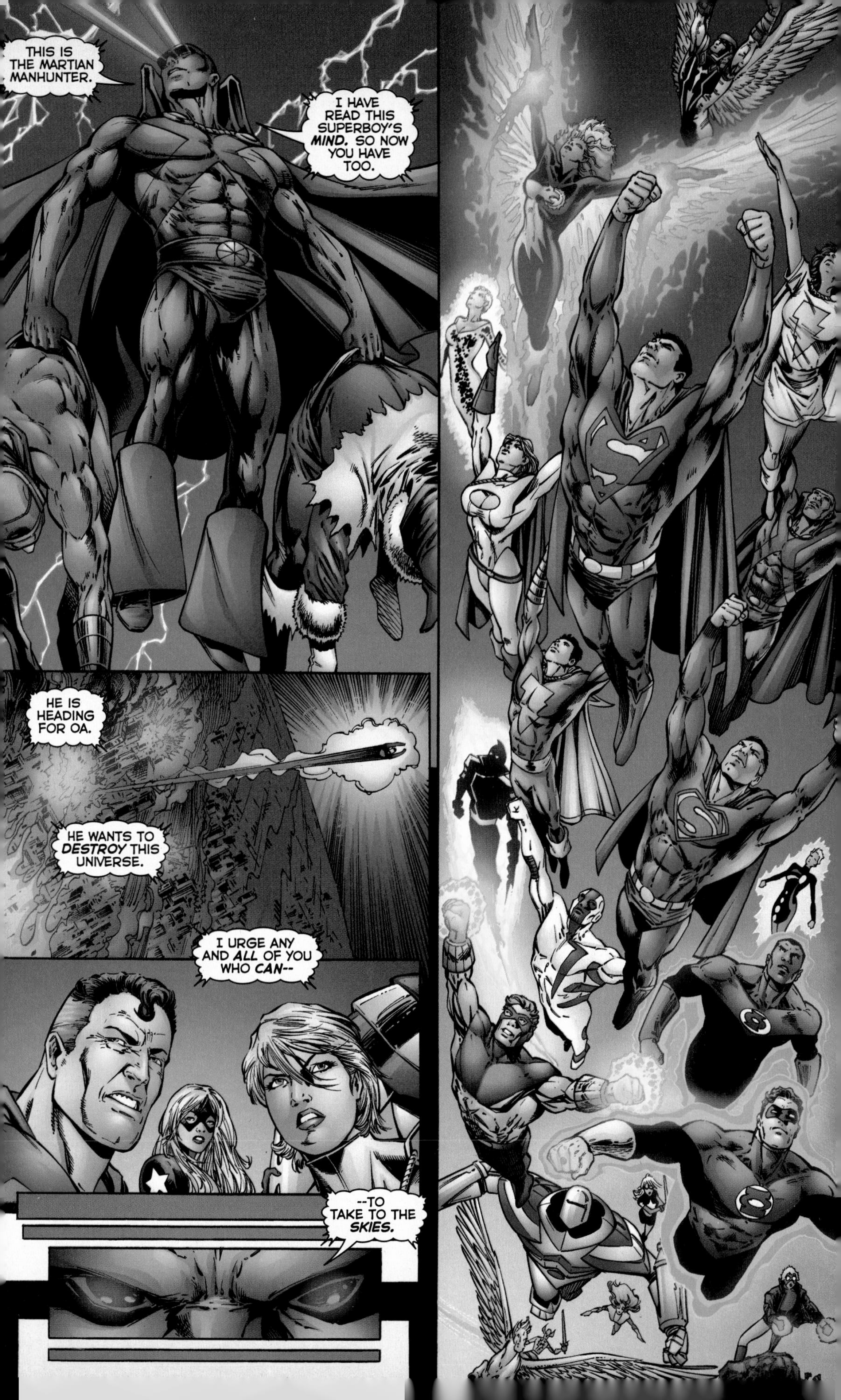

THIS IS THE MARTIAN MANHUNTER.
I HAVE READ THIS SUPERBOY'S *MIND.* SO NOW YOU HAVE TOO.
HE IS HEADING FOR OA.
HE WANTS TO *DESTROY* THIS UNIVERSE.
I URGE ANY AND *ALL* OF YOU WHO *CAN--*
--TO TAKE TO THE *SKIES.*

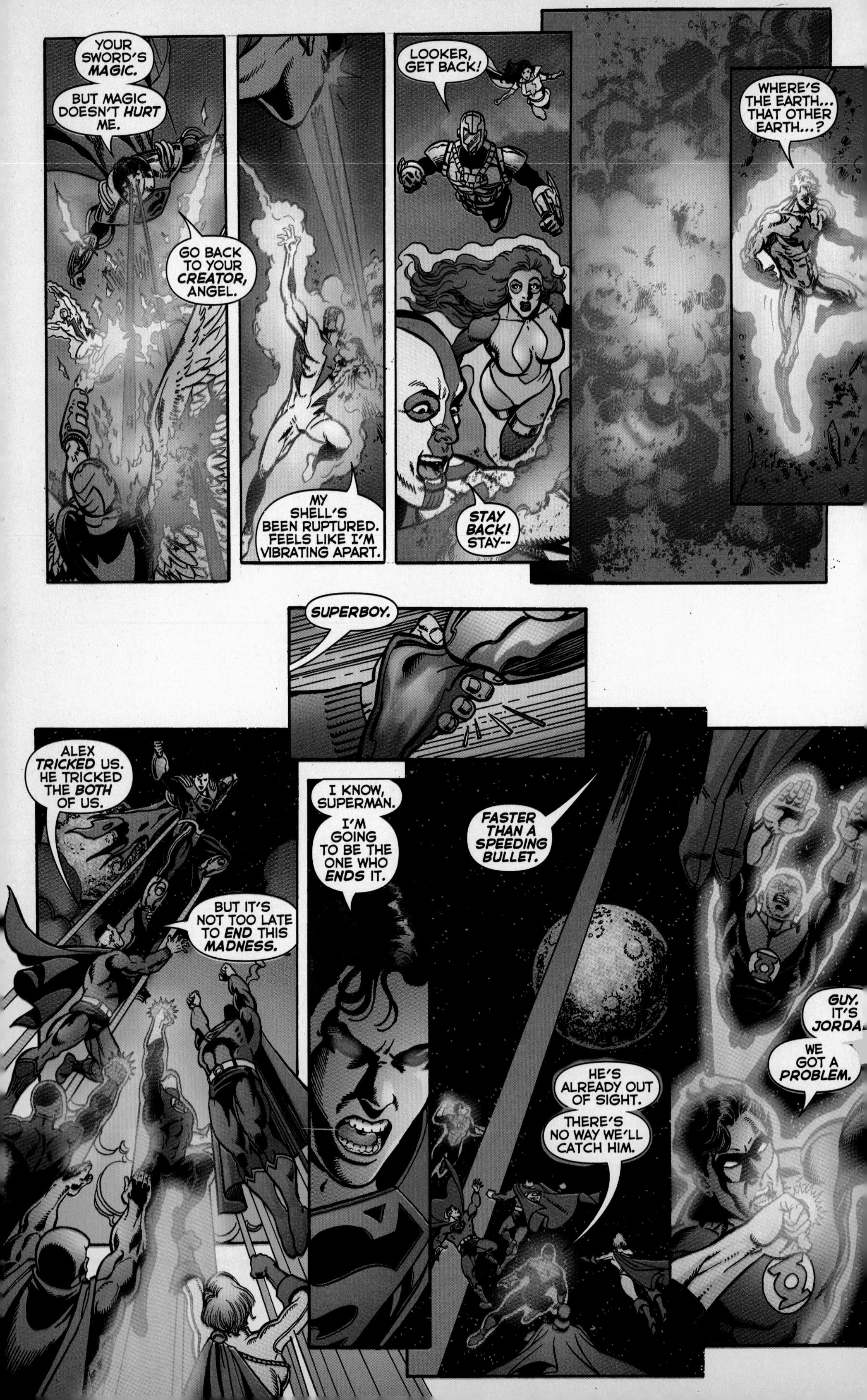
YOUR SWORD'S MAGIC.
BUT MAGIC DOESN'T HURT ME.
GO BACK TO YOUR CREATOR, ANGEL.
MY SHELL'S BEEN RUPTURED. FEELS LIKE I'M VIBRATING APART.
LOOKER, GET BACK!
STAY BACK! STAY--
WHERE'S THE EARTH... THAT OTHER EARTH...?
SUPERBOY.
ALEX TRICKED US. HE TRICKED THE BOTH OF US.
BUT IT'S NOT TOO LATE TO END THIS MADNESS.
I KNOW, SUPERMAN.
I'M GOING TO BE THE ONE WHO ENDS IT.
FASTER THAN A SPEEDING BULLET.
HE'S ALREADY OUT OF SIGHT.
THERE'S NO WAY WE'LL CATCH HIM.
GUY. IT'S JORDA
WE GOT A PROBLEM.

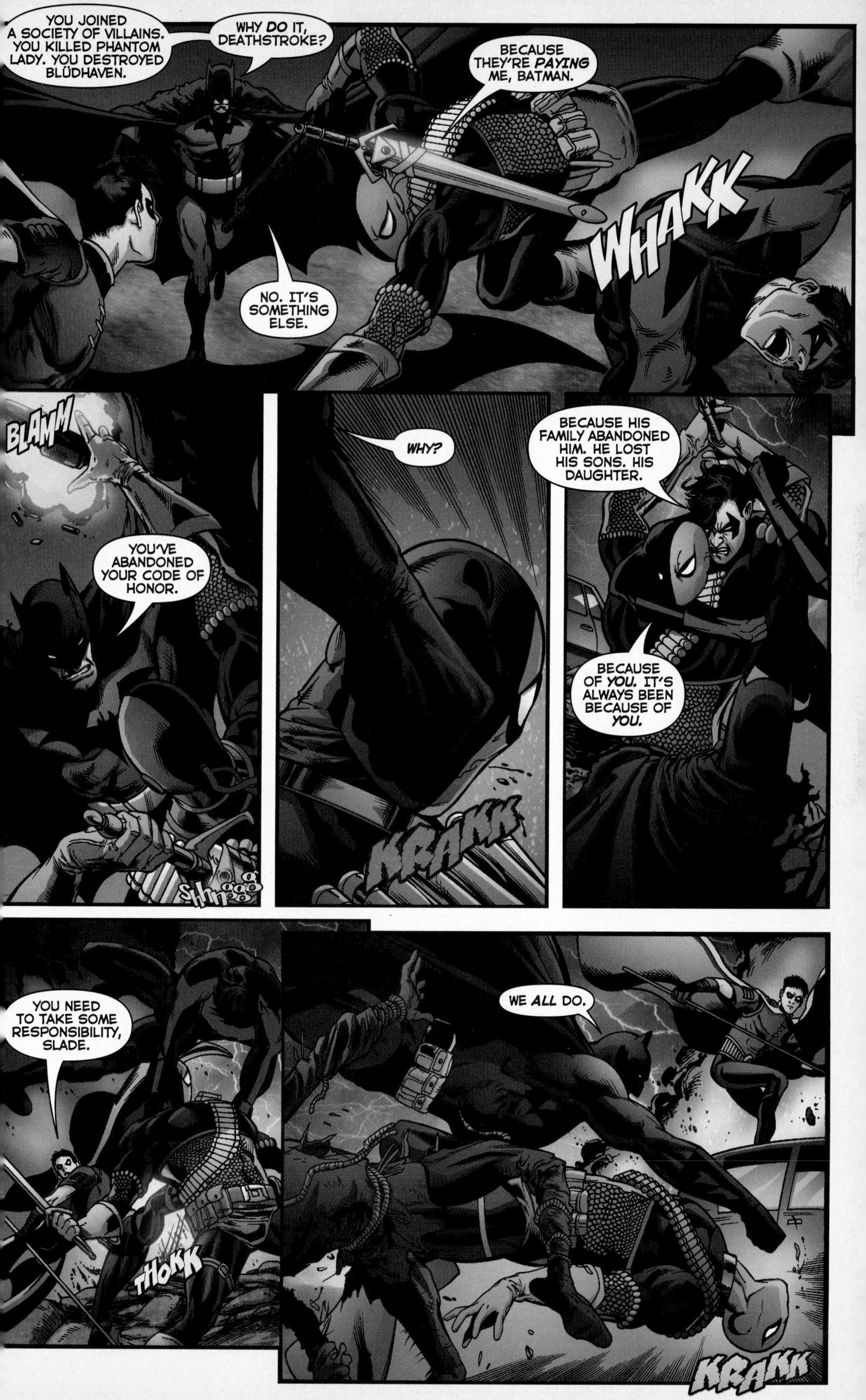
YOU JOINED A SOCIETY OF VILLAINS. YOU KILLED PHANTOM LADY. YOU DESTROYED BLÜDHAVEN.
WHY DO IT, DEATHSTROKE?
BECAUSE THEY'RE PAYING ME, BATMAN.
NO. IT'S SOMETHING ELSE.
WHAKK
BLAMM
YOU'VE ABANDONED YOUR CODE OF HONOR.
WHY?
KRAKK
BECAUSE HIS FAMILY ABANDONED HIM. HE LOST HIS SONS. HIS DAUGHTER.
BECAUSE OF YOU. IT'S ALWAYS BEEN BECAUSE OF YOU.
YOU NEED TO TAKE SOME RESPONSIBILITY, SLADE.
THOKK
WE ALL DO.
KRAKK

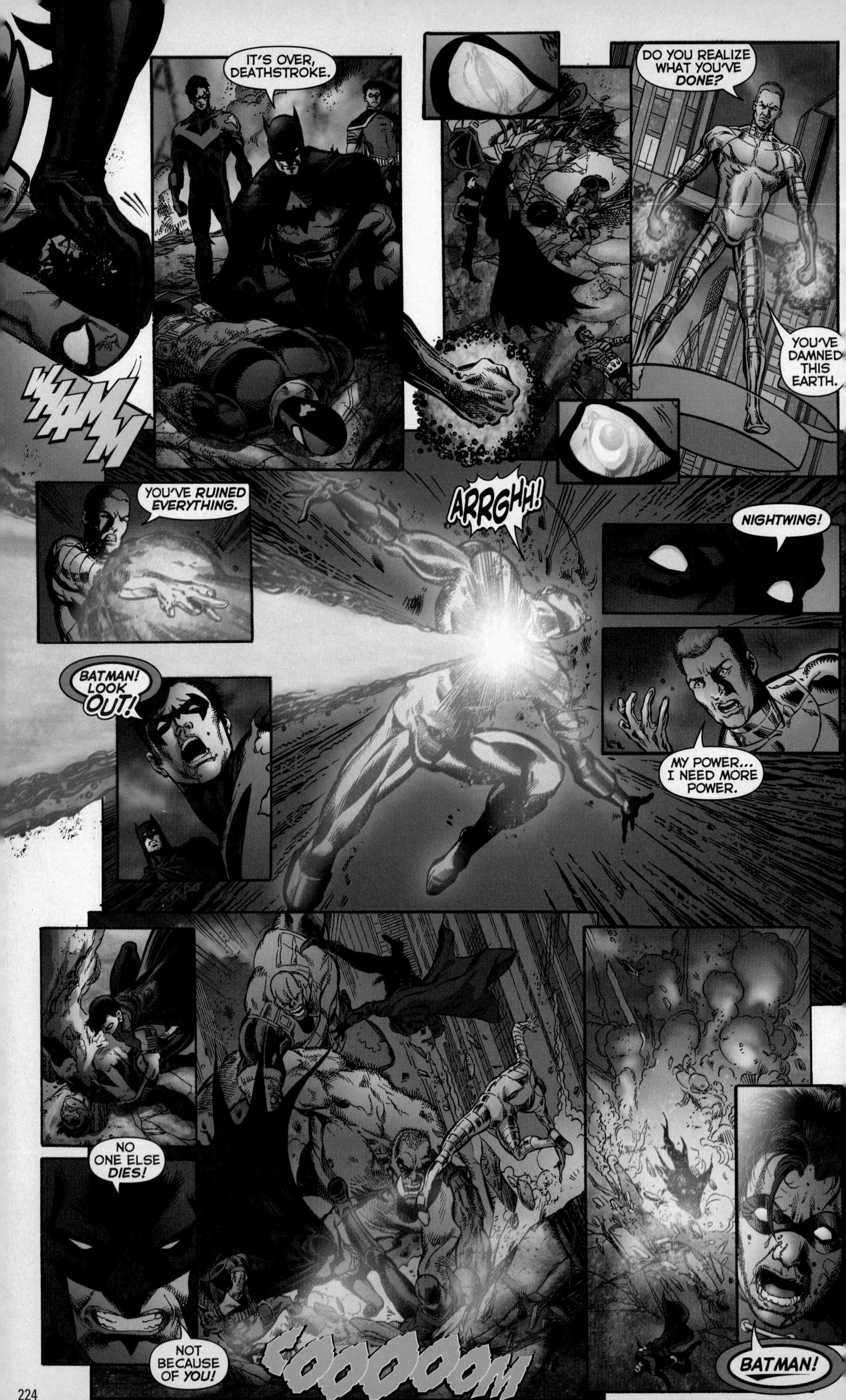

WHAM
IT'S OVER, DEATHSTROKE.
DO YOU REALIZE WHAT YOU'VE DONE?
YOU'VE DAMNED THIS EARTH.
YOU'VE RUINED EVERYTHING.
ARRGHH!
NIGHTWING!
BATMAN! LOOK OUT!
MY POWER... I NEED MORE POWER.
NO ONE ELSE DIES!
NOT BECAUSE OF YOU!
BATMAN!

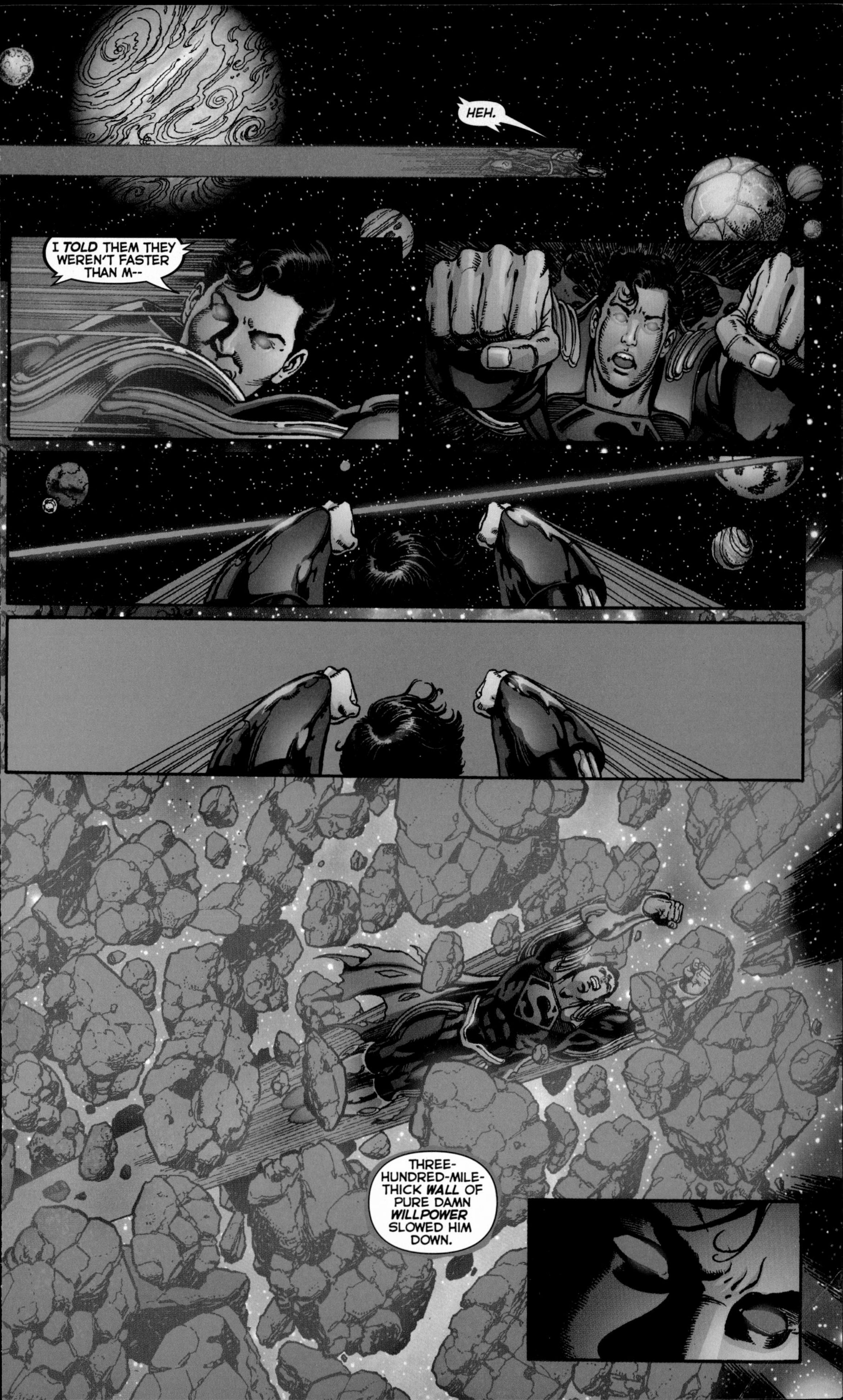
HEH.
I TOLD THEM THEY WEREN'T FASTER THAN M--
THREE-HUNDRED-MILE-THICK WALL OF PURE DAMN WILLPOWER SLOWED HIM DOWN.

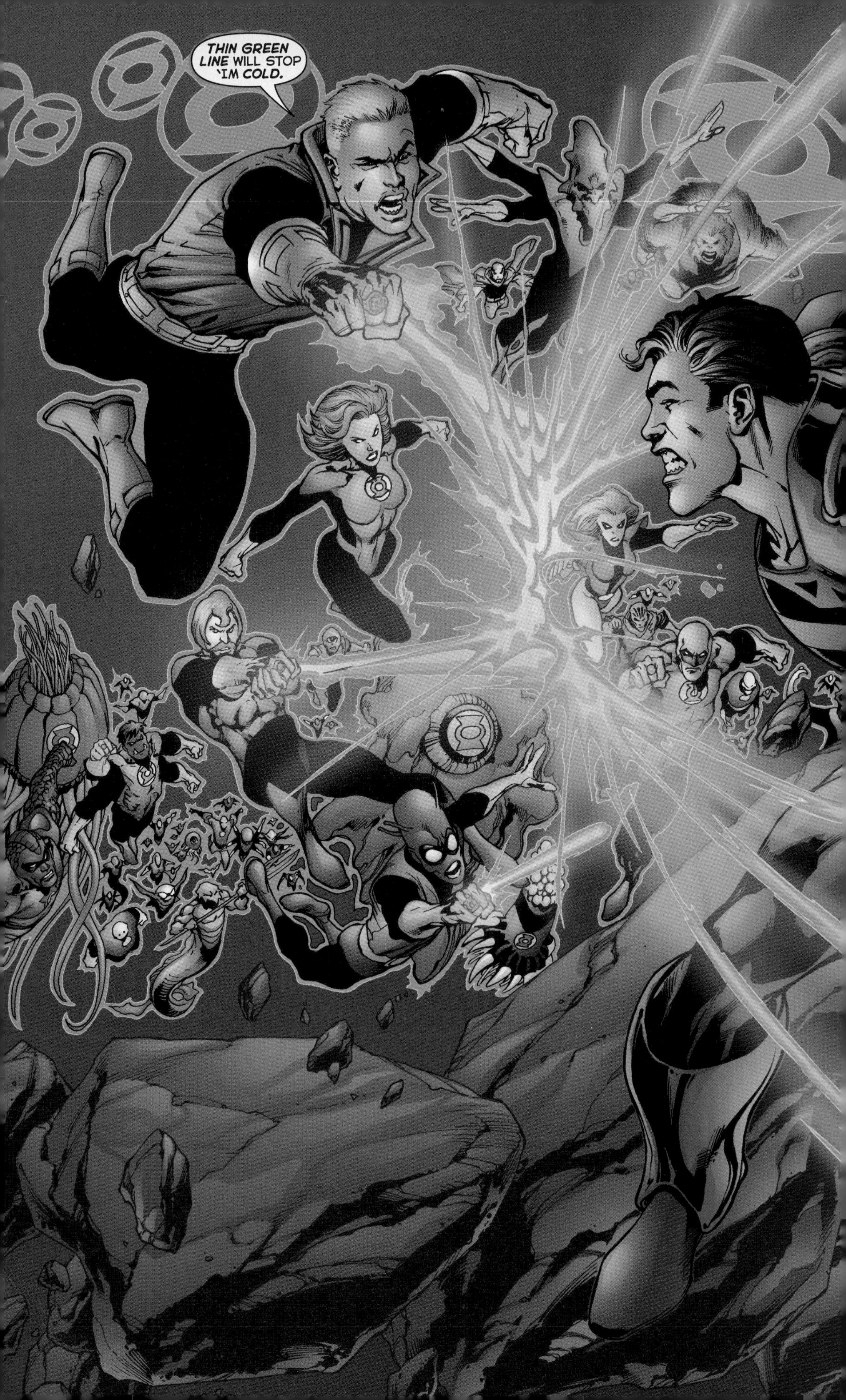
THIN GREEN LINE WILL STOP 'IM COLD.

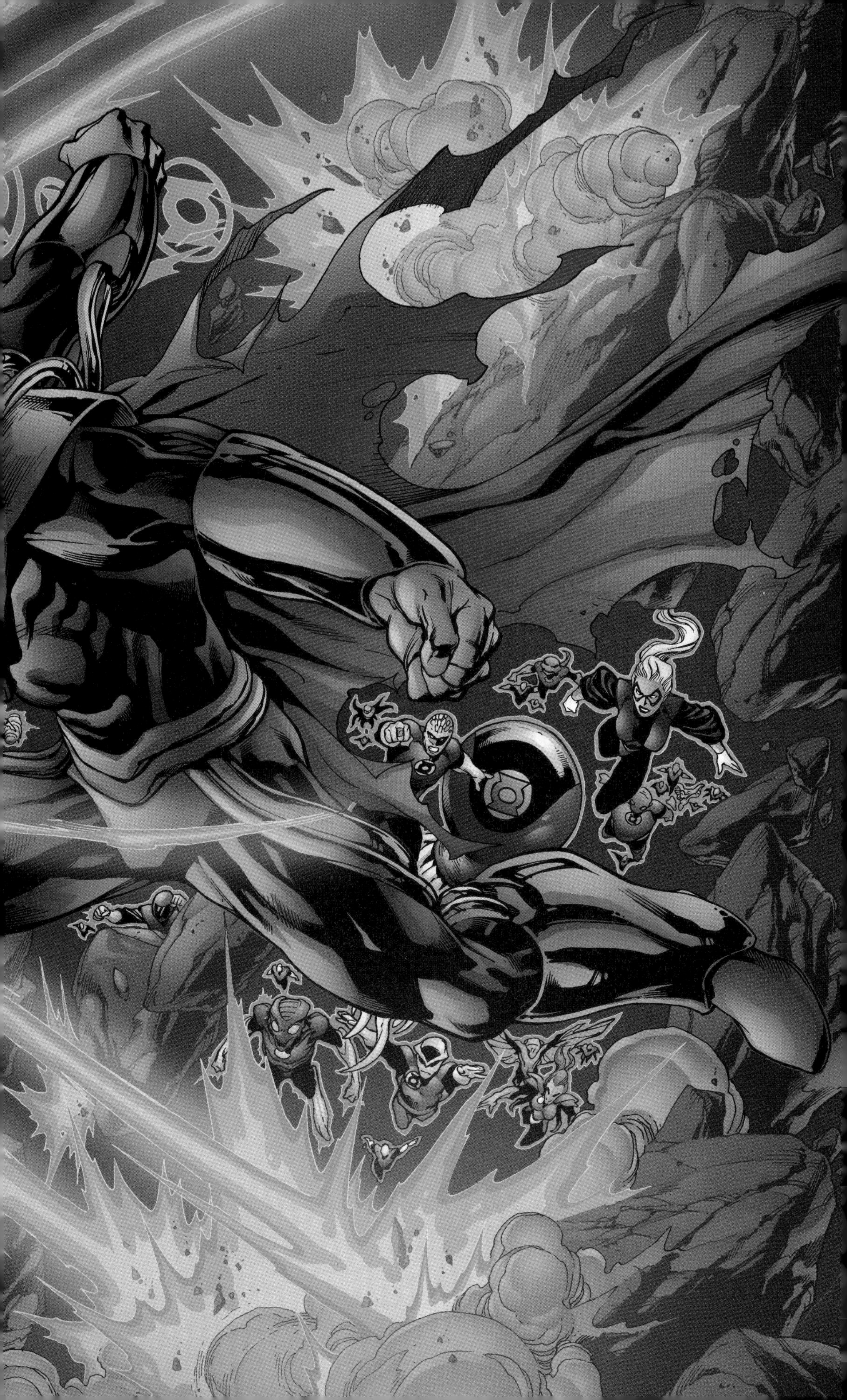

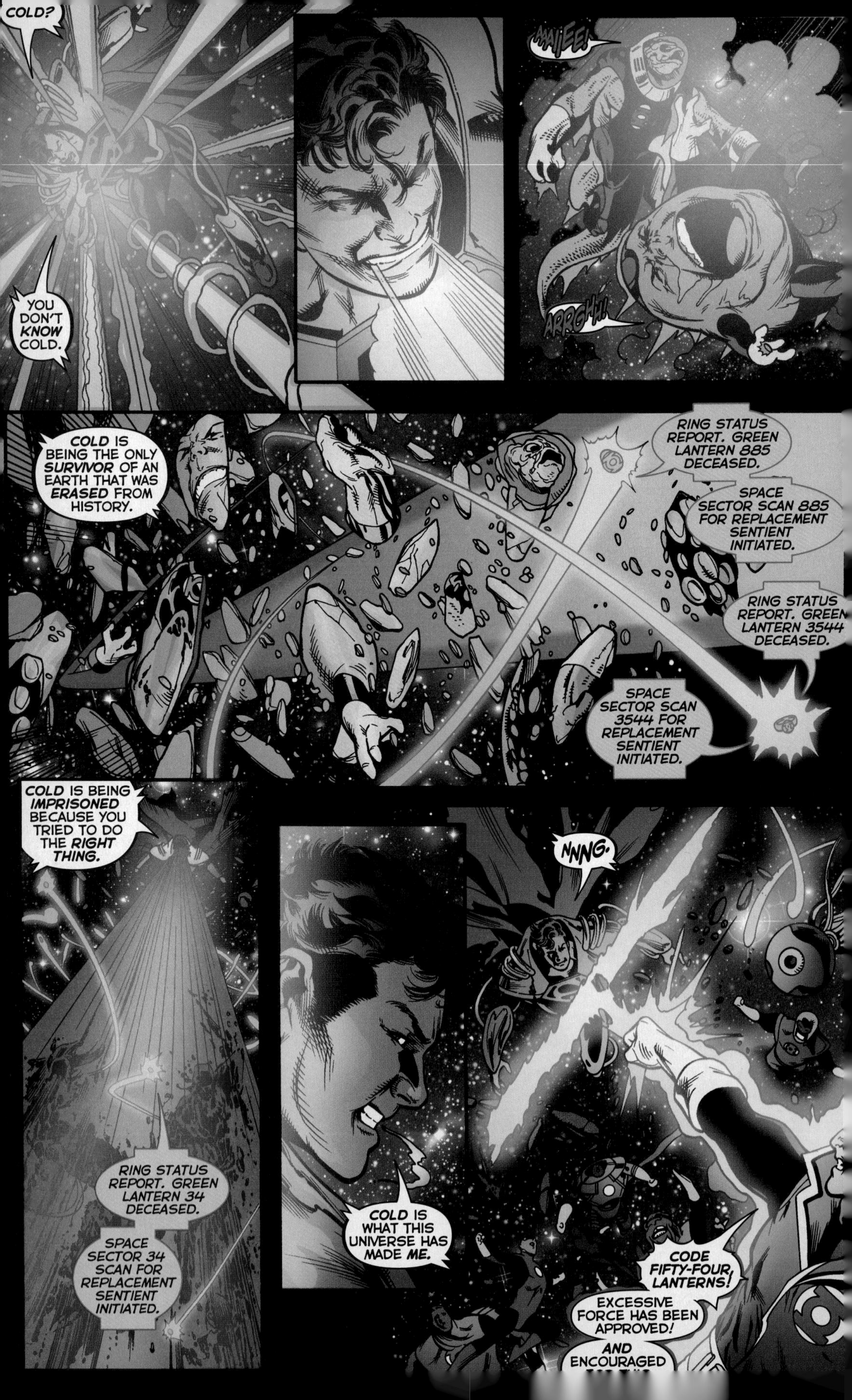
COLD?
YOU DON'T KNOW COLD.
AAAIIEE!
ARRGHH!
COLD IS BEING THE ONLY SURVIVOR OF AN EARTH THAT WAS ERASED FROM HISTORY.
RING STATUS REPORT. GREEN LANTERN 885 DECEASED.
SPACE SECTOR SCAN 885 FOR REPLACEMENT SENTIENT INITIATED.
RING STATUS REPORT. GREEN LANTERN 3544 DECEASED.
SPACE SECTOR SCAN 3544 FOR REPLACEMENT SENTIENT INITIATED.
COLD IS BEING IMPRISONED BECAUSE YOU TRIED TO DO THE RIGHT THING.
RING STATUS REPORT. GREEN LANTERN 34 DECEASED.
SPACE SECTOR 34 SCAN FOR REPLACEMENT SENTIENT INITIATED.
NNNG.
COLD IS WHAT THIS UNIVERSE HAS MADE ME.
CODE FIFTY-FOUR, LANTERNS!
EXCESSIVE FORCE HAS BEEN APPROVED!
AND ENCOURAGED

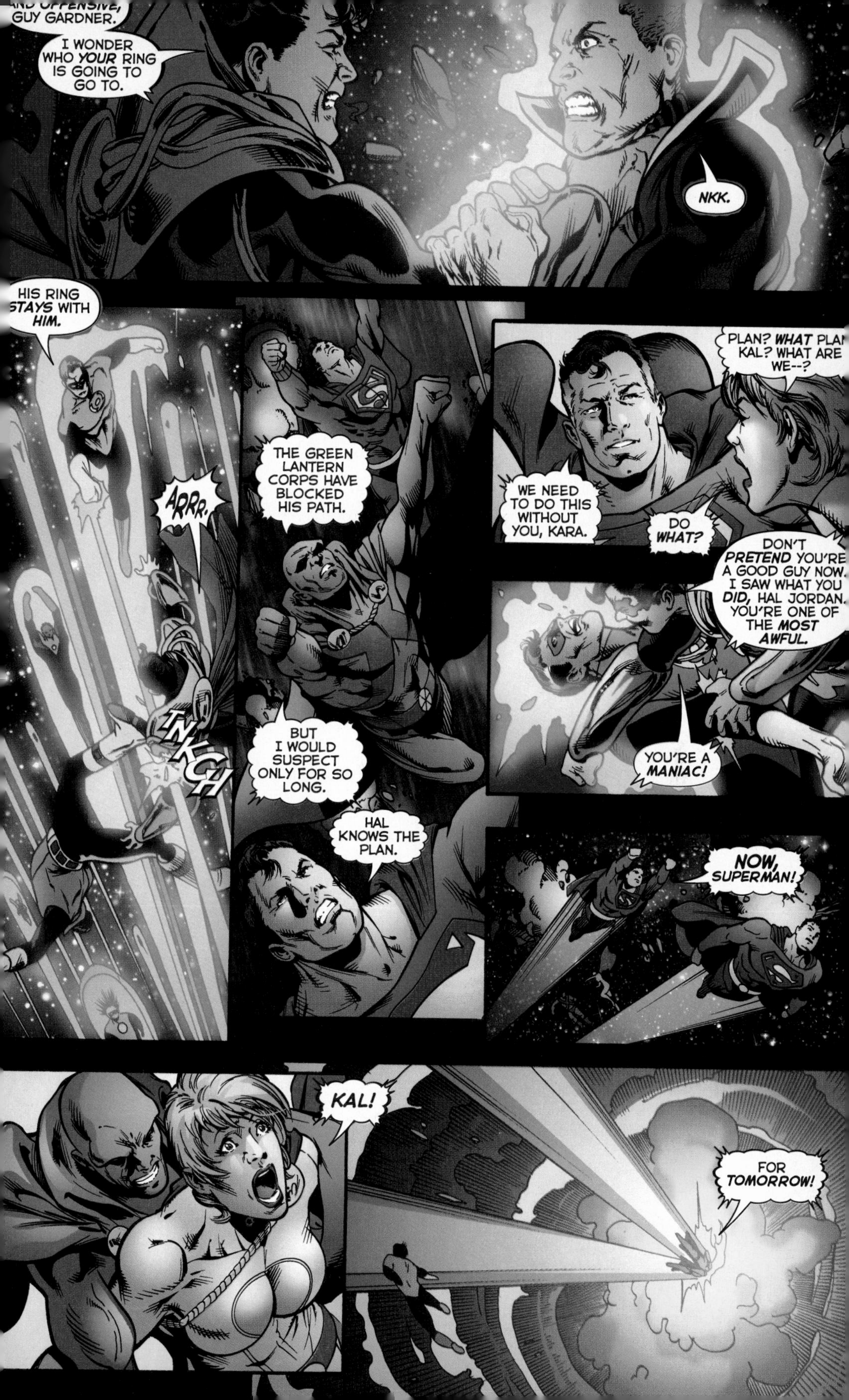
GUY GARDNER.
I WONDER WHO YOUR RING IS GOING TO GO TO.
NKK.
HIS RING STAYS WITH HIM.
ARRR.
INKCH
THE GREEN LANTERN CORPS HAVE BLOCKED HIS PATH.
BUT I WOULD SUSPECT ONLY FOR SO LONG.
HAL KNOWS THE PLAN.
PLAN? WHAT PLA
KAL? WHAT ARE WE--?
WE NEED TO DO THIS WITHOUT YOU, KARA.
DO WHAT?
DON'T PRETEND YOU'RE A GOOD GUY NOW. I SAW WHAT YOU DID, HAL JORDAN. YOU'RE ONE OF THE MOST AWFUL.
YOU'RE A MANIAC!
NOW, SUPERMAN!
KAL!
FOR TOMORROW!

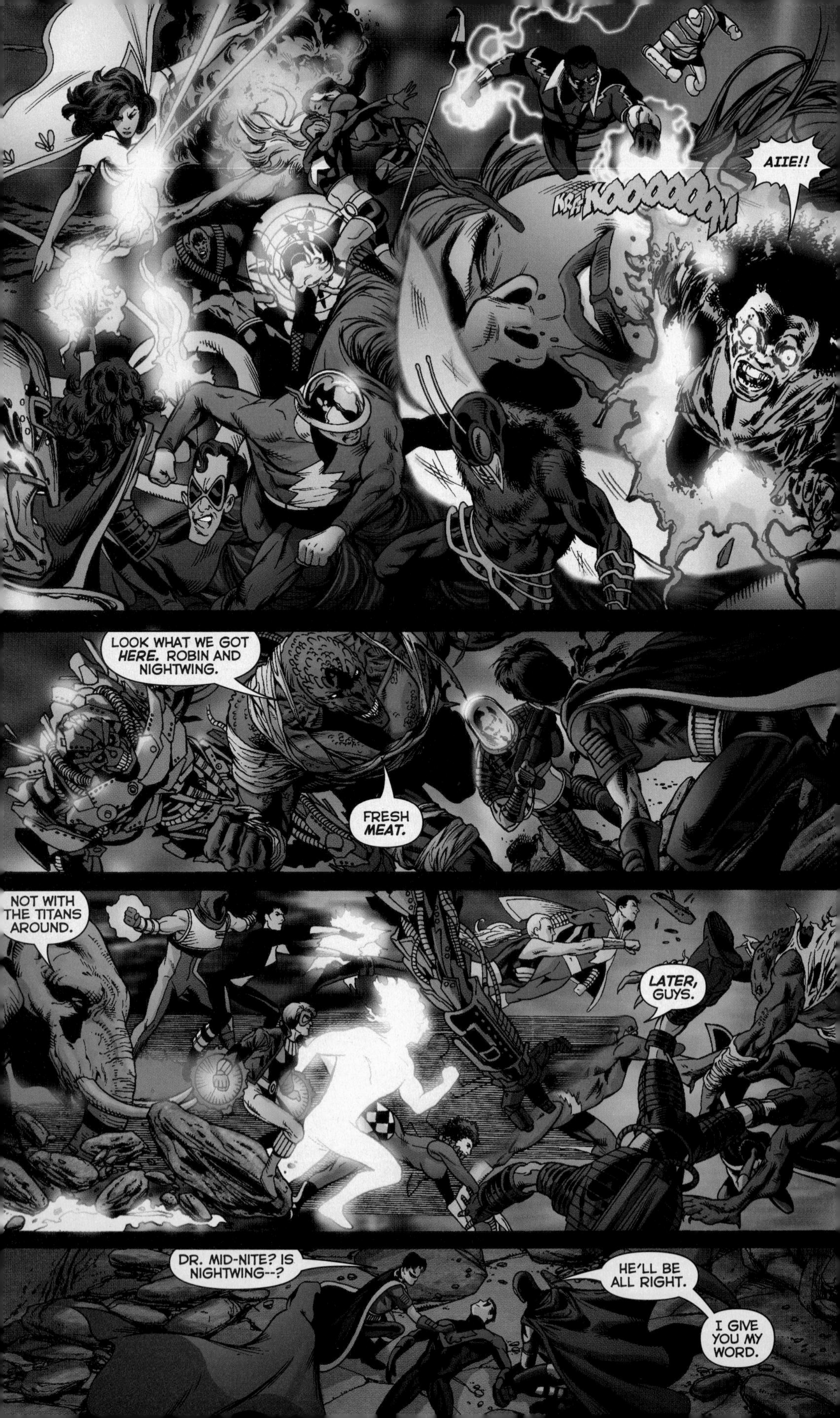
KRA-KOOOOOOM
AIIE!!
LOOK WHAT WE GOT *HERE.* ROBIN AND NIGHTWING.
FRESH *MEAT.*
NOT WITH THE TITANS AROUND.
LATER, GUYS.
DR. MID-NITE? IS NIGHTWING--?
HE'LL BE ALL RIGHT.
I GIVE YOU MY WORD.

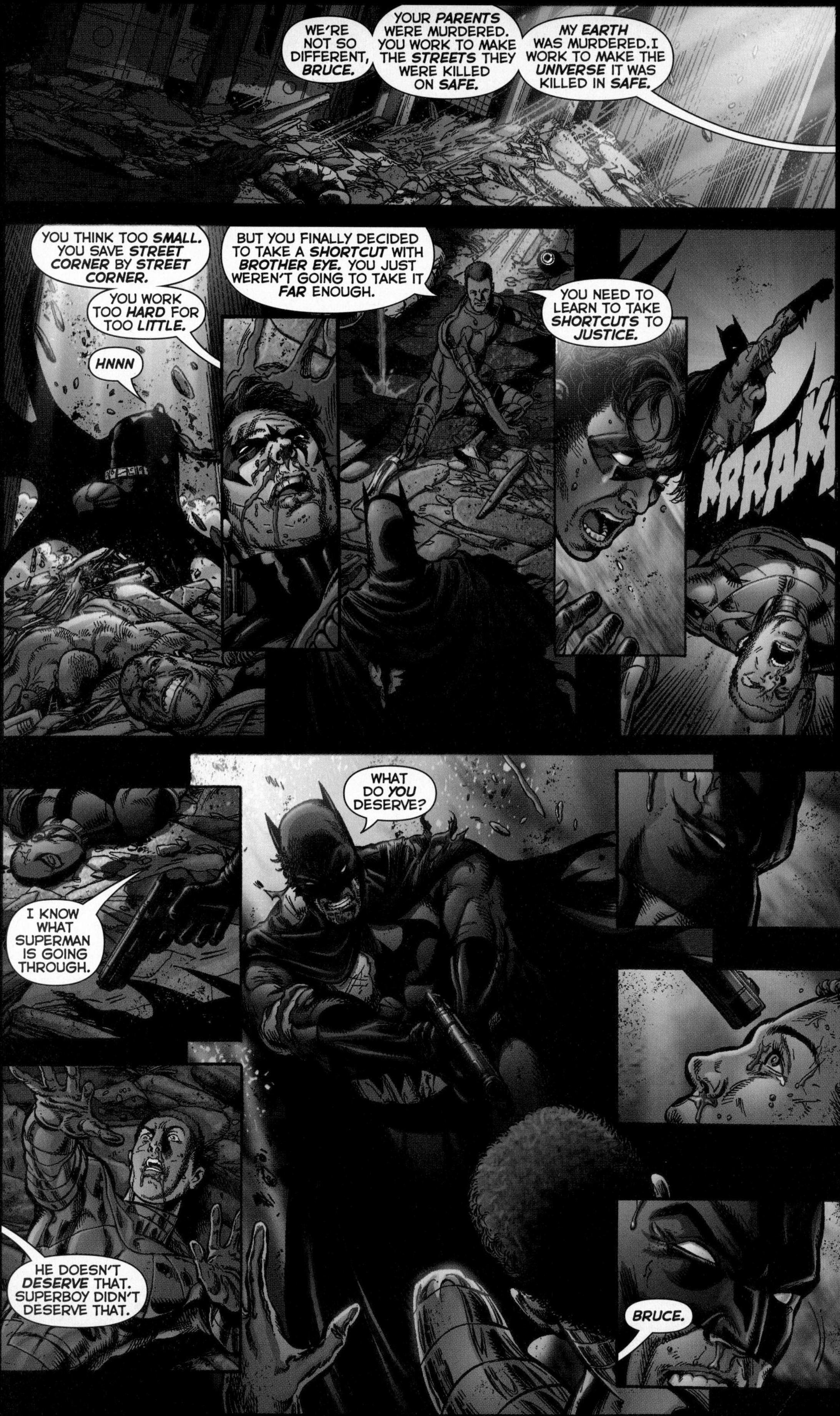

WE'RE NOT SO DIFFERENT, BRUCE.
YOUR PARENTS WERE MURDERED. YOU WORK TO MAKE THE STREETS THEY WERE KILLED ON SAFE.
MY EARTH WAS MURDERED. I WORK TO MAKE THE UNIVERSE IT WAS KILLED IN SAFE.
YOU THINK TOO SMALL. YOU SAVE STREET CORNER BY STREET CORNER.
YOU WORK TOO HARD FOR TOO LITTLE.
HNNN
BUT YOU FINALLY DECIDED TO TAKE A SHORTCUT WITH BROTHER EYE. YOU JUST WEREN'T GOING TO TAKE IT FAR ENOUGH.
YOU NEED TO LEARN TO TAKE SHORTCUTS TO JUSTICE.
KRRAM
WHAT DO YOU DESERVE?
I KNOW WHAT SUPERMAN IS GOING THROUGH.
HE DOESN'T DESERVE THAT. SUPERBOY DIDN'T DESERVE THAT.
BRUCE.

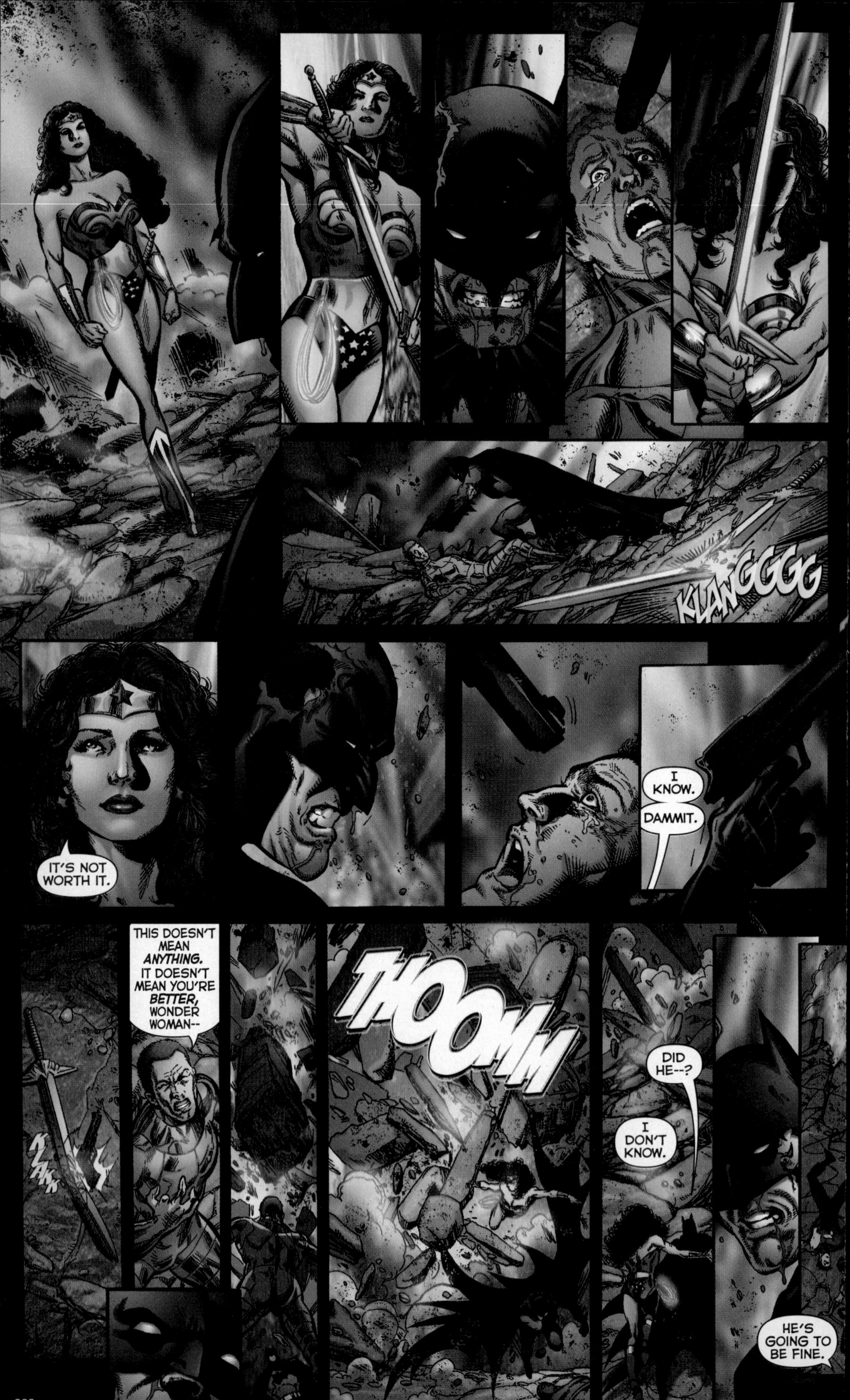

KLANGGGG
IT'S NOT WORTH IT.
I KNOW.
DAMMIT.
THIS DOESN'T MEAN *ANYTHING.* IT DOESN'T MEAN YOU'RE *BETTER,* WONDER WOMAN--
KLAKK
THOOMM
DID HE--?
I DON'T KNOW.
HE'S GOING TO BE FINE.

WHERE ARE YOU TAKING ME?

WHERE?!

YOU CAN'T SEND ME BACK INTO THE SPEED FORCE.

YOU'RE NOT *FAST* ENOUGH.

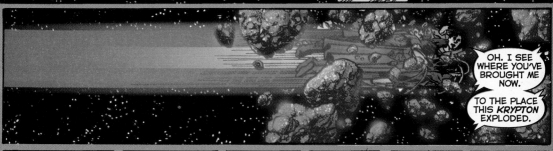

OH. I SEE WHERE YOU'VE BROUGHT ME NOW.

TO THE PLACE THIS *KRYPTON* EXPLODED.

BUT *THIS* KRYPTONITE ISN'T *FROM MY* UNIVERSE.

IT WON'T HURT *ME.*

ALL YOU'RE GOING TO DO IS KILL *THIS* SUPERMAN.

I MEAN, DID YOU *THINK* THESE *ROCKS* WOULD *STOP* ME?

HAHAHAHAHA

DID YOU *REALLY?*

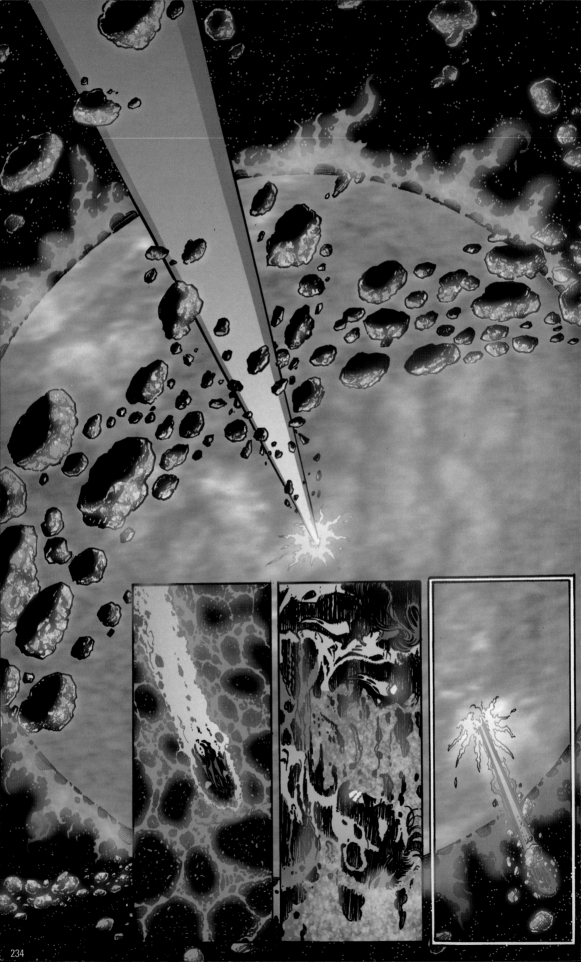

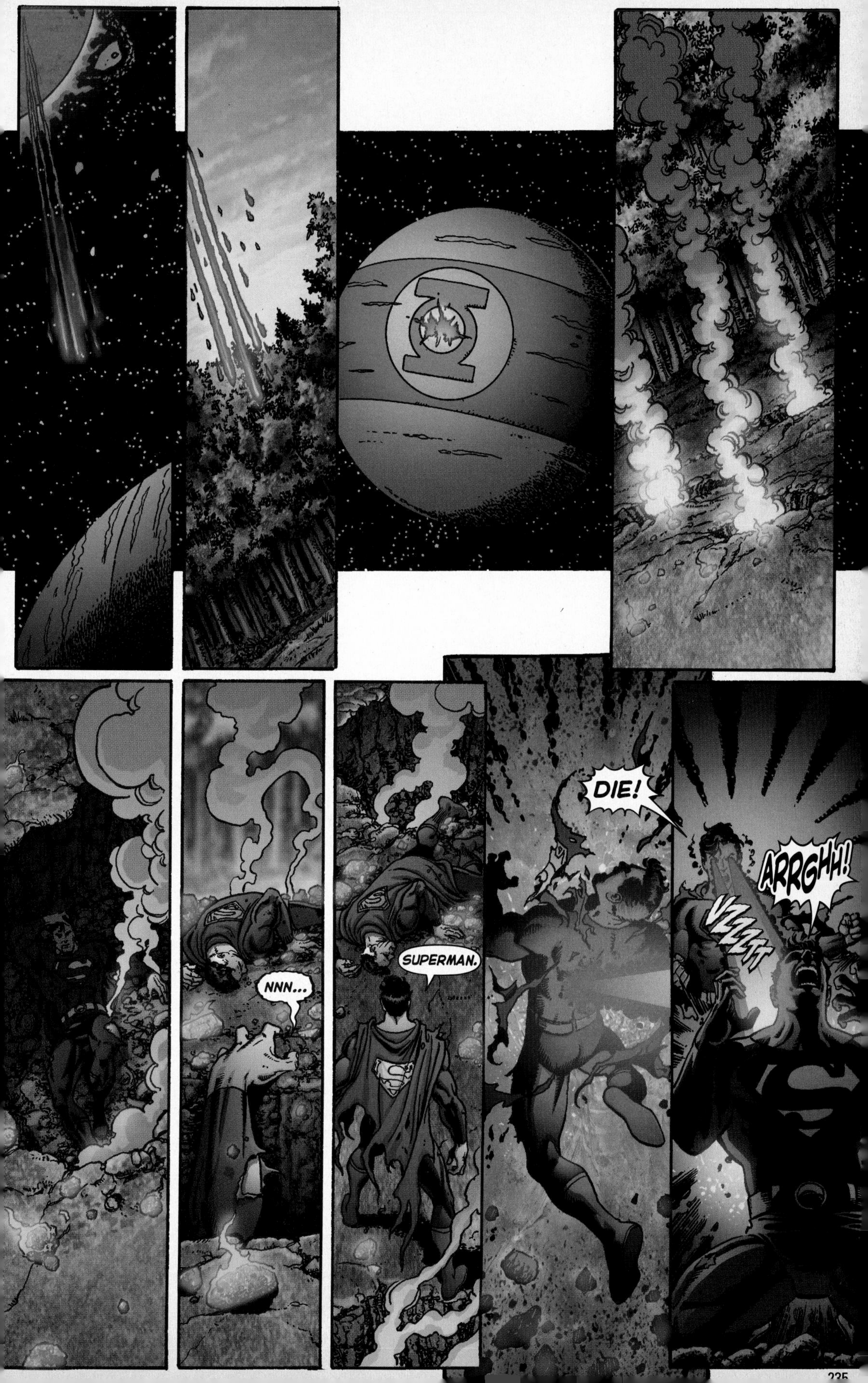
NNN...
SUPERMAN.
DIE!
ARRGHH!
VZZZZT

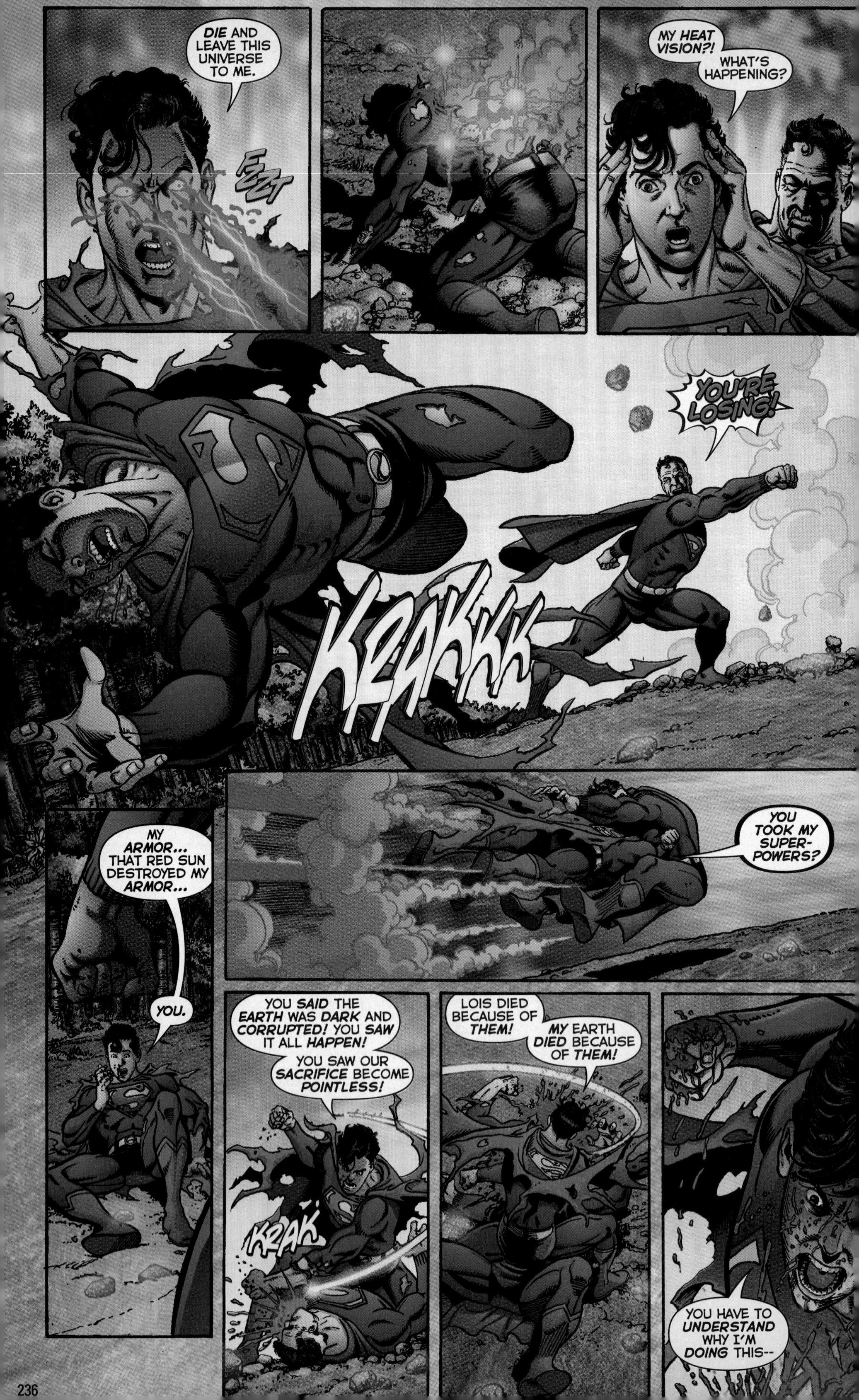

DIE AND LEAVE THIS UNIVERSE TO ME.
FZZT
MY HEAT VISION?!
WHAT'S HAPPENING?
YOU'RE LOSING!
KRAKKK
YOU TOOK MY SUPER-POWERS?
MY ARMOR... THAT RED SUN DESTROYED MY ARMOR...
YOU.
YOU SAID THE EARTH WAS DARK AND CORRUPTED! YOU SAW IT ALL HAPPEN!
YOU SAW OUR SACRIFICE BECOME POINTLESS!
KRAK
LOIS DIED BECAUSE OF THEM!
MY EARTH DIED BECAUSE OF THEM!
YOU HAVE TO UNDERSTAND WHY I'M DOING THIS--

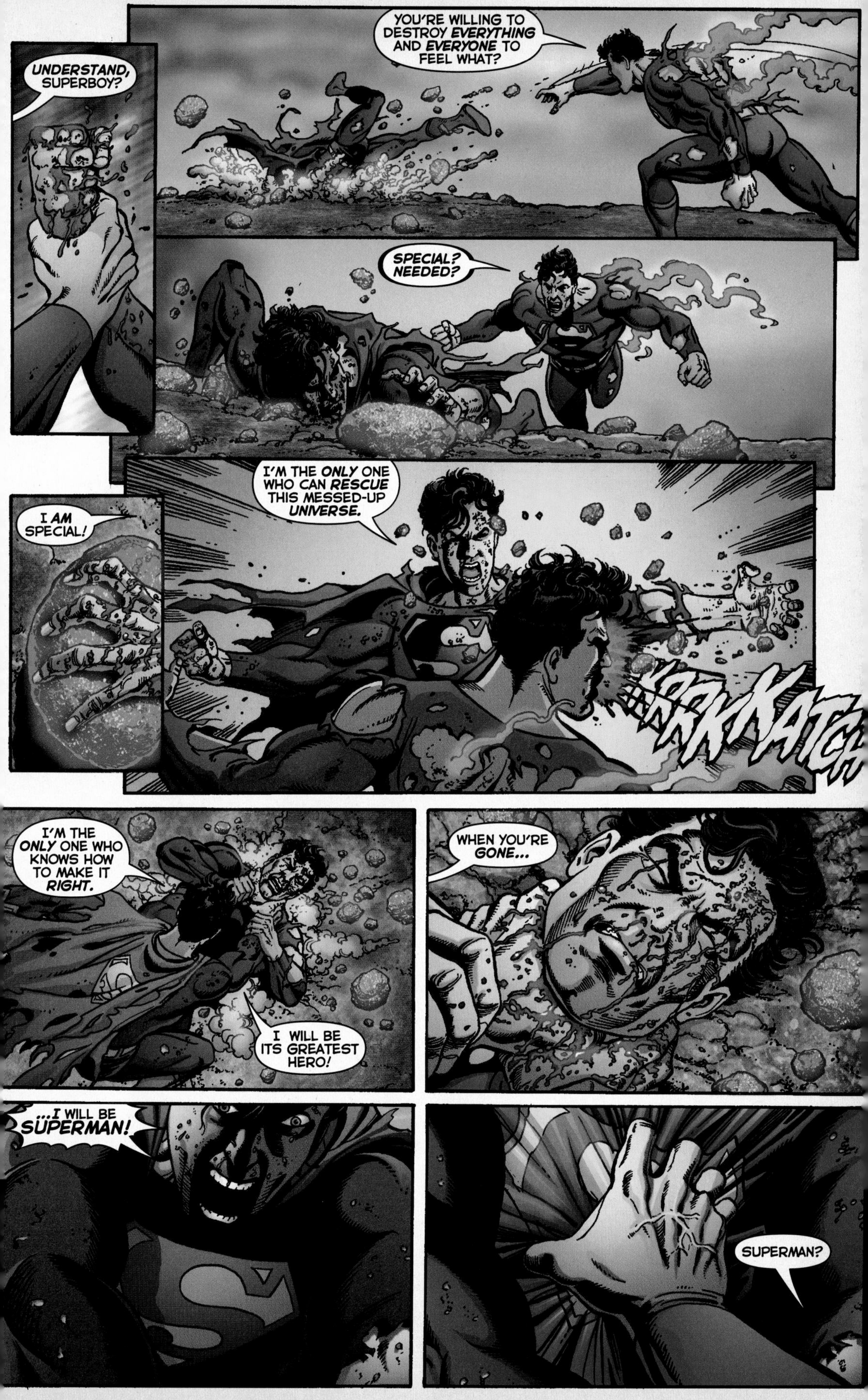
UNDERSTAND, SUPERBOY?
YOU'RE WILLING TO DESTROY EVERYTHING AND EVERYONE TO FEEL WHAT?
SPECIAL? NEEDED?
I AM SPECIAL!
I'M THE ONLY ONE WHO CAN RESCUE THIS MESSED-UP UNIVERSE.
KRAKKATCH
I'M THE ONLY ONE WHO KNOWS HOW TO MAKE IT RIGHT.
I WILL BE ITS GREATEST HERO!
WHEN YOU'RE GONE...
...I WILL BE SUPERMAN!
SUPERMAN?

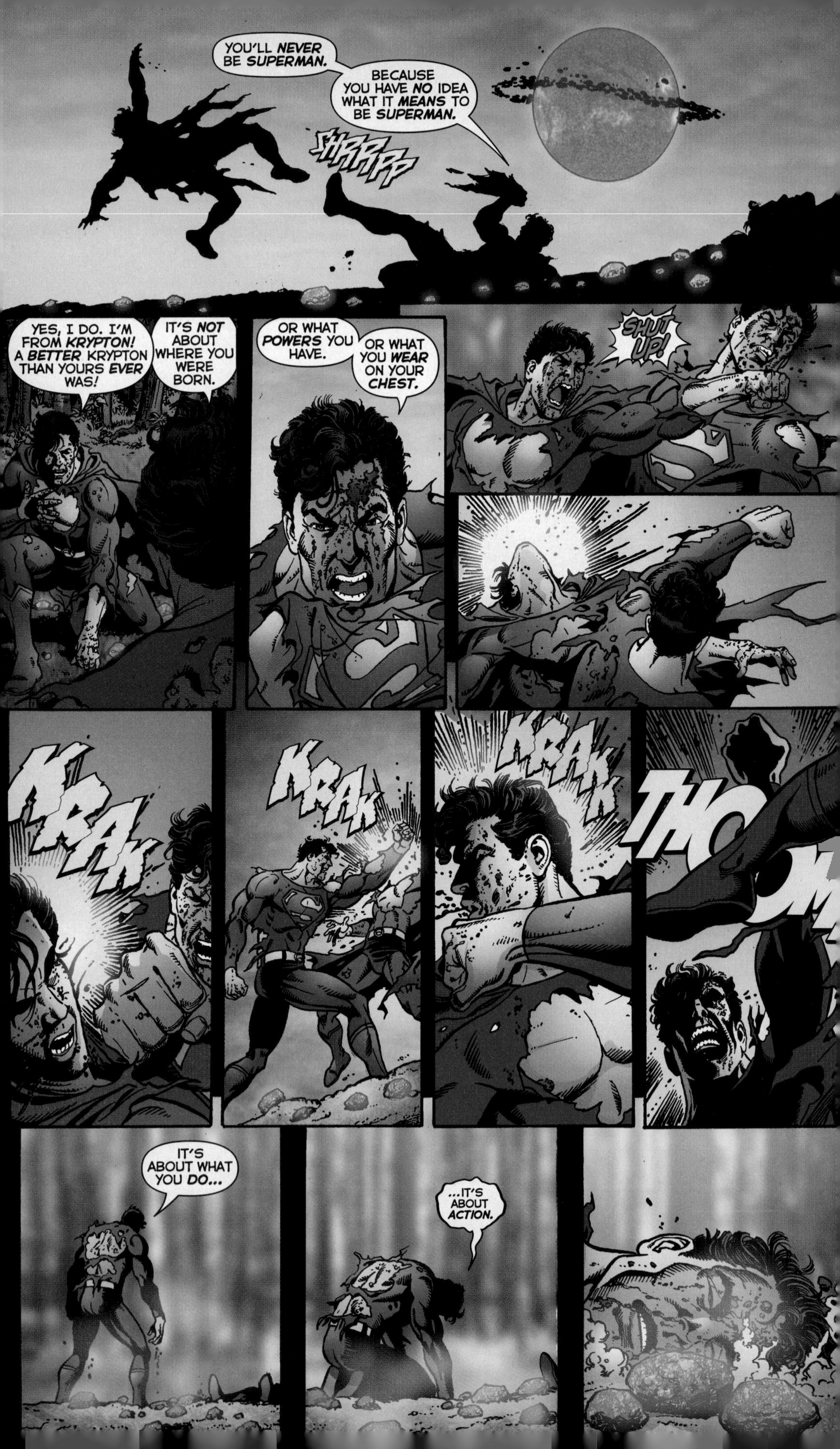

YOU'LL NEVER BE SUPERMAN.
BECAUSE YOU HAVE NO IDEA WHAT IT MEANS TO BE SUPERMAN.
SHRRPP
YES, I DO. I'M FROM KRYPTON! A BETTER KRYPTON THAN YOURS EVER WAS!
IT'S NOT ABOUT WHERE YOU WERE BORN.
OR WHAT POWERS YOU HAVE.
OR WHAT YOU WEAR ON YOUR CHEST.
SHUT UP!
KRAK
KRAK
KRAK
THOOM
IT'S ABOUT WHAT YOU DO...
...IT'S ABOUT ACTION.

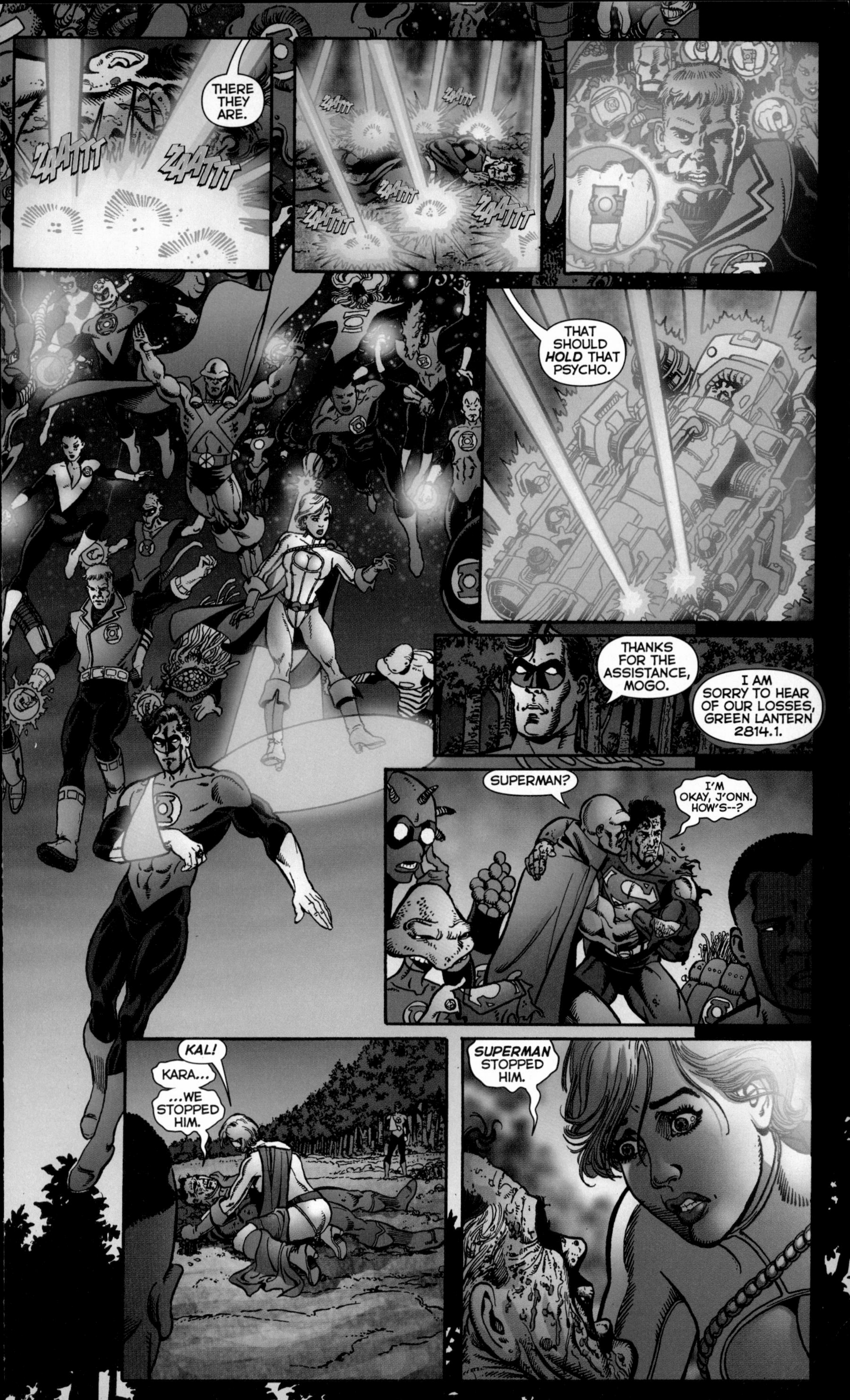

THERE THEY ARE.
ZAATTT
ZAATTT
ZAATTT
ZAATTT
ZAATTT
ZAATTT
ZAATTT
THAT SHOULD HOLD THAT PSYCHO.
THANKS FOR THE ASSISTANCE, MOGO.
I AM SORRY TO HEAR OF OUR LOSSES, GREEN LANTERN 2814.1.
SUPERMAN?
I'M OKAY, J'ONN. HOW'S--?
KAL!
KARA...
...WE STOPPED HIM.
SUPERMAN STOPPED HIM.

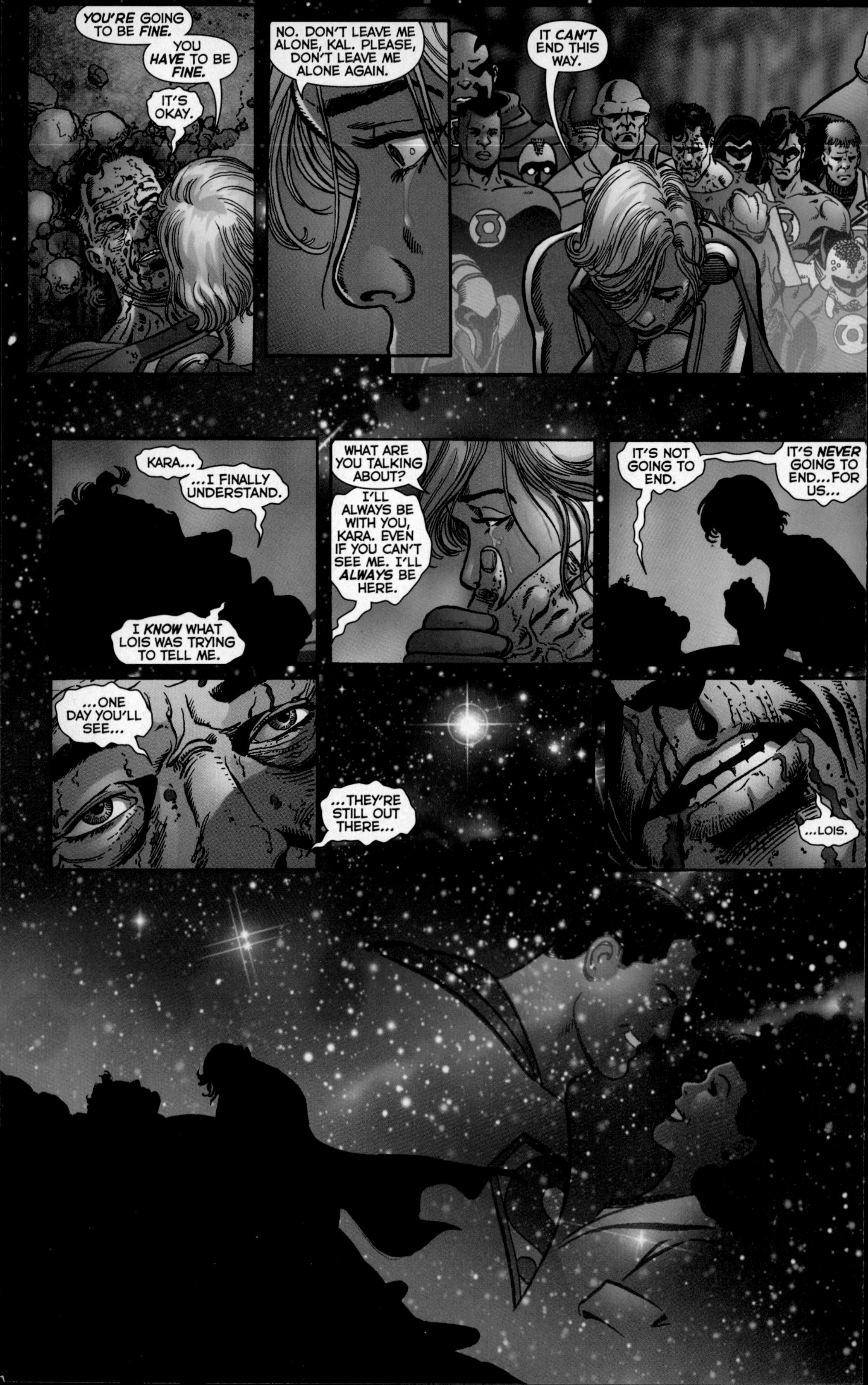
YOU'RE GOING TO BE FINE.
YOU HAVE TO BE FINE.
IT'S OKAY.
NO. DON'T LEAVE ME ALONE, KAL. PLEASE, DON'T LEAVE ME ALONE AGAIN.
IT CAN'T END THIS WAY.
KARA...
...I FINALLY UNDERSTAND.
I KNOW WHAT LOIS WAS TRYING TO TELL ME.
WHAT ARE YOU TALKING ABOUT?
I'LL ALWAYS BE WITH YOU, KARA. EVEN IF YOU CAN'T SEE ME. I'LL ALWAYS BE HERE.
IT'S NOT GOING TO END.
IT'S NEVER GOING TO END...FOR US...
...ONE DAY YOU'LL SEE...
...THEY'RE STILL OUT THERE...
...LOIS.

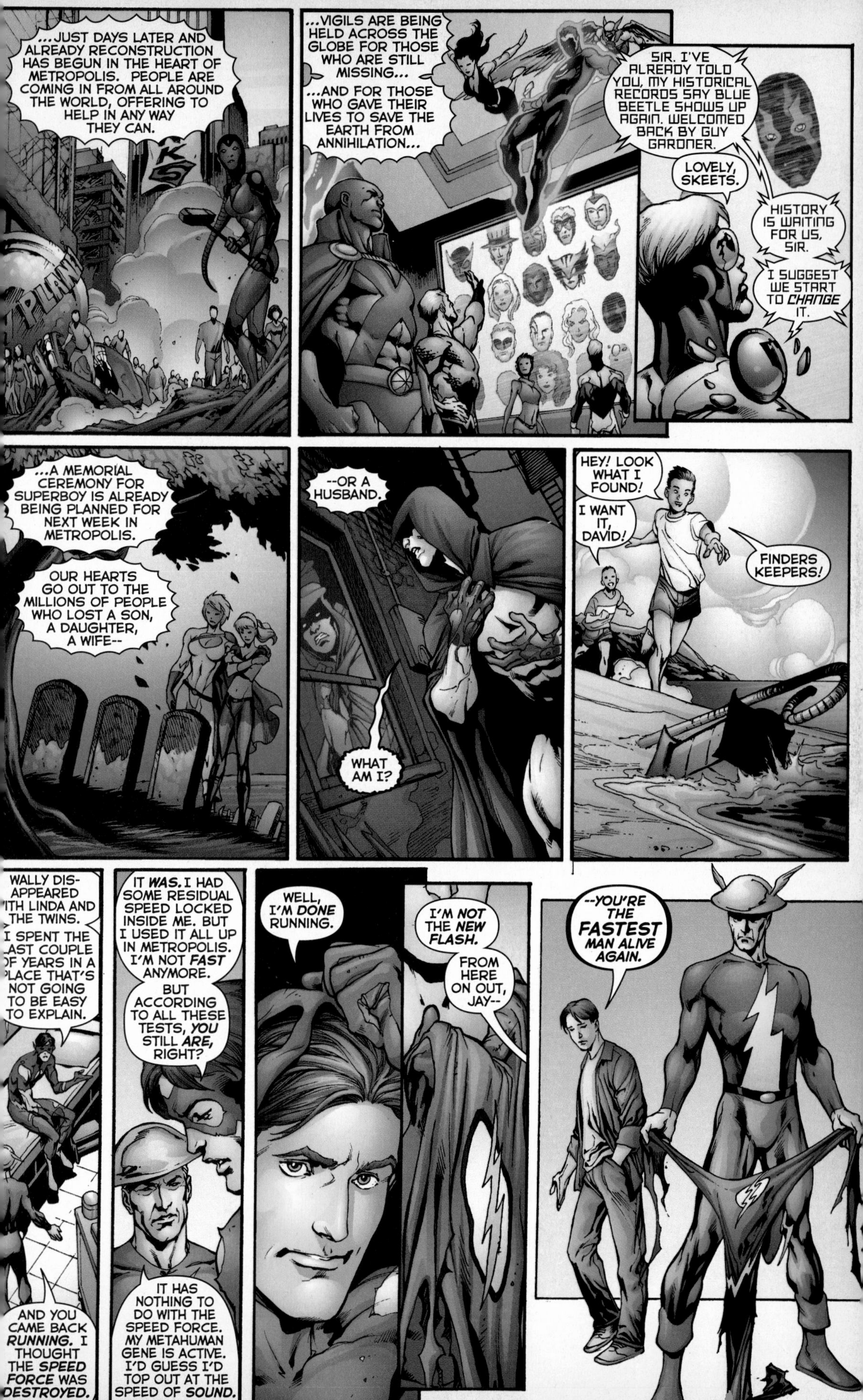
...JUST DAYS LATER AND ALREADY RECONSTRUCTION HAS BEGUN IN THE HEART OF METROPOLIS. PEOPLE ARE COMING IN FROM ALL AROUND THE WORLD, OFFERING TO HELP IN ANY WAY THEY CAN.
PLANET
...VIGILS ARE BEING HELD ACROSS THE GLOBE FOR THOSE WHO ARE STILL MISSING...
...AND FOR THOSE WHO GAVE THEIR LIVES TO SAVE THE EARTH FROM ANNIHILATION...
SIR. I'VE ALREADY TOLD YOU, MY HISTORICAL RECORDS SAY BLUE BEETLE SHOWS UP AGAIN. WELCOMED BACK BY GUY GARDNER.
LOVELY, SKEETS.
HISTORY IS WAITING FOR US, SIR.
I SUGGEST WE START TO *CHANGE* IT.
...A MEMORIAL CEREMONY FOR SUPERBOY IS ALREADY BEING PLANNED FOR NEXT WEEK IN METROPOLIS.
OUR HEARTS GO OUT TO THE MILLIONS OF PEOPLE WHO LOST A SON, A DAUGHTER, A WIFE--
--OR A HUSBAND.
WHAT AM I?
HEY! LOOK WHAT I FOUND!
I WANT IT, DAVID!
FINDERS KEEPERS!
WALLY DIS-APPEARED WITH LINDA AND THE TWINS. I SPENT THE LAST COUPLE OF YEARS IN A PLACE THAT'S NOT GOING TO BE EASY TO EXPLAIN.
AND YOU CAME BACK **RUNNING.** I THOUGHT THE **SPEED FORCE** WAS **DESTROYED.**
IT **WAS.** I HAD SOME RESIDUAL SPEED LOCKED INSIDE ME. BUT I USED IT ALL UP IN METROPOLIS. I'M NOT *FAST* ANYMORE.
BUT ACCORDING TO ALL THESE TESTS, **YOU** STILL **ARE,** RIGHT?
IT HAS NOTHING TO DO WITH THE SPEED FORCE. MY METAHUMAN GENE IS ACTIVE. I'D GUESS I'D TOP OUT AT THE SPEED OF **SOUND.**
WELL, I'M *DONE* RUNNING.
I'M **NOT** THE **NEW FLASH.**
FROM HERE ON OUT, JAY--
--YOU'RE THE **FASTEST** MAN ALIVE AGAIN.

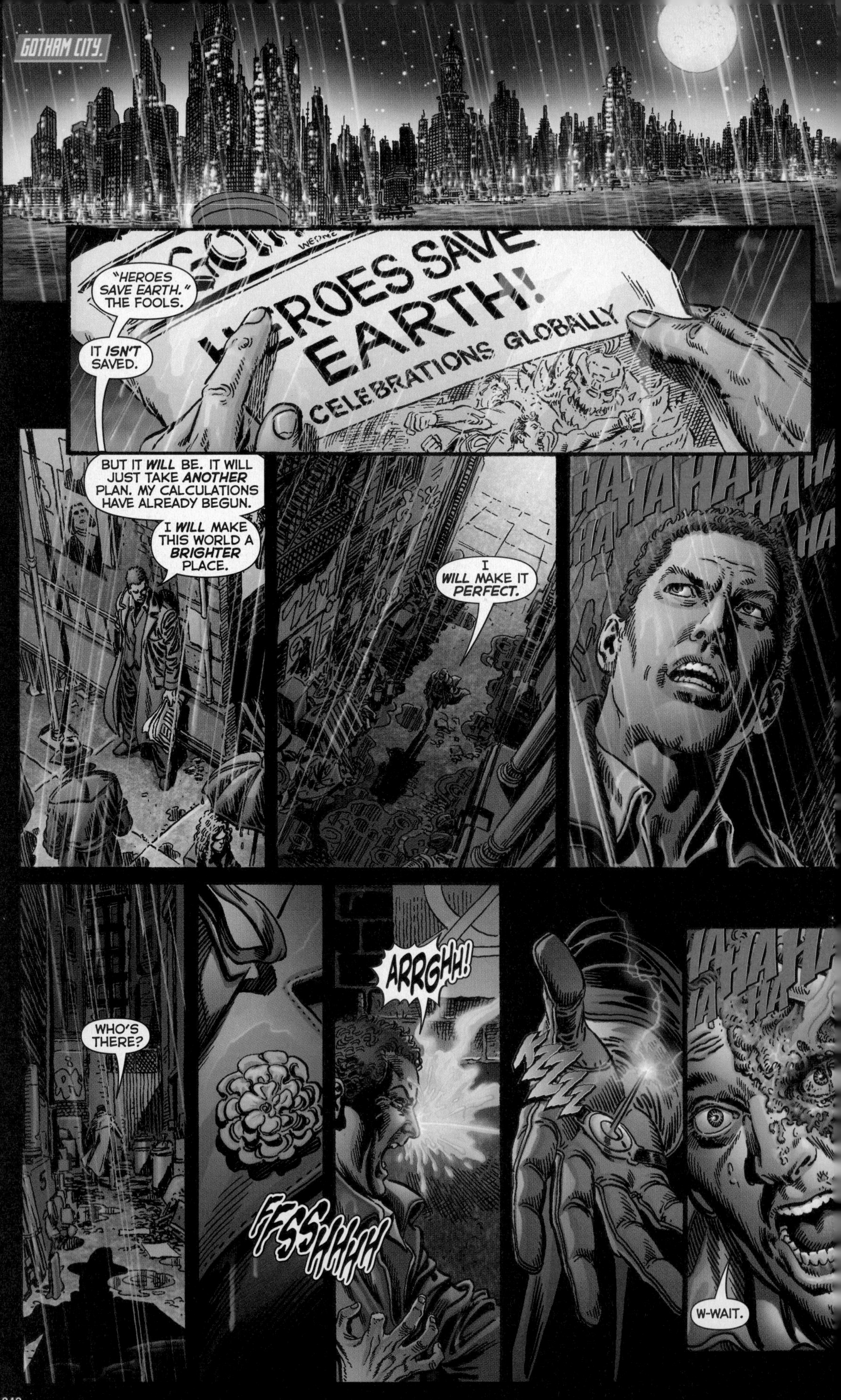
GOTHAM CITY.
"HEROES SAVE EARTH." THE FOOLS.
HEROES SAVE EARTH!
CELEBRATIONS GLOBALLY
IT ISN'T SAVED.
BUT IT WILL BE. IT WILL JUST TAKE ANOTHER PLAN. MY CALCULATIONS HAVE ALREADY BEGUN.
I WILL MAKE THIS WORLD A BRIGHTER PLACE.
I WILL MAKE IT PERFECT.
HAHAHAHAHAHA
WHO'S THERE?
ARRGHH!
FFSSHHHH
W-WAIT.

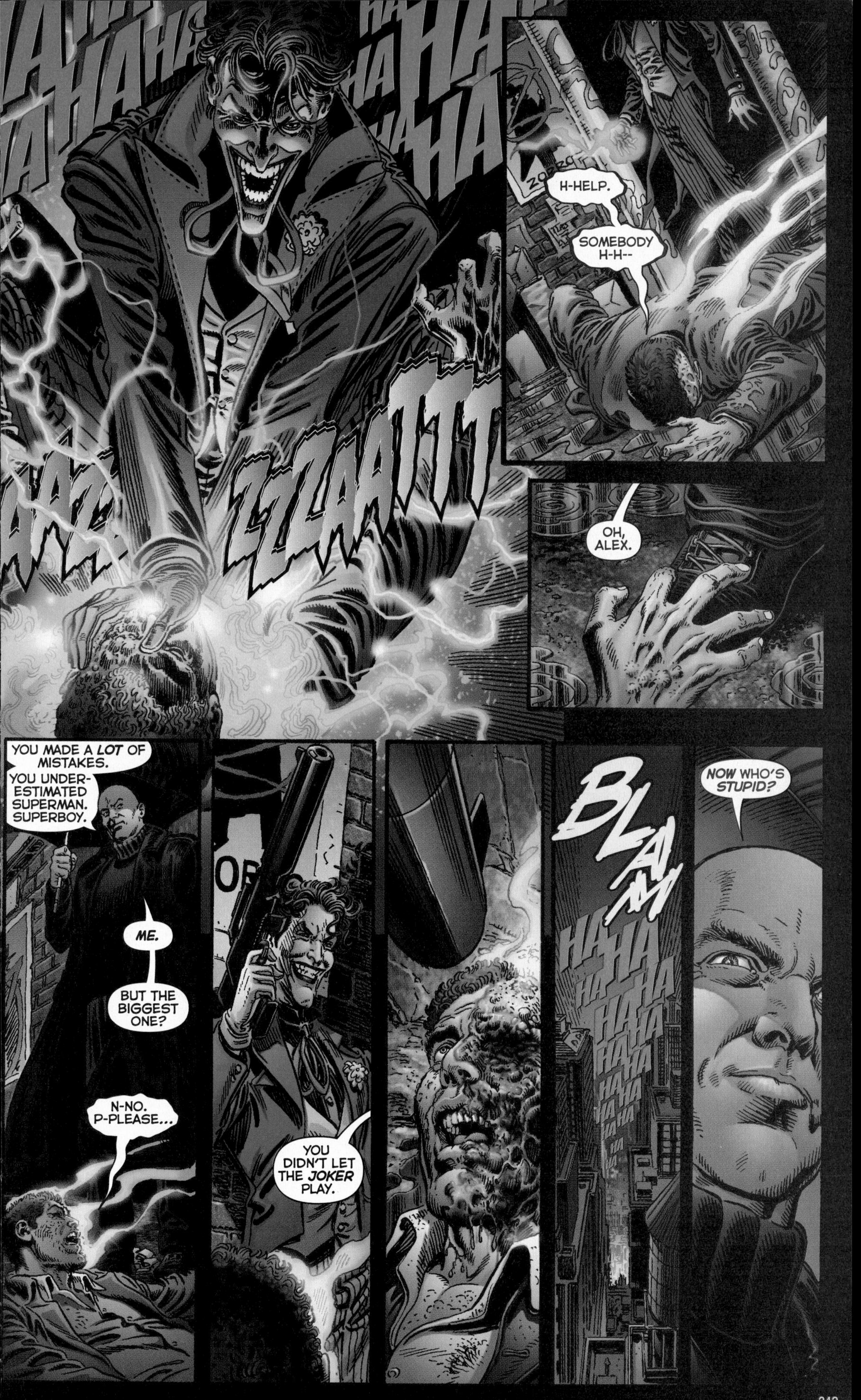
HAHAHA HAHAHA HAHAHA
ZZZAATTT
H-HELP.
SOMEBODY H-H--
OH, ALEX.
YOU MADE A LOT OF MISTAKES. YOU UNDER-ESTIMATED SUPERMAN. SUPERBOY.
ME.
BUT THE BIGGEST ONE?
N-NO. P-PLEASE...
YOU DIDN'T LET THE JOKER PLAY.
BLAM
HAHAHAHAHAHA
NOW WHO'S STUPID?

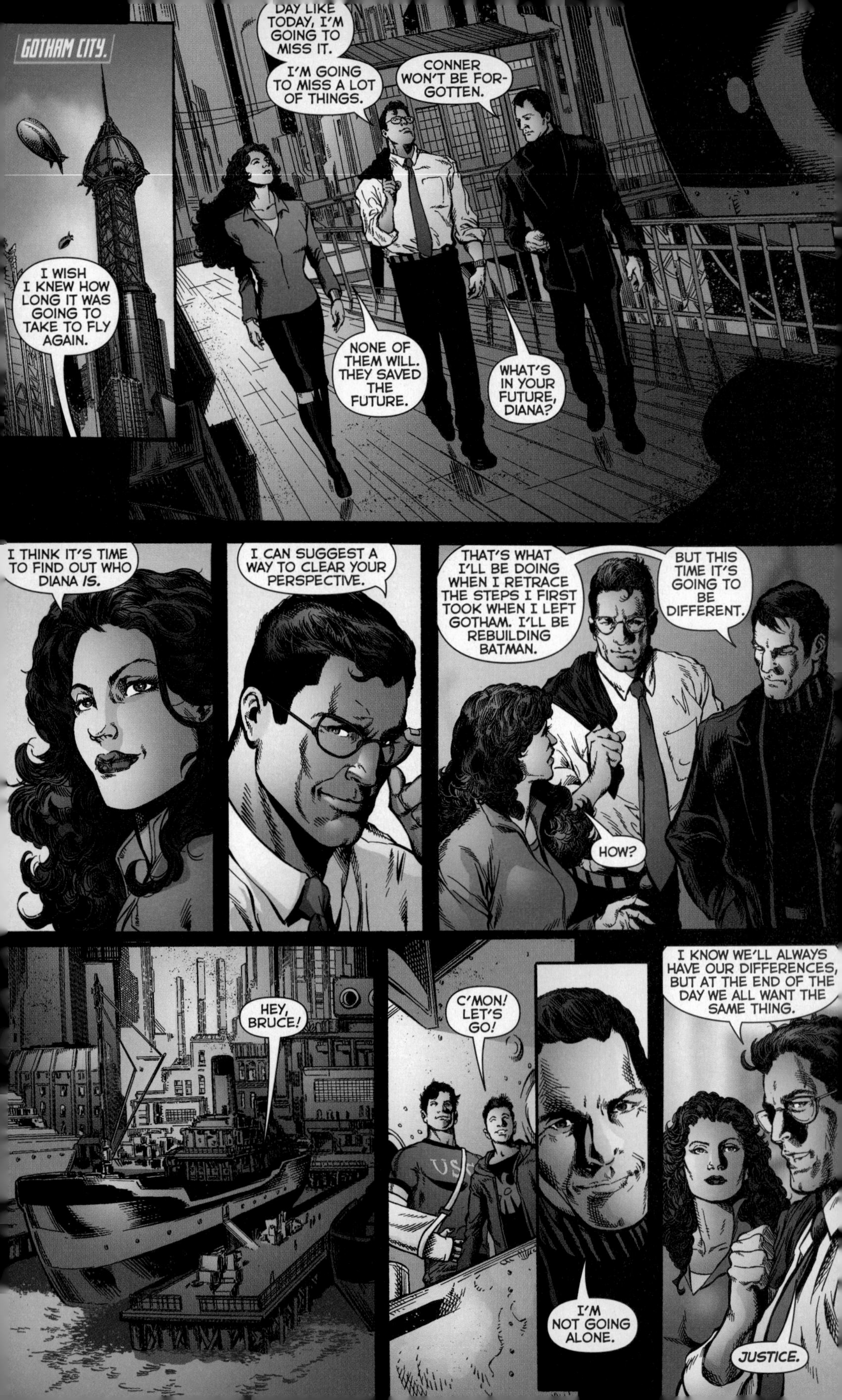
GOTHAM CITY.
DAY LIKE TODAY, I'M GOING TO MISS IT.
I'M GOING TO MISS A LOT OF THINGS.
CONNER WON'T BE FOR-GOTTEN.
I WISH I KNEW HOW LONG IT WAS GOING TO TAKE TO FLY AGAIN.
NONE OF THEM WILL. THEY SAVED THE FUTURE.
WHAT'S IN YOUR FUTURE, DIANA?
I THINK IT'S TIME TO FIND OUT WHO DIANA *IS*.
I CAN SUGGEST A WAY TO CLEAR YOUR PERSPECTIVE.
THAT'S WHAT I'LL BE DOING WHEN I RETRACE THE STEPS I FIRST TOOK WHEN I LEFT GOTHAM. I'LL BE REBUILDING BATMAN.
BUT THIS TIME IT'S GOING TO BE DIFFERENT.
HOW?
HEY, BRUCE!
C'MON! LET'S GO!
I'M NOT GOING ALONE.
I KNOW WE'LL ALWAYS HAVE OUR DIFFERENCES, BUT AT THE END OF THE DAY WE ALL WANT THE SAME THING.
JUSTICE.

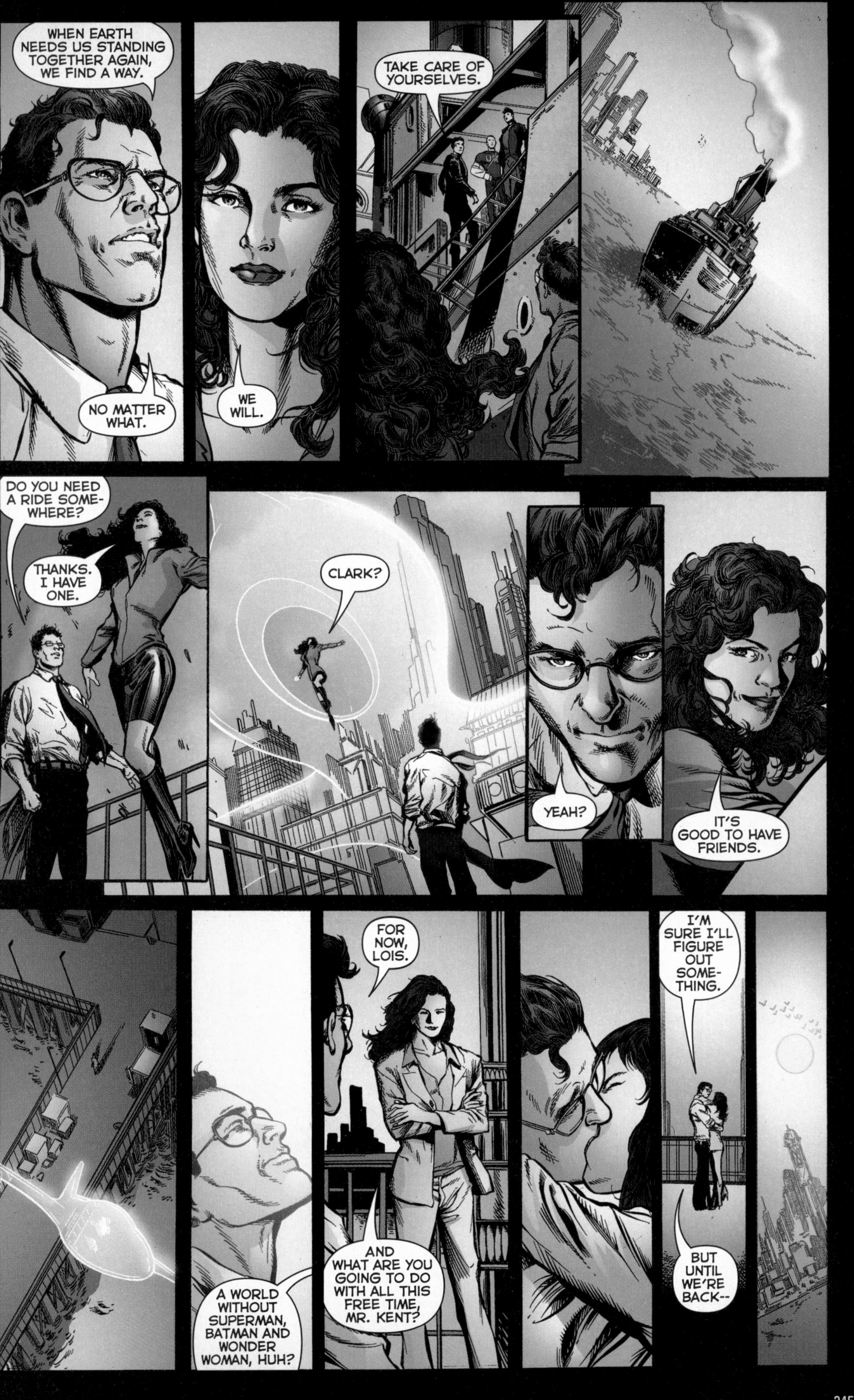
WHEN EARTH NEEDS US STANDING TOGETHER AGAIN, WE FIND A WAY.
NO MATTER WHAT.
WE WILL.
TAKE CARE OF YOURSELVES.
DO YOU NEED A RIDE SOME-WHERE?
THANKS. I HAVE ONE.
CLARK?
YEAH?
IT'S GOOD TO HAVE FRIENDS.
A WORLD WITHOUT SUPERMAN, BATMAN AND WONDER WOMAN, HUH?
FOR NOW, LOIS.
AND WHAT ARE YOU GOING TO DO WITH ALL THIS FREE TIME, MR. KENT?
I'M SURE I'LL FIGURE OUT SOME-THING.
BUT UNTIL WE'RE BACK--

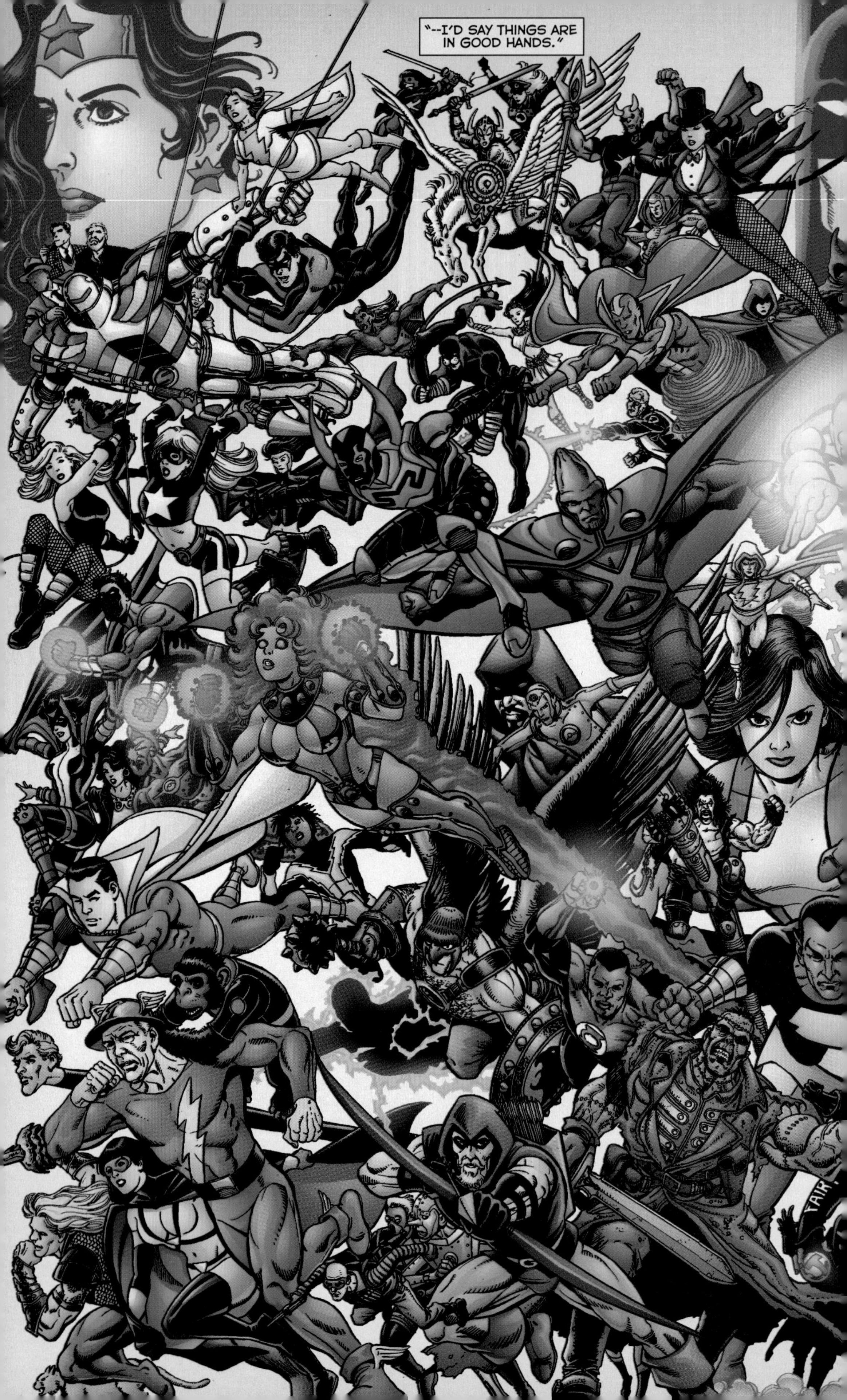
"--I'D SAY THINGS ARE IN GOOD HANDS."

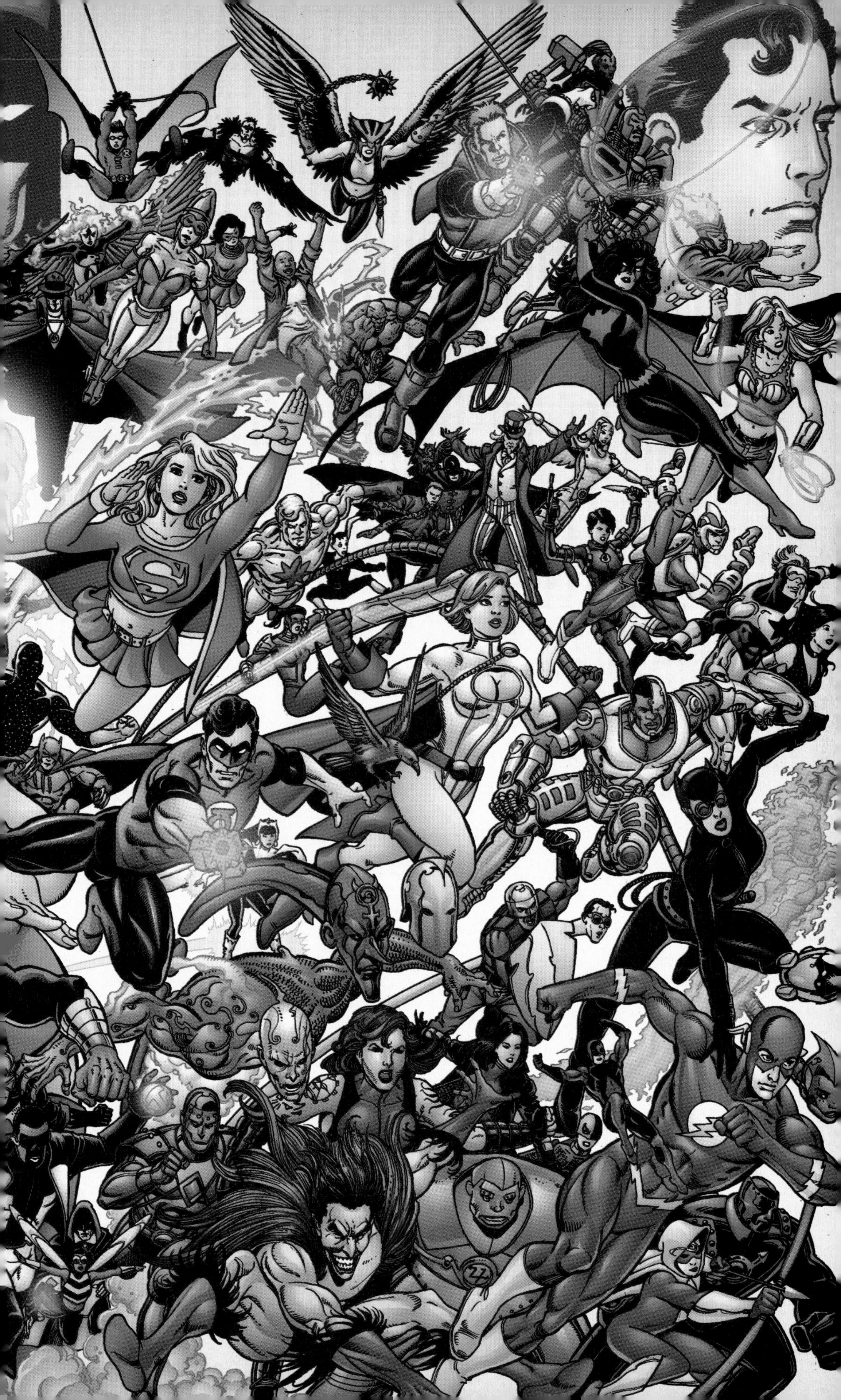

CENTER OF UNIVERSE.

THEY'RE ASKIN' ME TO DELIVER THE SPEECH AT TONIGHT'S CEREMONY, JORDAN. THIRTY-TWO LANTERNS K.I.A. HASN'T BEEN A MASSACRE LIKE THAT SINCE--

I KNOW WHEN.

OH. YEAH. I'M NOT ONE FOR PUBLIC SPEAKIN'.

YOU'LL DO FINE, GUY.

QUANTUM CONTAINMENT FIELDS SURROUNDING A *JUNIOR* RED-SUN EATER, COURTESY OF DONNA TROY. *FIFTY* GREEN LANTERNS WATCHING HIM AT ALL TIMES.

YOU THINK IT'LL HOLD?

I PRAY IT DOES.

I'VE BEEN IN WORSE PLACES THAN THIS.

AND I'VE GOTTEN OUT.

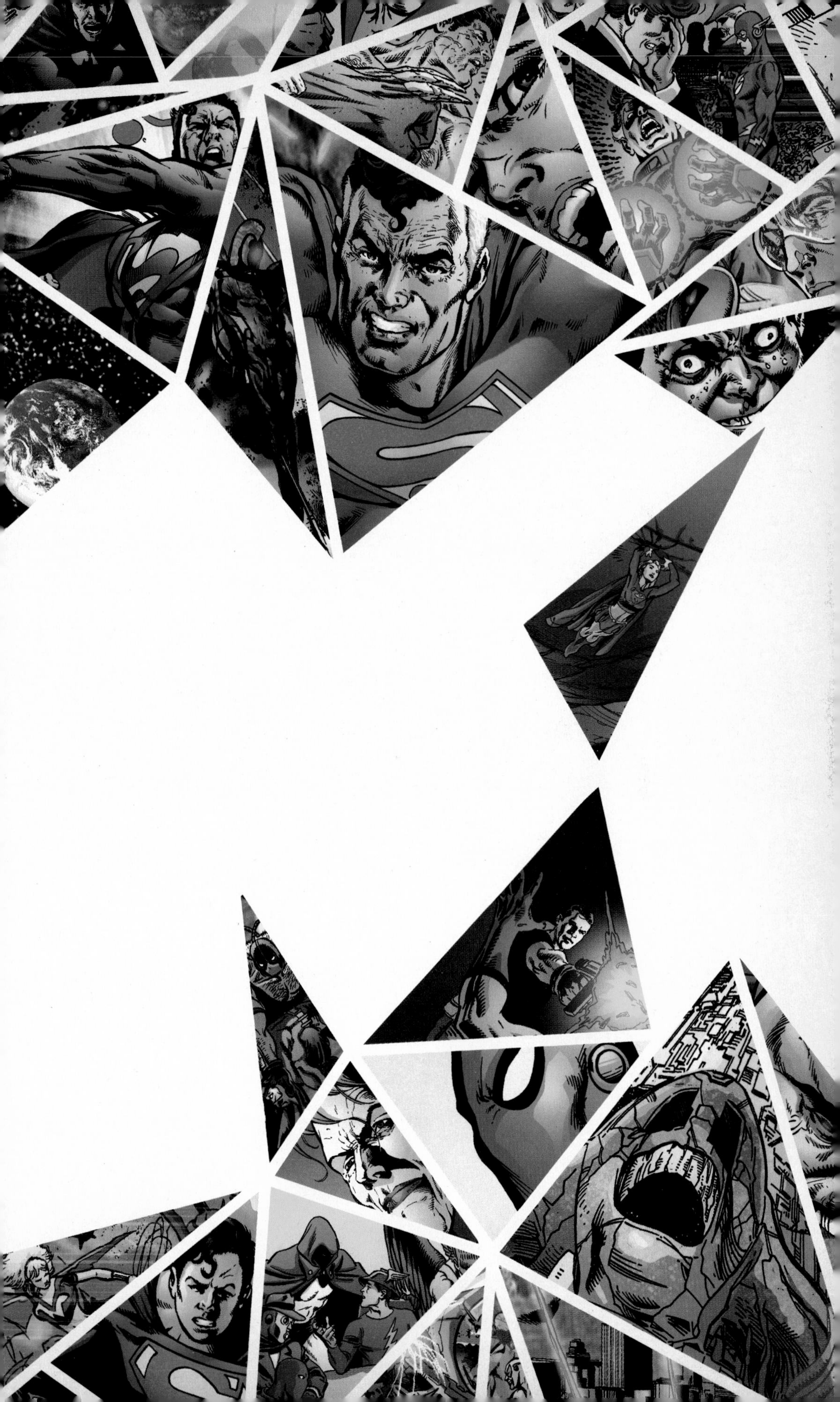

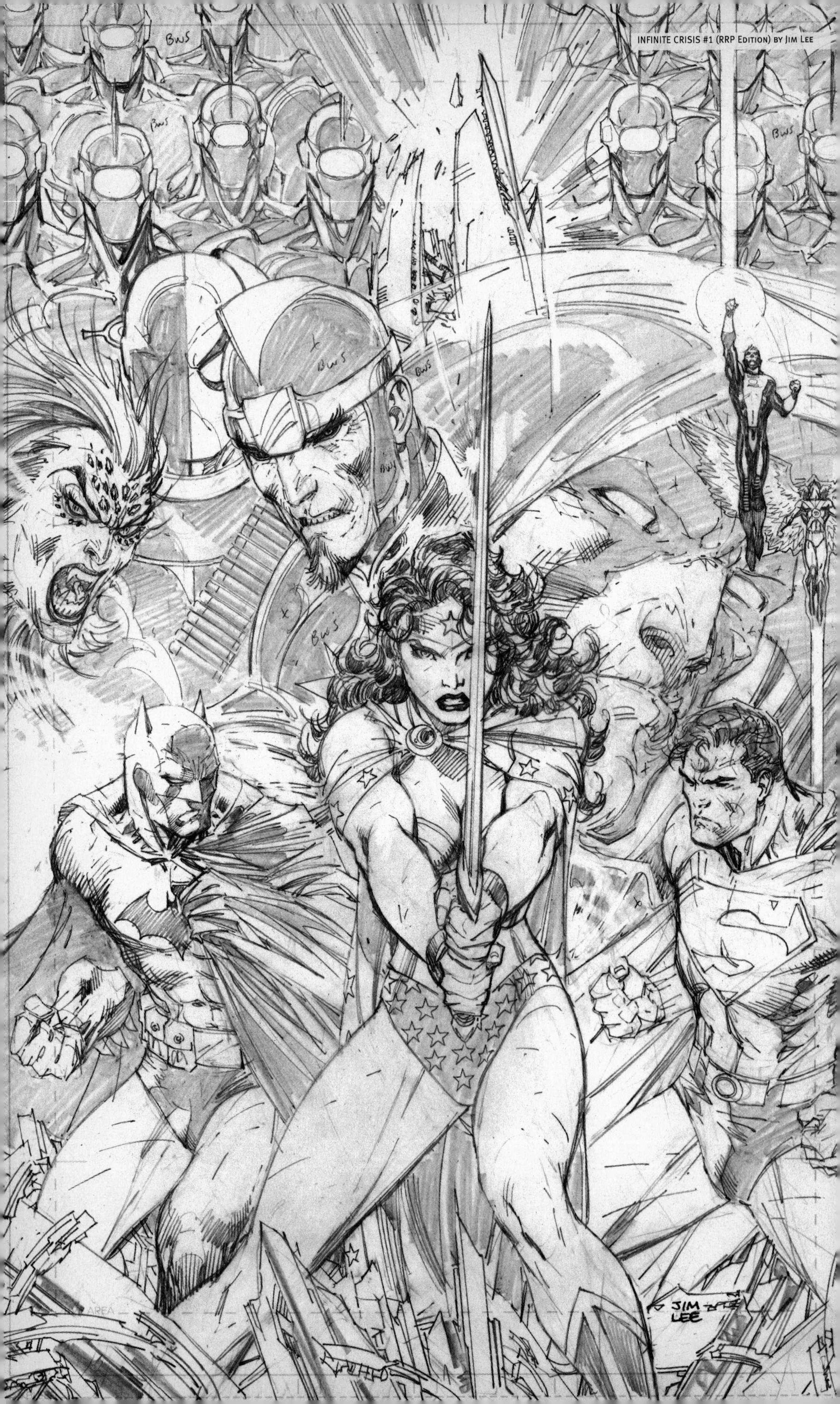
JIM LEE
INFINITE CRISIS #1 (RRP Edition) by Jim Lee

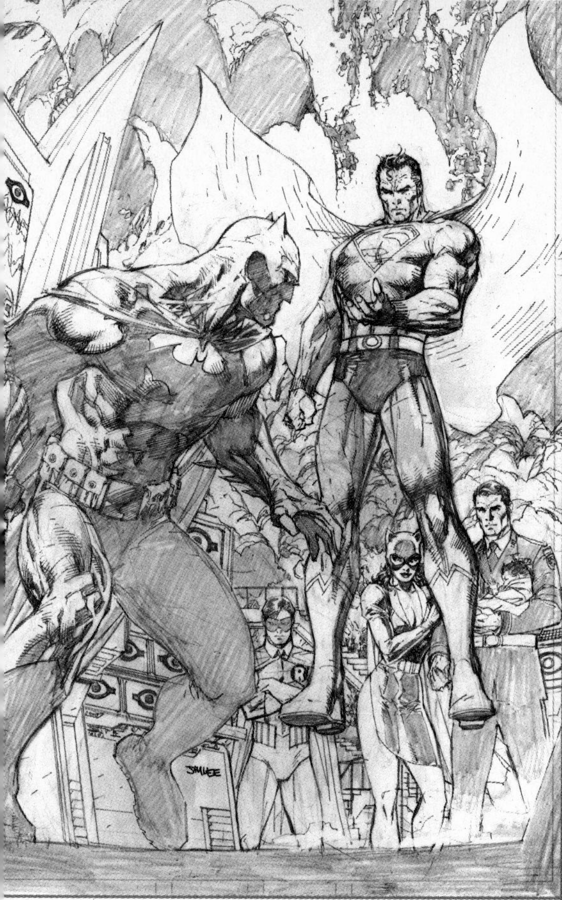
JIM LEE
INFINITE CRISIS #3 (SECOND PRINTING) BY JIM LEE

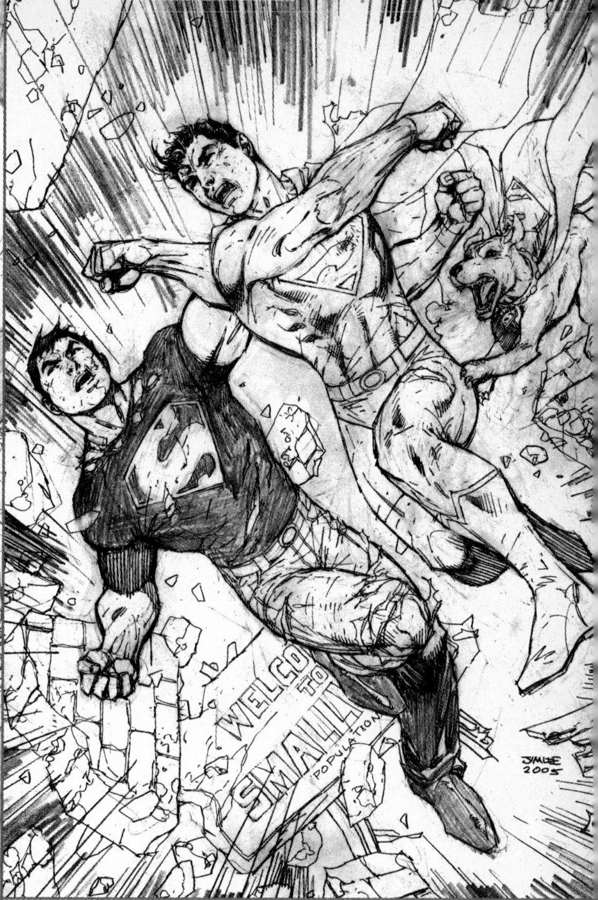
WELCO
TO
SMALL
POPULATION
JIM LEE 2005
INFINITE CRISIS #4 (SECOND PRINTING) BY JIM LEE

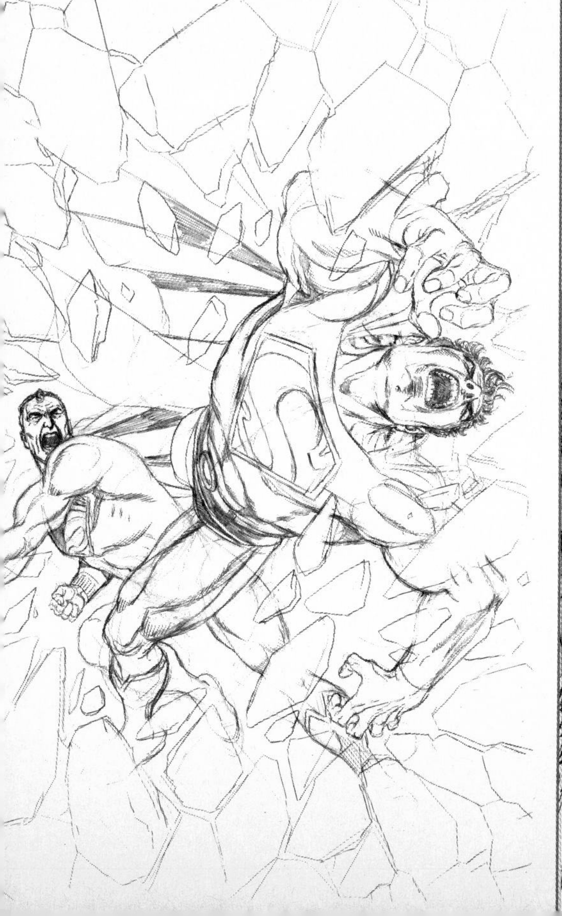
INFINITE CRISIS #5 (SECOND PRINTING) BY GEORGE PÉREZ

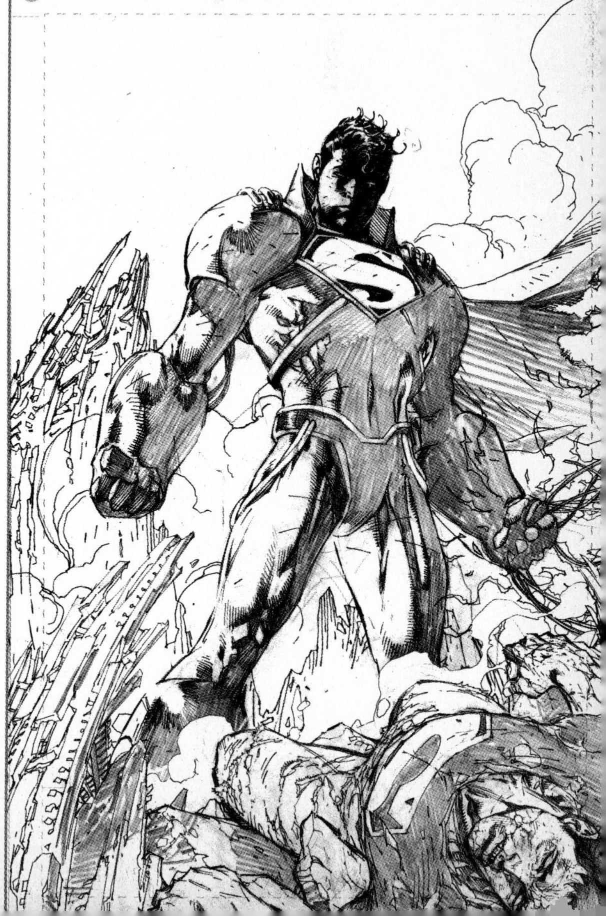
INFINITE CRISIS #6 (SECOND PRINTING) BY JIM LEE

INFINITE DISCUSSIONS

On the Friday before July 4th, after most DC employees had gone home early to enjoy the long holiday weekend ahead, Collected Editions Editor Anton Kawasaki gathered INFINITE CRISIS writer Geoff Johns (on speaker-phone), penciller Phil Jimenez, Group Editor Eddie Berganza, and Assistant Editor Jeanine Schaefer into a room to discuss the project one last time. With Chinese takeout and issues of the miniseries in hand, the group delved into one of the most talked-about events in DC's publishing history.

DC: So where did the idea for INFINITE CRISIS originate?

GEOFF: [Executive Editor] Dan [DiDio] always had the plan to do a sequel to the original CRISIS ON INFINITE EARTHS, and then he just got the rest of us involved. I remember him talking really early on about a big DCU miniseries for '05.

PHIL: I remember [Coordinating Editor] Ivan [Cohen] mentioned something about DC doing another major crossover — possibly a sequel to CRISIS ON INFINITE EARTHS — and I just told myself "I *have* to draw that."

I was in the middle of my Vertigo series OTHERWORLD, but there was a logical place in that story to break it and put it on hold while I worked on CRISIS. And so I pitched myself to Dan and told him why DC needed *me* to draw this story. Luckily he said he had planned to ask me to draw it all along.

DC: So why did you guys start this series the way you did?

EDDIE: Well, the JLA Watchtower had blown up at the end of Geoff's JLA arc. We had wanted the Trinity [Superman, Batman, and Wonder Woman] together but wondered what the threat would be.

GEOFF: [DC President & Publisher] Paul [Levitz] had the idea of seeing their splinter visually. I was personally inspired by the great Alan Moore story ["For the Man Who Has Everything"], and that's where Mongul came in.

PHIL: In that story, which was before the original CRISIS, these heroes were the best of friends. *Here* they are completely at odds with each other. Bitter pills. One thing I really liked about this sequence was that, while the universe was going to hell in a handbasket, all of the DC miniseries like OMAC PROJECT, VILLAINS UNITED, DAY OF VENGEANCE and RANN-THANAGAR WAR had pushed our world into such chaos — and our greatest heroes were having a philosophical debate in the ruins of the headquarters.

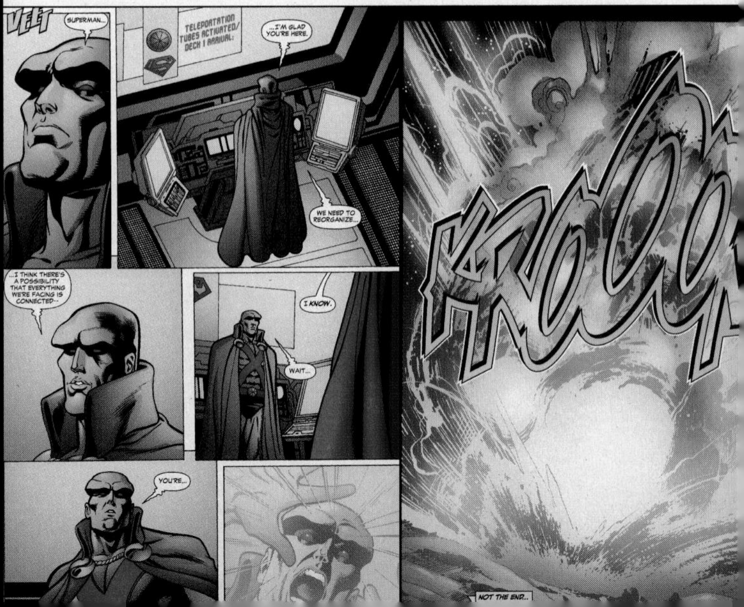

SUPERMAN...
TELEPORTATION TUBES ACTIVATED/ DECK 1 ARRIVAL:
...I'M GLAD YOU'RE HERE.
WE NEED TO REORGANIZE...
...I THINK THERE'S A POSSIBILITY THAT EVERYTHING WE'RE FACING IS CONNECTED--
I KNOW.
WAIT...
YOU'RE...
NOT THE END...

DC: We kept saying this would be DC's darkest day...

PHIL: Our greatest icons were bawling each other out on the moon while Uncle Sam, the spirit of America, is getting shot in the back by Deathstroke. It set up our heroes in this dark place — really self-involved jerks — and it gave us a great starting place to take our heroes back to their iconographic status.

EDDIE: I loved the way it was intercut, with the juxtaposition of scenes between the Freedom Fighters being massacred and just these three icons debating. That scene with Uncle Sam — the embodiment of America — face down in oil... was amazing. So symbolic.

JEANINE: Actually the oil thing resulted from a mistake. That was supposed to be water. We originally set it up that Uncle Sam was on a pier and it was destroyed, but we never showed that. And then the colorist mistakenly colored the water in that panel as blood, and then Sam was like... lying in this pool of crimson, and it was just awful, and we were like... "AAHH!! Make it oil! Make it oil!"

PHIL: And I even drew Uncle Sam getting beaten up, which we never figured out how to fit in at first.

EDDIE: Yeah, we wound up taking it out initially because it was such an ambitious overlay that we didn't know if it would work. The book allowed us to try out some cool things that, when they worked, were amazing — like the massive space spread.

DC: Originally, INFINITE CRISIS had all these vastly different storylines going on, and then it was decided that some of these stories would be explored in the four lead-in miniseries. So how different was the original script to issue #1 from what made it on paper?

GEOFF: Well, earlier on, I had planned to open with the Freedom Fighters scene, with them being massacred. But we changed it and had the big three there at the beginning instead. And after thinking about it, the cross-cutting made it more exciting anyway.

EDDIE: Yeah, Dan felt [the opening scene] wasn't kinetic enough.

GEOFF: I thought it worked out great in the end.

PHIL: The Bizarro page was fun...

GEOFF: I had something specific in mind for that, but different versions of how it would play out.

PHIL: I found composing it really hard to get all of Bizarro in. I drew about 18 panels — all in different pieces — just working out different compositions. And we trimmed it down to...how many?

EDDIE: We needed to get the beats just right for that scene. I remember spending a lot of time on that, trying to figure out how it would work.

PHIL: It was Eddie and Geoff who took the very panels I'd drawn and composed the scene — which was perfect. It really showed the horror of Bizarro's attack on Human Bomb, and the weird, Frankenstein Monster-esque reaction he has to it...

DC: Was the idea of these characters from the original CRISIS ON INFINITE EARTHS returning always the main thrust of the story?

EDDIE: No, that was different. The "missions" changed a lot. Originally it was all supposed to be a big "test" for Superman, some kind of big test that would involve other heroes.

GEOFF: We didn't know it was going to be those characters. I believe it was Jeph Loeb who suggested the four characters from CRISIS returning.

DC: There are so many amazing images in here — pages crammed with tons of characters and information. Phil, how do you even go about approaching some of these scenes? The space spread, for example [on pages 18 and 19]?

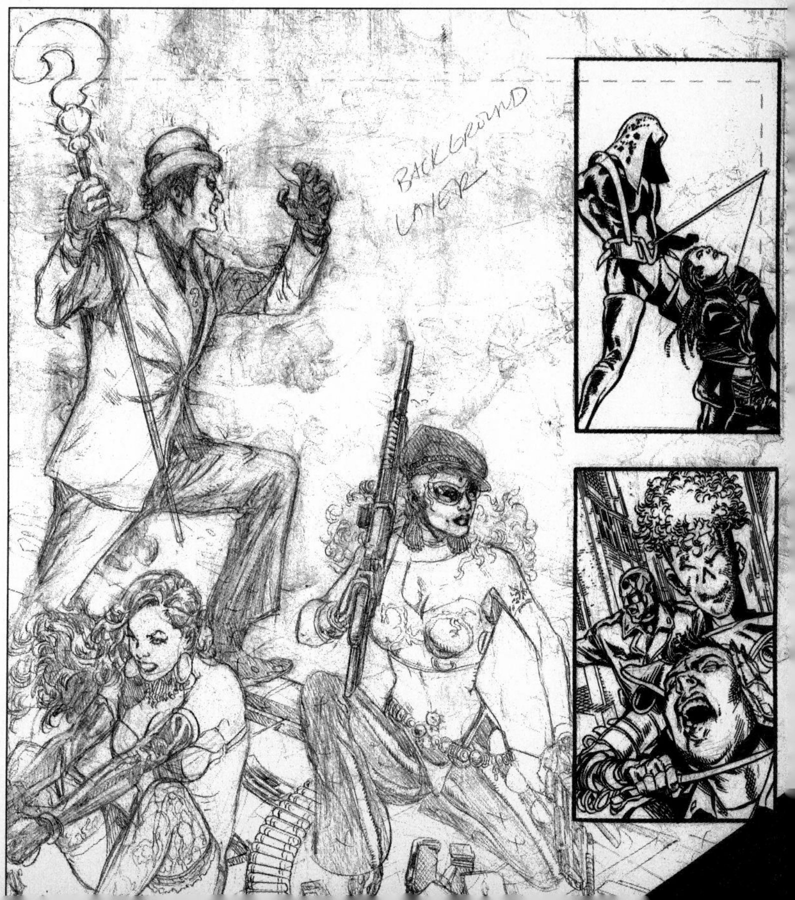
BACKGROUND LAYER

RIGHT: UNUSED PANEL

PHIL: As ever, the first place I start is reference. We had established all of these alien races and their spacecraft in books like RANN-THANAGAR and INVASION!...

DC: Oh my god... INVASION!

PHIL: ...and I wanted to use this preexisting material. So Jeanine helped me gather copious amounts of reference — the morphing Durlan ships, the sphere-shaped Dominator warcraft, etc., and then I began, as always, with a basic black and white marker layout to figure out the composition.

I developed a way of working with colorist Jeromy Cox on OTHER-WORLD. We created multiple lay-ers of art — figures and objects on one layer, background on another — that allowed him to separate all the pieces and do these amazing color effects. It was brilliant. So we tried to use that process on CRISIS. For the spread of the space war, I drew on a total of six boards instead of two. I created three spreads — one was for the background, another for space-ships, and then finally the charac-ters. This allowed the colorist to color each board separately and then combine them all in Photo-shop later.

DC: I liked the fact that my favorite DC family, the Bakers, made an appearance in the opening of issue #2.

PHIL: I travel to San Diego a lot for the San Diego Comic Con, and — having been there so often, and having friends who live there — I realized that the artists who had drawn ANIMAL MAN previously had drawn a very Midwestern house and city block. So I tried to get actual San Diego street refer-ence, planting the established house amid the palm trees and sunny skies of southern California. Also, I included several items from various Grant Morrison ANIMAL MAN stories in one of the panels.

DC: Right, right. The Thanagar hawk helmet. That orb bomb thing. These were part of the INVASION! crossover with Hawkman. I *loved* that issue.

Okay now...a few pages later, we see a scene that's directly spun out of Geoff's Power Girl story from JSA CLASSIFIED.

PHIL: It's always good to draw Giganta.

GEOFF: Eddie insisted on the red skies in that scene — an homage to the original CRISIS. But if you'll notice, the skies gradually lighten up until Earth-Two Superman shows up and meets Power Girl again — and then the sky is crystal clear blue.

PHIL: Huh. The color change didn't even occur to me.

GEOFF: That Superman shot is probably my favorite image in the whole book.

DC: Later on we look in on the Society and see what they've been up to. Anything you want to say about how Dr. Psycho looks here, Phil?

PHIL: I was going to draw him the way he was originally intended to look Post-Crisis, and that's that. I don't know who this other normal-looking diminutive person with a goatee is who's been running around the DCU lately...

DC: This version is certainly creepier. Oh, and while it may not look like it here, I just wanted to point out how all those villain headshots on the screens were drawn by Phil on a separate board and added in later.

Finally, we have Alex relate the story of the original CRISIS to Power Girl (and, therefore, the readers). Was it always intended to have original CRISIS artists George Pérez and Jerry Ordway draw that scene?

EDDIE: They were always meant to be a part of this project somehow.

GEOFF: Boiling down the history in three pages — that was fun.

DC: Can we talk about creating the orb and those information panels for Alex?

JEANINE: Those were supposed to be the mirror of Donna Troy's.

PHIL: [laughs] That's right! We established in THE RETURN OF DONNA TROY miniseries that Dark Angel, Donna's nemesis, was actually the evil Harbinger of the Anti-Monitor gone rogue. And her evil "Orb of History" disappeared. And Jeanine suggested that the orb actually be Alex's "World View," a sort of twisted version of the History of the DC Universe sphere, which was a catalogue of heroism. But we still don't know how he got it...

DC: This series really captured all the stuff I love about big "events" in comics.

GEOFF: In the '90s there was always a several-month window to shake up the status quo. And we're getting back to that now.

PHIL: In hindsight, the '90s comics of the DCU were, I think, an artistic reaction to Image Comics at the time. It was a way to compete with those guys.

GEOFF: People always complain about that era. You can say what you want about the Batman stuff, but it's still an interesting story. All this stuff is what people really remember, like Bane breaking Batman's back.

PHIL: Like Doomsday.

GEOFF: Yeah. When did we have that many good villains?

Speaking of...

I love the Joker. We did this bit in issue #2, because we always knew we wanted that last scene in the end with him. And so we only showed him here briefly.

DC: Eventually we catch up with Batman again, in his cave — trying to make sense of all that's going on. Usually we see him in control, with an answer and a solution to everything. But here he clearly has no clue what to do.

JEANINE: I was *very* distressed by Batman here. He was being so

mean to Alfred. There was a part of me that really wanted Geoff to rewrite this scene, even though I knew it was working *because* I was so uncomfortable.

GEOFF: Bruce refusing Alfred was the last straw.

JEANINE: I was upset that Alfred was so upset. It was like he was telling Bruce "I'm ashamed of you."

DC: By the end of issue #2, we're given the possibility of Earth-Two actually returning. Was there ever a point in this whole process where Earth-Two was actually going to return for good — and we'd have more than one Earth again?

EDDIE: No. Earth-Two was *always* a tease.

JEANINE: I always liked Earth-Three best. I wanted that to come back instead.

DC: Evil Earth? I love the Crime Syndicate! Actually, I noticed while looking over the original art boards that there's a panel with them in it from #6 that I missed in the miniseries — because a drawing of the Trinity is layered on top of them. It's hard to catch!

Issue #3 certainly opens with a shock — the destruction of Atlantis.

GEOFF: Yeah, the Atlantis stuff changed because of what was happening over in the AQUAMAN title.

JEANINE: Scenes kept getting shifted around. There were a lot of last-minute changes because of what was happening in other books.

GEOFF: Personally, I would have liked to have just removed the Atlantis scene, and just see more fighting go on elsewhere.

PHIL: Oh, I don't know. I liked it there because it was the *only* time Aquaman's "world" was shown. I thought that was important, in a book like this, to show the scope of the DCU.

GEOFF: True. I just would have liked to have more pages to tell more story, period. It could've been 1000 pages long.

PHIL: I would like to have seen the Legion of Super-Heroes... somewhere.

GEOFF: We talked about having, at one point, Superboy [Conner] coming back with the Legion. After being beat up by Superboy Prime in issue #4, he would go to the future somehow and come back with the *entire* Legion. But the Legion were "off-limits" to use.

PHIL: And then Rip Hunter would have gone *back* in time and brought characters from the past to fight. A new "Forgotten Heroes" — with all of our pre-21st century characters, like Jonah Hex, Balloon Buster, Viking Prince, etc. And Anthro. No crossover is ever complete without Anthro.

GEOFF: Sure, if we had twelve issues to work with, we would have.

PHIL: Perfect dream world: the return of the Legion would have included the best versions from every incarnation of the Legion. The Giffen/Levitz run, the five-year-later gap, the reboot, the Abnett and Lanning run. Lightning Lad and Live Wire, Shikari and Dawnstar, Sensor Girl and...well, Sensor Girl. But you get the idea. Just a swarm of the greatest Legionnaires from the past 40 years.

DC: Don't make me cry, Phil.

Moving on, issue #3 has a major turning point, with Earth-Two Superman coming to Batman and offering to have everything start over again. Create a world with a less grim Batman — one who actually settled down and got married.

GEOFF: Yeah, the most important stuff in that issue was always the Batman/Superman stuff. And also the scenes with Superboy Prime and Power Girl.

BELOW: AN EXAMPLE OF TWO SEPARATE LAYERS THAT WERE LATER COMBINED DURING THE COLORING STAGE

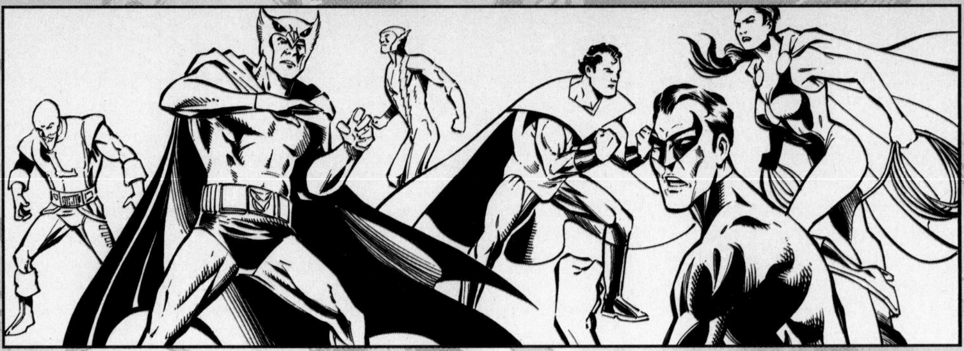

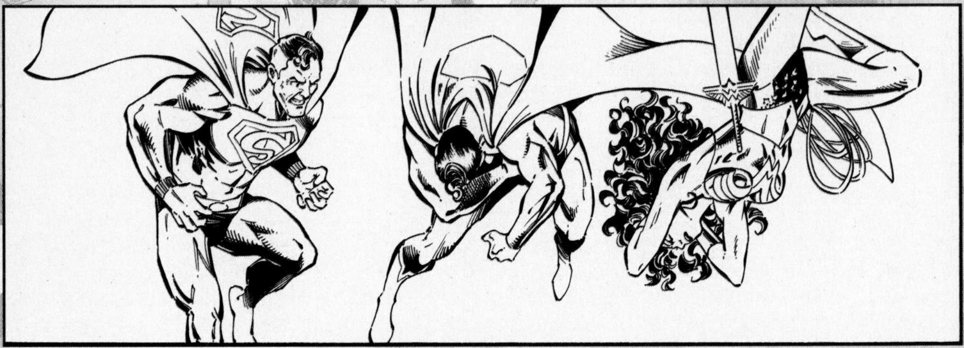

PHIL: How did George [Pérez] get involved?

EDDIE: He was happy to help out — be a part of the new CRISIS. So was Jerry.

GEOFF: This issue had great moments: I liked Batman admitting that Grayson was the person most important to him. The Lexes, Batman confronting Supes with the Kryptonite ring...

PHIL: Eddie and I worked over this scene to get the best moments out of it. That was definitely the best part of all this...the collaboration of it. Eddie and I have worked together now for over ten years, and it's easily been one of the most rewarding parts of the job. We have very similar sensibilities and cultural touchstones, and a wonderful shorthand. He gets what I try to achieve — which is a sense of scope and scale in these books.

JEANINE: It was really quite inspiring to work on. This was the book that I feel was truly a collaborative effort. Even though it was, well, [laughs] difficult, editorially, working with all these guys and seeing them all work together was completely amazing.

EDDIE: We played with the Superboy moment later on, that's for sure.

PHIL: Take note of the crystal in Lex's neck [on page 100], when Superboy rips open his LexCorp

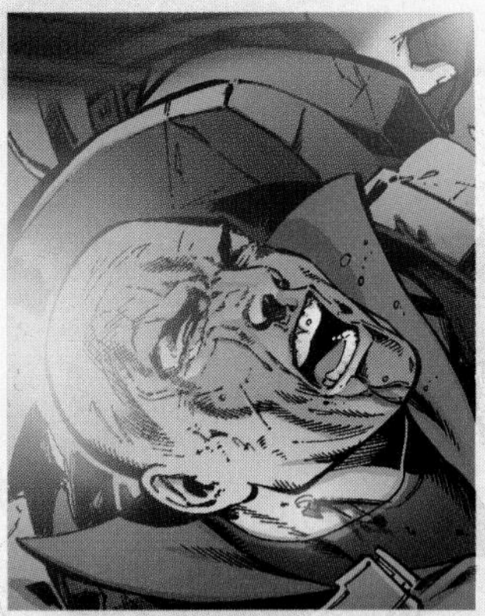

armor and he's revealed in his *Super Friends* costume. Not many people caught that in all the action and mayhem. It was simply supposed to be a tiny shard of glass that he would discover and use later, but the sliver became the size of a Gray's Papaya hot dog in later issues.

DC: Anything you want to say about issue #4?

GEOFF: I remember this issue was the dynamite. My favorite issue of the bunch and, I think, of most people.

DC: There was a sales spike too.

JEANINE: It's because of the monkey on the first page. Monkeys *always* sell.

GEOFF: One of the most fun things for me was writing the Brotherhood of Evil.

PHIL: I really had a blast drawing them as well. The coloring on that scene, especially Chemo, was *amazing*.

DC: How was the coloring on this project decided? Why two colorists?

JEANINE: Jeromy and Phil work so well together that there was no question about getting him, but we realized it was just too huge a project for one colorist. Guy [Major] worked on ACTION COMICS with Eddie and me, and Jeromy and Guy have worked together before, and it all seemed to click. They worked so smoothly together that sometimes we didn't know which pages were whose when they came in.

DC: This issue was definitely one of the most talked about, because of that bloody fight with the Superboys and all of the Titans.

PHIL: Yeah, that's when people were really taking this book seriously.

GEOFF: I rewrote that Titans fight so many times... Originally we thought of having more major characters die here, but that would have been too distracting at this moment in the story, and that wasn't the point. So we specifically picked minor characters to die. But it still really shocked people, due to the violence. I originally picked Argent to die, but Eddie liked her. So she wasn't touched. Phil wanted Red Star to buy it, but Jeanine loves him...

JEANINE: Yes!

GEOFF: ...so he survived. None of us thought Terra would work because she was too confusing, and people would be reminded of that if she died.

PHIL: Hey, I love Red Star too! I'm the one who designed his fire powers, remember? My reason for Red Star was to have fans have that moment like "Holy —! They just killed RED STAR." For Superboy to kill someone that powerful suggested he wasn't just a bully beating up on the little guys — which, in fact, he was.

GEOFF: But the important thing was that Superboy Prime lost it. I wanted him to kill a character that

most people wouldn't recognize so they'd focus on Superboy Prime's actions.

DC: I think instead they were saying "Holy —! Superboy just punched Pantha's head off!" [laughs] I'll never forget that original panel you drew of that, with her head literally flying by in the background.

PHIL: It was kind of genius. Robotman and Wildcat are just watching this...cathead...fly across a Metropolis parking lot.

JEANINE: And then there's the amazing moment with the Flashes.

PHIL: Can I just say... those Pérez pages are just beautiful.

EDDIE: Really stunning.

GEOFF: I really wanted to do one last great Flash scene somewhere, ever since I left [as writer of that book].

DC: Let's talk about issue #5, which opens at a church. Originally there was supposed to be a 2-page spread of all of these heroes, which didn't make the original issue because you guys ran out of time, but we're now including it in this collection.

GEOFF: There're a lot of primates in that scene!

EDDIE: Paul wanted the church scene spread. He wanted us to show heroes seeking something else in the midst of all of this

chaos. We actually had planned to have this scene earlier in the series, but moved it to later because not enough stuff had happened yet. And then after what [Superboy] Prime had done...

JEANINE: I was a bit mixed on the scene at first. But Geoff handled it with such a human touch, which I think is at the heart of this series. It became about faith rather than religion.

GEOFF: But too often religion is ignored in comic books. It's a part of many, many people's lives.

PHIL: Part of the composition question became: "Which of our characters would go here and feel comfortable?" Huntress, obviously, who wears her religion on her costume. But who else? It made me start considering the religious and spiritual backgrounds of our characters. It became very interesting to ponder. Would the gay characters go there, naturally? Is it a forum in which they would seek solace? I'm not sure it would be my first instinct....

DC: Yeah, I can see why that might be complicated. How do we feel about old Lois dying a few pages later?

EDDIE: Sad.

JEANINE: So sad.

DC: And I don't think anyone was expecting Wonder Woman of Earth-Two to show up here also.

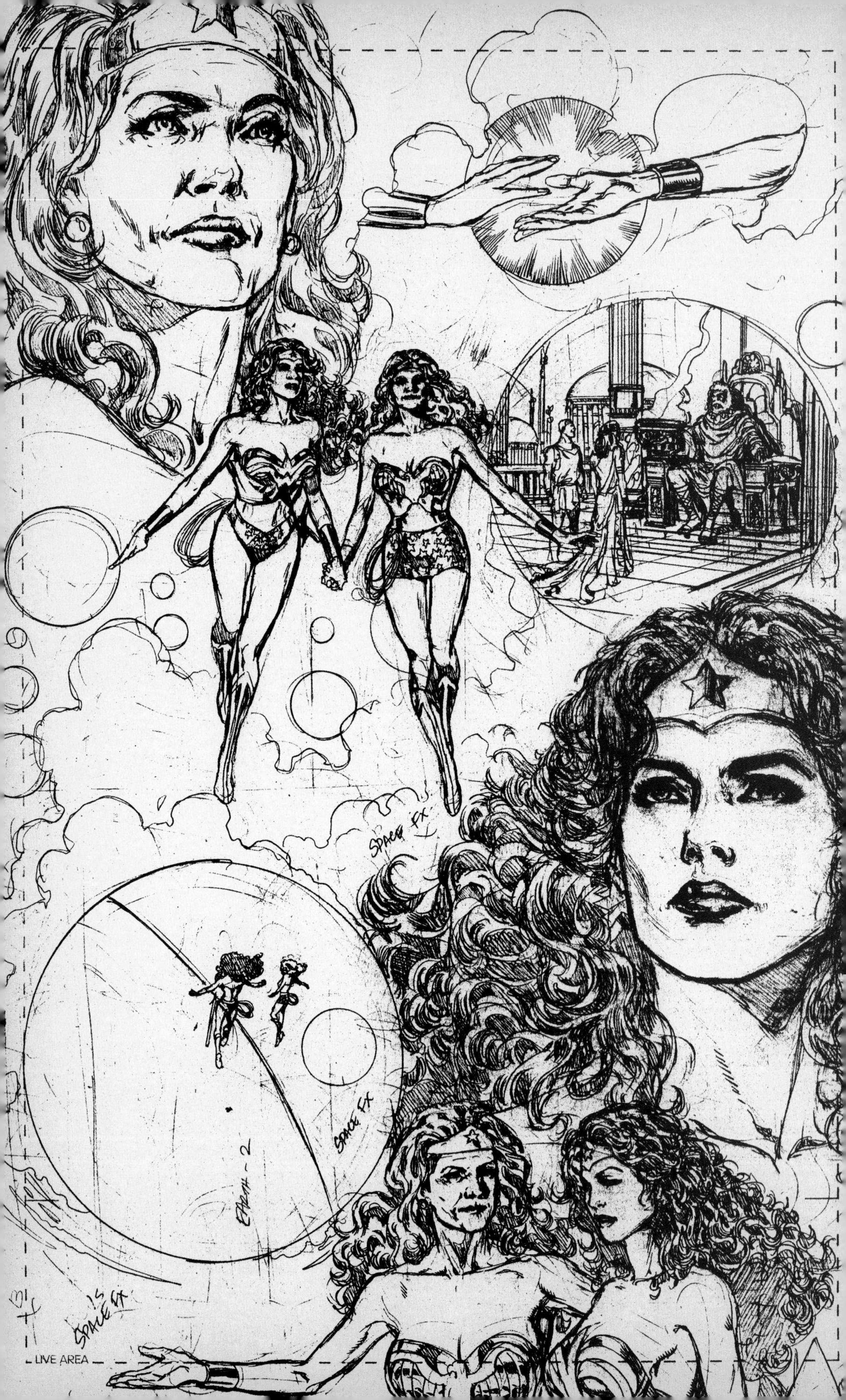
SPACE FX
SPACE FX
EARTH - 2
LIVE AREA

PHIL: Originally there was a longer sequence with the two Wonder Womans that was reconfigured because Dan said it was too "bookendy" — He felt that it took readers right out of the story.

Ultimately, I agreed with him. I think the scene was too self-indulgent, and so it was reworked. I even drew an alternate page, which Eddie liked more than I did. Regardless, we ended up dropping a lot of the less important work and ending on the beat of Diana's arrival on Earth-Two.

EDDIE: I loved the entrance of the Earth-Two Wonder Woman.

PHIL: And it was a nice farewell to her too. Geoff wanted to remind readers of the possibilities of humanity for Wonder Woman — who, in many ways, had become more godlike and distant, and less human. And if you're going to connect with people and teach them, you have to be one of them. The Earth-Two Wonder Woman is definitely one of us, and a great reminder for Diana as she moved to her next phase, in Allan Heinberg's run.

GEOFF: I really wish I had more pages for the Superman fight scene that Jerry drew.

DC: That was crazy to watch. When Alex starts messing with all the Earths, we see Superman splitting into all these variations we've seen over the decades — a visual that was then repeated in all of the DC Universe books that month with various characters.

GEOFF: We wanted to show as many Supermans as possible. John Wells and Kurt Busiek helped with picking some of them.

DC: I was just disappointed Sunshine Superman wasn't there!

JEANINE: Oh, he was there, but we couldn't fit him in on the page. He's off to the side, but Jerry drew him too close to the trim so he was unfortunately cut.

EDDIE: Interesting side-note: Andy [Lanning] actually did the multiple Earths page.

DC: Near the end, we see a double-page spread of Nightwing in an empty Titans Tower. In a series with so many jam-packed pages of art, this was quite a unique spread.

GEOFF: We needed an extra moment of Nightwing alone. We wanted to do the opposite of the "giant heroes gathering scene," something that would emphasize the large emptiness and quiet of the moment.

DC: Just in time for Superboy Prime's return at the end of the issue...

PHIL: Prime's costume was actually designed months before, in concert with DC Direct, as they needed a long development time for the action figure. Geoff, the DC Direct guys and I created a backstory involving the Anti-Monitor's armor. Originally, when Prime returned from the Speed Force, his body wasn't going to be able to harness yellow sun radiation in the same way, and so he used the Anti-Monitor's armor to better absorb the energy.

DC: In the opening of issue #6, why are these particular characters here together?

GEOFF: I chose this group because most of them are connected to Batman somehow. Sasha [Bordeaux], former bodyguard. Black Lightning and Metamorpho from The Outsiders... Green Arrow and Batman had a huge falling out earlier in JLA. So now it was like "Why the hell am I here?" And it was about Batman trusting people again and people trusting him. Which is why the Green Lanterns are present as well. This opening was the most fun for me in #6.

EDDIE: Wish we had more space to include moments like this.

EDDIE: That spread was like a puzzle. George had sooo much fun with Bizarros and such. And the super-sons and daughters. There's even a little homage to Andy's Legion. And the Tangent world that was one of my first big deal crossovers.

DC: And then finally, the magic characters show up! Can't have a Crisis without a big magic characters scene...

GEOFF: If you look closely, you'll notice some secret characters managed to make an appearance.

EDDIE: Shh!!

GEOFF: I went through the list, going through [DK's DC Comics] Encyclopedia for all the magic characters I could use.

DC: Was there anything you wanted to show in this series that you weren't allowed to?

JEANINE: Well, Geoff's idea was to have Red Hood be the Jason Todd of Earth-Two. So he'd be this kid, who wanted to be Batman's sidekick. He sneaks into the Batcave, and the first thing he sees as he boots up the bat-computers is... Batman murdered. And so he uses Bruce's stuff, training himself to take over for him. I think there was even talk of his possibly being Deathstroke's Robin.

DC: That's genius.

GEOFF: I really wanted to tie it in to the bigger story in a direct way. Superboy never punches a wall in our book, by the way.

DC: Really? Yeah, I guess not. [Editor's note: IN INFINITE CRISIS SECRET FILES, it was explained that whenever Superboy Prime punched at the wall of their "heaven," a subtle change would occur in DC's timeline — thus explaining the many continuity glitches that happened since the original CRISIS.]

PHIL: Do we want to talk about Black Adam and Psycho-Pirate?

JEANINE: Favorite line: "Booster. You have no idea how to talk to kids." [laughs] Like yeah, Bruce, you should be giving advice...

PHIL: The OMACs show up again after that, but we never quite got to use them the way we wanted to. I had helped create the OMACs, and I loved the idea that each one had a special way of defeating heroes and villains. Not simply electrocuting them, but using special offensive or defensive weapons against a particular hero.

GEOFF: We wanted more issues!

DC: A favorite moment for fans was the double-page spread Pérez drew of all of those alternate Earths!

GEOFF: All the Black Adam stuff really hit people. It was [editor Pete] Tomasi who suggested pushing the eyes through to the back of his head. Yes, it's violent, but it works.

EDDIE: How did you guys feel about the violence? Really, after Pantha, there was no turning back.

GEOFF: This kind of stuff works for this kind of story, for what it calls for.

PHIL: If you're going to do this kind of epic, world-shattering story, you have to show consequences — especially when it comes to violence.

DC: Speaking of world shattering...we finally come upon... "New Earth."

GEOFF: We always knew we were going to do something with New Earths. They're important to [weekly follow-up series] "52." Big revelations here.

DC: The ending of this issue really hit a lot of people hard, with the death of Superboy.

GEOFF: We originally talked about killing Nightwing. That was always Dan's plan.

EDDIE: But we didn't want [Nightwing] to die.

GEOFF: We wanted to have issue #6 be about bringing the Trinity back. Dan focused on offing Nightwing, but we all felt it was just the wrong character.

PHIL: Though I can't think of a character who would have a greater impact than Nightwing dying.

GEOFF: True, but it's Dick Grayson. My *mom* knows who he is. Nightwing would've been a mistake. Superboy was the best choice.

PHIL: Just in terms of links to other characters, though. Dick has so many connections to other characters. In many ways, even more than Superman or Batman, Nightwing is the soul, the linchpin, of the DCU. He's well respected by everyone, known to the JLA, the Titans, the Outsiders, Birds of Prey — everyone looks to him for advice, for friendship, for his skills. He's the natural leader of the DCU. His loss would devastate everyone and create ripples through the DCU. If it wasn't him, it had to be a hero that really impacted so many.

GEOFF: Well, what other character? Not Wonder Girl. Enough women have died in the DCU. Superboy was my favorite Titan. And I literally had to offer him as a sacrificial lamb.

DC: You killed your favorite Titan? That must have been hard to write.

JEANINE: I literally had tears in my eyes when the pages came in.

GEOFF: I really fought to have Conner in TEEN TITANS. He gave the title a dynamic the book never had before.

JEANINE: It's one of the reasons [his death] worked so well and became such a powerful scene. I remember talking to Geoff when the decision was made, and he was, correctly, really adamant that it *matter*.

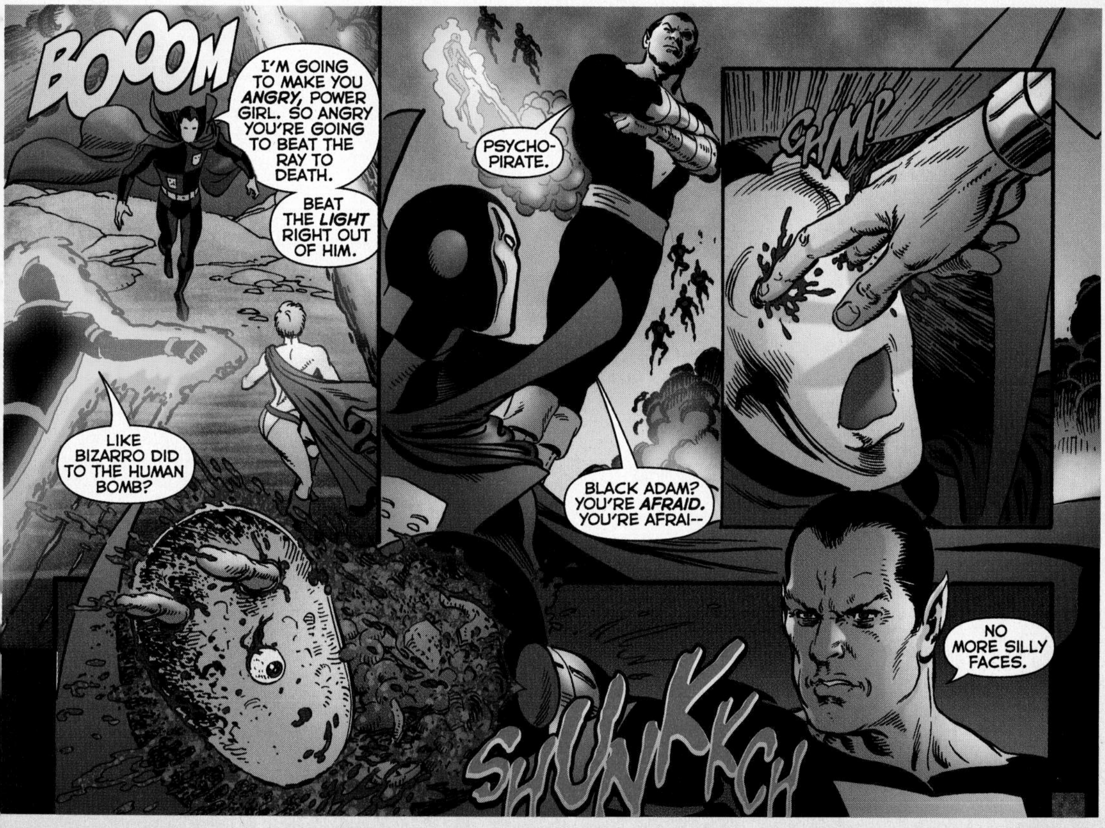

BOOOM
I'M GOING TO MAKE YOU ANGRY, POWER GIRL. SO ANGRY YOU'RE GOING TO BEAT THE RAY TO DEATH.
BEAT THE LIGHT RIGHT OUT OF HIM.
LIKE BIZARRO DID TO THE HUMAN BOMB?
PSYCHO-PIRATE.
BLACK ADAM? YOU'RE AFRAID. YOU'RE AFRAI--
NO MORE SILLY FACES.
SHUNKKCH

GEOFF: And Phil did such a great job with facial expressions there, depicting everyone's sorrow.

EDDIE: We were hoping to save both Nightwing AND Superboy. But at the end of the day, if we were going to do something really impactful, we really had to go *all* the way. It just worked for the whole story.

JEANINE: "Deaths are meaningless." But you couldn't *not* care about this.

DC: Okay, let's talk about the final issue, and then we wrap this up.

GEOFF: I wanted more pages for that opening fight scene... really show the scope of all this. We're finishing that spread, right?

EDDIE: You mean the inking?

DC: Yeah, it wasn't finished in time for the original comic, but we're "finishing" it for the collection.

PHIL: I don't know; I didn't mind all the red and just my pencils. It was certainly different.

DC: Well, we'll show the original in the collection so readers can compare!

GEOFF: I like the Doomsday stuff. Superman died fighting him before, but now we have *two* Supermans...

DC: So who really died in these scenes?

PHIL: Well, Peacemaker's probably dead. Madman could have survived, although I think Spellbinder and the Trigger Twins didn't walk out of that alley after being shot to death by Crimson Avenger and Wild Dog. Those New Bloods are gone — poor Razorsharp and Ballistic and Mongrel. It's hard when you're created to be the next generation of heroes. It's a lot of pressure, and it often leaves you dead. Although some of these people we think die here may not really be dead...

DC: We're also adding two new pages to this issue to "fix" the awkward way the Green Lantern spread originally fell. Damn you periodicals people for not paying attention and making us poor Collected Editions guys work harder! But I'm actually really happy that we could include these pages, and even more happy that they're not just "filler" and actually *add* something to the story.

GEOFF: Well, we always wanted to have *more* pages all around. We wanted to expand the Metropolis fight scene stuff, for sure — which we felt was shortchanged.

PHIL: What's it like to kill off the *original* super-hero?

DC: The Earth-Two Superman?

GEOFF: Well...

EDDIE: For me, I felt more for Superboy's death. George [Pérez] had a hard time letting [the Earth-Two Superman] go, hence the little silhouette in the sky.

PHIL: Think about it — we wouldn't have *jobs* without Superman and the guys who created him.

EDDIE: It was going to be a really brutal fight, and George came through amazingly with the final fight.

JEANINE: Also, just to clarify? There were a ton of people who were outraged that Batman would pull the trigger on Alex at the end of that Metropolis fight. There was a sound effect there, a "CHAK," and it was read as the gun not being loaded. But it was Batman *reloading* the gun, *not* firing it.

DC: Well, we're removing it for the collection so there's definitely no confusion.

PHIL: I have to say that the Mogo stuff was the one scene I didn't draw that I was really sad about. How amazing is a sentient planet coming to the rescue?

GEOFF: There are a lot more stories coming out of this than people realize. Everyone seemed to like how the Joker scene came out. "Don't screw with the Joker!"

DC: Any final thoughts?

PHIL: Start collecting reference for crossovers six months before you ever start them. EVER.

GEOFF: It was exhausting but fun. The fact that it turned out so well was really because we got along so well, and I thank Dan and everyone else for getting me involved.

JEANINE: This is what making comics is all about...

EDDIE: A *true* collaboration by people who truly love this medium — we gave up a piece of our lives for this...and it was worth it!

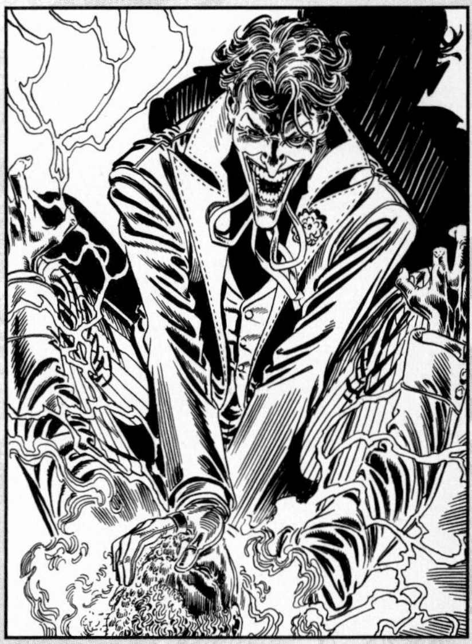

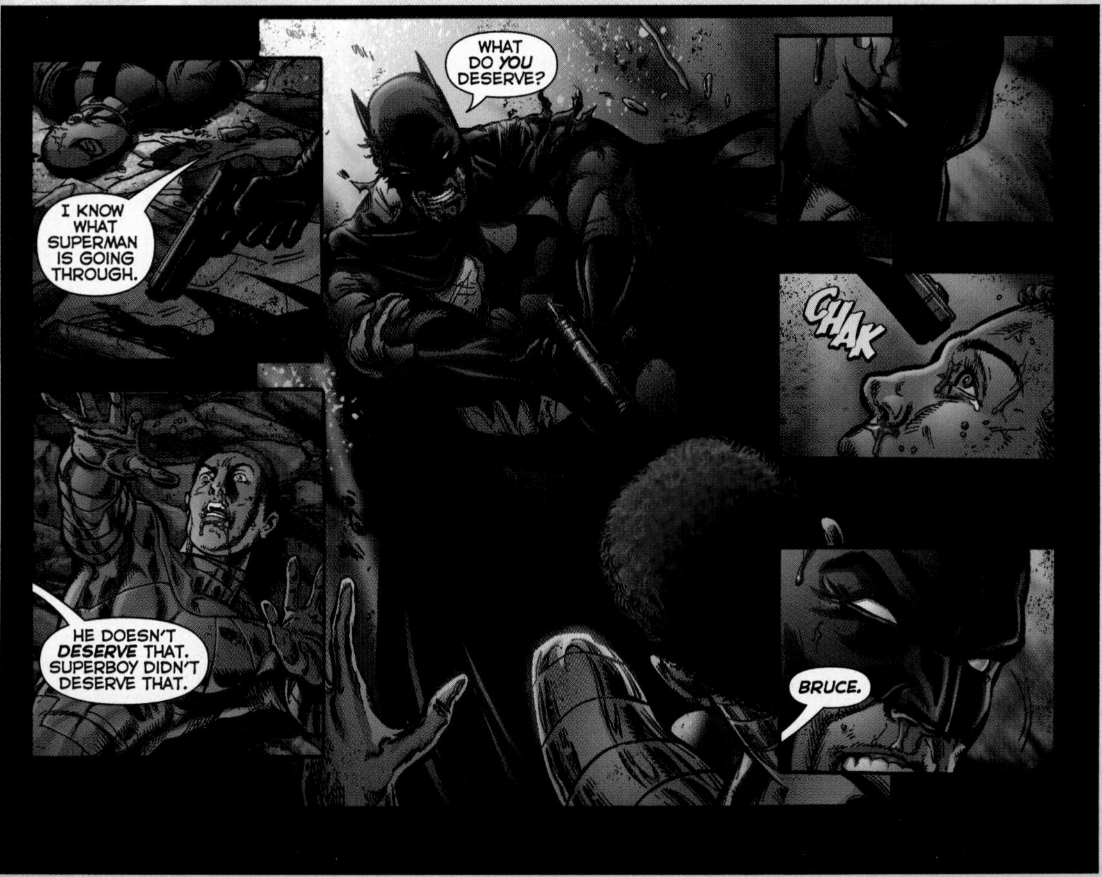
I KNOW WHAT SUPERMAN IS GOING THROUGH.
WHAT DO YOU DESERVE?
HE DOESN'T DESERVE THAT. SUPERBOY DIDN'T DESERVE THAT.
CHAK
BRUCE.

LOOK FOR THE FOLLOWING COLLECTIONS LEADING UP TO
INFINITE CRISIS:

THE OMAC PROJECT

Spinning out of the hit IDENTITY CRISIS, this volume shows you where it all started, collecting COUNTDOWN TO INFINITE CRISIS — written by Greg Rucka, Geoff Johns, and Judd Winick, with art by Jesus Saiz, Rags Morales, Phil Jimenez, Ivan Reis, and more! Plus, the crackerjack thriller **THE OMAC PROJECT** BY RUCKA AND SAIZ.

DAY OF VENGEANCE

BILL WILLINGHAM   JUSTINIANO   RON RANDALL

RANN-THANAGAR WAR

DAVE GIBBONS   IVAN REIS   JOE PRADO

VILLAINS UNITED

GAIL SIMONE   DALE EAGLESHAM   VAL SEMEIKS

JLA: CRISIS OF CONSCIENCE

GEOFF JOHNS   ALLAN HEINBERG   CHRIS BATISTA

AND BE ON THE LOOKOUT FOR
THESE COMPANION VOLUMES:

SUPERMAN: INFINITE CRISIS

JOE KELLY, MARV WOLFMAN, JEPH LOEB, ED BENES, LEE BERMEJO, HOWARD CHAYKIN, IAN CHURCHILL, TIM SALE

INFINITE CRISIS COMPANION

GREG RUCKA, BILL WILLINGHAM, DAVE GIBBONS, GAIL SIMONE, JESUS SAIZ, JUSTINIANO, IVAN REIS, DALE EAGLESHAM

SEARCH THE GRAPHIC NOVELS SECTION OF
WWW.DCCOMICS.COM FOR ART AND INFORMATION
ON ALL OF OUR BOOKS!